Norse Greenland: Viking Peasants in the Arctic

How could a community of 2000–3000 Viking peasants survive in Arctic Greenland for 430 years (ca. 985–1415), and why did they finally disappear? European agriculture in an Arctic environment encountered serious ecological challenges. The Norse peasants faced these challenges by adapting agricultural practices they had learned from the Atlantic and North Sea coast of Norway.

Norse Greenland was the stepping stone for the Europeans who first discovered America and settled briefly in Newfoundland ca. AD 1000. The community had a global significance which surpassed its modest size.

In the last decades scholars have been nearly unanimous in emphasising that long-term climatic and environmental changes created a situation where Norse agriculture was no longer sustainable and the community was ruined. A secondary hypothesis has focused on ethnic confrontations between Norse peasants and Inuit hunters. In the last decades ethnic violence has been on the rise in Eastern Europe, the Middle East and parts of Africa. In some cases it has degenerated into ethnic cleansing. This has strengthened the interest in ethnic violence in past societies. Challenging traditional hypotheses is a source of progress in all science. The present book does this on the basis of relevant written and archaeological material respecting the methodology of both sciences.

Arnved Nedkvitne is Professor Emeritus of Medieval History from the universities of Trondheim and Oslo. His main field of study has been pre-modern Norwegian social and economic organisation. Relevant monographs include: *The Peasant Economy of the Atlantic and North Sea Coast of Norway 1500–1730* (Oslo 1988, translation of the Norwegian title), *Lay Belief in Norse Society* (Copenhagen 2009) and *The German Hansa and Bergen 1100–1600* (Cologne 2014).

Norse Greenland: Viking Peasants in the Arctic

Arnved Nedkvitne

LONDON AND NEW YORK

First published 2019
by Routledge
2 Park Square, Milton Park, Abingdon, Oxon OX14 4RN

and by Routledge
52 Vanderbilt Avenue, New York, NY 10017

First issued in paperback 2020

Routledge is an imprint of the Taylor & Francis Group, an informa business

© 2019 Arnved Nedkvitne

The right of Arnved Nedkvitne to be identified as author of this work has been asserted by him in accordance with sections 77 and 78 of the Copyright, Designs and Patents Act 1988.

All rights reserved. No part of this book may be reprinted or reproduced or utilised in any form or by any electronic, mechanical, or other means, now known or hereafter invented, including photocopying and recording, or in any information storage or retrieval system, without permission in writing from the publishers.

Trademark notice: Product or corporate names may be trademarks or registered trademarks, and are used only for identification and explanation without intent to infringe.

British Library Cataloguing in Publication Data
A catalogue record for this book is available from the British Library

Library of Congress Cataloging in Publication Data
Names: Nedkvitne, Arnved, 1947- author.
Title: Norse Greenland : Viking peasants in the Arctic / Arnved Nedkvitne.
Description: Abingdon, Oxon ; New York, NY : Routledge, 2019. | Includes bibliographical references.
Identifiers: LCCN 2018003796| ISBN 9780815366294 (hardback : alk. paper) | ISBN 9781351259606 (e-book)
Subjects: LCSH: Vikings—Greenland—History. | Peasants—Greenland—History.
Classification: LCC DL65 .N43 2019 | DDC 998/.2—dc23
LC record available at https://lccn.loc.gov/2018003796

ISBN 13: 978-0-367-58580-8 (pbk)
ISBN 13: 978-0-8153-6629-4 (hbk)

Typeset in Times New Roman
by Swales & Willis Ltd, Exeter, Devon, UK

Contents

List of figures   xi
Preface   xii

Introduction   1

1 The problem   1
2 Earlier research   2
   Rediscovery and mapping of the Norse ruins (1721–1920)   2
   The stone ruins are described and categorised 1921–ca. 1970   4
   The university tradition enters Norse Greenland archaeology from the 1970s   7
   Natural sciences in Norse Greenland scholarship from the 1970s   8
   The present dominance of the ecological model   9
3 My contribution   10

1   The initial settlement in AD 985/6   14

1 The Icelandic sagas as historical sources   14
   Islendingabok and Landnámabok   14
   Who wrote the Vinland sagas and for what purpose?   15
   Categories of sagas which are relevant for Norse Greenland   18
   How reliable was the oral tradition on which the saga authors built?   19
   Sagas used as "narratives" or "remnants"   20
2 The first Greenlanders   21
   When did they go?   21
   What motivated them?   22
   Were the first immigrants Norwegians or Icelanders?   27

        The chieftain and his clients 30
        Was the Western Settlement organised differently
          from the Eastern? 31
        Population size at Eirik Raudi's time and later 32
   3 Conclusion 35

2   Political organisation   42

   1 Ethnic identity 42
      Language 42
      How did they name their ethnic group? 43
      The Norse narrative tradition in Greenland 45
      Courtly culture imitated in Greenland? 47
   2 Violence in a pre-state society 48
      The Groenlendinga tháttr as historical source 48
      The sense of honour 49
      Were feuds less common in Greenland than in
         Iceland? 49
   3 Jurisdiction in pre-state Greenland 50
      Was there a Greenland law? 50
      Legal proceedings at the Gardar Thing *53*
      How disputes in practice were settled 54
   4 The Brattahlid chieftain as pre-state political leader 56
   5 Ties to the Norwegian king before 1261 59
      Collective obligations to the Norwegian
         crown before 1261 59
      Were individual Greenlanders members of the king's
         hird? 61
   6 Attempts to organise a state administration
     after 1261 63
      The submission in 1261 63
      The courts of justice 66
      The royal manors at Foss and Hvalsey 67
      A state which failed its subjects 73

3   Church and religion   81

   1 Christianisation 81
      The pagans 81
      Collective and individual conversion 82
      The Norwegian king and the Christianisation of
         Greenland 82
   2 Church organisation before the parish AD
     1000–1124 85
      Private chapels 85
      Minsters in Greenland? 87

Flexible burial customs 89
Bishops in Greenland before 1124 90
Power in the Greenland church before 1124 91
3 The parish 1124–1340 92
The tithe 93
The number of parish churches at population
 maximum 94
How many parish churches remained ca. 1360? 95
How often did the Greenlanders attend mass in
 their parish church? 101
Who owned the parish churches? 102
What did the parish churches look like? 103
The parish church as centre for the diffusion of
 literacy 107
The Norse Greenlanders' aesthetic models 110
The parish as framework for social life and
 mentalities 113
4 The Gardar diocese 114
The bishop 114
Did the bishops live and work in Greenland? 115
The Gardar diocese and the archbishop
 in Nidaros 121
The Gardar diocese and the pope 123
5 The monasteries 128
Economy 129
Religious functions 131
6 The supernatural and the natural world 132
Christian miracles and magic 132
Geographic exploration 135
A theoretical interest in the natural world 140
Combining religion and practical rationality 141
7 The Greenland church in its final decades
1340–1410 141
The bishops 141
The church organisation after the bishops had left 142
Laymen's religious rituals in their parish churches 143
Laymen's religious practices in their homes 144

4   Trade and shipping   161

1 The imports 161
Necessities: iron and timber 161
Luxuries conferring status 166
How important were imports to the Norse
 Greenlanders? 169

2 The exports 170
  Walrus tusks and walrus rope 170
  Walrus tusks as raw material for objects of art 172
  The Norse Greenlanders' "nordrseta" in the Disco
    region 174
  Hides and skins 179
  Falcons and polar bears 180
  Lamp oil 182
  Foreign trade and the Greenlanders' material
    needs 183
3 Ships and boats 183
  Ocean-going ships 183
  Inshore ships of middle size 185
  Small boats for use in the fjords 186
  Driftwood as raw material in boatbuilding 189
  Were ships and boats built in Norse Greenland? 191
4 Crossing the Greenland Ocean 193
  Bergen: the commercial centre of
    the Norse realm 193
  Tackling the problems 196
  Those who failed to reach their destination 198
  How many ships reached Greenland annually? 200
5 The merchants 203
  Country of origin 203
  Part time and professional merchants 205
  Retailing foreign goods in Greenland 207
6 The political framework for trade and shipping 209
  Pre-state Greenland 209
  Under the Norwegian state 1261–1380 211
  Under Danish rule 1380–1410 211
  The hypothesis about "the royal monopoly ship" 214
  Merchants and state 217

5 Subsistence food production — 230

1 The basis: animal husbandry 232
  The local resources 232
  Milk from cows 233
  Milk from goats and sheep 243
  Meat from domestic animals 244
  Pigs 245
  Horses 246
  Conclusions and sources of error 247
2 Providing fodder for domestic animals 248
  Indoor or outdoor winter feeding? 249

Gathering winter fodder in outfields and common
       land 250
   Improving the meadow 252
   Summer pastures 256
   Sæters 256
   Tradition and flexibility 260
 3 Animal husbandry in crisis? 261
   Landowners exploiting peasants? 261
   Soil erosion and soil exhaustion 265
   The climate 268
   Rising sea level 271
   Conclusion: a sustainable agricultural production 271
 4 Hunting and fishing as flexible supplements 271
   Hunting and fishing open to all? 272
   Seals: less dominant than assumed? 274
   Reindeer: the most attractive game 279
   Whales 285
   Hunting expeditions to the east coast 288
   Cod and other sea fish 289
   Char and other fish in lakes and rivers 295
   How important was fish for the Norse
       Greenlanders? 297
   Edible plants 298
   Peasants and hunters 301
 5 Did the quality of the diet decline? 302
   From terrestrial to marine food in the diet 302
   Was the Norsemen's "marine food" fish or seal? 309
   From cattle to sheep and goats? 311
   The Norwegian model 311

6   One land – two societies   327

 1 Inuit attitude to violence 327
   Who exploited Greenland's resources most
       efficiently? 327
   How exposed were the Inuit to starvation? 331
   Violence to demonstrate power 336
   Sadism 337
   Fear of being killed 338
   The social background 339
 *2 Norse encounters with the Inuit from beginning
    to end 339*
   Did the Inuit exterminate the Dorset? 340
   The Norse and the Inuit AD 985–1341 341
   Ivar Bárdarson's account 1341–1363 342

How did the Norse defend themselves? 349
When did the Western Settlement cease to exist? 350
The Inuit close in on the Eastern Settlement
   1379–1406 355
The last ship 356
When did the Eastern Settlement cease to exist? 361
Inuit memories of a vanished society 363
Was the end of the Eastern Settlement violent? 366
Was the end preceded by a slow decline in
   population? 368
Four new methods and four new conclusions 369

3 "We found a rich land, but are not destined to enjoy it" 370

Bibliography	*378*
Appendix I	*399*
Appendix II, Introductory map and maps 1–10	*403*
Index of matters	*416*
Index of names (places and persons)	*424*

Figures

1.1	Agricultural land at farm E89a	24
1.2	Farm E96 in its landscape	25
1.3	Ruin of farm E167 in the Vatnahverfi	26
2.1	Map of Brattahlid manor	58
3.1	Wooden fish used as rosary	101
3.2	Trencher for eating	110
3.3	View from Kingittorsuaq island	138
3.4	Runestone from Kingittorsuaq island	139
4.1	Stone shed at Nuussuaq peninsula	176
4.2	Ground plan of the shed at Nuussuaq peninsula	177
4.3	Sexæringr from the Atlantic coast of Norway	187
5.1	Modern painting of W51 Sandnes farm	231
5.2	E232, example of *sæter*	257
5.3	Map of farm with one household	262
5.4	Map of farm with two households	263
6.1	Modern painting of farm W53c as an example of a "centralised farm"	353
6.2	Crucifix from farm W53d in the Austmannadal	354

Preface

The contemporary debate on climate change has increased the interest in the Arctic region, including the Viking peasants who settled in Greenland in AD 985, increased their number to 2000–3000, and disappeared mysteriously four to five centuries later. In Eastern Europe, the Middle East and Africa there have been ethnic conflicts in recent decades of a type which most people thought belonged to the past. This has made the ethnic tensions between Norse and Inuit relevant for contemporary issues. Was it climate change or ethnic conflict which destroyed the Norse community on Greenland?

The last monograph on Norse Greenland was published in 1982 by the Danish archaeologist Knud Krogh. In the following 35 years research has made great progress. The overwhelming majority of Greenland scholars are today archaeologists educated at universities, a few are anthropologists and historians. Representatives from natural sciences like physics and medicine are engaged in specific tasks. The university tradition has made presentations less descriptive and more focused on analysing problems. This development has made interdisciplinary cooperation more important and fruitful.

Around 1980 the Danish dominance in Greenland scholarship was still overwhelming. Today scholars from many countries participate, most prominent among the new nationalities are the Americans. Norwegian and Icelandic historians are particularly well qualified to write monographs since they are trained to analyse similar societies, and can read sagas, Icelandic Annals and other written sources in the original language. The scholarly progress in the last decades reinforces the need for a new synthesis of Norse Greenland history.

The National Museums in Copenhagen and later in Nuuk have accumulated resources on Norse Greenland in the form of knowledge, artefacts, written reports and literature for nearly two centuries. The most prominent representative of this tradition is today museum curator Jette Arneborg in Copenhagen who in the last 25 years has been the centre of an international research network. Through her I have been given access to numerous excavation and registration reports on paper, others are accessible online. Particularly useful has been the Nationalmuseum's "Nordboarkiv". Historians mainly get access to archaeological sources through articles and books and their bibliographies and footnotes. But supplementary information obtained through written material and conversations is of great value for scholars without excavation experience.

Enhedssekretær Else Rasmussen at the Medieval Department was very helpful with practical problems during my two stays at the Nationalmuseum in Copenhagen.

Souschef Georg Nyegaard at the National Museum in Nuuk gave me the same kind of help during my stay in Nuuk in 2014. I copied reports, theses and articles which were available at the museum and archive. A sincere thank you to him and the staff of the museum!

Arnved Nedkvitne,
Oslo, June 2018

Introduction

Greenland is geologically and geographically a part of North America, but politically it is today a part of Denmark. The historical reason for this Scandinavian link was Norse immigrants who settled in Greenland in AD 985 and lived there until at least 1410, i.e. for more than 425 years. This community numbered at its peak 2000–3000[1] and brought with them social practices and ideas from their land of origin, which ultimately was the North Sea and Atlantic coast of Norway. Its members were the first Europeans to set foot on American soil, which they called Vinland, and they linked the two continents through their shipping. But the Norse disappeared for some unknown reason, and America had to be rediscovered by Columbus.

1 The problem

How could a community of 2000–3000 Viking peasants survive for more than four centuries in Arctic Greenland, and why did they finally disappear? These two questions are equally exciting and challenging. They have been discussed for centuries in Scandinavian historiography and were put in a global context by the American physiologist Jared Diamond in his book *Collapse* from 2005. The disappearance of the Norsemen ca. AD 1415 is one of the great mysteries in world history.

The question which has attracted the greatest interest among scholars and laymen is the second one, the demise of Norse Greenland. In the last decades scholars have been nearly unanimous in emphasising that long-term climatic and environmental changes created a situation where Norse agriculture was no longer sustainable. A secondary hypothesis has focused on ethnic confrontations between Norse peasants and Inuit hunters. Grand social hypotheses like these are often called "models". Scholars mainly formulate them on the basis of the available empirical material, but the models are also influenced by social conditions in the author's society. Sources about Norse Greenland are scarce, which has made the "models" more influenced by the author's own society than is usually the case. I have called these alternative models "ecological" and "ethnic".

Scholarly analyses of the subject started in the 19th century. That was before Nordic archaeology had become a social science with scientific methods of its own taught at universities. The relevant sources were at that time the written ones.

2 Introduction

Several of them mention and describe violent confrontations between Norse and Inuit. It comes as no surprise that the common opinion in the 19th century was that the Norse had been the victims of violence.[2]

From ca. 1920 large archaeological excavations took place. The nature of the archaeological sources makes it unlikely that they will provide any evidence of violent confrontations. In the 1970s came the "Green Wave" in politics and social sciences, and the interest in ecological problems increased. In the last decades sophisticated scientific methods have given more detailed information about Norse Greenland agriculture and food consumption. Hypotheses about ethnic conflicts based on written sources were now marginalised, but not abandoned.

But other contemporary developments have prepared the ground for hypotheses in a different direction. Ethnic violence has been on the rise in Eastern Europe, the Middle East and parts of Africa. It has occasionally degenerated into ethnic cleansing and genocide. This has strengthened the interest in ethnic violence in past societies. The time has come for a critical examination of the generally accepted ecological hypotheses.

2 Earlier research

The last reliable information about the Norse Greenlanders is dated 1410, and three centuries later research in the history of this lost society started.

Rediscovery and mapping of the Norse ruins (1721–1920)

The Norse lived in two settlements, in the sources called the Western (in the fjords near Nuuk) and the Eastern (in the fjords near Qaqortoq). Around 1600 this localisation had been forgotten, and the commonly held idea was that the Western Settlement was on the west coast and the Eastern Settlement on the east coast of Greenland. Cartographers thought the two settlements were connected by a sound or strait cutting through the inland ice.[3]

In July 1721 the Norwegian missionary Hans Egede founded a colony near what today is Nuuk. At that time Norway was part of Denmark. It was one of Egede's tasks, given to him by his employers in Bergen and Copenhagen, to find out where the Norse had lived and whether the Norse community still existed. Egede was told in 1722 by the Eskimos that there were ruins where Europeans had lived in the fjords east of Egede's colony.[4] In the summer of 1723 he received orders from Copenhagen to explore the coast.[5] He at that time assumed that by sailing southwards on the west coast he would find the strait which would lead him to the east coast.[6]

He started his journey on 9 August 1723.[7] On 19 August 1723 they reached what we today know was the ruins of the Eastern Settlement east of Qaqortoq,[8] and carried on southwards until he came close to today's Nanortalik on 25 August 1723.[9] He had a great deal of confidence in the local Eskimos and writes that he could get no information from them "about this strait which should be the entrance to the Eastern Settlement, even if I diligently asked and searched for such information." Egede wanted his journey to continue around Cape Farewell and up the east coast in the Eskimos' small boats, but they strongly warned him against it, because they had to get back home before winter made such travel impossible.[10] This was no empty pretext; their homeward journey was problematic. They returned to the colony on 14 September 1723. Egede's conclusion was that the "strait leading to the Eastern Settlement . . . drawn on maps does not exist."[11]

Authorities in Copenhagen accepted Egede's judgement but did not abandon their hopes of finding the missing Norsemen. In 1728 a ship from Copenhagen brought 11 horses which were to be used in crossing the Greenland glacier from Nuuk to the East coast, probably as pack horses. Egede wrote in his diary, "this can in practice not be done". All 11 horses died the following winter. The commanding officer from Copenhagen travelled to the inland glacier to evaluate if it would be possible to cross the ice, and his conclusion was that it was not. "Just as the Eskimos had told him beforehand", Egede wrote in his diary. It gave more reliable results and was cheaper to ask the Eskimos and trust their answers.[12]

The Norse ruins on the west coast became better known, and in 1794 Henrik Peter von Eggers claimed correctly that the Norsemen's Eastern Settlement was the ruins in the fjords east of Qaqortoq.[13] In the following decades this opinion won increasing support.[14] Only the south-west coast of Greenland had a topography which would have permitted a Norse settlement of cattle farmers.

In 1380 Norway with its North Atlantic dependencies Greenland, Iceland, Faroes, Shetland and Orkney entered a personal union with Denmark. In 1814 the great powers transferred Norway to Sweden but let Greenland, Iceland and Faroes remain in Danish hands. Danish authorities feared that Norway could reclaim Greenland. A countermeasure was to give Danish scholars the responsibility for researching and writing the history of Greenland.

During 1838–1845, the Danish state edited *Grønlands historiske mindesmærker* (= GHM, *Remnants from Greenland's history*) in three volumes of 2500 pages. All known written sources of Norse Greenland's history were printed with Danish translations. Skills in Old Norse were no longer necessary to read the sources, and permissions for archaeological excavations in Greenland had to be obtained from Danish authorities. Norway's first university was founded in 1811, and in 1838 research in Norwegian history was still in its infancy, and there was no room for research on medieval Greenland.

The editors of GHM stated in their introduction that medieval Greenland was "an Icelandic colony".[15] The marginalisation of Norway and the focus on Iceland remained part of Danish research on Norse Greenland as long as Iceland was part of the Danish kingdom up to 1944, and even longer.

In the first decades after GHM had appeared in 1845, Danish politicians and historians had their eyes more fixed on Schleswig-Holstein, which was transferred to Prussia after a war in 1864. After 1880 research on Norse Greenland was resumed, and the first priority was to map the Norse ruins and identify them with farms mentioned in the written sources.

4 *Introduction*

The first systematic attempt was made by "first lieutenant in the navy" Gustav Holm in 1880.[16] He visited 40 "ruin groups" consisting of 300 ruins. His method was to find a stone wall and follow it, making a drawing of the wall. He also collected artefacts he found in the ruins,[17] and made a long list of artefacts which he found at 14 different "ruin groups". He considered this a good result "in consideration of the short time we could spend on it".[18]

In 1895 "first lieutenant" Daniel Bruun resumed this work.[19] He drew maps showing where ruins could be found and introduced a numbering system which is still in use. He worked one summer season with ca. 20 workers and covered a large number of ruins.[20] Seen with modern eyes, his and Holm's methods were archaeological vandalism.[21]

Hermann Schirmer was a Norwegian architect with special competence in medieval Norwegian churches. He was the first to argue in 1886 that Gardar cathedral was the church ruin at Igaliku, number E47 in Bruun's system.[22] The Icelandic philologist Finnur Jonsson in 1899 registered all extant place names from medieval Greenland and compared them to maps of ruins then available.[23] His conclusions are still authoritative.

Ca. 1900 maps were drawn with Norse ruins inserted and the most important farms named in the written sources identified. The pattern was not significantly changed by later research.

The stone ruins are described and categorised 1921–ca. 1970

In the period after 1645 Denmark was reduced from a first-rate to a second-rate power in Northern Europe. It lost its provinces in southern Sweden during 1645–1658, which today have 1.7 million inhabitants; in 1814 it lost Norway which today has some 5 million inhabitants; in 1864 it lost Schleswig-Holstein with a population today of 2.8 million; and in 1944 it lost Iceland which today has 0.32 million inhabitants. Today's Denmark has 5.6 million inhabitants, so if they had kept their lost provinces they would have had a total population of some 15.4 million today. This is part of the background to their Greenland policy during 1921–1981.

In 1921 Denmark declared that the whole of Greenland and its territorial waters was to be governed by Denmark. The Danish declaration on Greenland was not accepted in Norway, and in 1931 the Norwegian government declared uninhabited parts of Eastern Greenland to be Norwegian territory. It appointed a local governor (*sysselmann*), whose name was Helge Ingstad. At the international court in the Hague in 1933, Danish sovereignty was confirmed, and the Norwegian government accepted the verdict.[24]

Nationalmuseet in Copenhagen was founded in 1807 but did not regard Greenland as its responsibility. In 1921 Nationalmuseet was given responsibility for the Norse ruins.[25] Until 1941 Poul Nørlund[26] and Aage Roussell[27] conducted and published several large excavations on behalf of Nationalmuseet, and Christian Vebæk excavated several smaller sites.[28] Nørlund and Vebæk were historians by education, Roussell an architect.

The main focus of their work was the stone ruins. They showed little interest in the Norse peasants' adaptation to the Greenland environment and how they produced their food. Without previous methodological analysis they claimed that the northernmost Western Settlement had been ruined by the Inuit as described in the written sources, while the Eastern Settlement fell victim to a deterioration in the climate.[29]

The political situation in the 1920s and 1930s made it politically desirable to have publicity about the excavations, and the simplest way of doing this was to excavate the sites best known from the written sources: Brattahlid, Gardar, Herjolvsnes, Hvalsey and Sandnes. The Danish archaeologists were inexperienced in Norse archaeology and without archaeological schooling. Despite this they started with the two most important and interesting sites, the bishop's see at Gardar and Eirik Raudi's farm at Brattahlid. As could be expected, "much damage was done to these unique sites for rather scanty archaeological return".[30] Simple methods were used; they found a stone wall or its foundations and followed it, and the aim was to establish the extent of the building and its rooms. They removed soil inside the ruins searching for objects and exposing the floor.[31]

Roussell wrote his PhD on the architecture of churches and farmhouses and the function of houses and rooms. He excavated Sandnes, the most interesting site in the Western Settlement and all five farms in the interesting Austmannadal, which were more or less destroyed as future excavation sites in the process.[32] Roussell's ambition was to create a typology of Norse farm houses, but "most modern workers do not feel that [Roussell's] three generalised farm types provide any very useful markers for archaeological phasing of the settlements".[33] Today the monographs on Brattahlid, Gardar, Herjolvsnes and Sandnes are mainly used as sources for factual information. Their catalogues of objects are well organised.

Excavations inside buildings were not done stratigraphically, as would have been done today. Later archaeologists lack information on layers and phases in rooms and buildings, which would have made it possible to create a chronology.[34] Nationalmuseum archaeologists can today present regrettably few theories about changes based on archaeological material. They often write about change, but this is mostly based on written sources.

Archaeologists employed by Nationalmuseet had as their main task to register and protect ruins, and for that purpose their methods were adequate. Later archaeologists have wanted to use the written presentations of their excavations as sources for research, and from that perspective their work has been criticised. The excavators only took notes and made drawings which they needed for their own publications. They did not see it as their task to create material which could be useful for future generations.[35] Excavated material was to a limited degree brought back to Nationalmuseet in Copenhagen. From Gardar very little of the original documentation from the 1926 excavation exists today.[36] Roussell excavated Hvalsey in 1935, but he never wrote a monograph on it; he published only what he needed to verify his hypotheses on house types in his PhD from 1941.[37] The Nationalmuseum archaeologist Knud Krogh in 1974 and 1975 made several smaller excavations which are not documented anywhere.[38]

6 *Introduction*

The lack of preserved empirical material and documentation often makes it impossible to check the conclusions of the excavators, and in all scientific work such control should always be possible. Archaeologists who today want to raise new and different problems cannot do this because the excavator only left material which was relevant to problems which interested him.[39] Skaaning Høegsberg wrote his master thesis about Gardar and complained that Nørlund's monograph had to be his main source. Later archaeologists know which material Nørlund chose to use in his monograph, but not what he left out. They often have no alternative but to accept Nørlund's conclusions.[40]

Nationalmuseet in this period did its best to keep foreign archaeologists out of Greenland. In 1925, an American group applied to Nationalmuseet for permission to carry out excavations in Greenland. The application was rejected with the explanation that "our Norwegian friends" might apply for a similar permission.[41] Nationalmuseum archaeologists sought parallels in Iceland which up to 1944 was Danish, or stressed Norse Greenland's differentness, instead of discussing obvious Norwegian parallels.[42]

The result of these self-imposed limitations was that "Norse Greenland archaeology came to be a field open only to a handful of people. This allowed the research tradition to fall hopelessly behind the development in Scandinavian archaeology".[43] Archaeological stratigraphy was known and practised in most other Danish digs from the 1930s. "While the radiocarbon revolution swept over world archaeology ... the archaeology of Norse Greenland remained in theoretical and methodological backwaters".[44]

The large excavations organised by Nørlund and Roussell in the 1930s were made public in comprehensive editions, which are still used by scholars seeking empirical material. This tradition fell into decline in the following years. Christian Vebæk who was then the leading Norse Greenland archaeologist at Nationalmuseet, published results from Vatnahverfi excavations in a monograph in 1943,[45] and in the following 25 years he excavated a large number of Norse sites, but only published his results in conference papers and popular journals. Unpublished notes were organised into short monographs immediately before his death in 1994 with the help of his colleagues.[46] One gets the impression that money was readily available for excavations in Greenland, but that it was more important to demonstrate activity rather than to produce scientific knowledge.

Baltzer Heide (Århus University) is less critical of the early Nationalmuseum archaeologists than Skaaning Høegsberg (Århus University) and McGovern (CUNY):

> People may think what they want about the state-controlled archaeology which was to a certain extent practiced on Greenland through the Nationalmuseum in the 20th century. But it was one of the reasons why not only many excavations were organised, but even more important, we have many published excavations.[47]

When politicians want something done, they will grant money. But money alone cannot create scientific quality.

In this period the "find the stone wall and follow it" method was also common in Norway. What made the situation in Greenland particularly grave was that all the most valuable sites were attacked at once.

Archaeology was a latecomer among the subjects taught at universities. To my knowledge none of those who participated in excavations in Greenland before 1960 held degrees in archaeology. The criticism referred to in this section comes with the advantage of hindsight, formulated by scholars with a better education and who have benefitted from the academic freedom of research at universities.

The university tradition enters Norse Greenland archaeology from the 1970s

The first to break the Nationalmuseum's monopoly in Greenland research was Helge Ingstad with his book *Landet under leidarstjernen* from 1959.[48] He showed that the environment which the Norse left in western and northern Norway resembled the conditions which they met in Greenland. Ingstad had grown up in western Norway and could "read" the landscape with the eyes of a Norwegian coastal peasant.[49] He held a university degree in law, but not in archaeology or history.

Ingstad's next book *I vesterveg til Vinland* (1965) presented a world sensation. He and his wife Anne Stine Ingstad found in 1959 a Norse site from ca. AD 1000 at the northern tip of Newfoundland. He had used the Icelandic *Saga of Eirik the Red* and *The Greenlanders' saga* as sailing guides from Norse Greenland to the region which the sagas named "Vinland". Historians have always used sagas about Norwegian kings and Icelandic chieftains living after ca. 1130 as historical sources. But literary scholars around 1960 claimed that sagas about Icelanders who had lived before ca. 1050 (*Islendingasögur*) could be read as fiction only. Ingstad showed that even these sagas could be used as historical sources after having been submitted to source criticism.[50]

Helge Ingstad managed to convince Canadian authorities that an international team of archaeologists led by his wife Anne Stine Ingstad were the right ones to organise the excavations.[51] She was *magister* in Nordic Archaeology from the University of Oslo[52] and belonged to the first generation who was educated in Nordic archaeology at a university. In 1977 she published a monograph on the excavations in Newfoundland, which was accepted as a doctoral thesis at the University of Oslo.[53]

The new university archaeologists had as standard practice that when excavating important sites, part of the site should be left untouched. They knew that archaeological methods improved rapidly and it was therefore important to make it possible for future archaeologists to practice new methods. Anne Stine Ingstad followed this practice. When she returned to the site in 1975, she learnt that the Newfoundland representatives of the Canadian Directorate of Cultural Heritage (Parks Canada) had excavated the remaining parts. They had used the same methods and arrived at the same conclusions as Ingstad.[54]

8 Introduction

Thereafter, Nationalmuseet in Copenhagen became more open to cooperating with universities in America and Norway on Greenland. Professor Thomas McGovern of the City University of New York was invited to participate in the "Inuit-Norse Project" 1976–1977.[55] His influence did much to bring Norse Greenland archaeology to the fore with international debate in the 1980s and 1990s.[56] According to McGovern, the Norse peasants brought with them to Greenland some rigid ideas of how the natural environment should be exploited, but their practices were in the long run not sustainable.[57] He has been the main advocate for an "ecological crisis" on Norse Greenland. McGovern's special field is the analysis of animal bones. He is not schooled in social analyses, and he has a problematic relationship with written sources, partly because his knowledge of Scandinavian languages is limited.[58]

The Norwegian archaeologist Christian Keller was invited to participate in a Nordic project during 1974–1977, which was led by the Nationalmuseum archaeologist Knud Krogh and concerned settlement and vegetation in the Qorlortup valley behind Brattahlid.[59] In Norway there has been comprehensive research on *saeters* and Keller made the methods available to Greenland Norse archaeology.[60] In his PhD from Oslo he described the function and chronology of different church types on a safer empirical basis than had been done so far.[61]

Natural sciences in Norse Greenland scholarship from the 1970s

A major trend in archaeology in recent decades has been the proliferation of new methods borrowed from the natural sciences. The scientist who developed the radiocarbon (14C) method for dating received the Nobel Prize in 1960, and in the following period it became a standard tool for archaeologists.[62] It was used to date Greenlandic archaeological finds in the first part of the 1990s at the GUS excavations. As far as I can see, this was the first time it had been used.[63]

Bent Fredskild initiated a series of studies of variations in vegetation and climate, analysing pollen in lakes and bogs.[64] Drilling out samples from the inland ice made it possible to measure changing temperatures. Layers at the bottom of the fjords were analysed to verify hypotheses about temperatures, ocean currents, winds and the vegetation along the shores.[65]

Analyses of 13C isotopes in excavated human bones can measure what percentage of a human's protein consumption had been from "marine food", which on Norse Greenland was fish, seal, walrus and whales. The first analysis was contained in Niels Lynnerup's PhD in medicine from 1995, published in 1998.[66]

The basic method in all science is to formulate two or more hypotheses and then analyse which of them are best supported by the available empirical material. The proliferation of new methods and results from many sciences make it problematic to practise this ideal. Nobody understands or can compare the sources of error in all these analyses. Often the archaeologist who knows the total material best, will ask natural scientists to produce empirical material which is relevant to the hypothesis that interests the archaeologist the most, in our case often a deteriorating climate. This will concentrate the debate on ecological problems.

Introduction 9

Contributions from the natural sciences have made our picture of Norse Greenland richer in detail. Falsifying old and new hypotheses has become more demanding. But the new methods have not changed the previous basic understanding of Norse society.

The present dominance of the ecological model

Since the 1970s interest in Norse Greenland has been greatly inspired by the contemporary political debate on climate change. Scholars have connected history and politics by claiming that Norse Greenland and other North Atlantic communities had serious ecological problems after ca. 1250 due to falling temperatures and an exploitation of resources which was not sustainable. Similar developments are today taking place globally. Lessons can be learnt from medieval Greenland on how to meet similar crises in the future on a global level. Funding has therefore been readily available for advocates of the "ecological model" who make such claims.

The Leverhulme Trust has been particularly generous with funding for such projects, and scholars at the City University of New York are important beneficiaries.[67] The central person has been Professor McGovern. His research on the North Atlantic islands seems to be largely funded by the Leverhulme Trust, and he argues indirectly in his scholarly publications for more funding: "Thanks to major support from the Leverhulme trust and NSF"; and "Thanks to sustained funding support and sustained international collaboration we are now in a position to better identify common patterns and local variability in a surprisingly flexible and adaptable set of Norse Atlantic island economies".[68] McGovern's 35 years of cooperation with Scandinavian scholars has made him change opinion on central points, but for that he should thank them and not the Leverhulme Trust!

In an article from 2007 McGovern and two co-authors presented a large number of hypotheses for how Norse Greenland theoretically may have developed from beginning to end. But they do not even try to verify the hypotheses. The article from 2007 ends with vague, unverified hypotheses where climate is the first element mentioned.[69]

In an even later article from 2011 McGovern claimed that a long-term fall in temperatures created significant problems for "domestic mammal herding, caribou hunting and the hunt for non-migratory seals".[70] The natural scientist Jarred Diamond in his book *Collapse* (1977) gave the most extreme version of the "environmental crisis hypothesis". He is inspired by McGovern, who in the mentioned article from 2011 wrote that "Diamond's account now appears not so much wrong as overdue simple". In 2007 and 2011 McGovern still adhered to the ecological crisis theory.

In 2012 six leading archaeologists from Scotland, America, Denmark, Iceland and Norway claimed that Norse Greenlanders in the warm period AD 985–1200 developed practices in food production which enabled them to adapt to the Greenland environment.[71] From the end of the 13th century, temperatures fell and the climatic variations became more dramatic. The Norse tried to compensate by

10 *Introduction*

eating more seal. These claims are presented as unverified hypotheses about what probably "would have" happened "if" the deterioration were sufficiently serious. "Although the end of the Western Settlement is not completely understood, a likely proximate cause was isolation combined with late winter subsistence failure, plausibly connected to climate change".[72] Relations to the Inuit are mentioned in a short paragraph as "sporadic conflict with the maritime adapted Thule Inuit".[73] The article ends in the traditional way by claiming that:

> Surviving climate change is a current cultural, economic, and technological challenge and one that the Norse Greenlanders met for nearly 500 years . . . Norse Greenland may serve to broaden the perspectives and knowledge base of modern planners seeking sustainable futures in a contemporary world affected by rapid climate change and the historical conjunctures of economic stress and culture conflict.

The last contribution to the debate is Christian Koch Madsen's PhD thesis from 2014. It is basically a quantitative analysis of ruins and he claims that the number of farmsteads in the Eastern Settlement started to shrink after 1250 because of lower temperatures and "the effect of the deterioration of the vegetation surrounding their farmsteads".[74] But this does not explain a "complete collapse". For this he suggests hypotheses which he does not try to verify.[75] Conflict with the Inuit is not one of them.

The present book was finished and sent to relevant academic publishers in June 2016. They passed it on to external readers for evaluation. Electronic manuscripts are easy to share. I found it necessary to make the date when I sent my electronic manuscript to the publishers my date of completion, and I have not included in my discussions works published after that date.[76] None of the Norse Greenland archaeologists had at that time expressed doubts about the "ecological" hypothesis as the main key to understanding the demise of Norse Greenland.

A counter-hypothesis to the ecological model is that the Norse successfully adapted to the Greenland environment and changing climate, and that the final ruin was due to ethnic conflicts. The two hypotheses have never been confronted on the basis of available empirical material. This will be done for the first time in Chapters 5 and 6 of this book.

3 My contribution

Norse Greenland archaeology has in the last century produced valuable results on Norse architecture and housing. The main task of the Nationalmuseum is to register and protect the ruins; this priority is therefore natural. I have not included a chapter on housing; the main challenges in Norse Greenland scholarship lie elsewhere. Today Norse Greenland scholarship has stagnated because the archaeologists are unable to break out of the barriers created by the "ecological model". Historical scholarship has methods which can further progress the research tradition.

Introduction 11

The Norwegian background has so far been neglected. But Norse Greenlanders received their main overseas impulses from the Norwegian Atlantic and North Sea coasts, in some cases via Iceland. The immigrants carried this know-how with them, and it largely determined how they organised their society in Greenland. Knowledge about the Norwegian background promises to deepen our understanding.

Written sources provide knowledge which is not available through archaeology, on chronology, administration, jurisdiction, armed conflicts, religious practices, shipping and relations with the Inuit. Archaeologists use written sources but in a descriptive and superficial manner. A close reading combining several types of sources using modern saga criticism and other methods available to schooled historians, promise to generate new results.

Confronting hypotheses is the basic method in all scientific work. The archaeologists have not made systematic efforts to practise it because the "ecological model" has been used exclusively to the detriment of alternative hypotheses. The ecological model has in practice been used as a "premise" and not as an "hypothesis". Alternative hypotheses are sometimes mentioned, only to be rejected without methodological discussions. Accepted methodology demands that a hypothesis is accepted as verified if it is better supported by the empirical material than the counter-hypothesis. New empirical material or better scientific methods can change the outcome of the verification process.

Sociological methods seek to understand the different fields of activity in a society in context: agriculture, household work, trade, political power, church organisation, religious mentalities and secular culture. Sociological methods are particularly important in analyses of pre-state societies where there is no state which creates ties between these different social fields.

The present book is an overdue revision of the current understanding of Norse Greenland, and I look forward to a discussion of its conclusions with established archaeologists.

Notes

1 Population figures will be discussed in Chapter 1, pp. 32–35.
2 Bruun 1918 (b), p. 132.
3 The earliest cartographic work where this strait is shown is from 1592 (*Danish Arctic Expeditions 1605 to 1620*, volume I, p. 156).
4 Egede/Bobé, p. 33, date 24 October 1722.
5 Egede/Bobé, p. 92.
6 Egede/Bobé, p. 95, date 15 August 1723.
7 Egede/Bobé, p. 93.
8 Egede/Bobé, pp. 96–97.
9 Lund Jensen 2014, p. 40 says he turned when he came to Sermersoq.
10 Egede/Bobé, pp. 97–98.
11 Egede/Bobé, p. 103.
12 Egede/Bobé, pp. 210, 222, 225 and 226.
13 Eggers 1794, p. 295; Holm 1883, p. 122; Steenstrup 1886, pp. 32–33.
14 Holm and Garde 1889, pp 142–143.

15 GHM I, p. IV.
16 Holm 1883, pp. 57–145.
17 Holm 1883, pp. 64 and 69.
18 Holm 1883, p. 70.
19 Bruun 1896, pp. 171–495.
20 Bruun 1896, p. 186
21 Bruun 1896, pp. 202, 287, 299, 324, 347, 351, cf. 492.
22 Schirmer 1886.
23 Jonsson 1899, pp. 267–329.
24 This information can be found in any Danish or Norwegian encyclopedia, for example *Den store danske encyklopædi. Danmarks nationalleksikon*, Copenhagen 2001, entry word "Østgrønlandssagen" and *Store norske leksikon*, Oslo 2005, entry word "Grønlandssaken".
25 http://natmus.dk/besoeg-museerne/nationalmuseet/udstillinger/danmarks-middelalder-og-renaessance/danmarks-middelalder-og-renaessance/nordbosamlingen/.
26 Herjolvsnes: Nørlund 1924; Gardar: Nørlund and Roussell 1930; Brattahlid: Nørlund and Stenberger 1934.
27 Sandnes: Roussell 1936; survey of all known ruins: Roussell 1941. Roussell also excavated Hvalsey.
28 Cf. Vebæk, all dates, in the Bibliography.
29 Roussell 1936, p. 10; Nørlund 1942, pp. 139–141, English translation, pp. 146–148; Mathiassen 1936(b), pp. 84–84. Mathiassen is not clear on whether he thought the Inuit destroyed only the Western Settlement, or both.
30 McGovern 1979, p. 35.
31 Skaaning Høegsberg 2005, p. 21.
32 McGovern 1979, p. 36
33 McGovern 1979, p. 38.
34 Skaaning Høegsberg 2005, pp. 21–22.
35 Skaaning Høegsberg 2005, pp. 6–7.
36 Skaaning Høegsberg 2005, p. 85.
37 Skaaning Høegsberg 2005, p. 127.
38 Skaaning Høegsberg 2005, p. 17.
39 Skaaning Høegsberg 2007, pp. 85 and 95.
40 Skaaning Høegsberg 2005, p. 145.
41 Archives of the Danish Nationalmuseum, 2nd department. Here quoted after Keller 1989, p. 104.
42 Keller 1989, pp. 103–105.
43 Keller 1989, p. 105.
44 McGovern 1979, pp. 39–40.
45 Vebæk 1943, pp. 1–119.
46 Vebæk 1991(b), 1992, 1993.
47 Heide 2012 volume 1, p. 184.
48 English translation *Land under the Pole Star*, London 1966.
49 An example of this is his discovery of the irrigation system at Gardar (cf. Chapter 5, pp. 254–255).
50 See also Chapter 1, pp. 19–20.
51 Solberg 2002, p. 33.
52 This degree was on a higher level than today's Master's, but lower than a PhD.
53 Ingstad, A. S. 1977.
54 Ingstad, B. 2010, pp. 328–330; cf. Wallace 2000, p. 208.
55 McGovern 1979, p. 1; Keller 1989, pp. 98–99 and pp. 102–103.
56 Keller 1989, p. 103.
57 McGovern 1979, chapter 4; McGovern 1985; McGovern 2000, pp. 338–389.
58 This makes him repeat incorrect translations; McGovern 1979, p. 225.

59 Keller 1989, pp. 96–97.
60 Cf. Chapter 5, pp. 256–260.
61 Keller 1989, pp. 200–205.
62 Wikipedia, entry word "Radiocarbon dating".
63 Cf. McGovern 1979, p. 39.
64 Fredskild 1973, 1982, 1992.
65 Cf. Chapter 5, p. 269; Mikkelsen et al. 2001, pp. 67–68.
66 Lynnerup 1998, pp. 44–50, cf. pp. 7 and 129.
67 Dugmore et al. 2012, p. 3662.
68 McGovern 2011, pp. 292–293
69 McGovern et al. 2007a, pp. 12–36.
70 McGovern 2011, p. 299.
71 Dugmore et al. 2012, p. 3660
72 Dugmore et al. 2012, p. 3661
73 Dugmore et al. 2012, p. 3662
74 Madsen 2014(a), pp. 4, 8, 32, 36, 39 and 255.
75 Madsen 2014(a), p. 255.
76 There is one exception. Lisbeth Imer published in 2017 a useful catalogue of rune inscriptions excavated in Greenland, with extensive and informative comments. I have added references to her book in my use of the runic material. She does not discuss the ecological adaptation and final ruin of the Norse settlement.

1 The initial settlement in AD 985/6

In AD 985 the Norse language was spoken by the whole or parts of the population in what is today Norway, Iceland, Greenland, Faroes, Shetland, Orkney and the Hebrides. This created a cultural community where the main tie was the common language. If a clan or an individual in Norway or Iceland had to emigrate for some reason, it was natural for them to choose a country where their own language was spoken and where they also might have relatives. Practically all sources which are relevant to the initial Norse settlement of Greenland were written by Icelanders. They had personal ties to Greenlanders and understood the social mechanisms there. It is natural to start this chapter with a discussion of how reliable Icelandic sagas are as sources of the early history of Greenland.

1 The Icelandic sagas as historical sources

Islendingabok and Landnámabok

The oldest written descriptions of the initial colonisation of Greenland were authored by the Icelandic priest Ari Thorgilsson Frodi (1068–1148) in two books, *Islendingabok* and *Landnámabok*.

Ari built on oral sources, and he tells us from whom his oral information about Greenland has been received: "this was told to Thorkell Gellison when he was in Greenland by a person who followed Eirik Raudi from Iceland".[1] Thorkell was Ari's uncle. After his return to Iceland, Thorkell told Ari about Greenland.[2] The oral information had been transmitted from a person who had been part of Eirik Raudi's initial settlement group, to Thorkell Gellison and then to Ari who put it in writing. Ari's *Islendingabok* has been preserved; it is short but reliable.

Ari also wrote the first version of *Landnámabok* and even included sections on Greenland. *Landnámabok* was further developed and expanded in new versions in the 12th and 13th centuries. It was transcribed several times, and it is not known how much of it was composed in Ari's time. The oldest extant manuscripts, Sturlubok and Hauksbok, were written in the decades around 1300. Factual information connected to names and places in these manuscripts probably belonged to the oldest version and should be considered as reliable.

Other information may have been fiction and must be evaluated individually. The Vinland sagas expanded the information in *Landnámabok* on Greenland, adding information from others.

As long as the oral tradition on the initial settlement remained in Greenland, it should be seen as reliable, since there would be many persons who could confirm or correct what was being said. The person who told the story had also participated in the first emigration fleet. When Thorkell transferred this information to Iceland, it started a new life there as a written tradition. What Ari wrote about the initial settlement should be seen as the general opinion in Greenland when Thorkell stayed there. When was that?

Thorkell was born in Iceland ca. 1030. If he had talked to a person who arrived in Greenland in AD 985, Thorkell must have visited Greenland early in his life, ca. 1050. He returned to Iceland and lived there as an elderly man until ca. 1090. Ari would then be ca. 20 years old when he listened to his uncle's tales.[3] This is the hypothesis I find to be the most verifiable as it includes all extant information in a coherent narrative. Ari's extant *Islendingabok* is not dated but is assumed to have been written ca. 1130.

The main point is that Ari's narrative is based on an oral transfer of information from Eirik Raudi's time where all transmitters are known and where the resulting narrative was controlled by the general oral opinion in Greenland less than a century after the events.

Who wrote the Vinland sagas and for what purpose?

The initial settlement in Greenland is given its most extensive description in the two so called "Vinland sagas". Modern philologists have dubbed them "Eirik Raudi's saga" (*Eiriks saga Rauda*) and "The Greenlanders' saga" (*Groenlendinga saga*). Many have pointed out that these names are misleading since both take place in Greenland as well as Vinland, and Eirik Raudi is an important character in both.

Philologists agree that both sagas were composed ca. 1220–1250, but the year is not important in our context. It has been discussed whether the author of Eirik Raudi's saga knew and possibly owned The Greenlanders' saga or the other way round. The arguments both ways are weak.[4] Narratives about the past were widely disseminated orally in the Middle Ages; only the tip of the iceberg was written down in extant manuscripts. The simplest way of explaining similarities and differences between the two Vinland sagas is that the authors built on separate oral traditions. This was supplemented with written sources which were available to them. The philologist Sigurdur Nordal claimed that "These two sagas ... are so independent of each other that the most natural explanation seems to be that they were written at about the same time but in different parts of the country". He arrives at this conclusion by comparing details in the two saga accounts. The historian of literature Jonas Kristjansson seems to accept Nordal's view.[5] Handwritten manuscripts could remain in a family's or lineage's possession for decades without outsiders reading them.

One cannot be sure whether the authors had visited Greenland. *Fostbroedra saga* is another of the *Islendigasögur*, and part of the action takes place in Greenland ca. AD 1020. The author here assumes that it took a couple of hours to row from a chieftain's farm called Langanes in Einarsfjord to another chieftain's farm Brattahlid in Eiriksfjord in the middle of the night. An unusually large rowing-boat was used with room for the owner Thordis, her son and 15 servants, and the saga author relates that they rowed in the same boat all the way. The editor of the saga in *Islenzk Fornrit* points out that this demonstrates ignorance of the geography in this central part of Norse Greenland, since this would only have been possible if there had been a canal through the isthmus between the two fjords near Gardar, and such a canal did not exist. The story had been transmitted in oral tradition for 200 years, and the Icelander who wrote it down ca. 1220–1250 did not have a clear picture of the landscape.[6]

Why were the Vinland sagas written? "The Greenlanders' saga" says that travelling to Vinland gave both riches and honour (*at su ferd thykkir bædi god til fjar ok virdingar*),[7] and the Norwegian *King's Mirror* says that people voyaged from Norway to Greenland for three reasons: honour, gain and curiosity.[8] The main motive for writing the Vinland sagas must have been to give honour to those who had participated.

Eiriks saga Rauda claims that Vinland was discovered by chance by Leiv Eiriksson on a return voyage to Greenland from a visit to Norway. He lost his way and found a land where there grew wild wheat and grapes, but finally found his way to his father Eirik Raudi on Brattahlid. Eirik Raudi and another of his sons, Thorstein Eiriksson, next attempted to explore the new land, but contrary winds prevented them from reaching it.[9] The third expedition was organised by the Icelander Thorfinn Karlsefni who visited Eirik on Brattahlid, and there married Gudrid, the widow of Eirik's son. It was a large-scale expedition of 3 ships, 160 people and many domestic animals. The attempt was abandoned because of the permanent threat from the native population. Thorfinn Karlsefni's is the only planned expedition which reached Vinland described in "Eirik the Red's saga".

"Eirik the Red's saga" covers 43 pages in Islenzk Fornrit IV; of these 16 describe Thorfinn Karlsefni's Vinland journey. Thorfinn and Gudrid returned from Greenland to Iceland after their journey to Vinland. "Thorfinn had many and honourable descendants", says the saga. Among them were three Icelandic bishops. There are several indications that the saga was written by a cleric, the most likely hypothesis being that one of Gudrid and Thorfinn's clerical descendants in Iceland was the author, drawing on oral traditions in the family. The saga was evidently written to increase the honour of both Thorfinn and Gudrid.

"Eirik the Red's saga" was composed ca. 1220–1250. The oldest extant manuscript was copied 1330–1334 by the Icelandic judge Hauk Erlendsson into a codex which belonged to him and which today is called Hauksbok.[10] He was another of Thorfinn and Gudrid's descendants.[11] He also transcribed *Landnámabok* into Hauksbok, and here he gave Thorfinn Karlsefni the honour of having "found Vinland the good" (*Karlsefnis er fann Vinland hit goda*).[12] "Eirik the Red's saga" in Hauksbok is called "The saga of Thorfinn Karlsefni".[13] This is likely to have been the saga's original name. The next extant transcript is found in *Skálholtsbók* from ca. 1420, and here the title is *Eiriks saga Rauda*, which has remained its title ever since. The reason for this change of title probably was that Karlsefni's descendants between 1340 and 1420 became less prominent in Iceland. Eirik Raudi and his descendants attracted more interest.[14]

"The Greenlanders' saga" was also composed in the 13th century, but no transcript of the saga as a whole has survived. The compiler of the codex *Flateyjarbok* from ca. 1390 copied sections of the 13th-century version at two different places in his own account.[15] Modern editors have assumed that by combining the sections which contain information on Greenland and Vinland in the *Flateyjarbok*, they can reconstruct the 13th-century saga. The resulting narrative is printed in IF IV, pp. 241–269 with the modern title *Groenlendinga saga*. We do not know whether all parts of the original saga were copied in the *Flateyjarbok*, or whether some of the sections on Greenland and Vinland copied in *Flateyjarbok* are taken from other accounts. The compiler in 1390 evidently had access to a collection of manuscripts, some of which were relevant for the history of Greenland and Vinland. He states that a more detailed narrative about Eirik Raudi's early struggles in Iceland exists in *Sögu Eiriks*.[16] *Groenlendinga saga* as printed in IF and other modern editions may be a shortened version of a lost "Eirik's saga" (*Sögu Eiriks*) from the 13th century. This means that the sagas today called "Eirik Raudi's saga" and "The Greenlanders' saga" originally may have been called "Thorfinn Karlsefni's saga" and "Eirik's saga".

The main honourable achievements described in "The Greenlanders' saga" are:

- Eirik Raudi discovers and settles West Greenland.
- Bjarni Herjolvsson from a different Greenlandic clan discovers Vinland by chance.
- Leiv Eiriksson leads the first planned expedition to Vinland.
- Thorvaldr Eiriksson leads the second planned expedition to Vinland.
- Thorfinn Karlsefni leads the third planned expedition to Vinland. He is connected to the Brattahlid clan through his wife Gudrid who is Thorstein Eiriksson's widow.
- Freydis Eiriksdottir leads the fourth planned expedition to Vinland. In "Eirik Raudi's saga" she is called the illegitimate daughter of Eirik.[17] She is portrayed in a very negative manner: she murdered two Icelanders and their crew in Vinland.[18]

The core narrative of "The Greenlanders' saga" calls attention to Eirik Raudi and his four children Leiv, Thorvaldr, Thorstein and Freydis who belonged to the "Brattahlid clan".

The final chapter of the "Greenlanders' saga" says that "Karlsefni gave a more complete account than anybody else about these voyages, some of which have now been told".[19] Karlsefni was first in the chain of oral transmitters on which the author of the 13th century relied, but the author knew that there was more to be told. This confirms what he wrote earlier that more on this subject was to be found in *Sögu Eiriks*. What today is named "Eirik Raudi's saga" focuses more on Karlsefni's achievements than "The Greenlanders' saga"; it is therefore probable that both sagas originated from him.

Karlsefni and his wife Gudrid seem to have brought the main oral account of the Vinland and Greenland voyages to Iceland, and there it took different shapes in different social environments. One of the extant versions focuses on Karlsefni, the other on Eirik Raudi's children. Gudrid first marriage was to Eirik Raudi's son and her second to Thorfinn Karlsefni. Both Vinland sagas give very positive descriptions of Eirik Raudi, Thorfinn Karlsefni and his wife Gudrid. The heroic pictures painted of heads of lineages must be taken into account when using all sagas as historic sources.[20]

But this must also have motivated the saga authors to tell a story which corresponded to what the potential readers held to be true. The aim was to present their own ancestors as honourable, and then their achievements had to be real and not fiction. The narrative and its social environment must have corresponded to the reality as understood on Iceland at the time of writing ca. 1220–1250. The main accounts in the Vinland sagas are realistic by modern standards; the supernatural events are short stories which can be removed without the main narrative losing its logical progress.

Categories of sagas which are relevant for Norse Greenland

The basic principle in source criticism is to compare information from different and independent sources. Historians will not pick out a coherent narrative from a longer saga and ask whether this section is true from beginning to end. They will pick out isolated information about a person, a building, rites, customs, institutions, beliefs or objects, and compare it to other information about the same phenomenon. If two or more sources confirm one other, and are not contradicted by a third source, the information is considered as reliable. Much relevant information found in sagas stands alone. How should such information be used?

The sagas which are relevant in our context were written by clerics and lay magnates in the period ca. 1120–1350, but their subject matter includes events as far back as the 9th century. Sagas are categorised according to when events described in the saga took place. "Sagas of contemporaries" (*samtidssagaer*) describe events in the period 1100–1350 and were mostly written less than two generations after the events. These are reliable sources similar to English and continental chronicles. Often independent sources will be available for comparison. *Groenlendinga tháttr*, *Sturlunga saga*, *Sverris saga*, *Hákonar saga Hákonarsonar* and the youngest parts of *Morkinskinna* and *Heimskringla* belong to this category.

The other main category of sagas describes events taking place in the period ca. 995–1100. Here the stories were transmitted in an oral tradition for 100–300 years before being written down. During these centuries the stories were transformed in the way oral narratives usually are. The bulk of such sagas are Icelandic family sagas (*Islendingasögur*); in our context the Vinland sagas and *Fostbroedra saga* are most relevant. The author of *Groenlendinga saga* mentions through which persons his oral account has been transmitted and he assures us that the first oral transmitter Thorfinn Karlsefni was a reliable person. The fact that the saga author gives his readers source criticism of this kind, gives confidence that he did his best to describe the past as it was, even if the information had been transmitted several times in an oral tradition. But even if the aim were realism, it cannot be trusted that their knowledge was adequate to achieve it.

Many king's sagas also have narratives going back before 1100. In the introduction to his history of the ancient kings of Norway (Heimskringla), Snorri Sturluson (d. 1241) describes his methods. He attributed highest reliability to oral skaldic poetry composed immediately after the events and later transmitted in oral tradition. The metric form with its stringent rules was a guarantee of reliable transmission. But the bulk of the saga authors' information came from oral prose narratives transmitted from generation to generation. Snorri relied mostly on stories transmitted through men and women whom he could identify and who had possessed "great wisdom and good memory". He names men and women who had communicated reliable information in an oral tradition from the 10th century down to his own time of writing, ca. 1230.

How reliable was the oral tradition on which the saga authors built?

"The problem is that it is not possible to distinguish between what is fiction, and what is reality [in the Vinland sagas]", wrote the Nationalmuseum archaeologist Knud Krogh in 1982.[21] Was he right?

The most spectacular confirmation of realism in the Vinland sagas was Helge Ingstad's localisation of the Norse settlement at *L'Anse aux Meadows*. He found it using the Vinland sagas as a sailing guide from Greenland to Newfoundland. His "independent source" was the coastal landscape. Information about this sailing route had lived in an oral tradition for a couple of centuries when the saga authors wrote it down ca. 1220–1250.

The sagas name farms along the Greenland fjords and coast. Archaeologists have identified the ruins of several of them. The Vinland sagas date the first settlement in Greenland to AD 985, which corresponds to the results of the archaeological excavations.

The information that the Vinland explorers came to a place where they found wild grapes, in Norse called *vinber*, has been met with scepticism and contributed to undermine confidence in the Vinland sagas.[22] But the priest Adam of Bremen also wrote ca. 1070 that Vinland was so named because there were wild grapes there from which wine can be made.[23] Adam had visited the court of the Danish king Svend Estridsson and obtained his information there.[24] This was only 60–70 years after the events and at least 150 years before the Vinland sagas were written. There was an oral tradition about this which both Adam and the saga authors knew. A close reading of the two "Vinland sagas" shows that "Vinland" is a name for the area south of Labrador (Markland), a large area without clear boundaries which included the Gulf of St. Lawrence. Reports from the first European explorers in the 16th century confirm that wild grapes at that time grew around the Gulf of St. Lawrence in the Quebec area, and it is perfectly possible that the Norse Greenlanders found them there.[25]

The kings' sagas give a detailed description of King Harald Hardrádi's career as military commander in the service of the Byzantine emperor in his youth ca. 1034–1044. A contemporary Byzantine aristocrat gave a description of Harald's career from his point of view, and the two descriptions can be compared. They agree on Harald's position as leader of the Varangian guard. The wars and other events in which he participated can be identified. But the saga authors often misunderstood place and events and exaggerate Harald's achievements.[26] The narrative had been transmitted in an oral tradition for ca. 180 years when the saga authors inserted it into their sagas.

Criteria can be found for which information is most likely to survive in oral transmission. If oral information is connected to concrete objects like a landscape, a town, a building which was still standing, or concrete events like a battle, it is more likely to be remembered. Narratives which are disconnected from the main action are likely to be less reliable and so are conversations. Events involving famous people are often well preserved in oral tradition, but the chronology between these events is less reliable. Chronology is often unimportant in oral tradition and may be added as an organising principle when the narrative is written down.

The sagas which are relevant in our context have an ambition to tell a story which has taken place, and great events, persons and institutions can be trusted to be real. The details may also be real, but here conscientious source criticism is necessary. Even detailed events which never took place can be interesting for historians because they demonstrate the author's and his audience's understanding of the world which surrounded them. But before going one step further accepting that an event described in a saga really took place, a stricter source criticism has to be applied.

Sagas used as "narratives" or "remnants"

The Vinland sagas and other sagas used in this book were written in the 13th and 14th centuries about events taking place in the 10th to 12th centuries. At the time of writing Norse Greenland still existed, and Icelandic saga authors would know how this society normally worked in their own age. It was unavoidable that the saga author's knowledge about contemporary Greenland influenced his narrative about events 200 years earlier.

Historians will therefore use the sagas both as "narratives" about what happened in the 10th to 12th centuries, but also as "remnants" giving information about social relations in Greenland at the saga author's time. Source criticism has to include an effort to distinguish between the two time layers in the text. This has to be done by comparing to other sources and by analysing the saga as a whole.

2 The first Greenlanders

When did they go?

Ari Frodi (1068–1148) was the first Norse author to mention Greenland, and he wrote that Eirik Raudi occupied and settled Eiriksfjord on Western Greenland "14 or 15 years before Iceland was christened", that is AD 986 or 985.[27] The two Vinland sagas were written in the 13th century, and both say AD 985,[28] *Eyrbyggja saga* says AD 986.[29] The oldest extant Icelandic Annals were written in the 1280s, and they say that "Eirik Raudi voyaged to Greenland and settled Eiriksfjord" in AD 986.[30]

Landnámabok is preserved in the Sturlubok version[31] which says AD 985 and the Hauksbok version[32] which says AD 984.[33] The last date of 984 stands alone and is probably due to a copying error. All other dates seem to be based on Ari who gives the two alternatives of AD 985 or 986. I can see no reason to prefer the one before the other, but the dating in the Vinland sagas of AD 985 is used by most authors. For practical reasons I have chosen to use the same date in this book.

The Vinland sagas give a schedule for the settlement.[34]

AD 981 summer: Eirik Raudi leaves Iceland to explore Greenland

AD 982 summer: exploration continued

AD 983 summer: exploration continued

AD 984 summer: return to Iceland

AD 985 summer: Eirik accompanied by 14 ships settles in Greenland

Some of those who left Iceland with Eirik Raudi in AD 985 settled in the Western Settlement.[35] This information is confirmed by radiocarbon dates:

> The most comprehensive archaeological excavations in the last decades have been done at a Norse farm dubbed "The farm under the sand" (GUS) located in the Western Settlement. Claus Malmros in 1991 dated the first house there to ca. 1005, and in view of the large margins of error for radiocarbon dates this may include 985.[36] Two samples from the "lower cultural layers" of the "landnáma farm" E17a Narsaq gave the results AD 980–1035 and AD 905–990.[37] The lowest cultural layer at E34 gave a find which was dated to AD 895–1150.[38] Bent Fredskild analysed the vegetation history of the Brattahlid area, and he accepted the date AD 985 for the first *landnám*, but pollen analyses are too approximate to reveal smaller departures from this date.[39] Another analysis concluded that "pollen assemblage from Anavik in the Western Settlement reveals an early date for the *landnám* (ca. AD 1000) comparable with that from Eastern Settlement".[40] For Vatnahverfi "precise dating" using scientific methods confirms that the first Norse settlers arrived "at the end of 10th century". From the start many farms occupied areas which were marginal for agriculture.[41]

Arneborg claims that "there is not full correspondence between the written and archaeological data" on these points but admits that this is only a hypothesis since the archaeological dates have such large margins of error and are few in number.[42]

What motivated them?

When the emigration from Norway to Iceland started ca. AD 870 and to Greenland AD 985, the Norse area consisted of pre-state societies governed by chieftains and petty kings. Each chieftain had clients whom he was responsible for protecting.

The pre-state chieftains frequently feuded with each other. The members of a clan which had been defeated could end up without protection against an aggressive neighbour. This gave them the choice between a humiliating submission or leaving the region. The emergence of a proto-state in Norway in the 10th century increased the pressure on the Norwegian chieftains and their clients. This is the picture given in the earliest description of the emigration from Norway written by Ari Frodi (1068–1148). Chieftains refused to submit to the Norwegian crown, and "many of them fled the country". That was how Iceland, the Faroes and Shetland were settled, and some also went to Orkney and the Hebrides. The main wave of emigration to Iceland started in AD 870 and by AD 930 Iceland was "fully settled" (*albyggt*).[43]

The Icelandic saga authors writing in the period 1130–1300 knew how a pre-state Norse society functioned, not least because in Iceland it had a prolonged life until 1264. Their descriptions of the social mechanisms are realistic even if the individual stories in many cases were more or less fiction. The destiny of Thorolv, Egil Skallagrimsson's uncle, is an example. Thorolv served the Norwegian king but was at the same time an independent chieftain. The king wanted Thorolv to dismiss his retainers and become a soldier in his retinue (*hird*). Thorolv saw this as degradation and refused. The king then dismissed him from his service, and Thorolv returned to his farm. The king now regarded him as a dangerous adversary.[44] He attacked and killed Thorolv at his farm. Thorolv's father and brother took revenge by killing 50 of the king's men. Next they sailed to Iceland with their servants and clients, and Thorolv's brother settled as chieftain on the farm Borg.[45] The story was probably transformed in oral transmission before it was written down, but illustrates how the expanding power of kings made life dangerous for chieftains and their retainers.

The Vinland sagas explain Eirik Raudi's road to Greenland in a similar way. His father was a chieftain on Jæren in Norway. They had to leave because of manslaughter charges, and we should assume this was part of a feud where they ended up as the inferior party. They sailed to Iceland and settled at the farm Drangar. The saga author informs us that at this time Iceland was almost fully settled, which means that Eirik's father did not leave Norway because there was plenty of available land in Iceland. People living close to him at Drangar did not welcome new arrivals. After the death of his father Eirik married and moved to his father-in-law's farm at Haukadal. Here he cleared new land, which we must imagine was inferior to the land his household had left behind in Norway. He again became party to a feud and killed several men. At the local Thing assembly Eirik was sentenced to leave Haukadal and moved to his third location in Iceland. He handed over his high seat pillars to a neighbour, probably as a symbol of submission. When he later demanded to have them returned, he found himself in a new feud, killing two of his opponents, but he again ended up as the inferior party. This time he was outlawed at the Thing assembly and decided to found a new settlement in Greenland.[46]

Modern historians and archaeologists tend to present Eirik as a violent and murderous person. *Landnámabok* and the Vinland sagas open up a different interpretation. Eirik was a rational man who acted according to the norms of his society. He and his father were petty chieftains and had the sense of honour necessary to fulfil their social function. This involved them in blood feuds against superior enemies, but their mentality made it hard for them to submit to the victors. In Norway in the final phase of the Viking age the situation grew worse for such chieftains because of additional pressure from the increasingly powerful kings. Eirik was a chieftain with friends and allies in his feuds in Iceland, and when he finally sailed to Greenland there were 25 ships in the fleet. He evidently was a good network builder and for his contemporaries his revenge murders must have appeared as rational actions showing courage and strength. The details in Eirik's story may not be true, but they illustrate social mechanisms which are confirmed by other sources.

The brothers Thorleif Kimbi and Snorri Thorbrandsson grew up in Alptafjord in Iceland. They had an ancestor who was one of the first settlers in Iceland (*landnámsmadr*), and they were foster-brothers to the powerful Icelandic chieftain Snorri godi (ca. 963–1031).[47] This made them part of the Icelandic elite. They became involved in a feud on Iceland,[48] and as part of the peace agreement the two brothers left Iceland and settled in Greenland.[49] Snorri sailed with Eirik Raudi to Greenland in AD 985 and he "took land" in a Greenland fjord which he named Alptafjord after the fjord he had left in Iceland.[50] The statement that Snorri in Greenland was *landnámsmadr* and "took" Alptafjord, is likely to mean that he functioned as chieftain in that fjord. The two brothers cleared a farm and named it Kimbavágr after the elder brother Thorleif Kimbi who lived there permanently.[51] The younger Snorri seems to have shared one farm in Iceland and another in Greenland with his four brothers, and he travelled between the two countries. In ca. AD 1005 he followed Thorfinn Karlsefni from Iceland via Greenland to Vinland on a ship they owned in common.[52] Snorri's life ended in a skirmish with natives in Vinland.[53]

Another immigrant was Thorbjörn Vivilsson. He had been a respected chieftain[54] in Iceland, and he created a network of friends by inviting them to frequent banquets. But one day he realised that he could no longer afford this generosity, and this meant he would lose his position as chieftain. "I will rather change farmstead than destroy my honour (*soemdinni*). I will rather leave the land than bring dishonour over my lineage (*ætt mina svivirda*)". He sold his farm and bought a ship, and 30 people followed him to Eirik Raudi in Greenland. Eirik gave him the farm Stokkanes in Eiriksfjord, and he became one of Eirik's clients.[55]

24 The initial settlement in AD 985/6

Figure 1.1 Agricultural land at farm E89a, Appendix II map 6.

In the Norse period there was a farm here. The lush vegetation here at the head of the bay and along the shore on the left-hand side is shown by the yellow colour. When the original heather was burned, the new grass would give a good pasture. If it was manured over a long period, the result would be a meadow. Eirk Raudi called the new land Greenland, because he wanted it to have a good name to motivate people to settle there. This picture shows that this name was not only a PR stunt.

Source of photo: Farming in Norse Fjords. Report to the "National Museum of Denmark, Department of Middle Age and Renaissance", Copenhagen, April 2014, p. 36.

Copyright: The National Museum of Denmark.

Not only chieftains but also peasant households fled to Greenland after a feud. The Icelandic brothers, Helgi and Berg, became involved in a serious blood feud. They visited a Norwegian town, probably Bergen or Trondheim, and Berg was murdered on the street there by an enemy from Iceland. It was to be feared that Helgi now could meet a similar end. The captain of their ship arranged room for him on a ship bound for Greenland.

> He lived there and grew up to become a highly respected man. People were sent to Greenland to kill him, but his destiny was to be another. He lost his life on a hunting expedition, and people thought it was a great loss.[56]

This is told in one of the *Islendingasögur* where the action takes place ca. AD 1000, but information about who killed whom, and where people lived, is often reliable. An individual who emigrated from Iceland to Greenland to avoid being killed in a feud is a theme also found in sagas which are pure fiction.[57] In the first part of the 14th century Icelanders must have been familiar with this motive for settling in Greenland.

A peasant household which lost the protection of its chieftain could be forced to move, sometimes in the opposite direction, from Greenland to Norway. Skufr lived at the farm Stokkanes in Eiriksfjord and the chieftain at Brattahlid was his protector. The Icelander Thormod arrived in Greenland to avenge a murder and received help from Skufr and a widow and her son who lived at another farm. Thormod drew his supporters into conflicts with the Brattahlid chieftain. Skufr and the widow lost their protection and had to sell their farms and move to Norway.[58]

In the works of the Nationalmuseum archaeologists the political motives for moving to Greenland are almost absent. Knud Krogh explicitly claims that the motive for emigration to Greenland was not to escape political conflicts, even if this is the impression given by the Icelandic sagas. The real reason was the search for better resources.[59] Other archaeologists are less explicit. They mention the political hypothesis, but they give economic motives more attention. They do not verify or falsify the two hypotheses in a methodologically correct analysis. The archaeologists have never falsified the political hypothesis.[60]

Figure 1.2 Farm E96 in its landscape, Appendix II map 7.

In the foreground was the site of the farm buildings, even if little of the ruins is now shown above ground. Nearest to the photographer was a long house 15 × 12m, possibly the dwelling. Behind it can be seen a darker area with a lusher vegetation, which may have been the farm's meadow. If so the Norse manured it through four centuries. Even today Norse farms can be identified in the landscape by their luxuriant vegetation near the ruins. E96 like most Norse farms had easy access to a fjord. In winter and spring local fjord ice and large ice floes drifting from the North Pole would make sea communications difficult or impossible. This picture was taken in July when coast and fjords had navigable waters even in the Eastern Settlement.

Source of photo: Farming in Norse Fjords. Report to the "National Museum of Denmark, Department of Middle Age and Renaissance", Copenhagen, April 2014. p. 40

Copyright: The National Museum of Denmark.

26 The initial settlement in AD 985/6

The ecological hypothesis has some evidence to speak for it. If a farmer had more than one son, only the eldest could inherit the farm. The younger had to buy or rent a farm elsewhere or cultivate a new one. In the period 800–1349 the population in the Norse[61] region increased, and there must always have been young men on the lookout for a farm. Ari wrote ca. 1130 that Eirik Raudi discovered the land and called it Greenland, because it would "encourage people to go there if it had a good name".[62] "Green" was evidently meant to be understood as "suitable for agriculture". He explored the land for three years before choosing where to settle and took for himself the site which was best suited for cattle farming. Food resources that could be exploited without excessive toil were a precondition if the settlement was to endure, but is it a sufficient explanation? The population of Norway continued to grow until the Black Death in 1349 and in Iceland until 1402, so it was not necessary to leave the country to find farmland for cultivation in AD 985.[63] The written sources indicate that the contemporaries saw available agricultural land as a necessary but not sufficient precondition for moving to Greenland.

Figure 1.3 Ruin of farm E167 in the Vatnahverfi, Appendix II map 6.

A minority of Norse farms lacked direct or short access to the sea. Many of them were in the Vatnahverfi where they on the other hand had access to unlimited pasture in the outfield. On this farm a house for storing goods has been exceptionally well preserved; it measures 7.5 × 5 m. The vegetation in front of the house is particularly lush with willow. This is likely to have been part of the meadow which in the Norse centuries was covered with grass and manured. It is often said that the area where the Norse settled was more fertile when they left than when they arrived. The photos from E96 and E167 provide evidence of this.

Source of photo: Field report to Nationalmuseets Grønlandsforskningscenter, SILA report no. 25. Published by Nationalmuseets Center for Grønlandsforskning, Copenhagen 2007, p. 25.

Copyright: The National Museum of Denmark.

The Norwegian archaeologist Christian Keller claims that the Norse colonisation of Greenland was motivated by a search for export products, in practice walrus tusk.[64] But if priority was to be given to incomes from trade, secure supplies of food and other necessities had to be accessible at markets in return for the money gained from trading. This kind of food market never existed for the Norse Greenlanders. They obtained food security through their own agriculture and hunting.[65] Access to commercial goods was a desirable, but secondary priority.[66]

Summing up, the Icelandic written sources claim that the first settlers in Greenland in AD 985 and the first decades thereafter belonged to households or clans which had been humiliated in the feuds and disputes which were part and parcel of pre-state Norse society.

Available agricultural resources were a necessary but not sufficient motive for moving to Greenland. The archaeologists have focused on the economic motive without even trying to falsify the alternative political motive. If written and archaeological sources are seen in context, the political motive is best supported by the available empirical material.

Were the first immigrants Norwegians or Icelanders?

The first Norse Greenlanders sailed from Iceland, but that may have been because the only shipping lane to Greenland known at that time went from or via Iceland. It does not necessarily mean that the passengers were Icelanders in the sense that they were born there.

Ari Frodi wrote that Iceland was settled (*byggdisk*) from Norway after AD 870. This means that the first settlers to Greenland in AD 985 had ancestors who may have stayed in Iceland for a maximum of 115 years.[67] The most fruitful definition of an Icelander or Norwegian is in our context land of birth. There is only one example of an immigrant coming from the British Isles to Greenland. He came from the Hebrides which, at that time, had a Norse population.[68] All other immigrants mentioned in the written sources came from Iceland or Norway. No immigrants from Denmark or Sweden are mentioned.

Landnámabok and the Vinland sagas name ten men who followed Eirik Raudi and "took land" in named fjords or valleys in Greenland. A man who took land was called *landnámsmadr*, and he decided which peasants should be permitted to settle in his fjord. These peasants became his clients, and he became their chieftain.

Iceland has far better sources than Norway for identifying named immigrants to Greenland. *Landnámabok* gives short factual information about the first settlers on Iceland ca. 870–930 and their nearest descendants. In AD 985, the largest farms on Iceland were owned by descendants from the *landnámsmenn* and the most prominent Icelanders had ancestors who were *landnámsmenn*. I have compared the names of the ten men who followed Eirik to Greenland in AD 985 to the rich Icelandic name material.

Three of the 11 men who according to *Landnámabok* became *landnámsmenn* in Greenland are likely to have been born on Iceland:

Herjolv Bárdarson came from Norway as one of the first settlers on Iceland (ca. AD 870). One of his descendants was also called Herjolv Bárdarson and he sailed to Greenland with Eirik Raudi (AD 985). He settled at Herjolvsnes, is called in *Landnámabok* "a highly respected man" (*hinn gofgasti madr*) and became *landnámsmadr* and chieftain over Herjolvsfjord.[69] Archaeologists have registered several farms in the fjords behind Herjolvsnes.[70] Herjolv had a son called Bjarni. As long as his father lived on Iceland, Bjarni owned a ship and traded between Iceland and Norway, living every second winter in each country. When his father moved to Greenland Bjarni also settled there and inherited Herjolsnes. This was the first farm which ships reached in Greenland, and made the farm well known among merchants and gave the chieftain opportunities for a first choice of imported goods. Bjarni is said to have been a member of the *hird* of the Earl Eirik who was the ruler of Norway 1000–1014, and in *Groenlendinga saga* he is credited with having discovered Vinland;[71] the source value of this information can be discussed.

Snorri Thorbrandsson and his brother Thorleif came from an Icelandic *landnám* family. They were not chieftains on Iceland but became *landnámsmenn* and chieftains in Greenland. Their life was described earlier.[72] The sequence of names in *Landnámabok* shows that their fjord Alptafjord must have been north of Herjolvsnes but south of Einarsfjord.[73]

Thorbjorn Glora, who settled in Siglufjord, is mentioned immediately after Snorri in Alptafjord,[74] which indicates that they settled in neighbouring fjords. Siglufjord is a fjord in Iceland, and it is therefore likely that Thorbjorn Glora also named his Greenlandic chiefdom after the fjord he had left in Iceland.[75]

Three of the *landnámsmenn* who became chieftains in Greenland are likely to have been born in Norway:

Eirik Raudi was born in Norway (see earlier). He was a celebrity in Iceland, and his changes of residence are described in unusual detail in *Landnámabok*.[76] His father is mentioned in *Landnámabok* as the first settler at the farm Drangar on Iceland.[77] Eirik married an Icelandic woman, and her father and mother are mentioned in a separate section in *Landnámabok*. They were descended from an Icelandic *landnámsmadr*.[78]

Thorkell Farserkr was the chieftain in Hvalseyfjord. He is described as the "first cousin" (*systrungr*) of Eirik Raudi. *Systrungr* means that Eirik's mother was the sister of one of Thorkell's parents.[79] Eirik's parents were married before they left Norway; his mother must have been born in Norway and this is likely to have been so for his first cousins.[80] Thorkell was chieftain over a wide area between the outer parts of the two central fjords Eiriksfjord and Einarsfjord. He may have functioned as a guard to the most densely populated fjords with the two most important farms Brattahlid and Gardar.

Einarsfjord was named after Einar who according to *Landnámabok* voyaged with Eirik to Greenland and took land there.[81] Gardar in Einarsfjord was the second largest farm in the Norse settlement and it can safely be assumed that the first chieftain Einar settled there. Einar is not mentioned elsewhere in the *Landnámabok* or in sagas, which must mean that Einar did not have an ancestor who had been *landnámsmadr* on Iceland. Why was he given the position as the second most prominent man in Greenland with the second largest farm? He may have been Norwegian and invited by Eirik to participate in the colonisation of Greenland.[82]

Eirik Raudi married his only – illegitimate – daughter[83] to the man who ca. AD 1005 owned Gardar. He was called Thorvard and was probably Einar's son.[84] This was network building between chieftains of neighbouring fjords. The chieftain in Einarsfjord in the 1020s was called Thorgrim Trolle Einarsson who lived at the farm Langanes somewhere along the Einarsfjord. He was rich and followed by many men,[85] and was the second most powerful chieftain in Greenland, after the chieftain on Brattahlid.[86] His name indicates that he may have been the son of the first settler Einar and brother of Thorvard mentioned earlier.

Groenlendinga saga tells us that Eirik's daughter and her husband Thorvard killed 34 of their Icelandic companions on a voyage to Vinland. When they returned to Greenland her brother Leif, who was chieftain in Eiriksfjord, condemned what they had done.[87] It is possible that they were forced to pay such high damages to the surviving relatives that they lost Gardar. Later the chieftains in Einarsfjord had to live at another farm, Langanes.[88] A hundred years later Gardar was made the first bishop's see in Greenland.

Nothing is known about the ancestry of the five last *landnámsmenn* in Greenland:

Ketil took land in Ketilsfjord [Tasermiut].
Hrafn took land in Hrafnsfjord.[89]
Sölvi took land in Sölvadal [Unidentified].
Hafgrimr took land in Hafgrimsfjord and Vatnahverfi.[90]
Arnlaug took land in Arnlaugsfjord [Northern Sermilik?].[91]

If these five had belonged to prominent families in Iceland, some information about their ancestry is likely to have been given in *Landnámabok* or sagas. The Icelandic editors of *Landnámabok* find it remarkable that so few of the 11 named *landnámsmenn* in Greenland in AD 985 belonged to households which are mentioned in *Landnámabok* or saga texts.[92] One explanation may be that they had spent their whole life in Norway and never lived in Iceland. They may have come from Norway at Eirik's invitation shortly before the voyage, Eirik planned the settlement in Greenland four summers ahead (981–984), and that would have given him time to send enthusiastic invitations to friends with problems in his motherland and inform them about the meeting point and meeting time. It is not self-evident that it would have been possible to assemble 25 ships owned by Icelanders only and whose owners were willing to leave the island. An alternative hypothesis is that the five last *landnámsmenn* mentioned earlier were Icelanders outside the elite families.

30 The initial settlement in AD 985/6

After ca. 1050 the Norwegian crown gained control of armed violence in mainland Norway and feuding decreased. In Iceland the feuding continued until 1264 when the pre-state period ended there. If the main cause of immigration to Greenland was political, one should expect that immigration from Norway ceased or declined strongly after ca. 1050, but that it continued from Iceland until 1264. Norway had a far larger population than Iceland.

The Icelandic saga tradition claimed that the great wave of immigrants to Greenland came in AD 985 and in the years immediately afterwards. The Icelandic Sturlunga saga covers the period 1050–1264 and includes information about feuds and settlement of feuds in Iceland. It has only one example of Icelandic immigration to Greenland in this period. A peasant in Iceland with the byname "Murder-Hauk" (Viga-Haukr) and one of his relatives Magnus Markusson from Isafjordsysla in Northern Iceland ended up as the weaker party in an inheritance dispute.[93] Hauk decided ca. 1203 to emigrate to Greenland. He sailed via Norway with his family, probably because there was no direct shipping between Northern Iceland and Greenland. From Norway he hired his passage to Greenland.[94] Wherever he went he was highly esteemed (*thotti hann mikill madur hvar er han kom*). His ally Magnus Markusson also went to Greenland. None of them returned to Iceland.[95] The Icelandic *Sturlunga saga* gives reliable descriptions of the life of the Icelandic elite and their clients ca. 1120–1260. As Greenland is mentioned only once as a refuge, it should be taken as evidence that it was rarely used as such.

Both Norwegians and Icelanders emigrated to Greenland 985–1050, the empirical material does not permit a quantification of the two groups. But it seems that the motive for emigration was the same for both groups: defeat in dispute. In the period 985–1050 this was a serious problem in both countries. Since Norway had a far larger population, the Norwegian part of the immigrants may have been significant.

The chieftain and his clients

In his *Islendingabok* from ca. 1130 Ari Frodi says that Eirik Raudi "took land where it later has been called Eiriksfjord, and gave the land the name Greenland".[96] Eirik lived at and owned the farm of Brattahlid.[97] In the first phase he decided who should be permitted to build farms elsewhere in Eiriksfjord. An Icelandic Annals has this notice under AD 986: "*Tha for Eirekur hin raudi til Grænlands og bygdi Eireks fiord*".[98] *Byggja* means "provide with houses and people". When one of Eirik's friends from Iceland called Thorbjorn arrived at Brattahlid with his household, Eirik Raudi gave him land (*gaf Eirikr Thorbirni land*) at the opposite side of Eiriksfjord, where Thorbjorn built an honourable farm (*soemligr boer*) for himself.[99] In the quotation above Ari distinguishes between Eiriksfjord where Eirik "took land", and Greenland over which he had symbolic power since he had given it a name.

In the following period the households to which Eirik had given land in his fjord became his clients and he their chieftain. It was a Norse tradition that a chieftain invited his clients and allies for a feast at least once a year. Eirik Raudi followed this custom and invited them to *joladrykkju*.[100] "The Saga of the Foster Brothers" is a literary saga written at the beginning of the 13th century,[101] but where part of the action takes place in Greenland ca. 1020 when Eirik Raudi's grandson Thorkell was chieftain over Eiriksfjord.[102] He also invited his friends (*vinum sinum*) to celebrate Christmas at Brattahlid where beer was served (*joladrykkju*).[103]

A married couple living in Eiriksfjord are called Thorkell's clients (*Gamla ok Grimu, thingmanna thina*). When the couple hid and protected a man who had been outlawed at the Thing, it was seen as Thorkell's duty to make the couple respect the verdict. In the neighbouring Einarsfjord another chieftain held power, and he could not intervene directly against Gamla and Grimr but had to go via their chieftain. People from Einarsfjord wanted to search Gamla and Grimr's house, but Thorkell insisted that if it was to be done, he himself was to do it.[104] Tormod Kolbrunarskald in the same saga killed the chieftain of Einarsfjord, and Tormod's friends then found it safest to move the wounded Tormod from Einarsfjord to Eiriksfjord where it was harder for the killed man's relatives to reach him.[105]

The clients in Old Norse were called their chieftain's *thingmanna* or "Thingmen". If a client had a dispute or lawsuit which ended up at the Gardar Thing, the chieftain had an obligation to represent him and be his advocate. If the chieftain became involved in a lawsuit, his *thingmanna* had a legal obligation to follow him to the Thing and support him. There the party which could muster the largest number of armed men often determined who was to sit on the jury and the outcome of the case. There are no indications from Greenland that the chieftain owned the farm of his clients. This could happen but was not part of the system. The chieftain–client relationship in Norway, Iceland and Greenland was one of mutual judicial support in a stateless society, but it was not one of economic exploitation.

Was the Western Settlement organised differently from the Eastern?

The key role of chieftains in the Eastern Settlement is seen in how the districts were named. *Landnámabok* enumerates 11 units of settlement in the Eastern Settlement. Eight of them were named after the first chieftains: Eiriksfjord, Herjolvsfjord, Ketilsfjord, Hrafnsfjord, Sölvadal, Einarsfjord, Hafgrimsfjord and Arnlaugsfjord. The three other fjords were Alptafjord, Siglufjord and Hvalseyfjord. Alptafjord is known to have been named after the fjord on Iceland where the first two settlers, who were brothers, came from.[106] Since there were two initial chieftains, such a naming may have been a compromise. Siglufjord was also a fjord in Iceland. Why Hvalseyfjord was not named "Thorkellsfjord" after the first chieftain, is not known.[107]

After this enumeration of 11 chieftains who settled in the Eastern Settlement, *Landnámabok* adds that "some voyaged to the Western Settlement" (*en sumir foru til Vestribyggdar*) without mentioning a single name.[108] This indicates that none of the latter were chieftains. In sagas which took place in Greenland in the settlement period and later, chieftains from the Eastern Settlements appear but none is from the Western Settlement.

Later sources contain ten names of fjords in the Western Settlement, only two of which have a man's name as its first part.[109] In western Norway both landscape features and personal names were used in place names, but landscape names were by far the most common. The naming of the ten fjords in the Western Settlement corresponds to what Norse peasants were used to.

Eirik the Red's saga claims that Eirik named many places in the Western Settlement.[110] The present Ameragdla fjord was called Lysufjord,[111] and so was the main farm there.[112] The church in Lysufjord was called Sandnes and must have been built at the farm "Lysufjord".[113] Eirik Raudi was born in a region of Norway called Jæren, and close to Jæren was a long and narrow fjord named Lysufjord. Sandnes (sandy headland) is a headland at the bottom of the Gandsfjord which reaches into the central part of Jæren. It is the most convenient place to beach and load ships which depart from central Jæren. It has today grown into a town.[114] Sandnes in Lysufjord/Ameragdla was also a port for inland farms northwards towards Kapisillit and eastwards to the Austmannadal. Eirik may have named both Lysufjord and Sandnes after places he knew from his motherland.

Eirik's son Thorstein owned half of the farm Lysufjord and lived there, the other half being owned by a peasant who may have been one of Eirik's clients.[115] Thorstein possibly was meant to function as a representative of the Brattahlid clan in the Western Settlement. Judicial protection for peasants in the Western Settlement may have been given by the chieftain at Brattahlid and organised from Thorstein's farm. He may have acted as an arbitrator, or as an advocate if a case was submitted to the Gardar Thing.

The Norse Greenlanders' main source of money income was the walrus hunt which took place between Sisimiut and the Nuussuaq peninsula in March-April. At that time the Eastern Settlement was normally blocked by ice and the hunting ground could only be reached from the Western Settlement.[116] In Norway and Iceland it was common for chieftains to have servants or tenants who produced desirable products for them at some distance from the chieftain manor.[117] The walrus tusks may have found their way from the Western to the Eastern Settlement through similar mechanisms.

The English historian David Rollason has pointed out that kingdoms in the early Middle Ages often had a centre which he calls a "heartland", where the most powerful people in the realm lived and from where they controlled their subjects. In the periphery were areas where the control was weak, and often the people there would recognise their subordination only by swearing loyalty or paying a tribute. He finds this practice in Northern England which served as one of the models for state building in Scandinavia.[118]

The judicial ties between the central and peripheral settlements in Greenland were activated at the Gardar Thing. The economic ties were connected to the walrus hunt where organisers lived in the centre and hunters in the periphery.

Population size at Eirik Raudi's time and later

Ari Frodi (1068–1148) claimed that 25 ships sailed from Iceland with Eirik Raudi in AD 985, but only 14 reached Greenland. The rest were either driven back to Iceland or were shipwrecked.[119] Is it possible to estimate how many people there might have been on these 14 or 25 ships? In the sagas there are figures which

The initial settlement in AD *985/6* 33

may help us calculate how many men there normally were per ship. I have found it useful to distinguish between ships which sailed for purposes of settlement, exploration and trade. The saga authors writing ca. 1220–1250 would know how many people there usually were on these occasions in their own time. There was no dramatic increase in ship sizes between AD 985–1220.

Settlement:

> Thorbjörn the father of Gudrid was followed by 30 people (*manna*) on his ship when he emigrated from Iceland to Greenland a few years after Eirik Raudi. *Manna* could mean both "males" and "people".[120]
>
> *Eiriks saga Rauda* writes that on the largest expedition to Vinland there were three ships, one captained by the Icelanders Karlsefni and Snorri, the second by two other Icelanders Bjarni and Thorhall and the third by Eirik's son Thorvaldr and son in law Thorvard. These ships had 160 people on board,[121] or 50–60 people per ship.
>
> *Groenlendinga saga* writes that when Thorvaldr Eiriksson sailed from Greenland to Vinland he had 30 men on one ship.[122]
>
> When Thorfinn Karlsefni sailed from Greenland to Vinland to build a settlement, he had 60 men and 5 women plus domestic animals,[123] but it is not said on how many ships.
>
> When Thorgils sailed from Iceland to Greenland to settle there, he had 36 persons on his ship belonging to 2 households. Of these, 25 were thralls or slaves.[124]

Exploration:

> When Thorstein Eiriksson sailed to explore Vinland, his crew was 20 men, and they had a small cargo (*litit fe*) of just weapons and food. They did not find Vinland.[125]
>
> When Thorstein Eiriksson sailed to fetch the body of his brother Thorvaldr in Vinland, he had 25 men on one ship.[126]
>
> When Leiv Eiriksson sailed to find and explore Vinland, he had 35 men on one ship.[127]

Trade:

> When Thorfinn Karlsefni arrived in Greenland to trade, he had 40 men on the ship.[128]
>
> When the Greenlandic chieftain and merchant Thorgrim Trolle prepared to sail from Iceland to Greenland with his merchandise, he had 40 men on board. He was on his way from Norway where he had bought his goods.[129]
>
> The Norwegian merchant Thorir had 15 men on his ship which was wrecked off the Greenland coast ca. AD 1000.[130]

These figures indicate that when the purpose was exploration, the size of the crew would be 20–35 men. But when the purpose was settlement, they had to include more people who were not skilled sailors, and the number of people per ship would be 35–60. On 14 ships there would then be a maximum of (14 × 60) = 840 people on board and a minimum of 490. Some of the ships which were driven back to Iceland in 985 may have reached Greenland the following year. On all the 25 ships which sailed from Iceland there may have been a maximum of (25 × 60) = 1500 people. The first settlers who followed Eirik in AD 985 or 986 may have numbered between 500 and 1500 people.

Another starting point for such a calculation is that 11 chieftains emigrated with Eirik to Greenland. How many people would each chieftain bring with him on one or several ships? Egil Skallagrimson's saga written ca. 1220 gives a detailed description of his father's voyage from his chiefdom in Northern Norway to Iceland where he settled ca. AD 900. He was followed by his clients on several ships. Among them were ten free men to whom he gave land close to his own farm. These farms were operated in the following period as independent economic units, even if they were undoubtedly protected judicially by Skallagrim.[131] This seems to have also been the pattern in the initial settlement of Norse Greenland.

A total of 11 chieftains who each brought 10 households to Greenland gives 110 households. A peasant household along the Norwegian coast would normally have 6 members, so 110 households equals 660 members. To this must be added the chieftains' own households, which were significantly larger. It is realistic to think that each of them included at least 20 persons. These "guesstimates" suggest that nearly 1000 people may have settled in the Eastern Settlement in AD 985. Others settled in the Western Settlement, but how many is pure guesswork. The first wave of immigrants at Eirik Raudi's time is likely to have numbered just over 1000 people.

In the following period the population grew, and there are some figures for the period when the population is assumed to have been at its peak. During the time in office of bishop Thordr of Gardar, 1288–1314, a list was written in Iceland of the parishes in Greenland. The original list has been lost, but three copies of it have survived.[132] In two of the copies information about the number of farms in the Eastern and Western Settlements was also inserted.

One of the extant copies was written by the learned peasant Bjørn Jonsson from Skardsá in Iceland who died in 1655. His transcript says that in the Eastern Settlement in Greenland there were 190 farms (*bygda*) and in the Western Settlement 90 farms (*Svo er talid ad clxxxx byggda se i eystri byggd, xc i vestri*).[133] In this quotation the word *byggd* is used twice with different meanings. The basic meaning of the word is a place where houses are built. The first time Bjørn uses it, "farm" is evidently meant. The second time "settlement" is meant, Bjørn writes about the Eastern and Western Settlements. So, 190 plus 90 farms gives a total of 280 farms. As will be explained later, more than one household could live on a Norwegian farm with a name of its own. The archaeological material shows that this was also the case in Greenland. It is therefore necessary to distinguish between "name-farm" and "household farm".[134] Bjørn has a rather loose terminology where *byggd* means a location with many houses, which makes it likely that he meant "name-farm". Figures from the Western Settlement below suggest that on the 280 name farms there may have been ca. 340 household farms. If all 340 had been peasant farms which normally had ca. 6 occupants, ca. 2050 people are likely to have lived on the 340 farms.

A second extant copy of the list of parishes from 1288–1314 was made by Arngrimur Jonsson the Learned who died in 1648. He added a short notice on the number of farms in the Western Settlement, but not in the Eastern (*Villas habet 110, Paroecias 4*). It should be assumed that this Latin sentence was in the original from 1288–1314.[135] "Villa" meant in both classical and medieval Latin "rural dwelling with annexes and a yard", which could designate both peasant farms and manors.[136] Translated into Norwegian terminology, this would mean "household farm". The sentence made more explicit would then mean "In the Western Settlement there are 110 household farms in 4 parishes".

Bjørn's and Arngrimur's lists are therefore compatible. In the Western Settlement there were 90 name farms and 110 houshold farms, which is on average 1.2 household farms per name farm. If all the 110 household farms had been peasant farms, it would be a reasonable estimate that 660 people lived in the Western Settlement. Bjørn's and Arngrimur's figures are different but comparable, and the ultimate source for their information was bishop Thordr of Greenland. This indicates that Thordr had a list of all household and name farms on Norse Greenland. All households had to pay the tithe, and such a list was useful and even necessary when dues were collected. This is yet another example of the Gardar church being well organised with a competent staff.

In Iceland a chieftain's farm could have 100 residents..[137] Icelandic chieftain households were probably much larger than the Greenlandic ones for defence purposes. Eleven chieftains sailed to the Eastern Settlement in Eirik Raudi's fleet in 985.[138] The parish churches were originally privately owned by chieftains, and their number is another indication of the number of chieftains. Bjørn's and Arngrimur's transcripts mentioned above name 12 parish churches in the Eastern Settlement. The two figures for immigrant chieftains and parish churches indicate that the number of chieftains may have been around 11–12 in the three first centuries. The population on these chieftains' farms may have been a couple of hundred.[139]

The population of Norse Greenland seems to have reached its peak in a "long" 13th century. If a population of ca. 340 household farms of which 11–12 were chieftains' farms are added together, an estimate of at least 2000 inhabitants in both settlements is the closest one can get on the basis of available sources. A possible population decline in the settlements' final century will be discussed in Chapter 6.

3 Conclusion

The archaeologists who have dominated research on Norse Greenland for the last century emphasised the search for agricultural resources as the main motive for emigration to the North Atlantic islands. Economic resources were evidently a necessary precondition for a settlement, but analyses in this chapter indicate that it is not a sufficient explanation. There is no reason to reject the written sources which put the main emphasis on political conditions. Feuding set chieftains against one other and chieftains against king and made life dangerous in Norway and Iceland.

36 *The initial settlement in* AD *985/6*

Written sources indicate that the first wave of settlers included nearly 25 ships with ca. 1000 people. Around 1300, this number may have more than doubled. These numbers and individual biographies suggest that the settlers must have come from both Iceland and Norway. They imitated the chieftain–client organisation which at that time was practised in both Iceland and Norway. From the start a geographic pattern emerged where the Eastern Settlement was the centre and the Western settlement a periphery.

Notes

1. Islendingabok IF I, chapter 6, p. 14 note 3; English translation: chapter 6, p. 7.
2. Islendingabok IF I, chapter 1, p. 4, and chapter 6, p. 14; English translation: chapter 1, p. 4 and chapter 6, p. 7.
3. *Islendingabok* IF I, chapter 6, p. 14 note 3.
4. Kristjansson, J. 2007, pp. 270–273; *Medieval Scandinavia*, entry word "Vinland sagas".
5. Nordal 1953, pp. 248–249; Kristjansson, J. 2007, pp. 270 and 273.
6. *Fostbroedra saga* IF VI chapter 23, p. 244 and footnote 1; English translation: CSI chapter 23, pp. 384–385; *Medieval Scandinavia*, entry word "Fostbroedra saga".
7. *Groenlendinga saga* IF IV chapter 7, p. 264; English translation: CSI chapter 7, p. 29; Penguin edition, p. 17.
8. *Konungs skuggsjá*, Old Norse, p. 29; English translation, p. 142; Norwegian translation, p. 67.
9. *Eiriks saga Rauda* IF IV chapter 5, pp. 212–213; English translation: CSI chapter 5, p. 9 and Penguin edition chapter 14, pp. 35–36.
10. Introduction to *Eiriks saga Rauda* IF IV, p, LXVII.
11. *Eiriks saga Rauda* IF IV, pp. 236–237 and 269; English translation: CSI chapter 14, p. 18 and Penguin chapter 14, pp. 49–50.
12. *Landnámabok* IF I, p. 241, Hauksbok version chapter 175. Found can also mean "reached".
13. Introduction to *Eiriks saga Rauda* IF IV, p. LXIX; "Grænlands annal", p. 3, cf. pp. 21 and 36.
14. *Eiriks saga Rauda,* "Formáli" to Skálholtsbok text, IF IV, pp. 333–334; cf. wikipedia.org/wiki/Skálholtsbók.
15. *Flateyjarbok*, volume I, pp. 477–480 and volume II, pp. 20–32.
16. *Groenlendinga saga* IF IV chapter 1, p. 241.
17. *Eiriks saga Rauda* IF IV, p. 221 *dottur Eiriks rauda laungetna*; English translation: CSI chapter 8, p. 12 and Penguin chapter 8, p. 40.
18. *Groenlendinga saga* IF IV chapter 8, pp. 264–267; English translations: CSI chapter 7, pp. 29–31 and Penguin chapter 7, pp. 17–20.
19. *Flateyjarbok* volume 2, p. 32; Groenlendinga saga IF IV, p. 269; *hefir Karlsefni görst sagt allra manna atburdi um farar thessar allar, er nu er nokkut ordi a komit.*
20. This said, it cannot be completely excluded that the Greenlanders' saga (= *Sögu Eiriks*) which focuses on the Brattahlid clan, was written in Greenland, for example at the cathedral of Gardar.
21. Krogh 1982, p. 26.
22. *Eiriks saga Rauda* IF IV chapter 8, p. 223; English translation: CSI chapter 8, p. 13 and Penguin chapter 8, p. 40.
23. "*ibi vite sponte nascantur, vinum optimum ferentes. . . nonfabulosa opinione, sed certa comperimus relatione Danorum*". Adam of Bremen, book 4 chapter 39, cf. 38; Schmeidler 1917, p. 275; English translation: Tschan, p. 219; Norwegian translation, p. 218.

24 Adam of Bremen, book 4 chapters 38–39; Schmeidler 1917, pp. 231–232; English translation: Tschan, p. 219; Norwegian translation, p. 218; cf. Adam of Bremen, book 4 chapter 35; Schmeidler 1917, p. 269; English translation: Tschan, p. 215; Norwegian translation, p. 214.
25 Sigurdsson 2004, p. 276, cf. pp. 272–281.
26 Storm 1884, pp. 354–386.
27 *Islendingabok* IF I, pp. 13–14; English translation: chapter 6, p. 7; Norwegian translation: p. 54.
28 *Eiriks saga Rauda* IF IV chapter 2, p. 202; *Groenlendinga saga* IF IV chapter 1, p. 243.
29 *Eyrbyggja saga* IF IV chapter 24, p. 60; English translation: CSI chapter 24, p. 157; Norwegian translation: Norrøn saga III, p. 45.
30 IA, X Oddveria Annals, p. 464, and: I Reseniani, II Vetustissimi, V Skálholt, VII Lögmann and VIII Gottskalk; KLNM entry word "Årbøcker".
31 Written by Sturla Tordsson who died 1284.
32 Written by Hauk Erlendsson who died 1334.
33 *Landnámabok* IF I, pp. 132–133, S90 and H78; English and Norwegian translations: chapter 90.
34 *Eiriks saga Rauda* IF IV chapter 2, pp. 200–202; English translation: CSI, chapter 2, pp. 2–3 and Penguin chapter 2, pp. 26–28; *Groenlendinga saga* IF IV, chapter 1, pp. 242–243.
35 *Landnámabok* IF I, pp. 134–135, S92 and H79, *en sumir for til Vestribyggdar.* English and Norwegian translations: chapter 92. The first version of this source was written ca. 1130; *Medieval Scandinavia*, entry word "Landnámabok".
36 Malmros 1992, pp. 27 and 30.
37 Vebæk 1993, pp. 73–74.
38 Nyegaard 2014; sections 4.3 and 4.5.
39 Fredskild 1973, p. 122.
40 *Landscapes circum-landnám*, p. 15.
41 Grønnow 2008, pp. 12–13.
42 Arneborg 2004, pp. 228–229.
43 *Islendingabok* chapter 1, p. 4, and chapter 3, p. 9; English translation: chapter 1, p. 3 chapter 3, p. 5. *Heimskringla*, "The saga of Harald Fairhair", chapter 19.
44 *Egils saga* IF II chapter 16, pp. 38–41; English translation: CSI and Penguin same chapter division as IF; Norwegian translation: Norrøn saga I, pp. 48–49.
45 *Egils saga* IF II chapters 22 and 24–27, pp. 51–54 and 60–72; English translation: CSI and Penguin same chapter division as IF; Norwegian translation: Norrøn saga I, pp. 56–58 and pp. 63–71.
46 *Landnámabok* IF I, pp. 130–132, S89 and H77; English and Norwegian translations: chapter 89. *Eiriks saga Rauda* IF IV chapter 2, pp. 197–200; English translation: CSI chapter 2, pp. 2–3 and Penguin chapter 2, pp. 26–27; *Groenlendinga saga* IF IV, pp. 241–242.
47 *Landnámabok* IF I, p. 127, S86 = H74; English and Norwegian translations: chapter 86. *Eyrbyggja saga* IF IV chapter 12, p. 20; English translation: CSI chapter 12, pp. 138–139.
48 *Eyrbyggja saga* IF IV chapter 45, p. 130; English translation CSI chapter 45, pp. 190–193.
49 *Eyrbyggja saga* IF IV chapter 48, p. 135; English translation CSI chapter 48, p. 195.
50 *Landnámabok* IF I, pp. 134–135, S92 and H79; English and Norwegian translations: chapter 92. S92 calls the chieftain of Alptafjord Helgi Thorbrandsson, but this must be a mistake for Snorri or Thorleif who seem to have shared the chiefdom in the first period. Cf. Jonsson 1899, pp. 286–287.
51 *Eyrbyggja saga* IF IV chapter 48, p. 135; English translation: CSI chapter 48, p. 195

38 *The initial settlement in* AD *985/6*

52 *Eiriks saga Rauda* IF IV chapters 7 and 8, pp. 219 and 221; English translation: CSI chapters 7 and 8, pp. 11–14 and Penguin chapters 7 and 8, pp. 38–40.
53 *Eyrbyggja saga* IF IV chapter 48, p. 135; English translation: CSI chapter 48, p. 195; *Eiriks saga Rauda* IF IV chapter 11, p. 229; English translation: CSI chapter 11, p. 16 and Penguin chapter 11, p. 46 says that it was "Thorbrand Snorrason" who was killed in a skirmish with natives in Vinland. This is probably a mistake made by a copyist for "Snorri Thorbrandsson".
54 *Eiriks saga Rauda* IF IV chapter 3, p. 203. In one manuscript he is called chieftain (*godordsmadr*), in another peasant.
55 *Eiriks saga Rauda* IF IV chapter 3, p. 205 and IF IV chapter 4, p. 209; English translation: CSI chapter 3, pp. 5 and chapter 4, p. 7, and Penguin chapter 3, p. 30 and chapter 4, p. 33.
56 *Gisla saga Surssonar* IF VI chapter 38, pp. 117–118; English translation: CSI volume 2, chapter 38, p. 48; Norwegian translation: Norrøn saga III, p. 328.
57 *Kroka-Refs saga* IF XIV chapter 6, p. 131; English translation: CSI volume 3, chapter 6, p. 404; The saga was written in Iceland at the beginning of the 14th century (alternative English translation of the saga, Bachman 1985, p. XI).
58 The story is told more in detail in Chapter 2, pp. 62–63; *Fostbroedra saga* IF VI, p. 237, cf. 224–225 and 257; English translation: CSI pp. 379–378, cf. 373–374 and 390; Norwegian translation: Norrøn saga II, pp. 238, cf. 228–229 and 248.
59 Krogh 1982, p. 66 and 71.
60 McGovern 1979; Arneborg 2003(a), pp. 163 and 165; Arneborg 2004, pp. 275–276.
61 The term "Norse" is discussed in Chapter 2, pp. 43–45.
62 *Islendingabok* IF I chapter 6, p. 13; English translation: chapter 6, p. 7; Norwegian translation, p. 54.
63 On the Black Death, cf. Chapter 6, p. 360 and Index of matters, "Black Death".
64 Keller 2010.
65 Cf. Chapter 5, p. 230.
66 Cf. Chapter 4, pp. 161–169.
67 Methods borrowed from natural sciences for calculating the origin of the Icelandic population from Norway or the British Isles are speculative and are not relevant in our context.
68 He was also the first known Christian in Greenland. *Landnámabok* S91 and H79, IF I, pp. 132–134; English and Norwegian translations: chapter 91 = *Groenlendinga saga* IF IV chapter 2, p. 245; English translation: CSI chapter 1, pp. 19–20 and Penguin chapter 1, p. 3.
69 *Landnámabok* IF I, pp. 132–135, S91 and H79; English and Norwegian translations: chapter 91.
70 Appendix II, map 8.
71 *Groenlendinga saga* IF IV, chapter 1, pp. 244–248; English translation: CSI chapter 1, pp. 20–21 and Penguin edition, chapter 1, pp. 4–5.
72 Cf. Chapter 1, p. 23.
73 *Landnámabok* IF I, pp. 134–135, S92 and H79; English and Norwegian translations: chapter 92.
74 *Landnámabok* IF I, pp. 134–135, S92 and H79; English and Norwegian translations: chapter 92.
75 Cf. pp. 89–90.
76 Cf. Chapter 1, pp. 22–23; *Landnámabok* IF I, pp. 130–135, S89–S92 = H77–H79; English and Norwegian translations: chapters 89–92.
77 *Landnámabok* IF I, p. 197, S158; English and Norwegian translations: chapter 158.
78 *Landnámabok* IF I, p. 163, S122 = H94; English and Norwegian translations: chapter 122.
79 Fritzner volumes III and IV, entry word "systrungr".
80 *Landnámabok* IF I, pp. 134–135, S 93 and H80; English and Norwegian translations: chapter 93.

81 *Landnámabok* IF I, pp. 134–135, S 92 and H79; English and Norwegian translations: chapter 92.
82 *Landnámabok* IF I, pp. 134–135, S 93 and H80; English and Norwegian translations: chapter 93.
83 The daughter may have been born before Christianisation when illegitimacy in the Christian sense did not exist.
84 *Groenlendinga saga* IF IV chapter 1, p. 245 note 3; English translation: CSI chapter 1, p. 20 and Penguin chapter 1, pp. 3–4.
85 *Fostbroedra saga* IF VI chapter 21, p. 224; *Thorgrimr trolli Einarsson bjo i Einarsfirdi á Longunesi. Thorgrimr var godordsmadr, mikill hofdingi, rikr ok fjolmennr*; English translation: CSI chapter 21, p. 373.
86 *Fostbroedra saga* IF VI chapter 23, p. 237; *thann hofdingja, sem annarr er mestr a ollu Groenlandi.* English translation: CSI chapter 23, p. 380.
87 *Groenlendinga saga* IF IV, pp. 264–268; English translation: CSI chapters 7 and 8, pp. 30–31 and Penguin chapters 7 and 8, pp. 17–20.
88 *Fostbroedra saga* IF VI chapter 21, p. 224; English translation: CSI chapter 21, p. 373.
89 Appendix II, map 7 identifies Hrafnsfjord with Alluitsup/Agdluitsup. Ivar Bárdarson says that at the estuary of this fjord lies warm wells (*Det gamle Grønlands beskrivelse af Ivar Bárdarson*, pp. 23–24). This is the case at Unartoq fjord. Finnur Jonsson claims it to be beyond doubt that Hrafnsfjord is Uunartoq fjord (Jonsson 1899, p. 284).
90 Vebæk 1982, p. 207. He claims that Hafgrim built his farm at Eqaluit, but his evidence for this is not clear.
91 *Landnámabok* IF I, pp. 134–135, S92 and H79; English and Norwegian translations: chapter 92. If *Landnámabok* enumerates the fjords from south-east to north-west, Arnlaugsfjord should be what Ivar Bárdarson calls Bredefjord and Isafjord and which today have the official names of Ikersuaq and North Sermilik, or part of that fjord system.
92 IF I, pp. 134–135 footnote 2.
93 *Sturlunga saga* Old Norse chapters 173 and 174, pp. 231 and 233; English translation II, pp. 210 and 212; Danish translation I, p. 269 and 272.
94 *Sturlunga saga*, Old Norse chapter 174, p. 233, cf. p. 912; English translation II, pp. 212; Danish translation I, p. 272. According to the Old Norse edition, this took place in 1203 or shortly afterwards.
95 *Sturlunga saga*, Old Norse chapters 173–175, pp. 231–233; English translation II, chapter 13, p. 212; Danish translation I, pp. 269 and 272.
96 *Islendingabok* IF I, chapter 6, p. 13; "*nam thar land, es sidan er kalladr Eiriksfjördr.*"; English translation: chapter 6, p. 7.
97 *Landnámabok* IF I, pp. 134–135, S92 and H79; English and Norwegian translations: chapter 92.
98 IA, X Oddveria, p. 464.
99 *Eiriks saga Rauda* IF IV chapter 4, p. 209; English translation: CSI chapter 4, p. 7 and Penguin chapter 4, p. 33.
100 *Eiriks saga Rauda* IF IV chapter 7, p. 220; English translation: CSI chapter 7, p. 11 and Penguin chapter 7, p. 39
101 *Medieval Scandinavia*, entry word "*Fostbroedra saga*".
102 *Fostbroedra saga* IF VI chapter 20, p. 223; *Thorkell Leifsson var thá höfdingi yfir Eiriksfirdi*. English translation: CSI chapter 20, p. 373.
103 *Fostbroedra saga* IF VI chapter 22, pp. 226–227; English translation: CSI chapter 22, pp. 374–375. Chieftains over other fjords are likely to have done the same.
104 *Fostbroedra saga* IF VI chapter 23, pp. 245–246; English translation: CSI chapter 23, p. 383.
105 *Fostbroedra saga* IF VI chapter 23, p. 237; English translation: CSI chapter 23, p. 380.

40 The initial settlement in AD 985/6

106 Cf. Chapter 1 note 50.
107 *Landnámabok* IF I, pp. 134–135, S92–93 and H79–80; English and Norwegian translations: chapters 92–93.
108 *Landnámabok* IF I, pp. 134–135, S92 and H79; English and Norwegian translations: chapter 92.
109 Agnafjord and Lodinsfjord; Jonsson 1899, pp. 315–318.
110 *Eiriks saga Rauda* IF IV chapter 2, pp. 200–201; *Han for that sumar i hina vestri obyggd og gaf vida ørnefni*.
111 The most common meaning of *lysa* and *lysi* in Old Norse is "light" or something which gives light; a secondary meaning is the fish hake (*merluccius*). Finnur Jonsson thinks it means the latter. But hake has never been an important fish for food in the Norse tradition, and today does not exist in Greenland. Names with first syllable "Lys-" are found for fjords and other localities at several places in Norway, and its meaning is taken to be "light", as it was more open to sunshine than the surrounding area (*Norsk stadnamnleksikon*, p. 299).
112 *Eiriks saga Rauda* IF IV chapter 6, pp. 214 and 417; English translation: CSI chapter 6, p. 9 and Penguin chapter 6, p. 36.
113 Jonsson 1899, p. 315; cf. Chapter 3, pp. 92–106.
114 *Norske gaardnavne*, volume 10, Oslo 1915, p. 180, Høiland parish.
115 *Eiriks saga Rauda* IF IV chapter 6, p. 214 and 417; English translation: CSI chapter 6, p. 9 and Penguin chapter 6, p. 36.
116 Chapter 4, p. 174.
117 Chapter 5, Introduction, pp. 230–232.
118 Rollason 2003, pp. 22–24.
119 *Landnámabok* IF I, pp. 132–133, S90 and H78; English and Norwegian translations: chapter 90.
120 *Eiriks saga Rauda* IF IV chapter 3, p. 205; English translation: CSI chapter 3, p. 5 and Penguin chapter 3, p. 30.
121 *Eiriks saga Rauda* IF IV chapter 8, p. 222 note 1; English translation: CSI chapter 8, p. 12 and Penguin chapter 8, p. 41; Norwegian translation: Norrøn Saga V, p. 213.
122 *Groenlendinga saga* IF IV chapter 5, p. 254; English translation: CSI chapter 5, p. 26 and Penguin chapter 5, p. 12; Norwegian translation: Norrøn Saga V, p. 232.
123 *Groenlendinga saga* IF IV chapter 6, p. 261; English translation: CSI chapter 6, p. 28 and Penguin chapter 6, p. 15; Norwegian translation: Norrøn Saga V, p. 237.
124 *Flomanna saga* IF XIII chapter 20, p. 276; English translation chapter 20, pp. 288–289.
125 *Eiriks saga Rauda* IF IV chapter 5, p. 213; English translations: CSI chapter 5, p. 9 and Penguin chapter 5, p. 9; Norwegian translation: Norrøn Saga V, p. 209.
126 *Groenlendinga saga* IF IV chapter 6, p. 257; English translations: CSI chapter 5, p. 26 and Penguin chapter 5, p. 12; Norwegian translation: Norrøn Saga V, p. 234.
127 *Groenlendinga saga* IF IV chapter 3, pp. 248–249; English translation: CSI chapter 2, p. 21 and Penguin chapter 2, p. 6; Norwegian translation: Norrøn Saga V, p. 229.
128 *Eiriks saga Rauda* IF IV chapter 7, pp. 219 and 421; English translation: CSI chapter 7, p. 11 and Penguin chapter 7, p. 39; Norwegian translation: Norrøn Saga V, p. 212.
129 *Fostbroedra saga* IF VI chapter 16, pp. 201–202; English translation: CSI chapter 16, pp. 365–366; His ship is said to arrive in northern Iceland "from the ocean" (*af hafi*), and it continued to Greenland with its goods.
130 *Groenlendinga saga* IF IV chapter 4, p. 254; English translation: CSI chapter 3, p. 24 and Penguin chapter 3, p. 9.
131 *Egils saga* IF II chapters 28 and 29, pp. 73–74; English translation: CSI and Penguin same chapter division as IF; Norwegian translation: Norrøn saga I, pp. 73–74.
132 Cf. Chapter 3, pp. 94–95.
133 "Grænlands annal", in: Halldorsson 1978, p. 39 = GHM III, p. 228; Cf. Jonsson 1899, p. 273.

134 The difference between name farms and household farms is explained in more detail in Chapter 5, pp. 232–233.
135 This Latin quote is from Arngrimur's list, printed in Jonsson 1899, p. 322.
136 Niermeyer 1993, entry word "villa".
137 Miller 1990, pp. 124–125.
138 *Landnámabok* IF I, pp. 134–135, S 92 and H79; English and Norwegian translations: chapter 92.
139 Jonsson 1899 pp. 321–322, note 1.

2 Political organisation

The Norse Greenlanders had an ethnic identity which they preserved throughout their 425-year history, and which is a necessary background for understanding political organisation and political changes. The central element in any ethnic identity is a common language.

1 Ethnic identity

Language

The only source for the language spoken on Norse Greenland is extant rune inscriptions.

The Icelandic philologist Finnur Jonsson in 1924 claimed that the Norse Greenlanders wrote their runes in a language which he named "the Icelandic dialect in Greenland". His empirical basis for this hypothesis was that "I can find no deviations from the ordinary Icelandic of about 1300", but he admitted that there were some exceptions, and he thinks one of the rune-sticks may have been written by a Norwegian.[1]

The Nationalmuseum archaeologist Poul Nørlund claimed in 1942 that "the Greenlanders had their own particular dialect and partly their own rune forms. They were more conservative than Icelanders and Norwegians and preserved their forms from the first *landnám* long after they had been abandoned by other Norse".[2] This would imply that the Greenlanders had little contact with Norway and Iceland. At Nørlund's time large excavations were undertaken at Herjolvsnes, Brattahlid, Gardar and Sandnes. The archaeologists neglected stratigraphic analyses, and therefore really did not know how old the excavated objects with runic inscriptions were. They assumed (or guessed?) that all finds were from the final period ca. 1300 and later. If the Greenlandic runes were written in forms which in ca. 1300 were no longer used in Norway, they assumed that this was because the Greenlanders who lived ca. 1300 were conservative.

Marie Stoklund in 1993 chose to date Greenlandic crosses with runes to the time when the relevant type of runes was in use in Norway, which made her date several of them before 1300.[3] In 1953 a rune inscription was found in Narsaq which Stoklund claimed must be dated to ca. 985–1025 for runologic reasons.[4]

The Kingittorsuaq rune-stone was traditionally dated to the end of the 13th century, but in Norway some of its features would have been dated to the first part of the century.[5] Stoklund's method made her stretch the runic chronology on Greenland over all four centuries from ca. 1000 to ca. 1400. She admits, however, that the neglect of stratigraphy during past excavations makes it difficult to determine whether a runic form is present because it was copied from contemporary Norway, or whether it was a conservative remnant of forms which had long ago been abandoned in Norway.[6] Uncertain stratigraphy makes it possible that the Narsaq inscription is considerably later than ca. 1000.[7] Stoklund's main conclusion was nevertheless that Greenlanders developed dialect and rune orthography parallel to developments in Norway.

Høegsberg claimed in 2009 that there are significant differences in types and numbers of inscriptions between Greenland and Iceland.[8] In some late Greenlandic inscriptions the "th"-rune has been replaced by "t". This is a change which occurred in Norwegian but not in Icelandic. Høegsberg suggests that this could mean that the Greenlanders linguistically had closer contacts to Norway than to Iceland. Does this mean that the spoken language in Greenland followed Norway more than Iceland? Høegsberg comments that "in a discussion of identities this is an exciting possibility".[9] The runes are our only source for an answer to this problem, and they support the hypothesis of a close Norwegian connection as does the development in trade and shipping, where the main contacts after 1200 went to Norway, mainly Bergen. This is likely to have been the case even in the two first centuries.[10]

How did they name their ethnic group?

The immigrants to Greenland from Iceland and Norway called themselves *norrön* (= Norse). This word had a narrow meaning of "Norwegian", and the Icelandic *Sturlunga saga* writes that on a ship which in 1189 sailed from Norway to Iceland, there were *mart islenskra manna og svo norrænna, godra drengja*.[11] *Norrön* here clearly means "people from mainland Norway". But *norrön* also had a wider meaning including people not only from Norway, but also from Iceland, Greenland, the Faroes, Shetland and Orkney. Norse people in this wider meaning had in common that they spoke a language which had its origin in Norway but was also spoken elsewhere in the North Atlantic. They were different from Danes and Swedes.[12]

Norsemen living in Greenland called themselves "Greenlanders", and were different from "skraelings" (Eskimos) who also lived in Greenland. Norse-speaking people who were not Greenlanders they called *austmenn*, people from the east. The *Groenlendinga tháttr* is consistent in its distinction between "Greenlanders" and "*austmenn*", and some of the latter were Icelanders.[13] An official charter issued in Bergen in 1389 refers to a decision made at the Thing assembly for all Greenlanders concerning *austmenn*, which even in this case included both Norwegians and Icelanders.[14]

The only extant document written in Greenland is from 1409 and was written by the *officialis* at Gardar cathedral. He confirmed that a marriage between two

Icelanders had been announced the previous year in a Greenland church. "There were many respectable people present, both foreigners and natives (*utlendskum oc innlendskum*)". In this case all the "foreigners" were Icelanders.[15]

Fostbroedra saga was written by an Icelander but partly takes place in Greenland. Here the Greenlander Bjarni calls the Icelander Thormod *einn utlendr madr* (a foreigner).[16] Later in the same saga King Olav appears in a dream to the Greenlander Grimr and gives him a message concerning a person whom he first calls "a foreigner (*utlendr madr*)" and next Icelander (*islenzk madr*). Grimr found and talked to this Icelander and claimed to know his real name, "you are called Helgu-Steinarr in your own land (á *thinu landi*)".[17] The saga author and his audience considered Greenland and Iceland as two different "lands", in the meaning of "region" or "realm".

People living in Norway, Greenland, Iceland, the Faroes, Shetland, Orkneys and Hebrides felt that they belonged to an "ethnic" or "cultural" community mainly based on a common language which they called Norse. But at the same time, they were considered to live in different "lands" and regarded each other as "foreigners". Today's Norwegians were called "austmadr" or "norrön", the others *grönlenzkr*, *islenzkr*, *færeyskr*, *hjaltlenzkr*, *orkneyskr* and *sudreyskr*.[18]

In 1838–1845 Danish authorities published *Grönlands Historiske Mindesmærker* (GHM), and as part of that work they had to decide how to name the Norse inhabitants of Greenland. Hans Egede had called them Norwegians (*norske*) both in his diary from his years in Greenland and in his correspondence with authorities in Copenhagen published in 1741. His superiors in Copenhagen on the other hand called them "Danes" when they wrote back to Egede.[19] Norwegians and Danes were subjects of the same king who was Danish. After 1814 Denmark and Norway were separate states and this double naming was no longer possible. GHM introduced *nordbo*[20] which meant "citizen of the Nordic countries" which were Denmark, Sweden, Norway, Iceland and the Faroes.[21] When scholarly research on the Norse Greenlanders started 40 years later in the 1880s, "nordbo" had become the Danish name for the Norse Greenlanders.[22]

The director of the Nationalmuseum in Copenhagen Poul Nørlund explained in 1942 that he called "Greenland's medieval Nordic colonists" *nordboer*, even if they in medieval sources are called "Norse" and "Greenlanders". He does so in order to distinguish them from their "tribal relatives (*stammefrender*) in Norway" who in medieval sources also were called "Norse".[23] Another Nationalmuseum archaeologist Knud Krogh has pointed out that the term *nordbo* for Norse Greenlanders gives misleading associations.[24] The terms used in English (Norse Greenlanders) and Norwegian (*norrøne grønlendere*) are in harmony with medieval usage, and Knud Krogh thinks one should start using it in Danish as well.[25] But Jette Arneborg, who has been the most prolific Nationalmuseum archaeologist in recent decades, keeps to *nordbo*. In a Danish dictionary from 2005, "nordbo" is said to have a wide meaning of "person from one of the Nordic countries" and a narrow meaning of medieval "Norse Greenlander".[26]

In scholarly analyses it is always important to have well-defined and clear concepts. The Danish term "nordbo" indicates that the Norse Greenlanders came from all the Nordic countries, Denmark included. The international term, in Norwegian "norrön", in English "Norse", indicates that they belonged to a cultural sphere whose centre was in Norway but which also included Iceland, Greenland, the Faroes, Shetland and Orkney. If the purpose is to analyse social ties as they were experienced in 985–1410 by contemporaries, the analytic concept "Norse Greenlanders" is most fruitful. This is the term used in this book.

The Norse narrative tradition in Greenland

Story-tellers were popular at social gatherings in all Norse lands, Greenland included. The Greenlandic chieftain Thorgrim Trolle participated in the annual Thing assembly at Gardar. He had a reputation for telling stories "well and entertaining". One evening someone put a chair outside the booth where Thorgrim was staying, and Thorgrim sat down and told a story. Most of the other people present at Gardar sat down around him, probably on the ground, and listened. On this occasion he told the story of how he himself had participated in an honour killing in Iceland.[27]

In the 12th and particularly the 13th century such stories about warrior heroes and kings were written down in poems and sagas. The authors were mostly Icelanders, but there are indications that some of the works may have been authored in Greenland. "The Greenlandic poem of Atli" gives the best evidence.

In AD 437 the Huns conquered Burgundy and killed its king. Sometime afterwards a poem was composed in southern Germany about these events. In the 9th century the first poem was composed in the Norse language retelling the story.[28] The oldest extant Norse transcript is in a codex from ca. 1270–1280,[29] which contains two Norse versions. Finnur Jonsson concluded that one of them must have been composed in Norway, evidently for a pre-state elite household.

> The action takes place in Burgundy close to the Rhine, and its king is called the ally of the French. We are presented to a court of warriors with expensive equipment for men and horses, living in a castle. The forests were large and dark with brown bears and wolves. The Huns' hall was built of timber, and they had chariots with wheels (*hvelvogn*). This version must have been close to the lost German text. The landscape and fauna described was familiar to a Norwegian public, but brown bears, timber houses and wheel chariots did not exist in Iceland and Greenland. The Norwegian version of Atlekvida has been dated to the latter half of the 10th century.[30]

The other version has the heading "The Greenlandic poem of Atli" (*Atlamál hin Groenlenzku*), which means that the scribe who wrote the extant manuscript AD 1270–1280 thought that this version had been composed in Greenland. He does not say why he thought so, but Finnur Jonsson and other philologists have found reasons for accepting it.[31]

The Greenlandic Atlamál has 105 stanzas, the Norwegian version only 43.[32] The Greenlandic version is longer because the author is more at pains to explain things in detail for people who had never heard the story before, and who did not know how a king's hird functioned. The author moved the action from Burgundy to Jutland in Denmark, which was more familiar to a Greenland public (stanza 4). The fauna is Greenlandic. One person dreams of a threatening polar bear (*hvitabiorn*) and an eagle and wolves brought omens of bloody events to come (stanzas 18–19 and 24). Polar wolves today exist north of Melville Bay, but the King's Mirror written ca. 1250 claims that they also existed near the Norse settlements.[33] Riches are measured in cattle and slaves (stanzas 94–95). A white bear (*hvitabiorn*) is seen as a warning of a "storm from the east", that is from the inland glacier (stanza 18). In Norway storms normally come from the North-West. The struggle between Gunnar and Atli is described as a feud between two Greenlandic chieftains and not as a war between the King of Burgundy and the Huns. Gunnar was accompanied by two other warriors and two male servants in his meeting with Atli, but he let ten (?) other male servants (*huscarlar*) stay at home. This means that Gunnar had 12 male servants in all. All five rowed in the same boat, and the women stood at the "fjord" when the boat left the shore. The five rowed as hard as they could, Gunnar included (stanzas 30 and 37). It gave a loud sound when they knocked at Atlis' gate (*grindr*) (stanza 38). Atli and his 30 men then approached them so that only the [stone?] fence was between them (stanza 42). Atli's wife at the end of the poem claims that her husband was not much worth since he never won his cases at the Thing assembly (*thingi*) (stanza 101).

The landscape and environment are Greenlandic. Finnur Jonsson thought the poem was written in the second half of the 11th century, after Norse Greenland had become a stable society.[34] I can see no reason to question the claim that this poem was composed at this time in Greenland for a Greenlandic public.

Another poem is also likely to have been composed in Greenland. Its name was *Nordrsetudrápa*. Its subject was a journey to and a stay in the Disco region, which the Norse called *nordrseta*, literally "stay in the north". The poem itself has been lost, but Snorri Sturluson used a few lines of it in his *Edda* which is extant.[35] The skald is called Sveinn, and Finnur Jonsson thinks it is likely that he lived in Greenland at least when he composed the poem.[36] No modern scholar has known the skaldic poetry better than Finnur Jonsson, and he dates the poem to the 11th century. At that time the trade in ivory from walrus hunted in the Disco Bay region is likely to have started, and they could not be sure whether they would meet Inuit competitors there. *Nordrseta* must have been a glorious and profitable enterprise.[37]

The few extant lines do not give a clear picture of the whole poem. The poem was written in an intricate Old Norse language, and I have used Finnur Jonsson's and GHM's translations of the lines into Danish.[38] The lines translated into plain English without poetic circumlocutions (*kenning*) are:

1 Storms from snow-white mountains created large waves in the frosty region
2 Ugly winds started to blow
3 The wind blew against the boat/ship (*vid*)
4 The woman learnt me to play a hidden game [of love?].
 The river at last reaches the sea.

Quote no. 4 must be the final lines of the poem.[39] The poet dedicates his poem to a nameless woman, and the poem has come to its end, just like a long river which finally reaches the sea.

We can only speculate about the social context of this poem. It is likely to have been performed in the hall of a chieftain in the Western or Eastern Settlement, praising as heroes men who had been on hunting expeditions to the Disco Bay region. In Norway and Iceland men were first and foremost praised for their participation in battles in this early period. We do not know how representative the *Nordrsetudrápa* is, but it is an indication that the Greenlanders to a larger degree sought honourable challenges in struggles against the elements.

Few written texts authored in Norse Greenland are known, but sagas, poems and other literature may have been destroyed when the settlement was ruined.

Courtly culture imitated in Greenland?

In the period ca. 1220–1319 the Norwegian king Håkon Håkonsson and his successors made concerted efforts to create a court culture. Poems like those quoted above were one part of it, music another. Relevant instruments were inexpensive in this period, and learning to play them was not overly demanding.[40]

On the farm E34 just north of Brattahlid two "bridges" were found for string instruments with two and three strings respectively.[41] A similar "bridge" was found in Oslo, this one for seven strings, dating to ca. 1225–1250.[42] There is no doubt that the instruments in Oslo and E34 belonged to the same type. The "bridge" in Oslo has been classified as belonging to a lyre, in the Middle Ages often named "crowd". Norse laymen often included it under the imprecise and wide term "harp".[43]

Lyres of this type could be "plucked" like a modern guitar, and the musician would then vary the length of the vibrating strings with one hand and "pluck" them with the other. An alternative way of playing a lyre was to use a bow on the strings, like a modern violin; this was common in Norway in the 13th century.[44] The "bridges" from E34 had a flat upper side, which means that the two or three strings were on the same level, and if a bow was drawn over them all strings would sound at the same time. The player must have varied the length of one of the vibrating strings with one hand to create a melody. The other two strings would then give an accompanying "bourdon" tune. The musician would draw the bow with his other hand.[45] This is shown on a sculpture from Nidaros cathedral from ca. 1325–1350.[46]

Plucked and bowed lyres were used by professional jongleurs (*leikare*) as well as amateurs in Norway. Playing it gave status: King David was the great

48 *Political organisation*

model, and Earl Ragnvald of Orkney and possibly King Harald Hardrádi practised the art.[47] It is beyond doubt that the musician who played the lyre on E34 in Eiriksfjord was an amateur, and he may have belonged to the family of the chieftain on Brattahlid close by. At feasts a row of men and women may have danced holding hands and singing, accompanied by a musician who played the lyre. The secular culture on Greenland shows close parallels to aristocratic culture in Norway and Iceland and was related to an international court culture.

Summing up, the Norse Greenlanders shared their ethnic identity with other speakers of their Norse language. Their dialect varied little from Norwegian and Icelandic but seems to have been closer to Norwegian. They imported a narrative tradition from Iceland and Norway, and a courtly culture from Norway. Greenland was geographically isolated, but their secular culture was part of a larger Norse cultural community. This ethnic unity is an important background for understanding the political ties to Norway.

2 Violence in a pre-state society

The Groenlendinga tháttr as historical source

The *tháttr* (short story) called *Groenlendinga tháttr* or *Einars tháttr Sokkasonar* gives the longest and most coherent extant narrative of events taking place in Norse Greenland. Historians consider the *tháttr* to be a reliable source, but the Nationalmuseum archaeologist Jette Arneborg has dismissed it as slanted and unreliable.[48] This conclusion is not the outcome of a methodologically correct source criticism, as her only argument is that she does not find the narrative "reasonable".[49] It "surprises" her to read that the Greenlanders took the initiative to establish a bishop's see at Gardar, that they sought the cooperation of the Norwegian king and accepted that he appointed a Norwegian for the job. If the content of a source "surprises" the scholar, this is no argument for dismissing it. It may tell the scholar that her previous understanding should be modified.

The final and main part of the events in Greenland probably took place in 1131–1132. One of the foreign skippers involved was the Icelander Hermundr Kodransson who after these events returned "to his ancestral farm" in Iceland, and died there as an old man in his nineties in 1197.[50] He is likely to have brought the oral narrative to Iceland, where the *tháttr* is thought to have been composed in writing at the end of the 12th century.[51] We know through whom the oral narrative passed before it was written down, and this information inspires confidence.

The author gives several place-names in the Eastern Settlement. None of the names or topographic details contradicts what is known about the geography of the area, or information from other written or archaeological sources. Many personal names are given, and some of them can be checked against other sources.[52] This is a very realistic and detailed saga without supernatural interventions. The author gives rational and intelligent explanations of how the events are linked. The narrative corresponds to what is generally known about judicial procedures in Norway and Iceland at this time. This is a reliable source.

The sense of honour

A long time before Norse Greenland was settled, "honour" had governed Norsemen's social attitudes. Honour is usually defined as a person's value in the eyes of his society and in his own eyes.[53] All members of a peasant or warrior community were measured by those who knew him or her. The code of honour determined which qualities were honourable and what a person could do to increase his or her honour. If conflicts arose, efforts would be made to solve them peacefully, but if that was not possible the offended person had to resort to violence. Accepting a humiliation was dishonourable and would result in social degradation.

Icelandic saga writers evidently saw Greenlanders as having the same sense of honour and acceptance of violence as Icelandic society. Norwegian and Icelandic merchants carried weapons when they visited Greenland. Greenlanders carried axes when they travelled outside their farm, and they were meant for self-defence. At the Gardar Thing both Greenlanders and foreign merchants carried an axe. When they entered the church near the Thing meeting place, they had to leave them outside. In a tense situation the son of the Brattahlid chieftain called Einar Sokkesson left the church accompanied by the bishop, but when he exited from the churchyard he grabbed the axe of a Greenlander and killed a Norwegian merchant called Ossur who stood there leaning on his own axe.[54] Later attempts to settle the dispute degenerated into an open struggle at the Thing between Greenlanders and Norwegians where both axes and swords were used and several men were killed.[55]

In *Fostbroedra saga* a Christmas banquet is described which the grandson of Eirik Raudi called Thorkell arranged at Brattahlid for his clients and friends. The guests arrived from neighbouring farms with their weapons but had to leave them with one of Thorkell's slaves for safe keeping. The host evidently did not take any risks. The banquet lasted for several days with beer served, and Greenlanders were not used to alcohol. When the feast was over, the Greenlanders and the Icelander Thormod Kolbrunarskald had their axes and swords returned, and Thormod immediately used his axe to kill one of his host's slaves who had behaved disrespectfully. When Thorkell saw this, he reacted impulsively and ordered his men to kill Thormod.[56] The order was not executed because Thormod was protected by his status as one of the Norwegian king's retainers.

The Greenlanders were trained in using their weapons. The Greenlander Falgeir sought revenge on the Icelander Thormod for the death of his uncle. Falgeir attacked Thormod bravely and wounded him severely before being killed himself.[57] Thormod had serious problems carrying out his revenge on Greenland. The 13th-century Icelandic author of the saga evidently saw the Greenlanders as capable of handling weapons well. The Greenlanders shared the Norse sense of honour and were trained to use weapons if honour demanded revenge.

Were feuds less common in Greenland than in Iceland?

In Iceland feuds were frequent and a significant problem. Helge Ingstad pointed out that the sources give no evidence of feuds between Greenlanders.[58] Sagas give the impression that Greenlanders were more inclined to peaceful settlements and

50 *Political organisation*

less aggressive than Icelanders and Norwegians in pursuing revenge killings. The Norwegian Ossur damaged the ship of bishop Arnaldr of Gardar who was also a Norwegian. The Brattahlid chieftian wanted the conflict settled peacefully, but bishop Arnaldr declined and six men were killed in a feud.[59] The two Vinland sagas describe Eirik Raudi's feuds in Iceland, and they also mention that Eirik's father had similar conflicts in his Norwegian land of origin. But Eirik and his sons did not make feuds on chieftains who lived in Greenland, according to these sagas. Sagas describe feuds taking place in Greenland, but in all of them one of the parties was either Icelanders or Norwegians.

Eirik Raudi's daughter Freydis led an expedition to Vinland, and on a second ship sailed 35 Icelanders. In Vinland conflicts arose between the crews of the two ships, and Freydis then used her superior manpower to murder all the Icelanders. She tried to keep this a secret, but her brother Leiv Eiriksson heard about it. He grew furious and distanced himself from what his sister had done.[60]

The chieftain Thorgrim Trolle in Einarsfjord in Greenland sailed with his merchandise from Norway via Iceland to Greenland. In Iceland he was drawn into a feud between two Icelanders, and he helped a friend of his to have his Icelandic opponent killed. An Icelandic friend of the killed man, Thormod Kolbrunarskald, then travelled in disguise to Greenland to take revenge on Thorgrim Trolle. This was a formidable success, as the hero Thormod managed to kill the chieftain and four of his five nephews.[61]

All our information about feuds in Greenland are from sagas, and all of them were written by Icelanders. The information had previously been transmitted in an oral tradition in Iceland. This survival mechanism for the sources makes it understandable that only feuds where Icelanders participated were remembered. This may also be the whole explanation.

But Greenlanders also had two social mechanisms which may give an additional explanation for the absence of feuds between Greenlanders: the Thing for all Greenlanders at Gardar and the leading position of the Brattahlid chieftain. These were not well suited to settle conflicts between foreigners and Greenlanders but may have functioned between Greenlanders on Greenland.

3 Jurisdiction in pre-state Greenland

Was there a Greenland law?

Originally the laws in the Norse area were transmitted in an oral tradition. The future lawmen were trained from childhood to memorise laws. Their good memory made them the best transmitters of historical knowledge as well.

The point of departure for legislation on the North Atlantic islands was the law of the regional Thing (*lagting*) for Western Norway, called the Gulathing. According to Ari's *Islendingabok*, a Norwegian-born Icelander called Ulfljot was given the task of finding the best and most relevant laws for Iceland. In AD 930 or somewhat earlier he was sent to Norway where he contacted his uncle Thorleif the Wise, who was a law expert living in the region which belonged to the Gulathing.

Ulfljot took most of his paragraphs from the Gulathing law, but he discussed with Thorleif the Wise how some paragraphs could be added or removed and others changed in order to adapt the laws for Iceland. Icelandic tradition claimed that Ulfljot spent three winters in Norway memorising and adapting the relevant parts of the Gulathing law.[62] When he returned with his laws to Iceland, he took the initiative to establish the Althing at Thingvellir and became its first lawman (*lögsögumadr*).[63]

Some Icelandic philologists and historians have claimed that Ari exaggerated the influence from Western Norway; the Icelanders composed their laws themselves without or with minimum help from outside. They have not presented empirical evidence for this hypothesis.[64] On the background of what has been said earlier, it is methodologically correct to accept Ari's account on this point.

The first legal experts on Greenland probably did as Ulfljot: they memorised relevant laws and adapted them to conditions in Greenland. The two laws at their disposal were those of Gulathing and the Icelandic Althing. They may have chosen one of them or combined both.

In Norway the laws on how to implement Christianity had been put in writing by the 1020s, with the secular laws possibly being put in writing from the 1040s. The Icelanders started the writing of their secular laws in 1117.[65] Greenlanders probably also put their laws in writing in the 12th century, but nothing has been preserved. This comes as no surprise since all written material seems to have been destroyed when Greenland Norse society perished.

Groenlendinga tháttr is the only source to state explicitly that a separate Greenland law existed and it also gives a concrete example.

> A Norwegian crew stranded and died on the East Coast of Greenland, and their goods were found by Greenlandic hunters. A dispute arose between the Greenlanders using "Greenland law" and Norwegians using "Norwegian law". The first law said that the goods of shipwrecked seafarers belonged to the people who found it, while the latter law said that it remained the property of the survivors or their heirs. The son of the Brattahlid chieftain said to the jury at the Gardar Thing that it was possible that Norwegian law gave shipwrecked merchants, Greenlanders included, a right to their goods if they stranded in Norway. "But here [in Greenland] we keep to the laws which are valid here",[66] and Greenland law gave the shipwrecked goods to the finder.

The oldest extant Norwegian urban law confirms that the property of an Icelander (and Greenlander?) who died in Trondheim belonged to the heirs, except a fixed sum of six *eyrar* which was to cover the expenses for burial and a gift to the church.[67]

The claim that Greenlandic law gave shipwrecked property to the finder also seems to be correct. The Greenlanders who had appropriated the goods mentioned above said that they had divided the goods *at groenlenzkum lögum*.[68] Bishop Arnaldr of Gardar who had received the main part of the shipwrecked goods, also claimed that he and the hunters had respected what Greenland law said about such cases. Four times the saga author repeats claims that the dispute had to be solved according to Greenlandic and not Norwegian law.[69]

After the merchant Ossur was killed, another merchant Ketil was thought to be the best spokesman for the Norwegians because he knew Greenlandic law (*thvi mer eru kunnig groenlenzk lög*).[70]

It is improbable that the saga author would have told his Icelandic (and Greenlandic?) audience that there was a "Greenlandic law" if it had been common knowledge that the Greenlanders copied the law which at any time was used at the Icelandic Althing. It is also improbable that the author would have repeated four times that Greenlandic law and Norwegian law were different if it was common knowledge that Greenlanders used the Gulathing law.

One could suspect that the saga author, who probably was an Icelander writing shortly before 1200, had a message. The Norse Atlantic islands had the right to treat Norwegians less favourably than vice versa. Shipwrecked goods at the North Atlantic islands belonged to the finder; in Norway to the shipwrecked crew. The saga author ends his narrative by saying that king Harald Gilli (1130–1136), who reigned when the conflict took place, thought that the Greenlanders had been in the right.[71] Harald Gilli was the grandfather of King Sverrir who reigned when the *tháttr* was written, and the author may have inserted this claim to defend Greenlanders' interests.

In ca. 1360 Ivar Bárdarson claimed that Auros parish church north-west of Herjolvsnes had the right to shipwrecked goods (*vragh*) within its parish, which confirms that in Greenland local people had the right to such goods.[72]

The Greenlanders submitted formally to the Norwegian crown in 1261, but the agreement has not been preserved. In 1270–1271 the Faroese did the same, and here the royal ordinance (*rettarbot*) has been preserved. "We have granted and confirmed that here [in the Faroes] should be used the same law that is used at the Gulathing. But the section which concerns farming,[73] shall remain as it is in your old law-book".[74] Here it is said that the Faroese had an old law-book. It had probably started as a modification of the Gulathing law, and in the following period additions, omissions and changes had made it develop into something different and Faroese. The Gulathing law as practised in Norway had in the centuries before 1270–1271 been transformed gradually to suit the needs of a state society, and the king in 1270–1271 wanted the Faroese codex to adopt these changes. He made one exception in that he saw no need to make agriculture and the relations between tenant and landowner more "Norwegian". The first codices for the Faroes and Iceland seem to have in common that they were modified versions of the Gulathing law. Greenland's law-book may have developed in a similar way until 1261 and was changed when Greenland became part of the Norwegian realm in 1261.

In 1274 the Norwegian king introduced a new national law for his realm, which now included Greenland. We must assume that a copy arrived in Greenland some years later, even if our sources say nothing about it.[75] This did not prevent the Thing at Gardar from making additions to their law-book. Shortly before 1389 the *alþinge á Grønlande* decided that no *austmenn* (= Norwegians and Icelanders) should be permitted to buy food for their own consumption if they did not also buy Greenland merchandise for export.[76] Such ordinances were included in the law-book and were used in the same way as law paragraphs. The law of the Greenlanders continued to be changeable and flexible even after 1274.

GHM claimed in 1845 that Iceland was the "motherland" of the "Greenland colony", and Icelandic law was used in Norse Greenland all through its existence.[77] Greenlanders after 1261 became subjects of the Norwegian crown, but still had to obey Icelandic laws. The Icelandic law before 1264 was *Grágás*.[78] After 1281 the Icelandic "Jonsbok" was in force in Greenland, according to Daniel Bruun.[79] These claims lack an empirical basis.[80]

Summing up, the Gardar Thing had procedures for judging and settling disputes between Greenlanders. The law which was used connected Greenland to Norse legal culture represented by the Gulathing law and possibly Icelandic legislation. Norse principles were modified to meet Greenlandic needs. This "Greenlandic law" is likely to have been written, but it is not said explicitly that it was.

Legal proceedings at the Gardar Thing

Even serious crimes like murders were considered in Norse Greenland as private conflicts between the murderer and the victim's relatives. It was the latter's responsibility to prosecute the perpetrator at the Thing and mobilise allies to have the verdict implemented. *Fostbroedra saga* was authored ca. 1220–1250 and the action takes place in the 1020s. It tells that after the chieftain Thorgrim had been killed, his nephews raised a case at the Gardar Thing against the murderer Thormod, who was outlawed.[81]

In Norway at this time local Thing assemblies were *althing*, open to all, as was the Icelandic central Thing, also named *Althing*. In Greenland there seems to have been only one Thing, and in a verdict from 1389 it is called *althinge*.[82] This means that all Greenlandic men, in practice those who could handle a weapon, were entitled to participate. Descriptions of Thing meetings in *Fostbroedra saga* and *Groenlendinga tháttr* confirm this. In *Groenlendinga tháttr* there is a description of how Norwegian merchants came from both settlements to the Gardar Thing, and there is no reason to doubt that Greenlanders from both settlements also were present.[83]

The Norwegian regional *lagting* and the Althing for all Iceland were held at fixed dates, but Thing assemblies on a lower, local level could also be summoned when needed. At the Gardar Thing both procedures seem to have been used. The Brattahlid chieftain summoned a Thing at Gardar to discuss his plans for a Greenland diocese,[84] and the Norwegian merchant Ossur summoned another meeting to settle his dispute with Bishop Arnaldr.[85] The final, bloody meeting between the two parties took place "at midsummer", which sounds like a fixed date.[86] The Icelandic Althing also met at midsummer.[87] A likely interpretation is that there was an annual Thing assembly at midsummer, but meetings at other times could be summoned if it was urgent to settle a dispute.

Archaeologists have not been able to locate the site of the Thing assembly, but the written sources give some indications.[88] The site is normally called "at Gardar" (*i Gordum*),[89] but on one occasion the assembly is said to have taken place "on the isthmus" (*sætt gera á Eidi*).[90] This is the isthmus between Einarsfjord and Eiriksfjord, the two central fjords in the Eastern Settlement. From this can be concluded that the Thing was held on – or close to – the farm of Gardar on the slope (*i brekku einni*)[91] up towards the ridge which separates the two fjords. The men who spoke stood low in the slope, the audience sat (*settusk nidr*) further up the slope. The text says that one of the speakers "went up to" the audience which sat on the slope.[92]

The participants lived in *budir* or booths which seem to have had permanent walls of stone and turf, and roofs of tent canvas.[93] The Brattahlid chieftain and his people had their booth at the top of the slope where the audience used to sit.[94]

At the better known Gulathing in Western Norway and the Althing in Iceland verdicts were given by a jury (*dòm*). The members were appointed according to certain procedures. At the Thing in Norway and Iceland there would be a legal expert who in Norway was called *lögmadr*, in Iceland *lögsögumadr*, in English lawman. He was elected at the Thing.[95] If asked he would recite for the jury the relevant paragraphs in the law, but he had no authority to judge. The arrangement was probably the same in Greenland. There are no indications that the chieftain at Brattahlid functioned as lawman prior to 1261.

How disputes in practice were settled

In modern Western societies law is considered to be an absolute norm which has to be respected. In the *Groenlendinga tháttr* the Norwegian bishop Arnaldr shared this attitude; he wanted "Greenland law" implemented regardless of the consequences. The problem was that Greenland lacked a state power which could implement court verdicts by force. Pre-state procedures for settlements of disputes had to build on consent between the two parties and others with power to make their influence felt.

The chieftain at Brattahlid had no formal role in the procedures, but he was often a key figure. The saga author starts by telling us that the Brattahlid chieftain Sokki and his son Einar "had much power on Greenland, and in many respects they were the people's leaders".[96] The foreign merchants took the bishop of Greenland to court over a disputed inheritance. The Brattahlid clan were the protectors of the Greenland church, and the bishop reminded Sokki of this obligation.[97]

The Brattahlid chieftain was present at the court case at Gardar with a large retinue of armed men, and they had more manpower than their opponents. The leader of the foreign merchants said that if they had been able to muster more men at the Thing, the Greenlanders would have given their claim a more serious treatment.[98] Powerful chieftains in practice determined the composition of the jury. The verdict at the Greenland Thing about the heritage was in favour of the bishop. The Norwegians felt the jury had been partisan, and from then on the case left the legal path and degenerated into a feud.

The leader of the Norwegian merchants started the feud by damaging with an axe a valuable ship which was the main object in the disputed inheritance. The chieftain's son Einar retaliated by murdering the perpetrator. The Norwegians sought damages for the killing and submitted their claim to a jury at a new Thing assembly. But Einar followed by his armed retainers forced the jury to disband without passing a verdict. Instead the Brattahlid chieftain proposed himself as arbitrator in his son's case. He was much used as arbitrator (*a gera um mal manna*), and it may seem that the Brattahlid chieftain was so used to the role of arbitrator that he took it as a matter of course that this would be so even when his son Einar was accused of murder. But the Norwegian merchants rejected the proposal and instead retaliated by murdering Einar. Four other Greenlanders and three foreigners were also killed in the following skirmish.[99]

The Brattahlid chieftain wanted to continue the blood feud and united the Greenlanders for a final attack on the foreign merchants who stayed in their three ships in Einarsfjord. They were unable to leave because of ice and contrary winds. But the Greenlanders now thought that the Brattahlid chieftain pushed his case too hard. A "wise man and good peasant" among them told Sokki that he lacked the authority to lead the Greenlanders into a new bloody struggle, and proposed himself as arbitrator.[100] That ended the matter; Sokki lacked military power to go it alone. He felt this to be a loss of prestige, and he received no damages for his dead son in blood or money.

The story illustrates the basis of the Brattahlid chieftain's power and its limits. He could mobilise a larger military force than anybody else. If he feared the jury might pass an unwanted verdict, he could disband it by force. If he proposed himself as arbitrator, that would normally be "an offer you can't refuse". But if he defied the majority of armed peasants at the Thing, he overreached himself. In this case the peasants felt that bishop and chieftain were too inflexible. Sokki should have permitted a peasant jury to decide the damages which his son was to pay to the murdered Norwegian's relatives.

This pre-state way of settling disputes shifted between several methods which were adapted to different situations: verdict by a jury at the Thing, direct negotiations, mediation by a third party or arbitration. If all these procedures failed, a blood feud was a likely outcome. The Norwegians first tried to obtain their heritage through the law courts, but when they experienced that the jury was biased, they started a feud. In the next round they tried to obtain damages for the murder of Ossur through a jury at the Gardar Thing, but then the chieftains at Brattahlid disbanded the jury by force and Sokki proposed himself as arbitrator. When the Norwegians understood that neither jury nor arbitration would give them acceptable damages, they shifted to blood feud. This was a costly way of settling a dispute. When eight men had been killed, the Greenland peasants decided to shift the process back to arbitration. This time the arbitrator was a peasant who wanted peace, and he ended the conflict.

The party which could mobilise most armed men at the Gardar Thing could determine who would sit on the jury, disband the jury and control how the verdict was implemented. In armed confrontations it was much easier for a native

Greenlander to mobilise men for his cause. For foreigners these unpredictable shifts and the strong position of the Brattahlid chieftain was problematic and may explain why all known feuds in Greenland were between foreigners and Greenlanders.

4 The Brattahlid chieftain as pre-state political leader

In the initial period political authority on Greenland seems to have been based on the moral authority of the Brattahlid clan. Eirik Raudi was the most honoured (*mestri virdingu*) man on Greenland, "and all obeyed him".[101] His authority seems to have bordered on the supernatural. His son Thorstein wanted his old father to follow him on an expedition to Vinland, "because people thought he had best luck and wisdom (*forsjá*)".[102] His son Leiv Eiriksson and grandson Thorkell Leivsson appear as honoured leaders until the 1020s in the Vinland sagas and the *Fostbroedra saga*. After Thorkell, Eirik Raudi's descendants disappear from the extant sources. His lineage may have died out shortly afterwards. Main characters of the *Groenlendinga tháttr* from the 1130s were also Brattahlid chieftains, but may have belonged to another lineage. They also enjoyed great respect. In this situation no costly military or civilian administration was needed. There are no traces of taxation in the period before 1261.

Brattahlid was in the eyes of Eirik's contemporaries the best farm in Greenland, and modern historians agree. The Nationalmuseum archaeologist Poul Nørlund excavated the ruins of the Brattahlid farm in 1932. He estimated that the central part of the farm, the infield, was 16–18 hectares. This is slightly more than the fenced-in infield/home field at the episcopal farm of Gardar. At Brattahlid should be added the peripheral areas belonging to what Nørlund called "the South farm" and the "mountain farm". Eirik's Brattahlid had the largest infield of all farms in Greenland. It lies in a more sloping terrain than Gardar, which means that Brattahlid had better natural drainage. At Gardar the terrain is flatter and parts of the home field could become wet and boggy and therefore yield less grass per hectare.[103]

The infield was mainly used to harvest hay for winter fodder, and having the largest infield therefore meant that the farm could keep many domestic animals through the winter. The chieftain on Brattahlid could keep more people including armed retainers than any other chieftain in Norse Greenland. But if a sufficient number of other chieftains in other fjords allied against him, he could end up as the inferior party in a military conflict. This was illustrated earlier, where Sokki had to abandon his efforts to take revenge for his son because other Greenlanders refused to follow him.

In the 12th and 13th centuries the Brattahlid chieftain's economic basis was undermined. In the Norse area the largest agricultural unit is called a "name farm" (*navnegård*); Brattahlid is such a name. At a "name farm" there could live one or several households, each with a separate dwelling for humans and byres for cattle. Such household units are in English most conveniently called a "household farm" (*bruk*).[104] Only archaeology can tell how many "household farms" there were at Brattahlid.

In the settlement period there was only one household, that of Eirik Raudi. It seems to have remained that way at least for the first 150 years (985–ca. 1135). The development in the following two centuries is not clear, but in the last century of Norse settlement (ca. 1300–1410) there were four "household farms" on Brattahlid. Eirik's initial farm was divided into what Nørlund called the "North farm" and the "River farm",[105] on the map shown as numbers 539 (E29a) and 540 (E29). Outside the map to the south and west the "South farm" and "Hill farm" were established. Both were probably in the first period part of Brattahlid's outfield.[106]

- On the "North farm" was situated the central buildings of Eirik Raudi's initial farm: dwelling with hall for the chieftain, byre for cattle, and the church.
- The "River farm" had a dwelling "in the last period in the 14th and 15th century". In the "Conclusion" Nørlund is more precise, claiming that the house "cannot have been built until late in the thirteenth or perhaps even in the fourteenth century, and which, judging by the thinness of the refuse heaps, can only have been inhabited for a rather short span of time, at any rate compared with the North house".[107] Eirik Raudi's initial farm was divided into two farms, as part of the process whereby the parish priest was given a separate farm owned by the bishop's organisation.
- The "South farm" and the "Hill farm" may have been separated from the outfield of Eirik's old farm at the same time.

Ivar Bárdarson distinguished ca. 1360 between *Brattahlid* farm where the lawman lived, and the parish church which he called (*Lijder kircke*).[108] The church organisation owned *Lijder* parish church and the parish priest lived at the "North farm", which was the oldest and best part of Brattahlid.[109] The king's lawman must then have lived at the River farm, which Nørlund thought was established at the end of the 13th century shortly after Greenland had submitted to the Norwegian king in 1261. The parish church was transferred from the private church-owner to the bishop's control, and Brattahlid farm was divided between the lawman and the parish priest.[110]

The splitting up of Brattahlid farm visualises deep political changes. The first chieftains controlled the church, the courts of law and the peasant militia from their large farm. Greenland's largest farm was now divided and was no longer owned and inhabited by a chieftain who had ambitions to be Greenland's most powerful man. After 1261 a powerful, independent chieftain was not wanted by the new state power.

Resources from Brattahlid which could be mobilised for political functions were further reduced because the sea level rose during the Norse centuries, and land was submerged. Antoon Kuijpers suggests that the shore line at Brattahlid may have regressed 100 metres in the last 1000 years, but he does not say by how much during the four Norse centuries. The land nearest the shore does not belong to the most fertile part.[111]

58 *Political organisation*

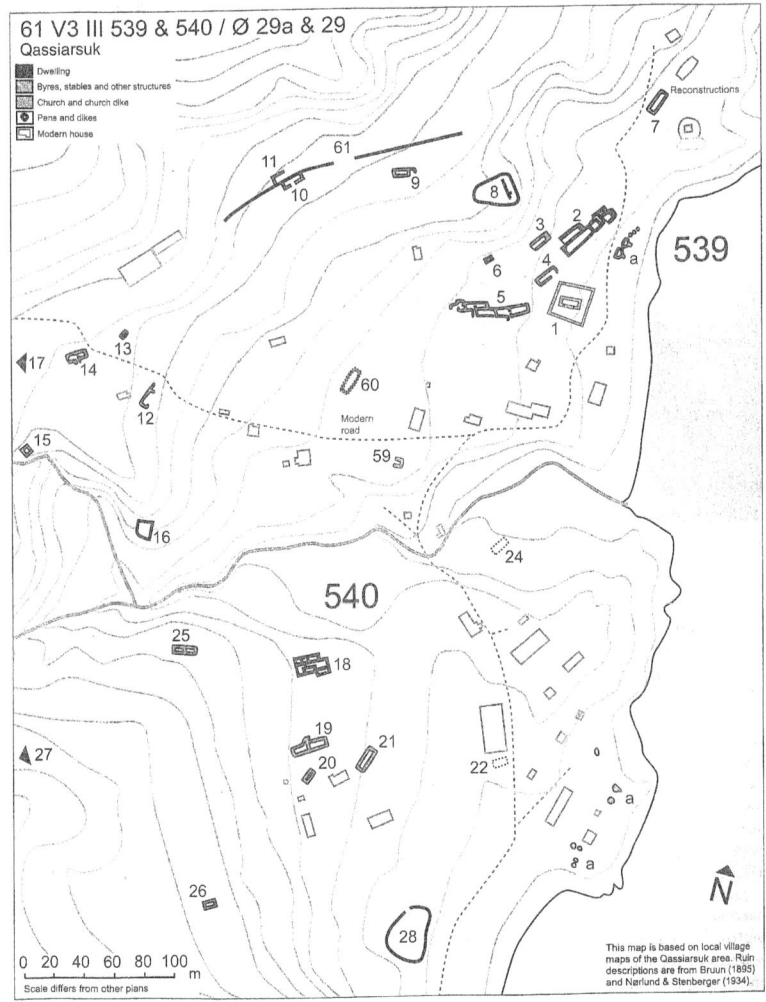

Figure 2.1 Map of Brattahlid manor, the seat of Greenland's mightiest chieftain, Appendix II, map 5.

Brattahlid in the final century of the farm's existence included two household farms and a church (cf. Chapter 5, pp. 232–233).
The household farm on which the church was situated (E29a = 539) had the buildings shown on the map. The archaeologists have identified the function of the following buildings:

   1 Church and church dike, mainly built of large stones. The church measures ca. 15 × 7.5 m and the dike, ca. 24 × 28 m.
   2 Dwelling and hall, ca. 48 × 9–15 m.

5 A large byre complex, ca. 52 × 8–12 m.
61 Dike separating infield from outfield.
8 A large pen, ca. 28 × 9–18 m. Cattle and goats were kept there at night in summer to be milked every evening and morning. In daytime they were pastured in the outfield, outside the dike.
14 Stable or byre. Built of turf and stones, ca. 15 × 6 m. The ruin has been excavated and shows standing stall stones.
59 Tjodhilde's church.

The remaining smaller houses were used for a variety of purposes which are difficult to determine: stables for sheep and goats, storage of food and outhouses for many kinds of equipment. Boat houses may have been swallowed by the rising sea level.

The second household farm was without a church (E29 = 540). The archaeologists have identified the function of the following buildings:

18 Dwelling, ca. 22 × 12 m.
19 Byre, built of turf and stones, ca. 26 × 7 m, with thick turf walls. The ruin shows standing stall stones.
21 Indistinct turf-built stable.
25 Stone- and turf-built stable, ca. 15 × 5 m.
27 A large pen, built of large blocks.
28 A large pen, ca. 40 × 30 m.

The remaining smaller houses were used for a variety of purposes which are difficult to determine.
At both household farms the byre was a short distance from the dwelling. This made the walk shorter for the women who had to milk their cows morning and evening on cold winter days.

Source and copyright: Guldager, Ole, Steffen Stummann Hansen and Simon Gleie, Copenhagen 2002, pp. 76–80.

5 Ties to the Norwegian king before 1261

The Greenlanders belonged to the same ethnic community as Norwegians and Icelanders. This must have made it easier for Greenlanders to accept becoming part of the Norwegian state. Were there political ties which united Greenland to Norway, Iceland and other northern islands even before it became part of the Norwegian state in 1261?

Collective obligations to the Norwegian crown before 1261

Adam of Bremen's "History of the church province of Hamburg" was written during 1073–1075, and the author obtained most of his information about Scandinavia when he visited the court of the Danish King Sven Estridsson. This is the oldest source which mentions power relations on the Norse Atlantic islands.

After Norway (*Nortmannia*), which is the northernmost province, no human dwellings exist, only horrible visions and the infinite ocean which surrounds the whole world. There exist outside Norway (*Nortmannia*) many important islands which now almost all are subordinated to the Norwegians' (*Nortmannorum*) command.

> (*Is habet ex adverso Nortmanniae insulas multas non ignobiles, qua nunc fere omnes Nortmannorum ditioni subiacent*).[112]

"Subiacere" is translated in dictionaries as "being subordinated to".[113] "Nortmannia" and "Nortmannos" are not Latin, Adam has taken it from his native language which was Low German. Here the common spelling for "Norwegian" was *Nor-man* which also could mean "person from the north". But "north" was in Middle Low German *nort*, and it was therefore unproblematic for Adam to choose a variant spelling *Nort-man*. He does not describe in what way Greenland was subordinated to the Norwegians and he suggests not all islands were.[114] Perhaps neither Adam nor his Danish informers had precise information. This evidence tells us that at the Danish court around 1070 Greenland was considered as subordinated to the Norwegian king.

Orderic Vitalis was an English monk who around 1135–1140 wrote a history of the Anglo-Norman church. He has the following to say about Greenland:

> [The Norwegians] practice their religion in accordance with Christian laws, preserve peace and chastity by the strictest laws, and punish crimes with savage penalties. The Orkney islands, Finnmark, Iceland and also Greenland, north of which no land can be found, and many other places as far as *Gollanda* [= Götaland in Sweden] are subject to the king of Norway, and wealth is carried there from all over the world.[115]
>
> (*Orcades insulæ et Finlanda, Islanda quoque Grenlanda . . . regi Noricorum subiciuntur.*)

Orderic was well informed, and his views are normally representative of his contemporaries. Orderic's words give a strong indication that the English elite at this time considered the Atlantic isles, Greenland explicitly included, as subordinated to the Norwegian king.

Historia Norwegie was written in Norway ca. 1150 or somewhat later, probably at one of the bishop's sees.[116] It has a chapter called "On the tributary islands". Both the Orkneys and the Hebrides pay "no mean tribute to the kings of Norway",[117] and it is later repeated that these islands "are legally bound to pay tribute to the Norwegian kings".[118] The Faroe islanders also "pay tribute to our kings at set times (*certis temporibus*)".[119] Iceland is given a section among the tributary islands, but it is not said that they paid tribute.[120] Greenland is not mentioned among the tributary islands, neither is it said to pay tribute, but it is not forgotten since it is mentioned in other contexts.[121] This is a strong indication that the Greenlanders did not pay tribute. In 1261 the Greenlanders promised to pay to the king taxes and fines for manslaughter, and this is presented as a novelty.[122]

Historia Norwegie does not say that Greenland was without ties to Norway, but it verifies that the island did not pay tribute.

Knut Helle has examined taxation to the Norwegian crown from all Norse Atlantic islands before 1261. He finds an older form of taxation, where taxes were paid at irregular intervals "on occasions of particularly strong Norwegian influence or when Norwegian support was particularly wanted by the local ruler". This payment was an "acknowledgement of submission or as price of peace and protection". He calls this irregular taxation "tribute".[123] The Norwegian crown did its best to impose a regular form of annual taxation, with mixed results until the second half of 13th century. Shetland seems to have paid more or less regular taxes to Norway from 1195, Orkney from 1210.[124] The Greenlanders did not need Norwegian support against external enemies before 1261, and Greenlandic chieftains did not seek Norwegian help against local competitors.

There are no indications that the Greenland community had collective, political obligations to the Norwegian crown before 1261. But in neighbouring Denmark there was an idea that Greenland and other northern islands were subordinated to "the Norwegians", and in England that it was subordinated to the Norwegian king. The origin of this idea may have been that Greenlanders had the same ethnic identity as the Norwegians, and that this ethnic group originated in Norway. This may have been combined with information that individual members of the elite on these islands had sworn loyalty to the Norwegian king.

Were individual Greenlanders members of the king's hird?

In Iceland many chieftains, their sons and other warriors were members of the Norwegian king's retinue (*hird*) and swore loyalty to him. The king then could demand loyalty from them even if Iceland before 1264 was not part of the Norwegian state organisation. An Icelandic *hirdmann* could stay with the king in Norway for several years, and when he returned to Iceland he was supposed to keep his pledge of loyalty. In internal power struggles in Iceland it was an advantage to be the king's *hirdmann*, because the king could then mobilise his Icelandic network in their support. Since the *hird* was based on individual and not geographic loyalty it was possible for a king to have loyal followers in territories which had not submitted to him. Did the king have a similar network in Greenland?

In Iceland the power of many lineages varied from one generation to the next. In Greenland the Brattahlid clan is likely to have been the most powerful from the start in AD 985 to 1261. This limited the king's possibilities of building a network of loyal *hirdmenn*; if it was to be effective it had to pass via or include the Brattahlid chieftain.

While his father Eirik Raudi was still alive, Leiv Eiriksson visited the *hird* of King Olav Trygvason (995–1000). It is not said how long he stayed there, but after a time the king ordered him to return to Greenland and Christianise the island. Leiv accepted reluctantly to make an attempt. The context makes it likely that Leiv was a member of King Olav's *hird*, even if it is not said explicitly.[125] When he returned his father Eirik was not amused. The saga says that this was because he disliked the new faith, but it is also possible that he disliked that his son and heir ran errands for the Norwegian king.

It did not become a tradition that Brattahlid chieftains were members of the king's *hird*. A hundred years later around 1130 the chieftain's son Einar was given the task of persuading the Norwegian king to establish a new diocese on Greenland.[126] The Brattahlid clan had no previous connections at the *hird*, and Einar had to give courtiers gifts to get access to the king. Nothing is said of Einar becoming a member of the *hird* or swearing loyalty to the king.[127] Later sources give no evidence that members of the Brattahlid clan were *hird* members.

Earl Eirik was the ruler of Norway between 1000–1015. Bjarni was the son of the chieftain at Herjolvsnes, and one summer he sailed to Norway and was made a member of Earl Eirik's *hird* (*Bjarni gerdisk hirdmadr jarls*). The following summer he returned to Greenland.[128]

Snorri Sturlusson in his Heimskringla claims that "St. Olav (1015–1028) sent messages and acquired many friends on Iceland, Greenland and the Faroes".[129] *Fostbroedra saga* gives graphic accounts of how the Norwegian king could use members of his *hird* to obtain power in Greenland. The story below is not meant as a presentation of historical facts, but as an illustration of social relations created by *hird* membership.

It all started on Iceland where one of St. Olav's *hirdmenn* was killed by a chieftain from Greenland called Thorgrim Trolle. King Olav then sent another of his Icelandic *hirdmenn* Thormod Kolbrunarskald to Greenland to take revenge.[130] Thormod sailed to Greenland on a ship owned by a skipper called Skufr. "Skufr lived on Greenland and had his ancestors there, he was a great merchant, a wise man and had many friends. He was a friend of King Olav and had sworn loyalty to him. Skufr sought the king's hird and was there during the winter".[131] He owned the farm Stokkanes in Eiriksfjord opposite Brattahlid, which means that he was the Brattahlid chieftain's client.[132] Skufr was to be Thormod's main support on Greenland, they were both the Norwegian king's *hirdmenn*.

The chieftain in Eiriksfjord was at this time Eirik Raudi's grandson Thorkell "who was a powerful chieftain, rich with many friends. He was a good friend (*vinr mikill*) of St. Olav".[133] Thorkell was a friend of St. Olav, but had not sworn loyalty to him as [a] member of his *hird*. Skufr now became St. Olav's oral messenger on Greenland, asking Thorkell to give the king's *hirdmann* Thormod all the protection and support he needed. Thorkell obeyed and offered Thormod board and lodging at Brattahlid.[134]

Thormod participated in the Christmas celebrations at Brattahlid, and there killed one of Thorkell's slaves. Thorkell was furious and ordered his servants to kill Thormod. Skufr then reminded Thorkell that killing the king's *hirdmann* was a serious matter. This made Thorkell accept a money compensation which Skufr paid. Afterwards Thormod moved to Skufr's household.[135]

Thormod attended the Gardar Thing as part of Skufr's household, and there managed to kill Thorgrim Trolle. Skufr asked Thormod not to escalate the conflict further, [as] he feared that his role as Thormod's protector would endanger his own position and possibly life. Thormod answered that he feared the killed man's relatives would take revenge.[136] He killed four of the dead man's nephews, three servants and one slave.[137]

Skufr paid a poor couple to take care of Thormod during the first winter, but they expressed fear that this might put their lives in danger.[138] Skufr now understood that Thormod had drawn him into deadly conflicts with so many people that he had to leave Greenland. His relations to his chieftain Thorkell were strained. He sold his farm, land and cattle and prepared his ship for emigration to Norway. A widow and her son who had helped Thormod, also emigrated.[139]

St. Olav thought that he through members of his *hird* had "taught the Greenlanders not to attack my men",[140] but the cost was nine killed Greenlanders and several others had to leave their farms.[141] Members of the king's *hird* had stronger protection than ordinary people.

Skufr was in a squeeze because he traded in Norwegian towns where he depended on the goodwill of the king, and in the Eastern Settlement where he depended on the Brattahlid chieftain. Thormod made this balancing act impossible, and Skufr ended his life in Norway as a warrior in St. Olav's *hird*.[142] For the Brattahlid chieftain protecting his clients and servants had a higher priority than the king's wishes – he had not sworn loyalty to King Olav. When Thormod killed one of his household slaves, he ceased to give active support to Thormod.

The Norwegian king did not manage to recruit many or important Greenlanders to his *hird* in the period before 1261. In Iceland the prime motive for joining the king's hird was that it gave protection against adversaries in feuds, which were rare or non-existent in Greenland. When Greenland society needed official communications with Norway, this seems to have been done by sending representatives authorised by the Gardar Thing or by the Greenland church. In the first decades after AD 985 Greenlandic merchants needed protection when they stayed in Norway, often for the whole winter, but after 1200, Greenlanders no longer sailed to Norway for trading purposes.[143]

The mafia-like murders of St. Olav and his *hirdmenn* were not those of a state organisation. A state had an administration which controlled the violence of its subjects and made its own violence legitimate through laws. That was the next stage.

6 Attempts to organise a state administration after 1261

The submission in 1261

In 1247 a representative from the pope arrived in Bergen. He had been invited by king Håkon to consecrate him as king. Håkon also asked the cardinal for help to make Iceland and Greenland parts of the Norwegian realm. The cardinal was positive, and he asked bishops and magnates present at the consecration to support the king's efforts. In 1247 the papacy was still at the height of its power.

King Håkon sent a delegation to Iceland with an order to the people there to submit to the king and pay taxes to him. The level of taxation was to be negotiated; the taxes were clearly more important as a symbol of submission than as a source of income for the crown. The messengers were one Icelandic bishop and one of the most powerful Icelandic chieftains who had been present at the consecration. The mission was not successful.

The king sent the bishop of Gardar to Greenland with the same message.[144] Bishop Olav had been consecrated in Norway the preceding year in 1246, and Icelandic Annals confirm that he sailed from Norway via Iceland to Greenland in 1247.[145] No secular chieftain from Greenland is mentioned, which must mean that none had been present at the consecration. King Håkon relied exclusively on the church. Bishop Olav's mission brought no immediate results. But the king did not abandon his plans, and in 1257 he sent three ambassadors to Greenland. They were Norwegians and were named Odd from Sjoltar, Paul Magnusson and Knarri-Leiv. The last person was evidently the skipper. They stayed in Greenland for four winters. This gave them three summers to execute their job.[146] They undoubtedly made speeches and participated in discussions at the Gardar Thing and in parish churches.

Their message was that the Greenlanders should pay taxes and fines to the Norwegian king. The Greenlanders and the messengers reached an agreement, which must have been done at the Gardar Thing. The envoys returned to Norway in 1261, but there are no traces of them in the Icelandic Annals so they may have sailed directly to Bergen.[147] Bishop Olav sailed from Greenland in his own ship the following year 1262. The envoys may have ordered him to Norway to swear allegiance to the king. But the bishop's ship was wrecked on the Icelandic coast, and he stayed there for two winters and did not continue to Norway until 1264.[148] He stayed there until he returned to Greenland via Iceland in 1271.[149] He died at his see in 1280.[150]

The Greenlanders agreed to pay taxes; the saga uses the word *skattgildi*, tax-payment.[151] *Skat* at this time normally meant regular, annual payments.[152] Since shipping to Norway was irregular, this may have been understood differently in Greenland. In a law from 1273 (*Hirdskrá*) the Norwegian realm (*Noregs vælldi*) is said to include Norway proper (*innan landz*) but also lands paying taxes (*skatlondum*).[153] Payment of *skat* was a symbolic expression of political subjection to the crown. King Håkon's saga does not say how much the Greenlanders paid.

The king should also have the right to fines for all manslaughters, but not for other crimes.

> They were to pay fines to the king for all manslaughters irrespective of whether the killed persons were Norwegians (*norænir*) or Greenlanders (*Grænlenzkir*) and equally whether they were killed in the [Eastern or Western] settlements

or in *Nordr-setu* (the Disco Bay region). Even if the manslaughter happened far north under the Pole Star (*allt nordr undir Stjörnuna*), the king was entitled to *thegn-gildi* after them.[154]

"Far north under the Pole Star" must mean north of the Disco Bay region. The fine is here called *thegngildi*. *Thegn* in Old Norse is a term used for the king's free subjects, and *thegngildi* was a fine to which the king was entitled because he had lost one of his subjects.[155] The payment of *thegngildi* was therefore a symbolic expression that the Greenlanders were now the king's subjects, and that Håkon ruled the west coast of Greenland as far as the Norse Greenlanders sailed northwards. Damages to the relatives of the murdered person were to continue as before.

Then follows in Håkon's saga a poem composed by the Icelandic court (*hird*) poet Sturla Thordarson:

It pleased you, warrior, to extend your realm northwards to the cold world quite up to under the Pole Star. Wise and just men will praise it. No other king than you have held sovereignty over a realm there. People will tell your glory and fame (*dyrd*) further than the sun shines.[156]

The symbolic and prestige value of Greenland for the crown is evident both in the poem and in the saga text. There are no indications that the economic transfers were important.

It has been claimed that this agreement from 1261 also included a promise from the king to send two ships a year to Greenland.[157] This will be discussed in Chapter 4, pp. 214–217.

What was the attitude in Greenland to the Norwegian ambitions? The leader of the Greenland church seems to have been a politically passive person who supported the king's plans when he was in Norway or was confronted by the king's envoys in Greenland. We can understand the bishop's problem – the Gardar bishops had to visit Norway to be consecrated and keep up contacts with church colleagues in Bergen and Nidaros. Then they could be exposed to pressure from the king and royalists among ecclesiastical colleagues. The Gardar bishop could not isolate himself from them if he and his church were to function normally.

The king had in 1247 given Bishop Olav the task of bringing Greenland under Norwegian sovereignty, but the bishop did nothing effective to execute these plans when he was left alone in Greenland. Perhaps the bishop tried but failed; perhaps he did not even try. His passivity when left without Norwegian pressure indicates that the Greenlanders were not eager to become the Norwegian king's subjects; they wanted to leave things as they were. After ten years King Håkon understood that the bishop was of no use to his project. When the king's three representatives turned up in Greenland in 1257, Olav probably gave them his support.

In Iceland there were violent and murderous struggles between chieftains in the decades prior to 1264, and this gave the Norwegian king allies in the secular elite. In Greenland this motive did not exist. All Greenlanders must have understood

66 *Political organisation*

that refusing the king's demands would mean isolation from the larger Norse cultural community, and this was clearly important to them. In 1261 the trade in walrus tusks was still flourishing, and the export/import trade went via Bergen.

The courts of justice

The lawman is the only state official mentioned by title by Ivar Bárdarson (ca. 1360), and the only information on him is that he "usually" lived at Brattahlid.[158] In Norway the lawman (*lagmann*) was at this time a state official who judged according to a law-book issued by the king. He could judge alone, in which case he would then base his verdicts on an authority which was independent from peasant society. An alternative was that a peasant jury judged, after having received counsel from the lawman. In both cases the lawman had a decisive influence on the outcome.

At the end of the 14th century or somewhat later, a long narrative poem was written about an Icelander called Skald-Helgi.[159] The poem belongs to an Icelandic literary genre called *rimur* and is fiction.[160] Helgi is said to have lived in the 11th century and was lawman in Greenland.[161] The poem may be used as a source for the ideas which Icelanders had about lawmen in Greenland in the final decades of the settlement's existence.

Skald-Helgi moved to Greenland as an adult. "The people there elected him to be their *lagmann*, and his function was to give law and justice to the land. They thought nobody was as well qualified to it as he".[162] The valid law in Greenland ca. 1400 was the law-book of the Norwegian king Magnus Lagabøte issued in 1274, and there it is assumed that the lawman was appointed by the king. But the central government in Bergen would have problems checking the Greenlandic candidates' competence and it is perfectly possible that they left it to the Gardar Thing to elect him. But some kind of authorisation from the crown may have been needed. It is also possible that this was historic knowledge, since the lawman had been elected in the 11th century.

Ivar Bárdarson states that the lawman lived at Brattahlid, and this is also said about Skald-Helgi who "moved to Brattahlid, and lived there until his old age".[163] Both sources were written in the second half of the 14th century. No third source contradicts this information. Historical methodology demands that for a source to be trusted it should be confirmed by another independent source. These two sources combined makes it likely that after the subordination to Norway the judge in Greenland was the lawman who normally lived at Brattahlid. One of the "household farms" on Brattahlid may have been state property and rented to the office holder.[164]

In the first centuries the Brattahlid chieftain was not lawman but had a decisive informal influence on the proceedings at the Gardar Thing.[165] After 1261 state authority may have put an end to this practice. Instead, the king appointed a judge who resided at Brattahlid. It cannot be excluded that this judge was elected at the annual Gardar Thing.

A judge after 1261 had to be able to read the law-book, but power of judgement and the ability to apply the law to concrete problems were also required.

This made education by an experienced person necessary. In the pre-state period in Iceland an experienced lawman would teach a talented and interested boy or youth who lived at his farm; the young man would often be his son.[166] In Greenland such education may normally have taken place at Brattahlid, and one of the tasks of the lawman may have been to educate his successor.

As mentioned earlier, the legitimacy of verdicts no longer rested with a jury which was appointed and said its verdicts at the Gardar Thing, but with the lawman personally. The Greenland lawman may have held court sessions at his residence Brattahlid, and parallel changes also took place in Norway at this time. The archaeologist Poul Nørlund excavated Brattahlid in 1932. At the peripheral South farm he found many bases for turf and stone walls which he interpreted as belonging to booths for temporary stays. He also found tent rings with fireplaces. They were so numerous that Nørlund thought they belonged to a place of assembly, most likely a Norse Thing or market place. Some may have been made by Inuit at a later date. An alternative hypothesis is that they were made by people who came to attend court sessions chaired by the lawman.[167]

Settling disputes was a major source of income for chieftains in pre-state Norse societies. The pre-state chieftain at Brattahlid was often used as an arbitrator,[168] and in Iceland powerful chieftains received a gift for this. If the losing party did not obey a verdict at the Thing, the winning party could ask a powerful chieftain for help, and then the helper expected a gift. The Norwegian king was given the right in the treaty of 1261 to fines for all murders in Greenland, which was a new right. The understanding must have been that the king's officials in return would give help to have the perpetrator punished. The loss of incomes from jurisdiction after 1261 could have been serious to the Brattahlid chieftain, but if the person who resided there after 1261 was the lawman who received the fines, there may have been continuity even in Brattahlid's incomes.

The royal manors at Foss and Hvalsey

The subject of Ivar Bárdarson's account was the church, but he mentions three farms in the Eastern Settlement as connected to the Norwegian crown, Brattahlid, Foss and *Thiødhillestad*.[169] Brattahlid's function has been discussed already. Foss and *Thiødhillestad* he calls *hoffgaard*,[170] a word best translated as "manor". The word does not necessarily imply that a state official resided there, and Ivar does not explain the farms' function.[171]

Ivar tells that Foss was "a large manor which belongs to the king". The name means "waterfall", and it was situated close to a lake which was rich in fish, and it had a church which was "costly".[172] Foss was, according to Ivar, east of Einarsfjord but west of Rampnessfjord (Southern Sermilik?).[173] This points to the site E91 at the head of the Amitsuarsuk fjord. Here are numerous Norse ruins, a waterfall and a fish-rich lake, and it lies between the two fjords just mentioned. Gustav Holm in 1880 found several large ruins here.[174] After an expedition led by Daniel Bruun in 1894, one of the participants Frode Petersen argued that this was Ivar Bárdarson's royal farm Foss. No one has later argued for alternatives.[175] Bruun published a drawing and a map of the site in 1918.[176] Helge Ingstad visited the site with his motorboat in 1953. He confirmed a rich fishery of Arctic char, salmon and cod. One of the waterfalls there is the largest in Southern Greenland.[177] Why did the king choose this site?

Foss had a good harbour. Reefs close to the head of the fjord prevented large ice floes from drifting to the shore, creating a protected basin for larger ships. In the opposite direction Foss must have been appreciated for giving good access to the densely populated Vatnahverfi. Goods could be rowed across the lowest lake closest to the fjord, carried up to the next lake Qolortorsuup on horseback or sledges, and transported on that lake to the farms E73 and E74, and further to other farms in Vatnahverfi.[178] The king probably chose this site mainly because it gave good access to the southern part of Vatnahverfi and farms along the Agdluitsup fjord system and had a harbour for ocean-going ships.

Along the shores of the lower lake it must have been possible to cultivate a large meadow close to the farm.[179] Today the land further away from the farm houses is covered by shrub mostly of willow, which is not ideal for summer pasture. The Norse may have burned it down, which would have given more grassland for pastures. Short walking or rowing trips along the Amitsuarsuk fjord from E91 brought them to what is today several small ruin groups, among them E310, E309 and E308. It is not clear which were sæters for E91 and which were independent farms.[180] A walk of ca. 2 km into the Vatnahverfi area brought them to Lake Qorlortorsuup. There they could row the animals to several sæters along the shore. It must have been possible to keep a large livestock and feed many people at E91 Foss.[181]

Ivar Bárdarson describes a lake full of large fish close to Foss.[182] Arctic char can swim without problems from the head of the Amitsuarsuk fjord up the river to a first lake at whose shores is the ruin group E91. Char is unlikely to have swum further up from this first lake to the second lake (Qorlortorsuup) since there was a steep 60 m long waterfall between them.[183] A large number of fish must have remained in the first lake at Foss' doorstep most of the year. Fish in lakes whose shores were privately owned belonged by law to the landowner.

Ivar tells that Foss had a "costly" church, but he does not say that it was large. It is likely to have had a parish which included the southern Vatnahverfi and the Agdluitsup fjord system. In Norway it was possible for royal chapels to have parish rights.[184] Its "costly" equipment must have given it royal prestige. The church must have been built after Greenland became part of the Norwegian realm in 1261, which means that it must have had the same rectangular ground plan as other Gothic parish churches in the Norse tradition, with Hvalsey as the best known example.[185] Anavik (W7) is a smaller parish church with a gothic ground plan, and its external measures were 13.9 × 6.8 m, nave and chancel included.[186] In 2006 Möller and Madsen registered 12 Norse house ruins at the site of E91, 3 of which they labelled as "dwellings", and all of them had a rectangular form. One of them could have been a church with external measures 15 × 12 m.[187] The archaeologists have so far not falsified Ivar's claim of a "costly church" at E91.

The largest of the three "dwellings" had external measures 23 × 21 m.[188] It was given the following description: "Ruin 14. Dwelling. Indistinct on sloping terrain. Very difficult to draw a limit to the midden below. Part of the measured building was probably midden".[189] This may have been byre and barn for cattle and not a dwelling since it had a large midden. The ruin has never been excavated, and it is therefore not possible to calculate the number of cattle which it could accommodate. If this was a byre and barn which was 23 m long, half of it may have been byre. The wall may have been ca. 1.5 m thick. This makes the internal length of the byre ca. 10 m. The stalls for the cows may have been ca. 1.2 m each along the wall, which would make room for eight cows along each wall. Since the cows here would stand along both walls tail to tail, the byre would give room for ca. 16 cows. This was above the average for Norse farms which was ca. 10 cows, but there were larger farms both in the Western and Eastern Settlements.[190] How these estimates are done is explained in more detail in Chapter 5, pp. 233–237. Since ruin 14 has not been excavated this is little more than a "guesstimate"; future excavations will give more precise information.

Ruin 4 was 20 × 10 m, the building site had been raised almost 1.5 m over the surrounding area probably to make the house drier, and it was divided into rooms. This may have been the dwelling.[191]

Of the 12 house ruins 6 are small, and Madsen categorises them as "economy buildings".[192] He hypothesises that most of them were "small livestock buildings", and from that he concludes that E91 was a farm "based on a sheep/goat economy".[193] Other hypotheses are not discussed. An alternative hypothesis could be that the six small buildings were mostly used to store goods which the state received as taxes, land rents and fines but also commercial goods which waited for a cargo ship to or from Bergen. This transforms E91 from a sheep and goat farm to a royal manor. The latter hypothesis combines written and archaeological sources, whereas the first hypothesis leaves out the written sources without explaining why.[194]

Who lived at Foss? Ivar says that the king "hired out" the farm – he uses the Danish word *forlene*. According to the largest Danish dictionary for the relevant period, *forlene* means "leave one's property to somebody for a limited time for free or for payment".[195] In our context this should be taken to mean that the king gave a person the right to use Foss in return for some kind of service to the crown.

Ivar says the following about the king's second *hoffgaard*, paraphrased in English with modern punctuation:

Next to Einarsfjord lies Hvalseyfjord. There is a church called Hvalseyfjord church. She owns the parish rights to the whole fjord, and also to the whole Ramstadefjord which lies next to it. In this fjord is a large manor, which belongs to the king, and is called Thiødhillestad.

Nest Einerfjord ligger Hvaltzøer fiord, ther ligger en kircke som heder Hvalsøør fiord kircke, hun eger all fiordenn, och saa alle Ramstadefiord som nest ligger, udi denne fiord er en stuor hoffgaard, som konningen hører till och hieder Thiødhillestad.[196]

The royal *hoffgaard* lies "in this fjord" (*udi denne fjord*). Grammatically "this fjord" should refer to the last-named fjord, which is Ramstadefjord. Finnur Jonsson as a good philologist interpreted it that way – *Thiødhillestad* was in Ramstadefjord which is today's Kangerluarsuk.[197] The problem is that *Thiødhillestad* is said to be large, and none of the farms in Ramstadefjord are large, as far as the archaeologists know. I have checked all farm ruins in the Kangerluarsuk fjord in Nationalmuseet's "Nordboarkiv" and it seems that none of them has been excavated.

An alternative hypothesis should therefore be discussed. According to Ivar, *Thiødhillestad* was in Hvalseyfjord parish. The largest ruin complex in that parish is today's Hvalseyfjord church and Hvalsey farm ruins. Are they remnants from Ivar Bárdarson's "royal manor"?

As mentioned earlier, "this fjord" should grammatically refer to Ramstadefjord. But "*och saa alle Ramstadefiord som nest ligger*" is an inserted clause. If that inserted clause is removed, "this fjord" will refer to the last-mentioned fjord in the main clause, which is Hvalseyfjord. The scribe may have confused the fjord last mentioned in the main clause and the fjord last mentioned in the inserted clause. If this is so, the royal manor is at the Hvalseyfjord. Can *Thiødhillestad* be the farm on which today's Hvalseyfjord church ruin is located?

Finnur Jonsson has given arguments for this hypothesis, without realising it. Another manuscript says there was a royal manor here called *Holastadr*.[198] *Holl* in Old Norse meant rounded hill. *Stadr* in 14th-century Iceland meant "a farm with a church located on it". The name Holastadr can be paraphrased as "a farm with a church on it, close to a rounded hill". This is a good description of the Hvalsey farm as it can be seen today. Finnur Jonsson thinks it likely that Holastadr and Tjodhildstadr were two names for the same royal *hoffgaard*.[199]

Norse tradition often named a parish church after its parish, which could be a fjord. Hvalseyfjord church would be understood as "the parish church of people living along the Hvalseyfjord". The farm on which the church stood could have another name. Ivar calls the innermost parish church in Eiriksfjord *Lijder* church, but the farm on which it stood, Brattahlid.[200] Hvalseyfjord church may have stood on *Thiødhillestad* farm. This farm may have been a royal manor.

Was Ivar's "large royal manor" a modest farm in the peripheral Ramstadefjord on which Ivar lavishes unrealistic praise? Ivar normally formulates himself in a sober manner, it is not his style to talk a medium sized farm into a "large manor" (*stuor hoffgaard*). For me it is easier to accept that the scribe who wrote Ivar's narrative in Bergen[201] formulated an ungrammatical sentence.

Hvalseyfjord church and the farm on which it stood changed name through the Norse centuries. *Landnámabok* is the oldest source in which Hvalseyfjord is mentioned. It called the farm of the first settler Thorkell Farserk *Hvalseyiarfirdi*.[202] When it was named, it was the only farm in the fjord. In the following period many new farms were established, each with its own name. Hvalseyfjord farm may have been renamed *Tjodhildstadr*, while the original farm name Hvalseyfjord remained as the name of the church and its parish.[203]

Shortly after 1261 the king may have acquired the farm and built a new church there. In 1408 a marriage took place "in Hvalsey on Greenland" (*i Hvalzæy á Grænlande*). Concluding a marriage contract was at this time a secular ceremony which could take place in church or in a secular house; in this case "in Hvalsey" seems to mean at the farm Hvalsey.[204] The name of the farm seems to have changed from "Hvalseyfjord" to "Tjodhildestadr/Holastadr" to "Hvalsey".

How large was the "large manor" in the Hvalseyfjord? There are two Norse ruin groups close to Hvalseyfjord church. There is one around Hvalseyfjord church and farm (E83), and another 1 km further east (E83a). One household cannot have milked and fed domestic animals in byres and stables so far apart. One hypothesis is that the two groups of houses may have been operated by two households, but both "household farms" may have belonged to the same "name farm".[205] An alternative hypothesis is that both groups of houses belonged to the same chieftain who had his dwelling close to the church, but had servants working in the houses further east. Aage Roussel excavated E83 and E83a in 1935, and he argued convincingly for the last hypothesis.

His most convincing argument is that on E83a there are seven house ruins, but none of them are dwellings – all are byres, stables or other agricultural buildings. There are traces of food having been made in byres and stables. Roussell says that in the Nordic tradition it was not unusual for servants to sleep in the byres and stables of domestic animals. I can confirm that this was also the case in Norway. The soil for agriculture was good around E83a.[206] On a Norse Greenland farm butter, cheese, meat and skimmed sour milk were produced to be consumed weeks or months later. It did not present problems for a chieftain to produce some of this a kilometre away from his main dwelling. At "sæters" the production took place even further away.[207]

How many cattle could the owner of Hvalsey/ *Thiødhillestad/Holastadr* keep in the byres on his farm? At E83 close to the church, byre ruin 1 had internal measures 6 × 3 m, and byre ruin 7 had internal measures 12 × 3m, with room for 5 and 10 cows respectively, 15 cows in all.[208] At 83a ruin 20 accommodating byre and barn had internal dimensions 47.6 × 3.6 m.[209] Normally half the length was byre, that is 24 m. There are indications that some of this space may have been used as sleeping quarters for milkmaids and other servants. The cattle may have occupied ca. 20 m standing along both walls. This gives room for 33 cows. E83 and 83a could together keep 48 cows. This makes Hvalsey the second largest farm in Norse Greenland, smaller than Gardar with 110 cows, but larger than the 2 Brattahlid farms with 32 and Sandnes with 34.[210] The Danish archaeologist Skaaning Høegsberg has claimed that E83 and E83a would have been able to feed a livestock of the same size as Brattahlid's.[211] The results above indicate that the livestock at Hvalsey was larger. Are the impressive ruins at Hvalsey remnants of the state's presence?

For what purposes did the Norwegian state use its manors Foss and *Tjodhildestadr*? On the Norwegian mainland there was after ca. 1160 a local official called *syslemann*. He organised the peasant militia, collected state taxes

72 Political organisation

and other dues, was state prosecutor, and for this he received a specified remuneration. Less specified were the duties and remunerations of the *lendmenn*. They were powerful local magnates who received land from the king for a limited period without paying rent, and in return they performed a variety of administrative tasks when needed. Their title means "men who have received land".

A letter issued by the king in 1374, more than a decade after Ivar Bárdarson had left the island, gives some concrete information on the crown's activities in Greenland. Sigurdr Kolbeinsson had been in Greenland as the king's representative (*ombudzman*), and his task had been to seek and gather everything to which the crown had a right. While Sigurdr was in Greenland a man called Bárdr Dies had died and left an inheritance of land and goods. Sigurdr had bought it privately and brought the goods back to Bergen. The king claimed that he should have bought goods and land for the crown making use of the crown's right to "first buy". The king accused him of disloyalty (*svikrede*), and ordered the goods now stored in Bergen to be confiscated.[212] Sigurdr Kolbeinsson was a witness in Bergen two years later where he evidently was a merchant and house-owner.[213] This must have been his main occupation. When in Greenland he had a double role as merchant and the king's representative, and it was not always straightforward to distinguish between the two roles. Where did he live during his stay in Greenland? My guess would be the crown's manors Foss or Hvalsey. On other occasions native Greenlanders may have been given the right to use one of the manors in return for services to the state.

In 1389 some merchants on their way from Iceland were driven by contrary winds to Greenland. When they finally arrived in Bergen the following year they explained that they had offered to freight "the crown's goods" from Greenland to Bergen, but the king's representative (*umbodzman*) in Greenland refused to hand the goods over to them because they did not have a letter permitting them to receive the goods.[214] The king evidently had a representative who stayed in Greenland for a longer period. In this case it is not clear whether he was a Greenlander living permanently there or a merchant from Bergen who stayed in Greenland for a limited number of years. He collected the crown's incomes but did not have his own ship to bring them to Bergen. He depended on visits by ships owned by merchants.

The two documents from 1374 and 1389 give the impression that the crown had an administration in Greenland, but it did not consist of professional officials. The occupants of Foss and Hvalsey may have been allowed to deduct a fee from what was produced on the farm. The merchants who freighted the king's revenues to Norway were probably remunerated on arrival in Bergen. The lawman may have been given a similar fee from Brattahlid farm, and in addition he would have received a fee from the parties in court cases.

Hvalsey and Brattahlid have in common that they were given rectangular churches around 1300 of the type which today can be seen at Hvalsey.[215] There may have been a similar church at Foss. The external measure of Hvalsey church is 16 × 8 m,[216] of the last Brattahlid church 15 × 8 m,[217] and of ruin 17 at Foss

15 × 12 m.[218] Hvalsey and Brattahlid have the same rectangular form and length. Did the initiative to build them come from the Norwegian king?

Three of the excavated chieftains' farms had banqueting halls which, according to the archaeologists, were not in daily use: Hvalsey of 41 m², Herjolvsnes of 62 m² and Gardar of 132 m².[219] Brattahlid's hall was of a different type and in daily use, perhaps for court sessions?[220]

I have argued above that the Norwegian king after 1261 was politically and administratively more active than has so far been assumed, and that these efforts were concentrated in the three farms Brattahlid, Hvalsey and Foss. The hypotheses that E83 Hvalsey and E91 Foss had administrative functions for the state, are new.

A state which failed its subjects

In its first decades Norse Greenland was governed by at least ten independent chieftains. This could have led to social instability and violence, but they apparently succeeded in organising a society with a low level of violence under the leadership of the Brattahlid chieftains and with the Gardar Thing as the judicial forum. The chieftains in Greenland had only judicial functions, and their function did not imply that they owned their clients' land. After the first decades the power of the local chieftains seems to have declined and faded out. The Greenlanders may have felt that they had become superfluous.

The first Greenlanders must have seen pre-state Norway and Iceland as dangerous places where violence was out of control. During 1050–1250 a state-building process made Norway internally safer and externally stronger. This state intensified a political campaign around 1250 to subject the North Atlantic islands. In Iceland there were in the decades prior to 1264 violent and murderous struggles between chieftains, and this gave the Norwegian king allies in his efforts to control the country. In Greenland the Norwegian plans do not seem to have been well received, and heavy pressure was needed to make this happen in 1261.

The most basic tasks of a pre-modern state were internal pacification and defence against external enemies. The Greenlanders organised the first task without a state. Before the 1260s they did not have external enemies. The Norse Greenlanders probably did not understand how a state could be useful to them. This they learnt the hard way in the following century.

Relations with the Inuit grew increasingly tense, and the Norse Greenlanders were without a state which could organise a defence. Shipping from Norway was no problem as long as walrus tusks were in high demand in Bergen. After ca. 1300 the Greenlanders missed a state which felt responsible for keeping the shipping lanes open.

In 1380 Norway entered a union with Denmark. The eyes of the joint king who resided in Copenhagen, were directed towards Schleswig-Holstein, Southern Sweden and Northern Germany. The Norse ethnic identity with its centre in Norway was undermined. Norse Greenlanders were left alone to struggle against the Inuit and isolation, and they were ill prepared for this challenge. The Norse

Greenlanders were in the last phase part of a state which was unable or unwilling to provide the most basic of all state services: protection of life and property against violence. The consequences will be the subject of Chapter 6.

Notes

1 Jonsson 1924, pp. 275 and 289.
2 Nørlund 1942, p. 48; English translation, p. 51.
3 Stoklund 1993(a), pp. 538–540.
4 Stoklund 1993(a), pp. 529–530; Stoklund 1993(b), p. 47.
5 Stoklund 1993(a), p. 534.
6 Stoklund 1993(a), pp. 534 and 539.
7 Imer 2017, p. 251.
8 Skaaning Høegsberg 2009 I, p. 184.
9 Stoklund 1993(a), p. 536; Skaaning Høegsberg 2009 I, p. 186.
10 Chapter 4, pp. 193–196.
11 "many Icelandic men and also Norwegian, good men". *Sturlunga saga*, Old Norse chapter 95, p. 122; English translation II, chapter 13, p. 118; Danish translation I, pp. 140–141.
12 Heggstad et al. 2008, entry-word "*norrönn*"; Fritzner volume I, 1891, entry-word "*norrönn*". The examples are taken from there.
13 *Groenlendinga tháttr* IF IV, p. 290 and other places.
14 DN XVIII no. 33 ; DI III no. 367 (p. 440f).
15 DI III no. 597 = GHM III pp. 148–150. The document only exists in a transcript from 1625.
16 *Fostbroedra saga* IF VI chapter 23, p. 237; English translation: CSI chapter 23, p. 380.
17 *Fostbroedra saga* IF VI chapter 24, p. 256; English translation: CSI chapter 24, p. 390.
18 Chapter 4, pp. 203–205.
19 Egede/Bobé, pp. 84–85 and 312.
20 GHM I, p. III.
21 *Ordbog over det danske sprog*, volume 14, column 1340.
22 Holm 1883, pp. 57–145.
23 Nørlund 1942, p. 10.
24 Krogh 1967, p. 12; Krogh 1982, p. 19.
25 Krogh 1967, p. 12; Krogh 1982, p. 19.
26 *Ordbog over det danske sprog*, volume 4, column 281.
27 *Fostbroedra saga* IF VI chapter 23, p. 231; English translation: CSI chapter 23, p. 377.
28 Holm-Olsen, L. 1975, p. 345.
29 *Medieval Scandinavia*, entry word "Codex Regius".
30 Jonsson 1894 I, pp. 305–306.
31 Jonsson 1894 I, pp. 312–313.
32 *Norrön Fornkvædi* 1965, pp. 282–310; first edition 1867.
33 *Konungs skuggsiá*, Old Norse, p. 30; English translation, p. 143; Norwegian translation, p. 68.
34 Jonsson 1894 I, p. 313.
35 *Den norsk-islandske skjaldedigtning*, volume A1, p. 418 and B1, pp. 387–388.
36 Jonsson 1894 I, p. 530.
37 Chapter 4, pp. 174–179 and Chapter 6, pp. 342–345.
38 *Den norsk-islandske skjaldedigtning*, volume B1, pp. 387–388; GHM III, pp. 237–239.
39 GHM III, p. 237; Jonsson 1894 I, p. 530.
40 The most comprehensive description of the role of music in Norwegian court culture in the High Middle Ages is found in Vollsnes 2004.

41 Arneborg 2004, p. 273.
42 Kolltveit 1997, pp. 69–70.
43 Kolltveit 1997, p. 74.
44 Kolltveit 1997, pp. 75–76.
45 Kolltveit 1997, p. 78.
46 Kolltveit 1997, p. 76.
47 Vollsnes 2004, pp. 54–61.
48 Arneborg 1991 (b), pp. 145 and 148; Arneborg 2004, pp. 248–250.
49 Arneborg 1991(b), pp. 148.
50 *Groenlendinga tháttr* IF IV chapter 6, p. 292, footnote 1; English translation: CSI chapter 6, p. 382; Norwegian translation, p. 259.
51 *Medieval Scandinavia*, entry word "Einars tháttr Sokkasonar".
52 Bishop Arnaldr, Hermundr Kodransson, Ketil Kalvsson, Kolbeinn/Kolbjörn Thorljotsson (IF IV, pp. 290–292).
53 Pitt-Rivers 1965, p. 21.
54 *Groenlendinga tháttr* IF IV chapter 4, p. 282; English translation: CSI chapter 4, p. 377.
55 *Groenlendinga tháttr* IF IV chapter 5, p. 287; English translation: CSI chapter 5, p. 380.
56 *Fostbroedra saga* IF VI chapter 22, pp. 227–228; English translation: CSI chapter 22, p. 375.
57 *Fostbroedra saga* IF VI chapter 23, p. 240; English translation: CSI chapter 23, pp. 381–382.
58 Ingstad, H. 1959, p. 338; reprint 2004, pp. 266–267; English translation, pp. 210–211.
59 Cf. "Jurisdiction in pre-state Greenland" below.
60 *Groenlendinga saga* IF IV chapters 8 and 9, pp. 264–268; English translations: CSI chapters 7 and 8, pp. 30–31, and Penguin chapters 7 and 8, pp. 17–20.
61 *Fostbroedra saga* IF VI chapter 23, pp. 232–233, cf. 224–225 and chapter 24, p. 257; English translation: CSI, p. 378, cf. 373–374 and chapter 24, p. 390; Norwegian translation: Norrøn saga II, p. 238, cf. pp. 228–229 and 248. Torgrim Trolle had two sisters; one had four sons, the other one son.
62 *Islendingabok* IF I chapter 2, pp. 6–7; English translation: chapter 2, pp. 4–5; cf. Jóhannesson 1956, English translation 1974, pp. 38–39.
63 *Islendingabok,* authored by Ari Frodi, IF I chapter 3, pp. 8–9; English translation: chapter 3, p. 5; cf. *Medieval Scandinavia*, pp. 384–385.
64 KLNM, entry word "Ulfljotslög".
65 Nedkvitne 2004, pp. 75–76; Kristjansson, J. 2007, p. 118; Miller 1990, p. 224.
66 *Groenlendinga tháttr* IF IV chapter 3, p. 280; English translation: CSI chapter 3, p. 376.
67 Bjarkøyretten. Old Norse: "Ældre Bjakø-rett" §133, printed in NGL I, p. 328; Norwegian translation: § 112.
68 *Groenlendinga tháttr* IF IV chapter 2, p. 279; English translation: CSI chapter 2, p. 376.
69 *Groenlendinga tháttr* IF IV chapter 3, p. 280; byskup kvazk fe tekit hafa eptir groenlenzkum lögum eptir slika atburdi; English translation: CSI, chapter 3, p. 276.
70 *Groenlendinga tháttr* IF IV chapter 5, p. 284; English translation: CSI chapter 5, p. 378.
71 *Groenlendinga tháttr* IF IV chapter 6, p. 291; English translation: CSI chapter 6, p. 382.
72 *Det gamle Grønlands beskrivelse af Ivar Bárdarson*, p. 23.
73 Bunadar bolckerer.
74 NGL IV, pp. 353–354 = RN II no. 92.
75 The Norwegian National law of 1274 was sent to Iceland in modified form in 1280. A later undated and anonymous Icelandic notice claims that the same law-book was sent

76 *Political organisation*

to Greenland the following year. The information is not reliable. The National Law of 1274 was certainly sent to Greenland, but was it the original Norwegian law of 1274 which was then modified in Greenland or a version modified in Norway for use in Greenland?

76 DN XVIII no. 33.
77 GHM III, p. 457–458.
78 *Grágás*, ed. Gunnar Karlsson and others.
79 Bruun 1918(b), p. 129.
80 The empirical evidence for this law community between Greenland and Iceland is said to be the Icelandic law-book *Grágás* which was in force until 1264 (GHM III, pp. 430–435). What does it say? *Grágás* discusses the role of Icelandic courts of justice if an Icelander is killed in Greenland, or if an Icelander is to seek damages for a man killed in Greenland. These cases could be taken to court in Iceland or in Greenland, and *Grágás* clarifies procedural rules for the Icelandic courts' role (Vigslodi chapters CII–CIII). Another paragraph in *Gragás* says that if a man dies in Greenland and his inheritors are Icelanders, they should seek his possessions left there in the same way as if the man had died in Norway (Arfatháttr chapter XIV). This is not evidence that the Icelandic law-book was in force in Greenland.
81 *Fostbroedra saga* IF VI chapter 23, p. 237; Bodvarr ok Falgeirr bjuggu mál til á hendr Thormodi, ok vard Thormodr sekr skogamadr um vigit. English translation: CSI chapter 23, p. 380.
82 DN XVIII no. 33; DI III no. 367 (p. 440f).
83 *Groenlendinga tháttr* IF IV chapter 5, pp. 284–285; English translation: CSI chapter 5, pp. 378–379; Norwegian translation: Norrøn saga V, p. 255.
84 *Groenlendinga tháttr* IF IV chapter 1, p. 273; English translation: CSI chapter 1, p. 272.
85 *Groenlendinga tháttr* IF IV chapter 3, p. 280; bjo Ossur mal til tings theira Groenlandinga, og var that thing i Gordum; English translation: CSI chapter 3, p. 376.
86 *Groenlendinga tháttr* IF IV chapter 5, p. 285; English translation: CSI chapter 5, p. 379; Norwegian translation: Norrøn saga V, p. 255.
87 Jóhannesson 1956. English translation 1974, p. 38.
88 Nørlund discusses whether the Thing booths may have been on the northern part of Gardar's infield, close to the fjord, but he rejects the idea (Nørlund and Roussell 1930, pp. 28 and 126–130). I agree with him, because this is contradicted by the written sources presented later in this chapter.
89 *Groenlendinga tháttr* IF IV chapter 3, p. 280; English translation: CSI chapter 3, p. 376.
90 *Groenlendinga tháttr* IF IV chapter 5, p. 285; English translation: CSI chapter 5, p. 379.
91 *Groenlendinga tháttr* IF IV chapter 5, p. 286; English translation: CSI chapter 5, p. 380.
92 *Groenlendinga tháttr* IF IV chapter 5, p. 286; English translation: CSI chapter 5, p. 380.
93 *Fostbroedra saga* IF VI chapter 23, pp. 230–231; Hann lætr tha tjalda bua sina med miklum soma ok buask um vel. English translation: CSI chapter 23, p. 376.
94 *Groenlendinga tháttr* IF IV chapter 5, p. 287; English translation: CSI chapter 5, p. 380; *Einar andadisk uppi brekkunni vid bud Groenlendinga.*
95 KLNM entry word "lögsögumadr".
96 *Groenlendinga tháttr* IF IV chapter 1, p. 273; Their fedgar atti mikit vald a Groenlandi, ok varu their thar mjok fyrir monnum; English translation: CSI chapter 1, p. 372.
97 *Groenlendinga tháttr* IF IV chapter 4, p. 281; English translation: CSI chapter 4, p. 377.
98 *Groenlendinga tháttr* IF IV chapters 3 and 5, pp. 280 and 284; English translation: CSI chapters 3 and 5, pp. 376 and 379.

Political organisation 77

99 *Groenlendinga tháttr* IF IV chapters 3 and 5, pp. 280 and 284–287; English translation: CSI chapters 3 and 5, pp. 376 and 379–380.
100 *Groenlendinga tháttr* IF IV chapter 6, pp. 288–289; English translation: CSI chapter 6, p. 381.
101 " . . . *ok lutu allir til hans*." *Groenlendinga saga* IF IV chapter 2, p. 245; English translation: CSI chapter 1, p. 20 and Penguin chapter 1, p. 3.
102 *Eiriks saga Rauda* IF IV chapter 5, pp. 212–213. *Forsjá* can also mean "ability to predict the future". The expedition was a failure.
103 Cf. Chapter 5, pp. 252–254.
104 More on this in Chapter 5, pp. 232–233.
105 Nørlund and Stenberger 1934, pp. 24–25.
106 Nørlund and Stenberger 1934, plate 1 and p. 25.
107 Nørlund and Stenberger 1934, pp. 72 and 143.
108 *Det gamle Grønlands beskrivelse af Ivar Bárdarson*, p. 27.
109 *Det gamle Grønlands beskrivelse af Ivar Bárdarson*, pp. 27–28, cf. below "Violence in a pre-state society"; GHM II, p. 558; *Rimnasafn*, p. 161, cf. below "Violence in a pre-state society" and "Attempts to organise a state administration".
110 Nørlund and Stenberger 1934, p. 26.
111 Nørlund and Stenberger 1934, p. 24; Kuijpers and others 1998, p. 64.
112 Adam of Bremen book 4 chapter 35, Schmeidler, p. 269; English translation: Tschan, p. 215; Norwegian translation, p. 214.
113 Niermeyer 1993, entry word "subjacere".
114 Adam of Bremen, Book 4 chapter 35, cf. chapters 36–39; English translation: Tschan, p. 215; Norwegian translation, p. 214.
115 *(The) Ecclesiastical History of Ordericus Vitalis* volume VI, Book X, pp. 220–221.
116 *Historia Norwegie*, pp. 23–24.
117 *Historia Norwegie*, p. 65.
118 *Historia Norwegie*, p. 69.
119 *Historia Norwegie*, p. 69.
120 *Historia Norwegie*, pp. 69–75.
121 *Historia Norwegie*, p. 55, cf. Chapter 3, pp. 82–85.
122 *Hákonar saga Hákonarsonar* chapter 311; Norwegian translation, p. 333.
123 Helle 2005, p. 16.
124 Helle 2005, p. 14.
125 *Eiriks saga Rauda* IF IV chapter 5, pp. 210–211; *Fór Leifr til hirdar Olafs konungs Tryggvassonar. Lagdi konungr á han goda virding.* English translation: CSI chapter 5, p. 8 and Penguin chapter 5, p. 34; Norwegian translation: Norrøn saga V, p. 208.
126 See "The Brattahlid chieftain as pre-state political leader".
127 *Groenlendinga tháttr* IF IV chapter 1, pp. 273–275; English translation: CSI chapter 1, p. 373.
128 *Groenlendinga saga* IF IV chapter 3, p. 248; English translation: CSI chapter 2, p. 21 and Penguin chapter 2, p. 5; Norwegian translation: Norrøn saga V, p. 228.
129 *Heimskringla*, "The saga of St. Olav", chapter 124.
130 *Foesterbroedra saga* IF VI, pp. 206–210 and 213–214; Norwegian translation: Norrøn saga II, pp. 219–224.
131 *Foesterbroedra saga* IF VI chapter 18, p. 214; Norwegian translation: Norrøn saga II, p. 224 (*Hann var vinr Olafs konungs ok honum handgenginn.*).
132 *Foesterbroedra saga* IF VI chapter 20, p. 224; Norwegian translation: Norrøn saga II, p. 227.
133 *Foesterbroedra saga* IF VI chapter 20, p. 223–224; Norwegian translation: Norrøn saga II, p. 227.
134 *Foesterbroedra saga* IF VI chapter 20, p. 224; Norwegian translation: Norrøn saga II, p. 227.

78 Political organisation

135 *Foesterbroedra saga* IF VI chapter 22, p. 228; Norwegian translation: Norrøn saga II, pp. 230–231.
136 *Foesterbroedra saga* IF VI chapter 23, p. 237; Norwegian translation: Norrøn saga II, pp. 235–236.
137 *Foesterbroedra saga* IF VI, p. 237, cf. 224–225 and 257; Norwegian translation: Norrøn saga II, pp. 238, cf. 228–229 and 248.
138 *Foesterbroedra saga* IF VI chapter 23, pp. 243 and 248; Norwegian translation: Norrøn saga II, pp. 240 and 243.
139 *Foesterbroedra saga* IF VI chapter 24, pp. 248 and 251; Norwegian translation: Norrøn saga II, pp. 243–245.
140 *Foesterbroedra saga* IF VI chapter 13, pp. 183–185; Norwegian translation: Norrøn saga II, pp. 213–214.
141 *Foesterbroedra saga* IF VI, p. 237, cf. 224–225 and 257; Norwegian translation: Norrøn saga II, pp. 238, cf. 228–229 and 248.
142 *Foesterbroedra saga* IF VI chapter 24, p. 257; Norwegian translation: Norrøn saga II, p. 248.
143 Chapter 4, pp. 203–204.
144 *Hákonar Saga Hákonarsonar* Old Norse chapter 257, p. 252; Norwegian translation: p. 265.
145 IA, nearly all annals mentions these two events.
146 *Hákonar Saga Hákonarsonar* Old Norse chapter 311, p. 321; Norwegian translation: p. 333.
147 *Hákonar Saga Hákonarsonar* Old Norse chapter 311, p. 321; Norwegian translation: p. 333.
148 IA, V Skálholt, pp. 193–194.
149 IA, IV Regii, p. 138.
150 IA, IV Regii, p. 141 and V Skálholt, p. 195.
151 *Hákonar Saga Hákonarsonar* Old Norse chapter 311, p. 321; Norwegian translation: p. 333.
152 Helle 2005, p. 11.
153 Hirdskrá from 1273 §2, printed in NGL II, p. 392; Included in Magnus Lagabøte's National Law II.4 from 1274.
154 *Hákonar Saga Hákonarsonar* Old Norse chapter 311, p. 321; Norwegian translation: p. 333.
155 KLNM, entry word "thegngildi".
156 Hákonar Saga Hákonarsonar Old Norse chapter 311, p. 321; Den norsk-islandske skjaldedigtning, B2, p. 118 verse 20.
157 GHM III, p. 200.
158 *Det gamle Grønlands beskrivelse af Ivar Bárdarson*, p. 28; on Ivar Bárdarson as source, cf. Chapter 6, pp. 342–349.
159 Olason 1993, pp. 340–342.
160 Printed: GHM II, pp. 419–575; *Rimnasafn*, pp. 105–165.
161 Den norsk-islandske skjaldedigtning, volume B I, p. 286.
162 GHM II, p. 532; *Rimnasafn*, p. 148.
163 GHM II, p. 558; *Rimnasafn*, p. 161.
164 Cf. Chapter 2, pp. 56–59 and Chapter 2, p. 66 where it is argued that the "River farm" was crown property.
165 Cf. Chapter 2, p. 66.
166 Cf. Chapter 2, pp. 66–67.
167 Nørlund and Stenberger 1934, pp. 106–115.
168 *Groenlendinga tháttr* IF IV chapter 5, pp. 284–285; English translation: CSI chapter 5, pp. 379–380.
169 On Ivar Bárdarson's account as historical source, cf. Chapter 6, pp. 342–349.

170 *Det gamle Grønlands beskrivelse af Ivar Bárdarson*, pp. 24 and 27.
171 Fritzner volume 2 1891, entry word "hofgardr"; Kalkar 1886–1892, entry word "Hofgård".
172 *Det gamle Grønlands beskrivelse af Ivar Bárdarson*, pp. 24–25.
173 Cf. Chapter 3, p. 98.
174 Holm 1883, pp. 123–124; For a map, see appendix II, map 6.
175 Petersen 1896, pp. 417–418; Jonsson 1899, p. 287.
176 Bruun 1918(b), p. 181.
177 Ingstad, H. 1959, pp. 402–404; reprint 2004, pp. 318–319; English translation, pp. 248–249.
178 Appendix II, map 6; Petersen 1896, p. 416; Madsen 2014(a), p. 210.
179 Madsen 2014(a), p. 48.
180 On sæters, cf. Chapter 5, pp. 256–260.
181 Madsen 2014(a), pp. 209–211.
182 Cf. Chapter 5, p. 296.
183 Petersen 1896, p. 416; Petersen writes 200 feet, each foot being 32 cm.
184 Cf. Chapter 3, p. 98.
185 Cf. Chapter 3, pp. 105–106.
186 Roussell 1941, pp. 105–107; wall thickness 0.9–1.2 m.
187 "Ruin 17. Dwelling? Oblong ruin made of stone and turf, collapsed walls with many visible stones. The building site is raised 0.5–0.8m above the surrounding terrain. It is 15 m long and 12 m broad" (Møller and Madsen 2007, p. 22).
188 Madsen 2014(a), p. 312, map p. 371.
189 Møller and Madsen 2007, p. 22.
190 Cf. Table 5.6.
191 Möller and Madsen 2007, pp. 21–22.
192 External measures (2 × 2 m), (6 × 3 m), (7 × 4 m), (8 × 4 m), (8 × 3 m) and (3 × 4 m).
193 Madsen 2014(a), p. 77.
194 Madsen quotes Ivar Bárdarson's text about Foss word for word once as an introduction to one of his chapters, but this is not followed by an analysis of the text; Madsen 2014(a), p. 180.
195 *Ordbog over det danske sprog*, volume 5, Copenhagen 1923, entry word "forlene".
196 *Det gamle Grønlands beskrivelse af Ivar Bárdarson*, p. 26–27.
197 Jonsson 1930, p. 62.
198 Jonsson 1899, p. 292; This manuscript is called AM 772b and is an Icelandic list of Greenlandic parishes written by Th. Thorlacius (Jonsson 1899, p. 322).
199 Jonsson 1930, pp. 61–62; Jonsson 1899, p. 292.
200 *Det gamle Grønlands beskrivelse af Ivar Bárdarson*, p. 27–28.
201 Cf. Chapter 6, p. 347.
202 *Landnámabok* S93 and H80 (*i tuni i Hvalseyiarfirdi*); English and Norwegian translations: chapter 93.
203 Cf. Chapter 2, p. 32. The first farm in Lysufjord seems to have been named Lysufjord. When the number of farms in Lysufjord proliferated, the farm was renamed Sandnes. Lysufjord remained the name of the fjord only.
204 DI III, no. 632; DN IV, no. 376.
205 On the concept of "household farm", cf. Chapter 5, pp. 232–233.
206 Roussell 1941, p. 40.
207 Cf. Chapter 5, pp. 256–260; Arneborg et al. 2009 argue that there was a dwelling on E83a. I find Roussell's arguments more convincing.
208 Arneborg 2006, pp. 71–72; cf. Chapter 5, pp. 233–243 for how the calculations are done. One cow occupied ca. 1.2m along the wall.
209 Madsen 2014(a), p. 93.
210 Cf. Table 5.6.

211 Skaaning Høegsberg 2005, pp. 127–129.
212 DN XV no. 29; The case is analysed more closely in Chapter 4, p. 212.
213 DN III no. 407; cf. Chapter 4, p. 207.
214 DN XVIII, no. 33.
215 Arneborg 2004, p. 251.
216 Roussell 1941, p. 119.
217 Nørlund and Stenberger 1934, p. 30.
218 Møller and Madsen 2007, p. 22.
219 Arneborg 2004, p. 242.
220 Skaaning Høegsberg 2005, p. 126.

3 Church and religion

1 Christianisation

I ask the pure monks
to protect me on my journey,
and the Heavenly King
to hold his hand over me.¹

These verses were recited by the first known Christian in Greenland. He was on the ship of the chieftain Herjolv who sailed with Eirik Raudi to Greenland in AD 985 and settled at the farm which was later called Herjolvsnes. The bard originated from the Hebrides and this set him apart from the majority of immigrants who came from Iceland and Norway. Christianity came earlier to the Hebrides.

The pagans

The saga tradition claims that the overwhelming majority of the first settlers were pagans, "people on Greenland were pagans at that time" (*heidit var folk á Groenlandi i thann tima*).² The bard from the Hebrides is the only Christian who is mentioned in written sources before AD 1000. The first chieftain of Hvalseyfjord was Thorkell Farserkr. He received a pagan burial in a barrow close to the farm houses. "Later he has often appeared as a ghost walking between the houses", wrote the 13th-century author of *Landnámabok*.³ *Fostbroedra saga* written in the 13th century tells of a woman who lived in Eiriksfjord ca. 1020, and who had a likeness of Thor with his hammer carved on a magic chair.⁴

The archaeologist Aage Roussell claimed that he had identified in the landscape at Sandnes in the Western Settlement a mound which is likely to have been a pagan barrow. He classified as "possible burial mounds" another site at Sandnes and one at Hvalsey.⁵ None of these has been verified as a pagan burial mound. On a loom weight made of soapstone from Brattahlid, someone carved a Thor's hammer.⁶ On another loom weight at Gardar was carved something which looks like a cross, but also could be interpreted as Thor's hammer.⁷ Icelanders in the 13th century thought that all or most of the first Greenlanders were pagan, and archaeological material confirms that there may indeed have been pagans living there. But the lack of verified pagan burials indicates that the pagan cult was short-lived.

Collective and individual conversion

Modern people tend to see religion as a private matter, and this makes it a minor problem that people living in the same society have different religions. Greenland and Iceland in AD 1000 were organised in clans led by local chieftains. Religion was at this time mainly understood as rituals which strengthened social cohesion between members of each clan, but religious rituals performed at the Gardar Thing also strengthened social ties between all Greenlanders. This would only work if all chieftains and the majority of the common people shared the same religion.

Ari Frodi in his *Islendingabok* from ca. 1130 describes a discussion which took place at the Icelandic Althing in AD 1000. Should each individual, each household or each clan be permitted to choose whether they wanted to keep their traditional pagan faith or convert to Christianity? The leader of the Althing was the *lögsögumadr* and he argued strongly that two religions would give two "laws" (*lög*), and in this concept he no doubt included both rituals and social norms. "Let us all have the same law and the same religion. It will prove true that if we tear apart the law, we will also tear apart the peace".[8] The Thing assembly agreed. Collective conversions had to be superficial by modern standards; in practice, baptism. For the Greenlanders it must have been important that they wanted to be part of the Norse cultural community, and this would in the future depend on Greenland being Christian.

The saga tradition claims that Eirik Raudi remained a pagan all his life, but his son and heir Leiv Eiriksson was baptised before his father died, and so was his wife. The first Christian church building mentioned in the written sources is the so-called "Tjodhild's church", named after Eirik Raudi's wife. She let the church be built in AD 1000 or shortly afterwards, "not too near the dwelling house" where the still pagan Eirik Raudi lived.[9] In 1961 a church and a churchyard which suited the saga description was localised. It was excavated by the Nationalmuseum archaeologist Knud Krogh who was in no doubt that this was Tjodhild's church.[10] He excavated 155 buried corpses, most of them in an east-west position with their bones in their natural position. Others were reburials, bones that had been put into a hole in the churchyard in a chaotic way. He suggested that some of these corpses first had received a pagan burial, and that later their Christian descendants may have removed their bones from a pagan mound and reburied them in this Christian churchyard.[11] C14 dates have been made of skeletons, and they confirm that the corpses may have been buried around AD 1000, but these dates have such wide margins of error that no precise conclusion can be drawn.[12]

My guess is that when Leiv inherited the chiefdom, he made the Gardar Thing pass a resolution that all Greenlanders should be baptised.

The Norwegian king and the Christianisation of Greenland

The most detailed descriptions of how Greenland was Christianised were transmitted in an Icelandic tradition which originally was oral and put in writing in several sagas in "the long 13th century". It claims unanimously that Greenland was Christianised from Norway on the initiative of King Olav Trygvason (AD 995–1000) and that Leiv Eiriksson was his instrument.

Eiriks saga Rauda was written in Iceland ca. 1220–1250.[13] The author is likely to have been a priest, or a layman with a particular interest in religion. Its description of the Christianisation is the most detailed in the Icelandic tradition. Eirik Raudi's son Leiv sailed to Norway and stayed at the court (*hird*) of Olav Trygvason one winter and evidently became a member of the king's *hird*. One day the king asked whether he planned to return to Greenland the following summer. Leiv confirmed this "if it is your will". The king answered that "this would be a good thing, and you shall go there in my service and command them to become Christians". Leiv answered that this should be as the king decided, but he thought it would be a difficult task. The king said that he knew "no man who is better qualified for the task than you, and your good luck will help you". Leiv retorted that "I think I will need the help from your good luck as well".[14] This conversation is of course constructed by the saga author ca. 1220–1250 but is likely to illustrate how relations were between the Norwegian king and Greenlandic chieftains in his *hird*. They were expected to use their personal prestige and network in the king's service.[15] On his return to Greenland Leiv "immediately ordered all people in the land to accept the Christian faith and the concept of sin in accordance with King Olav's message". He argued that the new social practices (*sid*) would give higher prestige and honour. Eirik Raudi accepted late the order to abandon his old religion (*sid*), but his wife Tjodhild did so promptly (*skjott*). She had a church made where she and the others who accepted the Christian religion said their prayers. Tjodhild refused to have intercourse with Eirik after she had been baptised, and that was much against his wishes (*skapi*).[16]

Other Icelandic sagas have shorter versions of the same story. The first extant saga to mention by whom Greenland was Christianised, was written ca. 1190 by an Icelandic monk at the North Icelandic cloister of Thingeyrar, Oddr Snorrason. It is a saga of King Olav Tryggvason, and Oddr's source was an oral tradition in Iceland and among the clergy, but he also used written sources that are now lost.[17] Greenland is mentioned in one short sentence: "The names of the lands which he Christianised are Norway, Shetland, Orkney, Faroes, Iceland and Greenland" (*En thessi eru heiti landa theira er han cristnadi Noregr, Hialtland, Orkneyar, Færeyiar, Island, Grönland*). He adds that the missionaries which King Olav brought to these countries from England were held in low esteem by the people because they could not preach in the "Danish tongue".[18] The Anglo-Saxon priests could not speak with the rhetorical force which the Greenlanders were used to from their leaders. Danish, Swedish and Norse were considered one *tunga* because people could understand each other when speaking, but separate norms for writing correctly made them three languages.[19]

Fagrskinna (ca. 1220) written in Norway paraphrases information from Oddr's saga in one sentence. Olav Tryggvason "was the first king of Norway to hold the true faith in God, and by his direction and power all the kingdom of Norway became Christian, as well as Orkney, the Faroes, Shetland, Iceland and Greenland".[20]

Snorri Sturluson in his *Heimskringla* ca. 1230 summarises information from *Eiriks saga Rauda*:

> Leiv, the son of Eirik Raudi who first settled on Greenland, arrived in Norway from Greenland this summer. He sought King Olav, was christened (*tok vid kristni*), and stayed all winter with the king . . . In spring King Olav sent Leiv Eiriksson to Greenland to command people there to be christened. Leiv sailed to Greenland that summer . . . He brought with him a priest and teachers, and went to his father at Brattahlid and lived there.

His father disliked that Leiv had brought "this swindler"[21] to Greenland, who was the priest. But he credited his son with having saved a shipwrecked crew on his way to Greenland, and he thought the two acts balanced each other.[22]

Groenlandinga saga only mentions the Christianisation of Greenland to date other events:[23] "*andadisk Eirikr Raudi fyrir kristni*[24] could mean "Eirik died before Greenland was Christianised" or "Eirik died before he was christened". The efforts of Olav Trygvason and Leiv Eirikssson to Christianise Greenland are not mentioned evidently because it was not relevant to the main story of the saga.

Kristni saga was probably written by the Icelandic *lagmann* Sturla Thordarson (died 1284) and its subject was the Christianisation of Iceland.[25] He included one sentence on the Christianisation of Greenland: "The summer when King Olav Tryggvason sailed to Vendland [AD 1000], he sent Leiv Eiriksson to Greenland to order them to accept the Christian faith".[26]

The Icelandic tradition unanimously claims that Greenland was Christianised by the Norwegian king. Was there a tradition at Trondheim cathedral which said that Greenland was Christianised from Iceland? This claim is represented by a single work, *Historia Norwegie*, which is likely to have been written by a cleric in Trondheim. The dating is uncertain, but it may have been written before the archbishopric in Trondheim was established in 1153, or at least before the routines of the new church province had been established. Both Trondheim and Gardar had before 1153 the archbishop of Lund as their superior, but there were no institutionalised contacts between Trondheim and Gardar. *Historia Norwegie* mentions the Christianisation of Greenland in one short sentence: "This country was discovered, settled and strengthened (*roborata*) in the catholic faith by the people of Thule".[27] "Thule" is a common name for Iceland in Latin texts. "*Roborare*" meant in Medieval Latin "confirm existing rights or a previous deed",[28] or "strengthen".[29] The author claims that Icelanders played a role in making the Greenlanders better Christians. He does not say that Greenland was Christianised from Iceland. He may have meant that many Icelandic priests had worked in Greenland. Lack of information on who the author was, when he wrote, from whom he obtained his information, and his obscure formulation give *Historia Norwegie* a lower source value than the Icelandic saga tradition.

A third hypothesis has been formulated by the Norwegian archaeologist Christian Keller who argued in favour of early religious impulses from Celtic Britain. His empirical material was the churchyards of seven small churches which were among the earliest in Greenland.[30] The church architecture points to Norway more than Celtic Britain as they were rectangular with an outer protective wall of turf and have their parallels in roughly 50 turf churches in Northern Norway.[31] What makes Keller's seven churches special is the walls surrounding their churchyards, which are circular. For this no direct parallels have been found in Norway. This may be because archaeologists have not looked for them, but there are several examples in Norway of the wall of a churchyard being circular on one side, or having an elliptical form.[32] "For the time being, however, the most obvious place to seek for the provenance of the circular churchyard is in Celtic Britain".[33] How did this idea arrive in Greenland? Norsemen may have seen them in Ireland, and the idea travelled in their heads via Western Norway to Greenland.[34] Priests who had been born and received their education in the British Isles were among the first missionaries whom King Olav sent to Greenland via Norway. The circular churchyards cannot be used as empirical evidence that Celtic missionaries sailed to Greenland directly from the British Isles, nor that religious ideas which were specifically Celtic found their way to Greenland.[35]

Summing up, the Icelandic saga tradition permits us to conclude that Greenland was Christianised on the initiative of the Norwegian king. The extant sources do not support hypotheses of independent missionary initiatives from Iceland or Celtic Britain.

2 Church organisation before the parish AD 1000–1124

King Olav Tryggvason brought missionary priests from Anglo-Saxon England to Norway where they organised the Norwegian church, a few of them being sent from Norway to the North Atlantic islands. They organised the Norse churches according to the Anglo-Saxon model which they knew.

Private chapels

In the Anglo-Saxon model many aristocrats and other landowners owned small churches, and the congregation would mainly be the church-owners' relatives and clients. Such private churches are normally called chapels.[36] In the Eastern Settlement seven small churches have been identified archaeologically, all of them close to ruins of Norse farms:[37]

- E29 Brattahlid. This is the so-called Tjodhild's church mentioned in *Eiriks Saga Rauda* and excavated archaeologically. The saga dates it to shortly after AD 1000, and 14C dates with their wide margins do not contradict the saga.[38] A drawing picturing what the church may have looked like is shown in Meldgaard 1982, p. 162. External measurements are 5×5 m = 25 m²,[39] and according to Melgaard it measured 3.5×2 m or 7 m² internally.[40]
- E33 and E35. A few kilometres to the north of Brattahlid two small and evidently private churches have been found on two farms. External measurements

для E35 are 6 × 5 m = 30 m². The peasants living there probably belonged to the Brattahlid clan and may have been relatives of Eirik and his sons.[41]
- E48 Gardar (Igaliku). This church is situated less than 500 m to the north of the main farm and the cathedral. At Brattahlid we are told that the first church was built at a short distance from the dwelling because some of the inhabitants were still pagan. Similar considerations may have prevailed in Gardar in the early period.
- E64 Iterolaq. This farm lies in the Einarsfjord at the entrance to the region called Vatnahverfi. External measurements: 6 × 4.5 m = 27 m².[42]
- E78 Eqaluit. This farm also lies in the Einarsfjord at the entrance to Vatnahverfi. External measurements: 5.5 × 3.5 m = 19 m².[43]
- E162 Narssaq in Uunartoq. External measurements are about 8 × 5 m = 40 m²; inside measurements may have been half or less.[44]
- E39 Kangilleq. External measurements 10 × 6 m, Guldager calls it a "presumed church" with churchyard.[45] Clemmensen was the first to make this claim in 1911.[46] Bruun thought it was a stable with a surrounding pen, Krogh did not include it among archeologically identified churches.[47] The external measurements are larger than in the other small churches. At present it is most correct not to include it in the discussion below.

Above seven small churches have been registered,[48] for five of them external size is known and they measure between 19 and 40 m². For E29 both external and internal measurements are known, external 25 m² and internal 7 m². This means that the internal size may have been ca. one-third of the external size. The five churches whose external measurements are known may have had internal sizes between 6 and 13 m². Later in Table 3.3 is a list of registered churches with parish rights and known internal measurements. The parish churches, the cathedral excluded, had internal sizes between 32 and 86 m², significantly more than the presumed private chapels of 6–13 m².

None of the seven small churches is known to have been a parish church; one of them, E29, is known to have been a private chapel, so it is likely that all of them were. In one such small church there would have been room for an officiating priest and family members belonging to the church-owner's household, but hardly more than that.

The date of building is known for only one of them, Tjodhild's church (E29), which is said in Eirik's saga to have been built shortly after AD 1000. It is also the only one to have been dated archaeologically, and the date ca. AD 1000 has been confirmed. Excavated churchyards suggest that the two churches at farmsteads E33 and E35 were in use during the 11th, 12th and 13th centuries.[49] Private chapels were the first churches to be built after Christianisation in the 11th century before parishes were organised.

When did these private chapels go out of use? Unpublished archaeological data indicate that the farms on which E64 and E78 stood ceased to be harvested around AD 1200.[50] E33 and E35 went out of use in the 13th century, as mentioned earlier. Private chapels may have gone out of service in the 13th century because they lost their burial rights to the parish churches. This confirms the commonly held hypothesis that most or all the small churches were private chapels built before the organisation of the parishes, and that some of them continued to be in private use mainly for burials into the 13th century.

Of the seven small private churches identified so far, all are in the Eastern Settlement, none in the Western or Middle Settlements. Three churches were in Eiriksfjord, three in Einarsfjord and one in the Uunartoqfjord. In the earliest period the richest and mightiest households had their farms in the Eastern Settlement, and preferably in Eiriksfjord and Einarsfjord.[51]

The private churches "are rather difficult to spot . . . it is likely that the figure will increase with closer survey".[52] They were built of timber, with a thick protective and insulating wall of turf on the outside. In the earliest period, there was plenty of driftwood along the shores and these small churches were simple and inexpensive to build. Nationalmuseum archaeologists have taken it as a matter of course that these Greenlandic wood-and-turf churches had Icelandic models.[53] But the archaeologist Christian Keller points out that ca. 50 churches of the wood-and-turf type have been identified in Northern Norway, probably more than in the rest of the North Atlantic put together. The building technique was used at secular buildings in Norway long before Christianisation. It may have reached Greenland from Norway via Iceland, or directly from Norway. The latter alternative is most likely, since the written sources verify that Christianisation had its point of departure there.[54]

Chapel priests in Anglo-Saxon tradition had the status of servants.[55] In Norway the contract for servants lasted one year, and it was specified in the laws on which date the change of master was to take place. Icelandic priests met at a synod once a year, and a priest's contract with a church-owner lasted from one synod to the next. The church-owner paid him his wage.[56] The Greenlanders may have copied this arrangement.

Some private churches did not have a fulltime priest. The church-owner made an agreement with a priest to celebrate mass and offer pastoral service a certain number of days per year. The *Groenlandinga tháttr* describes a murder at a farm in Einarsfjord called Langanes ca. AD 1131 while bishop Arnaldr was present at the church there. No parish church had that name, so it must have been a chapel, possibly E64. The bishop thought the victim had got what he deserved, but nevertheless consented for him to be buried at the local cemetery, "since this church has no permanent priest" (*at thessi kirkju, at eigi er heimilisprestr*).[57] The bishop distinguished between churches with permanent and part-time priests, and it was more honourable to be buried at the cemetery of a church which had a permanent priest.

A mass honoured God and was seen as a gift to him. A priest in a small church could do work which benefitted the soul of the clan leader and his next of kin who were present in the church, but the priest could also include a prayer for the souls of the whole clan.

Minsters in Greenland?

In the Anglo-Saxon model laymen could also receive pastoral services in larger churches, called minsters. They were manned by several priests who would sing masses and preach to a congregation in the minster. The priests sang intercessory prayers for people who were not necessarily present in the church. The clergy at the minster also travelled around within a larger area visiting rural communities which did not have a priest of their own. They could then sing masses and preach in private chapels, in the open air, or in the hall of a wealthy man and would receive payment from the laymen for whom they provided pastoral services.[58] Many minsters were financed and controlled by the king, others by aristocrats.[59] They provided all services which the church gave to laymen, and serviced an area which was much larger than the later parishes. In Norway the kings built "main churches" (*hofudkirkjur*) which had similar functions, but it is not known whether priests in these "main churches" were itinerant.[60] In Greenland no minster is described in the written sources and none of the Nationalmuseum archaeologists discusses them. Are there any indications that they existed?

The most likely place to look is Gardar. The farm's owners murdered 34 Icelanders in Vinland shortly after AD 1000, so the farm may have been confiscated to pay compensations.[61] On the initiative of Leiv Eiriksson or a later Brattahlid chieftain, Gardar may have become the site of a minster where several itinerant priests had their base. If this was so, a large church must have been built there at an early date, in practice the first decades after AD 1000.

The most extensive excavations at Gardar were made by Nationalmuseum archaeologists Poul Nørlund and Aage Roussell in 1926 and published in 1930. They concluded that Gardar in the earliest period was an ordinary farm. They found a churchyard which they thought had belonged to the chapel of this early farm but could not localise the chapel. Gardar remained a privately owned farm until the first bishop took over in 1126. He started the construction of the first large stone church, and on the south side of it he added several buildings around an enclosure where he and his clergy had their living quarters. In a second stage in the building process ca. 1200, the chancel was prolonged and received side chapels, and more housing for secular purposes was added.[62] In Nørlund's schema there is no place for a large church which could have been a minster before the bishop arrived in 1126.

In 2007 the Aarhus archaeologist Mogens Skaaning Høegsberg re-examined this chronology on the basis of Nørlund's and Roussell's own material; no major excavations had taken place in the meantime. It is not clear that the construction of the stone church was done in two stages only (1126 and 1200). It may have been done in many stages, but at present it is not possible to date when the building started or the following construction process.[63] The first church on the site was made of stone and had a nave which seems to have been $8 \times 8 = 64$ m² internally. Its chancel was $4 \times 4 = 16$ m².[64] For a comparison, the still standing parish church at Hvalsey measures internally $16 \times 8 = 128$ m², nave and chancel included.[65] This first stone church in Gardar was constructed on the Anglo-Saxon model with a chancel narrower than the nave, and had a dignified appearance. It may have been built before 1124[66] and if so it may have been used as a minster.[67] Høegsberg's hypothesis gives a place for a minster in the period before the bishop arrived in

1126. Neither Nørlund's nor Høegsberg's hypotheses are verified, but the main point here is that a minster at Gardar cannot be ruled out.

Ivar Bárdarson related ca. 1360 that Sandnes (*Stensnes*) in the Western Settlement had a "large church . . . that church was for a while cathedral (*domkircke*) and a bishop's seat".[68] Is it possible that this was a distant memory of a time when there was a minster at Sandnes? Nationalmuseum archaeologists Roussell and Arneborg agree that the excavated church may have been in use from around AD 1000 until the depopulation of the Western Settlement.[69] The interior of the chancel was 4 × 4 m, the same size as at the first church at Gardar. The naves of the two churches seem to have the same length, 8 m, but Sandnes church was only 5 m wide and Gardar 8 m. This makes the nave of Gardar church 64 m^2 and Sandnes 40 m^2. Both churches had a west wall of wood, and the other walls were of stone with wood panelling on the inside and protective turf on the outside. If both churches were minsters, it comes as no surprise that the Western Settlement had a smaller one; in other respects the two churches are similar. It is impossible to date them, but they belong to the same Anglo-Saxon model with a chancel which is narrower than the nave and may have been built at the start of the 11th century with English missionaries as architects.[70]

The farms of Gardar and Sandens also have in common that they ca. 1000–1010 belonged to children of Eirik Raudi. Gardar was owned by the husband of Eirik's daughter Freydis and may have been confiscated by Leiv Eiriksson.[71] Eirik's son Thorstein owned half of the farm Sandnes and settled there with his wife.[72] He died shortly after he arrived, and Leiv Eiriksson, who in the sagas is portrayed as an advocate for the new faith, may have donated Sandnes or Gardar or both for a minster to be built there.[73] In this way pastoral care worked with modest resources shortly after the majority of laymen had been baptised.

Flexible burial customs

Greenlanders made great efforts to have the dead buried in consecrated soil. Thorvaldr Eiriksson died and was buried in unconsecrated ground in Vinland. When his brother learnt this, he manned a ship and sailed to Vinland to bring the corpse back to the churchyard on Brattahlid.[74] The *Groenlendinga tháttr* describes how a ship crew was shipwrecked and died on the east coast of Greenland. A few years later their corpses were found and boiled so that the bones could be separated from the rotten flesh. The bones were transported to Gardar and buried there.[75] Bjørn Jonsson in his "Grænlands annal" tells the story of "Corpse-Lodin" (*Liika Lodin*) who seems to have made it a religious task to search for shipwrecked crews along the east coast of Greenland and give them a Christian burial.[76]

Eiriks saga Rauda was written ca. 1220–1250 probably by a clergyman, and he describes the death of Eirik Raudi's son Thorstein at Sandnes in the Western Settlement ca. 1010. Thorstein died in his bed, but some hours later he returned to life, sat up in his bed and told those in the room that "I want to be taken to church, along with the other people who have died here".[77] The saga author then adds his own comments:

It had been the custom in Greenland since Christianity came there, to bury people in un-consecrated ground at the farms where they died. A stake was driven into the ground above the dead person's breast and later, when priests arrived, the stake would be pulled out and holy water poured down the hole and they would sing prayers over them with funeral rites performed. This could take place much later. The bodies of Thorstein and the others were taken to the church at Eiriksfjord, and it was sung over them by priests.[78]

People who were not buried properly, could haunt the living as ghosts. Thorstein belonged to the Brattahlid clan, and their church was at Brattahlid.

The tombstone of the Norseman *Øssur Asbjærnarsson* was found in the Middle Settlement south of Arsuk Island. A tombstone indicates a permanent burial with necessary rituals. Albrethsen and Arneborg have estimated that the Middle Settlement had 23 farms, but no church has been localised.[79] To my knowledge church law did not forbid a consecrated churchyard without a church. Burial sites could also be consecrated individually, as mentioned earlier. A visiting priest could be sent from a minster in the early period and an itinerant brother from the Augustinian cloister in Ketilsfjord in a later period.[80]

The Norse considered what is today called the Middle Settlement as part of the Eastern Settlement. In the earliest period it may have been visited by a priest from the minster at Gardar. In the 13th century the Eastern Settlement had been divided into parishes, except the Middle Settlement. There farms may have been too few and too scattered for a parish organisation. Perhaps Gardar continued to send itinerant priests to the Middle Settlement as they had done before 1126? This is an unverified hypothesis, but the Greenland environment made flexible adaptations necessary.

Bishops in Greenland before 1124

In the period 1000–1124 the Christians on Greenland had no bishop of their own but were subjects of archbishops who until 1053 lived in Bremen or Hamburg. They were responsible for missions in Scandinavia.[81] In 1053 Scandinavia had been Christianised, and the pope made the archbishop of Hamburg/Bremen formally responsible for the church in the north; Greenlanders and Norwegians are among those mentioned.[82] By 1056 the archbishop had already consecrated Isleif to be the first bishop on Iceland, and "made him bring a letter to the peoples of Iceland and Greenland, where he respectfully greeted their churches and promised that he soon would visit them".[83] The meaning was that he would visit these churches through envoys from Bremen. They arrived and Icelandic sources mention some of them.

Adam of Bremen worked at the cathedral, and in the 1070s he wrote a description of the church province. The cathedral was "visited by people from all parts of the world, particularly from the Nordic countries. Icelanders, Greenlanders and Orcadians were the most distant visitors. They asked the archbishop to send preachers to them, and so he did".[84]

Education of priests took place in Greenland at local churches with experienced priests as teachers. Ordaining them should in principle be done by a bishop; after 1056 there were bishops both in Iceland and Norway. In 1104 the pope made the Nordic countries a separate church province with a seat in Lund, then in Denmark.[85] One of the priests in Greenland was also authorised to perform the ordination.

The first bishop who is known to have worked in Greenland was Eirikr Gnupsson Upsi. He was an Icelander from a farm close to present day Reykjavik.[86] For AD 1112 an Icelandic Annals noted: "*Ferd Eiriks byskops*", meaning "The journey of Eirik bishop". He left from Iceland, but it is not said where his destination was, although it was probably Greenland.[87] Nine years later in 1121, seven of the Icelandic Annals have the following notice, with minor variations: "Bishop Eirik Upsi of Greenland journeyed to find Vinland".[88]

Had Eirikr been consecrated as permanent bishop of Greenland? That is improbable based on what happened in 1124. A more likely hypothesis is that Eirikr was a missionary bishop or a *hird* bishop, that is a bishop without a geographically limited bishopric in the Norwegian king's or the archbishop in Lund's service. He may have been consecrated by the archbishop in Lund, or one of the bishops in Iceland or Norway. At Ivar Bárdarson's time (ca. 1360) there was a tradition that a bishop had lived at Sandnes. Helge Ingstad thought that the bishop may have been Eirikr Upsi.[89] During AD 1112–1121 Sandnes church may have been a "minster". His task in Greenland would have been to improve and control the work of Greenland priests and do missionary work. The frontier against the pagans was now Vinland, and Eirikr may have felt an obligation to Christianise the *skrælingar*. Eirikr and his crew never returned.

Power in the Greenland church before 1124

A Greenland diocese (bishopric) was founded in 1124, and the procedure gives a good impression of who held power over the Greenland church before the first bishop was in place. The process is described in detail in the so-called *Groenlendinga tháttr*, and source criticism confirms that this is a reliable source.[90]

The initiative came from the chieftain at Brattahlid. He convened the Gardar Thing and argued that he did not want the land to be without a bishop any more. All peasants (*boendr*) consented.[91] Several of them owned private churches, and the priests were their servants. The main duty of the new bishop would be to improve and control the quality of the clergy's work, and for this to function the church-owners had to cooperate. If the Brattahlid clan was behind minsters at Gardar and Sandnes, their voice would have a special authority in church matters.

The next step was to make the Norwegian "King Sigurdr the Jerusalem Crusader" cooperate. The Brattahlid chieftain had not made a deal with the king beforehand. His son Einar was the Greenlanders' envoy to the king and he brought with him much walrus tusk and ropes made of walrus hides, which were used as gifts to gain access to the king and create goodwill with the king and his councillors. Einar argued before the king that a bishop was necessary for the land (*naudsyn landsins*), and the king agreed that it would certainly be the best for them.[92]

At this time the king was the political head of the church on the Norwegian mainland,[93] therefore when a new bishop was to be appointed, the king chose the candidate and the archbishop consecrated him. The Greenlanders accepted being treated likewise. In this case the king chose one of his *hird* priests as the first bishop of Greenland and ordered him to travel to Lund to receive his consecration. "I will send you to Denmark to Archbishop Asser in Lund with my letter and seal".[94] The king did not intervene in religious questions, his main concern being to have bishops he could trust in his realm.[95] On the way back the new bishop and the son of the Brattahlid chieftain again visited the Norwegian king.[96] Jette Arneborg has called this an odd/incredible narrative because it gives the Norwegian king a central role in the process.[97] What is certain is that the *tháttr*'s narrative is not in harmony with Nationalmuseum historiography!

This procedure falsifies the hypothesis that Greenland was part of one of the Icelandic dioceses before 1124. In 1106 northern Iceland was separated from Skálholt diocese under the name of Hólar diocese. Even here the initiative came from the secular church-owners in the planned diocese. The bishop of Skálholt accepted the proposal, selected a priest from his own diocese and gave him a letter to the archbishop in Lund asking him to consecrate the candidate, which he did.[98] If Greenland had been part of an Icelandic diocese before 1124, the Icelandic bishop would have been involved. The *tháttr* says explicitly that Greenland was *byskupslaust* before the Gardar bishopric was organised.[99]

The Greenland church before 1124 was under the religious control of an archbishop who never visited the island and under the political control of a king who did not visit the island either. But the control of the Norwegian king was more real, since the Greenlanders' trade and shipping mainly went to mainland Norway.[100]

3 The parish 1124–1340

The first permanent bishop was consecrated in 1124 and arrived in Greenland in 1126. This marked the start of a process to reorganise the Greenland church. Before 1126 power over the Greenland church was divided between the local church-owners, the Brattahlid chieftain, the Norwegian king and the archbishop in Lund. The Greenland church was reorganised between 1126 and 1300. At the end of the period power was divided between the parish priests, the Gardar bishop, the archbishop in Trondheim and the pope. Power and control had been transferred from laymen to the church's own officials consisting of consecrated priests. This was part of a European process which started at the end of the 11th century and created the strong and independent West European church organisation of the 12th and 13th centuries.

Most important for laymen was the parish. What do we know about its function in Greenland society? How closely did the Greenland parish follow practices and changes in Norway and Iceland? To answer these questions, it is necessary to understand how the parish was financed.

The tithe

Iceland had a bishop with a permanent seat at Skálholt from 1056, and in 1096 he took the initiative to introduce annual tithe on the island.[101] In mainland Norway the saga tradition gives King Sigurdr the Jerusalem Crusader (1103–1130) the honour of having introduced the tithe. It was a tax paid to the church of one-tenth of production in agriculture, fishing and in Greenland probably also hunting. This was a significant income and created a material basis for a parish organisation. The tithe was divided into four parts – one part was given to the parish priest, one was for the maintenance of the parish church, one was for the bishop and the final part was distributed among the parish poor.[102] In Norway the great building boom for new parish churches occurred ca. 1150–1250, and in the following period 1250–1350 many of these churches were enlarged and improved.[103]

In Greenland we have no direct information about the tithe, but we can register developments which would have been impossible without it. The purpose of introducing the tithe was to finance a parish system led by a bishop. The first Greenland bishop arrived in Greenland in 1126, which was a few years after the tithe had been imposed on Icelanders and Norwegians. The *Grænlendinga þáttr* only mentions that the peasants at the Gardar Thing decided to establish a bishop's see, but they must at the same time have decided to establish a parish system and finance it through the tithe – these three elements were part and parcel of the same initiative. Each peasant household had to be registered as parishioners of a particular church to which they paid their tithe, and the parish priest had to provide pastoral services in return. The relationship between church, priest and parishioners became institutionalised.

All parish churches had a churchyard, and the parishioners had a legal obligation to bury their dead there, if possible. Some families gave these graves a formal, appearance assuring the dead of a long memory. Five extant runic messages have been found on graves. A stone from Gardar had an inscription which was formulated as a prayer, "Vigdis M.'s daughter rests here, God gladden her soul". Others were more simple and informative, "Ingibjorg's grave" from Brattahlid, and "Here rests Roar Kolgrimsson" from Herjolvsnes and "Thorfinna".[104] If the churchyard was far away it seems to have been possible to bury the dead near the farm. The tombstone of *Øssur Asbjærnarsson* was found just south of Arsuk Island in the Middle Settlement where no parish church or churchyard existed.[105] In the churchyard of Herjolvsnes church 58 coffins were localised where a wooden cross had been buried inside or on top of the coffin. The idea was possibly to identify the person as Christian and the hope may have been that all those buried in the churchyard would revive collectively on doomsday and start their eternal life.

In Norway and Iceland the first churches which attained parish status were privately owned, and there can be little doubt that this was so even in Greenland. Building a parish church was an investment. The tithe was income for the church-owner. For part of this income he hired a priest for his church.[106] The church-owner had a legal duty to provide religious services, which in Iceland meant at least 13 masses a year, so one priest could serve two or three churches.[107] All parish churches had to provide the necessary sacraments: baptism, confession with Holy Communion and burial. Those who had paid their tithe had a legal right to these services free of charge.[108]

The number of parish churches at population maximum

The original of the list of Greenlandic churches to be discussed here had the heading "So many churches are there on Greenland" (*Svo margir eru kirkjur á Grænland*). This original has not survived. But copies of the list were made and have survived. The oldest was made in *Flateyjarbok* ca. 1390, and names 12 churches in the Eastern Settlement and 3 in the Western.[109] Later Arngrimur Jonsson the Learned (died 1648) copied the same list, naming 12 churches in the Eastern[110] and 4 in the Western Settlement.[111] Björn Jonsson from Skardsá (died 1655) counted the churches from the original manuscript and noted the numbers in his "Grænlands annal", but without naming them. "There are 12 churches on Greenland in the Eastern Settlement, and 4 in the Western Settlement".[112]

There is a discrepancy in the number of churches in the Western Settlement: Armgrimur says four, the same number as Björn. Flateyjarbok states three. Arngrimur also has a name for the fourth church which is left out in Flateyjarbok, "Straumsnes in Straumsfjord". Against this background it should be seen as verified that the original manuscript said four churches in the Western Settlement. The Icelandic philologist Finnur Jonsson found that Arngrimur's transcript was the best.[113]

When was the lost original of this list authored? The transcript which was made in Flateyjarbok ca. 1390 gives some indications. Here this list is part of a section about Greenland.[114] First the clerk copied *Grænlendinga tháttr*, then he copied a list of names starting with the words "Those have been bishops on Greenland".[115] It starts correctly with Bishop Arnaldr, but it ends with Bishop Thordr who was bishop of Gardar 1288–1314. This makes it highly likely that the original list of bishops was authored during his term of office. The list of parishes in Greenland in Table 3.1 follows immediately after the list of bishops. It is therefore likely that Flateyjarbok copied the list of bishops and the list of parishes from the same original, which was written during bishop Thordr's term of office.

The list of parishes in Table 3.1 is likely to reflect the situation ca. 1288–1314. Thordr made a temporary stay in Iceland on his way to Greenland in 1289. One hypothesis could be that an interested Icelandic cleric composed the lists then, based on information from Thordr, and that the lists continued to be read by Icelanders until the 17th century.

At this time the population of Norse Greenland must have been near its maximum.[119] The information that there were 110 farms and 4 parishes in the Western Settlement is from Arngrimur's list and gives 27 farms in an average parish. It is most likely that he meant "name farm". If so 6–10 persons may have lived at each farm, and 160–270 in an average parish.[120] Among the 16 churches with parish rights was also Gardar cathedral; the cathedral clergy gave pastoral services. In Norway it was not unusual for a cathedral to have a parish.

Table 3.1 Parishes in Norse Greenland ca. 1288–1314

In the Eastern Settlement:

1.	Herjolvsnes ad sinum Herjulvsfiord	(also IB)
2.	Vatnsdalur in sinu Ketelsfiørd	(also IB)
3.	Vik in eodem sinu	(also IB)
4.	Vogum in Siglufiørd	(also IB)
5.	Høfdu (= E66 Undir Höfda) in Austfiørd	–
6.	Gardar in Einarsfiørd	(also IB)
7.	Hardsteinaberg	(= IB's Dyrnes)
8.	Brattahlid in Eireksfiørd	(also IB)
9.	Solarfiøll	(also IB)
10.	Hvalseyarfiordur	(also IB)
11.	Gardanes in Midfiørdum (E1)	–
12.	Isefiørdur[116] (E4?)	–

In the Western Settlement: Villas habet 110, Paroecias 4[117]

1.	Sandanes ad sinum Lysufiord	–
2.	Hop in Agnafiord	–
3.	Anavik in Ragnafiord	–
4.	Straumsnes in Straumsfiord[118]	–

Source: The table combines the church names in Arngrimur's and Flateyjarbok's transcripts of the original list from 1288–1314. The names are the same, but the order is slightly different. Flateyjarbok's transcript is printed in Olafur Halldorsson 1978, p. 79. Arngrimur's transcript is not extant, but several copies of it exist, and Finnur Jonsson has on this basis reconstructed Arngrimur's original list. (Finnur Jonsson 1899, pp. 321–322, cf. pp. 273, 297–298, 304 and Finnur Jonsson 1930, p. 63–67). In brackets information about whether the parish in question is also mentioned by Ivar Bárdarson in his account from ca. 1360 (IB) (*Det gamle Grønlands beskrivelse af Ivar Bárdarson*, printed in Finnur Jonsson 1930, pp. 19–29).

Date of table: The reign of Bishop Thordr of Gardar, cf. earlier discussion.

The names in the table: They are those of the parishes (*paroecias*), but the church and the parish normally had the same name.

How many parish churches remained ca. 1360?

Ca. 1360 Norse Greenland had passed its demographic peak. Information about the number of parish churches ca. 1360 is found in the account of the clergyman Ivar Bárdarson. Its source value will be discussed in detail later, and the conclusion there is that it satisfies the tests normally used in historical source criticism.[121] Ivar had resided at Gardar for many years and evidently participated in visitations of parish churches. He explicitly describes a parish system in Greenland, and he calls Dyrnes "the largest parish on Greenland".[122]

Ivar's oral account was written down by a cleric at Bergen cathedral. The cathedral administration wanted to know which churches were under the bishop's jurisdiction, the geographic extent of parishes, and other rights which gave an income. This is a list of churches which the bishop would visit, and it names which rights the *visitator* should ask about when he came there. He mentions Herjolvsnes and Foss churches, but he says nothing about their incomes. The reason must be that they were not under the bishop's jurisdiction. Many private chapels were built in the period before parishes were organised.[123] Ivar makes no mention of them since they were not under the bishop's jurisdiction, probably many of them no longer existed.

Ivar Bárdarson repeatedly says that fjords, land or hunting rights are owned by, belong to or "lie to" a church. Earlier research assumed that this meant ownership of land and other properties. Many authors have on this basis assumed that the parish churches were the largest landowners in Norse Greenland.[124] The Norwegian archaeologist Christian Keller in his PhD argued through a linguistic analysis that when Ivar uses the word "owns" (*eijer*) he normally meant "have parish rights" to the land mentioned, in practice the right to collect the tithe. When he uses the word "lies to" (*ligger thiill*) or "belongs to" (*hører til*) he meant that the parish church had ownership rights in the modern sense to farms, hunting or fishing.[125] Whether property rights or parish rights were meant was no problem for the *visitator* from Gardar as the local priests would know. The context in most cases makes this evident even for a modern reader.

Ivar in practice describes a visitation journey starting from the southernmost church at Herjolvsnes and ending in the northernmost fjord with a Norse population.[126]

> Ivar mentions Herjolvsnes several times, but not its church whose existence is verified archaeologically to the end of the settlement shortly after 1410.[127] To the east of Herjolvsnes he mentions a populated fjord called Skagefjord (= *Narssap sarqa*?), it evidently belonged to Herjolvsnes. The same must have been the case for *Igdlukasip tunua*. Herjolvsnes church no doubt had a parish, but the bishop does not seem to have had judicial rights over it. Keller suggests that Herjolvsnes may have had a special judicial status as marketplace administered according to the "merchant law" (Bjarkøyrett).[128] Herjolvsnes would then have been under crown administration. If this had been so, Ivar is likely to have mentioned it. An alternative hypothesis is more likely. Herjolvsnes was in the early period the seat of a chieftain who next to the Brattahlid chieftain was the most respected on Norse Greenland. Before ca. 1160 and possibly quite up to the second half of the 13th century all parish churches on Greenland were privately owned,[129] but in 1360 only Herjolvsnes seems to have remained in private hands, its tithe included.
>
> The next fjord is Ketilsfjord (= *Tasermiut*) which was "fully settled" and had three churches with parish rights. The church nearest the sea was Auros, which probably was situated at E137, E108 or E109. It has not been localised archaeologically.[130] Its parish stretched along the fjord to the coast where it owned islands and islets. It reached Herjolvsnes, meaning that it had borders to Herjolvsnes parish. Auros parish probably reached the sea at the estuary of Ketilsfjord, and continued northwards up to the fjord estuary today called Qornoq. It was the only church which had a right to ships wrecked within its parish.[131]

The second Ketilsfjord church was called Pettersvig and was assumed by Nørlund and Vebæk to be a church ruin identified at E140. This was rejected by Krogh.[132] Its parish included the farms which were collectively called Verdsdal, and the farms along the rich fish lake Tasersuaq.

Further into Ketilsfjord was a "large cloister" for Augustinian canons. At E105 the ruin of a large stone church has been identified but not excavated.[133] The Augustinians were consecrated priests and could provide pastoral services. Their parish included farms from the cloister to the head of the fjord, and the west and probably east sides of the fjord out towards the coast, but it is not clear how far.

IB says that "Next to Ketilsfjord lies Rampnessfjord and far into that fjord is a Benedictine nunnery". If "next to Ketilsfjord" is to be taken literally, the nunnery should be "far into" the Southern Sermilik fjord, and E131 or E138 would then be the most likely sites. No church ruins have been registered there, perhaps because nobody has looked for it? The nuns would have a priest who gave them pastoral services, and he could also serve a parish. If the nunnery really was in Sermilik fjord, what would then be the borders of its parish? *"Dit closter eger alt ind i botnen och ud fra Vage kircke"*. This means that the parish started at the head of Sermilik fjord and extended out towards the coast until it met the border of the parish of Vágar church. Where that was is not said, probably because it would be difficult to explain to the cleric at the cathedral in Bergen who wrote this down. A likely place would be in the neighbourhood of the bay today called Tunungassoq.

The next church on Ivar's westwards journey was Vágar. Ivar does not state the Norse name of the fjord, but Arngrimur's list used in Table 3.1 above says Vágar was in Siglufjord. Ivar mentions hot springs in this fjord, which confirms that Ivar's Vágar was in today's Uunartoq fjord. Neither does Ivar state where in Uunartoq fjord Vágar was, but archaeologists have found two churches there at E162 and E149. Both are situated in bays, which is the meaning of the word *vágar*. The church at E162 is small and of the same type as Tjodhild's church. The outside dimension is $8 \times 5 = 40$ m², the inside perhaps half or less.[134] It can only have functioned as a private church for the household at E162 and would have no room for a parish congregation.[135] The church at E149 is a rectangular stone church large enough for a congregation, and the inside dimensions were $13 \times 5 = 65$ m².[136] Vágar parish church is most likely to have been at E149. Vágar's parish is said to include "all land from the church and to the coast", which means on the west side all Norse farms out to Akuliaruseq and on the east side all farms around today's Quvnermiut. "In the [Uunartoq] fjord there are many islets which the nunnery owns ("eger") in common with the cathedral, and they have hot springs".[137] The hot springs still exist on Uunartoq Island. No Norse farms have been found on the islands; "own" in this case cannot refer to parish rights; and its value for cathedral and nunnery can only be ownership of the hot springs.

Nørlund and Vebæk thought that the nunnery was at E149 and Vágar parish church at E162.[138] Krogh was sceptical and Arneborg finds that the empirical material does not support Nørlund's and Vebæk's identifications. She gives no alternative solution to the problem.[139] My "close reading" of IB attempts to do this.

Between Ivar's Rampnessfjord [= Southern Sermilik] and Einarsfjord [= Igaliku fjord], there was "a large manor called Foss which belongs to the king, and there stands a costly church dedicated to St Nicholas and which the king rents out".[140] The king owned both manor and church and rented out both. Foss is most likely to have been at today's ruins E91.[141] In Norway the king owned several royal chapels, and some of them functioned as parish churches for neighbouring peasant households.[142] Ivar does not say explicitly that Foss had a parish, and he does not describe the boundaries of its parish. But Ivar normally only draws the borders of parishes which were controlled by the bishop and were to be visited by him. No other church is known along the Agdluitsup fjord, and the farms north of Foss in Vatnahverfi also needed a parish church, but Ivar does not mention other churches in this area which may have had parish functions. Foss is likely to have been a royal chapel with parish rights.

The next fjord was the long and well-settled Einarsfjord. Ivar says that the cathedral at Gardar (E47) had a parish which included the whole fjord and Renø (Reindeer island = Akia).

Sailing north-westwards the next parish church was Hvalseyfjord church at E83. Its parish included all Hvalseyfjord, the neighbouring *Ramstadefjord* (= Kangerluarsuk) and *Langhøø* island (= Tugtutoq).[143] Hvalsey farm seems to have belonged to the king,[144] but Hvalseyfjord church and parish were under the bishop's administration.

Dyrnes church (E18) was located at the sound today called Narsap Saava passing Narsaq. Its parish extended into and up Eiriksfjord (= Tunulliarfik) to the border against *Solefields/Undir Solarfjöllum* (= Sillisit)'s parish. Ivar says that Dyrnes parish on the opposite western side extended into Northern Sermilik up to *Mitfjord* (*Diverness kircke æger alt ind udi Mitfjord*). Where was Mitfjord? Finnur Jonsson claimed that this was the three small fjords in the Northern Sermilik fjord today called Tasiussaq, Tasiussarsuk and Kangerdlua.[145] Ivar calls Dyrnes the largest parish in Greenland, which he probably meant in extent and not population.[146]

Solefields (= Sillisit) church and parish (E23) were located at the Eiriksfjord between Dyrnes' and Brattahlid's parishes.[147] But Ivar also says that (*Solefieldz kircke . . . æger alt Mitfjord*). If this information is correct, it must mean that some of *Solefield*'s parishioners lived in the *Mitfjord* of the Northern Sermilik fjord as described earlier and had to walk over land to get to their parish church in Sillisit at the Tunulliarfik (= Eiriksfjord). *Solefields* (= Sillisit) church has been located archaeologically as a rectangular stone church, which makes it likely that the church which was standing ca. 1360 was built around AD 1300.[148] But other hypotheses are also possible, and it is not certain that in 1360 there were still Norse households living along the

Northern Sermilik, and Ivar's claim of parishioners there was possibly no longer real. What is beyond doubt is that ca 1288–1314 there were two parish churches at the Northern Sermilik, but ca. 1360 there were none.

The final parish church mentioned by Ivar is *Leijder* church located on Brattahlid farm (E29). Its parish started at the head of Eiriksfjord and ended on the east side at the Qooroq fjord, on the west side it ended somewhere north of *Solefields* (= Sillisit) church. *Leijde*r was a rectangular stone church.[149] Brattahlid parish church was under the bishop's jurisdiction.[150]

Key information about the 12 parish churches has been summarised in Table 3.2.

A comparison between Tables 3.1 and 3.2 will show that between ca. 1300 and ca. 1360 the total number of churches with parish rights had been reduced from 16 to 12. Seven had disappeared, three had been added.

The most striking change was that all four churches in the Western Settlement had disappeared. Ivar Bárdarson gives an explanation for this, that the Inuit had chased or killed the Norse inhabitants.[151]

In the Eastern Settlement the northernmost fjord system is a long fjord which is today named Ikerssuaq and Northern Sermilik, extending from the coast to the Inland Ice. Archaeological excavations have confirmed that there are Norse ruins along the whole of this northernmost fjord, but so far it has not been verified that any of these farms were still inhabited as late as ca. 1360; the ruins have not been dated.[152] In this fjord were two churches ca. 1288–1314, "Gardanes in the Midfjord" and Icefjord *Isafjørdur*.[153] Archaeologists have found a church ruin at E1 and have identified it as Gardanes. Some have claimed there is a church ruin at E4 and have identified it as *Isafjørdur*, but that is unlikely.[154] E1 and E4 lie close to the bays which today are called Tasiussaq and Tasiussarsuk at the south-eastern side of the fjord.

Table 3.2 Parishes on Norse Greenland ca. 1360

	Name	Owner of the tithe	Existed 1288–1314?
1	Herjolvsnes	Chieftain	Yes
2	Auros	Bishop	Yes (= Vatnsdalur)
3	Petersvig	Bishop	Yes (= Vik)
4	Augustinians	Bishop	No
5	Nunnery	Bishop	No
6	Vágar	Bishop	Yes
7	Foss	King	No
8	Gardar	Bishop	Yes
9	Hvalseyfjord	Bishop	Yes
10	Dyrnes	Bishop	Yes (= Hardsteinaberg)
11	Solefield	Bishop	Yes (= Undir Solarfjöllum)
12	Brattahlid	Bishop	Yes

Source: Ivar Bárdarson's visitation journey as described earlier.

At Ivar's time ca. 1360 Gardanes and *Isafjördur* churches no longer functioned, but Ivar mentions two bays in this northern fjord, *Ijdrevigh* ("Outer Bay") and *Indrevigh* ("Inner Bay"). This may be where Gardanes and *Isafjördur* churches had formerly been.[155] The fact that this northern fjord system had lost its parish churches is a strong indication that the population there had declined or disappeared.

North of Ikersuaq/Northern Sermilik in 1360 there were no Norse churches or farms (*och alt ubijgt*). The so called "Middle Settlement" around today's Ivittuut and the Western Settlement had been abandoned.

The abandoned parish churches mentioned in Table 3.1 moved the northern limit for Norse churches southwards from Anavik in the Western Settlement to Brattahlid in the Eastern Settlement. This may be due to the Inuit threat as claimed by Ivar. But it may also be interpreted as a reaction to a colder climate as the northernmost church was ca. 1300 at 64°50'N but 60 years later it was at 61°15'N.

One of the seven disappeared parish churches was not geographically marginal like the other six. E66 South Igaliku was in Einarsfjord not far from Gardar cathedral. Ca. 1360 the cathedral was the only remaining church with parish rights in that long and populous fjord, and South Igaliku's parishioners must have been transferred to the cathedral. The bishop drew parish borders, and it may have been more important for him to give his cathedral a large and rich parish than to give farms along the fjord easy access to their parish church. The closing down of E66 South Igaliku may also have had practical reasons, as many of its parishioners lived in Vatnahverfi, and it is possible that the population there was declining at this time.[156]

The transfer of ownership of parish churches from private laymen to the bishop's organisation had been nearly completed by ca. 1360. Only Foss, which belonged to the king, and Herjolvsnes, which seems to have belonged to the chieftain there, were still owned by laymen. This made it possible for the bishop to use the resources of the parish churches to serve other church purposes. Ca. 1360 two of them were also cloisters; this use of the tithe for cloisters had taken place after 1288–1314.[157] The cathedral may have had a parish from its foundation in 1126. Of the 12 parish churches which functioned ca. 1360, six combined it with other functions for church, king and chieftain.[158] The Greenland church had shrunk geographically ca. 1300–1360, but it now had a complex organisation after a Norwegian model with cloisters for men and women, royal chapel(s) and a cathedral.

The church landscape in the Vatnahverfi region visualises how the church organisation changed from Christianisation to its final stage ca. 1360. Shortly after Christianisation private chapels at E78 and E64 were built. They functioned until ca. 1200 when they went out of use.[159] Ca 1300 a parish church had come in their place which now served Vatnahverfi, South Igaliku (E66).[160] Ca 1360 South Igaliku had ceased to function as a parish church, and the peasants of Vatnahverfi now used services from the cathedral and a royal chapel.

In the 13th century the Greenland church faced a serious challenge which forced it to close all churches north of Eiriksfjord, probably due to the Inuit advance. But it could also celebrate a significant triumph through the transfer of

Church and religion 101

most parish churches from secular owners to the church organisation. This placed a greater responsibility for leadership on the bishops. When they left Greenland and settled in foreign countries this undermined the political leadership at a time when it was needed more than ever. We shall return to this matter in Chapter 6.

How often did the Greenlanders attend mass in their parish church?

In *Fostbroedra saga* we meet a poor elderly couple who lived at an isolated, small farm in Eiriksfjord. The wife complained that "I rarely come to church to hear the preaching of learned men, because it is a long journey, and we are few people at home".[161] One person had to stay at home to look after the animals. The parish organisation had been created in countries with a higher population density. Were there so many parish churches in Norse Greenland that peasants could receive the pastoral services the church thought they needed?

There was no duty to attend church every Sunday or regularly in the Nidaros province. In 1268 it was incorporated into Norwegian secular law that "All Christians who have reached the age of discretion should be shriven at least once a year in Lent, confessing their sins to the priest, and later take Holy Communion on Easter Day". A similar provision was taken into the Icelandic secular law in 1275. It should be assumed that the same was done in Greenland, since Greenland and Iceland after 1261–1264 were part of the Norwegian realm.[162] One visit a year was an absolute minimum in the last part of the settlement's existence.

Figure 3.1 Wooden fish 10.5 × 2.2 × 1.2 cm from W52 Umiviarssuk, museum catalogue no. U. 593; Appendix II, map 2.

On Norse Greenland sticks with notches have been excavated which traditionally have been interpreted as counting-sticks for economic purposes. This fish probably had the same function as a rosary. The ten notches on its back show that it was used as an aid in counting something. The runes on one side says "Mary. You are mindful of the word of your servant" and on the opposite side "in which you gave me hope" (Imer 2017, p. 316). These words indicate that what was to be counted were prayers to St. Mary. In the sacrament of penance, the confessor would often for minor sins impose a certain number of prayers, the most common being The Lord's Prayer and "Hail Mary". Gradually laypeople started to say these prayers on their own initiative when they had committed a minor sin. In this way the concept of sin was internalised; the sinner penalised himself. The owner of this fish accepted the concept of sin and did what she/he was expected to do to avoid penalties in the next life. Cf. Roussell 1936, p. 207 and plate 6.

Photo: CC-BY-SA John Lee, Nationalmuseet.

Copyright: The Nationalmuseum in Copenhagen.

Peasants must have seen visits to the parish church as desirable for religious reasons, because it gave religious merits to participate in the celebration of mass and other religious rituals. For many it must also have been a social occasion. Limits to church attendance must have been created by practical problems.

All Norse fjords in the Eastern settlement had a parish church. For most households it must have been possible to reach the church and return home in one day if the weather was favourable and the voyage started early in the morning. In the Western Settlement the population was more scattered and the parish churches fewer. To my knowledge nobody has measured how long it would take to row to the parish church from the most remote farms, but some experience with a modern motorboat along the Greenland fjords indicates to the present author that at least some peasants would have problems making a return voyage to their parish church in one day. Some religious feasts lasted several days, and in summertime they could sleep in a tent close to the church, or with neighbours.

One priest could service several churches, which meant that on many holidays mass was not celebrated. In the Middle Settlement neither of the two extant lists from ca. 1288–1314 and 1360 mentions a parish church, and none has been found archaeologically.[163] The peasants there received their pastoral services from itinerant priests who are likely to have been based in the early period in "minsters", later in the Augustinian cloister. Such "mass free Sundays" also existed in Norway, and then the household could gather in the living-room for prayers and some kind of sermon. At midsummer Greenlanders from both settlements assembled at the Gardar Thing close to the cathedral. For some this may have been their only opportunity to attend mass, hear sermons and receive the sacrament of penance.

In the pagan and early Christian period, Greenlanders assembled for religious and social purposes at their chieftain's farm, and from the 12th century at their parish church.

Who owned the parish churches?

The tithe was imposed and the building of parish churches started in Greenland in the decades after 1126. As in Iceland and Norway they were built and owned by laymen. From the 1160s the archbishop in Trondheim demanded that parish churches be owned by the church organisation led by bishops. The former church owners would then lose control of the income and expenditure of the church and the right to appoint parish priests. In Norway an open conflict erupted from the 1170s, but by 1247 the church's claims seem to have been met. The exception was that the bishops permitted the king to keep his own chapels.[164]

In Iceland the church went further than in Norway, since in many cases it demanded not only the ownership of the churches, but also of the farms on which the church stood. Confronted with the opposition of the powerful Icelandic chieftains, the church at first met with little success.[165] In 1264 Iceland submitted to the king of Norway where the church's demands had already been met. The king tended to support the Icelandic bishops and in 1297 the king, the archbishop and the bishop of Skálholt agreed that many of the most valuable church farms in Skálholt diocese were to be transferred to the bishop's control.[166] The Norwegian and Icelandic background makes it likely that the transfer of churches in Greenland could not take place until after 1261 when the island became part of the Norwegian realm and could enlist the support of the king.

Our only source for ownership of church farms in Greenland is Ivar Bárdarson's account from ca. 1360. At that time 10 of the 12 churches with parish rights in Greenland belonged to the church organisation led by the bishop.[167] But this did not mean that the farm on which a parish church stood was church property. The church organisation led by the bishop owned the church building of *Hvalsøør fiord kircke* and its tithe, but in my interpretation the king owned the farm on which it stood.[168]

The only parish church which had incomes in addition to its tithe was Auros church, which claimed the right to wrecked ships within its parish.[169] The parish churches may have had little time to accumulate wealth. Their tithe had probably been transferred from private to church ownership not many decades before 1360, between 1261 and 1360. The Norwegian archaeologist Christian Keller has made out that it was a catastrophe for Greenland society that the ownership of parish churches was transferred from local chieftains to the church. This undermined the chieftains economically and politically.[170] It is correct that the chieftains lost their incomes from the tithe, but they kept their farms where no doubt most of the food they consumed was produced.[171] All chieftains must have emerged weaker from the process, but how weakened they were must have varied.

What did the parish churches look like?

In a Greenlandic parish there may have lived ca. 160–270 people, and a parish church had to provide room for those of them who could be expected on a normal church feast day. The earliest private chapels could not meet this demand.[172] In Iceland there is a transition ca. 1100 or shortly afterwards from small churches where there was only room for the officiating priest and the family of the church owner, to larger churches. This was a visible expression of the introduction of a parish organisation in the decades after 1097.[173] It has not been possible to date archaeologically when the building of parish churches started in Norse Greenland, but it must have been after 1126.[174]

Table 3.3 Churches with parish rights and known internal measures, size in m².

Gardar II		Cathedral without chapels	154[175]
Herjolvsnes	E111	Whole church	86[176]
Gardar I	E47	Nave: 8×8, chancel: $4 \times 4 =$	80[177]
Hvalseyfjord	E83	Whole church	68[178]
Augustinians	E105	Nave: 8×6, chancel: $3 \times 6 =$	66[179]
Vágar	E149	Whole church: $13 \times 5 =$	65[180]
South Igaliku	E66	Whole church: $13.5 \times 4.6 =$	62[181]

(continued)

Table 3.3 (continued)

Brattahlid/Lijder	E29 II	Whole church: 12.6 × 4.7 =	59^{182}
Sandnes	W51	Nave: 8 × 5, chancel: 4 × 4 =	56^{183}
Anavik	W7	Whole church: 12 × 4.5 =	54^{184}
Gardanes	E1	Whole church: 11 × 4 =	44^{185}
(Isafiördur?)	E4	Whole church: 9.2 × 4.2 =	39^{186}
Undir Solarfjöllum	E23	Whole church: 8 × 4 =	32^{187}

Sources: Included in this table are churches which are mentioned in Tables 3.1 and 3.2 with parish rights. These two tables both name 12 parish churches in the Eastern Settlement, but it is only partly the same churches. In the Western Settlement the list in Table 3.1 has four parish churches. Together the two tables name 19 different farms with churches with parish rights. A total of 12 farms have been located archaeologically and their churches measured, and they are listed in the present Table 3.3. In this table there are 13 different churches because both Gardar I and Gardar II are included. I have only used measurements which are stated in the text referred to. If both external measurements and the thickness of the walls are stated, I have combined the two. I have not measured millimetres on drawings made by archaeologists. References for the size of the churches are found in the footnotes.

The parish churches were 32–86 m² and all of them were larger than the private chapels of ca 6–13 m².[188] Measured in floor size the difference in size is so wide that it is possible to distinguish them archaeologically. Churches below 15 m² are private chapels, churches above 30 m² are large enough for use as parish churches.

The picture which many people have in their minds of a Greenlandic parish church is Hvalseyfjord. How representative is it? It will appear from Table 3.3 that it was slightly above middle size among the Greenland parish churches. Since the farm on which it was built may have belonged to the crown and representatives of the king may have resided there, this comes as no surprise.

How large were Greenlandic parish churches compared to their Norwegian counterparts? Eidsfjord parish church at the head of the Hardanger fjord near Bergen may have been a model for Hvalseyfjord. They were built at approximately the same time with the same rectangular ground plan, the chancel had the same width as the nave, both were of stone, and lime mortar was used to paint them white on the outside and inside.[189] External measures were for Eidsfjord 22 × 11 metres = 242 m²,[190] for Hvalseyfjord 18 × 8 metres = 144 m².[191] Eidsfjord's size is representative of stone churches in peripheral rural districts of medieval Norway. If Eidsfjord church had been in Greenland, it would have belonged to the largest parish churches.

The categorisation of medieval churches as Romanesque or Gothic is the most used point of departure for discussions of chronological and social contexts for these churches. In Norwegian parish churches the distinction between the two styles can be made both on the basis of the ground plan, and whether the windows had rounded or pointed arches. In Greenland the building material made it impossible to construct pointed arches,[192] so the only criterion left is the ground plan.

The Greenland parish churches had walls made of stone with turf outside and wainscot inside. This normally makes it possible for archaeologists to reconstruct the ground plan. They categorised the ruins of Greenland stone churches into three types:

1 The chancel is narrower than the nave, the west wall is made of wood.
2 A rectangular building where the west wall is made of wood, the three other walls of stone, turf and wainscot.
3 A rectangular building where all four walls are made of stone, turf and wainscot.

Table 3.4 lists the churches with parish rights and their known ground plan according to these three types.

Table 3.4 Churches with parish rights and known ground plan

Norse name	Ruin number	Ground plan[193]	References[194]
Herjolvsnes	E111	type 1	1288–1314, IB
Augustinian monastery	E105	type 1[195]	—, IB
Gardar I	E47	type 1	1288–1314, IB
Brattahlid I	E29	type 1[196]	1288–1314, IB
Sandnes	W51	type 1	1288–1314, —
Vágar	E149	type 2	1288–1314, IB
South Igaliku	E66	type 2	1288–1314, —
Gardanes	E1[197]	type 2	1288–1314, —
Hvalseyfjord	E83	type 3	1288–1314, IB
Undir Solarfjöllum	E23	type 3	1288–1314, IB
Brattahlid II	E29	type 3	1288–1314, IB
Anavik	W7	type 3[198]	1288–1314, —
Isafjørdur	E4?[199]	type 3	1288–1314, —

Sources for church types are taken from the footnotes listed in Table 3.3. The exception is Brattahlid I where the reference is given in the footnote.

Parish churches where the chancel is narrower than the nave are modelled on an Anglo-Saxon pattern. In Norway they are dated to ca. 1140–1250 and are called Romanesque.[200]

On Greenland churches of type 1 have the same ground plan as Norwegian Romanesque churches. At Brattahlid a parish church of type 3 was built over a predecessor of type 1.[201] Churches of type 1 seem to have been the earliest ones even in Greenland. They are found at the chieftains' seats of Brattahlid (E29) and Herjolvsnes (E111), the bishop's seat of Gardar (E47) and the monastic church in Ketilsfjord (E105), which is likely to have been built at the bishop's initiative.[202] The fifth church of the Anglo-Saxon type is Sandnes, which in the early period may have been a "minster" owned at least partly by the Brattahlid clan.[203] All churches of this early Anglo-Saxon type may have been built by or at the initiative of the top elite in Greenland society. All of them may have been built before the parish churches were transferred from private to church ownership at the end of the 13th century. Perhaps these five churches were meant to demonstrate the prestige of their owners.

Ca. 1250–1350 new parish churches in Norway were built and old ones rebuilt with nave and chancel of the same width and all four walls built of stone. In Norwegian literature they are labelled Gothic.[204] Greenland churches of type 3 have the same ground plan as Gothic parish churches in Norway. They are therefore likely to have been built in the same period ca. 1250–1350. Hvalseyfjord church has the same "Gothic" ground plan as Eidsfjord parish church near Bergen, which has been dated to ca. 1300 by Norwegian archaeologists.[205] It is difficult to connect the five churches of type 3 to social status. Hvalseyfjord and Brattahlid II were built on high status farms, but Undir Solarfjöllum, Anavik and the doubtful church Isafjördur (E4) seem to have been built on ordinary farms for a congregation of peasants. These churches are built like a box, which would have been less expensive, and status must have been created through decorations.

The three parish churches of type 2 are Vágar (E149), South Igaliku (E66) and Gardanes (E1). They have in common a rectangular ground plan, which connects them to the "Gothic" parish churches of type 3. But the two also have in common a west wall made of wood, and this connects them to the five churches of type 1 which all have this kind of west wall. Type 2 may have been a transitional form between type 1 and type 3 and they are difficult to date. It cannot be excluded that types 1 and 2 were contemporary, but type 1 had a higher social status.

Summing up, in the period from ca. 1126 to the end of the 13th century the elite built the parish churches at their own cost and they wanted their churches to give them prestige. Later the responsibility for building parish churches was taken over by bishops who made the peasants pay for them. Prestige may have become less important and the quality declined.

Wooden houses with an outer, protective wall of stone and/or turf are known in Western Norway from the Late Roman and the Migration periods.[206] Later the technique was used in North Norwegian, Icelandic and Faroese churches.[207]

In Greenland wooden walls were thin because wood was scarce. The stone wall was used both for protecting the inner wall of wood and for additional insulation. In Norway the builders used lime mortar to stabilise the stones in the wall. In Greenland lime was scarce, and normally replaced by clay. Gardar, Anavik (W7) and Vágar (E149) churches are examples of this. As long as the clay remained under a roof, it served its purpose and stabilised the wall. But if the roof rotted, water washed the clay away and the walls crumbled.[208] It can not be ruled out that the walls of Hvalsey church were stabilised with lime mortar. If they were, this may explain why it is the only standing Norse church. The protective wall could consist of turf only. This would work if a roof kept the turf dry. When the roof rotted rain decomposed the turf wall. This may be the reason why archaeologists have failed to localise several of the parish churches.[209]

Seen from the outside, most churches in Greenland had walls of grey stone or turf. Only Hvalseyfjord church is known to have been painted with white lime just like Norwegian stone churches.[210] The old Greenlandic name for the ruin's site is Qaqortuq, which means the colour white. "So perhaps the first Inuit who visited the place gave it a name from what they saw: a whitewashed church".[211]

I argued above that Hvalsey farm, but not the church, belonged to the king. Perhaps the cost of building Hvalsey church and providing the lime was born by the king?

The inside walls of Gardar cathedral were decorated with cloth. This is known because in 1347 King Magnus Eiriksson and his queen donated cloth worth 100 marks in Norwegian money "to ornate this precious church".[212] Cloths or carpets no doubt also hung on walls of parish churches. The floor of Tjodhild's church at Brattahlid was covered with red sandstone.[213] In Vágar parish church (E149) the floor consisted entirely of gravel.[214] If the church was built on dry and porous land, a gravel floor was a lowcost solution.

Much of the church equipment was imported. A mould made of soapstone for casting crucifixes was found in Gardar cathedral and may have been Greenlandic, but the metal used must have been imported iron or bronze.[215] At Sandnes a wooden "Pax" was found and Roussell who organised the excavation thought that an imported crucifix of metal originally had been a central part of it.[216]

Metal from broken bells has been found in several church ruins in the Eastern Settlement.[217] Church bells may have arrived in Greenland via Bergen from England. An English merchant arranged for a church bell to be cast in England, sold it to King Håkon V of Norway (1299–1319) who donated it to one of his royal chapels a short distance south of Bergen.[218]

The church also imported church art in wood.[219] The bishop's staff of walrus tusk, which was put in the grave of bishop Olav in 1280, was possibly carved in Trondheim and given to him when he was consecrated. In the ruins of Gardar cathedral a fragment of a glass window was found.[220]

The architecture of the parish churches demonstrates the Greenlanders' will to be part of a West European religious community where they found their main concrete models in Norway. But Greenland was a peripheral and poor part of the Norse realm, and their attempts to imitate the churches they had seen in Western Europe must be seen against that background.

The parish church as centre for the diffusion of literacy

In Iceland and Norway the parish priests needed boys to help them in the liturgy. For this purpose they taught a few youngsters such reading skills that they were able to sing a known Latin liturgical text. There can be no doubt that the same happened in Greenland. The boys had to learn letters and words and how to pronounce them, but it was not necessary to understand the meaning of the Latin text. This skill could help them to learn how to read a text in the vernacular, which they in turn could teach to their sons and daughters. A social mechanism was created for spreading literacy in the peasantry.[221] Parish churches are likely to have been the main centres for the spread of literacy in local communities, even in Greenland.

Finnur Jonsson assumed that all runic inscriptions with Latin words in them had been written by members of the clergy.[222] There must, however, have been laymen who had a superficial knowledge of Latin. In some runic inscriptions Latin and the vernacular are mixed. Other inscriptions seem to be based on the rich supply furnished by the liturgical texts of the Roman Catholic Church, but they are rather garbled so that only some elements can be recognised.[223] Perhaps the carvers were schoolboys who had been taught to read and sing Latin texts they did not understand?

Runes have survived in the soil because they were written on wood and stone, and an analysis of literacy in Greenland depends on them. In the Norse cultural area runes were used earlier than Roman/Latin letters. In Norway Old Norse started to be written with Roman letters on parchment shortly after AD 1000. This influenced the way runes were written. Ca. 1100 a new runic alphabet with 23 different runes was created, where each rune with few exceptions corresponded to a Roman letter with the same sound value. This makes it likely that all who could write Old Norse with runes could also write Old Norse using the Roman alphabet.[224] The number of rune inscriptions increased ca. 1200.[225] At this time the liturgy in Norse parish churches was more formalised, and it should be assumed that this was also the case for the education of the parish priests' helpers in the liturgy. More literate choirboys meant more people who could write runes.

In European churches it was usual that writing exercises in a school context were made with Roman letters on wax tablets, and there is no reason to believe this was done differently in Greenland. No such tablets have survived. But some or most of these schoolboys also seem to have acquired the ability to carve runes, which normally was done on wood or steatite stones. Many of these exercises have survived.

Some inscriptions are just one letter, others are several letters in a row, but which do not make a known word. Others are a name, both men's and women's, so it is likely that the rune carver wrote his own name as an exercise. Sometimes he wrote the name of the object he wrote on, like "bone", "club", "loom weight" or "bottom" [of a vessel]. The runologists agree that these inscriptions can only be explained as writing exercises, some written by beginners, others by grown up peasants to keep their skills alive, or for pastime.[226]

The origin and source of writing skills in Greenland was the church. In the group of ca. 30 inscriptions which had a meaning, between 40 and 50% were religious.[227] The simplest were the name of a saint, most common being "Mary", but also other saints, archangels and different names of God. The three most popular prayers were "Pater noster", "Ave Maria" and "Credo", and words from these were also found. Short quotations from church liturgy or the Bible also occur. These inscriptions could be seen as writing exercises where words from well-known texts are used.[228] Some were evidently meant as prayers.[229]

Some inscriptions were carved in Roman letters in the Latin language. Latin is almost exclusively found in religious texts.[230] Latin rune texts look like quotations, and so it should be concluded that the rune carver did not know sufficient Latin to formulate his own sentences.

Runes were also used for secular purposes. *The Greenlandic poem of Atli* describes how runes were used for sending messages.[231] Gudrun understood that her husband planned to murder her two brothers, and she cut runes on a rune-stick to warn them. The rune-stick was carried by a messenger, and he turned out to be a traitor and changed the runes so that they became incomprehensible. The wife of one of the brothers was loyal to her husband and was skilled in runes. The messenger asked her to read them, but she did not catch the meaning. She knew that Gudrun was skilled in the art and understood that someone had falsified them on the way.[232] This demonstrates the problem of sending messages on rune-sticks. They had to be carried physically by a messenger, and therefore the messenger might as well communicate the message orally.[233]

Runic messages could be sent for posterity. The priest Ingemund and his crew were shipwrecked on the uninhabited east coast of Greenland. They were found 14 years later, and Ingemund had written about their destiny with runes on a wax tablet.[234] In the churchyard of Herjolvsnes was found a coffin which only contained a rune-stick: "This woman who was called Gudveig, was laid overboard in the Greenland Ocean".[235] Who was the recipient of this message? Perhaps God on doomsday?

Runes were used in trade. In Bergen and Trondheim a large number of wooden tags have been excavated with runic inscriptions referring to ownership, like "Olav owns". They must have been attached to a consignment of goods on board a ship on its way to Bergen. On arrival the tags had served their purpose and were thrown away. Runes were also used to make ownership public in Greenland. On a meat-fork (W54) was written "Ljotr owns me" (*ljotrmk*), and on a spindle whorl "made Sigrid".[236] The Greenlanders knew that runes could be used to make ownership public, but rarely used it in trade.[237] Only one such tag has been excavated in Greenland, and it was without runes.[238] The explanation may be that such tags were not convenient when the main part of the cargo was walrus tusks. A priest living at Hitarnesi on Iceland where a cargo ship from Greenland had been wrecked in 1266, told the annalist Bjørn Jonsson (1574–1655) that even 350 years later he sometimes found tusks marked with old runes in red. "The Greenlandic peasants had done this because the tusks were different in quality and size. People wonder that these marks have not disappeared after so long [a] time in sea and sand".[239] The red runes mentioned by Bjørn are more likely to have been owners' marks. They are useful if the tusks belonged to several people and served the same purpose as the wooden tags. The Norse Greenlanders used writing in trade, but in a simple way which served their needs.

In Norway peasants used charters to defend ownership of land in court, which was a motive for farmers to acquire literacy skills.[240] The smallest dioceses in the Nidaros province were the Faroes and Greenland. Three charters witnessing possession of land written on the Faroes before 1412 are extant,[241] but there are none from Greenland. There are no indications that Norse Greenlanders learnt to read or write to defend their land. But one should be careful not to draw firm conclusions, as nothing written on parchment in Norse Greenland has been preserved.[242]

In Norway writing was used in trade, jurisdiction, state administration, the church and for sending and storing messages. In Greenland only church and religion were fully relevant. But it was not necessary for peasants to be literate to function well in their religious community, since the priest communicated with them orally. Literacy was less useful in Norse Greenland than in the rest of Scandinavia. The more complex a society is, the more useful literacy will be. Norse Greenland was less complex than other societies in the Norse region and in Western Europe.

110 *Church and religion*

The Norse Greenlanders' aesthetic models

The *Fostbroedra saga* describes how the chieftain Torgrim Trolle arrived at the Gardar Thing. "He had a stately ship and the crew was brave and well armed . . . When the ship arrived, people went to the shore to look more closely at their splendid equipment and weaponry".[243] This "stately splendour" in ships and weaponry could not be copied by ordinary peasants. They mainly found their aesthetic models in churches.

Figure 3.2 Trencher of wood for eating, 23 × 17 × 2.4 cm from W51 Sandnes; Appendix II, map 2.

Cf. the main text. The cross in the middle is a Maltese cross, but they probably chose it for decorative and not religious reasons. The Cross is surrounded by three concentric circles. From them double diagonal lines run to the corners. The other side is without decorations and has knife marks showing that this was the side used to cut food. Cf. Roussell 1941, pp. 284 and 285.

Photo: CC-BY-SA Lennart Larsen, Nationalmuseet

Copyright: The Nationalmuseum in Copenhagen.

The cross was the church's most potent symbol. The peasants ate from wooden trenchers, and a cross was incised and figured prominently on some of these. In Scandinavian peasant society it was common to say a short prayer before each meal, asking God to bless the food, and after the meal to thank God for the food. I would see the cross on the trencher as part of the same thinking: food was a gift from God. On a well-preserved trencher from Sandnes there is on one side irregular incisions from knives showing that this was the side where the owner put his food. The other side was decorated and without incision marks, and the central figure was a cross.[244] It should be assumed that the trencher when not in use was put on a shelf for decoration with the cross-side out.

Not all uses of the cross were religious. A small cross 13 × 13 mm, which had been perforated to be hung around the neck, was found at Herjolvsnes. It was made of jet stone and decorated with circles, and was both a piece of jewellery and a religious symbol.[245] If the cross was incised into the handle of a kitchen vessel, it should be seen as an ornament, but if found on sherds of soapstone with no apparent use, it could be no more than graffiti.[246] A cross was carved in the bottom of a barrel found at Sandnes. It may have been an owner's mark, perhaps that of a church.[247] It is often difficult to determine how a cross was meant.

Runes were used as ornaments. Erik Moltke observed in 1936 that Greenlanders had a fondness for embellishing their utensils with runes, but he was not sure why they did it, but he and Stoklund were inclined to think that they did it for protection. The name *Helgi* was carved on an armchair. No saint had that name, so why carve this name on an armchair? *Maria* was carved on a spindle whorl,[248] so did the Greenlanders think that a spindle whorl needed protection from St. Mary? The word *Maria* written on a wooden cross no doubt was meant as a prayer to St. Mary. When written on a spindle whorl one has to consider the hypothesis that it was meant as a decoration, written by a semi-literate, who perhaps only knew how to carve her own name and that of St. Mary. Another possibility is that *Maria* was the name of the owner.

Using runes as ornaments was a distinctive feature for Norse Greenland. Ca. 800 loom weights were excavated from Bryggen in Bergen, and 150 of them were decorated with crosses and other symbols. None of them carried runes.[249] Weavers in Bergen had the same desire as in Greenland to decorate their equipment; however, the difference was that in Bergen runes were not seen as decorative, but in Greenland they were. One hypothesis could be that a smaller part of the population was literate in Greenland, and the use of runes for practical purposes was rarer. This gave the ability to carve runes and the runes themselves a high social prestige which they did not have in Bergen where runes and Roman letters were more part of everyday work. In Norse Greenland literacy was also more closely connected to church and religion, which must have further increased the prestige of runes. A room with objects decorated with runes may have given it social status and aesthetic qualities in the eyes of the illiterate women who used the textile equipment.

Runes were an inexpensive way of decorating objects and were therefore not necessarily more used on rich farms. A list of excavated inscriptions divided by farms shows that the largest number of finds have been made on the farms which have been excavated most thoroughly, and the largest farms with churches are the best excavated ones.[250] This makes the result predictable. A comparison can nevertheless be made:

- The three large church farms with most inscriptions: 27 (Gardar E47), 17 (Sandnes W51), 13 (Herjolvsnes E111).
- The three well excavated middle-sized farms with most inscriptions: 16 (GUS), 11 (E34 in Qorlortup valley), 6 (Narsaq E17a).
- One small farm has been well excavated: 7 (Umiviarsuk W52a).

The large church farms had more inscriptions than the smaller farms, but the difference is not dramatic. Two factors have the potential for making the use of writing egalitarian:

- Writing skills were spread by the parish priest, and all Norse Greenlanders belonged to a parish. The parson would probably give education to boys he found most fit for it, and they did not necessarily live at the church farm.
- Runes had a function even for illiterates, as they could serve as ornaments.

But the survey above nevertheless indicates that one was more likely to find literate people on the church farms.

Geometric figures were used as ornaments in churches. In the chancel of Gardar cathedral and in the bishop's residence archaeologists found square and rhomboid slabs of soapstone ca. 7–8 cm in diameter, which seem to have been meant as flagstones for the floor.[251] Borders or ribbons carved on metal, soapstone or wood, consisting of long rows of circles and semi-circles, were used extensively for decorating architecture and objects in churches. A shard from a church bell found near Herjolvsnes parish church gives one example,[252] and the Gardar bishop's crozier in walrus ivory another.[253]

For a peasant it was demanding to carve such borders. The simplest way of doing it was with repeated and identical straight lines.[254] The geometric figures in churches were imitated, but they were simplified. One, two or three parallel lines were often incised as borders all around vessels used in the kitchen.[255] Parallel straight lines were also used on spindle whorls[256] or combs,[257] and circular lines on tub bottoms.[258] Equally simple to make were rows of small holes carved with a knife.[259] Slightly more complicated were rows of circles,[260] or rows of X's.[261] The most complex border found in Greenland is one where two lines of treble ropes are incised alternately one end over the other.[262] Square wooden trenchers for eating were decorated with lines along the edges and with smaller circles.[263]

Leaf ornaments in a church context are best preserved on the bishop's staff found in a grave at Gardar, probably from 1280.[264] Another example is a round disk with a diameter of ca. 19 cm found close to the Gardar cathedral. In the middle it had a cross surrounded by double circles, but most of the disc consisted of intricate leaf ornaments. The disc may have hung on a wall inside the church, instead of mosaic windows. Such leaf ornaments were copied for secular use,[265] for example on a piece of wood for winding up yarn.[266]

Summing up so far, Norsemen surrounded themselves with everyday objects to which they did their best to give an aesthetic appearance. In the kitchen, tubs in wood and large vessels of soapstone were decorated with circles and more or less complex borders along the edges.[267] At meals on their table they had wooden trenchers decorated with a pattern of squares, circles and sometimes crosses on the underside.[268] Their spoons could be decorated with geometric leaves.[269] When the meal was over, the front side of the trenchers decorated kitchen shelves. In the corner for spinning and weaving the spindle whorls were decorated with runes, lines in a geometric pattern or points carved with a knife.[270] Loom weights were often polished.[271] Yarn could be wound up on pieces of board decorated with leaf ornaments.[272]

Humans and animals are far more demanding to carve or paint for peasant amateurs than geometric ornaments, and the attempts resulted in simple sculptures in wood or soapstone, and graffiti carved on soapstone.[273] A crucifix from the Austmannadal, probably carved by a Greenlander, stands above the rest.[274] "The best piece of soapstone sculpture" preserved from Gardar cathedral is a bird's head.[275] Since it was made of soapstone it is assumed to have been carved in Greenland. Nørlund suggests that it was meant to be an eagle, which was the symbol of St. John the Baptist, and it definitely looks more like an eagle than any other bird. A wooden fish with runes carved at its flanks was found at GUS.[276]

Dragons and other fabulous animals were often depicted in medieval churches. At Sandnes an arm from a chair ending in dragon's head was found.[277] It could have been part of a prestige chair for the bishop when he visited the church, or for the secular chieftain of Sandnes, placed in the chancel visible for the congregation. In one of the living-rooms on Sandnes farm was found what seems like a simpler copy of it.[278] In a farm in the Austmannadal which belonged to Sandnes parish, was found what seems like another copy possibly used as a tally-stick.[279] On a plank later used for a coffin at Herjolvsnes churchyard was carved a dragon as graffiti.[280] In their churches the Greenlanders found both figurative and non-figurative ornaments and the latter were better adapted to the artistic skills of the peasantry.[281] The Norse Greenlanders had an aesthetic sense which was largely formed by what they saw in church.

The parish as framework for social life and mentalities

The parish with its parish priests was a powerful instrument for transforming social life and mentalities at grass roots level. The church imported to Greenland a model for how Christians should organise their social life to obtain a good life after death. The ownership of parish churches transformed local power relations and in the church they were presented with new values and ideas of visual beauty and "splendour".

Despite long distances and scattered settlements, the church managed to create an organisation which more or less reached out to all Norse Greenlanders. This was done through a flexible adaptation of the general parish model to the rather special Greenland environment. All elements in their church organisation can be found in Norway and other parts of the Nidaros church province, but in many respects they were weighted and used differently.

How deeply the church's values penetrated the minds of the Norse Greenlanders can best be seen when they had a real choice. When they decorated their rooms, equipment or utensils, they found their models in the church. Those who had literacy skills seem to have learnt them directly or indirectly through the parish priest. The West European parish was an effective instrument for transforming and indoctrinating people at grass roots level, and there is no reason to doubt that this was also the case in Norse Greenland.

4 The Gardar diocese

Laymen knew that the parish made them part of a much larger community which included all western Christendom. This community was based on the participation in religious rituals which were identical in all churches under the pope's supervision. The Catholic Church created a large organisation to ensure that this conformity was a reality. Very few Greenlanders would ever see the pope in Rome or the archbishop in Trondheim; the latter's work was on the organisational level. But the Gardar bishop would be a real person who visited their parish church at more or less regular intervals. He visited the archbishop when he was consecrated and on other occasions. The bishop was the link between the parish and Catholic Christians overseas.

The bishop

As mentioned earlier, there may have been a "minster" in stone at Gardar when the first bishop arrived in 1126. The church's next building stage was stone houses to the south of the church around an enclosure. These may have been built for secular activities and as dwellings for the clergy of a "minster" before 1126, or for the new bishop after 1126.[282] Similar constructions have many parallels at European cathedrals. The cathedral was later extended and then attained the length of 27 m as listed in Table 3.5. Mogens Høegsberg is the last to have examined the church ruin, and he thinks this is likely to have happened after AD 1200, but before a bishop was buried there in 1280.[283]

Before 1126 responsibility for controlling local churches had been divided between the church owner and occasional missionary bishops. None of them was in a position to do this effectively. After 1126 the Gardar bishop would exercise his control at visitations to the parish churches, ideally every third year, and in addition he would meet the priests at a synod once a year. In Norway priests' synods were combined with secular Thing meetings,[284] and one should assume the same at Gardar. The rich Icelandic material shows that the bishop controlled that priests could celebrate mass in correct Latin,[285] distribute the sacraments correctly and explain to laymen how the church helped them obtain salvation and a good life after death.[286]

Both before and after 1126 the education of future priests to a large extent took place at the different parish churches, with the parish priest as teacher. This gave practical exercise in the skills necessary to serve a congregation. Gardar cathedral lacked a chapter of canons and a cathedral school, but some of the schoolboys may have received individual education and practical training there. Regardless of how they were taught, it was the bishop's duty to examine the candidates before he consecrated them as priests.[287] This task could be delegated to a local priest in Greenland if no bishop was present there.

Before 1126 secular church-owners treated their priests as servants. The new bishop with a permanent seat at Gardar could not be deposed by secular Greenlanders and he met Greenlandic priests at annual synods. This changed relations between secular and ecclesiastical power. Before the first bishop Arnaldr accepted the office, he made the son of the Brattahlid chieftain swear that he would defend the properties and rights of the church.[288] As mentioned earlier, Arnaldr had a serious conflict with foreign merchants about property. He pressurised the Brattahlid chieftain into supporting him, reminding him of what his son had promised in the Norwegian king's presence. The outcome was that the chieftain's son was killed.[289] This suggests that the Gardar bishop was strongest from the start.

Did the bishops live and work in Greenland?

A basic condition for success was that the Gardar bishops really lived at their see in Greenland, so this has been a controversial question.

> The reliable *Groenlendinga tháttr* says repeatedly that the first bishop Arnaldr from the start resided in Gardar.[290] He was consecrated as bishop in Lund in 1124,[291] and in 1126 he arrived in Iceland on his way to Greenland. An Icelandic Annals comments that this year there were three bishops on the Icelandic Althing (*Thrir byskupar á Althinge*), they were Thorlak of Skálholt, Ketill of Holar and Arnaldr of Greenland.[292] The *tháttr* describes in detail the conflict he had with Norwegian merchants in the first part of the 1130s. He is there described as an intransigent but effective defender of the economic interests of his cathedral. These qualities were needed when creating a new organisation. He seems to have worked continuously in Greenland for 24 years (1126–1150). The Icelandic Annals usually mention visits by Greenland bishops, but none is recorded in this period. This does not exclude that Arnaldr may have visited Norway sailing directly without a stopover in Iceland. In 1152 "was founded a bishop's see in the town of Hamar, and Arnaldr bishop of Greenland was there the first bishop".[293] The most likely interpretation is that Arnaldr had been effective in building the new bishop's see in Greenland, and the king and the prelates saw him as the right man for a similar task in Hamar. A less likely and more pessimistic interpretation is that Arnaldr had become an old man and wanted to return to his homeland. According to the Icelandic Annals Arnaldr's successor to Gardar was consecrated in 1150, so on that occasion both of them are likely to have been present in Nidaros. Arnaldr was consecrated to his new bishopric in Hamar in 1152, so that year he must have been in Norway.

In 1150 Jon Knutr was consecrated new bishop of Greenland.[294] It is not recorded in the Icelandic Annals that Jon Knutr journeyed to Greenland via Iceland in 1150 or later. Most likely this means that he sailed directly from Norway to Greenland without a stopover in Iceland. During 1161–1188 Norway had an exceptionally strong archbishop called Eystein Erlendsson who forcefully and successfully built the new church province of Nidaros. It is unimaginable that he would have permitted bishop Jon to sit somewhere in Norway neglecting his duties in Greenland. In 1186, 36 years after his consecration, Jon was evidently ill, and sailed to Iceland. The Icelandic Flatø Annals write under 1186 that there were "three bishops on Iceland" (*Thrir biskupar á Island*). Two of them must have been the Icelandic ones, the third Jon of Gardar.[295] The way it is mentioned shows that this was a novelty. The following year in 1187 another Icelandic Annals recorded the "death of Jon Knutr *Groenlendinga byskups*".[296] He seems to have died in Iceland.

If we are to believe Bishop Gudmund's saga, Archbishop Eystein asked the Icelandic priest Ingemund, who was in Norway when Jon Knutr's death became known there, to become the new bishop of Gardar, but he declined the offer.[297] Early in 1188, just before he died, Archbishop Eystein ordained Jon Smyrill, also called *Sverrisfostri*, as new bishop of Greenland,[298] and he seems to have been Norwegian. The same year Jon sailed to Iceland and stayed in the eastern fjords of Iceland through the winter to 1189.[299] In both 1188 and 1189 Icelandic Annals wrote that there were "three bishops on Iceland" (*Thrir byskupar á Island*).[300] This is not said for 1190, so he must have continued his journey to Greenland in 1189. Jon stayed in Greenland from 1189 to 1202.

In March 1202 the church's great opponent King Sverrir died; he was excommunicated when he died. His son and successor concluded a peace agreement with the church in the summer of 1202. Bishop Gudmund of Holar arrived in 1202 from Norway,[301] and the same year an Icelandic Annals writes that Jon bishop of Greenland came to Iceland for the second time (*Jon Gronlendinga byskup kom annat sinn til Islandz*). Jon of Greenland and Pál of Skálholt were no doubt eager to hear from Gudmund of Hólar what was happening in Norway after the death of King Sverrir. The following year in 1203 "three bishops met in the eastern fjords of Iceland, Pál of Skálholt, Gudmund of Holar and Jon of Greenland" (*Tha funduz 3 byskupar i Austfiordum*). The meeting seems to have taken place before Easter 1203, and afterwards Jon of Greenland visited Bishop Pál in Skálholt where he arrived on Maundy Thursday. "Both bishops consecrated priests. They told each other true tales (*tölur truligar*) and had learned conversations. Bishop Pál received him with great honour (*soemd*) and held honourable banquets (*virduliga veizlu*) for him. The departure was generous and Jon received both gifts and other honours. Bishop Jon advised people on how to make wine from crowberries, which he had learnt from King Sverrir".[302]

Bishop Jon of Greenland had the byname "Sverrir's foster son" (*Sverrisfostri*), and the story about the crowberries makes it likely that this "Sverri" was the

Norwegian king with that name. His other byname *Smyrill* (Falcon) gives aristocratic associations. His aristocratic reception by the bishop of Skálholt confirms the impression of a high status person. The hard conflict between King Sverrir and the church may explain why the archbishop only gave him the poorest diocese in the Nidaros province. He may have wanted to move him to the periphery of the church province to prevent his contact with King Sverrir.

Jon left Iceland for Norway and continued to Rome in 1203.[303] He may have been the only bishop who remained loyal to Sverrir at the time of the latter's death, and he may have acted as ambassador for the new king to the pope, to explain the peace agreement between the new king and the Norwegian church.

When he returned from Rome, there are no traces of him returning to Greenland via Iceland, but one cannot discount that Jon may have sailed directly from Norway to Greenland. The final notice about him is from 1209, "Death of Jon bishop of Greenland".[304] He may have died in Norway or in Greenland. Jon was in office 21 years, at least 13 of them in Greenland.

The next bishop Helgi is the only known Icelander to have become bishop of Greenland. His father owned a ship which sailed between Eyafjördr on northern Iceland and Norway in 1185.[305] The same year an Icelandic priest named Ingemund sailed from Eyafjördr to Norway on another ship. The archbishop offered Ingemund the position as bishop of Greenland, but he declined.[306] There may have been ties between a family with clerical traditions in Eyafjördr and the cathedral in Nidaros. Helgi's predecessor died in 1209, but we do not know when Helgi was consecrated. He arrived in Greenland as bishop in 1212.[307] The next information about him is a notice in Icelandic Annals in 1230: "Death of Helgi Grönlendingabyskup".[308] He probably stayed in Gardar for 18 years, his term of office was a maximum 21 years.

His successor Nikulas was consecrated in 1234.[309] He had previously been archdeacon in Stavanger.[310] In 1236 he was still in Stavanger in the company of the Archbishop of Nidaros,[311] and he did not sail to Greenland until 1239.[312] He died in 1242.[313] He lived at Gardar for three of his eight years in office.

Olav was the next bishop, and he was consecrated in 1246.[314] In 1247 an envoy from the pope visited Bergen to crown King Håkon. Cardinal and king agreed that Greenland and Iceland should submit to a king "like all other countries in the world". Bishop Olav was present at the king's coronation, and was afterwards sent to Greenland with this message on behalf of king and cardinal.[315] He sailed from Bergen via Iceland to Greenland later the same year (1247).[316] As mentioned earlier, Olav's mission brought no results, and the king had to send three secular envoys to Greenland during 1257–1261 to obtain the submission to the Norwegian crown.[317] Bishop Olav stayed at his cathedral during 1247–1262, but the three secular envoys evidently ordered him back to Norway. In 1262 he sailed from Greenland on his way to Norway, but his ship came no further than Iceland. "Olav bishop of Greenland wrecked his ship at Iceland in Herdisarvik and he stayed here two winters" (*Olafr Grænlendinga byskup braut skip sitt vid Islandi i Herdisarvik ok var her ij vetr*).[318] In 1263 the Icelandic Annals proudly tell that there were "three bishops on Iceland" (*Thrir byskupar á Islandi*).[319] In 1264 Bishop Olav left Iceland for Norway (*Utanferd Olafs Grönlendinga byskups*).[320] He stayed in Norway for seven years, and was present in Trondheim when the new archbishop Håkon was consecrated in 1267.[321] One cannot discount that he was kept back by the king who may have doubted his loyalty, but there is no direct evidence for it. In 1271 he sailed from Norway via Iceland to Greenland "for the second time" (*Tha for Olafr byskup annat sinn til Grönlandz*).[322] This expression means that he did not sail to and fro more than the two times mentioned in the annals. In 1280 king Eirik was crowned in Bergen. The Norwegian church province had 11 bishops at this time, 9 of them were present in Bergen (Nidaros, Bergen, Stavanger, Oslo, Hamar, Skálholt, Holar, Faroes, Hebrides/Man), and only two were absent (Greenland and Orkney).[323] There may have been several reasons why Bishop Olav was absent, but the main one is to be found in the annals from that same year 1280: "Death of bishop Olav of Greenland".[324] There can be little doubt that he died in Greenland. A bishop's grave has been excavated in Gardar cathedral, radiocarbon dating indicating that it was Olav.[325] His first stay there was 15 years, his second 9, and he held his office for 34 years, 24 of them in Greenland.

During 1280–1288 the office of bishop was vacant, because at this time there may have been conflicts about the control of the parish churches opposing the cathedral administration and secular church-owners. This may have made it less attractive for competent candidates to become bishop of Gardar.[326] An alternative explanation is that news about Olav's death may have reached the archbishop several years after the event.

On 10 October 1288 a mass was held in Nidaros Cathedral where a new archbishop was consecrated, and he afterwards consecrated three new bishops, Thordr of Greenland, Arni of Skálholt and Thorstein of Hamar.[327] It was too late to sail to Greenland that year, but in 1289 he sailed there via Iceland (*Thordr byskop for til Grönlandz*).[328] For the next 20 years Thordr seems to have performed his duties on Greenland.

On 22 June 1308 the bishop of Bergen sent a letter to his colleague in Greenland, and started by telling him the news, "whether you have heard it or not", that king Eirik had died nine years earlier in 1299.[329] This must mean that no ship had sailed from Bergen to Greenland for at least nine years. It was difficult for the bishop in Bergen to know whether ships had sailed from Trondheim or anywhere else along the coast. A ship must have left for Greenland shortly after the letter was written on 22 June. The ship evidently stayed in Greenland through the winter to sell and buy goods, but in the summer of 1309, it returned to Bergen. Bishop Thordr in Gardar seems to have seized this opportunity to return with the ship to Norway; the Icelandic Gottskalk Annals note for 1309: *Thordr byskup af Grænlandi for til Noregs*.[330] Perhaps he was nervous that he should get stranded on the polar island?

Shortly after his arrival in Bergen, Thordr issued a testimony in favour of the archbishop on 26 November 1309.[331] On 26 December 1310 he issued another testimony in a conflict between members of the Bergen clergy,[332] and yet another on 1 February 1311.[333] On 9 May 1311 he issued a *vidimus* of a papal letter of protection for a local hospital.[334] Four extant letters in less than two years is quite a lot as we know that the overwhelming majority of letters from this period have been lost. But the letters concern routine matters, and Thordr does not seem to have been given tasks or responsibilities which implied independent decision-making. After 1311 no letters issued by him have been preserved. In 1314 Icelandic Annals noticed "Death of Thordr bishop of Greenland".[335] Thordr was in office 26 years, 20 of them spent in Greenland.

The archbishop consecrated the successor Arni the same year as Thordr died in 1314 (*Vigdr Arni byskup til Grænalandz*).[336] Bishop Arni sailed to Greenland the following year 1315.[337] For the next 28 years we have no information about him. If he had visited Norway via Iceland, it would have been noted in the Icelandic Annals. If he had stayed in Norway for a longer period, some information about his functions while there would have survived, because after ca. 1300 charters in larger numbers than previously are preserved in mainland Norway. There can be little doubt that he stayed in Greenland and did his duties from 1315 probably until 1349.

Arni's term of office had a mysterious ending. The Icelandic Annals tell us that old bishop Arni was still alive in Greenland in 1343, but Archbishop Pål Bårdsson in Nidaros did not know this. The archbishop assumed that Arni was dead, and consecrated Jon Skalli as the new bishop to Gardar in 1343 (*Vigdr... Jon byskup Skalla til Grænlandz ok lifdi Arni byskup á Grænlandi at ovitande Paali erchibyskupi*).[338] The Skálholt Annals add that Jon Skalli did not get his bishopric (*ok komast eigi*) for this reason.[339] Jon Skalli may have been consecrated in spring or summer. Ivar Bárdarson was sent to Greenland in 1341, and seems to have returned to Bergen in 1343, probably in the autumn. He must have brought fresh news from Greenland, perhaps informing Jon Skalli that Arni was still alive in Greenland.[340] In 1346 Jon Skalli was in Nidaros,[341] in 1354 in Oslo,[342] but he never functioned as bishop of Greenland. The most likely explanation for this incident is lack of information. The archbishop in Nidaros did not know that Ivar Bárdarson had been sent from Bergen to Greenland in 1341 and so may not have heard from old Arni for many years and assumed that he was dead. It may seem that for some reason it was urgent to get a new and energetic bishop in Greenland, and this may have had something to do with dramatic events in the Western Settlement. Bishop Arni seems to have remained in

Greenland until he died. In 1368 a new bishop (Alfr) arrived in Greenland, and the Skálholt Annals then comment that Greenland had been without a bishop for the previous 19 years. This means that Arni died in 1349, the year of the Great Plague, but not necessarily from the plague (*Herra Alfr byskups kom til Grænlands, hafde dar verid biskupslaust um xix ár*).[343] Arni was bishop for 35 years, 34 of them spent in Greenland.

The fate of Gardar cathedral and its bishops after 1349 in the final decades of the settlement's existence will be discussed at the end of this chapter.

The two first bishops Arnaldr and Jon Knutr had exceptionally long terms of office, together 63 years (1124–1187). Arnaldr arrived at his see in 1126 and seems to have stayed there until ca. 1150, or around 24 years. How long it lasted from Jon Knutr's consecration in 1150 to his arrival in Greenland is not known, but he returned from Greenland in 1186, the year before he died. There is no reason to doubt that nearly all of his 37 years in office were spent in Greenland. Continuity and presence in this initial period must have created a framework for long-term planning, accumulation of experience and good routines. Arnaldr and Jon Knutr seem to have been Norwegian. On the Norwegian mainland before 1130 the backgrounds of 28 bishops are known: 11–12 seem to have been English, 7–8 German, 1 Irish, 1 Danish, 1 Icelandic and 3–4 Norwegian.[344] In the founding years for new bishoprics foreigners from more advanced countries were seen as providing valuable expertise.

The most important changes in the Norse Greenland church organisation were the creation of Gardar diocese with its parishes in the 12th century, and that laymen had to hand over control and ownership of these parish churches to the bishop probably in the 13th century. This would hardly have been possible without the presence of bishops in Greenland.

The first Gardar bishop was consecrated in 1124; the last bishop who functioned and lived in Greenland died in 1378. The Greenland diocese functioned for 254 years. The Norse Greenlanders had nine functioning bishops in this period, and they were in office for 231 years or 91% of the time, the remaining 9% being interregna. The archbishop in Nidaros must have been eager to consecrate a new candidate as soon as the problematic communications permitted, and he did not want the office to be vacant.

A bishop was present in Greenland for 192 of these 254 years, which means that the Norse Greenlanders had their bishop with them for 76% of these years. The fact that the parish churches for most of this period were visited by the person with the highest religious authority in Greenland, must have meant that it was easier to impose catholic orthodoxy in line with what was practised elsewhere in the Nidaros province, and more difficult for unorthodox religiosity to win support.

A bishop was in office for 231 years in the period we are analysing here, and for 192 of these years they lived in Greenland. The nine bishops spent 83% of their time in office in Greenland. None of the nine used Gardar as a stepping stone to a more attractive see elsewhere. Arnaldr was given a new diocese in the final years of his life, and the remaining eight died as bishops of Gardar. Three seem to have died in Norway (Arnaldr, Jon Smyrill, Thordr), one in Iceland (Jon Knutr) and the remaining five probably in Greenland.

The general understanding of the morale of the West European clergy is that it was high during 1100–1300. In the following period there was a serious decline among the prelates, but on the parish level the situation was more varied. In the Gardar diocese a decline among the bishops is evident after 1378.[345]

Summing up, the Gardar diocese functioned for 254 years (100%), of which 23 years (9%) were interregna when there was no functioning bishop, 39 years (15%) he was absent in Norway, Iceland or Rome, and 192 years (76%) he was present at his see in Gardar. The bishops seem to have executed their office conscientiously,

Danish archaeologists have expressed low opinions of the bishops of Gardar's sense of responsibility for their diocese. Jette Arneborg claims that "There is no evidence that Bishop Arnald ever went to Greenland",[346] and that Helgi was the first bishop who went there – in 1212.[347] An analysis of the *Groenlendinga tháttr* and Icelandic Annals according to the methods of historical science verifies that this is wrong.[348] She also claims that "From 1123 to 1378 – a period of 255 years – the Norse Greenlanders had a bishop among them only for 106 years, if the annals are to be believed".[349] A competent historian would not write "if the annals are to be believed"; he would analyse the relevant sources and conclude from that whether the annals are to be believed and if there are other sources which can supplement the annals. This has been done in the biographies above.

The Greenland bishops took their task seriously and created a functioning framework for a strong church organisation and for the religiosity of laymen.

The Gardar diocese and the archbishop in Nidaros

From Christianisation ca. AD 1000 to 1104 Greenland was part of the church province (archbishopric) of Bremen; between 1104 and 1153 it belonged to a Nordic church province with a seat in Lund, then in Denmark.[350] In 1153 Norway and the Norse-speaking North Atlantic islands were made a separate church province with an archbishop in Trondheim. The 11 subordinate dioceses were Gardar, Oslo, Hamar, Stavanger, Bergen, Trondheim (= Nidaros), Skálholt, Hólar, Faroes, Orkney/Shetland and Hebrides/Man.[351] The size of Gardar cathedral can for practical reasons

Table 3.5 Length of cathedrals in the Nidaros church province

Trondheim	100 metres
Kirkwall	74 metres
Oslo	70 metres
Stavanger	64 metres
Hamar	57 metres
Skálholt	49 metres
Faroes	27 metres
Gardar	27 metres

Source: Nedkvitne 2009, p. 175; http://da.wikipedia.org/wiki/Kirkjubøur.

best be compared to other cathedrals in the Nidaros province through its length (see Table 3.5 for lengths of cathedrals in the Nidaros church province).

Gardar and the Faroes had the smallest populations, and their cathedrals were by far the smallest. The Faroese cathedral has remained unfinished to this day.

At each cathedral a new bishop was in principle to be elected by an assembly of the senior clergy at the cathedral called the chapter of canons. But Greenland and some of the other cathedrals were modest institutions without chapters. In 1297 the archbishop and the chapter in Nidaros agreed on how bishops should be appointed in the 11 dioceses. The archbishop and the canons in Trondheim were to elect new bishops in Greenland, the Faroes, the Hebrides/Man and the two Icelandic bishoprics. The other cathedrals had a local chapter and they were to elect their own bishops, but their candidate was to be approved by the archbishop and his chapter.[352]

According to the Icelandic Sturlunga saga this was also the practice. The Icelandic priest Ingemund worked as a parson near Nidaros when Bishop Jon Knutr of Greenland died in 1187. "Archbishop Eystein wanted to consecrate Ingemund as bishop of Greenland", but Ingemund declined the offer.[353] The author assumed that the archbishop had the authority to appoint a new bishop in Greenland. In 1343 in Trondheim Archbishop Pål consecrated a new bishop of Gardar, without knowing that the old bishop Arni was still alive in Greenland.[354] Pål appointed a new bishop without consulting anybody in Greenland. No source contradicts that the archbishop before 1349 had this power.

The newly appointed bishop of Gardar was consecrated in Nidaros cathedral before taking office. Shortly before Archbishop Eystein died on 26 January 1188 he consecrated Jon Smyrill as the new bishop of Greenland.[355] One hundred years later on 10 October 1288 a mass was held in Nidaros Cathedral where a new archbishop was consecrated, and he afterwards consecrated three new bishops, Thordr of Greenland being one of them.[356] There is no evidence that the Greenland bishops during 1153–1349 were consecrated by anyone other than the archbishop or in churches other than the cathedral in Nidaros. In the agreement from 1297 it is said that archbishop and canons should elect the Gardar bishop jointly, but it is unclear whether the Nidaros canons in practice played a role.

These routines were practised until the Black Death in Norway in 1349. The Norwegian parson Peder Clausson Friis (died 1614) wrote a "Description of Norway". One of his informants was an old judge who before the Reformation had gone to school in Trondheim and served at the catholic cathedral.[357] He knew oral traditions there and had probably read documents from the catholic archbishop's archive. Friis' information that "all bishops of Greenland were consecrated in Trondheim" evidently came from this judge, and confirms the other sources mentioned earlier.[358]

The Archbishop of Nidaros owned a warehouse in Bergen to which his incomes from the regions north of Bergen were sent and goods sold to foreign merchants. The bishop of Gardar benefitted from the economic services of the archbishop's servants in Bergen. Goods were sent from Gardar to the archbishop's warehouse, probably with a notice of which goods should be sent in return with the first ship. The archbishop's representative must have kept an account-book on these exchanges.[359] The archbishop never taxed the Greenlandic church.

Few Greenland bishops kept up face to face contacts with their colleagues in mainland Norway after they had arrived at their see, but the Gardar bishop could return to Norway for a limited period. Bishop Olav stayed in Norway for seven years during 1264–1271. According to the Icelandic Annals, 1271 was the "second time" he sailed to Greenland, the first being in 1247 after he had been appointed. But the 1260s were turbulent times for the Greenlanders, and the king probably ordered Olav to Norway. Bishop Jon Smyrill may have stayed in Iceland, Rome and Norway from 1202 until his death in 1209. This absence also had a political background.[360] Our main sources for these voyages are the Icelandic Annals, the Icelandic *Sturlunga saga* and the sagas of Icelandic bishops. They mainly register the voyages between Norway and Greenland if the bishop made a stopover in Iceland. No source tells that a Greenland bishop sailed directly from Greenland to Norway and back, but they may have done so.

Gardar bishops corresponded with Norwegian colleagues when available shipping permitted. On 22 June 1308 in Bergen a ship was ready to sail for Greenland and Bishop Arni of Bergen used this opportunity to send a letter to his colleague Bishop Thord of Gardar. Arni told him the names of bishops and other prominent Norwegians who had died during the previous nine years, and asked Thord to pray for their souls in Gardar cathedral. He also sent gifts, mostly European luxury clothing which must have distinguished the bishop and other prelates from other Greenlanders. The clergy at Gardar cathedral did their best to keep to Norwegian standards, and with support from their colleagues they may have succeeded, at least until the Black Death. The bishop of Bergen calls these goods gifts to a "friend".

The clergy at Gardar cathedral after 1261 helped to open communication channels between Greenland and the Norwegian court, which at this time mainly resided in Bergen. The priest Arnaldr Greenlander (*Arnaldr prestr grænlenzka*) followed bishop Olav when the latter sailed from Greenland to Norway in 1262. In 1271 Bishop Olav returned to Greenland, but Arnaldr stayed behind as chaplain (*hirdprestr*) at the court of King Magnus Håkonsson (1264–1280). Perhaps he functioned as Greenlandic ambassador and advised the king in matters Greenlandic after Bishop Olav left.[361]

The Gardar diocese and the pope

Only one Greenland bishop made a journey to Rome before 1378 – Jon Smyrill Sverrisfostri. It is not said what his business was in Rome, but it was probably political.[362]

The pope was the undisputed authority in questions of theological doctrine. He normally communicated his instructions to the archbishop in Nidaros, who passed them on to relevant dioceses. The archbishop could negotiate with the pope to obtain flexible adaptations of church doctrine. According to church law, people who were related within the sixth generation or less could not marry. Archbishop Eystein (1161–1188) explained to the pope that 12 days' journey from Norway there was an island with so few people that it was almost impossible for them to contract marriages which were legal. The island was said to have a bishop of its own and therefore must have been Greenland. Eystein asked for a dispensation.

Church and religion

Pope Alexander III authorised a bishops' synod in Nidaros to limit the prohibition to those related within the fourth generation or less, which means that it included second cousins.[363] Greenlanders evidently had so little contact with people living in Norway and Iceland that it was impracticable to find marriage partners there.

But the pope's flexibility had limits. In 1237 the archbishop told the pope that in some churches in the Nidaros province it was problematic or impossible to obtain bread of wheat and wine of grapes to be used at Holy Communion. People therefore made bread of whatever material was at hand and used beer or other beverages instead of wine. The archbishop was anxious that this would make the sacrament of penance invalid. The pope answered that only bread of wheat and wine of grapes were to be used at Holy Communion.[364] This prescription may have been impossible to practise in Greenland and the Faroes.

The Norwegian King Sverrir (1177–1202) was born and had been educated as a priest on the Faroes. He taught his foster son Jon, who was to become bishop of Greenland, how to make wine from crowberries. When Bishop Jon stayed in Iceland in 1203 he taught this to an Icelandic colleague. A man called Eirik, who lived close to Skálholt cathedral, made some wine that same summer and it was good.[365] On Greenland crowberries are so plentiful that they can make hills appear black.[366] It cannot be dismissed that Greenlandic priests used wine from crowberries in Holy Communion despite the pope's prohibition. The supply of wine from grapes may in Greenland have depended on colleagues in Norway who felt responsible for the community in Greenland. In 1308 the bishop of Bergen sent "a cask of grapes" (*eit fat med vinberium*) to the bishop in Greenland. Grapes would probably rot on their way from southern Germany or France to Greenland, so it is therefore likely that wine made of grapes was what was meant.[367]

From the end of the 13th century a new development emerged whereby the pope and his Curia in Rome showed less interest in organisational and theological questions and more in collecting taxes for the Curia's own use. In 1247 King Håkon made the pope send Cardinal Wilhelm of Sabina to Bergen to crown him as king. According to the English monk Matheus Parisiensis who visited Norway at this time, the king paid the Roman Curia 15,000 marks for the service, and the cardinal demanded 5000 marks from the Norwegian church. One third of the latter sum went to the king.[368] In return the king received help from the cardinal in mobilising the bishops of Iceland and Greenland in his campaign to bring the two islands under Norwegian sovereignty.[369] This cynical description contrasts with the idealised version in the saga of *Hákon Hákonárson*.

We are relatively well informed about the pope's taxation of Greenland since accounts exist in the Vatican Archives. In 1274 a church council in Lyon permitted the pope to collect a tax of 10% of all church incomes for six years. The tax was not to be paid by laymen, only by members of the church organisation. The archbishop in Nidaros was ordered to visit personally all dioceses in his province to organise the taxation.[370] The archbishop answered that Gardar was so remote beyond the sea that this could not be done there. He therefore asked the pope for permission to have this done by representatives, and in 1276 the permission was granted.[371] The archbishop sent a new letter in 1279. "The island on which the bishopric of Gardar is situated, because of the treacherous ocean in which this island is situated, is rarely visited by ships".[372] Not until recently had the archbishop been able to send a man there. He asked the pope to approve the arrangement, which the pope did. The pope also excommunicated clerics who neglected to pay, but the archbishop's representatives sailing to Gardar and other islands in the ocean were authorised to absolve them when they had paid.[373] The pope's hidden threat was to deny disobedient priests the right to distribute the sacraments and celebrate Holy Mass. Giving such an order would have been impossible without the archbishop in Nidaros as an intermediary. This cooperation between pope and archbishop made Greenland's integration into the international church effective from a financial perspective as well.

In 1282 the envoys to Greenland, the Faroes and Iceland had returned. The tax from Greenland had been paid in hides of cattle and seal, and tusks and ropes from walrus.[374] The archbishop claimed in a letter to the pope that the goods could hardly be sold in Nidaros for an adequate price.[375] He probably meant that if the Roman curia wanted an adequate price for the goods which had been collected with so much effort, they had to organise a transport to Flanders or other markets where the goods were in higher demand. The archbishop asked the pope for advice and was told to sell the goods for silver or gold, and send the profits to Rome with the taxes from the other Norwegian dioceses.[376] Later the same year the archbishop was told to leave the money to eight named merchants from Lucca who would bring it to Rome.[377] The archbishop asked for very detailed instructions because he feared he would be held economically responsible if he acted on his own and something went wrong.

In August 1326 the pope, who at this time lived in Avignon and was French, demanded another temporary tax, which included Greenland. It was to be used for warfare against the pope's enemies in Italy. Again the tax was imposed only on the clergy, and the amount was to be 10% of their incomes for six years (see Table 3.6). The pope ordered the Archbishop in Nidaros to organise the collection, but also sent letters directly to Gardar and the other bishops in the Nidaros province about the arrangement.[378] Two tax collectors from the French-speaking part of today's Switzerland were sent to Scandinavia.[379] Their account-book is still in the Vatican archive, and was printed by the Norwegian historian P.A. Munch in 1864;[380] relevant letters were also printed in DN VI in 1863.[381] These accounts make it possible to quantify the taxes paid from Greenland and other dioceses.

Table 3.6 Sums the pope demanded from each diocese in "the six years tithe" issued in 1326.[382]

Diocese	Norwegian marks[383]	Reference to Munch 1864[384]
Oslo	5002	p. 19
Hamar	1553	p. 20
Nidaros	4208	p. 21
Bergen	2700	p. 22

(continued)

Table 3.6 (continued)

Diocese	Norwegian marks[383]	Reference to Munch 1864[384]
Stavanger	1494	p. 23
Orkney	1135[385]	pp. 25–26
Greenland	254	pp. 25 and 45

Source: Munch, P.A. ed. 1864. The tax collectors' account-book registers the dioceses one by one. First it estimates the amount which each diocese should pay for all six years. This assessment was probably made in cooperation with the archbishop. Next it registers how much was actually paid in the year 1327 when the collectors made their first tour of Norway, which should be regarded as a first instalment on the total sum. The table shows the estimates for all six years. All five dioceses on the Norwegian mainland were assessed; of the North Atlantic dioceses only Orkney (Shetland included) was assessed, probably because it was by far the richest one.

Greenland was not assessed in the same way as the richer dioceses in Table 3.6. The archbishop of Nidaros was present in Bergen on 11 August 1327 at the same time as the papal collectors. He paid them walrus tusk weighing 127 "Norwegian lispound" on behalf of the Greenland church.[386] This was evidently considered as a one-time payment fulfilling the Greenland church's obligations for all six years. The papal collectors kept the walrus tusk until 6 September, when they sold it to a Flemish merchant called Johannes d'Ypres.[387]

The 127 lispounds of walrus tusk paid from the Greenland church were sold for 254 shillings (*solidi*) *Tournois*.[388] The tax collectors used an exchange rate of one *solidus Tournois* to one Norwegian mark (*parve monete noricane*).[389] The total "six years tithe" for Greenland was paid with a value equivalent to 254 Norwegian marks. This was ca. 22% of the assessed tax from Orkney, ca. 9% of the tax from Bergen, 6% of that from Nidaros and 5% of that from Norway's largest diocese Oslo. This measures the income of the clergy in these dioceses and gives an idea of the relative value of production there. It is an estimate made by the archbishop and his staff, but they were in a better position than most of their contemporaries to make such an estimate.

How many walruses had to be killed in Greenland to pay the six years' tithe imposed in 1326? The papal tax collectors sold their 127 Norwegian lispound (*lisponsos ad pondus Norwegie*) of walrus tusk in Bergen to a merchant from Ypres in Flanders for 2 shillings *Tournois* per lispound.[390] This means that one shilling *Tournois* would buy half a lispound.

The archbishop also paid a minor part of the six years' tithe from his own Nidaros diocese in walrus tusk. This time the tusks were counted and there were 24 tusks in all. The collectors sold these to the same Flemish merchant and received half a Norwegian mark in money (*parva moneta noricana*) per tusk.[391] This means that one Norwegian mark would buy two tusks.

In the exchange rate used by the collectors, one Norwegian mark had the same value as one shilling of *Tournios* silver coins.[392] Using the results above this means that two tusks had the same value as half a lispound tusks, or four tusks had the same value as one lispound tusks. One Norwegian lispound weighed 6.17 kg.[393] One tusk therefore weighed $(6.17/4)$ kg $= 1.54$ kg.[394]

The whole six years' tithe from the Gardar diocese was 127 lispound. One lispound contained on average four tusks.³⁹⁵ This means that the six years' tithe from Greenland contained 508 tusks. To produce these tusks 254 walruses had to be killed. We lack information on how many walruses one hunter produced in one season in the Disco Bay region. We therefore cannot calculate how many men had to be sent north to produce these tusks. In theory the tithe was to be paid over six years, which meant killing 42 walruses per year.

During this year the Greenland church also had to pay three lispound tusks in unpaid debts from Peter's Pence, corresponding to 12 tusks or 6 killed walruses. A total of 254 + 6 = 260 walruses had to be killed to satisfy the demands of the tax collectors of the Roman Curia. But this demand in 1327 was extraordinary. The tithe was a temporary tax to be paid over six years, but Peter's Pence was for an unknown number of years.

The church claimed the right to tax its own personnel and the state claimed the sole right to tax all its subjects. In practice this meant that the church had to obtain state approval to tax its clergy. This approval came at a price: the papal tax collectors had to give half of the six years' tithe to the king.³⁹⁶ The pope in Rome and the state in Norway cooperated to tax the clergy. The Greenland clergy must have disapproved of this development.

It would be interesting to know if the archbishop put a heavier burden on the Greenland clergy than on the clergy on the Norwegian mainland, but no information exists on the clergy's total income. Comparing the clergy's tax payments and population size would provide some indication. Norwegian historians have estimated population figures for Norway in the period immediately before the Black Death. The Gardar diocese paid 6% of what Nidaros diocese paid in papal taxes. The population of Nidaros diocese was ca. 60,000. If payment per inhabitant was the same, Gardar would have had 3,600 inhabitants. The Gardar diocese also paid 9% of what the Bergen diocese paid. The population of the Bergen diocese may have been ca. 45,000. If payment per inhabitant was the same, Gardar would have had 4000 inhabitants.³⁹⁷ A total of 3600–4000 inhabitants on Greenland is somewhat more than the estimate made in Chapter 1, p. 35 of ca. 2500 inhabitants. The difference between 3600–4000 and 2500 is so small that it in our context it may be explained by the sources of error in the calculation. The extant sources indicate that the level of papal taxation in Greenland was not significantly different from the Norwegian mainland.

In 1343 bishops in the Nidaros province received yet another order from the pope to collect a tax of 10% on the clergy's incomes, this time for three years. In addition, each cloister, nunnery and cathedral chapter was to pay a fixed sum.³⁹⁸ The bishops on the Norwegian mainland decided to send a delegation which was to explain to the Avignon Curia that parts of the ordinance were impossible or difficult to implement. To cover the expenses for this delegation, the Oslo diocese was to pay 6 pounds sterling, Hamar 3 and the others 4 pounds. Gardar and the Faroes were exempted, as the bishops evidently wanted to protect them.³⁹⁹ They at this time knew that the Greenland church had special problems in relation to the Inuit. Ivar Bárdarson had returned from there in 1343.⁴⁰⁰

128 *Church and religion*

The pope in 1345 repudiated the bishops' complaint and extended the tax from three to five years.[401]

In 1346 a new archbishop of Nidaros was consecrated in Avignon, and he explained to the Curia that there were special problems collecting the tax from the north Atlantic isles. Ships sailed only once a year to some islands and to others every third year. We can safely assume that Greenland was among the latter. The Avignon Curia was unrelenting. It left it to the archbishop to decide when instalments should be paid from these islands, but the bishops on the Norwegian mainland were ordered to pay annual instalments.[402] In 1348 the pope sent a tax collector to Scandinavia to speed up the process.[403]

But now events more powerful than papal envoys made the conflict irrelevant. The Black Death struck Avignon in 1348 and Norway in 1349. No papal taxes are known to have been demanded or collected from Greenland after the Black Death even if such taxes were imposed on other Norse dioceses.

In a first period from 1124 to the second half of the 13th century, the main task of the Gardar bishop was to implement in his diocese the organisation, rituals, norms and theology practised in the international church. Around 1300 the Greenland church largely functioned as the other dioceses in the Nidaros province and western Christendom without external interference. From 1274 the pope's main emphasis shifted from ideology and organisation to taxation. The archbishop tried in some cases to protect economically weak dioceses like Gardar. The pope's economic exploitation of the Gardar diocese took a sinister turn when he started to sell the title of the Gardar bishop. We shall return to this towards the end of this chapter.

5 The monasteries

The first written evidence that cloisters (in plural) existed in Greenland is found in a letter which the bishop of Bergen in 1308 sent to his colleague in Greenland. "We also send some other things to the cloisters, and which Olav Bonde shall hand over to you. He will tell you how to distribute them".[404] Olav Bonde was evidently the skipper who was about to cross the North Atlantic. The second and last written evidence for these cloisters is found in Ivar Bárdarson's account from ca. 1360.

The source from 1308 uses *klaustr* as a common name for the two religious communities in Greenland, one for men and another for women. The best translation will be "cloister". When Ivar Bárdarson wrote about the Augustinian community for men, he used the same word *closter*. When he wrote about the Benedictine community for women, he called it *søster closter*, literally "cloister for sisters", which is best translated as "nunnery".

They use "cloister" as the common name for all religious communities. They also use "cloister" about communities for men only, but communities of women are given a special name, nunnery. I shall use the terms in the same way. The housing in which they lived, I shall call a "monastery".

Economy

Ivar Bárdarson tells that in Ketilsfjord, today's Tasermiut, there were three churches with parish rights, and the innermost belonged to a cloister.[405] "Further into the fjord . . . lies a large cloister in which live regular canons and which is consecrated to St. Olav and St Augustine".[406] Their official name was *Canonici Regulares*, and they lived according to a monastic rule written by St. Augustine and today they are often called Augustinians.[407]

Ivar's description combined with a study of a map, makes the estuary of the river Uiluit kua the most likely site to search for the cloister. The ruin of a stone church was found there (E105), and the localisation of the Augustinian monastery is today considered as certain. The ruins have not been excavated, but a "superficial examination" was made by Nationalmuseum archaeologist Poul Nørlund in 1926. He did not try to measure the dimensions.[408] A calculation of the internal space of the church has to be done on the basis of a drawing of the church made by Aage Roussell.[409] My result was a nave of $8 \times 6 = 48$ m^2, and a chancel of $3 \times 6 = 18$ m^2 which makes 66 m^2 in all. It was slightly larger than an average Greenland parish church.[410]

Ivar calls the whole monastic complex "large". The dwelling was really large, with exterior dimensions of 37×32 m. If the walls were ca. 2 m thick, the interior must have been ca. 33×28 m or ca. 900 m^2. It was divided into many rooms.[411] The Augustinian canons probably had one room each, and other rooms may have been for work and meetings. A nearby house had an exterior of 14.5×7 m, and the interior may have been 10.5×3 m or ca. 30 m^2. It was also divided into several rooms and may have been for the servants or for sheep and goats.[412] Another building had two rooms which may have been the byre and barn for cattle. The barn had an exterior measuring 7.3×3.5 m. The byre had walls of both stone and turf, which gave better insulation and had an exterior measurement of 6×5m, and the interior may have been 4×3 m.[413]

In Chapter 5, pp. 234–238 we will calculate how much space was needed to keep a cow in a byre. If the byre was more than 3 m broad internally, the cows could stand tail to tail in two rows along the longest walls. If it was narrower there would normally only be one row of cows. This byre was on the borderline. Each cow needed a stall which was ca. 1 m broad. This byre was 4 m long, which means that there was room for four cows in each row. The byre had room for a maximum of eight cows, possibly only four. The average number of cows at Norse farms seems to have been around ten,[414] which means that E105 was not even an average farm. This confirms the claim of the Nationalmuseum archaeologist Christian Vebæk that conditions for agriculture at the Augustinian monastery were "rather poor" (*ret ringe*) since the home field was small and the outbuildings few.[415] Many Norwegian monasteries were built on large farms, but this was not the case for the Augustinians in Ketilsfjord. They must have received significant incomes from other sources.

The other cloister on Greenland was a nunnery. "Next to Ketilsfjord lies Rampnessfjord and far into that fjord lies a Benedictine nunnery".[416] Ivar has given us no reason to doubt his good memory in other church matters so far, and we should take "next to Ketilsfjord" literally. This means that the nunnery was "far into" the Southern Sermilik fjord, and E131 or E138 would then be the most likely sites. Archaeologists to my knowledge have not looked for a church there, and we have to await further archaeological investigations before we can confirm whether Ivar is reliable on this point. The Nationalmuseum archaeologist Christian Vebæk thought he had found the nunnery at E149 in the Uunartoq fjord, but he has not convinced his colleagues.[417]

Nunneries elsewhere often demanded that novices brought with them a "dowry" from their parents' household. This was meant to correspond in size to the novice's dowry if she had married and was her part of the inheritance from her parents. It was therefore profitable for a nunnery to receive novices from rich households.

The most important permanent income for both cloisters may have come from their parish function. The tithe in Norway was divided into four parts: a salary for the parish priest, upkeep of the parish church and the other parts for the bishop and the parish poor. The cloisters would receive the first two parts of the tithe, and had the task of distributing the part which was meant for the parish poor. But the parishes of the two cloisters were not among the richest in Greenland.[418]

Only consecrated priests could become members of the Augustinian order.[419] In mainland Norway members of Augustinian houses could function as parish priests in nearby parish churches. They could also practise "termination", which meant that they were itinerant priests who preached and offered pastoral services for a fee.[420] In Greenland the Augustinians may have functioned as priests at the two other parish churches in Ketilsfjord and possibly other parish churches if needs arose, but extant sources say nothing about it. Well-off households often paid cloisters to sing requiem masses for dead relatives. This was thought to create religious merits and give them a better life after death. This may have been a significant source of income for both cloisters.

On the Norwegian mainland Augustinian and Benedictine cloisters had their main incomes from land rents. This was not so in Greenland: the two cloisters probably owned the farms on which they were situated, but not other farms. The nunnery and the cathedral owned in common several islets in *Siglufjord* (Uunartoq). None of them had Norse farms, but Uunartoq Island had hot springs in which people bathed to improve their health. This may have given the nunnery incomes which were probably modest.[421]

Both monasteries were situated in the southern periphery of the settlement, and it reinforces the impression of periphery that both the Augustinian cloister and the nunnery were in the inner, barren parts of their fjords. One explanation for these unfavourable locations could be that the cloisters were latecomers.

Many monastic orders had in their statutes that they should have at least 12 monks or nuns. The Augustinian rule had no such minimum requirement. Iceland had seven cloisters for men, of which five were Augustinian.[422] There may have been economic reasons for this preference for the Augustinian order in Iceland as well as Greenland. The Augustinians in Ketilsfjord may have been few in numbers.

Summing up, the Greenland cloisters seem to have been financed mainly through their parish rights supplemented with products from their home farm. The nunnery received extra incomes through "dowries" from novices, and the Augustinians possibly from offering pastoral services outside their own parish.

Religious functions

The declared aim of the medieval church was to save souls. One way of doing this was for nuns and monks to sing intercessory prayers in the chancel of their church, which was done seven times a day and once at night. It was a common belief among laymen that the prayers of morally superior nuns and monks were more likely to reach God and his saints than their own prayers.[423] These intercessory prayers gradually grew less important as the parish took centre stage, but they were not felt to be superfluous. The parish priest's task was to educate laymen through sermons and personal conversations during confession. There were two ways to salvation and they were felt to be complementary.

In the period before 1124 priests stationed in larger churches probably spent much of their time as itinerant priests, singing masses for local communities.[424] The rise of the parish marginalised this activity, but the Greenland geography did not permit all Greenlanders to travel to and from their parish church in one day. The Augustinians may have continued the tradition of itinerant priests.

The bishop was supposed to visit parish and monastic churches in his diocese every third year. This control of the nunnery may have been felt to be insufficient. Medieval churchmen had in general limited confidence in nuns' ability to govern themselves economically and religiously. In France and elsewhere on the continent it was not unusual for a nunnery to be supervised by monks in a neighbouring cloister.[425] The two Greenland cloisters were in the inner part of two neighbouring fjords with a short isthmus and a fjord between them. This may have been done on purpose to make it easier for the monks to supervise the isolated nuns and give them pastoral services.[426]

Who founded the Greenland cloisters? They both belonged to orders which were controlled by the bishop. Their main income ca. 1360 was from the tithe which at that time was controlled by the bishop. The best verified hypothesis is that the bishop took the initiative to both cloisters and gave them a parish with the tithe included.

When was this done? The church of the Augustinians in Ketilsfjord had a narrow chancel and a wider nave. In Norway this type was not used after ca. 1250, but it may have been in Greenland.[427] The cloisters are likely to have been founded after the bishop had obtained control of the tithe from the secular church-owners, which is likely to have happened after 1261.[428] Both cloisters received their parish rights between ca. 1288–1314 and 1360, but may in theory have existed before they received parish rights. The letter from the bishop of Bergen to his colleague in Greenland shows that both cloisters were founded before 1308.[429] They are likely to have been founded between 1288 and 1308.

Compared to Iceland and Norway, the Greenlandic cloisters were latecomers. There were five Augustinian cloisters in Norway, four of them founded under

Archbishop Eystein (1161–1188).[430] In Iceland the last Augustinian cloister was Mödruvellir founded in 1296, which may have been contemporary with the Greenlandic one.[431] Five Benedictine nunneries were founded in Norway. Three of them are from ca. 1150, one in each of the three main dioceses Nidaros, Bergen and Oslo. The fourth came in Eystein's time and the last ca. 1226.[432] Iceland had the nunneries Kirkjubær in Skálholt (1186) and Reynistadur in Holar (1295), the last one possibly being contemporary with the Greenlandic nunnery.[433]

After ca. 1150 laymen were mainly part of a religious community through the parish. The Greenland geography could easily have made a substantial part of the population feel excluded, but the cloisters counteracted this. Itinerant Augustinians visited peripheral local communities. Benedictine nuns and Augustinian canons sang intercessory prayers for laymen every day of the year. The Norse Greenlanders received the same church services and probably felt as integrated in a Christian community as laymen in the other Norse dioceses.

6 The supernatural and the natural world

Christian miracles and magic

In a prayer the Christian can ask God and his saints to fulfil a wish, but he knows that it is up to God whether the wish shall be fulfilled. The Christian religion also taught that God and his saints could intervene in the real world on their own initiative and change the natural course of events. This is not magic, it is a Christian "miracle".

In 1407 there was an incident in Greenland which definitely was not a Christian miracle, and which modern people would consider as superstitious. A man called Kollgrimr allegedly seduced a married woman with the help of black magic (*svarta kuonstrum*). Her father was a prominent Icelander. Kollgrimr was sentenced to death and burned (*brendur eptir dom*).[434] He had invoked non-Christian forces for help, and the belief that such forces could be used to harm others was widespread in the Middle Ages until the 17th century. To harm others in this way was a criminal offence according to general European church law. In Chapter 6, pp. 357–358 we will discuss whether Kollgrimr's case was handled in the Greenlandic court of justice according to contemporary legislation.

"Magic" is an analytical concept used by modern scholars, and an author has to formulate a definition of it which is fruitful for the relevant study. I shall call it "magic" if supernatural powers other than God and his saints are asked for help, for example the Devil or powers which exist somewhere in nature. Kollgrimr was accused of "magic" in this sense, but his alleged crime was within what most of his contemporaries thought was possible.

The best extant sources for how Norse Greenlanders experienced miracles and magic in their society are written accounts from Greenland based on oral narratives from people who had lived in or visited the settlements. Four such accounts exist.

The Icelander Hermundr Kodransson experienced ca. 1130 the events described in the *Groenlendinga tháttr*. He returned to Iceland and died there as a man in his nineties in 1197.[435] He is likely to have brought the oral narrative to Iceland, where the *tháttr* is thought to have been composed in written form at the end of the 12th century.[436]

The King's Mirror was written ca. 1250, probably in Bergen by a cleric connected to the royal *hird*, and it has a section on Greenland. The narrator (the father) says that he has "seen some of those who have voyaged to Greenland and heard their tales and what they say".[437] Later he confirms that "I have often met people who have been for a long time on Greenland".[438] His information on Greenland is detailed and concrete, and this gives credence to his claim that they come from the oral narratives of people who had experienced and seen what they told.

In the 1260s a Greenlandic priest called Halldor wrote a description of a voyage in a small boat called *sexæringr* from Gardar northwards, possibly as far as Melville Bay. They sailed through mists into unknown lands which the author claimed had never before been visited by Norsemen.[439]

The fourth narrator, Ivar Bárdarson, seems to have been born in Greenland, and the person who wrote down his oral narrative in Bergen ca. 1360 explains that Ivar worked for many years at Gardar cathedral and had seen what he describes (*hand hafde alt dette seet*).[440] All four narratives contain visual details which give confidence that the narrator had been in Greenland himself or reports faithfully facts which he had been told by people who had been there. None of the four sources describes magic or miracles in Greenland, and they have a secular understanding of the natural environment there.

In Hávamál the pagan god Odin is said to use runes as a means to obtain magic power; this part of the poem may have been composed in the pagan period.[441] Poul Nørlund,[442] Erik Moltke, Finnur Jonsson[443] and Marie Stoklund[444] thought runes were used for magical purposes in Greenland even after Christianisation, but none of the extant Greenlandic rune inscriptions can be verified to have a magical function. Inscriptions which have been called "magic" can be explained as normal Christian prayers or meaningless carvings done by people who were only semi-literate. The invocation of non-Christian divinities after Christianisation has only been claimed for one rune-stick found in Narsaq.[445] The claim is based on Moltke's interpretation of the inscription, which is strange to say the least. The Icelandic philologists Halldorsson and Helgason have interpreted the inscription as a play on words of a type which was common in the 12th and 13th centuries, and which has nothing to do with magic. Their interpretation has today strong support among runologists.[446]

Apart from Kollgrimr's story, all extant examples of miracles and magic in Norse Greenland are from sagas written in Iceland. Most Icelandic sagas (*Islendingasögur*) include miracles or magic, but the authors evidently thought they occurred more often in Greenland and Vinland. The reason for this may partly be that Greenland was at the periphery of the known world, and partly an idea that paganism lasted longer in Greenland than in other parts of the Norse realm. The authors of these *Islendingasögur* had probably never visited Greenland, and what they relate is the Icelanders' ideas of miracles and magic among Norse Greenlanders. Norse Greenlanders are sometimes described by modern authors as irrational in several ways, and it is claimed that the Christian religion had penetrated their mentalities superficially. How much of this is Icelandic prejudice against the Greenlanders appearing in sagas which are fiction?

The Icelandic skald Thormod was the liegeman of the Norwegian king and later saint Olav Haraldsson, and when he visited Greenland Thormod received supernatural help from him.[447] The most critical struggle for Thormod was a duel with the nephew of the chieftain he had just killed. Thormod at one point lost his axe and received a deep wound between his shoulders. He understood this could be the end and prayed to be given king Olav's strength and good luck. Then the opponent lost his axe too, and Thormod jumped over a cliff into the sea. The result was a fist struggle in the water, which ended when the opponent's belt burst, his trousers became wrapped around his legs, he could no longer swim and then drowned.[448]

In another critical situation Thormod had to seek refuge in the middle of the night on an islet where he hid under some seaweed. Five men searched for him, using spears to find whether he lay under seaweed, but without results. The woman who led the search party then called out: "If Thormod has more courage than a mare, he shall answer me now". This was a serious insult, and Thormod opened his mouth for an answer, but he could not utter a sound because an invisible hand covered his mouth. After this the pursuers left. At the same time a peasant at a nearby farm dreamt that a man came up to him and said: "I am King Olav Haraldsson. I want you to row to the islet close to your farm and save Thormod my liegeman".[449] Thormod escaped and shortly afterwards left Greenland for Norway.

King Olav was venerated as a saint after his death, and it would not be contrary to official theology that he could work miracles even in his lifetime. At the same time the saga author opens up for rational explanations. Thormod's opponent could have lost his axe and belt for natural reasons, and the invisible hand could have been a feeling which Thormod had. Readers who were sceptical about miracles could choose to interpret it that way.

Other supernatural interventions cannot be rationalised in this way. The sister of the chieftain whom Thormod had killed, commanded non-Christian supernatural help, and one night she woke up and said to her son: "I have roamed widely on my magic stick tonight, and learnt things which I did not know before". She now knew that Thormod was hidden at the farm of a poor, old couple.[450] The wife on this farm, Grima, "possessed ancient, pagan wisdom" (*fornfrod*). She had a chair on whose arms were carved large likenesses of the god Thor with his hammer, and whoever sat in it became invisible.[451] That very night she had a dream where she learnt that Thordis was on her way to them. Grima put Thormod in the invisibility chair, and he was not detected.[452] Thormod seems to receive magic help from the pagan god Thor. The author explains that the pagan religion in the 1020s was still present in Greenland. But the situation is ambiguous – perhaps it was St. Olav who helped his loyal liegeman Thormod through a Christian miracle?[453]

The most dramatic stories of supernatural interventions in Greenland are in the two Vinland sagas. The Icelander Gudrid and her father arrived at Herjolvsnes in Greenland where there were famine and epidemic diseases. The chieftain at Herjolvsnes invited a soothsayer to predict when this calamity would end. She needed an elaborate ritual to attract spirits who could help her see the future more clearly. An important element was a particular song which only Gudrid knew, and she participated in the ritual. The soothsayer predicted that the famine would end in the coming spring and so would the epidemic, and she was right.

The helping spirits are called *natturur*, and the word is etymologically the same as "nature". These were spirits existing in nature independently of Christianity. Laypeople living in the 1220s thought that such forces were a reality. The clergy wanted laymen to regard them as allied to the Devil, and it was against church law to seek help from them. But most laymen held a different opinion – these spirits were neither of God, nor Devil nor pagan gods like Thor and Odin, and if the aim of the ritual was good, it was no sin to seek their help.[454] In this case the ritual definitely had a good purpose, and those present are said to have taken comfort from the prediction. Gudrid at first refused to participate in the ritual "because I am Christian" but yielded to pressure from her host. Gudrid's father left the room because he did not want to witness such sorcery (*slik hindrvitni*).[455]

A ghost story which took place at Sandnes in the Western Settlement is included in both Vinland sagas. Thorstein was the son of Eirik Raudi. Gudrid from the first story had become his wife and they lived one winter at Sandnes. They were baptised but stayed with a couple who were still pagan. An epidemic struck the settlement. One evening the pagan hostess met several ghosts outside. Among them she saw herself and Thorstein. The ghosts were the people who were destined to die, and so they did that very night. The hostess after her death tried to rise from her deathbed, but her husband struck her down with an axe to her breast. Thorstein also returned from the dead, sat up in his bed and told his wife that he had arrived at a good place after death and predicted her future.[456] To keep the ghosts (*aptrgöngum*) away, they had to burn the corpse of one of those who had died in the epidemic, who was evidently not a good Christian.[457] Thorstein was a messenger from God and his saints.

The author explains that "at that time Christianity was still young on Greenland" (*Tha var enn ung kristni á Grænlandi*).[458] He then indirectly says that such supernatural spirits and ghosts did not appear in his own time ca. 1220–1250. These two episodes from the Vinland sagas have in common that they are not well integrated into the main narrative and may have been added at a late stage in the transmission by a person who had a religious message: we now live in a spiritually safer world.

There are no indications that the Greenlanders thought their country had a relationship to the supernatural world which was different from that of other parts of the Norse realm. But Icelanders who saw Greenland society from a distance may have thought that this was the case.

Geographic exploration

The Norse did not know for certain whether Greenland was an island or the southern promontory of the northern massif of land and ice which today is called the Arctic. Most people assumed the latter. Northern Russia east of the White Sea was thought to be connected with the uninhabited Eastern Greenland by a long northern coastline called *Hafsbotn*, or "the end of the ocean".[459] The west coast of Greenland was connected to today's Canada by another coastline also called *Hafsbotn* or *Marklandsbotn* (= the end of Markland). It went from Melville Bay, crossing what we today know is Smith Sound. From there was a coastline southwards where the Vinland explorers sailed and which they named Helluland and Markland, corresponding to Baffin's Land and Labrador. A geography probably written by the Icelandic abbot Nikolas in the 1150s but preserved in a manuscript from 1387, says that there was a sound between Markland (Labrador) and Vinland (Newfoundland), today called Strait of Belle Isle. Sailing westwards through this sound one would finally arrive at the World Ocean (*uthaf*). The *uthaf* was the ocean which surrounded the world's landmass. From the southern side of this sound (Strait of Belle Isle) a landmass was thought to continue southwards to, and then along, the coast of today's New England and ended up close to Africa.[460] The southern Atlantic between these two continents ultimately also reached the World Ocean. There was no agreement among the Norse about how many outlets there were to the World Ocean. Some authors thought that the sounds and islands west of northern Greenland which are part of today's Canada, also ultimately reached the World Ocean.[461]

Parts of this understanding of the northern coasts was backed up by rational arguments. The same animal species were to be seen in Scandinavia, Russia and the Norse settlements in western Greenland. Hares, wolves and reindeer are mentioned, but the list can be extended. The only way the medieval Norse could explain this was that these animals had walked from European Russia westwards along the coasts of *Hafsbotn* to the uninhabited eastern coast of Greenland. From there they walked southwards to Cape Farewell and then further to the Eastern Settlement. There was also an alternative theory that there might be an ice-free valley through the inland ice connecting the east and west coasts of Greenland. Greenlanders climbed the highest ice-free mountains on the west coast in vain attempts to find this valley or catch sight of the ocean on the other side of the inland glacier.[462] The medieval Norse did not know that animals could walk from the White Sea through Siberia to northern Canada crossing the Smith Sound to Greenland. They combined available geographic knowledge in a rational manner and used it to place Greenland on the world map.

Several voyages explored the North Atlantic between Greenland and Norway. In 1285 the Icelandic priests Adalbrandr Helgason and his brother Thorvald sailed to the uninhabited eastern coast of Greenland (*Grœnalandz obygdir*), and on the same voyage they discovered "New Land". Adalbrandr on other occasions sailed to Norway where he visited the king's court.[463] In 1289 the king sent a man to Iceland to make people search for and exploit the newly discovered land.[464] There was a will for systematic exploration.

In the 1260s the Inuit appeared in the Disco area, which was the Norse Greenlanders' most profitable hunting ground. The Norsemen's reaction is described in a letter written by the priest Halldor in Greenland to a Greenlandic colleague who lived at the court of King Magnus ca. 1270. It describes two journeys, the first in 1266 and the second in 1267 or later. The letter was copied by the Icelander Hauk Erlendsson (ca. 1265–1334) in his compilation called "Hauksbok". He lived most of his adult life in Bergen as a royal official and is a reliable source for events there ca. 1300.[465]

In 1266 a log was found in the sea close to the Norse settlements. It had been hewn with small axes and wedges which had been made of animal teeth and bones. They were hammered into the log. The Norse thought this had been done by the Inuit, since Norsemen would have used iron for splitting logs.[466] The Norsemen knew that logs drifted down eastern Greenland, rounded Cape Farewell and continued up the west coast past the Norse settlements. The arrival of the log made the Norse think that the Inuit had now settled on the east coast. They came closer to the settlements from both sides. Modern knowledge tells us that some of these logs came from Siberian rivers and the attempt to fell and split the log may have been done there.

Hunters who voyaged to the Disco region in the spring of 1266 were evidently asked by priests at Gardar cathedral to investigate what could be found out about the Inuit's whereabouts there. Some hunters sailed further north than anyone had done before. They found Inuit housing (*skrælingja-vistir*) only in *Kroksfjardarheidi* (= Nuussuaq) but did not meet them. The Inuit may have been in the fjords hunting reindeer, or gone into hiding when they saw the Norse approaching.

The priests and other people in the Norse settlements were in doubt as to how this should be interpreted. Hauk only writes that "People thought that *Kroksfjardarheidi* was nearest to where they came from".[467] This could be interpreted as a guess that the Inuit lived permanently north of *Kroksfjardarheidi*. But the Norse were not sure of this and wanted to find out more.

Later (*sidan*) the priests in Gardar organised a new expedition which was sent even further north than the expedition from 1266. This may have been in 1267 or a couple of years later. The purpose was clearly to find out if the Inuit threatened from the north-west coast the Norse Greenlanders' traditional hunting in the Disco region. They voyaged in a *sexæringr* (a boat with six oars) which could be rowed by three or six men. It also had a square sail and when sailing, the boat was easier to handle with three men on board. This is the most probable number of men on board the Greenlandic boat.[468]

All the participants seem to have lived in Gardar, since the account ends with the following sentence: *Sidan fori their heim aftur i Garda*. The journey took place in July when there was less ice than in March-April when the *nordrseta* usually took place. They first sailed to *Kroksfjardarheidi* (= Nuussuaq), which was the northern part of where the Norse normally had their *nordrseta*.[469] This was also where the previous expedition had seen Inuit housing. From there they sailed out to sea so that the coast sank beneath the horizon. Then a strong wind blew up from the south, it grew dark and they had to sail with the wind northwards. When the clouds broke up and it became lighter, they saw many islands and all kinds of animals for hunting: seals, whales and a large number of polar bears.

138 *Church and religion*

Figure 3.3 View from Kingittorsuaq island where the Norse runestone was found. One or several sexæringr from Gardar were sailed and rowed in the 1260s through this landscape.

Photo: Meldgaard 1995, p. 211.

Copyright: The Nationalmuseum in Copenhagen.

I would guess this was somewhere north of Upernavik. They reached *Hafsbotn* (the Ocean's end) where all land they could see was to the south of them. This was so for the ice-free land as well as the glaciers. This indicates that they had reached the southern edge of the frozen sea in the northern part of Melville Bay, somewhere in the neighbourhood of Savissivik. They found some old and abandoned Eskimo houses there, and archaeological excavations have confirmed that Dorset and then Inuit had lived in this area from ca. AD 800 up to the time when our sexæringr visited the area. The Norse dared not stay ashore for longer periods for fear of being attacked by polar bears. They then started the homeward journey and sailed or rowed for three days and nights and went ashore on some islands south of a mountain called *Snæfelli* (Snow mountain) and which evidently was known from earlier journeys. There they found Inuit housing which was still in

Figure 3.4 Runestone from Kingittorsuaq island. Its origin and later discovery are described in the main text.

Photo: CC-BY-SA Arnold Mikkelsen, Nationalmuseum

Copyright: The Nationalmuseum in Copenhagen.

use, but no Inuit in sight. They rowed from there on 25 July, and after "a long day of rowing" they were back in Nuussuaq. The Midnight sun still shone there, but it was below freezing at night.[470]

The most famous of all Greenlandic rune-stones was found in 1824 in a cairn at Kingittorsuaq close to Upernavik, far north of where the Norse normally had their *nordrseta*. It says that "Erlingr Sigvatsson and Bjarni Thordarson and Eindridi Oddsson on the Saturday before Rogation day (25 April) built this cairn". The three named Norsemen were present there on 25 April in an unknown year. This was probably the crew of a Norse sexæringr.[471] They must have been peasants or servants on a hunting or reconnaissance expedition from the Western or Eastern Settlement. The form of the runes made Stoklund date the Kingittorsuaq rune stone to the 13th century, most likely the second half of that century.[472]

Were the three men named on the rune-stone members of the expeditions mentioned above? The second expedition took place in July and the rune-stone was written in April, which excludes that members of the second expedition wrote it. The men on the first expedition did this as part of their normal hunting voyage. The date is not given, but these hunts normally took place in March-April. The three men who participated in this first expedition in 1266 are said to have been further north than Norsemen before them. The rune carver may have wanted to tell this to posterity.[473]

These expeditions show a will to analyse the Inuit problem by trying to map where the Inuit lived, and their conclusion was that this was one day's rowing north of Nuussuaq. The letter says nothing about action taken after these reconnaissance voyages. They had problems interpreting their information since they did not understand the Inuit's seasonal movements. As long as they lived north of *Kroksfjardarheidi* this was no problem. But when they started settling further south, the Norse had to reconsider their walrus hunts. The capacity to analyse the

A theoretical interest in the natural world

The King's Mirror's section concerning Greenland describes a curious natural phenomenon, "that which the Greenlanders call northern lights" (*that er groenlendingar calla nordrlios*).[474] This formulation could suggest that the word had its origin in Greenland. Old Norse dictionaries confirm that the word "northern lights" is only used in *The King's Mirror* and only about the phenomenon as it appeared in Greenland. Corresponding words in other Germanic languages (*Nordlicht, northern lights, nordlys* etc.) are according to the etymological dictionaries translations from Old Norse, or perhaps one should rather say Greenland Norse. In antiquity and Latin it was caller Aurora Borealis (northern sunrise). This word may be the only Greenland Norse contribution to a language which still exists. The Norwegian author of *The King's Mirror* suggests three explanations for the phenomenon but admits that he lacks empirical knowledge to verify any of them. This is a sensible conclusion, since modern science of course has verified quite different theories.[475]

The Greenlandic priest Halldor mentioned earlier wanted to tell his readers about another curious natural phenomenon, the midnight sun. He illustrates it using the experiences of the crew that sailed to Melville Bay shortly after 1266.[476] They had used the same measuring method as sailors measuring their ship's northern latitude. At midnight when the sun is in the north the sun was as high as at home in the settlement at nine o'clock in the evening. He also gives an imprecise measurement of how high the sun was there at midday. "If a man laid down in a sexæringr crosswise stretched out between the gunwales with his face towards the sun, the shadow of the gunwale which was nearest the sun would cover his face".[477] This means that at midday the sun in this northern location was lower than at Gardar. Compared to more southern latitudes the sun was higher at midnight but it was lower at midday. The lack of instruments for measuring makes his illustration of the phenomenon appear unscientific, but the main point in our context is that his intellectual curiosity and will to measure reveals a scientific mentality.

Another question which aroused the curiosity of *The King's Mirror* was why it was so cold in Greenland. The author was well aware that the earth is a sphere – he calls it "the earth sphere" (*iardar bollum*).[478] He divides it into five regions. At the extreme north and south it is so cold that nobody can live there; around the middle of the "earth sphere" is a belt which is so hot that it is uninhabitable as well. Between these regions are two temperate zones where people can live.[479] *The King's Mirror* explains that the middle region was hottest because the sun was nearest to the earth there.

The author of *The King's Mirror* and the Greenlandic priest Halldor both had a strong intellectual curiosity about unusual phenomena in nature, but in practice got no further than describing the natural phenomena they observed.

Combining religion and practical rationality

The educated elite in Greenland had a secular, rational attitude to the natural environment and social challenges. The sources give no information about attitudes among peasants, but there is no reason to assume that their attitude was different.

This means that Norse Greenlanders did not replace practical action with prayers for divine miracles and did not practice magic in the sense of seeking supernatural help from non-Christian forces.[480] But prayers to a benevolent saint could improve the chances of self-help being successful.

The church promised a good life after death for those who participated in the church's rituals and respected its ethics. The Sunday mass and other rituals united people in a local community which was both religious and secular. The Norse Greenlanders did what the church taught was necessary to get a good existence in the next life and combined it with a rational analysis of and curiosity about the nature and society in which they lived.

7 The Greenland church in its final decades 1340–1410

The scarcity of sources makes it difficult to follow the decline of the Greenland church in detail in the final decades of its existence. Our best information is on the bishops.

The bishops

Bishop Arni seems to have died in Greenland in 1349. Due to a misunderstanding the archbishop had already consecrated his successor Jon Skalli in 1343. It was impossible for the latter to go to or stay in Greenland when it became known that his predecessor still lived, but he did not go even after 1349 when Arni died,[481] as he was in Nidaros in 1351 and in Oslo in 1354.[482] This may have been because many bishops died in the plague in 1349, and he may have hoped for a more attractive appointment elsewhere. In 1357 he was moved to Holar on Iceland. Now the Gardar bishopric became vacant for a new appointment, but nothing happened.

Finally a candidate was found. Alfr was a Benedictine monk at the cloister of Munkeliv in Bergen. In 1365 he was consecrated bishop of Greenland, evidently in Nidaros.[483] In 1366 he was in Bergen and donated his houses there to his nephew. This may have been in preparation for his departure to Greenland.[484] He arrived in Greenland in 1368. The Skálholt Annals comment that Greenland then had been without a bishop for 19 years, since Arni died in 1349.[485] Alfr was the last bishop who was Norwegian by birth, appointed and consecrated by the archbishop in Nidaros and went to Greenland. According to the Gottschalk Annals Alfr died in 1378.[486] Three other annals claim that he died in 1375, 1376 and 1377 respectively, and give the additional information that his death became known outside Greenland with a ship which sailed directly from Greenland to Norway six years after Alfr's death.[487] Earlier research has trusted the Gottschalk Annals, which gives the most direct and unequivocal date, and I see no reason to question this. Alfr was the last in a line of nine bishops who during a 254 year period 1124–1378 had worked in Greenland and done what they no doubt saw as their duty to the Norse community there.[488]

When the news of Alfr's death came to Norway in 1384, six years after the event, the situation there was much changed from what it had been before the Black Death. The consequences of the plague had undermined the economic basis of the Norwegian elite. The state and church organisations had been seriously weakened and were less capable of putting into practice their own political program or offer resistance to external pressure. The major pressure came from Denmark which, at this time, was a great power in a Scandinavian and North German context. Bergen got its first Danish bishop in 1370.[489]

The pressure from the Roman Curia also hardened. In 1381 the chapter of canons in Nidaros elected a Norwegian for their next archbishop, as they were entitled to, and the candidate started on his journey to the Roman Curia to be consecrated by the pope. But "a man called Nikolas, he was Danish",[490] travelled quicker and made the pope consecrate him in 1382.[491] The new archbishop consecrated another Dane called Henrik as bishop of Greenland probably in 1386,[492] and that year both of them were in Nyborg in Denmark.[493] In 1388 Henrik was in Oslo,[494] in 1391 he was in Orkney as the pope's envoy,[495] and later the same year he was back in Rome.[496] In 1394 the pope transferred Henrik's bishop's title to Orkney, which was a far richer diocese.[497] None of the bishops consecrated after 1386 visited Greenland. The Papal Curia had instituted the rule that if a bishop's office became vacant while the previous bishop was at the Curia, the pope had the right to appoint his successor. After 1394 the pope transferred from Trondheim to Rome the right to appoint bishops of Gardar.

A consecrated bishop could work as temporary substitute for another bishop. In this way bishops consecrated to Gardar could earn their living without incomes from Greenland. The Gardar bishops had become irrelevant to their diocese. On 27 March 1411 a notice was entered in a protocol in the Vatican that the pope had appointed his confessor Johannes Petersson Treppe bishop of Gardar. Both were present in Bologna.[498] Later the same year Johannes Treppe functioned as substitute for the bishop of Roskilde in Denmark.[499] He seems to have been Danish. When the diocese of Gardar was instituted in 1124, the intention had been to improve the quality of the work done in the Greenland church by making it a more closely integrated part of the Western church. Some 277 years later, the title had been reduced to a source of income for clerics in foreign countries who felt no responsibility for the community in Greenland.

The church organisation after the bishops had left

When bishop Arni died in 1349 there had been a parish system in Greenland for more than two centuries. This organisation needed a strong bishop with authority when it was established and made itself independent from secular chieftains in the 12th and 13th centuries. In 1349 it functioned according to routine procedures accepted by all. The bishop's main duty was now to check that the church rituals were performed, and that the parish priests were competent to do this correctly.

At Gardar a spindle whorl was excavated with an inscription in Latin, "Thithricus me possidet". Thithricus is the German name Didrik, and the inscription being carved in Latin indicates that the owner of the spindle whorl was a priest, even if the spinning work must have been done by one of his servants. It is not impossible that a German priest worked at the Gardar cathedral. Even if Gardar did not have a chapter of canons, there must have several priests there. But a priest named Didrik lived in Iceland at the end of the 13th century, and it cannot be ruled out that our Didrik was a Norwegian or Icelander with a German name.[500] The spindle whorl has not been dated.

The first long period without a bishop was 1349–1368. For parts of this period, we do not know which years, Ivar Bárdarson administered or participated in the administration of the bishop's office. We do not know his formal position. Ivar was an envoy from the Bergen bishop but also seems to have been born in Greenland. His narrative makes evident that he travelled around Greenland on visitations, either as a substitute for the bishop or as part of the retinue of this substitute.

The Icelander Bjørn Einarsson stayed in Greenland for two winters during 1385–1387.[501] He wrote a diary which is now lost, but Bjørn Jonsson from Skardsá on Iceland (1574–1655) made an excerpt of it in his extant "Grænlands annal": "When Bjørn Einarsson 'Jerusalem-pilgrim' was in Greenland, the bishop of Gardar in Einarsfjord had just died [Alfr in 1378]. An old priest managed the bishop's see and made all consecrations which were the normal responsibility of a bishop (*vigdi öllum byskups vixlum*)."[502] At the Gardar see there must have been several priests, and one of them had evidently been given this authority. Perhaps he had the same authority as Ivar Bárdarson 20–30 years earlier.

The only written document which is known to have been made in Greenland was sealed on 19 April 1409 at Gardar cathedral. Eindridi Andresson, who held the title *officialis*, and the priest Pál Hallvardsson witnessed that they had made public in Gardar cathedral on three Sundays the coming marriage of an Icelandic couple, as prescribed by church law.[503] An *officialis* was a cathedral priest who had a special responsibility in Scandinavia for the church's jurisdiction in cooperation with the bishop. But he also functioned as the bishop's second in command and substitute when the bishop was absent.[504] Ivar Bárdarson and the old priest whom Bjørn Einarsson met, may also have held the title *officialis*. It was possible for the cathedral to function without a bishop if somebody else performed his day to day duties. The main organisational structures seem to have been intact to the very end.

Laymen's religious rituals in their parish churches

Did laymen receive the pastoral services which they felt they needed from the church in these final decades of the settlement's existence? Our sources are silent about this, but there is no reason to doubt that after 400 years of religious indoctrination, Heaven and Hell were a reality for the Norse Greenlanders as they were

144 *Church and religion*

for practically all medieval Europeans. There was no external reason why the Greenlanders should discontinue their religious rituals.

Most important was Holy Mass held in churches with parish functions on Sundays and other feast days at 10 a.m. In Iceland and Norway many stayed at the church until vespers or evensong at 4 p.m., which also made church holidays a social occasion.[505] Attending mass was thought to contribute to the remission of sins and increase the chances of salvation. From the end of the 12th century bishops' synods in the Nidaros province demanded that the parish priests added a sermon in Norse to their liturgy in Latin, and this was gradually put into practice in the following century.[506]

After 1268 in Norway and 1275 in Iceland it became compulsory for all laymen to confess their serious sins to their parish priest or another priest at least once a year. He would then impose on them an appropriate penance, and after that the sinner would receive holy communion.[507] Baptism and burial normally took place in the parish church and at its churchyard.[508] Marriage was a secular agreement between two families in the Norse Middle Ages, but the couple could choose to receive the parish priest's blessing in front of the church door or ask for a mass inside the church. The marriage was legally valid even without these church rituals.[509]

At a certain point in the mass the "pax" was sent around to the congregation for each of them to kiss it, symbolising that they pardoned their enemies.[510] A "pax" consisted of a piece of wood, in which was carved a shelf where a crucifix and other figures, often made of imported metal, were fastened with nails. The wooden shelf of a "pax" was excavated at Sandnes farm and had probably been used in Sandnes church.[511] An almost identical wooden frame has been preserved from Hedal church in Norway.[512]

The excavations at Herjolvsnes churchyard demonstrate that burials continued to take place there until the end of the settlement shortly after 1410, and there is no reason to doubt that laymen also received the other pastoral services in their parish churches to the very end.

Medieval archaeology and history have in the last decades shown increasing interest in religion and culture and have tried to analyse its social impact. In Denmark archaeologists from Århus have been more inclined to take in this trend than those from Nationalmuseet.[513] Arneborg expresses a low opinion of the importance of religion for laymen and clerics in Norse Greenland, but this view is not representative of contemporary scholarship.[514]

Laymen's religious practices in their homes

The Nationalmuseum archaeologist Poul Nørlund excavated the cemetery at Herjolvsnes in 1921, and among the finds were 58 wooden crosses. The largest of them was 69 cm high and 29 cm wide, the smallest 11 × 8 cm, and most of them were ca. 20–30 cm high. All of them were found in or on a coffin and were slender and light to carry. Of the 58 crosses found, 54 had a plug or a dovetail at the lower end, indicating that the crosses had an earlier function before they were buried with the corpse. The plug made it possible to carry the cross atop a pole in a procession. It is more likely that the plugs were meant to stand in a candlestick. Many crosses may have stood on a table in the deceased person's living-room, and it could have been placed in a corner without dominating the room. Marie Stoklund has suggested that many Norse living-rooms had what she calls a "devotional corner" (*andagtskrog*).[515] In church people used to say their Pater Noster and Ave Maria in front of paintings or sculptures of Christ or the saints. Many Greenlanders are likely to have done the same in front of unpretentious wooden crosses in their own living-room. In their lifetime they prayed in front of a cross, which later followed them to the grave.

Seven of the 58 crosses had runic inscriptions naming God, Jesus, the Holy Ghost, Maria, Mikael or St. John whom the owner of the cross invoked for protection.[516] "Maria and Mikael own me Brigit" says one inscription – the dead woman Brigit declares herself to be under the protection of St. Mary and the archangel Mikael.[517] "Jesus Christ help me, Jesus was born for us" – this prayer was meant to help the deceased in the next life.[518] Other carvings say "God Almighty protect Gudleif well" and "Thorleifr made this cross in praise and worship of God the almighty".[519]

Some peasant households would have an entire crucifix (Jesus on the cross) in their "devotional corner", inspired from altars in churches and chapels.[520] In the Austmannadal in the Western Settlement there were five farms. The easternmost of them was close to the inland glacier and had a main building with 21 rooms (W53d).[521] In the final phase its only living-room (room XXI) had a fireplace, wainscoting and benches along two of its walls.[522] In front of one of the benches were found many loom weights and other remnants of a loom. Women evidently worked there.[523] The benches were of a Norwegian type called a "soil-bench" (*moldbenk*). A plank 22 cm high was put on edge 45 cm from the wall, the room between the plank and the wall was filled with dry soil, and boards were laid on top.[524] The benches were of course meant for sitting, but also insulated the room. In one of these "earth-benches" the archaeologists excavated an "outstanding object", "a wooden slab with a crucifix in high relief".[525] In the final phase part of the house including the living-room was destroyed by fire.[526] If the person who put the crucifix in the earth-bench wanted to protect it from fire, she or he succeeded. It is today exhibited at Nationalmuseet in Copenhagen.

The meticulous carving makes it evident that this crucifix was meant as an object of devotion. It had a plug for fixing it to a candlestick like the crosses mentioned earlier.[527] The crucifix cannot have been meant for a church since there was no church on W53d. It probably had the same function as the crosses, but was more prestigious. The Nationalmuseum archaeologists Roussell and Nyborg thought it was made by a Greenlander, since the material was driftwood.[528] The Norwegian art historian Erla Hohler suggested it may have been imported from Norway.[529] All agree that it was made in the final century before the Western Settlement was abandoned ca. 1350.

Another wooden crucifix was found at the cemetery of Sandnes parish church at the bottom of a coffin under the thigh bone of the skeleton, with the front side down.[530] The historians Roussell and Hohler agree that the crucifix should be dated to ca. 1250–1300.[531] Roussell praises the quality of the work and finds it likely "that the craftsman has had his workshop at one of the episcopal seats in Iceland or in Norway".[532] He thinks the crucifix had an earlier life in Sandnes church. Stoklund, however, argues that it had its original place in the "devotional corner" of Sandnes farm, which was the richest in the Western Settlement.[533]

A cross cut from baleen or crucifixes incised on soapstone could be hung on the wall.[534] Crosses can also be found on shards of soapstone which had been perforated, showing that they had been carried around the neck or perhaps hung in the house. They should be seen as non-vocal prayers.[535] At a farm in Vatnahverfi (E167) fragments of two steatite plates were found on which were carved crucifixions; one of them included Mary and John. Both were square, the sides ca. 6–7 cm and they were perforated probably to be hung on a wall.[536]

Few Greenland peasants were literate, and their prayers were mostly formulaic like Pater Noster and Ave Maria.[537] Formulaic prayers in front of a cross or crucifix in their own living-room were no doubt felt to be collective, first because the whole household may have participated in the prayers but also because they knew that other Christians said the same prayers in front of similar devotional objects all over Christendom.

Christianity came to Greenland at the order of the Norwegian king, and the first priests were English. Some 400 years later, the Christian religion had become an important, perhaps the most important, part of Norse Greenlandic identity. Prayers in front of crosses and crucifixes in private living-rooms were voluntary and continued contact with western Christendom after shipping had ceased and Danish kings and bishops had lost interest in Norse Greenland.

When physical contacts between Greenland and Norway became irregular or ceased altogether, the Norwegian state could no longer function in Greenland.[538] The Christian religion created cultural ties, and they could continue and be strong even without physical contacts. In the settlement's final decades religion may have become the Norse community's strongest tie to a larger Norse and western community to which they felt they belonged.

Notes

1 *Landnámabok* S91 and H79, IF I, pp. 132–134; English and Norwegian translations: chapter 91. *Groenlendinga saga* IF IV chapter 2, p. 245, English translation: CSI chapter 1, pp. 19–20 and Penguin chapter 1, p. 3.
2 *Groenlendinga saga* IF IV chapter 2, pp. 245–246; English translation: CSI chapter 1, p. 20 and Penguin chapter 1, p. 4.
3 *Landnámabok* IF I, pp. 134–135, S93 and H80; English and Norwegian translations: chapter 93.
4 *Fostbroedra saga* IF VI chapter 23, pp. 242, 245 and 247: English translation: CSI chapter 23, pp. 382–385.
5 Roussell 1941, pp. 95–97.
6 Krogh 1982, p. 51
7 Skaaning Høegsberg II, 2009, p. 100
8 *Islendingabok* IF I, chapter 7, pp. 16–17; English translation, chapter 7, p. 9

9 *Eiriks saga Rauda* IF IV chapter 5, pp. 212 and 415–416; English translation: CSI chapter 5, p. 8 and Penguin chapter 5, p. 35.
10 Krogh 1982, pp. 33–41; Arneborg 2004, p. 236
11 Krogh 1982, pp. 41–52
12 Arneborg 2004, p. 237
13 Cf. Chapter 1, p. 15.
14 *Eiriks saga Rauda* IF IV chapter 5, p. 211; English translation: CSI chapter 5, p. 8 and Penguin chapter 5, p. 34.
15 Cf. Chapter 2, pp. 61–63.
16 *Eiriks saga Rauda* IF IV chapter 5, pp. 212 and 415; English translation: CSI chapter 5, p. 8 and Penguin chapter 5, p. 35
17 *Medieval Scandinavia*, entry word "Olafs saga Tryggvasonar".
18 *Saga Óláfs Tryggvasonar af Oddr Snorrason munk*, p. 155; English translation, chapter 52, p. 102; Norwegian translation, p. 108; *ukunnandi at fara med danscri tungu*.
19 Nedkvitne 2014(b), pp. 89–92.
20 *Fagrskinna*, ed. Jonsson, F., chapter 21, p. 113; English translation: p. 115. *Han helt fyrstr Noregskonunga retta tru til guds, ok af hans stjorn ok riki vard allt Noregsveldi kristit ok Orkneyar ok Færeyar, Hjaltland ok Island ok Grønaland*.
21 skémadr = skimadr, cf. Fritzner volume 3, 1896, entry word "ski" and "skimadr". A person with false appearance.
22 *Heimskringla*, "The saga of Olav Tryggvason", chapters 86 and 96, cf. 95.
23 It is used in this way three times: *Groenlendinga saga* IF IV pp. 245–6, 256 and 257–8; English translation: CSI pp. 19–20, 25 and 26, and Penguin pp. 3, 11 and 12
24 *Groenlendinga saga* IF IV chapter 5, p. 256; English translation: CSI chapter 4, p. 25 and Penguin chapter 4, p. 11.
25 KLNM, entry word "Kristni saga".
26 *Kristni saga*, Old Norse and English translation, p. 397; *tha sende han ok Leif Eiriksson til Groenland at boda thar tru*. English translation by Sian Grønlie, chapter 12, p. 47.
27 *Historia Norwegie*, p. 55.
28 Niermeyer 1993, entry word "roborare".
29 Latham 1965, entry word "robur".
30 Keller 1989, pp. 188 and 193.
31 Keller 1989, pp. 187 and 203–204.
32 Keller 1989, pp. 197–198.
33 Keller 1989, p. 191.
34 Keller 1989, p. 199.
35 Roussell 1941, pp. 120, 122 and 126.
36 Blair 2005, pp. 368–395.
37 Krogh 1982, p. 123; Keller 1989 pp. 184, 185 and 187; Vebæk 1991(b), pp. 7–18; Arneborg 2004, p. 250.
38 *Eiriks saga Rauda* IF IV, pp. 212 and 415; English translation: CSI chapter 5, p. 8 and Penguin chapter 5, p. 35.
39 Guldager et al. 2002, pp. 78–79.
40 Meldgaard, Jørgen 1982, p. 160.
41 Guldager et al. 2002, pp. 46–47 and 55–56.
42 Vebæk 1982, p. 210.
43 Vebæk 1982, p. 210.
44 Vebæk 1991(b), pp. 18–19; cf. below p. XXX.
45 Guldager et al. 2002, p. 44.
46 Clemmensen 1911, p. 325.
47 Bruun 1896, p. 308; Krogh 1976, p. 298, and 1982 p. 123.
48 E29, E33, E35, E48, E64, E78 and E162.
49 Nyegaard 2014; see Chapter 3, pp. 89–90.

50 Madsen 2014(b), p. 110. The author gives a reference to "J. Arneborg, unpublished data".
51 Cf. Chapter 1, p. 23.
52 Keller 1989, p. 187; Vebæk 1991(b), p. 18.
53 Krogh 1976, pp. 304, 306–307 and 309; Krogh 1982, pp. 38–39.
54 Keller 1989, pp. 202–204.
55 Blair 2005, pp. 368–395.
56 Kjartansson 2005, pp. 95–97. The source is from 1122–1133.
57 *Groenlendinga tháttr* IF IV chapter 4, p. 283; English translation: CSI chapter 4, p. 378
58 Blair 2005, pp. 153–165; Higham 2013, pp. 213–214.
59 Blair 2005, pp. 323–328.
60 Andersen 1977, pp. 319–323; in Iceland, Eythorsson 2005, pp. 64–66; Antonsson 2005, pp. 182–186.
61 Cf. Chapter 1, p. 29 and Chapter 2, p. 50; described in *Groenlendinga saga* IF IV chapters 6–8, pp. 264–268.
62 Nørlund and Roussell 1930, pp. 32–57.
63 Skaaning Høegsberg 2007, pp. 84–94.
64 Nørlund and Roussell 1930, pp. 46 and 44; Nørlund says the evidence is not clear, the nave may have been as large as $8 \times 11m = 88$ m^2. All measures are internal.
65 Roussell 1941, p. 119.
66 The first bishop was ordained in 1124 and arrived in Greenland in 1126.
67 In Norway wood was plentiful, and most churches were built in that material, but stone was considered to give more prestige. The first known church in stone was built by King Harald Hardrádi in Trondheim probably ca. 1050 (Ekroll 1997, p. 25). Anglo-Saxon missionaries in Greenland would know how to build in stone, and in Greenland wood was more expensive than stone.
68 *Det gamle Grønlands beskrivelse af Ivar Bárdarson*, p. 29.
69 Roussell 1936, p. 27; Arneborg et al. 2012(a), p. 29.
70 Roussell 1936, pp. 26–27.
71 Cf. Chapter 1, p. 29 and Chapter 2, p. 50.
72 *Eiriks saga Rauda* IF IV chapter 6, pp. 214 and 417; English translation: CSI chapter 6, p. 9 and Penguin chapter 6, p. 36.
73 Chapter 1, p. 29.
74 *Groenlendinga saga* IF IV chapters 5 and 6, pp. 256–257; English translation: CSI chapters 4 and 5, p. 26, and Penguin chapters 4 and 5, pp. 9–10
75 *Groenlendinga tháttr* IF IV chapter 2, p. 278; English translation: CSI chapter 2, p. 375
76 "Grænlands annal", pp. 56–57.
77 *Eiriks saga Rauda* IF IV chapter 6, p. 216; English translation: CSI chapter 6, p. 10 and Penguin chapter 6, p. 38.
78 *Eiriks saga Rauda* IF IV chapter 6, p. 217; English translation: CSI chapter 6, pp. 10–11 and Penguin chapter 6, p. 38.
79 Albrethsen and Arneborg 2004, pp. 12–17 and catalogue pp. 20 ff.
80 Cf. Chapter 3, pp. 88 and 130.
81 RN I nos. 3, 4 and 5; *Diplomatarium Danicum* 1. række, volume 1, nos. 25, 28 and 119.
82 RN I no. 34; DN XVII no. 849; Hamburgisches Urkundenbuch I, no. 75; DI XVIII no. 18; *Diplomatarium Danicum* 1.række, volume 2, no. 1; Andersen 1977, p. 312.
83 Adam of Bremen book 3, chapter 24; English translation, p. 134; Adam of Bremen book 4, chapter 36; English translation, p. 218; Norwegian translation, pp. 216–217.
84 Adam of Bremen book 3, chapter 24; English translation, p. 134; Adam of Bremen book 4, chapter 36; English translation, p. 218; Norwegian translation, pp. 216–217.
85 Andersen 1977, p. 181.
86 *Landnámabok* IF I, pp. 56–57, S17 and H17; English and Norwegian translations: chapter 17.
87 IA, VII Lögmann, p. 251.

88 "*Eirekur byskup upsi af Grænlandi for at leita Windlandz.*" IA, X Oddveria, p. 473; cf. annals nos. I, III, IV, VII, VIII and IX.
89 Ingstad, H. 1959, p. 210; reprint 2004, p. 168; English translation, p. 119.
90 See Chapter 2, p. 48.
91 *Groenlendinga tháttr* IF IV chapter 1, p. 273; English translation: CSI chapter 1, p. 372.
92 *Groenlendinga tháttr* IF IV chapter 1, pp. 273–274; English translation: CSI chapter 1, p. 373.
93 Andersen 1977, p. 311.
94 *Groenlendinga tháttr* IF IV chapter 1, p. 274; English translation: CSI chapter 1, p. 373.
95 Andersen 1977, p. 313.
96 *Groenlendinga tháttr* IF IV chapter 1, pp. 274–275; English translation: CSI chapter 1, p. 373.
97 Arneborg 2004, p. 249; "*en besynderlig beretning*".
98 *Jons saga helga eptir Gunnlaug munk,* Old Norse, pp. 213–260; Norwegian translation, pp. 88–92.
99 *Groenlendinga tháttr* IF IV chapter 1, p. 273; English translation: CSI chapter 1, p. 372.
100 Cf. Chapter 4, pp. 193–196 and 203–205.
101 *Islendingabok* IF I, chapter 10, p. 22; English translation: chapter 10, p.11; KLNM entry word "Tiende, Island".
102 Heimskringla, "The saga of Sigurdr, Eystein and Olav", chapter 11; Andersen 1977, p. 335; KLNM entry word "Tiend".
103 Ekroll 1997, pp. 11, 29, 49–50 and 52.
104 Stoklund 1993(a), pp. 532–533; Skaaning Høegsberg 2009 I, p. 181.
105 Krogh 1982, p. 131; Vebæk 1991(b), p. 16.
106 Kjartansson 2005, pp. 95–97. The source is from 1122–1133.
107 Kjartansson 2005, pp. 98–99.
108 Nedkvitne 2009, pp. 80–122.
109 *Flateyjarbok*'s list is printed in Halldorsson 1978, p. 79.
110 Jonsson 1899, pp. 273 and 297–304; Jonsson 1930, pp. 63–66.
111 Jonsson 1930, p. 67.
112 *xij kirkjur eru á Grænlandi i hinni eystri byggd, iiijar i Vestribygd*; "Grænlands annal", p. 37; On Björn and his annals: Halldorsson 1978, p. 147.
113 Jonsson 1899, p. 298.
114 *Flateyjarbok* volume IV, p. 241.
115 *Thessir hafa biskupar verit á Grænlandi.*
116 Jonsson 1899, pp. 321–322, footnote 1.
117 This Latin quote is from Arngrimur's list, printed in Jonsson 1899, p. 322.
118 Straumsnes church is only mentioned in Arngrimur's transcript. Jonsson 1899 p. 322, cf. p. 320; Jonsson 1930, p. 67.
119 Discussions of the demography of Norse Greenland are found in Chapter 1, pp. 32–35 and Chapter 6, pp. 368–369.
120 On the concept "name farm", cf. Chapter 5, pp. 232–233.
121 Cf. Chapter 6, pp. 342–349.
122 "*then største kirckesogn som paa Grønland ligger*". *Det gamle Grønlands beskrivelse af Ivar Bárdarson*, p. 27.
123 Cf. Chapter 3, pp. 85–87.
124 Keller 1989, p. 233, he refers to Gad, Berglund and McGovern.
125 Keller 1989, pp. 227–235; There is one exception, his description of Langhøø where he has reversed his normal use of the two terms *eijer* and *ligger thill* (*Det gamle Grønlands beskrivelse af Ivar Bárdarson*, p. 26).
126 *Det gamle Grønlands beskrivelse af Ivar Bárdarson*, pp. 19–28. Cf. maps in Appendix II.

127 Cf. Chapter 6, pp. 362–363.
128 Keller 1989, pp. 233–234. In bibliography: Ældre Bjarkø-Ræt.
129 Cf. Chapter 3, pp. 102–103.
130 Vebæk 1991(b), p. 13.
131 *Det gamle Grønlands beskrivelse af Ivar Bárdarson*, p. 23.
132 Vebæk 1991(b), p. 6; Krogh 1976, p. 298.
133 Krogh 1982, pp. 138–139; Arneborg 2004, p. 254.
134 Vebæk 1991(b), pp. 18–19.
135 Keller 1989, pp. 193 and 201; Arneborg 2004, pp. 250 and 255.
136 Vebæk 1991(b), pp. 25–26; Arneborg 2004, p. 250.
137 *Det gamle Grønlands beskrivelse af Ivar Bárdarson*, p. 24.
138 Vebæk 1991(b), p. 14.
139 Krogh 1982, pp. 139–140; Arneborg 2004, pp. 254–255.
140 Cf. above Chapter 2, pp. 67–69; Jonsson 1899, p. 287.
141 This identification is discussed in detail in Chapter 2, pp. 67–69.
142 Helle 1999, pp. 54–103.
143 Map: Ingstad, H. 1959, p. 72; reprint 2004, pp. 60–61; English translation, pp. 48–49. *Det gamle Grønlands beskrivelse af Ivar Bárdarso*, pp. 26–27
144 Cf. above, Chapter 2, pp. 69–71.
145 Jonsson 1930, p. 47.
146 *Det gamle Grønlands beskrivelse af Ivar Bárdarson*, pp. 27, 28 and 29.
147 *Det gamle Grønlands beskrivelse af Ivar Bárdarson*, p. 27.
148 Vebæk 1991(b), p. 15.
149 Krogh 1976, p. 300.
150 Cf. Chapter 2, p. 57.
151 *Det gamle Grønlands beskrivelse af Ivar Bárdarson*, pp. 29–30.
152 *Det gamle Grønlands beskrivelse af Ivar Bárdarson*, p. 29; Appendix II, maps 5 and 4.
153 Table 3.1; Jonsson 1899, pp. 321–322, footnote 1; cf. Jonsson 1930, pp. 65–66.
154 Cf. discussion in Table 3.3, footnotes.
155 *Det gamle Grønlands beskrivelse af Ivar Bárdarson*, p. 28.
156 Cf. Chapter 6, pp. 368–369; Madsen 2014(a), figure 8.9, p. 234.
157 On Foss see Chapter 2, pp. 67–69; on the cloisters see Chapter 3, p. 99, Table 3.2.
158 Herjolvsnes, Augustinians, Nunnery, Foss, Gardar and possibly Hvalsey.
159 Cf. Chapter 3, pp. 86–87.
160 Cf. Table 3.1.
161 *Fostbroedra saga* IF VI chapter 23, p. 247; English translation: CSI chapter 23, p. 385.
162 Nedkvitne 2009, pp. 118–119; The Fourth Lateran Council in Rome had passed a resolution on this already in 1215, but we do not know if this early resolution was observed in Norway.
163 Vebæk 1991(b), pp. 16, 17 and 18. Vebæk claims that churches 11 and 12 in Table 3.1 were in the Middle Settlement, but does not even try to verify his hypothesis.
164 Helle 1974, pp. 64, 87, 95 and 114–115; cf. "Talen mot biskopane", Norwegian translation, pp. 220 and 223–226.
165 Jóhannesson 1956. English translation 1974, pp. 186–190.
166 DI II no. 167; Thorlaksson 2012, pp. 261–279.
167 Table 3.2.
168 Cf. Chapter 2, pp. 69–71; *Det gamle Grønlands beskrivelse af Ivar Bárdarson*, pp. 26–27.
169 *Det gamle Grønlands beskrivelse af Ivar Bárdarson*, p. 23.
170 Keller 1989, pp. 183–290.
171 Keller 1989, pp. 289–290.
172 Cf. Chapter 3, p. 86.

173 Vesteinsson 2005, pp. 78–79.
174 Keller 1989, p. 201
175 Nørlund and Stenberger 1934, p. 37 note 3.
176 Nørlund and Stenberger 1934, p. 37 note 3.
177 Nørlund and Roussell 1930, pp. 46 and 44; this is the oldest church on the site, of unknown date.
178 Nørlund and Stenberger 1934, p. 37 note 3.
179 Roussell 1941, pp. 106–107; cf. Chapter 3, pp. 103 and 129.
180 Vebæk 1991(b), p. 25.
181 Clemmensen 1911, p. 341; Nørlund and Stenberger 1934, p. 37 note 3; Bruun 1896, p. 377.
182 Nørlund and Stenberger 1934, p. 30.
183 Roussell 1936, p. 26; calculated on the basis of Roussell's drawing of the church's ground plan.
184 Roussell 1941, pp. 105–107 and 119 gives outside measurements of 13.9 m and 6.8 m and wall thickness 0.9–1.2 m.
185 Albrethsen 1972, pp. 11–15; repeated in Vebæk 1991(b), p. 10; Guldager et al. 2002, pp. 88–89; Guldager agrees that E1 had a church. The eastern part of the relevant building was excavated and shows that the chancel and nave had the same width. The remains of the western part indicate that it was made of wood. It seems to have been a square church with a west wall of wood, type 2 in Table 3.4. Albrethsen gives the church's length as a maximum 12 m and the breadth as 5.6 m. He does not say whether this is external or internal measurements, but a drawing in the Nationalmuseum of Denmark shows that external is meant. The walls were ca. 0.8 m wide, which should make the internal dimensions 11 × 4 m if the west wall was made of wood. This makes the church 44 m^2 internally and 66 m^2 externally. Albrethsen identifies the church as Gardanes church, which is mentioned in Arngrimur's church list. Guldager supports Albrethsen's conclusions.
186 Clemmensen argues that ruin 1 at this site might have been a church, with external measurements of 12 × 7 m, and the walls were 1.4 metres thick. If these measurements are used, the internal measurements will be 9.2 × 4.2 = 39 m^2. Guldager does not conclude on the building's identity as a church. He gives external sizes of the relevant building as 11 × 6 m but does not say how thick the wall was. The building is rectangular with four stone walls (Clemmensen 1911, p. 323; Guldager et al. 2002, p. 67).
187 Guldager et al. 2002, pp. 116–117; external measurements are 10 × 6 m, and I have found no internal measurements. If the walls were 1 m thick, the internal measures are 8 × 4 = 32 m^2.
188 Chapter 3, pp. 86 and 103, Table 3.3.
189 Nørlund and Roussell 1930, pp. 47–48; Roussell 1941, pp. 104–105.
190 Ekroll and Stige 2000, p. 146.
191 Nedkvitne 2009, p. 292; the measures given in Table 3.3 are different because they are internal.
192 Roussell 1941, pp. 123–124.
193 Cf. description of types above, see p. XXX.
194 The farms marked 1288–1314 are taken from Table 3.1; the farms marked IB are taken from *Det gamle Grønlands beskrivelse af Ivar Bárdarson*, see Table 3.2.
195 Roussell 1941, pp. 106–107.
196 Nørlund and Stenberger 1934, p. 33; Keller 1989, p. 201.
197 Cf. Table 3.3 and the footnote on Gardanes there.
198 Roussell 1941, pp. 105–107.
199 Cf. Table 3.3 and the footnote on *Isafjørdur* there.
200 Ekroll 1997, p. 29.
201 Nørlund and Stenberger 1934, pp. 34–36; Keller 1989, p. 201.

Church and religion

202 Cf. Chapter 3, p. 131.
203 Cf. Chapter 3, p. 89.
204 Ekroll 1997, p. 52.
205 Ekroll 1997, p. 258; Ekroll and Stige 2000, pp. 146–148; Roussell 1941, p. 124.
206 Myhre 1982, pp. 98–118.
207 Keller 1989, p. 203.
208 Roussell 1941, pp. 104–105; Vebæk 1991(b), p. 25; Wikipedia "Hvalsey church", accessed 20.05.2018.
209 Keller 1989, p. 202.
210 Roussell 1941, p. 104.
211 Nyegaard 2009, pp. 7–18.
212 DN V no. 193 = GHM III, p. 116; "*Item legamus ecclesie cathedrali in Groenlande centum mercas denariarum in vestibus pro ornatu ecclesie preciosa*".
213 Roussell 1936, p. 38.
214 Vebæk 1991(b), p. 25.
215 Nørlund and Roussell 1930, p. 146.
216 Cf. Chapter 3, p. 107; Roussell 1936, pp. 24–25.
217 More on this in Chapter 6, pp. 351, 355, 366–367.
218 DN IV no. 128 = RN III no. 1112. The church was at Avaldsnes.
219 Cf. Chapter 3, pp. 107 and 145–146.
220 Nørlund and Roussell 1930, p. 37.
221 Nedkvitne 2004, pp. 58–59 and 199.
222 Jonsson 1924, p. 289.
223 Stoklund 1993(a), p. 530.
224 Spurkland 2001, pp. 166–167.
225 Imer 2017, pp. 34, 35 and 38.
226 Imer 2017, pp. 67–113.
227 Imer 2017, p. 105.
228 Imer 2017, pp. 58–108.
229 Imer 2017, p. 316.
230 Imer 2017, p. 107.
231 Cf. Chapter 2, pp. 45–46.
232 *The poetic Edda*, "Atlakvida hin Groenlenzku", stanzas 4, 9, 11 and 12.
233 Nedkvitne 2004, pp. 25–28.
234 *Sturlunga saga*, Old Norse, chapter 95, p. 122; English translation II, chapter 13, p. 118; Danish translation I, pp. 140–141; The shipwreck took place in AD 1189 according to the Old Norse edition.
235 Imer 2017, p. 234.
236 Stoklund 1993(a), pp. 531–532; Skaaning Høegsberg 2009 II, p. 144.
237 Stoklund 1993(a), p. 529; Hagland 1990, pp. 106–109; Nedkvitne 1989, pp. 348–350.
238 Skaaning Høegsberg 2009 II, p. 69.
239 "Grænlands annal", pp. 54–55; GHM III, pp. 244–245.
240 Nedkvitne 2005, pp. 97–106; cf. Nedkvitne 2004, p. 198.
241 DN I no. 590 = RN VIII no. 1239 (1403); DN I no. 591 = RN VIII no. 1243 (1403); DN II no. 626 = RN IX no. 860 (1412).
242 Chapter 5, pp. 261–265.
243 *Fostbroedra saga* IF VI chapter 23, p. 230; English translation: CSI chapter 23, p. 376.
244 Cf. Figure 3.2; Roussell 1936, p. 145 and p. 203, number S 545 = Roussell 1941, p. 285, from Sandnes..
245 Skaaning Høegsberg 2009 II, pp. 66 and 150; Nørlund 1924, p. 192 figure 135 says it is made of bone, but this is evidently a mistake. The picture shows that it is definitely not bone.
246 Skaaning Høegsberg 2009 II, p. 93 and 100; Vebæk 1992, p. 88; Vebæk 1993, p. 43.
247 Roussell 1936, p. 137.

248 Moltke 1936, pp. 223–226.
249 Imer 2017, p. 78.
250 Imer 2017, p. 30.
251 Nørlund and Roussell 1930, pp. 158–160; Arneborg 2004, p. 252.
252 Arneborg 2004, p. 253.
253 Arneborg 2004, p. 250.
254 Skaaning Høegsberg 2009 II, pp, 88–90.
255 Skaaning Høegsberg 2009 II, p, 87.
256 Skaaning Høegsberg 2009 II, pp. 91 and 93.
257 Skaaning Høegsberg 2009 II, pp. 105–117.
258 Roussell 1936, p. 138.
259 Skaaning Høegsberg 2009 II, pp, 93–94.
260 Skaaning Høegsberg 2009 II, p, 90.
261 Skaaning Høegsberg 2009 II, p. 150.
262 Nørlund and Stenberger 1934, figure 83.c, p. 123; Skaaning Høegsberg 2009 II, p. 98.
263 Roussell 1936, p. 145.
264 Arneborg 2004, p. 250.
265 Skaaning Høegsberg 2009 II, pp. 101–102 and 165.
266 Arneborg 2004, p. 262.
267 Nørlund and Stenberger 1934, p. 123: Skaaning Høegsberg 2009 II, pp. 87–90, 146 and 150.
268 Roussell 1936, p. 145.
269 Skaaning Høegsberg 2009 II, pp. 150.
270 Skaaning Høegsberg 2009 II, pp. 84, 91 and 94.
271 Nørlund and Stenberger 1934, pp. 130–131; Arneborg 2004, p. 271; Skaaning Høegsberg 2009 II, p. 101.
272 Arneborg 2004, p. 262.
273 Skaaning Høegsberg 2009 II, pp, 95–98, 100, 101, 103, 134 and 165.
274 Figure 6.1; Skaaning Høegsberg 2009 II, p. 162; cf. Chapter 3, pp. 145–146.
275 Nørlund and Roussell 1930, p. 162.
276 Arneborg 2004, p. 263.
277 Roussell 1936, p. 28; Skaaning Høegsberg 2009 II, p. 159.
278 Roussell 1936, p. 209; Skaaning Høegsberg 2009 II, p. 156.
279 Roussell 1936, p. 154; Skaaning Høegsberg 2009 II, p. 161.
280 Nørlund 1924, p. 47; Skaaning Høegsberg 2009 II, p. 151.
281 Skaaning Høegsberg 2009 I, p. 190; Høegsberg examined the finds from 5 farms and found 75 wooden objects with carvings. Of these, 72 were geometric and only 3 figurative.
282 Cf. Chapter 3, pp. 88–89.
283 Skaaning Høegsberg 2005, pp. 39, 51 and 54–55; The year 1280 is the result of radiocarbon datings combined with written evidence that bishop Olav died in 1280.
284 Andersen 1977, p. 333.
285 "Mass" is a divine service where Eucharist is part of the liturgy.
286 Nedkvitne 2009, pp. 46–55 and 94.
287 Nedkvitne 2009, pp. 49–50.
288 *Groenlendinga tháttr* IF IV chapter 1, p. 274; English translation: CSI chapter 1, p. 373.
289 Chapter 2, p. 55.
290 *Groenlendinga tháttr* IF IV chapters 1–3, pp. 276, 278, 279 and 280; English translation: CSI chapters 1–3, pp. 374, 375, 376 and 376.
291 IA, I Resiniani, III Høyer, X Oddveria.
292 IA, VII Lögmann, p. 252.
293 IA, IV Regii, p. 115; IX Flatø; X Oddveria.
294 IA, III Høyer; IV Regii; X Oddveria.
295 IA, IX Flatø; GHM III, p. 7.
296 IA, X Oddveria, p. 476.

297 *Sturlunga saga*, Old Norse chapter 92, p. 118; English translation II, chapter 11, p. 113; Danish translation I, pp. 135–136.
298 *Sturlunga saga*, Old Norse chapter 94, p. 120; English translation II, chapter 12, pp. 115–116; IA, I Resiniani, III Høyer, V Skálholt, VIII Gottkalk, X Oddverja.
299 *Sturlunga saga*, Old Norse chapter 94, p. 120 dates this stay to 1187–1188. The annals here should be considered as more reliable.
300 IA, V Skálholt, IV Regii.
301 IA, IV Regii, p. 122; V Skálholt, p. 181; VIII Gottskalk, p. 325.
302 *Páls saga byskups* IF XVI chapter 9, p. 311.
303 *Páls saga byskups* IF XVI chapter 9, p. 311.
304 IA, IV Regii, V Skálholt, VIII Gottskalk.
305 *Sturlunga saga* Old Norse chapter 92, pp. 117–118; English translation II, chapter 11, p. 113; Danish translation I, pp. 135–136.
306 *Sturlunga saga* Old Norse chapter 92, pp. 117–118; English translation II, p. 113; Danish translation I, pp. 135–136.
307 IA, IV Regii, V Skálholt, VIII Gottskalk.
308 IA, IV Regii, p. 128; V Skálholt, p. 187; VIII Gottskalk, p. 327.
309 IA, IV Regii, p. 129; V Skálholt, p. 188.
310 RN I nos. 628 and 656.
311 RN I no. 656.
312 IA, IV Regii, p. 130.
313 IA, V Skálholt, p. 189; VIII Gottskalk, p. 328; X Oddveria, p. 481.
314 IA, IV Regii; VIII Gottskalk.
315 *Hákonar Saga Hákonarsonar* Old Norse chapter 257; Norwegian translation, p. 265.
316 IA, IV Regii, p. 132.
317 *Hákonar Saga Hákonarsonar* Old Norse chapter 311; Norwegian translation, p. 333.
318 IA, V Skálholt, p. 193; cf. I Annales Resiniani, III Høyer, IV Regii, VIII Gottskalk; cf. *Sturlunga saga* Old Norse chapter 492, p. 759; English translation II, p. 489; Danish translation II, p. 326.
319 IA, IV Regii, V Skálholt, VII Lögmann, VIII Gottskalk.
320 IA, IV Regii, V Skálholt, VIII Gottskalk; *Sturlunga saga* Old Norse chapter 493, p.768; English translation II, p. 498; Danish translation II, p. 335 (*Tha for Olafur Grænlendingabiskup af Islandi*).
321 IA, IV Regii, p. 136.
322 IA, IV Regii, p. 138.
323 *Arna saga biskups* IF XVII chapter 56, pp. 79–80.
324 IA, II Vestustissimi, III Høyer, IV Regii, V Skálholt, VII Lögmann, VIII Gottskalk.
325 Nørlund and Roussell 1930, pp. 67–69; Arneborg 2004, p. 250; Skaaning Høegsberg 2009 II, p. 160.
326 Cf. Chapter 3, pp. 102–103.
327 *Arna saga biskups* IF XVII chapter 135, p. 188; IA, I Resiniani, II Vestusissimi, III Høyer, IV Regii, VII Lögmann, VIII Gottskalk, IX Flatø.
328 IA, I Resiniani, II Vestustissimi, III Høyer, IV Regii, VIII Gottskalk, IX Flatø.
329 DN X no. 9 = RN III no. 500.
330 IA, VIII Gottskalk.
331 DN VII no. 54 = RN III no. 500.
332 DN VII nos. 63 and 61 = RN III nos. 692 and 702.
333 DN VII no. 62 = RN III no. 705.
334 DN IX no. 84.
335 IA, V Skálholt, VIII Gottskalk.
336 IA, V Skálholt, VIII Gottskalk.
337 IA, IV Regii, X Oddveria; *Laurentius saga* IF XVII chapter 38, p. 330; Norwegian translation, chapter 33, p. 151; Danish translation, chapter 30, p. 99.
338 IA, VII Lögmann.

339 IA, V Skálholt.
340 Cf. Chapter 6, p. 343.
341 DN II no. 276.
342 DN IV no. 368.
343 IA, VI Skálholt, p. 228.
344 Andersen 1977, p. 333.
345 Cf. Chapter 3, pp. 141–142.
346 Arneborg 2000, p. 311.
347 Arneborg 1991(b), pp. 144–145. In her text this appears as a hypothesis which she does not even try to verify, but afterwards she writes as if it is verified.
348 Cf. Chapter 3, pp. 115–117, and the biographies of bishops pp. 115–120.
349 Arneborg 1991(b), p. 145.
350 Andersen 1977, p. 181.
351 DN VIII no. 1.
352 DN III no. 39.
353 *Sturlunga saga*, Old Norse chapter 92, p. 118; English translation II chapter 11, p. 113; Danish translation I, pp. 135–136.
354 IA, VII Lögmann.
355 IA, I Resiniani, III Høyer, V Skálholt, VIII Gottskalk; Sturlunga saga Old Norse chapter 94, p. 120.
356 *Arna saga biskups* IF XVII chapter 135, p. 188; *Sturlunga saga edition* II, p. 871; IA, I Resiniani, II Vestusissimi, III Høyer, IV Regii, VII Lögmann, VIII Gottskalk, IX Flatø.
357 Steinnes 1962.
358 "Norrigis Bescrivelse", p. 438.
359 Cf. Chapter 4, pp. 193–196; on the trade practices of foreign merchants in Bergen, cf. Nedkvitne 2014(a), pp. 401 and 432–442.
360 Cf. their biographies in Chapter 3, pp. 115–120.
361 GHM III, p. 238; "Grænlands annal", p. 53.
362 Cf. his biography in Chapter 3, pp. 116–117.
363 Vandvik. E. 1959., p. 65 = DN I no. 139.
364 DN I no. 16 = NGL IV, p. 108 = DI I no. 131.
365 *Páls saga byskups* IF XVI chapter 9, p. 311.
366 Ingstad, H. 1959, p. 342; reprint 2004, p. 270.
367 DN X no. 9 = GHM III, p. 96; RN III no. 500.
368 Chronica majora by Matheus Parisiensis, volume IV 1240–1247, pp. 650–652.
369 Cf. above Chapter 2, p. 117 and Chapter 3, pp. 117–118.
370 Munch 1864, p. 141 = DN VIII no. 11a; RN II no. 122.
371 Munch 1864, p. 143 = DN VI no. 36 = RN II no. 155.
372 *Insula in qua civitas Gardensis consistit, propter malitiam maris Occeani, infra quod ipsa consistit, raro navigio visitatur.*
373 Munch 1864, p. 146 = DN I no. 66 = RN II no. 218.
374 *in bovinis et focarum coriis ac dentibus et funibus balenarum.*
375 *vix ad competens pretium vendi possunt.*
376 Munch 1864, p. 153 = DN I no. 71 = RN II no. 292 and 295.
377 Munch 1864, pp. 154–155 = DN VI no. 46 = RN II no. 296.
378 Munch 1864, pp. 169–170, 171, 172–173 = DN VI no. 117, 118, 119c .
379 Munch 1864, p. 18.
380 Munch 1864.
381 These account notices were translated into Norwegian by Erik Gunnes and printed in RN IV. Gunnes was an excellent Latinist, but he did not fully understand how accounting was done. The Norwegian archaeologist Keller 1989 used Gunnes' translation. I have gone back to Munch's Latin edition.
382 The sums are the tax collectors' assessments of the money to be expected from each diocese for all six years.

383 Parve monete noricane.
384 The sums are also printed in Munch 1864, pp. 180–182.
385 The entire sum from Orkney for all six years was 256 marks sterling (Munch 1864, p. 45). One mark sterling was 13.3 shilling (Nedkvitne 2014(a), p. 175), which makes 256 mark sterling the equivalent of 3405 shilling English sterlings. The tax collectors write that their exchange rate was 3 shillings English sterling for one mark Norwegian coins (parva moneta noricana). This makes 3405 English shillings 1135 Norwegian marks.
386 Munch 1864, p. 25.
387 Munch 1864, p. 28.
388 Munch 1864, p. 25.
389 Munch 1864, p. 45.
390 Munch 1864, p. 25.
391 Munch,1864, p. 21..
392 Munch 1864, p. 45
393 KLNM entry word "lispund".
394 Bugge 1898, p. 137; Keller 1989, p. 279.
395 An irrelevant but potentially interesting piece of information is that according to *The King's Mirror* a tusk could become 1½ ells (alen) long, corresponding to ca. 0.75 m (*Konungs skuggsiá*, Old Norse, p. 29, cf. p.147; English translation, p. 140; Norwegian translation, p. 66). The information about the length of the tusks is only in some manuscripts, in others it is lacking (*Konungs skuggsiá,* Old Norse, p. 147).
396 Munch 1864, pp. 180–182.
397 Sandnes 1968, p. 281.
398 DN VI no. 170a = RN V no. 670.
399 DN IV no. 293 = RN V no. 80.
400 Cf. Chapter 6, p. 343.
401 DN VI no. 176.
402 RN V no. 895.
403 DN XVII nos. 898 and 899; RN V nos. 1021–1027.
404 DN X no. 9 = GHM III, p. 96 = RN III no. 500 (regest); *Tha luti flæiri sem ver sendum til klaustranna her skal Olafr bonde yðr j hendr fa. Ok skiptið eftir thui sem han segir yðr til.*
405 Table 3.2 and Chapter 3, p. 97; Appendix II, maps 7 and 8.
406 *Det gamle Grønlands beskrivelse af Ivar Bárdarson*, p. 23. *End fra thenne bij ligger en stourt closter, som canonici regulares er udi, som er vigt til Sanct Oluff och Sanct Augustinum.*
407 Lawrence 2001, pp. 160–166.
408 Nørlund 1926; Albrethsen 1970.
409 Roussell 1941, pp. 106–107; cf. Vebæk 1991(b), p. 6.
410 Cf. Table 3.3.
411 Albrethsen 1970, ruin II.
412 Albrethsen 1970, ruin III
413 Albrethsen 1970, ruin IX. The same ruin is described in Nørlund 1926 and is there called "ruin V".
414 See Table 5.6 in Chapter 5, p. 240.
415 Vebæk 1953, p. 196.
416 *Det gamle Grønlands beskrivelse af Ivar Bárdarson*, p. 23 *Nest Kiedeltzfiord ligger Rampnessfiord, och langt ind udi then fiord ligger et søster closter ordinis Sancti Benedicti.*
417 Vebæk 1991(b), p. 6; Krogh 1982, pp. 139–140; Arneborg 2004, pp. 254–255.
418 The boundaries of the parishes are described above in pp. 97–98; compare this to Nationalmuseet's map of ruins printed in Appendix II, maps 7 and 8.
419 Lawrence 2001, pp. 160–166.

420 Nenseter 2002, pp. 70–96, particularly pp. 95–96.
421 *Det gamle Grønlands beskrivelse af Ivar Bárdarson*, p. 24; Appendix II, map 7.
422 Nedkvitne 2009, p. 339.
423 Cf. Chapter 3, pp. 131–132 on intercessory prayers.
424 Cf. Chapter 3, pp. 87–89 on minsters.
425 Lawrence 2001, pp. 217–224.
426 Calculations with the help of a Greenland Tourism hiking map tells me that the distance across the isthmus is 20 km and the crossing of the fjord ca. 10 km. This can be done in one day, but there were farms along the way where the inspector could spend the night.
427 Cf. Chapter 3, 104–106.
428 Cf. Chapter 3, pp. 102–103.
429 Cf. Chapter 3, p. 128.
430 Nedkvitne 2009, pp. 340–341; Halsnøy near Bergen 1164, Elgeseter near Trondheim ca. 1180, Jonskloster in Bergen town bef. 1181, Kastelle in present day Bohuslän ca. 1181. The fifth was Utstein near Stavanger in 1263.
431 Nedkvitne 2009, pp. 339; Thykkvibær 1168, Helgafell 1184, Videy 1226 and Möðruvellir 1296.
432 Nedkvitne 2009, pp. 340–341.
433 Nedkvitne 2009, p. 339.
434 IA, VII Lögmanna, in 1407.
435 *Groenlendinga tháttr* IF IV chapter 6, p. 292, footnote 1.
436 *Medieval Scandinavia*, entry word "Einars tháttr Sokkasonar".
437 *Konungs skuggsiá*, Old Norse, p. 28; English translation, p. 138; Norwegian translation, p. 65; *hofum ver noccora set af theim oc heyrt theira roedur oc frasagur*.
438 *Konungs skuggsiá*, Old Norse, p. 32; English translation, p. 149; Norwegian translation p. 72; *hæfi ec tha mænn funnit idulega er langar stunnder hafa á Groenlande værit*.
439 "Grænlands annal", pp. 53–54 = GHM III, pp. 238–243; cf. Chapter 3, pp. 136–139.
440 *Det gamle Grønlands beskrivelse af Ivar Bárdarson*, pp. 29–30.
441 Hávamál, stanzas 138–144.
442 Nørlund 1942, p. 48; English translation, p. 51.
443 Jonsson 1924, p. 283.
444 Stoklund 1993(a), p. 531.
445 Stoklund 1993(a), pp. 528 and 530 (E17a1).
446 Stoklund 1993(b), pp. 47–50; Imer 2017, pp. 80–81. The exact stratigraphic location of the rune-stick is unknown. It has not been radiocarbon dated (Vebæk 1993, p. 73; Imer 2017, p. 251).
447 On Thormod's struggles on Greenland, cf. Chapter 2, pp. 62–63.
448 *Fostbroedra saga* IF VI chapter 23, p. 240; English translation: CSI chapter 23, pp. 381–382.
449 *Fostbroedra saga* IF VI chapter 24, pp. 254–256; English translation: CSI chapter 24, pp. 389–390.
450 *Fostbroedra saga* IF VI chapter 23, pp. 243–244; English translation: CSI chapter 23, p. 383.
451 *Fostbroedra saga* IF VI chapter 23, pp. 242, 245 and 247; English translation: CSI chapter 23, pp. 382–385.
452 *Fostbroedra saga* IF VI chapter 23, pp. 245 and 247; English translation: CSI chapter 23, pp. 384–386.
453 Nedkvitne 2009, pp. 276–284.
454 Nedkvitne 2009, pp. 280–281.
455 *Eiriks saga Rauda* IF IV chapter 4, pp. 206–209; English translation: CSI chapter 4, pp. 5–7 and Penguin chapter 4, p. 33.
456 *Eiriks saga Rauda* IF IV chapter 6, pp. 214–217; English translation: CSI chapter 6, pp. 10–11 and Penguin chapter 6, p. 38; *Groenlendiga saga* IF IV chapter 6, pp. 258–260; English translation: CSI chapter 5, pp. 26–27 and Penguin chapter 5, pp. 12–14.

158 Church and religion

457 *Eiriks saga Rauda* IF IV chapter 6, p. 216; English translation: CSI chapter 6, p. 10 and Penguin chapter 6, p. 38.
458 *Groenlendinga saga* IF IV chapter 6, pp. 257–258; English translation: CSI chapter 5, p. 26 and Penguin chapter 5, p. 12.
459 *Bárdar saga Snefellsáss* IF XIII chapter 18, p. 163; English translation, chapter 18, p. 262; The saga was written ca. 1300. It is pure fiction but may reveal something about the geographic ideas of the Icelandic author and his public. He assumes that it was possible to sail along the coasts of Hálogaland, Finnmark and Hafsbotn to the east coast of Greenland.
460 *Alfrœdi Islenzk* volume 1, p. 12 (Landafrædi, pp. 3–31); Also printed in Halldorsson 1978, pp. 79–80; Danish translation in GHM III, pp. 220–221; cf. Historia Norwegie, p. 55.
461 *Konungs skuggsiá*, Old Norse, p. 32; English translation, p. 148; Norwegian translation, p. 72; *Historia Norwegie*, p. 55.
462 *Konungs skuggsiá*, Old Norse, p. 30; English translation, pp. 143–144; Norwegian translation, pp. 68–69; cf. *Alfrœdi Islenzk* volume 2, p. 104.
463 IA, III Høyer; *Helgasynir sigldu i Grœnlandz obygdir*; IV Regii *Fundu Helgasynir nyia land Adalbrandr og Thorvalldr*; cf. *Arna saga biskups saga* IF XVII, chapter 42, p. 63, and in *Sturlunga saga* edition 1988, volume 2, p. 798.
464 IA, IX Flatø, years 1289 and 1290.
465 Hauksbok itself is lost, but its information on Greenland was copied by the Icelander Bjørn Jonsson (1574–1655) in his *Grænlands annal*. This part of the "Grænlands annal" is printed in Halldorsson 1978, pp. 53–54 and GHM III, pp. 238–241.
466 "Grænlands annal", p. 53.
467 "Grænlands annal", p. 53 and GHM III, pp. 240–241.
468 Cf. Chapter 4, pp. 186–188.
469 Chapter 4, pp. 174–179 on *nordrseta*.
470 "Grænlands annal", pp. 53–55 = GHM III, pp. 240–243.
471 Cf. Chapter 4, pp. 186–188.
472 Imer 2017, p. 243; Stoklund 1993(a), 537–540; cf. Arneborg 2004, pp. 266–267; cf. Chapter 2, pp. 42–43.
473 These voyages were described in Nørlund 1942, pp. 124–126; English translation, pp. 129–131.
474 *Konungs skuggsiá*, Old Norse, pp. 13, 31 and 32; English translation, pp. 101, 146 and 149–152; Norwegian translation, pp. 70 and 72–74.
475 *Konungs skuggsiá*, Old Norse, pp. 31–34; English translation, pp. 149–151; Norwegian translation, pp. 72–73.
476 Cf. Chapter 3, pp. 137–139.
477 "Grænlands annal", p. 54 = GHM III, pp. 242–243.
478 *Konungs skuggsiá*, Old Norse, p. 32; English translation, p. 148; Norwegian translation, p. 71. The English translator translates *iardar bollum* as "the entire sphere" and the Norwegian translator with "jordkula". "Bolli" normally means a "bowl" but the context makes it evident that a "sphere" or "kule" is meant.
479 *Konungs skuggsiá*, Old Norse, pp. 31–32; English translation, pp 147–148; Norwegian translation, p. 71.
480 Cf. Chapter 3, pp. 132–133; Chapter 6, pp. 349–350.
481 Cf. Chapter 3, 119–120.
482 Cf. DN XVII B, p. 283.
483 IA, VI Skálholt, p. 227.
484 DN XII no. 103 = RN VI no. 1141.
485 IA, VI Skálholt.
486 IA, VIII Gottskalk year 1378: "Obitum herra Alfs byskups aa Grænlandi".

Church and religion   159

487 IA, VII Lögmann year 1382; IX Flatø year 1383; *Oddaannalar og Oddverjaannall* 2003, year 1381, p. 180. Oddverjaannal says that a ship arrived in Norway from Greenland in 1381 and the travellers told that bishop Alfr had died six years earlier, which means that he died in 1375. VII Lögmann says that the ship arrived in Norway in 1382 with the same message, which means that Alfr died in 1376. IX Flatø relates that the ship with this message came to Norway in 1383, which means that Alfr died in 1377.
488 Cf. Chapter 3, pp. 115–120.
489 DN XVII B, p. 224.
490 *Oddaannalar og Oddverjaannall* 2003, p. 180.
491 DN XVII B, p. 209.
492 DN XVII B, p. 283.
493 DN IV no. 530.
494 DN III no. 477.
495 DN XVII A no. 175 = RN VIII no. 14.
496 DN XVII A no. 177 = RN VIII no. 56.
497 DN XVII A no. 180; cf. Table 3.5.
498 DN XVII A no. 356 and 357 = RN IX nos. 679–681.
499 DN XVI no. 62.
500 Jonsson, F. 1929, p. 74; Nørlund and Roussell 1930, pp. 147–149; Imer 2017, p. 186.
501 Cf. Chapter 4, pp. 212–214.
502 GHM III, p. 439; "Grænlands annal", p. 45.
503 DI III no. 597; only a transcript from 1625 is preserved.
504 KLNM entry word "official".
505 Nedkvitne 2009, pp. 85–92.
506 Nedkvitne 2009, pp. 52–55.
507 Nedkvitne 2009, pp. 114–122.
508 Nedkvitne 2009, p. 83.
509 Nedkvitne 2009, pp. 206–207.
510 KLNM entry word "fredskys".
511 Roussell 1936, pp. 24–25.
512 KLNM entry word "fredskys. Norge".
513 Skaaning Høegsberg 2009 I–II.
514 Arneborg 2004, pp. 247–257.
515 Stoklund 1984, pp. 101–103, 105, 107 and 113.
516 Stoklund 1984, pp. 110–112.
517 Jonsson 1924, p. 281.
518 Jonsson 1924, p. 287–288.
519 Jonsson 1924, pp. 277–279; Stoklund 1993(a), p. 533.
520 Skaaning Høegsberg 2009 II, pp. 101, 140, 141 and 162; cf. Chapter 3, pp. 144–146.
521 Roussell 1941, p. 180; an illustration of the neighbouring farm W53c is found in Figure 6.1, p. 353.
522 Roussell 1941, p. 182.
523 Roussell 1941, p. 184.
524 Roussell 1941, p. 182.
525 Roussell 1941, pp. 184 and 247.
526 Roussell 1941, p. 179.
527 Arneborg 2004, p. 248; Krogh 1982, pp. 89 and 137.
528 Figure 6.2; Roussell 1941, pp. 247–249 and 39.
529 Skaaning Høegsberg 2009 I, pp. 195–196.
530 Roussell 1936, p. 19.
531 Roussell 1936, p. 24; Skaaning Høegsberg 2009 I, p. 194.
532 Roussell 1936, pp. 23–24.

533 Stoklund 1984, p. 106.
534 Vebæk 1992, p. 77 = Skaaning Høegsberg 2009 II, pp. 77 and 101; Skaaning Høegsberg 2009 II, p. 140.
535 Skaaning Høegsberg 2009 II, p. 92.
536 Vebæk 1992, p. 77; Skaaning Høegsberg 2009 I, p. 155.
537 Nedkvitne 2009, pp. 113–122.
538 Chapter 4, pp. 214 and 217.

4   Trade and shipping

From the Norwegian western and northern coasts, the Norse Greenlanders brought with them ideas about how their household economy should be organised. Each household should produce its own food. If possible, the household would also produce for the market. Along the Atlantic coast of Norway many households would send one of their men to the cod fisheries in January-March, and after ca. 1100 the stockfish which they produced was marketed in Bergen. The money was mainly used to buy textiles, beer and imported flour, which supplemented the food and woollens they produced themselves. They were not so dependent on the goods they bought in Bergen that it would cause hardship if the foreign ships failed to arrive.[1]

1 The imports

Were imported commodities considered as necessary for a normal life? Or were they rather luxuries which gave status and symbolised social position?

Necessities: iron and timber

The King's Mirror has the following to say about goods imported to Greenland: "Everything which the Greenlanders need to help the country, they have to buy from other countries, both iron and all timber from which they make houses".[2]

The claim that the Greenlanders had to import all their iron implies that bog iron was not produced in Greenland. Bog iron was produced in two stages. First bog ore was heated and "smelted" in an oven, producing what in English is called "bloom", in Old Norse *blásturjarn* or *fellujarn*, which is unfinished, not refined iron. Afterwards the bloom had to be brought to a smithy where the iron was purified and forged into the products needed. "Smelting" and "forging" both produced a residual product called slag. With modern analyses it is possible to distinguish between the two types of slag.[3]

In 1930 the Danish archaeo-metallurgist Niels Nielsen claimed that bog iron was produced in Greenland.[4] Later the methods for verifying this hypothesis improved. In 1934 Nørlund admitted that "no place where bog ore was smelted has yet been found in Greenland".[5] In 2001 another Danish archaeo-metallurgist Vagn Buchwald explained the criteria for distinguishing between "production slags" and "purification slags" and concluded that no smelting of bog ore took place in Greenland. Only "purification slags" had been found which verifies that there were smiths and smithies in Greenland where iron implements were forged from imported blooms.[6]

This was a sensible division of labour. Extraction of bloom from bog ore demanded much firewood and was best done in Norway where wood was abundant. Iron was used for many purposes and therefore it was often most practical to forge the iron bloom or iron bars into implements on the farm in Greenland where they were to be used.[7] There was a smithy on all larger farms in Greenland. An iron bar was found at Herjolvsnes, which may have arrived from Norway, and was finished by being forged into useful implements at Herjolvsnes.[8]

Fostbroedra saga describes a Greenlandic peasant-merchant called Bjarni. "Bjarni forged for Thormodr [Kolbrunarskald] a broad axe according to Thormod's prescriptions". The saga author describes the axe in detail, and comments that it "bit well".[9] Much exercise is needed to become a skilled smith, and because of limited fuel resources it would be hard to acquire such experience in Greenland. At least this was so after the first few generations.[10]

Poul Nørlund who excavated Brattahlid and Gardar, had a low opinion of the technical skills of Greenland smiths:

> At the places so far investigated only few objects of iron have been found in Greenland ... the impression is that there has not been much chance of obtaining iron, and that the Norsemen there had no great knowledge of the art of the smith ... The iron objects at Brattahlid and elsewhere are strikingly small, some of the knives being almost diminutive ... When one does find a good and decoratively worked object of iron ... one entertains no doubt that it has been imported from Europe [read: Norway].[11]

In the region called Hardanger close to Bergen there was a rich production of iron from bog ore. Ca. 1567 a Bergen clergyman called Absalon Pedersson Beyer wrote that "People in Hardanger were in former times so rich, manly and skilled that they sailed to Greenland, Iceland and the White Sea Area bringing salt, iron and other goods. For this purpose they used large ships".[12] Iron and salt were produced by the Hardanger peasants themselves, benefitting from firewood in forests close to the sea. In 1217 a large *knarri* arrived in Vestmannaeyar in Iceland "and it had formerly served in the Greenland trade. The skippers (*styrimenn*) were called Grim and Sörli and were from Hardanger".[13]

Iron objects may have been more available than the archaeological material indicates. Used iron objects were taken care of and reworked by smiths. Ca. 1130 some Norse Greenland hunters found a wrecked trading ship on the east coast of Greenland. They removed the iron rivets from the hull and burned the ship. The rivets could be sold to smiths in the Norse settlements and recycled.[14] The Inuit searched the sites for iron after the Norse were gone. Finally, iron rusts easily in moist soil.

The King's Mirror claims that iron was a necessity for the Norse Greenlanders, and archaeology gives more precise information. Mogens Høegsberg has analysed finds from five of the largest farms in Norse Greenland (W51, E29, E47, E111, E167).[15]

Some 150 iron objects were registered,[16] the largest category being rivets, mostly for ship hulls (44 objects).[17] After a rough crossing from Norway or Iceland, repairs may have been needed. Ships' hulls were clinker built and rivets were used to fasten two planks together.[18] Ships may have brought a bloom or bar of iron from Norway, and the forging of a necessary number of rivets may have been done in a smithy in Greenland. Nails and rivets were found at all of Høegsberg's five sites.[19] A ship where iron rivets had been replaced by wooden pegs arrived in Iceland from Greenland in 1189, and some of the boards had also been bound together with sinews. This was so extraordinary that Icelandic Annals made specific mention of it. They came from the east coast of Greenland where the crew had evidently been hunting. The next year (1190) the ship left for Norway but disappeared at sea. The author does not say that the ship sank because of faulty construction but seems to suggest that this may have been the case.[20] Iron may have been necessary for making ocean-going ships safe.

The second largest category of iron objects was knives (38 objects).[21] In Norse peasant society it was normal for an adult male to have a knife in his belt. This was a multi-purpose tool for making, adapting and repairing objects of wood. The Greenlanders ate much meat, and knife and fingers were the usual aids when slaughtering and eating fish and prey. In an emergency it could also be used for defence against men and animals. Knives were found on four of Høegsberg's five farms.[22] At Brattahlid alone 7 knives or fragments of knives were found,[23] and 13 knives and knife handles were registered at Sandnes.[24] Whetstones were also found on all five of Høegsberg's farms,[25] and they were often perforated so that they could be hung on a rope from the belt beside the knife. Some 14 of them were found at Brattahlid[26] and 9 at Sandnes.[27] An iron ice-spur with spikes was found at Brattahlid, which would have been fastened under the shoes for walking on slippery ice.[28]

Sickles were in Norway mostly used for harvesting cornfields, and in Greenland they were useful when harvesting leaves and twigs for winter fodder. Scythes were used for mowing grass when producing hay for the winter.[29]

Knives, scythes and sickles could be replaced by imitations made of bone or tooth, but iron was much sharper. Effective iron tools saved labour, more hay could be produced, more animals kept through the winter, and more people fed. The iron tools must have improved standards of living.

Did the Norse Greenlanders have effective iron weapons in their confrontations with the Inuit? The Norse weapons of self defence were axes and swords according to the written sources,[30] and in one case spears[31] are mentioned. These weapons are described as widespread among peasants. After the Norse Greenlanders were gone, the Inuit searched the abandoned sites for iron, and particularly iron weapons, and they left little for the archaeologists. In 1936 one Norse iron axe had been excavated in Greenland.[32] An axe of whale bone has been found on Sandnes.[33] One spear head of iron was found at Brattahlid.[34] No swords have been found. At Gardar a mould of soapstone for casting arrow heads of iron or another metal was found,[35] and at Sandnes an arrow head of iron.[36] The arrows may have been primarily for hunting and not defence. The Norse Greenlanders must have felt that their iron weapons made their defence more credible and gave them better protection. Iron weapons were more effective than those of bone and teeth.

Iron tools were used in house building. From Gardar a hammer and a gimlet have been preserved.[37] An awl has been preserved from Brattahlid, which would have been used when working in wood, but also in skin.[38] Chisels or wedges were used to split wood when making boards, and two of them have been found at Sandnes.[39]

Metals were used in contexts where they could have been replaced by other materials or techniques. In Brattahlid churchyard coffins were held together with nails.[40] A fragment of a nail was found in the dwelling house at Herjolvsnes.[41] Equipment and furniture in the living-rooms were partly made of metals:

- A "handsomely worked" iron hasp for locking a casket, Nørlund is in no doubt that it was imported.[42]
- An iron key perhaps for a chest.[43]
- A candlestick of bronze.[44]
- A fragment of a beaker or ewer of tin.[45]
- For use in the kitchen section of the living-room a leg of a bronze cooking pot; the bronze pots could be replaced by soapstone pots made on the farm.[46]
- Moulds made of soapstone for casting spindle whorls in metal.[47]
- Slender needles of metal have disappeared, but small boxes for keeping them in have survived, and so have specialised whetstones for needles.[48]
- A 5 cm long iron pincer that was probably used for textile work but may also have been used for other purposes.[49]
- A wooden sheath for keeping shears; they may have been used to shear sheep or cut cloth.[50]
- Shears of iron.[51]

The uses of iron and other metals were extensive, in agriculture, for housebuilding, for shipbuilding, for weapons, in the kitchen, in the living-room and for knives which were multi-purpose tools. Iron was, and was felt to be, a necessity. An iron object could last for decades, and worn-out iron objects could be forged into new ones. All metals had to be imported, but their dependence on metals from abroad was long term. They could live without new deliveries for many years, and the problem would only be felt gradually.

In western and northern Norway in ca. AD 985 dwellings were built of wood, with an exterior insulation of stone and turf. From the inside the peasants must have seen their living-rooms as made of boards. This tradition was continued in Greenland, and one should assume that the Greenlanders saw wooden living-rooms as part of their Norse tradition.

No trees grow in Greenland which are large enough for making boards and planks. In Norway timber had a low market value compared to volume, but the cost of transporting it over long distances was high. It was nevertheless imported to Greenland by merchants. The Norwegian merchant Thorir sailed ca. AD 1000 from Norway to Greenland with a cargo which mainly consisted of timber.[52] The Nationalmuseum archaeologist Poul Nørlund excavated oak which he thought had been imported from Norway.[53] He is corrected by Jette Arneborg who claims that no timber which can be identified scientifically as Norwegian, has so far been found in Greenland. She does not discuss where Nørlund's oak may have come from.[54]

The King's Mirror claims that the Greenlanders had to buy from other countries "all timber from which they made their houses".[55] It was probably written in Bergen, where the author may have seen timber being shipped to Greenland. But Norwegian timber may have been less important in Greenland than the author imagined, since Greenlanders had alternative sources of wood. In the first period after their arrival Norse Greenlanders could satisfy their needs for housebuilding from drift-timber along the shores, and for fire-wood from shrub of willow and juniper. But the renewal of these resources was slow, and they may have been exploited beyond what was sustainable.

The problem is not described in medieval sources, but Hans Egede mentions it in his diary. He established his colony near Nuuk on 3 July 1721, but just two years later on 27 September 1723 he complained about problems with firewood for heating. At first they used drift-timber close to their settlement, but now they had to row increasingly long distances to find it.[56] The Medieval Norse may have used their driftwood more wisely, using turf and seal-oil for heating and driftwood for housebuilding. But their settlement lasted over 400 years, and the problem must have grown worse.

Bjørn Jonsson (1574–1655) claimed in his "Grænlands annal" that "all rich farmers in Greenland had large ships and smaller ones *(skutur)* built to be sent to the Disco region for among other things 'hewn wood' *(tegldum vidum)*". This must have been boards and planks which were hewn from drift timber where they were found. It is not clear how reliable Bjørn's information is more than 200 years after the Norsemen disappeared. He may have found it in the Hauksbok written ca. 1300, but that is only a hypothesis.[57]

In 1347 a ship sailed from Greenland to Labrador (Markland). It not said what they sought there, but Labrador had rich, unexploited forests. On the way back, the ship drifted to Iceland, where the annalists made a point of how small the ship was and how poorly it was equipped.[58] Such ships may have been in common use in the search for driftwood north of the Western Settlement. *Groenlendinga saga* claims that both Leiv Eiriksson[59] and Thorfinn Karlsefni[60] brought back timber from Vinland. This information may have been added by the saga author ca. 1220–1250, but it shows that Icelanders at that time saw timber as a commodity sought by Greenlanders on the other side of the Davis Strait. Hans Egede in 1724 sent a ship to America for provisions.[61] The Canadian scholar Valeri Pilgrim thinks that voyages for timber from Norse Greenland to Labrador must have been common, but her empirical evidence is limited to the notice in the annals from 1347.[62]

After the driftwood near the settlements had been depleted, a man who wanted to build a house had to send a boat or ship along the Greenland coast, or to Labrador or Norway. They would probably use axes to hew and wedges to split it into boards on the spot. One problem may have been that they lacked ships which were sufficiently large for long voyages with bulky goods, and another that the

166 *Trade and shipping*

voyages had to take place in the short summer sailing season when there was so much work to be done on the farm.

Heating and light were necessities. The Inuit used seal and occasionally whale blubber for heating and had no problems. The Norse also used seal and whale blubber, and in addition had turf, driftwood, shrub and bushes. The Norse did not need to import firewood but may have needed to import planks and boards for housebuilding.

The Norse Greenlanders could do without imported salt because of the cold climate. Domestic animals were slaughtered in autumn at the start of the cold season. Meat and fish was dried in the wind without salt in low temperatures. This has a long tradition along the north Norwegian coast. In *Groenlendinga tháttr* a large room dug into the earth is described where 60 slaughtered animals and much butter and dried cod was stored, at least for one year, perhaps for many. It is said to belong to an ordinary peasant.[63] One should take this to be fiction as the soil in Einarsfjord is not deep enough for a room that large. But the principle is real enough – the cold climate made it possible to store meat, fish and butter without salt.

Iron was the most necessary import. Imported timber for housebuilding was easier to replace. Iron objects and implements could function for years without being renewed, and so could the wood of the interior walls in their living-rooms and roof structures. If ships from Norway failed to appear, life would gradually grow more miserable, but it was not a question of life or death.

Luxuries conferring status

The King's Mirror says that imported grain products were not bought by "most people (*mæstr fiold*)". They did not know what bread was and had never seen it.[64] The same point is illustrated in episodes from two *Islendingasögur*. The Icelandic merchant Karlsefni stayed one winter at Brattahlid. He then told his host Eirik Raudi that "on our ship is both malt and grain", and he gave some of it to Eirik so that he could prepare a Christmas feast. Those present "thought they had never seen such generosity (*rausn*) in a poor land (*in fatöku landi*)".[65] The malt and grain were part of the commercial cargo to be sold in Greenland; it had not been brought to Greenland as a gift for Eirik Raudi.

According to another saga the grandson of Eirik Raudi did the same.

> When Christmas drew near, the chieftain Thorkell at Brattahlid brewed beer (*mungát*) since he wanted to arrange a Christmas feast. He did so to obtain honour, since feasts with beer are far between in Greenland. He invited his friends to stay there during the Christmas holidays.[66]

The author does not explicitly say that the chieftain on Brattahlid bought malt from a merchant who had just arrived from Norway, but that must have been his meaning. Both sagas were written ca. 1220 in Iceland, and it seems to have been common knowledge there that the chieftain on Brattahlid, and possibly other chieftains, brewed beer for the Christmas feast, but not at other times, if they could get hold of the necessary malt from Norway. These feasts strengthened the ties between the chieftain and his clients.

It was impossible for even the elite to make imported grain a permanent part of their diet. Nobody would starve if a ship from Norway did not arrive. Efforts were made to cultivate grain in Greenland, but with little success.[67] "Luxury" is what I shall here call imports which could be replaced by products produced in Greenland without hardship being caused to anyone, but nevertheless were imported because imports gave higher social status.

Clothing in Norse society was the most important way of making social status visible. Cloths of wool, linen and hemp could be woven in Greenland, but they were also imported. The archaeologists cannot distinguish between those made in Greenland and overseas by analysing the raw material, but since all dyes were produced overseas, it is possible to distinguish them by the colour.

Clothing has been found at several Greenlandic churchyards, particularly at Herjolvsnes. Most people were buried in their everyday clothing where functionality came first. The simplest way of colouring clothes was to mix wool from sheep of different colours: grey, brownish and black. Everyday clothes were coloured in this way.[68] They used hides from domestic and hunted animals for making clothing for special outdoors purposes. In *Fostbroedra saga* we are told that a slave on Brattahlid wore a short coat and trousers made of sealskin, probably to make them watertight.[69] Clothing for everyday use could be made from raw materials produced on the farm.

Linen cloth and linen canvas were made from flax grown in Greenland. No flax grows wild in Greenland, so it was a garden plant, and pollen has been found at Norse sites.[70] Archaeologists have found linen cloth at Gardar,[71] Hvalsey (E83),[72] GUS,[73] Sandnes (W51), Niaquusat (W48)[74] and Nipaatsoq (W54).[75] Equipment for combing flax was found at Narsaq (E17a).[76] Østergård interprets one find from GUS as the remnants of a linen shirt. She suggests that the finer qualities of linen cloth may have been imported, and only the coarser linen canvas was made in Greenland.[77]

A rope of hemp was found at Sandnes, and hemp and wool were mixed in one of the dresses found at Herjolvsnes.[78] It is most likely that products of hemp were imported from Norway where they were widely used. No hemp grows in Greenland today, and there is no evidence that it was grown there in the Norse period, but it cannot be ruled out that Norse Greenlanders kept it as a garden plant.

The elite coloured their wool clothes by using pigments. Woad coloured the cloth blue and was produced in England and elsewhere in northern Europe.[79] This colour gave the clothes a high status. It has been found archaeologically at Sandnes and Narsaq.[80] In 1308 the bishop of Bergen sent a gift to his colleague in Greenland: "a long coat (*skingr*) and an over-cloak (*syrkot*) and a hood coloured in light blue. Coat, cloak and hood have a lining made of grey fur from squirrel. And finally a short coat (*kyrtil*) made of the same kind of cloth".[81] This was clothing which would distinguish a bishop from the common people, and keep him warm. The short coat may have been for summer use.

A red-violet pigment[82] was made of a lichen which in Old Norse was called *korki*. This lichen does not grow in Greenland, so *korki* must be an import. It is found in customs accounts as exports from Bergen to England during 1303–1311 under the name *corke* or *litmose*.[83] The *korki* pigment found in Greenland probably arrived from Bergen. The red pigment extracted from a plant called "crap" was used in two textiles found in Norse Greenland.[84] There are no indications that the crap plant grew in Greenland, and Rogers thinks both textiles were coloured in Greenland using imported pigments.[85]

Norwegian peasants north of Bergen used imported textiles on special occasions, like Sundays and church feast days. Social distance between elite and peasants, differences within peasant society and different social occasions could be symbolised in this way. Even in Greenland some peasants may have owned imported, coloured clothing or clothing produced in Greenland but coloured with imported pigments. The model must have been the clothing of the Greenlandic elite and what they saw when they visited Bergen and Trondheim. Even the cut of everyday clothing followed what the Greenlanders saw in these towns. They had Norway and indirectly Western Europe as patterns for all kinds of clothes. This is yet another visual expression of their cultural identity.[86] Their aesthetic ambition demonstrates that the Norse Greenlanders did not live at a minimum level of existence.

Products made from metals, timber and cloth were the main imports to Greenland, and to these should be added minor products.

Jewellery was often made of imported bronze, and for special purposes of gold or silver. At Herjolvsnes two circular brooches of brass and two ornamental pins of copper were found.[87] At Nipaatsoq (W54) a buckle of brass was found which had been part of a belt, and a finger ring of silver.[88] Bishop Olav, who was buried in Gardar cathedral in 1280, had a finger ring of gold which had probably been given to him when he was consecrated in Norway.[89] All these pieces of jewellery must have been imports.

Most jewellery was not made of imported metals, but of polished stones like jet, walrus tusk or bones made in Greenland.[90] A polar bear in walrus ivory was found at Sandnes in the Western Settlement. It was 2.5 cm long and perforated, proving that it was worn as jewellery, perhaps by a Norseman who had participated in *nordrseta*. A tooth from a polar bear had cuts which suggest that it was also used as a pendant.[91] A similar use was probably made of a walrus 4 cm long made of ivory.[92] Small pendant crosses in bright colours were probably for women.[93] A chess piece today called "knight" was carved as a horse.[94]

Toilet articles and jewellery which were made in Greenland often had their models in Norwegian towns. Combs were common on all farms. They were used to remove parasites, but also to keep the hair in place. The form is mainly functional, but with some ornamental elements.[95] In Scandinavia before ca. 1200 most combs had teeth on one side only; later combs with teeth on both sides became increasingly common. The excavation methods make it difficult to date finds, but combs seem to have followed developments in Bergen, Trondheim and Oslo, even if many or most of them were made in Greenland.[96]

Numerous hairpins were found at the farms. Most had a drilled hole or eye for a ribbon. Hairpins and ribbons kept women's long hair in place. At the chieftain's farm of Brattahlid both straight and curved hairpins were found, and they were more decorated than at other farms with lines and dots, and one with geometric figures. Hairpins have also been found at Sandnes, Narsaq and at E167 in Vatnahverfi.[97]

Poul Nørlund led the excavations at Herjolvsnes, Gardar and Brattahlid, and he claims that "earthenware was neither made in Greenland nor in general use there. We say this with some justification, after excavating for three summers at the largest farms in the Eastern Settlement, with a yield of one potsherd per summer".[98] Imported Rhenish stoneware was found at Gardar, Herjolvsnes and E167 in Vatnahverfi, one sherd at each site.[99] The Greenlanders may have felt that they did not need imported stoneware since they could make cheap replacements in soapstone.[100]

Wooden bowls made with the help of lathes were imported to Greenland. One of those found at Brattahlid was made of oak, and probably had a South Norwegian origin.[101] Lathes were not used in Greenland, and the Greenlanders hollowed out their bowls by knife. Afterwards they increased the prestige of their bowls by incising circles on the interior bottom which imitated those produced when lathes were used.[102] Other wooden objects were made of local raw material like juniper and willow. These were sometimes so thick that small household utensils like spoons, scoops, ladles, dippers and stirrers could be made from them.[103] Some 58 crosses were excavated at Herjolvsnes, all of them made from driftwood.[104]

At Sandnes the archaeologists found a lump of stone coal of a type which does not exist in Greenland (*anthracite*),[105] but which existed and was a commercial commodity on the British Isles in the Middle Ages. In 1308 a Norwegian merchant exported coal from King's Lynn in England on a ship belonging to the King's Chapel in Bergen (*Apostelkirken*).[106] The same year the bishop of Bergen sent a gift of among other things imported luxury clothes to his colleague in Greenland.[107] Perhaps the coal in 1308 voyaged from King's Lynn to Bergen to Gardar?

How important were imports to the Norse Greenlanders?

"The Norse Greenlanders wanted to live like Nordic (read: Norse) peasants, and never adopted the Eskimo way of life. Consequently they could not survive without imports". This claim comes from the Danish archaeologist Else Roesdahl.[108] The only imports which could have consequences for "survival" were iron weapons and iron implements used in food production, and in some situations wood for housebuilding. Other imports made life more like that lived in the Norwegian motherland, and different from that lived by the Inuit, but were not essential for survival.

Imported food, clothes and other objects of prestige expressed social status. They made social differences visible. Eirik Raudi and his sons strengthened the loyalty of friends and clients through Christmas feasts where imported beer was drunk and bread made from imported grain eaten. A shift of emphasis from violence to symbolic expressions of social differences may have helped to pacify Greenland society without changing power relations.

2 The exports

Most of what the Norse Greenlanders produced, they consumed themselves. This "subsistence economy" will be the subject of Chapter 5. They marketed a limited part of their production in Norway, from where it was exported to other North Sea ports. Cattle and goats were kept for their milk and meat, and seals were hunted for their lamp-oil and meat. The exported hides from these animals were by-products of this subsistence farming and hunting.

Walrus, however, were hunted exclusively for their export products, which were tusks and ropes.

Walrus tusks and walrus rope

The North Norwegian chieftain Othere visited the court of king Alfred of England in the 890s and described his hunting expeditions in Finnmark and the White Sea region:

> His principal purpose for going there, in addition to the exploration of the country, was to get the walruses,[109] for they have very excellent ivory in their tusks, and he brought some of them to the king. From their skin can be made hides from which can be made excellent ropes for ships (*sciprapum*). The walrus is much smaller than other whales because it is no more than seven ells (ca. 3.5 metres) long.[110]

Norwegian merchants sold walrus tusks and ropes on the north European market before Greenland was settled in AD 985. Othere mentions the market towns of *Sciringesheal* at today's Oslofjord, *Hæthum* (Hedeby) in today's Schleswig-Holstein and he also visited England.[111]

Walrus hides were made into ropes which were appreciated by kings because they were well suited to be used on warships. *The King's Mirror* claims that rope from walrus hides was so strong that 60 men could not make it break by pulling it.[112] King Sverrir used walrus ropes (*svard*) to fasten the shields along the rails of his warships when he prepared for the battle of Fimreite in western Norway in 1184.[113] He probably thought this would make it more difficult for the enemy to remove the shields and board his ships. The Saga of Kroka-Ref is fiction written at the beginning of the 14th century. Before leaving Greenland for Norway and Denmark, Ref loaded his ship with "Greenland wares which were walrus ropes, walrus tusks and skins".[114] When Ref arrived in Denmark, the saga author enumerates the same Greenland wares as being on his ship, but adds that these commodities "were rarely seen in Denmark".[115] King Sveinn of Denmark particularly appreciated a gift of "walrus ropes to equip our ships".[116] On warships, reliable equipment could be a question of life or death.

The first mention of walrus products from Greenland is in *Groenlendinga tháttr* which was written ca. 1200, but where the relevant event took place ca. 1124. Then the Brattahlid chieftain sent his son to the Norwegian king on an important mission. He brought with him much walrus tusk and walrus ropes, which were used as gifts to gain access to and create goodwill with the king and his councillors.[117] We do not know if the saga author based himself on a reliable oral tradition from 1124, or if he added this rather marginal piece of information because he thought it was reasonable to assume that it happened like that. In our context this is not important. The source verifies that in the 12th century in Iceland walrus tusks and ropes were the most valuable commercial goods Greenland could offer.

In 1226 the verse novel "Tristram and Iseult" was translated at the Norwegian court from French into Norse. In the French original it is told how Tristram was abducted in France by the merchants on a Norwegian cargo-ship. In the Norse translation this passage was expanded, and the translator added a list of the commodities which the ship had on board. This list expresses what a person living in Norway, probably Bergen, thought a cargo-ship sailing from Norway to France was likely to carry. Among the commodities were walrus tusks (*tannvara*), goshawks, grey falcons, many white falcons, "and all kinds of Norse wares (*norröna vara*)".[118] Walrus tusks were at this time no longer hunted by Norwegians in the north. They came from Greenland and occasionally from Iceland to Bergen and were sent further to the European continent.

The King's Mirror from ca. 1250 contains the first list of goods exported from Greenland: "hides from billy-goats, hides from cattle, hides from seals, ropes called *svardreip* which people cut from the fish called walrus (*rostungr*), and the teeth (*tænnr*) of walrus".[119]

In 1266 a ship coming from Greenland and evidently on its way to Bergen, was wrecked at Hitarnesi in Iceland, and 41 men drowned.[120] The Icelandic annalist Bjørn Jonsson (1574–1655) wrote that this catastrophe was remembered in his own lifetime 350 years later. "Until this day are washed ashore some of the Greenlandic teeth from whales and walruses (*rostunga*) and which sank on that occasion. The Greenlanders had sent them out to be sold". Bjørn speculates that they had put this surprisingly high number of tusks lowest in the hull as ballast and used some kind of glue to keep the ballast stable.[121] This source makes it highly likely that walrus tusk was the main export from Greenland around 1266, and that great quantities were produced.

Some of the 78 chessmen of walrus-ivory found on Lewis in the Hebrides had also been stained red when they were sent from Trondheim to the British Isles ca. 1150–1200. In that case the dye-stuff is thought to have been "madder", and the purpose must have been the same as having white and black chessmen today.[122]

In 1282 the archbishop's envoy returned from Greenland to Nidaros with a tax which the pope had prescribed and which had been paid in tusks and ropes from walrus and hides of cattle and seal.[123] The pope instructed the archbishop to sell it at the price he could get in Norway, and give the profits to merchants from Lucca who would bring it to Rome.[124]

In the period 1303–1311 numerous customs accounts have been preserved from east English ports; they register imports from abroad, Norway included. No imports of walrus tusks or walrus ropes are registered.[125] No goods arrived in English ports directly from Greenland.

172   Trade and shipping

But walrus tusks were sent via Norway to other countries, for in 1316 the Norwegian crown imposed a customs duty on the export of several commodities, walrus tusks (*tanvaru*) included.[126] In 1327 the whole papal tithe from Greenland was paid in walrus tusks.[127] From Gardar it was sent to the archbishop of Nidaros' warehouse in Bergen and there sold to a Flemish merchant from Ypres. He probably transported it to Bruges or another market town in Flanders. Bruges' hinterland included northern France and the Rhine area.[128] After 1327 no exports of walrus products are mentioned in the written sources.

Walrus tusks as raw material for objects of art

The most valuable part of the walrus was its tusks. Some were worked on by Greenlandic craftsmen and used as decorations. Kroka-Ref's saga is pure fiction written at the beginning of the 14th century, but its description of artefacts made from walrus ivory is likely to mirror practices in the author's time. A Greenlander presented a skilfully made chessboard with chess pieces made of walrus tusk (*tanntafl*) to the Norwegian king and a "walrus skull (*rostungshauss*) with both tusks, it was carved and inlaid with gold, this was the greatest treasure".[129] The latter was probably hung on a wall as decoration. It is not said whether the ivory in these cases had been worked on in Greenland or Norway.

A total of 30 walrus skulls without tusks were excavated in the churchyard of Gardar cathedral. The archaeologist Nørlund suggests that some magic notion could be behind this. My hypothesis would be that the skulls with tusks originally hung in one of the bishop's living-rooms as decorations. After the Norse were gone, the Inuit removed the tusks, which were useful for other purposes, and buried the skulls where the soil was deep enough, in the churchyard.[130] Walrus skulls may also have hung in the dwellings of Greenlandic peasants as trophies. Decorating a walrus skull in the way described above must have demanded little skilled workmanship.

In the early period walrus was also caught in Iceland and Finnmark, and it is often impossible to determine where the craftsmen had worked. King Magnus Bareleg of Norway (1093–1103) fought his final battle in Ireland with a sword which had a hilt made of walrus ivory.[131] Ivory miniature sculptures of polar bears, walruses, a man's head and geometric reliefs have been found in Greenland, Trondheim and Bergen and several other places in the Norse realm.[132] Objects made from walrus ivory with religious motives are known from the Danish realm.[133]

Archaeological finds suggest that Trondheim was particularly important. The crozier of a bishop's staff was found in a grave which is assumed to be from ca. 1280 in Gardar cathedral. The crozier was made of walrus ivory.[134] The bishop had probably received a staff with a crozier when he was consecrated in Trondheim in 1246.[135] Another walrus relief which had possibly belonged to an abbot's staff, was found at the site of the cloister Nidarholm.[136] The fragment of a queen chess piece of walrus ivory was excavated in the town centre.[137] A sculptured walrus carved from walrus ivory dated 1225–1275 was found in a recent urban excavation. Several pieces of walrus tusk have been found in the ground, but so far no remains which indicate a craftsman at work carving walrus ivory objects.[138] The starting point for a possible walrus-ivory workshop in Trondheim must have been the archbishop who needed its products not only for croziers but also for other church purposes. Bishops were consecrated in Trondheim and could visit the town on other occasions. The framework was in place for a walrus-ivory workshop there. The art historian Gaborit-Chopin has made a stylistic comparison between the famous chess pieces from Lewis on the Hebrides on the one hand, and wooden sculptures from Norway and reliefs from the cathedral in Trondheim, on the other. She concluded that the ivory chessmen from Lewis are likely to have been made in Trondheim.[139]

The most illustrious of the extant objects made from Greenlandic walrus ivory are the Lewis chessmen from ca. 1150–1200. In this period the walruses must have been hunted in Greenland, and the tusks were shipped across the Atlantic to Trondheim. At a workshop there they may have been carved into chessmen. A merchant or a representative of the archbishop acquired at least four complete sets of chessmen, each set 16 "officers" and 16 "pawns". Today 8 "kings" and 8 "queens" are preserved. If there were originally four sets, this means that all the kings and queens are today in museums in London and Edinburgh.[140]

The ship with the chessmen is likely to have sailed the normal sea lane from Trondheim along the Norwegian coast to Bergen, where it turned west arriving in Shetland. From Shetland it turned south following the western coast of Orkney, Scotland and the Outer Hebrides. But at Uig Bay on Lewis in the Hebrides passengers and crew must have encountered problems, because the merchant went ashore, dug a stone-chamber in the sand and deposited his chessmen there. They were not rediscovered until 1831.

In the period 1050–1250 chess was seen as a "knightly skill", a mark of distinction which gave honour to those who mastered it.[141] The chessmen may have been on their way to the court of Dublin or to the earl of the Hebrides and Man.[142] The art historian Gaborit-Chopin finds that the figures have a compact form of high quality despite the artist's scarce use of artistic effects.[143] They lend associations to modern art. The aristocratic customers wanted their chessmen to be aesthetic. Walrus ivory carved by highly skilled artists during 850–1200 in Northern France, Britain and the Rhine area can today be seen in the Louvre and the British Museum.[144]

The artists preferred elephant ivory to walrus ivory because the former were larger and whiter and the carved objects were easier to give a homogenous appearance. The demand for and value of walrus ivory depended on how much elephant ivory was available. Shipping across the Mediterranean was reduced because of tensions between Muslim and Christian states between the 7th and 13th centuries. The value of walrus ivory as a result remained at a high level. In the second half of the 13th century the shipping lanes across the Mediterranean became safer and more numerous and the result was an "Überfluss an Elfenbein".[145] After ca. 1350 ivory fell in price, and walrus ivory was marginalised by elephant ivory. Walrus ivory was no longer seen by people who wanted prestige objects as a valuable raw material. This meant that they ceased to pay highly skilled artists to carve ivory, and the quality of the work declined.[146] The hunt for and transport of walrus ivory from Greenland involved much work and great costs. A point was reached when merchants and perhaps even the hunters found that it was not worth the effort.

Walrus products met the luxury demands of church and state, which could afford to pay a high price for it. When it was no longer felt to be a luxury, the market failed.

The Norse Greenlanders' "nordrseta" in the Disco region

The stock of walrus on the west coast of Greenland has been drastically reduced since the Middle Ages. This development reached a crisis point in the 20th century. In 1952 Norwegian authorities made walrus an endangered species and prohibited hunting on Svalbard. In north-western Greenland the walrus is still hunted with shotguns and speedboats.[147] The skull of a walrus with tusks is sold legally in shops to tourists for ca. 10,000 Danish crowns.[148]

In Greenland's west coast the largest and most stable concentrations of walrus were formerly found between Sisimiut and the Nuussuaq peninsula. *Kroksfjardarheidi* (= Nuussuaq) was in the 1260s the northern limit of the region which the Norse normally visited.[149] In this book "the Disco region" will be used about this part of the coast where the Norse had their best hunting ground. *Nordrseta* (stay in the north), will be used in the sense of "stay for hunting purposes in the Disco region", which corresponds with how the Norse Greenlanders used the word.[150]

In March-April large walrus populations stayed along the edge of the coastal sea ice in the Disco region.[151] This would be a suitable hunting season for the Norse, as at this time snow would still make agricultural work impossible in the settlements.[152] We only have one dating for Norsemen's travels to the far north: the Kingittorsuaq rune-stone which dates itself to 25 April. It was found near Upernavik, north of the Norse hunting fields, but the time may nevertheless be representative of the Norsemen's *nordrseta*.[153]

The "Polar Ice" from the North Pole, also called the "Great Ice" normally prevented boats and ships from leaving the Eastern Settlement in March-April.[154] The Western Settlement was ice free all year, and we should assume that hunting voyages to the Disco region departed from there.[155]

In the part of the west coast of Greenland which was relevant to the Norse, there were two types of ice in March-April. At Sisimiut–Nuussuaq there was coastal ice stretching into the Davis Strait and ending on an edge. The walruses assembled on this edge and this is where the hunt took place. Here Norsemen had their *Nordrseta*. In this region there were no ice floes in the Davis Strait, which blocked access to this ice edge.[156]

Was it realistic to row or sail from the Western Settlement up to the Disco region and back if voyage and hunting had to be done during a few weeks in spring? When Bjørn Jonsson (died 1655) wrote his "Grænlands annal", he used an "old booklet" (*gömlu kveri*) with information about distances in Norse Greenland, measured in how many days it would take to row it.[157] The information is so precise that it inspires confidence and is likely to have been written at a time when the Norse Greenlanders still visited the northern hunting grounds. From the Western Settlement it would take 15 days to row to *Bjarneyar*, which evidently was Disco Island.[158] The Norse could normally row in ice-free waters from the Western Settlement up to Sisimiut where the hunting grounds for walrus started. There they would meet ice floes originating from coastal ice between Sisimiut and Disco Island, but it would normally be possible to navigate between them.[159] At night they would sleep in tents or in booths made of turf and canvas.[160] It would take one month to row between the Western Settlement and Disco Island both ways. If they spent two-three months of the year on their *nordrseta*, this would leave more than one month for active hunting.

Which boats or ships were used in the northern hunts? It may have been important that they could be drawn onto an ice floe if the hunters were surrounded by ice which threatened to crush the boat and that the boat could be drawn ashore at night. This favoured small boats. The rowing distances in Bjørn Jonsson's "old booklet" are for a sexæringr rowed by six men.[161] If the boat was used for fishing, three men in one boat would give the best working conditions.[162] But in the walrus hunt the Norse went ashore when they killed the animals, so six men per boat would probably make a better hunting team.

The description of the journey from the Disco region and northwards in 1267 or shortly afterwards explicitly says that it was done in one or several *sexærings*.[163] They sailed at least part of the way, as all sexærings at this time could be sailed or rowed.[164] The Kingittorsuaq rune-stone names three men who were present there on 25 April, which could have been the crew of a sexæringr. On this latitude and with only three men they were probably on a journey of exploration and not hunting.[165]

A Norwegian sexæringr had three "rooms" for rowers but could also have one or several additional "rooms" meant for cargo only, in which case the boat had to be built longer. There is no evidence for such cargo rooms, but one cannot rule out that sexærings used in the Disco region could have one or two extra "rooms" to provide storage places for hunting equipment and tusks.[166]

The sexærings may not have been sufficient to bring the hunting products home, particularly if room had to be found for six men in each boat. The Norse Greenlanders also owned medium-sized inshore ships called *skuta* or *ferja*.[167] Bjørn Jonsson claimed that products from the Disco region were transported back to the settlements on *skutur* and not in the sexærings.[168] It was feasible to send an inshore cargo-ship from the settlements and northwards later in July-September when the whole west coast from Herjolvsnes to the Disco region was normally free from ice. In the meantime, tusks and other walrus products could be put in storehouses made of stone. One storehouse has been found at the western tip of the Nuussuaq peninsula. The exterior is 4.5 × 4.5 m, the interior 2.4 × 1.3 m, and it was originally almost 2 m high. Its position on the coast with a view to the open ocean must have made it easily visible and accessible for a *skuta* sailing northwards from the Western or Eastern Settlements.[169] This is the only storehouse for walrus ivory and other products found outside the settlements and it therefore gives no firm evidence that transports with *skutur* were institutionalised. But combined with Bjørn

Figure 4.1 Stone shed at the tip of the Nuussuaq peninsula in the Disco region.

In this shed walrus ivory and other hunter products are likely to have been stored while waiting to be transported south to the settlements. The main text describes how this was organised. Similar sheds were also common at most Norse farms. Food for the winter and all kinds of equipment were stored in them. The wind would blow straight through and keep meat and fish dry and cold.

Source: Meldgaard 1995, p. 206.

Copyright: The Nationalmuseum in Copenhagen.

Jonsson's claim, which is an independent source, it indicates that this may have been the case.

In the Norwegian cod fisheries in January-March sexærings and átt-ærings (eight oars) were used. The cod was hung for drying and was fetched by medium-sized inshore cargo-ships in May or later and transported to Bergen.[170] This is the same combination of sexærings and inshore trading vessels as may have been practised in Norse Greenland.

Along the Atlantic and North Sea coast of Norway boat and fishing tackle could be owned by a member of the elite or a rich local peasant-landowner, and the crew could be his servants, but this was far from always the case. The boat was an investment which a medium peasant could afford alone or in partnership with other peasants. The tackle was normally the private property of each crew member.[171] The threshold was low for those wanting to participate in fishing. This may also have been so in Greenland. Most hunters may have lived in the Western Settlement and belonged to peasant households there. Hunting and fishing did not necessarily create an economic basis for inequality.

It would have been different for the larger *skutur*, which later in the year may have freighted the catch south to the settlements. Bjørn Jonsson (1574–1655) thought they were owned by a peasant elite.

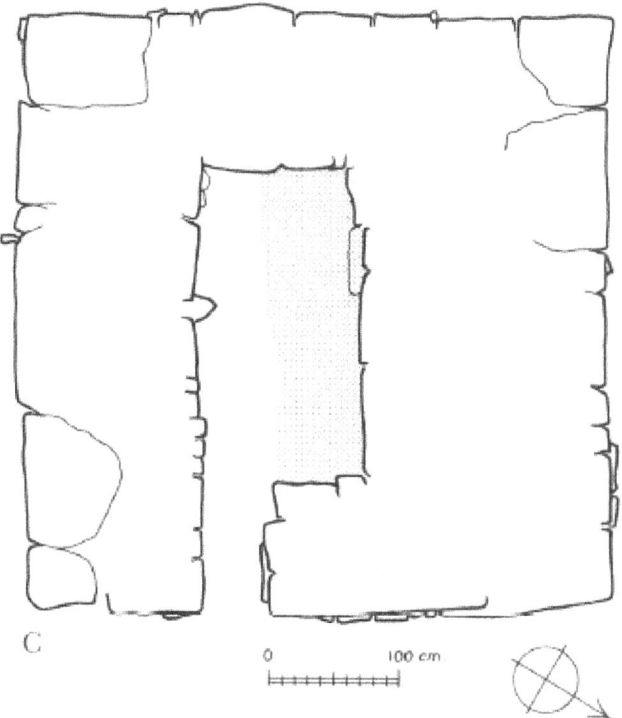

Figure 4.2 Drawing of the ground plan of the stone shed in Figure 4.1.

The Norse who sailed north of Nuussuaq ca. 1267, claimed that there were many polar bears there ("Grænlands annal", pp. 53–55). The stone shed had walls which were at their thickest 1.7 m, impossible for a bear to break down. The entrance was only 45 cm wide, which made it impossible for a bear to enter. In the shaded area in Figure 4.2 one or two wooden shelves are likely to have been constructed, 2.4 m long. The largest Narwhal teeth would be ca. 2.3 m, exceptionally 2.7 m. But the most common goods stored there must have been walrus ivory.

Source: Meldgaard 1995, p. 207.

Copyright: The Nationalmuseum in Copenhagen.

All large farmers (*storbændur*) in Greenland had large ships and *skutur* which were built to be sent in *nordrsetu*, from where they transported what was produced there, that is all kinds of hunted animals and hewn timber. Sometimes they participated in person.[172]

Bjørn tells his readers that his source is the *rimur of Skald-Helgi* and the *tháttr of Thordis*. The first was written sometime between 1350 and 1540 and is pure fiction, the second source is not otherwise known,[173] but a similar role for an economic elite in coastal Norway strengthens the credibility of the information on which Bjørn built his case. The walrus hunt seems to have been organised in such a way that both ordinary peasants and the coastal elite profited from it.[174]

Trade and shipping

Norse Greenland households obtained practically all their food through their subsistence food production, which will be discussed in Chapter 5. The trade described in this chapter made it possible for them to supplement it with imported commodities. This combination of subsistence and market production was also found along the Norwegian Atlantic and North Sea coasts. In the period before ca. 1050 one of the main exports may have been walrus products, but after that time dried cod (stockfish) exported via Bergen dominated. They considered these incomes as an indispensable part of their household economy.

Compared to the better-known situation along the Norwegian coast, how important were the Norse Greenlandic households' incomes from the commercial walrus hunt in the period before the decline started after ca. 1330? In the following estimates I will assume that prices and exchange rates were approximately the same in the 25-year period 1303–1328 since the sources do not permit us to follow annual price changes.

The two tusks of a walrus could ca. 1328 be sold for one mark in Norwegian coins in Bergen.[175] In 1328 one mark in Norwegian coins could be exchanged for three English shillings in Bergen.[176] Two tusks = 3 English shillings = 1 Norwegian mark.

In the years 1303–1311, the market price of one "hundred" stockfish in Bergen was 3.5 English shillings.[177] One "hundred" stockfish = 3.5 English shillings, or 0.86 hundred stockfish = 3.0 English shillings.

A "hundred" stockfish was at that time a large hundred of 120 fish. This means that 0.86 "hundred" stockfish contained 103 fish. 3 English shillings = 103 stockfish = 2 tusks.

Along the coast of Northern Norway peasants left their farm for ca. two months from ca. mid January to mid March and sailed to the Lofoten islands or other fishing villages. There they lived in huts, fishing cod and producing stockfish. A normal catch for a season in Lofoten would result in ca. 950 stockfish. This means that the value produced in an average season in Lofoten corresponded to the value of the tusks from ca. nine walruses. These walruses also gave walrus ropes which were in high demand. A Greenland peasant during a season in the Disco region had to hunt less than nine walruses to produce the same value as his Norwegian counterpart produced in Lofoten. All values are registered in Bergen.

I do not know how realistic it was for one Greenland peasant to hunt somewhat less than nine walruses during a season in the Disco region. If there were six hunters in one sexæringr, such a team had to kill ca. 50 walruses if each of them were to obtain the same income measured in coins as a Norwegian peasant-fisherman in one season in Lofoten ca. 1303–1328.

The products had to be transported from Greenland and Lofoten to Bergen to obtain this price, and the transport costs were evidently higher for the tusks. A larger part of the profits must have gone to merchants in the walrus trade. There are many elements of uncertainty in these estimates, but the empirical material makes it possible that the coastal population in Greenland obtained significant incomes from trading. Not only the elite but also peasant households may have profited substantially from a hunting season in the Disco region.

When did the Norse start to visit the northern hunting grounds, and when was the hunt abandoned? The first Norse settlers knew that there was a market for walrus tusk in England and on the North European continent. Eirik Raudi may have already discovered the large populations of walrus on his reconnaissance voyages before AD 985. The first written source mentioning *nordrseta* is fragments of a skaldic poem called *Nordrsetudrápa* which according to the Icelandic philologist Finnur Jonsson was composed in the 11th century.[178] In GUS in the Western Settlement archaeologists found stones suitable to be used for igniting fires and which had been brought there from the Disco region in the 11th century.[179] The Norse Greenlanders seem to have started their walrus hunts shortly after their arrival in AD 985.

In 1327 the Norse Greenlanders still visited the northern hunting grounds.[180] The next and last contemporary source which can shed light on the hunting voyages to the Disco region is Ivar Bárdarson's account written ca. 1360.[181] He gives no information about the northern regions or walrus hunts. Members of the church or other Norsemen evidently did not organise hunting expeditions there at this time. Ivar is better informed about hunting in the uninhabited coast at the other side of Cape Farewell, but here walruses are not mentioned either by Ivar or by others.[182]

Hides and skins

In enumerations of exports from Greenland walrus products are always included, and often they are the only item mentioned. The most reliable and complete list of exports from Greenland to Bergen is that from *The King's Mirror* (ca. 1250) which adds hides from billy-goats (*bucca voru*), hides from cattle (*nauta voru*) and hides from seals (*sæla huder*) to the walrus products mentioned earlier.[183] In a list of the commodities which the archbishop of Nidaros received as six years' tithe from Greenland in 1282 are included "hides of cattle and seal (*focarum coriis*), in addition to tusks and ropes from walrus.[184] The Saga of Kroka-Ref is fiction written at the beginning of the 14th century. Before leaving Greenland for Norway and Denmark, Ref loaded his ship with "Greenland wares which were walrus ropes, walrus tusks and skins".[185] When "skins" are specified in the examples above, it is cattle (two times), seal (two times) and billy-goat (once). There is no evidence of furs, but "skin" is a word which includes both "hides" and "furs". Icelanders and Norwegians saw these goods as normal exports from Greenland.

Sealskins were used in Greenland in clothing for special outdoors purposes, probably to make it watertight.[186] Exported sealskins may have been used for the same purposes. Sealskins are registered in East English customs accounts as exported from Bergen to England during 1303–1311, and Hansa merchants exported sealskins from Bergen to Boston in England in 1388, 1390 and 1391.[187] Sealskins were also produced in Norway, and it is not possible to separate Greenlandic and Norwegian products. Sealskins could be cut into stripes and used as ship-ropes. Around AD 890 sámi chieftains in Northern Norway had to pay two ship ropes of ca. 30 m each in taxes, one made of sealskin and the other of whale-skin.[188]

The fox is the most common fur animal in Greenland. In the numerous English customs accounts from 1303–1311 no furs of foxes are registered from Norway. In the Late Middle Ages, I have registered one ship carrying fox furs from Bergen to England; it was a Hansa ship in Boston in England in 1390.[189] Furs from foxes were not in high demand in the North Sea area. Tastes had changed during 1721–1736, when Hollanders and Danes bought hides of reindeer and seal, and furs of fox from the Inuit.[190]

Falcons and polar bears

The most numerous falcon species in Greenland is the migratory falcon (*Falco peregrinus*), which is common south of Thule on the west coast and Amassalik on the east coast between May and August-November. The other species is the Hunter Falcon (*Falco rusticolus*), which is larger and rarer. In summer they live along the whole Greenland coast, most of them in northern Greenland. In winter they move southwards mostly to southern Greenland but also to Iceland. They are also found in Norway. Some of the Hunter Falcons are white and fetched a higher price.[191]

Falcons were used in a type of sport hunting which was popular among European aristocrats but was unknown in Greenland.

> Falcons (*val*) are there large in size and numerous. In other countries they would have been seen as a great treasure. White falcons are more numerous than in any other land. The Greenlanders themselves do not know how to make use of them.[192]

The literary *Kroka-Ref's saga* describes the export of 50 falcons, of which 15 were white, from Greenland via Norway to Denmark.[193] The translator of the verse novel "Tristram and Iseult" narrates ca. 1226 that "grey falcons and many white falcons" were sent from "Norway" to France,[194] which meant that the ship came from a Norwegian port.

In 1224–1225 King Håkon Håkonsson wrote to King Henry III that he had sent two men to Iceland two years earlier to catch falcons, and they had now returned with 13 falcons, 3 of them white.[195] Several ships sailing from Norway to East England carried both falcons and sulphur, the latter being a typical Icelandic commodity. The owner of the cargo had evidently bought both falcons and sulphur from Icelanders in Bergen.[196]

Some falcons were ordered by the English court. In 1129–1130 a man in Lincolnshire had undertaken to provide the English court with 100 Norwegian hawks of which 4 ought to be white, and 100 gyrfalcons of which 6 ought to be white. He had so far only delivered 25 grey gyrfalcons (that is, none was white) and 8 hawks.[197] "Gyrfalcon" was a name for the largest falcon (*Falco rusticolus*). Other falcons were sold by merchants. In 1365 a Hanseatic merchant ship sailing from Bergen to East England had falcons as one of its commodities.[198]

Falcons were also imported into Western Europe from the Baltic.[199] I see no reason to analyse the trade in falcons from Bergen in detail since it is impossible to distinguish between falcons arriving via Bergen from Greenland, Iceland and the Norwegian mainland.[200]

Polar bears came from the polar region on ice floes along the Greenland East coast. In the Cape Farewell area there was a large island called Cross Island (*Kaarsö*). It was owned by the bishop of Gardar and with his permission Greenlanders hunted polar bears there.[201]

They were exotic animals which symbolised aristocratic status. Isleif was the first bishop of Iceland (1056–1080). He was elected by the Icelandic people, and then travelled to Emperor Henry III, who in 1056 was the political head of the Catholic Church, to receive his confirmation. "Isleif gave him a polar bear which had come from Greenland, and that bear was a great treasure".[202] In 1124 the Greenlanders decided that they wanted a diocese of their own, and sent the son of the Brattahlid chieftain to the Norwegian king who at that time was the political head of the church in the Norse realm. He brought with him a polar bear from Greenland as a gift to King Sigurdr.[203]

Shortly afterwards there was a conflict in Greenland, and one of the parties wanted to have the Norwegian king on his side. He brought a polar bear from Greenland, made a gift of it to the king, and complained about the unjust treatment he had suffered in Greenland. Later the other party also argued their case before the king who then understood that the first version was false. The first man "was given no reward for his animal".[204] A polar bear could give access to the king, but there was no guarantee that the king would consent to the request!

The English king had a royal zoo at the Tower of London and appreciated gifts of exotic animals. In 1252 he received a gift of a polar bear from the Norwegian king and included it in the Tower zoo. The sheriff of London was ordered to provide a muzzle and an iron chain for it, and a strong rope to hold it when it caught fish in the Thames.[205]

Most bears were killed and their skins taken. The Italian merchant Piero Quirino was shipwrecked on the Norwegian coast in 1431–1432 and visited among other places Trondheim cathedral. There he saw a very white bearskin (*una pelle d'orso bianchissima*), ca. 3.5 m long. At this time no bishop lived in Greenland, but the skin may have been a gift from one of the former bishops.[206]

Icelanders who go to Greenland where they buy a polar bear which they later give to a king to obtain a favour, is a topos in late sagas and *thættir*. The Icelander Bárd gave to king Harald Hardrádi a "polar bear, tame and fully grown" from Greenland. Later in the same saga another Icelander brought five polar bears from Greenland via Norway to Denmark for sale there.[207] The "Tháttr of Audun from the Western fjords" in Iceland is included in *Morkinskinna*. He was a poor Icelander who travelled to Greenland where he used all his money to buy a polar bear "which was a great treasure". In Norway he was intercepted by the retainers of King Harald Hardrádi. The king asked Audun to give or sell the bear to him and offered a good price, but Audun declined. He continued to Denmark where king Sveinn gave Audun a fully loaded ship, silver coins and a gold ring in exchange

182 *Trade and shipping*

for the bear.[208] The story demonstrates the high value which Icelanders ca. 1220 thought a polar bear from Greenland could receive at the Norwegian and Danish courts, and how clever Icelanders could benefit from this.

Bears could also be commercial goods. In 1304 one bear (*ursum*) arrived in Hull on a cargo-ship from Bergen. The skipper had the Norwegian name "Thorstein from Bergen" and customs demanded from foreign merchants was paid for the bear.[209] In this case it is an open question whether the bear was brown from Norway or white from Greenland.

The English customs accounts of 1303–1311 verify that polar bears and falcons were rare indeed in the trade between Bergen and England, and they do not seem to have been important in the trade between Greenland and Bergen either. But they may have been important as gifts to kings for whom they were objects of prestige.

Lamp oil

Scandinavian long-distance trade was before ca. 1100 focused on luxury consumption. The Greenland trade with its walrus products and exotic animals belongs to this category. In the following period commodities of mass consumption emerged which, in the Norse realm, was represented by stockfish exported from Bergen. Norse Greenland had potential here which failed to materialise.

From the 13th and 14th centuries people living in North European town houses replaced their open fireplaces on the floor with closed ovens. The living-room increasingly received light from larger windows, and after dark from lamps. Lamp oil grew into an article of mass consumption, and one possible raw material was seal blubber.

The 1303–1311 English customs accounts give rich information about merchandise transported from Norway to East England, but no seal blubber or seal oil is mentioned.[210] In 1383 two ships owned by Hansa merchants on their way from Bergen were plundered off the coast of Scotland probably on their way to Boston in Lincolnshire. The main cargo was stockfish, but there were also 144 barrels of *sele-smolte* on board.[211] *Sele-smolte* could mean both "seal blubber" and the oil produced from seal blubber.[212] I would guess that the 144 barrels contained the finished oil ready to be burnt in lamps.

This incipient trade could have encouraged Greenlanders to produce larger quantities of lamp oil as a "mass product", but this was not done. The great expansion in the export from Bergen of seal oil came after the Norse had disappeared from Greenland. In the 1470s Dutch merchants specialised in exporting seal oil and cod liver oil from Bergen.[213] After ca. 1575 Dutch whalers appeared in West Greenland and their main product was lamp oil from whales, walruses and seals. In Hans Egede's time (1721–1736) seal blubber was the main commodity which the Inuit sold to Hollandish and Danish merchants.[214]

If the Norse Settlements had still existed when the Hollanders started to buy larger quantities of seal oil in Bergen and later in Greenland, the Norse Greenlanders could have participated in the production of a new important mass commodity on the European market.

Foreign trade and the Greenlanders' material needs

Some 5000 years before the settlement of Greenland, Norwegian coastal peasants had started to live permanently at farmsteads where at least the interior of their living-rooms was made of wood. Simultaneously they started to produce grain consumed as bread, porridge and beer. Some 1500 years before the settlement of Greenland, Norwegian coastal peasants had started to use iron for weapons and for tools used in agriculture, hunting and fishing. Iron, wooden planks and grain were produced in Norway by the peasants themselves. The Norse Greenlanders settled in a different natural environment where iron and grain could not be produced, and planks only under certain circumstances.

In Norway meat was valued as a better and more prestigious food than grain products. For the Norse Greenlanders it cannot have been a sacrifice to replace bread and porridge with meat and milk products, but they evidently missed the beer. The lack of iron was more serious since it reduced their ability to defend themselves properly and made food production less effective and more labour intensive. Driftwood gradually grew scarcer, and wood for housing became a problem.

In the first centuries the Norse Greenlanders could pay for imports of these commodities. But in the decades after ca. 1330 the international demand for walrus products declined. The Inuit pushed southwards and made it risky for the Norse to continue their hunting expeditions to the Disco region. These two developments made the Norsemen cease their production of walrus products for export, and they could no longer pay for imports which they felt were necessary. The Norse Greenlanders must have experienced a gradual decline in their quality of life, and Norse Greenland became a less attractive place to live.

3 Ships and boats

What means of transport did the Norse Greenlanders use for bringing these goods to and from their island, and internally within Greenland? Practically all Norse farms were a short walking distance from a fjord or the sea, and the Greenlandic landscape made land communications problematic. Communication problems were in practice a question of whether ships and boats were available to serve the Norsemen's needs. Transport of merchandise was essential, but equally important was transport of people. This was necessary for the internal cohesion of Norse Greenland and the integration of Norse Greenland in the larger North Atlantic Norse community.

Ocean-going ships

Today in English and Scandinavian languages, "ships" are large and "boats" are small. This was different from Old Norse where *skip* was used irrespective of size, but "boats" were small even then. In this book I will follow modern usage and differentiate between "ship" and "boat".

Before the middle of the 10th century there was no difference in construction between ships used for trade and war. After that time the long and slender warships were built differently from cargo-ships, which were broader and higher in relation to their length.²¹⁵ Only cargo-ships visited Greenland. In the High Middle Ages (ca. 1100–1350) ships which crossed the Greenland Ocean (*Grœnalands haf*) were sometimes called "ocean-ships" (*hafskip*), and were different from inshore vessels.²¹⁶ They were also called *kaupskip* to distinguish them from warships or longships.²¹⁷ Icelandic sources sometimes call them *Grœnlandsfar*, that is ships which sailed to Greenland from Norway or Iceland.²¹⁸ *Knarri* was the only name for them which points to construction and not function.

The captain was often called *styrismadr*. When crossing the open ocean for several days and nights, there always had to be one man at the helm, and then there had to be two captains on board. The voyages to Greenland lasted at least one year, and then there was a real possibility that one of them could die or fall ill.

A ship crossing the Greenland Ocean between Norway and Greenland could have ca. 15–40 people on board, crew, merchants and other passengers included. When a ship on its way from Greenland to Norway was wrecked on the Icelandic coast in 1266, 41 "men" perished.²¹⁹ The Greenlandic chieftain Thorgrim Trolle had 40 armed men on his trading ship sailing from Norway to Greenland via Iceland according to an *Islendingasaga* written ca. 1220.²²⁰ The Norwegian merchant Thorir whose ship was wrecked with a cargo of timber on the Greenland coast, had 15 men on board.²²¹ During the conflict ca. 1130 between visiting merchants and Greenlanders, 30 men went ashore from the three merchants ships, and one should assume that most of the crew remained on board to defend the ships.²²²

One of the Viking Age trading ships excavated from the Roskilde fjord in Denmark (*Skuldelev 1*) was analysed with dendrochronology, which revealed that it was built in Sogn in Western Norway ca. 1060. This was the heart of the region where emigrants to Iceland and Greenland had their ancestors. A replica was built at the Roskilde Museum, and it could carry a cargo of about 24 metric tons. A minimum crew was five to eight men, but two shifts may have been needed when crossing the Greenland Ocean in rough weather. The Danish archaeologists who excavated the ship claim that it was a *knarri* similar to those sailing to Greenland, but lack of ship finds from Greenland makes this impossible to verify.²²³

If 40 men were normal on trading ships sailing to Greenland, and only a third were needed as crew, most people on board must have been merchants and other passengers. The *Fostbroedra saga* describes how an Icelander called Steinar in Bergen hired a room on a ship ready to sail for Greenland. He went down to the quay, greeted the skipper, and asked "if you will give me passage to Greenland this summer?" The skipper asked for the man's name and who were his relatives (*kyn thitt*). Steinar gave a false name and did not reveal his relatives. Family identity was clearly a means to determine whether a man was trustworthy and would not create problems on board. The skipper replied: "You are unknown to me, and I have to discuss this with the crew". This was an indirect way of declining the request. Steinar understood this and he answered that "It will be best if I work on board like a crew member, so that your crew (*hásetar*) need not work for me". This decided the matter, and the skipper promised Steinar passage. Steinar went back to his lodgings in the town and returned with a large load of baggage. The ship's cargo was in the middle of the ship. Steinar found free space in the aft between the cargo and the rudder. There he deposited his luggage and slept at night. Steinar kept his promise and undertook his share of the work during the journey. He helped to bail the ship and mend the *rá* when it broke.[224] There was no clear-cut distinction between crew and passengers on Norse ships at least until the early 14th century. Passenger traffic may have been an important part of the skipper's earnings.

Ocean-going cargo-ships had to be protected during the winter they spent in Greenland. By onshore winds from the west, polar ice could drift into fjords, damaging the hull of the ships. Ice all over the ship could become so heavy that the ship sank or capsized. Along the western and northern coast of Norway it was normal to draw inshore- and ocean-going ships ashore in winter, and shelters were built for them. In Greenland more than one or two ocean-going ships per winter must have been rare. The sources mention three merchant ships at one time ca. 1130, and 1385–1387 four ships were driven by unfavourable winds to Greenland and stayed there two winters.[225] A ruin identified as a shelter for ocean-going ships at Brattahlid was "an oval hollow" which was "dug into the shingle" "about 20 m long, about 10 m wide, and about 0.5 m deep".[226] *Skuldelev 1* which was built in Western Norway ca. 1060 and mentioned earlier was 16 m long. The boathouse at Brattahlid may have been built to protect a similar ship.[227] Other such constructions may have been washed away since the sea level has risen. At Brattahlid the shoreline has been pushed back ca. 100 m since AD 1000.[228] If a large ship were to be drawn ashore, many people would have to be mobilised.

Inshore ships of middle size

In the struggle between Greenlanders and visiting merchants ca. 1130, a wise Greenlander counselled against laying the "small ships" of the Greenlanders alongside the "large ships" of the Norwegians and Icelanders (*at leggja smáskipum at storskipum*).[229] The saga author evidently thought that the Greenlanders did not own large ocean-going ships. This was the situation when the *Groenlendinga tháttr* was written ca. 1200 and probably also ca. 1130.

But the Greenlanders owned middle-sized inshore ships. In Norway they appear under several names. *Skuta* was the most common name for them. *Ferja* was a middle-sized cargo-ship which could sail along the Norwegian and Danish coasts into the Baltic. *Byrdingr* was mostly used about cargo-ships which sailed along the coast from Bergen to Northern Norway.[230] These middle-sized ships were clinker built in the same way as the larger ocean-going ships. They were sailed if possible but could be rowed. One of the ships excavated in the Skuldelev fjord (*Skuldelev 3*) was such an inshore craft. It could carry ca. 4.5 tons of cargo, about one-fifth of the ocean-going ship *Skuldelev 1*.[231]

Norse Greenlanders used the same types of inshore craft as in Norway and Denmark. "Sigurdr Njálsson was [a] Greenlander. He often went hunting in autumn along the uninhabited eastern coast. He was a skilled seafarer. On his ship they were fifteen men". Later his ship is called *ferja*.[232] One should imagine seven men rowing at each side, and skipper Sigurdr sitting at the helm. The *tháttr* was written ca. 1200 about events which had taken place ca. 1130. Some 330 years later, ca. 1360, Ivar Bárdarson also describes hunting at the uninhabited coast east of Herjolvsnes, and he names several fjords and islands: Berrefjord, the fjord Öllumlengri, the port "Finn's booths" and Cross Island. It is not clear how far up the east coast these locations were. In 1942 no archaeological remains of Norsemen had been found north of Lindenow fjord.[233] These expeditions may have created a permanent demand for inshore ships of middle size.

Fostbroedra saga tells the story of the two Greenlanders Skufr and Bjarni who had been the guests of the grandson of Eirik Raudi at Brattahlid at Christmas. They owned a farm at the opposite side of the Eiriksfjord and crossed the fjord in their "ship" which is later called *ferja*. There was no quay, and when someone needed to enter the *ferja*, it was laid close to the shore and a gangway was laid from the shore to the ship's gunwale.[234] This was practical since the difference between ebb and flow is great in Greenland. The ship was evidently rowed by Skufr's and Bjarni's servants.

In the same saga it is told that a rich widow called Thordis in Einarsfjord had a dream telling her where her enemy was hidden. "She rose in the middle of night, took a *skuta* which she owned and entered it with fifteen men".[235] One should assume that Thordis was a passenger, her son sat at the helm and seven men rowed at each side. The crew of Thordis' *skuta* and Sigurdr Njálsson's *ferja* were the same size. Later that night they met the chieftain at Brattahlid who joined them in his own ship. He had 20 men on his ship because he wanted to outnumber Thordis.[236] It is not said how many of his men were oarsmen and how many were passengers, but his ship may have been of the same size as Thordis'. When the *ferja* was sailed, a smaller crew was needed. The plot in another saga, Kroka Ref's saga, is fiction from the early 14th century, but its information that seven men sailed along the Greenland coast in a *ferju* may be realistic.[237]

When the chieftain Thorgrim Trolle visited the Gardar Thing, he had several armed men on board his ship. It was run aground at the shore (*renndi at landi*), probably to be drawn ashore later.[238] It must have been a *ferja* or *skuta*.

The main conclusions from this section are that medium-sized inshore ships existed in Greenland which were manned by around 14 oarsmen and were meant for cargoes and passengers. They were used for transport of people along the Greenland fjords, for hunting expeditions to the east coast and possibly to bring walrus products from the Disco region to the settlements in autumn. All ships of this middle size were owned by Greenlanders.

Small boats for use in the fjords

Along the western and northern coast of Norway almost every farm had at least one small boat for fishing and transport of people, goods and domestic animals. They varied in size and could have four, six or eight oars. In Greenland there is only evidence for the type with six oars, the sexæringr. It was normally rowed by three men; one man would then sit on a thwart (a wooden seat) with one oar in each hand. It could also be rowed by six men, two men would sit on each thwart, each of them with both hands on one oar. This would make the journey speedier.

Figure 4.3 A sexæringr with a crew of five from Trøndelag on the Atlantic coast of Norway, photographed ca. 1900.

This is the only boat type mentioned in written sources for fishing in the fjords, for rowing to the walrus hunt in the Disco region and for voyages of discovery further north towards Melville Bay. It was indispensable for communication between farms in this thinly populated area. The boat had a crew of three to six men depending on the circumstances.

The sexæringr continued to be used in Norway until the motorboat took over after ca. 1900; the one in the picture was one of the last. There is no reason to think it had changed its shape since the Middle Ages. A single square large sail was the norm during the whole period. With a crew of five it could be both rowed and sailed effectively.

Copyright: Woxengs samlinger, Rørvik, Norway.

A widow living on a chieftain's farm travelled with five servants; they must have rowed a sexæringr.[239] In most examples quoted in this section the sexæringr was rowed. But in the account of the voyage towards Melville Bay it is said that the sexæringr was sailed part of the way.[240]

The sexæringr was used in the walrus hunt in the Disco region, fishing for cod and char in the fjords, communication between Norse farms[241] and to visit the Gardar Thing. The distance from the Western settlement to the Disco region and the walrus hunt is given in the number of days six men needed to row a sexæringr. Fishing on the fjords in the settlements seems to have been done with three men.[242]

Did the farms along the Greenland fjords include boathouses (*naust*) for rowing boats? The authors of *Fostbroedra saga* and *Flomanna saga* thought so.

Thormod Kolbrunarskald sought to kill four brothers living at a chieftain's farm in Einarsfjord. When Thormod arrived at the farm, three of the brothers were out fishing. It is said explicitly that the boat had three "rooms" for rowers, and that the three brothers rowed it. This means that it was a sexæringr. The forward rowing-room is called *hals*, this means that this boat could also be sailed, but when fishing on the fjord it was most convenient to use oars. Thormod hid close to the boat's *naust*, and in the evening the sexæringr with the three brothers returned. They would evidently have drawn the sexæringr ashore in front of the boathouse or into it, if Thormod had not killed them all.[243]

At another farm[244] Thormod went to the *naust* and saw that it was empty. He assumed that servants on the farm had rowed out fishing, and he hid under some seaweed. In the evening he heard the sound of oars, and the servants came ashore. One of them said: "There will be fine weather tomorrow, and we will set out to row again then. We will not drag the boat ashore, but let it float in the harbour this night". So they did and walked home. The saga author evidently inserted this conversation to explain why the boat was not drawn ashore, as was normally done. Thormod would have great problems drawing a sexæringr alone down to the sea. Now he "went to where the boat was moored, untied it, and sat down at the oars". One man could row a sexæringr, even if the speed would be slow.[245]

The hero of *Flomanna saga* walked across the southern tip of the Greenland inland glacier and the first sign of civilization he saw when he reached the Herjolvsnes area was a boathouse.[246] Few boathouses have been found in archaeological excavations in Norse Greenland.[247] As mentioned earlier, the sea may have swallowed many. Koch-Madsen thinks he has been able to identify seven in the Vatnahverfi. The median length of these boathouses was 7 m, and the sexæringr was normally 6–8 m long.[248]

The boat-types used in Greenland were Norwegian, and they could be bought there. Every ship crossing the Greenland Ocean had at least one small boat in tow, functioning as a lifeboat.[249] *Thorlakssudin* sank in the open ocean. All on board entered the lifeboat but some died before they reached the Norse settlements in Greenland.[250] The Icelandic skipper Bjarni Grimolvsson was driven off course when sailing from Vinland to Greenland, and his ship started to sink off Ireland. There were 40 men on board, but there was room for only half of them in the lifeboat – they reached Ireland and survived. The other half drowned when the ship sank.[251] We are told that the Greenlander Thorgrim Trolle's ship was served by two "after-boats", probably because he had 40 men on board.[252] In some cases a *skuta* may have been used.

Since merchant ships in Greenland often were anchored at a distance from the shore, the after-boat was also used to transport goods and people ashore, and in that function the boat was called a *kaupskipsbátinn,* "the boat of the merchant ship". The ocean ships were difficult to manoeuvre in narrow waters or close to the shore, so in such situations the boat(s) was used to tow the ship.[253] The *eptirbát* could be filled with merchandise – Leiv Eiriksson filled his with grapes when he returned to Greenland from Vinland.[254]

Skippers are likely to have bought many after-boats in Norway where suitable timber and boatbuilding skills were of a high quality. They were towed to Greenland and sold there.

Driftwood as raw material in boatbuilding

The terms used for ships and boats in Norse Greenland were imported from Norway: knarri, skuta, ferja, sexæringr and skipsbátr.[255] Ships and boats used in Greenlandic waters belonged to a Norwegian shipbuilding tradition. Did Greenlanders develop an expertise in building them or were they bought from Norway?

In Norway it was common practice to build ships and boats close to forests where the shipbuilder could select and fell timber with the size and form he needed. Greenland lacked forests with trees large enough for ship- and boat-building. If the Greenlanders were to build their ships and boats in Greenland, they would have to use driftwood originating from Siberian rivers.

The Norwegian explorer Fridtjof Nansen was to my knowledge the first scholar to comment on the use of driftwood for shipbuilding. He had personal experience with shipping in the Polar region and had lived one winter in Nuuk. He did not raise doubts about the quality of driftwood but did not think there were sufficient quantities of it. "Driftwood would not go very far in building boats, to say nothing of larger vessels". There was also "great scarcity of rivets and iron nails in Greenland".[256]

The Danish archaeologist Roussell had a high opinion of the quality of driftwood. "The timber suffers no injury from its long journey . . . there is no question of qualitative deterioration, enclosed by ice as it is for most of the voyage from Siberia . . . in a cold climate and impregnated with salt it can last for long".[257] He does not comment explicitly on its use in shipbuilding.

In the last decades some archaeologists have lowered the value of driftwood. The Danish archaeologist Joel Berglund claimed that driftwood found at GUS could be "riddled with holes made by shipworms", and that "wormholes are usually found in Siberian driftwood".[258] Berglund has not verified that the wood with wormholes found at GUS was driftwood, that the worms entered the wood while the logs floated in the North Atlantic, or that most driftwood had wormholes. The Canadian archaeologist Valerie Pilgrim in her MA thesis accepts Berglund's conclusion, and adds that "Driftwood is hard, inflexible and often cracked, making it a difficult material for use in boat building".[259] The empirical basis for the last claim is not clear. Berglund's and Pilgrim's claims, even if unverified, have made it necessary to discuss if driftwood has the same qualities as fresh wood.

Pre-modern Iceland had a boatbuilding tradition despite its lack of forests, and the raw material was driftwood or imported timber, mainly from Norway. They combined wood of different origins in the same ship. Ludvik Kristjansson in his *Islenzkir sjávarhættir* gives numerous examples from written sources that boats for fishing and transport were built from driftwood. He claims that "in the Middle Ages boats were mainly built from driftwood".[260] The boat-builder Jon Ragnar Dadason from Siglufjord in northern Iceland has informed me that he has built a boat of 6 m from drift timber, and knows boats with three, four and five pairs of oars built from such timber.

In Norway and Iceland there are still living boatbuilding traditions. My main oral source has been Jon Bojer Godal, who was a teacher in the building of traditional Norwegian boats and their use; but also Per Johnson who has run a sawmill on Svalbard where his main raw material was driftwood from Siberian rivers, Jon Ragnar Dadason mentioned earlier, and Gunnar Eldjarn who builds traditional boats in Tromsø.

The logs arriving in West Greenland would have been in salt water for several years. They would therefore have been impregnated with salt, which protects the wood and the future boat against rot and shipworms. Here driftwood has an advantage compared to freshly felled wood. Driftwood is also protected against shipworms because growth and reproduction of the worms only occur if temperatures are 11–25°C.[261] Water temperatures in the Arctic are almost always below 10°C. The wood with wormholes in GUS may have been infected in more southern waters. The Icelandic skipper Bjarni Grimolvsson tried to sail from Vinland to the Eastern Settlement but ended up in the ocean west of Ireland. There they found themselves in waters infested with maggots (*komu in madk-sjo*), and the ship started to sink under them. They had a shipboat "which was treated with tar made from seal-blubber, because then sea-worms can't penetrate the wood". The destiny of the 40 passengers was described earlier.[262]

A log which has lain for years on a beach may dry up and develop cracks. If a log should have wormholes or cracks, an experienced boat-builder will discover this before he starts working on it. Per Jonsson on Svalbard did not experience this as a problem.

Are boards made from driftwood less flexible when used in the rounded hull of a clinker built boat? Jonsson and Godal claim that numerous hulls of this type have been built from driftwood without later problems of this kind. Dadason has bought timber from Norway and Sweden but claims that "good drift wood fresh from the sea" is better. Only fresh wood which has come ashore after bad weather is used for boatbuilding in Iceland. Driftwood which has lain on the beach for years becoming dry is only used for housebuilding.

Boards in the hull may crack if the boat is sailed fast in rough and choppy seas. It is not the experience of boatbuilders that this is more likely to happen if the boards are made of driftwood. Dadason claims that this depends on the quality of the wood regardless of whether it is driftwood or newly felled wood.

Driftwood was also used for housebuilding and firewood. This made the demand for driftwood significantly higher than the availability. As mentioned earlier, Hans Egede arrived in the Nuuk area in 1721, and after two years he was complaining that they had to journey further and further away to find the driftwood they needed.[263] The Norse stayed for more than 425 years. Grenlandic boat-builders had to row along the shores looking for suitable logs or find them by disentangling large piles of driftwood. This could become time consuming. Availability of sufficient quantities of suitable wood must have been a problem. But the hypothesis that the quality of driftwood compared to fresh wood was a problem, is not supported by available empirical material. Boatbuilders with the right skills and training would know how to put driftwood to its correct use.

Were ships and boats built in Norse Greenland?

There are no indications that ocean-going ships were built in Greenland, but repairs were certainly made. At the farm Narsaq in the Eastern Settlement the archaeologists found part of a rib (53 × 10.5 × 10.5 cm) which must have belonged to "an ocean-going ship" (*hafskip*). The piece was made of larch (*Larix*), which at that time did not grow in Norway, but was abundant in northern Siberia. This makes it likely that the rib was made of driftwood,[264] and was the result of repairs made in Greenland or Iceland. Few fragments of ocean-going ships have been found in Greenland since these ships belonged almost exclusively to Norwegians and Icelanders,[265] and their ships were repaired and broken up at home if possible.

It must have been possible to buy inshore ships of middle size in Norway and tow them across the Greenland Ocean as *eptirbát*, but some *skutur* and *ferjur* were built in Greenland. Asmundr Kastandratzi in 1189 was on a hunting expedition just east of Cape Farewell at "Cross Island" and "Finn's booths", and afterwards crossed the Denmark Strait to Breidafjord in Iceland. He owned a ship which had a crew of 13, which may have been a *skuta* or *ferja*. At this time it was normal to join the boards of the hull together with iron rivets, but this ship only had wooden pegs and in some places the boards were bound together with animal sinews. The ship had evidently been made in Greenland where iron was expensive. The following year (1190) Asmundr continued towards Norway, but his ship perished at sea.[266] The contemporary *Sturlunga Saga* comments that many Icelandic men perished on Asmundr's ship, and that caused "great harm" (*mikill skada*).[267] The author indirectly blames Asmundr for having attempted to cross the Greenland Ocean in a ship which was not fit for purpose. It is not said whether Asmundr was an Icelander or Greenlander, but the context makes the latter alternative most likely.

In 1347 a ship sailed from Greenland to Markland (Labrador) and from there it drifted to Iceland. It was "smaller than the smallest ships which sail between Iceland and Norway" and there were 17 men on board. This may also have been a *skuta* or *ferja* built in Greenland. It lacked an anchor, which made it difficult to prevent the ship from drifting ashore when they approached a coast.[268] These Greenlanders sailed on a different ship to Bergen in the following year, and from there they are most likely to have returned to Greenland.[269] They may have feared that it was unsafe to cross the Denmark Strait in their own ship.

The ships from 1189 and 1347 are likely to have been built in Greenland. As long as they were used inshore, they functioned. But in these two instances they attempted to cross the Greenland Ocean and the Davis Strait and that was a challenge they were not built for. These medium-sized ships made it possible for

192 *Trade and shipping*

Greenlanders to organise long-distance hunting expeditions on their own without any help from Norwegian or Icelandic ships.

Several species of wood have been identified in archaeological remains of sexærings. Larch was driftwood from Siberia,[270] pine and oak point to Norway,[271] while spruce may have originated in both regions. Boats made from larch must have been built in Greenland and those of pine and oak in Norway. A piece of wood "which presumably has served as the foot of a mast on a small boat" was found at the chieftain's farm at Sandnes. I assume "small boat" in practice means sexæringr.[272] It was made of larch, which means that the small boat to which it had belonged was made of driftwood found in Greenland.[273] In an article from 1992 ten boat fragments from Narsaq in the Eastern and Sandnes in the Western Settlement are examined. Six were larch, two spruce and two could not be identified. None was made of pine. Small boats in use in Greenland seem to have been mostly made from driftwood.[274]

At the farm Umiviarsuit close to Sandnes a board was found which had once been part of the hull of a vessel of unknown size. On one side it had small holes into which had been put baleen strips plugged in with wood. This board had evidently been sewn together with another board with baleen thread.[275] This is the same sewing technique as used on Asmundr Kastandratzi's ship in 1189, but then animal sinews were used. The Icelandic Annals thought that this technique made large ships unsafe for crossing the Greenland Ocean, but it may have been safe for a sexæringr along the fjords or a *skuta* inshore.

Did Norse Greenlanders cross the Davis Strait to build small boats and even medium-sized ships on the western shore? The ideal environment for a boat-builder was where he could walk around in a forest, pick out and fell suitable trees, and build his boat or ship on the shore close to the forest. Such an environment could be found in Labrador. They could also bring with them iron bars or "bloom" iron from Greenland and forge the iron rivets they needed in Labrador.[276] The coast of the Western Settlement was ice free all year. It would have been feasible for boat-builders to sail to Labrador in early spring, work for some weeks and then return with their boat or ship.[277] But so far there is no evidence that it was actually done. Archaeologists have not found a single piece of wood in Greenland which they identify as American.[278] It must have been a problem that in the summer season all hands were needed at the farm.

There can be no doubt that the Greenlanders possessed the skills necessary to build a sexæringr from driftwood for communications along the fjords, transport of hay and domestic animals, fishing and hunting internally in the settlements. They could also build ships for inshore voyages. The Norsemen had packhorses, and in the hills behind Brattahlid, in the Sandnes-Austmannadal-Kapisillit area and Vatnahverfi overland transport was important. Communications did not prevent the Norse Greenlanders from producing the food they needed in Greenland and organising themselves internally. But for exchange of goods and people across the North Atlantic they depended on foreign shipping, in practice ocean ships built in Norway.

4 Crossing the Greenland Ocean

The Norse Greenlanders mastered sea communications internally in Greenland on their own. But crossing the North Atlantic or "The Greenland Ocean" (*Grænalands haf*) as it is called in Norse sources, brought challenges which they needed external expertise to overcome.

Bergen: the commercial centre of the Norse realm

Bergen had no competitor as the commercial hub of the Norse realm. Communications between the Norwegian church and the Gardar see went via Bergen; at least this was so in the two known cases from 1308 and 1341.[279] The Gardar see seems to have sent its goods to the archbishop's warehouse in Bergen, where buying and selling took place.[280]

Some peasants living at the estuary of the Trondheim fjord owned ships on which they traded with Greenland, but the merchandise which they brought from Greenland, was sold in Bergen.[281] Trondheim had an independent foreign trade until ca. 1310–1320, but the exchanges with Greenland went via Bergen. Walrus products had specialised markets, and the potential buyers were to be found in Bergen.

Bergen had direct shipping contacts with numerous ports around the North Sea and the Baltic.[282] Walrus ivory was transported from Bergen to markets in Flanders and further to Northern France, to England, to the Rhine area and to Denmark.[283] Imports from West European countries excavated in Greenland do not verify that there were direct shipping lanes between Greenland and these countries.[284]

Medieval navigators would often bring sailing directions in which was described in words how to sail between ports. One such *periplus* for the North Atlantic has been transcribed in the Icelandic *Landnámabok*. The oldest extant transcript is from the second half of the 13th century.

Two sailing routes are described between Norway and Greenland. One went via Iceland, which is likely to have been the oldest one since the saga literature describes Iceland as a first step in the settlement of Greenland. The point of departure was the promontory Stad which is situated on the coast of western Norway midway between Bergen and Trondheim. From there the skipper was to sail westwards and slightly northwards for seven days and nights arriving at Horn[285] on the south-eastern coast of Iceland. Stad was at 62°10'N and Horn at 64°10'N. From there they sailed along the southern coast of Iceland until they could turn northwards to Snæfellsnes on the west coast. If they sailed from Snæfellsnes straight west they would reach the uninhabited eastern coast of Greenland. This coast was followed southwards to Cape Farewell, but at a certain distance from the land to avoid the ice. There they turned north-west, and after one day and night of sailing they would arrive at the mountain Hvarf under which was the southernmost Norse farm Herjolvsnes and a port called Sandhöfn. By normal conditions the sailing time from Snæfellsnes to "Hvarf on Greenland"[286] was four days and nights.[287]

194   Trade and shipping

The alternative sailing route went from Bergen directly to "Hvarf on Greenland". Bergen developed into the commercial centre of the Norse realm at the end of the 11th century, and the direct voyage is likely to have its origin or at least have become dominant from that time. The ship would then sail from Bergen out of Herdlefjorden to the small island of Hernar just south of Fedje. This island lies in the open ocean, and from it one can sail in a straight line westwards to Greenland. One will then sail so far north of Shetland that it is possible to see land there by clear weather. Further on, the ship will sail so far south of the Faroes that the horizon will appear to stand half way up the mountains' side (*sva at sjor er i midjum hlidum*). The ship will sail south of Iceland so near that they meet birds and whales; another version of *Landnámabok* says 12 hours of sailing south of Iceland.[288] Hernar outside Bergen lies at 60°40'N and Cape Farewell is slightly further south at 60°N. This means that if they kept to the same latitude they would touch Greenland's east coast slightly north of Cape Farewell.

Landnámabok does not tell how many days and nights it would take to sail directly from Bergen to Hvarf, probably because the book's Icelandic public was mainly interested in distances from Iceland. But it took seven days to sail in a straight line from Stad in Norway to Horn in Iceland, and four days to sail from Snæfellsnes to Hvarf. The sailing time between Horn and Snæfellsnes along Iceland's southern coast is unknown. One should expect that it would take somewhat more than 12 days and nights of active sailing to cover the whole distance Bergen–Greenland. This is confirmed by a letter sent from Archbishop Eystein to the pope ca. 1161–1172, where the distance between Norway and Greenland is estimated at 12 days and nights.[289] These are days and nights of active sailing; in practice the journey in most cases lasted longer because the ship had to wait for favourable winds.

Landnámabok gives a framework and a point of departure for a discussion of the shipping to and from Norse Greenland. What is known from other sources about the destination of ships arriving in and leaving the island?

Ships sailed from Iceland to Greenland with emigrants, but there is no evidence that they sailed with merchandise. Between Greenland and Iceland there was no trade for the simple reason that the Icelanders produced no goods which the Greenlanders wanted to buy, and the Greenlanders did not produce goods which Icelanders wanted to buy. But there is evidence that ships sailed via Iceland and made a stopover there when they sailed between Greenland and Norway. Thorgrim Trolle was Greenlandic chieftain and merchant. He must have sailed from Norway to Langanes on north-eastern Iceland, and continued from there westwards to Hraunhöfn on the north coast. From there he crossed the Denmark Strait and arrived in Einarsfjord. His ship was fully loaded with merchandise, evidently from Norway. Thorgrim chose the shipping lane along the northern coast of Iceland because he had a companion who was from north Iceland, and who owned half the ship and its cargo.[290] The story was written 200 years after the events and may express what Icelanders ca. 1220 considered to be reasonable.

When ships sailed via Iceland they always seem to have had special reasons for doing so. In 1385 four Icelandic merchant ships sailed from Norway to Iceland, but they were driven by unfavourable winds to Greenland where they stayed for two winters and probably bought goods from Greenlanders. When they left Greenland, they had on board goods bought in Bergen to be sold in Iceland, and goods bought in Greenland to be sold in Bergen. They returned to Iceland in 1387 and continued to Bergen in 1388 where they sold the Greenland wares.[291]

The ship carrying the bishop of Greenland to Norway was wrecked at the Icelandic coast in 1262 with the bishop on board. It seems that his ship followed the shipping lane via Iceland described in *Landnámabok*. The ship must have sailed from Cape Farewell to Snaefellsnes on the west coast of Iceland, and from there southwards to Reykjanes and then eastwards along the southern coast of Iceland where it was driven ashore by unfavourable winds and currents and was wrecked at Herdisarvik on the southern coast of Reykjanes.[292]

In 1266 a ship with unknown owners followed the same route but was wrecked at Hitarnes between Snæfellsnes and Reykjanes. Some 41 people drowned, and the disaster was still remembered 350 years later.[293] It is striking that two ships sailing from Greenland to Norway were wrecked in the same region of Iceland within a period of four years. One could suspect that the Greenlanders were using a route which was unfamiliar to them. Herdisarvik and Hitarnes are near the largest Icelandic see of Skálholt. It is possible that the sailors' intention was to make a stopover at the coast near Skálholt because the bishop of Gardar and other prominent clerics from Greenland wanted to confer with their colleague at Skálholt. The 1260s were crucial years for Greenland as well as Iceland. The two countries consented to become part of the Norwegian realm, but it was not quite clear what this meant in practice. Skippers sailing from Greenland may have been more used to the direct route from Cape Farewell to Bergen, and they would not have been used to making stopovers in small Icelandic harbours.

The Greenlandic skipper and merchant Skufr sailed the direct route between Norway and Greenland both ways.[294] There are several examples where Icelandic merchants also sailed from Greenland directly to Norway if they had goods to sell, and they did not go via their homeland. The last ship which is known to have visited Greenland was Icelandic and sailed from Norway for Iceland in 1406, but was driven to Greenland.[295] In 1410 it left and sailed directly to Norway.[296] The Icelander Thorfinn Karlsefni loaded his ship with valuable goods in Vinland and Greenland ca. AD 1005, and sailed from Greenland directly to Norway where he sold the cargo.[297] The sagas used are realistic, even if parts of them are fiction.

Individual Icelanders who wanted to travel between Iceland and Greenland sometimes did so via Norway, probably because ships did not sail directly between Greenland and Iceland. As mentioned earlier, the Icelander Hauk had to take this detour ca. 1203, according to the reliable *Sturlunga saga*.[298] *Bárdar saga Snæfellsáss* tells of an Icelandic merchant who stayed at Brattahlid, then sailed to Norway and remained there two winters before returning to his farm in Iceland. The plot of this saga is fiction, but the author's ideas about merchants' travel patterns may mirror realities at the time of writing ca. 1300.[299] Audun is a character in an Icelandic *tháttr*. He was a passenger on a ship from Iceland to Norway, stayed one winter there, and next summer sailed to Greenland and stayed the second winter there.[300]

196 *Trade and shipping*

There are no indications that ships sailed from Greenland directly to the British Isles, Germany, Denmark or other destinations outside the Norse realm. Danish and American archaeologists still write about Greenland's trade and shipping going to "Europe". It would bring discussions to a more precise level if they started to use "Norway" and "Bergen". Bergen's foreign trade has been extensively discussed by Norwegian historians.[301]

Tackling the problems

The ships which crossed the Greenland Ocean in the period 985–1410 had one large square sail. This made it difficult, time consuming and often impossible to tack against the wind. It was not necessary to have the wind from behind in the sailing direction, but that was a great advantage. They often had to wait for favourable winds, sometimes for weeks. If the wind changed direction while the ship was on the open ocean, the skipper could be forced to do the same, and a ship on its way from Norway could end up in Ireland instead of Greenland. The Hollanders in the 16th century had many small sails on larger ships, which gave greater manoeuvrability in rougher seas.

The King's Mirror warns skippers to be prepared for damages and repairs on the open ocean and in foreign ports. On board should be 100–150 m of wadmal to repair the sail, many needles and sufficient quantities of thread. Large quantities of rivets of all types which were used in the ship, were necessary. So were axes, augers and all kinds of tools which are used in shipbuilding.[302]

Serious problems on the open ocean did not necessarily have fatal consequences if the crew had the necessary skills. *Fostbroedra saga* tells that on a voyage directly from Norway to Greenland the ship encountered a storm. The large beam called *rá* broke, which had the large square sail attached to it. This was the ship's only sail, and it blew over board. They luckily had strong ropes attached to *rá* and sail and could haul the sail back on board. Among the crew were men who could repair the *rá*, and they sailed on. The ships were not watertight, and it seems to have been standard procedure that the water had to be bailed out. One man stood in the bottom of the hull and filled a bucket with water, and he handed it up to another man who stood on the deck and poured it overboard. *Fostbroedra saga* makes us understand that this was heavy work, particularly on the long journey to Greenland. Passengers were expected to do the work of a crew member if they were physically able.[303]

Skippers sailing to Greenland used an instrument which was basically a vertical staff fastened to a horizontal staff to measure the sun's altitude when it was at its highest. After dark they could measure the altitude of the Pole Star. The measurements could be checked against tables of the altitude of these celestial bodies at different latitudes at different times of the year. In this way they controlled the ship's latitude. This was a predecessor to the Jacob's staff. They were also helped by a "sun-compass" until the 13th century, and a magnetic compass thereafter. These methods are well described in the two articles referred to in the footnote, and I see no reason to repeat it here.[304] Skippers had no means of measuring their longitude. They could measure how far north they were, but not how far west. Often unfavourable winds or clouds hiding the sun and the Pole Star would make precise navigation impossible. They could then "discover" Newfoundland or Labrador against their will.

The most serious problem when the cargo-ships approached the Greenland coast was the ice. In spring large and thick ice floes from the polar region would drift along the eastern coast of Greenland, turn round Cape Farewell and continue northwards along the western coast as far as Paamiut. The polar ice will normally block access to the Eastern Settlement until late summer. In autumn and winter the local fjord ice made it problematic to visit the fjords of both settlements.[305] The best description of the problems with the polar ice is found in *The King's Mirror*:

> When one leaves the Greenland Ocean and approaches the Greenland coast, there is so much floating ice that there is nothing like it anywhere in the world. Some of the floes are 4–5 ells thick (ca. 2 metres), and are found so far from the shore that it takes four days or more to cross the ice and reach the coast. But there is less of this ice the further north one travels [on the west coast]. Ships should sail northwards along the west coast until the ice ends, and the ship should not turn landwards until it reaches that point. But it often happens that people turn their ship towards the shore too early, and therefore get caught among the ice floes. Some of them have perished there, but others have escaped. The sensible thing to do if one gets caught in the ice, is to put the small lifeboats on the ice and draw them from one ice floe to the next until one reaches the shore. The ocean cargo-ship has to be left in the ice, and ship and cargo are lost.[306]

A skipper in 1389 relates that they met "great icebergs and ice floes and their ship was severely damaged".[307]

Hans Egede and his son Niels give additional information. Polar ice normally blocked the access to the Eastern Settlement from March until the last part of July. In June and July winds from the north "blow the ice from the coast, and from this time the western Greenland coast is quite free from ice".[308] "Ships should not seek the coast until the month of August, because at that time there will normally be no ice there".[309] Today's scholars confirm these descriptions, and modern shipping has unproblematic access to the former Eastern Settlement only from July.[310] The coast of the Western Settlement, however, is ice free all year.[311]

Approximate sailing dates are known for two Norse cargo-ships which left Bergen for Greenland. On 22 June 1308 the bishop of Bergen wrote a letter to his colleague in Greenland, and we should expect that the ship left Bergen shortly afterwards.[312] If winds and weather were reasonably favourable, they could expect to reach the coast outside the Eastern Settlement a month or so later at the end of July. The bishop of Bergen issued a safe conduct for the priest

Ivar Bárdarson on 8 August 1341 for a voyage to Greenland. Again we should assume that the ship left shortly afterwards. If wind and weather were reasonably favourable he would have arrived at Gardar around 1 September.[313] A ship arrived in Bergen from Greenland shortly before 24 July 1325. The Norwegian merchants must have left Greenland around 1 July, possibly from the Western Settlement which was then ice free.[314] Merchants always stayed in Greenland for at least one winter. The Greenlandic merchant Skufr arrived at his home farm in Eiriksfjord "late in the autumn" and stayed there three winters before he returned to Norway.[315]

Our best description of a merchant visit in the Eastern Settlement is found in *Groenlendinga tháttr*. Three ships arrived from Norway in the summer. The merchants traded in the following period and then hired lodgings at several farms during the winter. The following summer they prepared to leave from Einarsfjord. "Then ice drifted in and covered all fjords". It became impossible for the merchant ships to leave. "But just before the end of the month all the ice drifted away, and the merchants could leave Greenland". All three ships arrived safely in Norway.[316] The ice must have been polar ice and this indicates that they left at the end of July when the polar ice was about to disappear from the coast for the season.

Norse skippers tackled the challenge of crossing the open Greenland Ocean with the help of a compass and an instrument for measuring their northern latitude. Even more important was nautical experience, particularly of the annual variations in sea ice, and what to do if caught between ice floes around Greenland, and how to repair a damaged rá and sail on the open ocean. This was knowledge accumulated through generations.

Those who failed to reach their destination

Crossing the Greenland Ocean meant hard work for the crew, an uncomfortable meeting with rough seas for all, seasickness for many and it was dangerous. Thorbjørn was an emigrant from Iceland to Greenland.

> They sailed from Iceland, but when they reached the open ocean the wind abated, there was fog, and they did not know where they were. They had problems all summer. People fell ill and Orm and his wife Halldis died, and so did half of the others on board. The sea was heavy and they endured hardships and misery. They finally arrived at Herjolvsnes in Greenland just before the start of the winter.[317]

Seasickness over a long period can weaken the body's resistance to other diseases, and indirectly cause death. In a coffin at Herjolvsnes churchyard a rune-stick was found which said that "This woman, whose name was Gudveig, was laid overboard in the Greenland Ocean (*Grænalands haf*)". She may have suffered a similar fate to some of the passengers on Thorbjørn's ship.[318]

Many ships perished on the open ocean.[319] One of them was Asmundr Kastandratzi's ship which sailed from Greenland to Norway via Iceland.[320] The cargo-ship of the Icelandic diocese of Skálholt was called *Thorlaks-sudinne*. On its way to or from Norway it ran into rough weather and "sank in the open ocean" (*forgieck i hafue*) not far from Greenland. "All managed to enter the [life]boat, but many died later". In Greenland they met a merchant ship called *Olavssudin* which in 1383 returned to Norway with survivors from *Thorlaks-sudinne* on board.[321]. It must have been exceptional that the crew managed to row a small boat over the open ocean and along dangerous coasts in stormy weather and reach Norse settlers in Greenland. Ocean-going ships had at least one lifeboat in tow, in this case it saved lives. Sometimes a man would sit in the lifeboat, probably to steer it and prevent it from capsizing. If the boat capsized anyway, it could mean death by drowning for the man in the boat.[322]

The most dangerous part of the journey was to navigate close to the coast. When they crossed the open ocean they had to sail day and night, but when they tacked along the coast they often went ashore and slept in a tent at night.[323] The light northern summer nights would, however, permit sailing.

In 1126 three ships left Norway bound for Greenland via Iceland. Bishop Arnaldr's ship seems to have sailed the shipping lane to Horn on south-eastern Iceland.[324] From there they sailed along the southern coast, but the winds were contrary, and when they arrived at Eyjafjall they went ashore and spent the winter with a local chieftain. The other ships did not arrive in Iceland, but some said that the skipper had probably changed his mind and taken the direct route to Greenland. In reality the other ships had sailed past Iceland and reached the uninhabited East Greenland coast, but had been unable to turn south. They were driven ashore where one of their two ships was wrecked. They were unable to continue the journey, perhaps because of ice problems, starved to death and were found a few years later.[325]

Two ships on their way in the other direction from Greenland to Norway were wrecked on the coast of Iceland in 1262 and 1266 respectively.[326] A *knarri* on its way from Greenland was wrecked on the Norwegian coast in 1367.[327]

Ships which sailed from Norway to a destination in the northern fjords of Iceland could get an involuntary and rough meeting with Greenland instead. The Icelandic priest Ingemund in 1189 was to sail from Bergen to Eyjafjördr in northern Iceland where he had his home. He is likely to have sailed from Bergen to Langanes on north-eastern Iceland, from there the ship navigated at some distance along the rugged northern coast of Iceland, the intention being to turn south when they arrived at the same longitude as Eyjafjördr. They evidently had not been able to make this turn because of contrary winds or mist. The ship seems to have continued westwards until it was wrecked on the uninhabited eastern coast of Greenland, where their bodies were found 14 years later.[328]

Ingemund's brother Einar also had his ship wrecked on the East Greenland coast not far from Cape Farewell. This time the ship's port of departure or destination is not reported, but he was probably also on his way to Eyjafjördr. After the shipwreck those on board divided themselves into two households, one of them ran out of food and attacked Einar's group. Einar and two others escaped and tried to walk over the glacier. They died when they had only one day's journey left to reach the southernmost farms in Herjolvsnes parish. They were found the following year. The author assures his readers that the story is reliable because he had heard it from "Styrkár Sigmundsson from Greenland" who "knew much history and could be relied on to tell the truth".[329]

The sources used above to exemplify how dangerous the crossing of the Greenland Ocean was, are mostly taken from the reliable *Sturlunga saga* and Icelandic Annals, and the stories should be seen as verified. Some examples are taken from *Fostbroedra* saga which is a realistic *Islendingasaga*, and here it should be assumed that similar events were known to the author. But there are also stories which should be seen as manifestations of fears.

At this time whales were numerous along the Greenland coast and may have scared sailors and other travellers. In the Greenland Ocean there is said to be both male and female sea monsters which could predict the future. From their conduct the seamen could learn when there would be a storm, and whether people on board the ship would drown or survive. Sometimes the waves were like high mountains and could break against the ship from three sides at the same time, according to *The King's Mirror*. But, says the author sensibly, God must have saved some from this trap, otherwise nobody would have survived to tell us about it![330] The Greenlanders were not trained seafarers and feared the sea. This may have been different in the first decades when contacts with Norwegian shipbuilding and seafaring traditions were kept alive.

In the 14th and 15th centuries sagas were written which were pure fiction. In two of them, *Flomanna saga* and *Jökuls tháttr Buasonar*, shipwrecks on the east coast of Greenland are the starting point for what today would be called horror stories. People are left alone in an inhospitable natural environment, they starve to death, murder each other, ghosts appear, they walk across the inland ice in desperate attempts to save their lives, and they struggle with and kill dirty and stinking witches and sorcerers. The latter may have the Inuit as models, but if so these prejudices are those of the authors and their readers in Iceland who never had seen an Inuit, and not necessarily those of the Norse Greenlanders.

Crossing the Greenland Ocean was dangerous, but the seafarers had a rational attitude to these challenges. They concentrated their voyages on the month of August when ice did not prevent access to the Eastern Settlement. Members of the crew had skills and tools to repair the ship in open seas if necessary. They preferred the open ocean and avoided coastlines which were dangerous in rough weather. But beneath these rational preparations were fears which resulted in imaginary horror visions.

How many ships reached Greenland annually?

The Icelandic Annals only register voyages to and from Greenland if there is something special about them which attracted the interest of Icelandic clerics. This could be that the bishop of Gardar was on board, that a ship on its way to or from Iceland was driven by contrary winds to Greenland, or if a dramatic shipwreck which cost human life happened on the Greenland coast or on the way to or from Greenland. Normal merchant voyages are not registered. These annals are our main source for quantifying shipping to Greenland.

The most attractive exports from Greenland were walrus tusks, ropes and hides. They were durable and could be stored for many years without deterioration in quality. So the Greenland trade did not demand annual or regular visits from foreign merchants.

There are a few examples of more than one ship sailing to Greenland in the same year. The skippers Thorfinn Karlsefni and Bjarni Grimolvsson visited Brattahlid with their ships ca. AD 1005.[331] The Norwegian merchant Arnbjørn owned two ocean-going ships which he sailed to Greenland at the same time in 1126.[332] These seem to be normal trading voyages, and the motive for sailing two together may have been security as the risk of being shipwrecked was very real. The two ships in 1126 ended their voyage on the deserted east coast of Greenland. Ca. 1130 two Norwegian and one Icelandic merchant vessels sailed together to the settlements. Here security evidently was the motive since their main purpose was to initiate legal proceedings against powerful opponents at the Gardar Thing.[333] Even later several ships came to Greenland at the same time, but all of them were on their way to or from Iceland and were driven off course by unfavourable wind and weather to Greenland. This was so for two ships in 1382[334] and four ships in 1384.[335]

The source material for the Greenland trade is very scarce, and it is therefore not remarkable that only three examples are extant from the four Norse centuries of more than one ship arriving in Norse Greenland at the same time. But it is remarkable that all three are from sagas written ca. 1190–1220 about events taking place ca. 1005–1130. The reason for this may be that walrus products were most attractive to merchants in this early period. But source criticism warns against drawing conclusions. In most cases only one ship is mentioned, but this could be because only this ship was relevant to the story to be told; unnamed ships may have arrived the same year.

In the 12th century it seems to have become increasingly common for ships to take the direct route from Bergen to Cape Farewell, and then it was less likely that they were mentioned in written sources which were mainly Icelandic. Much of the later information concerned ships which were on their way between Norway and Iceland, but were forced to Greenland by unfavourable weather conditions.

Years could pass between each visit from merchant ships. In 1346 the Archbishop of Nidaros informed the pope that some of the North Atlantic dioceses could only be reached by ship every third year.[336] Greenland must have been one of them.

In 1308 bishop Arni of Bergen sent a letter to his colleague in Gardar, where he told him "whether you have heard it or not",[337] that king Eirik died nine years ago, and later the bishops of Oslo, Stavanger, Bergen, Hamar and the Faroes had died. He asked bishop Thordr of Gardar to include them in his prayers.[338] This does not necessarily mean that no ship had sailed from Bergen to Greenland for nine years. The sender had been consecrated bishop of Bergen three years earlier in 1305 and perhaps had not checked which letters his predecessor had exchanged with the bishop of Greenland. He also says explicitly that the purpose of naming these dead persons was to ask bishop Thordr to pray for their souls. The letter verifies that years could pass between each ship sailing to Greenland but not necessarily nine years.

In 1343 Icelandic Annals note that Archbishop Paul consecrated Jon Skalli as bishop of Greenland in Trondheim, without knowing that the previous bishop

Table 4.1 Year when Icelandic Annals ceased to be written

I	Resiniani	1295
III	Henrik Høyer	1310
II	Vetustissimi	1314
IV	Regii	1341
V–VI	Skálholt	1372
VIII	Gottskalk	1394
IX	Flatø	1394
X	Oddverja	1427
VII	Lögmann	1430

Source: IA and *Odda-annalar og Oddverja-annall*.

still lived on the island; he did not die until 1349.[339] Ivar Bárdarson sailed from Bergen to Greenland in 1341 and must have returned in late summer 1343,[340] and the consecration of Jon Skalli must have taken place in 1343 before Ivar's return. In 1378 bishop Alfr of Gardar died, but the news did not arrive in Norway until six years later.[341]

From this it can be concluded that in the years ca. 1300–1390, as much as six years could pass between each ship from Norway. The visits may have been more frequent in the 12th and 13th centuries when walrus products were in stronger demand.

Our main source for shipping to Greenland in the final century was the Icelandic Annals. Icelanders started to write down history in the form of annals around 1280.[342] The decline in registered shipping to Greenland could be due to Icelanders writing fewer annals (Table 4.1).

The Lögmann Annals were continued until 1430. They are detailed until the very end and were written at Skálholt cathedral where the clergy was well informed. The nine annals in Table 4.1 largely contain the same information and the annalists copied each other. For this reason the quantity of relevant information declined less than the number of annals.

The last extant information about Norse Greenland is from 1410, and it is found in the Lögmann Annals. But the Lögmann Annals continued to be written until 1430, without any information about Greenland. The conclusion to be drawn from this is that no relevant or important information about Greenland reached Iceland during 1411–1430.

Norse communities had the nautical technology and personal skills to cross the North Atlantic to Greenland during the whole period AD 985–1410. The Greenlanders mastered these skills in the first part of their stay in Greenland. But it was a major problem for their shipbuilding skills that they lacked suitable wood and iron. They gradually lost control of their own contacts to overseas ports and markets, and the initiative to organise crossings of the Greenland Ocean to Norway and Iceland came to depend on foreign merchants who were interested in trading in Greenland. This interest declined and disappeared in the 14th century and the Norse Greenlanders were isolated.

5 The merchants

There is no evidence that Greenland had maritime connections to countries other than Norway and Iceland. The Danish archaeologist Joel Berglund is the only scholar to have claimed that some of the merchants who arrived in Norse Greenland may have been English. He has not presented empirical material to verify his claim.[343] All merchants who are known to have visited Norse Greenland were Greenlanders, Icelanders or Norwegians.

Country of origin

The life of the first Greenlanders AD 985–ca. 1030 is described in *Eiriks saga Rauda*, *Groenlendinga saga* and *Fostbroedra saga*. All three were written ca. 1220.

At that time there was a tradition in Iceland that the first Greenlanders owned ocean ships and traded with Norway. The first settlement would have been impossible without such ships. In the next generation the son of the Brattahlid chieftain, Leiv Eiriksson and the son of the Herjolvsnes chieftain Bjarni owned such ships.[344] The Greenlandic chieftain Thorgrim Trolle traded between Norway and Greenland via northern Iceland. He had an Icelandic partner and they owned ship and cargo in common. When they decided to end their partnership, Thorgrim received the ship and his Icelandic partner the cargo.[345] Another Greenlander in the same saga is Skufr who was skipper on a ship which sailed directly between Greenland and Norway. "He had his household and relatives in Greenland, and was a great merchant (*farmadr mikill*), wise and friendly".[346]

In the confrontation between foreign merchants and Greenlanders ca. 1130, it is said that the Greenlanders only had small ships (*smáskip*) compared to the ocean-going ships of the visiting merchants.[347] In 1189–1190 an unsuccessful attempt was made to sail from Greenland to Norway via Iceland in a ship type which was normally used in hunts along the coast.[348] The Greenlanders no longer owned ocean-going ships, but they could still freight their cargo on Norwegian or Icelandic ships. In 1191 a ship with Danish pilgrims visited Bergen, and a participant named "Greenlanders" as one of the merchant groups visiting the town.[349] This is the last time the sources verify or indicate that Greenland merchants traded in foreign ports.

The *Groenlendinga tháttr* claims that the first bishop of Gardar owned an ocean-going ship. In the following period the Icelandic Annals write repeatedly that bishops of Gardar sailed to or from Norway directly or via Iceland. It is normally not said whether the ship belonged to the bishop. There is one exception, in 1262 a ship which is explicitly said to be the Gardar bishop's was wrecked at Herdisarvik in Iceland with bishop Olav on board.[350] After 1262 there is no firm evidence that the bishops of Gardar owned a ship. In 1266 a ship which had visited Greenland was wrecked at Hitarnesi in Iceland; the contemporary Icelandic Annals do not state who owned ship and cargo.[351] Some 350 years later Bjørn Jonsson (1574–1655) claimed that the bishop of Gardar had owned the ship, but that the cargo of walrus tusks was owned by Greenlandic peasants.[352] But if the wrecked ship really was the bishop's, the Icelandic Annals would probably have mentioned it, so Bjørn's information should be questioned.

In 1328 the Gardar bishop sent his clergy's papal tithe to the archbishop's warehouse in Bergen.[353] At this time he must have hired cargo space on a ship belonging to a Norwegian or Icelandic skipper. The Gardar see used the archbishop's representative in Bergen as an economic agent from the end of the 13th century.

Summing up, in the settlement's first decades, the Greenlanders participated in trade as both skippers and merchants. They ceased as skippers sometime in the 11th century but continued as merchants to the end of the 12th century. A Greenlandic merchant's main problem may have been that he did not own an ocean-going ship and had to rely on foreign ships which arrived at unpredictable intervals.

The first known Icelandic skippers to trade in Greenland were Thorfinn Karlsefni and Bjarni Grimolvsson, who sailed their two ships to Greenland while Eirik Raudi was still alive. "Thorfinn journeyed for purposes of trade, and he had a reputation as a good travelling merchant".[354] Thorfinn voyaged from Norway and returned there after his stay in Greenland and Vinland.[355]

One of the three merchant ships which confronted the Greenlanders ca. 1130 was Icelandic and had "a large crew". The skipper afterwards returned to Bergen and sold his goods, and then settled in Iceland.[356]

This source from 1130 is the last verifiable evidence that Icelandic ships traded in Greenland or that Icelanders came there as merchants. In the following period we only have uncertain indications that this may have been the case. The Icelandic law codex *Grágás* was valid until the acceptance of Norwegian sovereignty 1262–1264. It has a paragraph which says that if men sail from Iceland to Greenland or sail to find new land or to visit another Icelandic port, and then are driven by contrary winds to Norway, then they shall not pay the *landøre* tax in Norway.[357] A paragraph which was adopted and written into the law-book, could remain there long after it had become irrelevant. We do not know if and when this particular paragraph ceased to be used. Several Icelandic ships on their way to or from Iceland were driven by contrary winds to Greenland, and they then used the opportunity to buy Greenlandic merchandise there. Evidence for regular trade is lacking.

Icelandic merchants withdrew from the Greenland trade in the 12th century. The reason was evidently the lack of commodities which could be exchanged between Greenland and Iceland. The market for Greenland goods was in Bergen, and there the goods which the Greenlanders wanted in return could be purchased.

Norwegian merchants seem to have been active in Greenland from the very start. The Norwegian Thorir (*norroen madr at kyni*) sailed ca. AD 1000 from Norway with a cargo of timber and other commodities. His ship was wrecked on a reef at the Greenland coast, but he was saved by the Greenlander Leiv Eiriksson who was also on his way from Norway.[358]

Groenlendinga tháttr describes a conflict which resulted from a visit by two Norwegian and one Icelandic merchant ships ca. 1130. The uncle of one of the Norwegian skippers had formerly traded with Greenland but had lost his life when his ship was wrecked on the coast of east Greenland. Another of the Norwegian merchants had visited Greenland on earlier occasions. At this time Norwegian merchants seem to have dominated the trade.[359]

In the following period the sources are scarce, but several episodes 1200–1370 show that Norwegian merchants were active. In 1217 a large knarri (*knörr mikill*) which had formerly been a *Groenlandsfar* arrived in Iceland; the skippers were from Hardanger near Bergen.[360] A man called Gudbrand lived in the Trondheim region. Sometime between 1290 and 1297 he left for Greenland and he seems never to have returned. It is not said explicitly that he was a merchant, but he belonged to a well-to-do family and had a brother who was a member of the king's *hird*, so it is improbable that he went to Greenland to become a farmer.[361]

In 1324 a *knarri* owned by skipper Olav from the farm Leksa at the estuary of the Trondheim fjord sailed to Greenland. Shortly before 24 July 1325 he returned to Bergen with Greenland goods.[362]

In 1346 the Skálholt Annals write that "the knarri arrived from Greenland safely and with very much goods".[363] It is not said whether it arrived in Iceland or Norway, neither is the nationality of the ship and merchants specified, but it is most likely to have been Norwegian since there is no certain evidence that Icelandic merchants traded with Greenland after ca. 1130.

The narrative of Ivar Bárdarson was probably written around 1360. It describes the port Sand close to Herjolvsnes as an *almindeligh* port for "Norwegians and merchants". He may have meant "Norwegians and other merchants" or "Norwegian merchants". *Almindeligh* meant that it was open for all.[364] The wording indicates that Norwegians were most numerous among the merchants who arrived in Sand. Ivar seems to describe the situation as it had been when he stayed at Gardar in the 1340s and 1350s.

In 1366 a knarri (*knor*) was prepared for a journey to Greenland, with Sigurdr of Bautahlutanum as skipper *(formadr)*.[365] Bautahlutanum was an urban "warehouse with dwelling" (*gárdr*) in Bergen.[366] Shortly before 1374 a merchant named Bárdr Dies died in Greenland. He had lived in the *gardr* Holmedalen in Bergen.[367] This is the last datable mention of Norwegians in the Greenland trade.

During the first century of its existence the settlement in Greenland was part of a tightly knit Norse network of shipping and commercial exchanges in which skippers and merchants from Greenland, Iceland and Norway participated. At the beginning of the 12th century the Greenlanders and Icelanders seem to have ceased their commercial shipping to and from Greenland, and at the end of the century individual Greenlandic merchants also ceased their overseas visits on board Norwegian ships. After that skippers and merchants from the west coast of Norway, Bergen included, dominated or monopolised the exchanges.

Part time and professional merchants

All known traders living in Greenland were part time merchants. Thorgrim Trolle was the second most powerful chieftain in Greenland and owned the farm Langanes in Einarsfjord. He arrived at the Thing assembly at Gardar "in a stately ship and his crew was valiant and well armed".[368] Thorgrim is presented as a man who cherished aristocratic values and appearances. The Greenlander Skufr was an ordinary peasant who owned the farm Stokkanes in Eiriksfjord.[369] He was a more modest, wise and friendly man. He had a partner called Bjarni who administered the farm when Skufr was in Norway and they owned farm, ship and cargo in common.

Two Icelanders trading with Greenland have a social background which is known. Thorfinn Karlsefni was the heir to a large farm in Iceland. As a young man he practised as a merchant and traded between Norway and Greenland.[370] One of the skippers in the confrontation with the Greenlanders ca. 1130 was the Icelander Hermundr Kodransson who returned "to his ancestral farm" (*ættjarda sinna*) in Iceland after these events.[371] He also belonged to a prominent family.

Part time merchants were common along the Atlantic and North Sea coast of Norway throughout the period when Norse Greenland was settled ca. 985–1410. The peasant Olav lived at the estuary of the Trondheim fjord. He owned and lived at the farm Leksa and was a skipper on a *knarri* which he used to trade between Greenland and Bergen. Olav had his farm in Trondheim diocese, but sold his goods in Bergen diocese. This resulted in a conflict between the two bishops about where the tithe for his merchandise should be paid. The Bergen bishop claimed that it should be paid where the goods were sold, and the Trondheim archbishop that it should be paid where the merchants stayed in winter, had their property and had lived in childhood.[372] Olav must have been an independent merchant and not just an agent, otherwise he would not have been held responsible for paying the tithe of his goods. In the previous century in 1217 a "large knarri" with skippers from Hardanger, which is in the countryside near Bergen, arrived in Vestmannaeyar. It had formerly been used in trade with Greenland.[373]

From the 12th century onwards a social group emerged in Bergen which earned its entire income from urban professions. They did not replace, but rather supplemented the part time merchants. Ketil Kalvsson was the name of the skipper of one of the Norwegian ships in Greenland ca. 1130. He was the most experienced of the overseas traders. When the skipper of the other Norwegian ship was killed, Ketil offered to conduct the court case at Gardar Thing, "because I know Greenland law, and I am willing to do it". Ketil wanted a settlement more than the others because he regularly traded with Greenland. In 1158 an Icelander killed a man with an axe in Bergen. The murderer feared revenge and sought refuge in the house of a man called Ketil Kalvsson,[374] probably the same man who had sought to obtain a settlement in Greenland 25 years earlier. Professional, full time merchants were more dependent on the rule of law than most other people.

The occupants of the *gardr* (= warehouse with dwelling) *Betalutanom* in Bergen had a tradition for trade with Greenland and Iceland, and extant documents makes it possible to give an outline of their trade. In 1326 a transfer of property took place in the living-room on the first floor of *Bautaluta*.[375] In the period 1366–1388 the merchant, house-owner and skipper Sigurdr lived there and traded with Greenland and Iceland. In 1366 the Icelandic Gottskalk Annals has the following entry: "A knarri prepared for Greenland [from Bergen], and the skipper was Sigurdr of *Bautahlutanum*".[376] The following year 1367 the same annals reported that "the knarri" (*knoren*) had been wrecked north of Bergen.[377] This must have been "the knarri" that was mentioned in the same annals the previous year, and where Sigurdr was skipper. Shortly before 1374 the Bergen merchant Sigurdr Kolbeinsson sailed to Greenland to trade for his own profit, but he also agreed to act as the crown's representative collecting taxes and other duties.[378] The same Sigurdr Kolbeinsson two years later in 1376 witnessed the transcript of a letter in Bergen, so he must have lived permanently in the town.[379] Gustav Storm thinks Sigurdr Kolbeinsson and Sigurdr of Bautahlutin were the same person.[380] This may well be the case, as both were house-owners in Bergen who traded with Greenland. In 1378 *Sigurde i Betalutanom* was a member of a jury in Bergen[381] and was a house-owner there.[382] In 1388 a ship called *Bautahlutin* arrived in the eastern fjords of Iceland from Norway.[383] The ship was evidently owned by a merchant who lived in the *gardr* with that name. Perhaps old Sigurdr was still an active merchant?

Bárdr Dies was a merchant who died in Greenland shortly before 1374. His first name makes it likely that he was a Norwegian.[384] Norwegian law used at that time in Greenland said that if a man died and none of his heirs was present to take care of the inheritance, it should be valued and remain in the house where he died, waiting for an heir to appear. If none turned up within one year, the inheritance should be turned over to the king's representative, but the heirs could claim it back within ten years. After that time limit it was crown property.[385] It would be impossible for an heir to reach Greenland within 12 months, and for many it was problematic to reach Greenland at all. Under these circumstances the king's representative in Greenland Sigurdr Kolbeinsson [in Bautahlutanum] mentioned earlier bought Baard's merchandise and landed property. The merchandise was brought to Bergen and stored in a *gardr* on Bryggen called Holmedalen, which seems to have belonged to the deceased Baard. His land is likely to have been in Greenland. The priest Absalon Pederssøn Beyer lived in Bergen around 1560 and he wrote that many members of the local nobility there possessed letters documenting ownership of land in Greenland, but they had neither seen it nor received rent from it – for good reasons![386]

Ketil Kalvsson, Sigurdr of Bautahlutanum and Bárdr Dies are examples of professional urban merchants visiting Greenland from Bergen. But most professional merchants in Bergen were Germans of the Hanseatic league. None of them sailed to Greenland, but Norwegian nationals may have sold Greenlandic goods to them in Bergen.[387]

Retailing foreign goods in Greenland

How did the visiting, overseas merchants sell their goods in Greenland? The written evidence reveals an organisation adapted to the irregular character of Greenland's foreign trade.

In 1328 papal money collectors received a six years' tithe and Peter's Pence from Norwegian bishops. From the bishops of Oslo, Hamar, Stavanger, Bergen, Trondheim, the Faroes and Skálholt the sums were paid in coins minted in Norway. The bishop of Orkney paid in English sterling. The bishop of Greenland was the only one to pay in kind, in walrus tusks.[388] This indicates that money was less used in Greenland than in other parts of the Norse realm. The archaeologists have found no coins in Greenland.[389] Trade with foreign merchants was probably organised as barter.

According to the reliable *Groenlendinga tháttr* improvised markets were organised when a trading ship arrived from Norway. "They arrived in Eiriksfjord, and people came to them and traded".[390] It is not said where in Eiriksfjord this trading took place, but it is likely to have been at Brattahlid since the local chieftain had the right to buy first. Two of the three cargo-ships which voyaged together to Greenland ca. 1130 came to Eiriksfjord, and the third ship sailed to the Western Settlement.[391]

The cargo-ships could also sail along fjords and make stops at appropriate places. Thorgrim Trolle sailed from Norway to Greenland with a stopover in Hraunhöfn on the north coast of Iceland. They anchored the ship at a short distance from the shore and transported the goods they wanted to sell ashore in a rowing boat. "One day when the weather was good, they brought ashore valuable cloth, canvas and other precious objects and spread it out".[392]

Merchants and ship crews normally stayed one winter in Greenland. They then lived at farms which were willing to put them up. Thorfinn Karlsefni ca. AD 1000 was received by Eirik Raudi, and the three ship crews ca. 1130 were received by the Gardar bishop and peasants in both settlements. Merchants paid for their stay with gifts of merchandise.[393]

Were there institutionalised marketplaces in Norse Greenland? The strongest candidate is Brattahlid. Poul Nørlund thought he had found remnants of booths where Greenlanders lived when they traded with visiting ships from overseas. The booths are similar to those found on Iceland. The walls of turf and stone were permanent, and the roof of skins or woollen cloth were temporary. Fireplaces could be outside or inside. The booths resembled Eskimo tent rings,[394] and further investigations may conclude that they were not Norse. Some 125 m south of the booths he found ruins of what he thought was a shelter for an ocean-going ship, to be used by foreign skippers in winter.[395] Exchanges may have taken place as a market during a short period, or as individual trading over a longer period.

The Thing assembly at Gardar seems to have met at Midsummer every year.[396] It may have been difficult to use it as a marketplace for foreign merchants because they arrived in August after the Gardar Thing had ended, and Midsummer the following year would normally be shortly before they left.

Another candidate for a market place is Sandhöfn close to Herjolvsnes. It was the first port in Greenland for cargo-ships from Norway and Iceland. They would normally reach Greenland on the east coast a short distance north of Cape Farewell, then sail round the cape and northwest for one day and one night. Then they would see the mountain Hvarf (today Ikigait, 900 m high) and under it the farm Herjolvsnes (today also called Ikigait) and the port Sandhöfn with four large houses, one of them 40 m long.[397] Here ocean ships would have to change their direction and may have waited for favourable winds. Apart from the ruins, there is no evidence of market activity. Institutionalised marketplaces do not seem to have existed in Greenland.[398]

The Greenland trade had an improvised character. It was organised by merchants who were not professionals; it was a sideline for them and they did not visit Greenland every year. Commercial exchanges were improvised when a trading ship arrived from overseas. The Norse hunters did not have long-term commercial contacts with particular foreign merchants or merchant groups but used the trading opportunities which were available.

The organisation of the Greenland trade was different from the stockfish trade from Northern Norway and Bergen, which was the great commerce in the Norse realm in this period. It was organised by professional German Hansa merchants who owned houses in Bergen and had permanent commercial contacts with Norwegian stockfish producers. These visited their merchant in Bergen regularly, many of them every year. The merchants in Greenland organised their trade in a way which after ca. AD 1100 belonged to the past along the Norwegian coast.

6 The political framework for trade and shipping

The political framework which political rulers imposed on trade and traders changed during the Norse centuries. In the earliest period the sagas give a unique insight into how pre-state chieftains met the visiting merchants. After 1261 the Norwegian state administration gives historians a few sources on the relationship between state and merchants.

Pre-state Greenland

The most basic social requirement for merchants was judicial protection. They could become party to a judicial conflict, and in a society without state they would then need a local protector with authority. The Icelandic skippers Thorfinn Karlsefni and Bjarni Grimolfsson sailed to Greenland to trade ca. AD 1000. Both ships reached Eiriksfjord and moored at Brattahlid.

> Eirik Raudi and some other settlers rode down to the ships and the trading between them took place without problems. The skippers offered Eirik to have as much of the goods as he wanted. Eirik wanted to reciprocate their generosity, and invited both crews to be his guests at Brattahlid for the winter. The traders accepted the invitation and thanked him. Their goods were brought up to Brattahlid, where there was no lack of outhouses to store their goods. Nor did they lack other things which they needed. The merchants spent the winter comfortably.[399]

Even if it is not said explicitly, the chieftain at Brattahlid also must have given the visiting merchants judicial protection. The exchanges between Eirik and Thorfinn are presented as reciprocal gifts which gave both parties honour; the merchants gave goods and received lodging and protection. For both parties it was vital to appear as honourable men, therefore none of them made unreasonable demands or denied the other what he wanted.

This case was not unique. The skipper and merchant Skufr was a Greenlander and owned a farm at Stokkanes in Eiriksfjord across the fjord from Brattahlid. When he returned home from a journey to Norway, he moored the ship at his own farm. "Thorkell Leivsson was then the chieftain over Eiriksfjord ... He came to the ship immediately after it had been moored, and bought from the skipper and the crew those things which he needed".[400]

Whatever the chieftain at Brattahlid bought (*keypti*), he had to pay for. Skufr as a Greenlander did not need lodging and he had judicial protection as a member of Greenland society. Therefore the Brattahlid chieftain did not receive a gift, but he demanded the right to buy first.

Skufr and his partner Bjarni were clients of the Brattahlid chieftain in the 1020s. When Skufr visited Norway, he stayed one winter there, was the Norwegian king's liegeman and lived at his *hird*. Skufr was under the king's personal protection when in Norway, and under the Brattahlid chieftain's when in Greenland. This functioned well for many years, until the king ordered him to help the Icelander Thormodr in a blood feud in Greenland. This involved him first in a conflict with his chieftain on Brattahlid, and next with the community of Greenlanders represented at the Gardar Thing. At all crossroads Skufr was eager to bring about reconciliation, without success. His situation in Greenland gradually became untenable. Skufr and Bjarni sold their farm and domestic animals in Greenland and left for Norway.[401] Merchants were vulnerable to political violence.

The three Norwegian and Icelandic merchant ships which arrived in Greenland ca. 1130 also first sailed to Eiriksfjord.[402] They also must have sought and received judicial protection from the Brattahlid chieftain. In this case the protection did not work because the Brattahlid chieftain had promised to protect the Greenland bishop and his see. In the following conflict between bishop and merchants the Brattahlid chieftain gave priority to his duties towards the church, and the merchants were left without legal protection. The Brattahlid chieftain prevented the merchants from using the Gardar Thing, and the only alternative left to them was then to start a feud. Several of them were killed, and they were chased from Greenland.

The problem for overseas merchants in pre-state Greenland was not a lack of laws. Claims of inheritance and shipwrecked goods were at the heart of the conflict ca. 1130, and in the period before 1261 both Norwegian[403] and Greenlandic[404] laws and customs were relevant in these fields. The problem was that political backing was needed for the laws to be implemented.

Merchants who spent the winter in Norway had to pay *leidang*, which in peacetime was a sales tax of 2% on all merchandise.[405] The Norwegian king no doubt claimed the right to buy first even if this was not codified until 1274.[406]

In pre-state society the political rulers' demands on the merchants were presented as reciprocal gifts and services. It is impossible to quantify how heavy were the economic burdens on the Greenland trade beyond the 2% *leidang*. It may have been more important for king and chieftains to buy first and get hold of the best goods than it was to exploit the merchants economically.

Under the Norwegian state 1261–1380

Trade between Greenland and Norway became part of Norway's domestic trade after 1261. In 1294 the Norwegian king prohibited foreign ships from sailing north of Bergen.[407] The main purpose was to prevent Hansa merchants from sailing to northern Norway to buy stockfish, but the paragraph also made it illegal for Germans, Englishmen and Danes to sail to Greenland. This had no practical consequence since they had never traded there, nor expressed any wish to do so. Between 1316 and 1343 customs were collected from foreign merchants who made purchases in Bergen and exported several kinds of merchandise, among them walrus tusks. The rate was one-twelfth of the value.[408]

The crown after 1261 claimed the right to buy first in both Bergen and in Greenland. According to The National Law from 1274, "the King or his representative has the right to buy first all merchandise (*varningr*) and other necessities which are offered for sale by natives or foreigners".[409] For Bergen the king made the law more precise in 1358 and 1360:

> Norwegians and those who enjoy the same legal rights as Norwegians may freely unload [from their ship] their goods as is old custom. But before they sell, they shall tell the king's official which goods they have so that use can be made of the king's right to pre-emptive purchase of goods which the king needs for his own use.[410]

The price was to be the same as others were willing to give, but the merchants complained that they sometimes were forced to accept less.[411] This law was valid in town and countryside, in mainland Norway and in Greenland. In Greenland the king's representative was accused in 1374 of not having exercised the king's right to pre-emptive purchases properly.[412] The Greenlandic chieftains' right to buy first was not practised since it no longer was they who gave the overseas merchants legal protection.

After 1261 Norwegian law was valid in Greenland, and it gave shipwrecked merchants the right to salvage their goods and demand help for the salvage work from local peasants.[413] The heirs' right to the goods of merchants who died in Greenland was safeguarded if the claim was made within a certain time limit.[414] These laws reduced the potential for conflicts between visiting merchants and Greenlanders. The Norwegian state did not impose economic burdens which were specific to the Greenland trade during 1261–1380.

Under Danish rule 1380–1410

In 1380 the last Norwegian king Håkon VI died, and his son became king of both Norway and Denmark at the age of ten. The real ruler was his Danish mother queen Margrete. She lived in Denmark and her perspective was Danish. She was the real ruler of Greenland and Norway when Greenland society disappeared from view in 1410.

In the 1370s the consequences of the Black Death had impoverished the Norwegian state, and the efforts to administer Greenland met with formidable challenges. A low cost solution was to transfer parts of the state's administrative work to merchants. In 1374 the Bergen merchant Sigurdr Kolbeinsson (mentioned earlier) sailed to Greenland to trade for his own profit, but he also accepted "to be the king's representative and seek everything to which the kingdom and the king has a right". The state wanted to collect taxes and duties and buy landed property. They also expected Sigurdr to make use of the king's right to "first purchase". The king was not satisfied with Sigurdr' performance and accused him of neglecting his job, confiscating some of his property.[415] Using merchants to do the job of state officials was an experiment which had to be abandoned, partly because the merchants sought their own profits more than the state's, and partly because the number of merchants who visited Greenland plummeted. After 1374 all known ships which visited Greenland are said to have been driven there by contrary winds and currents.

In 1384 or 1385 four ships sailed from Norway to Iceland but were driven by unfavourable winds and currents to Greenland where they stayed for two winters.[416] The leader of the convoy was the Icelander Bjørn Einarsson. He wrote a diary which has been lost, but another Icelander Bjørn Jonsson (1574–1655) made a short excerpt from it in his "Grænlands annal", which still exists.[417]

The Greenlanders did their best to make it possible for the visitors to stay. They granted to Bjørn Einarsson *Eiriksfjardar syslu*, which must mean that they gave him the right to collect state taxes from Eiriksfjord. In his diary he wrote that he received "130 pairs of cured legs of mutton, with all [the meat?] that ought to belong to them".[418] It is not said that the three other ship crews received similar tax incomes from other fjords, but this is likely. The ship crews seem to have consumed this meat themselves, even if Bjørn does not say so in his diary. Judicially this meant that they consumed the king's tax-meat without his permission. They supplemented this food with a drifting, wounded or dead *steypireidur*, which means a large whale, perhaps a blue whale.[419] In the summer of 1386 or 1387 they arrived safely in Hvalfjord in Iceland.[420] In the summer of 1388 they sailed to Bergen,[421] sold their Greenland goods there, and stayed the winter of 1388–1389 in Bergen. But in May 1389 the syslemann in Bergen in his role as public prosecutor accused them in court of having traded illegally in Greenland.[422] The syslemann's accusation can be summarised in three points.

First, their voyage to Greenland had been planned and this was contrary to the law (*med retto forakt*). The syslemann does not tell which law he refers to, and I do not understand which law that could be. After 1294 it was forbidden for foreigners to sail north of Bergen for purposes of trade (*non tamen ultra Bergas versus partes boreales*).[423] But Icelanders were at this time not foreigners, and no law prevented subjects of the Norwegian king from sailing to any part of the Norwegian realm. Demanding that subjects of the Norwegian crown needed permission to trade in Greenland was to create a new right for the king. The authorities would probably demand a fee to issue the permission. The merchants did not deny that it was illegal to sail to Greenland without crown authorisation, but they claimed to have been in life threatening danger on the ocean because of great icebergs and ice floes, and their ships were severely damaged. The judges accepted their excuses and acquitted them on this point.

The second accusation was that they had traded in Greenland without the crown's permission (*þeir hafdo køft ok selt a Grønlande vttan orlof konungsdoomssens*). It is not easy to understand the legal basis for this accusation. It may be royal ordinances prohibiting Norwegians and foreigners from trading in the countryside, the first one in 1299. All trade was to take place in towns.[424] There were no towns in Greenland, neither was there any in Iceland, but traditionally the state had not applied those laws there. The syslemann now may have insisted that special permission from royal officials had to be obtained to trade in the Greenland countryside. This was in practice new legislation. The merchants did not deny that they had traded with the Greenlanders, and that this was illegal, but they claimed to have been pressured to do this. Bjørn Einarsson produced two witnesses who told the court that they had lived in Greenland before Bjørn arrived in 1384–1385. They were probably Greenlanders who had followed Bjørn's ships from Greenland. They confirmed to have been present at the Gardar Thing when the Greenlanders passed a resolution that *Austmenn* (= Norwegians and Icelanders) should not be permitted to buy food for themselves, if they did not also buy other Greenland goods for export. It is likely that merchants were rare in Greenland at this time, and that the Greenlanders wanted to benefit as much as possible from this unexpected visit. The judges accepted this explanation and acquitted them on this point too.

The third accusation was that the merchants had illegally bought the crown's goods (*þeir hafdo køft krvnonne godz a mote loghonum*). Here the syslemann had a point. Bjørn Einarsson wrote in his diary that they had received the king's taxes paid in kind as legs of mutton and consumed the meat in Greenland. But in court he denied this accusation. Quite on the contrary, the merchants claimed through their witnesses to have offered to transport the crown's incomes paid in kind on their ships to Bergen. The King's representative in Greenland declined the offer because Bjørn had no written permission to receive the taxes. The representative in Greenland is called *ombudsmann*, which means that he was not an official, but a person who collected the king's taxes as a sideline beside his main occupation. The syslemann then finished off by confirming that the merchants on arrival in Bergen had paid the customs duty called *sekkia gield*, not only on goods from Iceland but also on goods from Greenland, as they had a legal obligation to do so (*efter rette*). In reality this is the first time this customs duty is known to have been imposed on goods coming from Greenland. Earlier it was mentioned as a special customs duty on goods arriving in Norway from Iceland. It was paid at a rate of 5%.[425] After this the jury consisting of high officials and nobles from the Norwegian west coast acquitted the merchants. The Nationalmuseum archaeologist Poul Nørlund claims that *sekkia gield* "is likely to have been a very high duty".[426] He did not even care to check the sources before pronouncing his judgement!

A report on the court case was sent to the regent Queen Margrete. This was unusual, and one could suspect that this was done because officials in Copenhagen had initiated the case and wanted a copy of the verdict. The report was kept in Copenhagen and has survived to this day. One might think it had no value for the

214   *Trade and shipping*

crown since the accused were acquitted on all points. In reality it created new rights for the crown and could be used as precedence. These merchants trading in Greenland accepted as a legal obligation that nobody could sail to Greenland or trade with Greenlanders without having obtained the king's permission in advance. Skippers were obliged to transport taxes in money or in kind to Bergen. They had to pay *sekkia gield* which earlier had not been paid on goods from Greenland. If Norwegian legislative practices had been followed, Margrete should have issued an ordinance (*rettarbot*) where she introduced these new laws. She did not do that, probably because there would have been resistance in Norway and Greenland among those who formally had to approve it. Through this verdict she instead created a precedent which evidently was meant to have the same force as legislation.

The background for these new laws or norms evidently was that the crown no longer sent ships to Greenland or had an official who could take care of the crown's interests there. Then it made sense to demand that merchants bought licences in Bergen before sailing to Greenland and impose on them a legal obligation to transport the king's taxes to Bergen. Finally, the merchants had to pay a low customs duty and give the king the right to buy first when they returned to Bergen. The clue here is that officials could sit in Bergen and receive duties which symbolised that Greenland was Danish, without setting foot on the island.

The authorities in Copenhagen evidently did not understand that they had to provide the Norse Greenlanders with services in return for the tax incomes. The most important of these were defence against the Inuit who came ever closer, and shipping which could bring people, goods and cultural impulses to the increasingly isolated community. The legal framework created by the Danish crown made trade with Greenland more bureaucratic and less profitable.

The hypothesis about "the royal monopoly ship"

In his survey of Norse Greenland history which appeared in five editions 1934–1967, Poul Nørlund gives a survey of the quantitative development of the trade with Norse Greenland. Trade between Greenland and Norway flourished as long as the Greenlanders decided the conditions under which it was to take place. In 1261 this power was transferred to the Norwegian king. As part of the agreement the Norwegian king undertook to send two ships a year to Greenland. In practice he only sent one ship to which he gave the monopoly to trade with Greenland, and which was called "the knarri". Private merchants had to hire cargo space on "the knarri". The king transformed his own duty to provide shipping to the Greenlanders into a source for exploitation.[427]

Nørlund uses value-laden words when he describes this development. The king's motive was to give "his personal coffer" incomes, and the arrangement had "hair-raising consequences" (*gav sig hårreisende udslag*). The "royal monopoly ship" (*det kongelige monopolskib*) was wrecked on the Norwegian coast in 1367, and the king did not replace it. The Greenlanders revolted against "the monopoly management's" (*monopolstyrets*) efforts to "prevent free trade", but the "local Norwegian authorities" (does he mean in Bergen or in Greenland?) showed "an infamous passivity" (*lidet berømmelig uvirksomhed*).[428] This destruction of the

Greenland trade was organised by "Norwegian kings who resided in Denmark", some of whom were of "German extraction". A strange way of expressing the fact that Norwegians and Greenlanders after 1380 were involuntary subjects of Danish monarchs residing in Denmark.[429] These unverified hypotheses seem to have won acceptance in later Danish research by virtue of not having been opposed.[430] Helge Ingstad analysed the relevant sources and concluded that a "monopoly" and "monopoly management" never existed.[431]

Did the Norwegian king promise to send two ships annually to Greenland in 1261? On 2 April 1568 the Dano-Norwegian King Fredrik II resided in his castle in Copenhagen and was preparing a ship to be sent to Greenland where he hoped that a Norse community still existed. Since nothing had been heard from them for 150 years, he probably thought that they were still Catholics, and more important still, that they did not know that they were now the Danish king' subjects. He therefore gave the skipper a letter in Icelandic which was meant to be read aloud to the Norse Greenlanders if they were found.

The letter starts by stating that "Greenland from the time of Our first forefathers and previous kings always has belonged to and been the legal property and land of the Norwegian crown". The statement would have carried less weight if he had added that the crown had not given any state services to Greenland for almost two centuries. The king therefore also gave the Norse Greenlanders a carrot.

> When We obtained Our royal power of government, We learnt that there should have been made some settlement agreed by both sides that from Norway should sail two ships every year to Greenland, and bring there all good and useful goods which the land and the common people need. We have now learnt that this for some time has not been done because of the weather, the times and important events.[432]

The king promises to resume this practice, and therefore sends a ship with goods which was to be divided between them.

When Iceland submitted to the Norwegian crown in 1262, the king guaranteed that "six ocean-going ships shall sail to Iceland every year without exception".[433] The agreement with the Greenlanders had been made the previous year in Greenland by the Norwegian king's envoys. The Greenlanders could not know what would be negotiated between the king and the Icelanders the following year. Around 1261 shipping to Greenland seems to have been satisfactory; *The King's Mirror* witnesses that walrus products were still attractive merchandise. The situation in Iceland was different. Their main export was wadmal which did not have a European market, and the stockfish export was still modest.

The alleged promise of 1261 seems to have been invented in Fredrik II's chancery in 1568 for pragmatic reasons. There are no references to such a promise before 1568, no known ships owned by the king were sent to Greenland to trade, neither are two ships known to have sailed to Greenland together after 1261. In the court case in Bergen 1389 against merchants who had visited Greenland illegally, the "royal monopoly ship(s)" is not mentioned.[434]

216 *Trade and shipping*

An alternative hypothesis is more likely. Nørlund claimed that "the royal monopoly ship" was called "The Knarri". Until the end of the 13th century *knarri* was a usual name for trading ships built in the Norse tradition and it was used in overseas voyages to all destinations. Ca. 1300 *bussa* became the usual word for merchant vessels used in foreign trade built in the Norse tradition, and it is assumed that they were somewhat larger and higher than the *knarri*. But *knarri* continued to be the name for trading ships to Greenland; not a single *bussa* is registered there. *Knarri* gradually changed from being the name of all overseas trading ships built in the Norwegian tradition to becoming the name for trading ships sailing to Greenland. These were changes in terminology which took place independently of the state's trading policy. Below is a list of all instances when the word *knarri* is used in the Greenland trade:

- The first time a knarri is mentioned in the Greenland trade is in 1217 when a *knörr mikill* arrived in Vestmannaeyar in Iceland. It had formerly been a "Greenland voyager"; the skippers' homesteads were in Hardanger in the countryside near Bergen.[435]
- In 1257 King Håkon Håkonsson sent a delegation to Greenland to negotiate the island's submission to the Norwegian crown. One of the representatives is called *Knarri-Leiv*; he must have been the skipper on the *knarri* which brought them across the Greenland Ocean.[436]
- In 1270 a Greenlandic priest called Halldor wrote a letter to his colleague Arnaldr in Bergen and sent it on "the knarri".[437] Our text is a paraphrase by Bjørn Jonsson (1574–1655) and we do not whether "the knarri" was used in the original from ca. 1300. If it was, it could mean "the *knarri* which now is here in Greenland and is about to sail to Bergen".
- In 1325 are mentioned "those merchants of Trondheim who now came in the *knarri* from Greenland".[438] The definite form means that one *knarri* had just travelled from Greenland to Bergen, and this ship is referred to as "the knarri".
- In 1346 Icelandic Annals note that "the *knarri* came from Greenland safely with very much goods".[439] Here a knarri has not been mentioned in the previous text, and the definite form must mean that the readers would know which knarri was meant. This could support Nørlund's interpretation, but not necessarily.
- In 1354 King Magnus mentions "all men who want to journey in the *knarri* to Greenland". One ship had been prepared in Bergen to go to Greenland and this ship is referred to as "the knarri".[440]
- In 1366 an Icelandic Annal says that "A *knor* was prepared for Greenland, and the skipper was Sigurdr of Bautahlutanum". He was a Bergen citizen. The following year 1367 it is noted that "The *knor* was wrecked north of Bergen".[441] The definite form is used because the annalist refers to the *knor* which was mentioned the previous year.

These examples support the hypothesis that the use of this ship type in the period 1300–1367 was gradually limited to Greenland voyages. The Greenland skippers continued to use the ship type *knarri* because it was smaller than the *bussa*. It had to be drawn ashore in Greenland in winter, and then large ships could create problems.[442] Smaller ships were easier to manoeuvre between ice floes. With the exception of timber products, the goods transported to and from Greenland did not demand much space.

But the source references do not support the hypothesis that there was a *knarri* owned by the crown and which had a monopoly of trading with Greenland. It is not mentioned how cargo space was chartered, which indicates that it was done as usual. Hansa skippers in Bergen at this time announced publicly that they planned a voyage to a certain destination and invited merchants to charter cargo space on their ship.[443] A *knarri* sailed to Greenland when there was sufficient interest for it in Bergen.

Merchants and state

Before 1261 merchants visiting Greenland had to obtain the protection of a powerful chieftain who in return claimed the right to buy imported goods first. When merchandise produced in Greenland reached Bergen, the king's representative had the same right to buy them first, but it is doubtful whether he felt he needed many of them. Authorities in Bergen also imposed the so-called *leidang* tax of ca. 2% on all goods sold there.

After 1261 merchants in both Greenland and Bergen were protected by the king's representatives. The right to buy imported goods first now belonged to the representatives of the Norwegian king at both ends of the exchange.

From the 1380s authorities in Bergen received their instructions from Denmark. Merchants had to buy licences to sail to Greenland for trading purposes. When they returned to Bergen they had to pay a new customs duty of ca. 5% (*sekkia gield*) in addition to the *leidang* tax of 2%. They also had to transport the king's taxes from Greenland to Bergen. The authorities in this way made visible their sovereignty over Greenland without having a state administration there. The cost was that the Greenland trade became more bureaucratic and less profitable. The Danes were new to the administration of Greenland in the 1380s and did not understand how fragile the settlement was.

The market's interest for walrus tusks declined and bureaucratic barriers were created for merchants who despite this continued the Greenland trade. It became increasingly difficult to make a voyage to Greenland profitable. Fewer overseas merchant vessels appeared in the Greenlandic fjords. In other parts of the Norse region international trade developed differently. For peasant-fishermen on the Norwegian coast and on the North Atlantic islands, the decades ca. 1350–1500 were the most profitable in the history of the stockfish trade.[444]

But trade was not the most important source of income for the Norse Greenlanders. They obtained practically all their food through their subsistence food production. This will be the subject of the next chapter.

Notes

1 The Norwegian coastal economy in the Middle Ages is described in Nedkvitne 2014(a), chapter 6. It is done more extensively in Nedkvitne 1988.
2 *Konungs skuggsiá*, Old Norse, p. 29; English translation, p. 142; Norwegian translation, pp. 67–68.

3 Buchwald 2001, p. 8; Espelund 2007.
4 Nielsen 1930.
5 Nørlund and Stenberger 1934, p. 131.
6 Buchwald 2001, pp. 5 and 82–83.
7 Espelund 2007, p. 58.
8 Nørlund 1924, p. 192.
9 *Fostbroedra saga* IF VI chapter 23, p. 229; English translation: CSI chapter 23, p. 376; Norwegian translation: Norrøn saga II, p. 231.
10 Buchwald 2001, p. 83.
11 Nørlund and Stenberger 1934, p. 132. At Gardar he unearthed a knife of unusual quality, and he comments that "it is undoubtedly an imported specimen, from Europe" (Nørlund and Roussell 1930, p. 144).
12 "Om Norgis Rige", edition from 1968, p. 70; the date 1567 is from *Norsk biografisk leksikon*, first edition, volume 1, p. 82, entry word "Absalon Pederssøn Beyer".
13 *Sturlunga saga*, Old Norse chapter 185, p. 255; English translation I, p. 163; Danish translation I, p. 296 (*kom knörr mikill ok hafdi verid Grænlandsfar*).
14 *Groenlendinga tháttr* IF IV chapter 2, p. 278; English translation: CSI chapter 2, p. 375.
15 Skaaning Høegsberg 2009 II, p. 74.
16 Skaaning Høegsberg 2009 I, p. 138.
17 Skaaning Høegsberg 2009 I, p. 138.
18 Cf. Roussell 1936, p. 101.
19 Skaaning Høegsberg 2009 II, p. 67.
20 IA, IV Regii; *Oddaannalar og Oddverjaannall*, p.136 (AD 1189 and 1190); *Sturlunga saga*, Old Norse chapters 95 and 96, p. 122; English translation II, chapter 13, p. 118 and 119; Danish translation I, pp. 141 and 142.
21 Skaaning Høegsberg 2009 I, p. 13.
22 Skaaning Høegsberg 2009 II, p. 66; the exception was Herjolvsnes.
23 Nørlund and Stenberger 1934, pp. 132–133.
24 Roussell 1936, pp. 177–178, cf. p. 111.
25 Skaaning Høegsberg 2009 I, p. 65.
26 Nørlund and Stenberger 1934, p. 134; Nørlund 1924, p. 194; Østergård 2003, p. 112.
27 Roussell 1936, p. 180, cf. p. 112.
28 Nørlund and Stenberger 1934, p. 134.
29 Nørlund and Stenberger 1934, p. 133.
30 Cf. Chapter 2, p. 49.
31 *Fostbroedra saga* IF VI chapter 24, pp. 254–256; English translation: CSI chapter 24, p. 389.
32 Roussell 1936, p. 104.
33 Roussell 1936, pp. 104–105.
34 Nørlund and Stenberger 1934, p. 133.
35 Nørlund and Roussell 1930, p. 146.
36 Roussell 1936, p. 107.
37 Nørlund and Rousssel 1930, p. 144; Skaaning Høegsberg 2009 II, p. 65.
38 Nørlund and Stenberger 1934, p. 134.
39 Roussell 1936, pp. 109 and 175.
40 Nørlund and Stenberger 1934, p. 134.
41 Nørlund 1924, p. 226, no. 191.
42 At Brattahlid; Nørlund and Stenberger 1934, pp. 132 and 134.
43 At Sandnes; Roussell 1936, p. 178, object number S. 201; Skaaning Høegsberg 2009 II, p. 75.
44 At Gardar; Nørlund and Roussell 1930, pp. 144–145.
45 At Herjolvsnes; Nørlund 1924, p. 267, object no. 167.
46 At Brattahlid; Nørlund and Stenberger 1934, p. 135; fragments of another at E167; Skaaning Høegsberg 2009 II, p. 150 and I, p. 139 and T.

Trade and shipping 219

47 Six fragments were found at Gardar and at Brattahlid one fragment. Objects from Gardar: Nørlund and Roussell 1930, pp. 146–149; they suggest p. 149 that the metal used in the moulds was lead or bronze. Other archaeologists claim that the Greenlanders were hardly competent to found alloys.
48 Østergård 2003, pp. 111–112.
49 At Brattahlid; Nørlund and Stenberger 1934, p. 134.
50 At Sandnes; Roussell 1936, p. 110.
51 At E167; Skaaning Høegsberg 2009 II, p. 67.
52 *Groenlendinga saga* IF IV chapter 4, pp. 253–254; English translations: CSI chapter 3, p. 24 and Penguin chapter 3, p. 9.
53 Nørlund and Stenberger 1934, pp. 120–121.
54 Arneborg et al. 2008, p. 150.
55 *Konungs skuggsiá*, Old Norse, p. 29 *kaupa af adrum lonndum vid allan thænn sæm their skolo hus af gera*; English translation, p. 142; Norwegian translation, pp. 67–68.
56 Egede/Bobé, p. 104.
57 "Grænlands annal", "Um Nordursetufolk i Grænlandi", pp. 55–57 = GHM III, pp. 242–243; *Kroka-Refs saga* describes how a ship which sailed into a fjord in the uninhabited northern part of Greenland saw shores full of drift timber. The saga is fiction, but uninhabited Greenlandic fjords full of drift timber may have been a reality in the author's time (IF XIV chapter 6, p. 132; English translation: CSI volume 3, chapter 6, p. 405).
58 IA year 1347, V Skálholt and IX Flatø.
59 *Groenlendinga saga* IF IV chapter 4, p. 253; English translation: CSI chapter 3, p. 23 and Penguin chapter 3, p. 8
60 *Groenlendinga saga* IF IV chapters 7 and 9, pp. 264 and 268; English translation: CSI chapter 6, p. 29 and chapter 8, p. 32, and Penguin chapter 6, p. 17 and chapter 8, p. 21.
61 Egede/Bobé, p. 127, cf. pp. 128–129; 6 June 1724.
62 Pilgrim 2004.
63 Cf. Chapter 5, p. 297; *Groenlendinga tháttr* IF IV chapter 6, p. 290; English translation: CSI chapter 6, p. 381.
64 *Konungs skuggsiá*, Old Norse, p. 30; English translation, p.142; Norwegian translation, pp. 68–69.
65 Cf. Chapter 1, pp. 30–31; *Eiriks saga Rauda* IF IV chapter 7, p. 220; English translation: CSI chapter 7, p. 11 and Penguin, p. 39.
66 *Fostbroedra saga* IF VI chapter 22, p. 226; English translation: CSI chapter 22, pp. 374–375; Norwegian translation: Norrøn saga II, p. 229.
67 Cf. Chapter 5, pp. 298–300.
68 Østergård 2003, p. 79; cf. Arneborg 2004, pp. 260–261.
69 *Fostbroedra saga* IF VI chapter 22, p. 227; English translation: CSI chapter 22, p. 375.
70 Østergård 2003, pp. 76–77.
71 Østergård 2003, p. 78.
72 Østergård 2003, p. 82.
73 Østergård 2003, pp. 30–31.
74 Østergård 2003, p. 76.
75 Østergård 2003, p. 78.
76 Østergård 2003, p. 77.
77 Østergård 2003, p. 78.
78 Roussell 1936, p. 175, object number S148; Østergård 2003, p. 24.
79 Østergård 2003, p. 90; Wikipedia, entry word "woad"; Rogers 1993, pp. 56–58.
80 Rogers 2003, p. 90.
81 DN X no. 9.
82 Rogers 2003, p. 89.
83 Nedkvitne 1977, p. 46.

220   Trade and shipping

84 The sites are Herjolvsnes (E111) and Nipaatsoq (W54).
85 Rogers 2003, p. 90.
86 Arneborg 2004, p. 260; Skaaning Høegsberg 2009 I, pp. 174–176.
87 Nørlund 1924, pp. 1100 and 102, cf. Østergård 2003, p. 109.
88 Østergård 2003, pp. 109–110.
89 Nørlund and Roussell 1930, pp. 67–69; Skaaning Høegsberg 2009 II, p. 160; the identity of the bishop has not been fully verified.
90 For example Nørlund 1924, p. 192 = Skaaning Høegsberg 2009 II, p. 150.
91 Skaaning Høegsberg 2009 II, p. 103; Vebæk 1993, p. 33 (E17a).
92 Skaaning Høegsberg 2009 II, p. 166.
93 Skaaning Høegsberg 2009 II, p. 150; Nørlund 1924, p. 192.
94 Skaaning Høegsberg 2009 II, p. 167.
95 Roussell 1936, p. 121; Skaaning Høegsberg 2009 II, p. 105.
96 Roussell 1936, pp. 118–122; Skaaning Høegsberg 2009 I, pp. 161–165 and II, pp. 105–117.
97 Nørlund and Stenberger 1934, pp. 136–137 (Brattahlid); Roussell 1936, pp. 122–123 (Sandnes); Vebæk 1993, p. 33 (Narsaq); Vebæk 1992, pp. 79–80 (E167).
98 Nørlund and Stenberger 1934, pp. 118–119; more on Herjolvsnes: Nørlund 1924, p. 221; more on Gardar: Nørlund and Roussell 1930, pp. 150–152. On Daniel Bruun's find: Bruun 1896, p. 451, no. 181.
99 Skaaning Høegsberg 2009 I, p. 66; Nørlund 1924, p. 168; Roussell 1941, p. 243.
100 Skaaning Høegsberg 2009 I, p. 66.
101 Nørlund and Roussell 1930, pp. 120–121. The Norwegian origin of the bowl is Nørlund's opinion.
102 Roussell 1936, p. 142.
103 Roussell 1936, pp. 148 and 204; Nørlund and Stenberger 1934, p. 121. It is a problem that the archaeologists normally categorise such utensils as made of "wood" without telling us which kind of wood.
104 Stoklund 1984, p. 101.
105 Roussell 1936, p. 34, cf. Wikipedia entry word "anthracite".
106 RN III no. 540 = DN XIX no. 460; Nedkvitne 2014(a), p. 61.
107 DN X no. 9.
108 Roesdahl 1995, p. 33.
109 In Anglo-Saxon walrus is spelled *horshwælum*, litterally "horse-whales".
110 Othere's account to King Alfred. In Anglo Saxon: *The Old English Orosius*, pp. 13–16; Danish translation: *Ottar og Wulfstan*, pp. 21–22.
111 Othere's account to King Alfred. Anglo Saxon: *The Old English Orosius*, pp. 13–16; *Ottar og Wulfstan*, p. 24.
112 *Konungs skuggsiá*, Old Norse, p. 29; English translation, p. 140; Norwegian translation, p. 66.
113 *Sverris saga*, Old Norse, p. 95; Norwegian translation, p. 97.
114 *Kroka-refs saga* IF XIV chapter 14, p. 146; *grænlenzkum varningi, svörd ok tönn ok skinnavöru*; English translation; CSI volume 3, chapter 14, p. 413.
115 *Kroka-refs saga* IF XIV chapter 18, p. 157 (*fjar i svörd ok tannvöru ok skinnavöru og mörgum theim hlutum, er fásenir varu i Danmörk af grænlenzkum varningi*); English translation: CSI volume 3, chapter 18, pp. 418–419.
116 *Kroka-Ref's saga* IF XIV chapter 18, pp. 156–157 "*svörd til reida á skipum varum*"; English translation: CSI volume 3, chapter 18, p. 405.
117 *Groenlendinga tháttr* IF IV chapter 1, pp. 273–274. *Einarr hafdi med ser tannvoru mikla ok svörd, at heimta sik fram vid höfdingja*. English translation: CSI chapter 1, p. 373.
118 *Tristrams saga ok Isöndar*, Old Norse, p. 27; English translation, *The saga of Tristram and Isönd*, p. 21.
119 *Konungs skuggsiá*, Old Norse, p. 29; English translation, p. 142; Norwegian translation, p. 68.
120 IA, IV Regii, year 1266; VIII Gottskalk, year 1266.

121 "Grænlands annal", pp. 54–55; GHM III, pp. 244–245.
122 Robinson 2004, p. 62.
123 *In bovinis et focarum coriis ac dentibus et funibus balenarum.*
124 Munch 1864, p. 153 = DN I no. 71 = RN II no. 292 and 295.
125 Cf. Nedkvitne 2014(a); Chapter 1, Section 3.
126 NGL III no. 47 = RN III no. 972.
127 Munch 1864, pp. 25 and 28.
128 On the papal taxes in 1327, see Chapter 3, pp. 125–127.
129 *Kroka-Ref's saga* IF XIV chapter 11, p. 142; English translation: CSI volume 3, chapter 11, p. 410.
130 Nørlund and Roussell 1930, p. 138; cf. Krogh 1982, p. 163.
131 Heimskringla, "The saga of King Magnus Bareleg", chapter 24.
132 Illustrations in: Roesdahl 1995; Skaaning Høegsberg 2009 II, pp. 166 and 168; Krogh 1982, pp. 57, 153 and 159.
133 Roesdahl 1995, p. 25.
134 Nørlund and Roussell 1930, p. 72.
135 Cf. Chapter 3, pp. 117–118.
136 Roesdahl 1995, p. 21.
137 Stratford 1997, pp. 44–45; Robinson 2004, pp. 35 and 58.
138 Nordeide 1994, pp. 248–249, cf. Christophersen and others 1994, p. 35; Roesdahl 1995, picture on the cover and p. 20.
139 Gaborit-Chopin 1978, p. 116; Gaborit-Chopin 1992, p. 204.
140 Robinson 2004, p. 11.
141 Robinson 2004, p. 50.
142 Robinson 2004, p. 59.
143 Gaborit-Chopin 1978, p. 116.
144 Gaborit-Chopin 1992, pp. 204–205, 387 and 389; *Louvre–Guide* 1993, pp. 27, 34, 35.
145 Gaborit-Chopin 1978, pp. 9–14, particularly p. 11 and p. 14.
146 Gaborit-Chopin 1978, pp. 164–166.
147 Born 2005, pp. 49–51, 61 and 73–74.
148 Born 2005, p. 55.
149 Born 2005, pp. 15–17; "Grænlands annal", p. 53.
150 In the poem "Skald-Helga Rimur" the northern hunting grounds are called Greipar. The poem is printed in GHM II, pp. 419–575, Greipar is mentioned on p. 492, stanza 42. The two relevant lines are copied by Bjørn Jonsson in his "Grænlands annal", p. 50. This *rimur* is pure fiction written ca. 1350–1540. According to the editor Halldorsson this is the only time the name is used (Halldorsson 1978, p. 256). The author of the *rimur* may have invented the name. I have chosen not to use the name in this book.
151 Born 2005, p. 58.
152 Ingstad also thought that Norse Greenland hunters sailed to "Nordsetur" in spring, based on Inuit practices at the time when he wrote his book (Ingstad, H. 1959, p. 206; reprint 2004, pp. 164–165; English translation, p. 116). Arneborg 2004, p. 269 claims that these hunting expeditions were in the autumn, concentrated in October. She does not give references for this.
153 Cf. Chapter 3, p. 139.
154 Egede, Niels: *Description of Greenland*, p. 267.
155 Valeur 2000, pp. 14–17.
156 On ice conditions along the west coast of Greenland, cf. Chapter 4, pp. 197–198. See also Index of matters, entry word "ice".
157 "Grænlands annal", pp. 38–39; GHM III, p. 229.
158 The "old booklet" says that 12 days were needed to row around Bjarneyar. There is only one island north of the Western Settlement which is that large, which is Disco Island. The "old booklet" subdivided the journey northwards into three parts, from the northern limit of the Western Settlement (near Nuuk) to *Lysufjardar* six days, from

there to *Karlbuda* another six days, and from there to Disco another three days. Where Lysufjardar and Karlsbuda were, is not known, and it is less relevant in our context. Lysufjardar was a common name both in Norway and in Norse Greenland. It was also the Norse name for the Ameralik fjord in the Western Settlement.

159 Valeur 2000, pp. 14–17; cf. Arneborg 2004, p. 269 who thinks the hunters may have stayed all winter in their *nordrseta*. I see no reason to believe that.
160 *Groenlendinga tháttr* IF IV chapter 2, pp. 277; English translation: CSI chapter 2, pp. 375; *Groenlendinga saga* IF IV chapter 2, pp. 250–251; English translation: CSI chapter 2, p. 22 and Penguin chapter 2, p. 7.
161 "Grænlands annal", p. 39; GHM III, pp. 228–229; "six men on a boat with six oars".
162 Cf. Chapter 5, p. 292.
163 Cf. Chapter 3, p. 137.
164 "Grænlands annal", p. 54; GHM III, p. 242. On the sexæringr, cf. Chapter 4, pp. 186–188.
165 Cf. Chapter 3, p. 137.
166 Nedkvitne 1988, pp. 254–255.
167 Cf. Chapter 4, pp. 185–186.
168 "Grænlands annal", p. 55; Halldorsson 1978, pp. 259–262.
169 Ingstad, H. 1959, pp. 150–151; reprint 2004, pp. 119–121; English translation, p. 82; Meldgaard, J. 1995, pp. 204–207.
170 Nedkvitne 2014(a), chapter 6.
171 Nedkvitne 1988, pp. 205–207.
172 "Grænlands annal", p. 55 = GHM III, pp. 242–243.
173 Halldorsson 1978, pp. 159–160 discusses the reliability of Bjørn's information on this point.
174 Arneborg 2004, p. 268; cf. Skaaning Høegsberg 2009 I, p. 137.
175 Munch 1864, p. 21; cf. Chapter 3, p. 126.
176 Munch 1864, p. 45.
177 Nedkvitne 2014(a), pp. 707 and 711.
178 Cf. Chapter 2, pp. 46–47; *Den norsk-islandske skjaldedigtning*, volume A1, p. 418, and volume B1 pp. 387–388; the poet is called Sveinn, and the verses are quoted by Snorri Sturlusson in his Edda.
179 Arneborg 2004, p. 266. She quotes an archaeological source.
180 Cf. Chapter 3, pp. 126–127.
181 For a discussion of this source, cf. Chapter 6, pp. 342–349.
182 Cf. Chapter 5, pp. 288–289; *Det gamle Grønlands beskrivelse af Ivar Bárdarson*, pp. 21–22; cf. *Groenlendinga tháttr* IF IV chapter 2, pp. 276–277; English translation: CSI chapter 2, pp. 374–376; Norwegian translation: Norrøn saga V, pp. 249–251.
183 *Konungs skuggsiá*, Old Norse, p. 29; English translation: p. 142; Norwegian translation, p. 68.
184 Munch 1864, p. 153 = DN I no. 71 = RN II no. 292 and 295.
185 *Kroka-refs saga* IF XIV chapter 14, p. 146; *grænlenzkum varningi, svörd ok tönn ok skinnavöru*; English translation; CSI volume 3, chapter 14, p. 413.
186 *Fostbroedra saga* IF VI chapter 22, p. 227; English translation: CSI chapter 22, p. 227.
187 Nedkvitne 2014(a), pp. 631, 633 and 634.
188 *Ottar og Wulfstan*, p. 22.
189 Nedkvitne 2014(a), p. 632.
190 Egede/Bobé, p. 391.
191 Gensbøl 1999, pp. 262–263.
192 *Konungs skuggsiá*, Old Norse, p. 30; English translation, p. 144; Norwegian translation, p. 69.
193 *Kroka-Refs saga* IF XIV chapter 18, pp. 156–157; *Their höfdu fimm hvitabjörnu ok 50 falka ok 15 hvita*. It is not clear whether the 15 white falcons are included in the 50 or are in addition to them. This is not important since this is pure fiction, and the author meant to say there were "many". English translation: CSI volume 3, chapter 18, p. 419.

194 *Tristrams saga ok Isöndar* Old Norse, p. 27; English translation, p. 21.
195 DN XIX no. 167 = PRO – Ancient correspondence IV no. 116.
196 Nedkvitne 2014(a), pp. 610 and 621.
197 Pipe Rolls 1833, p. 111; Pipe Rolls 2012, p. 88. Norwegian summary in RN I no. 73.
198 Nedkvitne 2014(a), p. 621.
199 Nedkvitne 2014(a), p. 59.
200 Further information cf. "Index" in Nedkvitne 2014(a); RN I–IX, index; KLNM entry word "Falkar".
201 *Det gamle Grønlands beskrivelse af Ivar Bárdarson*, pp. 21–22.
202 *Hungrvaka* IF XVI chapter 2, p. 7; Kolsrud 1913, p. 259; *hvitabjörn er kommin var af Grönlandi*.
203 *Groenlendinga tháttr* IF IV chapter 1, p. 275; *Einarr hafdi haft med ser bjarndyri af Groenlandi ok gaf that Sigurdi konungi; fekk hann thar i mot soemdir ok metord af konungi*. English translation: CSI chapter 1, p. 373.
204 *Groenlendinga tháttr* IF IV chapter 6, p. 291; English translation: CSI chapter 6, p. 382.
205 *Calendar of the Liberate Rolls*, Henry III volume 4, pp. 70 and 84.
206 Wold 2004, pp. 188 and 200.
207 *Kroka-refs saga* IF XIV chapter 11, p. 142 and chapter 18, pp. 156–157; English translation: CSI volume 3, chapter 11, p. 410.
208 *Morkinskinna*, Old Norse ed. Unger, pp. 61–65; English translation, chapter 36, pp. 211–215.
209 DN XIX no. 430; Nedkvitne 2014(a), p. 600.
210 Nedkvitne 2014(a), pp. 57–60.
211 *Urkundenbuch der Stadt Lübeck* IV, no. 506.
212 Lübben A. ed, 1888. Entry word "sele-smolte".
213 Nedkvitne 2014(a), pp. 219 and 205.
214 Egede/Bobé, pp. 258–259.
215 Christensen, A. E. 2000, p. 92.
216 *Groenlendinga tháttr* IF IV chapter 2, p. 277; English translation: CSI chapter 2, p. 375.
217 *Fostbroedra saga* IF VI chapter 17, p. 206 written ca. 1220; English translation: CSI chapter 17, p. 367.
218 Icelandic Annals in the years 1185 and 1266.
219 IA, IV Regii 1266.
220 *Fostbroedra saga* IF VI chapter 16, p. 202; English translation: CSI chapter 16, p. 366.
221 *Groenlendinga saga* IF IV chapter 4, p. 254; English translation: CSI chapter 3, p. 24 and Penguin chapter 3, pp. 9–10.
222 *Groenlendinga tháttr* IF IV chapter 6, p. 289; English translation: CSI chapter 6, p. 381; Norwegian translation: Norrøn saga V, p. 258.
223 Christensen, A. E. 2000, pp. 92–93; Pentz 2014, pp. 208–209.
224 *Fostbrædra saga* IF VI chapter 20, pp. 222–223; English translation: CSI chapter 20, pp. 372–373.
225 *Groenlendinga tháttr* IF IV chapter 2, p. 279; English translation: CSI chapter 2, p. 376; IA, IX Flatø 1385 and 1387; VII Lögmann 1384 and 1386.
226 Nørlund and Stenberger 1934, pp. 116–117.
227 Pentz 2014, p. 209.
228 Kuijpers et al. 1998, p. 64; cf. Nørlund and Stenberger 1934, p. 117.
229 *Groenlendinga tháttr* IF IV chapter 6, p. 288; English translation: CSI chapter 6, p. 381.
230 Bjørgo 1965, here pp. 9, 11 and 18.
231 Christensen, A. E. 2000, pp. 93–94; Pentz 2014, pp. 208–209.
232 *Groenlendinga tháttr* IF IV chapter 2, pp. 276 and 278; English translation: CSI chapter 2, p. 374 and 375.

224 *Trade and shipping*

233 Nørlund 1942, p. 88; English translation, p. 93.
234 *Fostbroedra saga* IF VI chapter 22, pp. 227–228; English translation: CSI chapter 22, p. 375.
235 *Fostbroedra saga* IF VI chapter 22, p. 244; English translation: CSI chapter 23, pp. 383–384.
236 *Fostbroedra saga* IF VI chapter 22, p. 245; English translation: CSI chapter 23, p. 384.
237 *Kroka-Refs saga* IF XIV chapter 10, p. 140, cf. pp. 138–139; *ferju ok á sjau menn*; English translation: CSI volume 3, chapter 10, p. 409.
238 *Fostbroedra saga* IF VI chapter 23, p. 230; English translation: CSI chapter 23, p. 376.
239 *Fostbroedra saga* IF VI chapter 24, p. 253; English translation: CSI chapter 24, p. 389.
240 Cf. Chapter 3, p. 137.
241 *Fostbroedra saga* IF VI chapters 23 and 24, pp. 234, 237, 239, 241 and 252; English translation: CSI chapters 23 and 24, pp. 378, 380, 381, 382 and 388.
242 Cf. Chapter 4, p. 175 and Chapter 5, pp. 186–188.
243 *Fostbroedra saga* IF VI chapter 23, p. 239; English translation: CSI chapter 23, p. 381.
244 The previous farm is called Löngunes, the latter Langanes. The editors of IF think the same farm is meant, the chieftain's farm in Einarsfjord. IF VI, chapter 21, footnote 5.
245 *Fostbroedra saga* IF VI chapter 24, pp. 251–252; English translation: CSI chapter 24, p. 388.
246 *Flomanna saga* IF XIII chapter 24, p. 299.
247 Personal communication from Georg Nyegaard, Grønlands NationalMuseum, Nuuk.
248 Madsen 2014(a), p. 145, table 6.10; KLNM, entry word "Båt".
249 *Groenlendinga tháttr* IF IV chapter 2, p. 278; English translation: CSI chapter 2, p. 375; *Groenlendinga saga* IF IV chapter 4, p. 253; English translation: CSI chapter 3, p. 23 and Penguin chapter 3, p. 8.
250 Cf. Chapter 4, p. 199.
251 *Eiriks saga Rauda* IF IV chapter 13, p. 235; English translation: CSI chapter 13, p. 18 and Penguin chapter 13, p. 49.
252 *Fostbroedra saga* IF VI chapter 17, p. 206, cf. p. 202; English translation: CSI chapter 17, p. 367.
253 *Fostbroedra saga* IF VI chapter 17, p. 206; English translation: CSI chapter 17, p. 367.
254 *Groenlendinga saga* IF IV chapter 4, p. 253; English translation: CSI chapter 3, p. 23 and Penguin chapter 3, p. 8.
255 Bjørgo 1965, pp. 7–20 concerning the names used in Norway.
256 Nansen 1911, p. 305.
257 Roussell 1941, p. 23.
258 Berglund 2000, pp. 297 and 299.
259 Pilgrim 2004, p. 39.
260 Kristjansson, L. 1982, pp. 113–19, quotation p. 113; *á midöldum hefur efni i báta adallega verid rekavidur*.
261 Wikipedia, entry word "Teredo navalis".
262 *Eiriks saga Rauda* IF IV chapter 13, pp. 234–235; English translation: CSI chapter 13, p. 18 and Penguin chapter 13, p. 49.
263 Cf. Chapter 4, p. 165.
264 Andersen and Malmros 1992, pp. 121–122; cf. Vebæk 1993, p. 39.
265 See Chapter 5, pp. 203–205.
266 IA, I Resiniani years 1189 and 1190; III Høyer 1189 and 1190; IV Regii 1189 and 1190; V Skálholt 1190; *Oddaannalar og Oddverjaannall* 2003, year 1190, pp. 136–137.
267 *Sturlunga saga* Old Norse chapters 95 and 96, p. 122; English translation II, chapters 13 and 14, pp. 118 and 119.

268 IA, AD 1347, V Skálholt and IX Flatø; GHM III, p. 14.
269 GHM has included a notice for 1348 which Gustav Storm did not include in his comprehensive edition of the Icelandic Annals. He may have doubted the authenticity of the two manuscripts in which the notice was found. The notice says that in 1348 "the Greenlanders" sailed from Iceland to Norway on the same ship as an Icelandic chieftain (GHM III, p. 14). We can safely assume that it was the Greenlanders who had drifted to Iceland the previous year.
270 Cf. Chapter 4, p. 191; Pentz 2014, pp. 208–209.
271 Klepp 1983, pp. 42 and 86.
272 Roussell 1936, p. 101; registration number of the wood is S91.
273 Andersen and Malmros 1992, pp. 118–119.
274 Andersen and Malmros 1992, p. 122.
275 Roussell 1936, pp. 101, 169 and 170, object no. U86. The board is 111 cm long and 2 cm thick.
276 Cf. Chapter 4, p. 192.
277 Information from Jon Bojer Godal. The hypothesis is discussed in Pilgrim 2004.
278 Arneborg 2004, pp. 267 and 392 note 101; Pilgrim 2004, p. 39.
279 DN X no. 9 = RN III no. 500; DN V no. 152 = RN V no. 476.
280 Cf. Chapter 3, pp. 172, 122.
281 DN VII no.104.
282 Nedkvitne 2014(a), chapters 1 and 2.
283 On Flanders, cf. Chapter 3, pp. 125–126, 172, 193; Gaborit-Chopin 1978, p. 14; Gaborit-Chopin 1992, pp. 204–205, 387 and 389; *Louvre–Guide* 1993, pp. 27, 34 and 35.
284 Nørlund seems to claim this was the case (Nørlund 1924, pp. 144–145).
285 *Horn austanverdu*, that is "eastern Horn", on modern maps called "Vesturhorn".
286 Hvarf means "that which disappears", and probably is meant the land last seen on Greenland when one leaves the country. Ivar Bárdarson explains that it is the mountain above Herjolvsnes, today called Ikigait, and which is 900 m high, and that Sandhöfn was a port close to Herjolvsnes. This was the first stop which it was possible to make in Norse Greenland for merchant ships coming from Norway or Iceland (*Eiríks saga Rauða*, IF IV, p. 201, footnote 2; Ivar Bárdarson, p. 19; Berglund 1979).
287 *Landnámabok* IF I, pp. 32–33, S2 and H2; English and Norwegian translations: chapter 2. I have followed the Hauksbok version.
288 *Landnámabok* IF I, pp. 32–33, S2 and H2; S2 says "tylft" south of Iceland. Two tylft of sailing corresponded to one day and one night of sailing (KLNM entry word "tylft"). English and Norwegian translations: chapter 2.
289 Vandvik, E. ed. 1959 no.11 = RN I no. 139.
290 *Fostbroedra saga* IF VI chapters 16–18, pp. 202–211; English translation: CSI chapters 16–18, pp. 365–369.
291 Cf. Chapter 4, pp. 212–214.
292 IA, year 1262, in: I Annales Resiniani; III Høyer; IV Regii; V Skálholt.
293 IA, year 1266, in: IV Regii; VIII Gottskalk; cf. Chapter 4, p. 171.
294 *Fostbroedra saga* IF VI chapters 20 and 24, pp. 222–223 and 257; English translation: CSI chapters 20 and 24, pp. 372–373 and 390.
295 Cf. Chapter 6, pp. 357 and 359.
296 IA, VII Lögmann years 1406, 1410 and 1413.
297 *Groenlendinga saga* IF IV chapter 9, p. 268: English translations: CSI chapter 8, p. 32 and Penguin chapter 8, p. 20–21.
298 *Sturlunga saga*, Old Norse chapter 174, p. 233; English translation II, pp. 212; Danish translation I, p. 272 (Old Norse edition says 1203 or shortly thereafter); identical information in "Hrafns saga hin serstaka", printed in Old Norse edition of *Sturlunga saga*, p. 912.
299 *Bárdar saga Snæfellsáss* IF XIII chapter 5, p. 114; English translation chapter 5, p. 243.
300 *Audunar tháttr vestfirzka* IF VI chapter 1, p. 361; English translation chapter 1, p. 370.

226 Trade and shipping

301 Nedkvitne 2014(a) is the last contribution.
302 *Konungs skuggsiá*, Old Norse, p. 6; English translation, p. 94; Norwegian translation, p. 27.
303 *Fostbroedra saga* IF VI chapter 20, pp. 222–223; English translation: CSI chapter 20, pp. 372–373.
304 KLNM entry word "Navigation"; Ramskou 1966, pp. 27–29.
305 Valeur 2000, pp. 14–17.
306 *Konungs skuggsiá*, Old Norse, p. 28; English translation, pp. 138–139; Norwegian translation, p. 65.
307 DN XVIII no. 33; *storum sio iaklum ok isom ok fengo storan skada a theira skipom*.
308 Egede/Bobé, p. 209; 11 June 1728.
309 Egede, N. *Description of Greenland*, p. 267.
310 Kuijpers et al. 2014, p. 9; A table for the years 1867–1879 confirms that this was generally so, but the date for an ice-free Eastern Settlement varied, and the ports in 1868 were not accessible until November.
311 Valeur 2000, pp. 14–17.
312 DN X no. 9 = RN III no. 500.
313 DN V no. 152 = RN V no. 476.
314 DN VII nos. 103 and 104.
315 *Fostbroedra saga* IF VI chapters 20 and 24, pp. 223 and 248; English translation: CSI chapters 20 and 24, pp. 373 and 386.
316 *Groenlendinga tháttr* IF IV chapter 6, p. 290; English translation: CSI chapter 6, p. 382.
317 *Eiriks saga Raudi* IF IV chapter 3, p. 205; English translation: CSI chapter 3, p. 5 and Penguin chapter 3, p. 30.
318 Jonsson 1924, pp. 274–275; Imer 2017, p. 234.
319 *Konungs skuggsiá*, Old Norse, pp. 27–28; English translation, pp. 137–138; Norwegian translation, p. 64.
320 IA, years 1189 and 1190 in these annals: I Resiniani, III Høyer, IV Regii, V Skálholt; *Oddaannalar og Oddverjaannall 2003*, p. 136.
321 *Oddaannalar og Oddverjaannall 2003*, p. 180, years 1380 and 1381; IA, VII Lögmann; 1382; IX Flatø 1382; VIII Gottskalk 1382; VII Lögmann 1383; IX Flatø 1382. The exact year of each event differs between the annals; the dates in the text are my interpretation. Cf. IA, IX Flatø 1382 and 1383; VII Lögmann 1381 and 1382.
322 *Groenlendinga tháttr* IF IV chapter 6, p. 292; English translation: CSI chapter 6, p. 382.
323 *Groenlendinga tháttr* IF IV chapter 2, p. 277; English translation: CSI chapter 6, p. 277.
324 *Horn austanverdu*, that is "eastern Horn". On modern maps called "Vesturhorn".
325 *Groenlendinga tháttr* IF IV chapters 1 and 2, pp. 275–278; English translation: CSI chapters 1 and 2, pp. 74–75.
326 Cf. Chapter 4, p. 195.
327 IA, VIII Gottkalk, year 1367; *Forgeck knoren nordr fyrir Biorgvin*.
328 The departure from Eyafjördr in 1185: *Sturlunga saga*, Old Norse chapter 92, pp. 117–118; English translation II chapter 11, p. 113; Danish translation I, pp. 135–136; The shipwreck in 1189 and their discovery 1203: *Sturlunga saga*, Old Norse chapter 95, p. 122; English translation II, p. 118; Danish translation I, pp. 140–141; The annals says he was found in AD 1200 which is 11 years later: IA, IV Regii, V Skálholt, X Oddveria.
329 *Sturlunga saga*, Old Norse chapter 82, pp. 100–101; English translation II, p. 93; Danish translation I, p. 116. For the dating cf. Old Norse edition p. 101; *sagnamadr mikill ok sannfroedr madr*.
330 *Konungs skuggsiá*, pp. 27–28; English translation, pp. 135–137; Monsters in the Greenland Ocean are also mentioned in *Historia Norwegie*, p. 55.

Trade and shipping   227

331 *Eiriks saga Rauda* IF IV chapter 7, pp. 218–219; English translation: CSI chapter 7, p. 11 and Penguin chapter 7, p. 39.
332 *Groenlendinga tháttr* IF IV chapter 2, pp. 277–279; English translation: CSI chapter 2, pp. 374–376.
333 *Groenlendinga tháttr* IF IV chapter 2, p. 279; English translation: CSI chapter 2, p. 376.
334 IA, VII Lögmann, year 1282; the relevant annals are: *Oddaannalar og Oddverjaannall*, p. 180, years 1380 and 1381; IA, VII Lögmann year 1381; IX Flatø year 1382; VIII Gottskalk year 1382; VII Lögmann 1382; IX Flatø 1383.
335 IA, VII Lögmann, years 1384 and 1386; IX Flatø, years 1385 and 1387.
336 *Clèment VI, Lettres closes, patentes et curiales*, Paris 1960/1; Regest (= summary of the document) in Norwegian: RN V no. 895.
337 *hvart ther hafed thau spurt eda eigi.*
338 DN X no. 9; *bidium ver at ther minnizst thessarra hofdinga saler.*
339 IA, V Skálholt, VII Lögmann, IX Flatö, all year 1343.
340 Cf. Chapter 6, p. 343.
341 VIII Gottskalk, year 1378.
342 *Medieval Scandinavia*, entry word "Annals. Iceland".
343 Berglund 1979, p. 26; some vague suggestions by Poul Nørlund may be interpreted in the same direction (Nørlund and Roussell 1930, p. 144).
344 Cf. Chapter 1, p. 28. For biographic details on the two, see the index to this book.
345 *Fostbroedra saga* IF VI chapters 16 and 18, pp. 204 and 211; English translation: CSI chapters 16 and 18, pp. 366 and 369.
346 *Fostbroedra saga* IF VI chapter 18, pp. 214 and 224, cf. pp. 227, 248 and 257; English translation: CSI chapter 18, p. 370 and 373, cf. pp. 375, 386 and 390.
347 *Groenlendinga tháttr* IF IV chapter 6, p. 288; English translation: CSI chapter 6, p. 380.
348 Cf. Chapter 4, p. 191.
349 *Profectio Danorum in Hierosolymam*, Latin text, pp. 475–476; Norwegian translation, p. 115.
350 IA, V Skálholt, year 1262.
351 IA, IV Regii; VIII Gottskalk, year 1266.
352 "Grænlands annal", pp. 53–54.
353 Cf. Chapter 3, pp. 125–127; Chapter 4, p. 207–208.
354 *Eiriks saga Rauda* IF IV chapter 7, pp. 218–219; English translation: CSI chapter 7, p. 11 and Penguin chapter 7, p. 39; *Thorfinnr var i kaupferdum ok thotti godr fardreng.*
355 *Groenlendinga saga* IF IV chapter 7, p. 260 and chapter 9, p. 268; English translation: CSI chapter 6, p. 28 and chapter 8, p. 32, and Penguin chapter 6, p. 15 and chapter 8, p. 20.
356 *Groenlendinga tháttr* IF IV chapters 2 and 6, pp. 279 and 292 footnote 1; English translation: CSI chapters 2 and 6, pp. 376 and 382.
357 NGL I, pp. 437–438 = Norske middelalderdokument, Oslo 1973, p. 14.
358 *Groenlendinga saga* IF IV chapter 4, pp. 253–254; English translation: CSI chapter 3, p. 24, and Penguin chapter 3, pp. 9–10.
359 *Groenlendinga tháttr* IF IV chapter 5, p. 284; English translation: CSI chapter 5, pp. 378.
360 *Sturlunga saga*, Old Norse chapter 185, p. 255; English translation I, p. 163; Danish translation I, p. 296.
361 DN II no. 42 and 64. Cf. RN II nos. 868, 624 and 887.
362 DN VII, no. 103, cf. 104.
363 IA, V Skálholt, year 1346; *Kom knörrinn af Grænlandi med heilu, ok hardla miklu fe.*
364 *Landnámabok* IF I, pp. 32–33, S2 and H2; English and Norwegian translations: chapter 2; Ivar Bárdarson, p. 19.
365 IA, VIII Gottskalk, year 1366.
366 DN II no. 158 = RN IV no. 411.
367 DN XV no. 29.

368 *Fostbroedra saga* IF VI, pp. 224, 230 and 237; English translation: CSI, p. 373, 376 and 380.
369 *Fostbroedra saga* IF VI chapter 20, p. 224; English translation: CSI, p. 373.
370 *Eiriks saga Rauda* IF IV chapter 7, pp. 218; English translation: CSI chapter 7, p. 11 and Penguin chapter 7, pp. 38–39. *Eiriks saga Rauda* IF IV chapter 14, p. 236 footnote 1; English translation: CSI chapter 14, p. 18 and Penguin chapter 14, pp. 49–50; *Groenlendinga saga* IF IV chapter 7, pp. 260–261; English translation: CSI chapter 6, p. 28 and Penguin chapter 6, p. 15.
371 *Groenlendinga tháttr* IF IV chapter 6, p. 292 note 1.
372 DN VII, nos. 103 and 104 (1325).
373 *Sturlunga saga*, Old Norse chapter 185, p. 255; English translation I, p. 163; Danish translation I, p. 296.
374 *Sturlunga saga*, Old Norse chapter 82, p. 101; English translation II, p. 93; Danish translation I, pp. 116–117.
375 DN II no. 158 = RN IV no. 411. Here the name is transcribed *Lauta luta*. I have checked the original again and changed the spelling.
376 IA, VIII Gottskalk, year 1366; *Buin knor til Grænlands og var formadr Sigurdr af Bautahlutanum.*
377 IA, VIII Gottskalk, year 1367.
378 DN XV no. 20 = RN VII no. 430.
379 DN III no. 407.
380 IA, index, p. 625.
381 DN II no. 453 = RN VII no. 726.
382 Cf. DN II no. 158 = RN IV no. 411 and DN II no. 453 = RN VII no. 726.
383 IA, VIII Gottskalk, year 1388.
384 DN XV no. 20 = RN VII no. 430.
385 *Magnus Lagabøte's National Law* V.11.
386 *Om Norgis Rige*, edition from 1968, p. 50; GHM III, pp. 226–233.
387 Cf. Chapter 4, p. 182.
388 Munch 1864, pp. 19–28.
389 Christiansen 2004, p. 32.
390 *Groenlendinga tháttr* IF IV chapter 2, p. 279; *"Þeir komu í Eiríksfjörð og sóttu menn til fundar við þá og slógu kaupum"*. English translation: CSI chapter 2, p. 376.
391 *Groenlendinga tháttr* IF IV chapter 2, p. 279; English translation: CSI chapter 2, p. 376.
392 *Fostbroedra saga* IF VI chapter 16, pp. 204–205; English translation: CSI chapter 16, p. 366.
393 *Eiriks saga Rauda* IF IV chapter 7, pp, 219–220; English translation: CSI chapter 7, p. 11 and Penguin chapter 7, p. 39.
394 Nørlund and Stenberger 1934, p. 114.
395 Nørlund and Stenberger 1934, pp. 116–117.
396 Cf. Chapter 2, p. 53.
397 Berglund 1979, p. 29.
398 Christiansen 2004, p. 32.
399 *Eiriks saga Rauda* IF IV chapter 7, pp. 219–220; English translation: CSI chapter 7, p. 11 and Penguin chapter 7, p. 39.
400 *Fostbroedra saga* IF VI chapter 20, pp. 223–224; English translation: CSI chapter 20, p. 373.
401 *Fostbroedra saga* IF VI, chapter 24, p. 257, cf. pp. 214, 227–228 and 248; English translation: CSI, chapter 24, p. 390, cf. pp. 370, 375 and 386.
402 *Groenlendinga tháttr* IF IV chapter 2, p, 279; English translation: CSI, chapter 2, p. 376.
403 *Bjarkøyretten*, chapter 85, p. 112. St. Olav's ordinance about Norwegians' rights on Iceland and Icelanders in Norway, NGL I, pp. 437–438 = *Norske middelalderdokumenter* no. 1.

404 Cf. Chapter 2, pp. 50–56.
405 *Magnus Lagabøte's Urban Law* III.6.
406 *Magnus Lagabøte's National Law* VIII.9.
407 DN V no. 23.
408 NGL III no. 47 = RN III no. 972; Nedkvitne 2014(a), p. 312.
409 *Magnus Lagabøte's National Law* VIII.9.
410 NGL III no. 89 = RN VI no. 469; NGL III no. 91 = RN VI no. 651.
411 Nedkvitne 201 (a), pp. 314–315.
412 DN XV no. 29.
413 Nedkvitne 2014(a), pp. 300–301 and 309–310.
414 *Magnus Lagabøte's National Law* V.11; cf. Chapter 4, p. 207.
415 DN XV no. 29.
416 IA, VII Lögmann, years 1384 and 1386; IX Flatø, years 1385 and 1387.
417 "*Grænlands annal*", pp. 44–46.
418 "*Grænlands annal*", p. 45 = GHM III, pp. 436–439.
419 Widding 1976, entry word "steypireidur".
420 IA, IX Flatø 1385 and 1387, pp. 414–415; IA, VII Lögmann years 1384 and 1386, pp. 365–366.
421 IX Flatø says that Bjørn Einarsson continued to Norway in 1389. This must be wrong for 1388. The annals often give incorrect dates for real events.
422 DN XVIII no. 33; cf. GHM III, pp. 135–142.
423 DN V no. 23.
424 Nedkvitne 2014(a), pp. 322–324.
425 *Sekkjagjald* is first mentioned as a customs duty due from merchants arriving from Iceland in 1360. It is then said to have been imposed for the first time under king Magnus who became king in 1319 (NGL III no. 91 = RN VI no. 651). The main export from Iceland at this time was stockfish, and here *sekkjagjald* was paid with 6 fish for each 120, that is 5% (NGL III no. 118 = RN VII no. 1051; cf. NGL III no. 119 = RN VII no. 1117).
426 Nørlund 1942, p. 97; English translation, p. 102.
427 Nørlund 1942, pp. 83–98; English translation, pp. 87–104.
428 Nørlund 1942, pp. 97–98 and 136; English translation, pp. 102–103 and 142, in a milder form.
429 Nørlund 1942, p. 136; English translation, p. 142.
430 Arneborg claims that "Norwegian royal power" after 1261 maintained its "monopoly trade" (*monopolhandel*), and that this continued to the end of the Norse settlement (Arneborg 2004, p. 268).
431 Ingstad, H. 1959, p. 391; reprint 2004, p. 310; English translation, p. 242.
432 GHM III, pp. 199–200.
433 NGL I, pp. 460–461 = DI volume 1 no. 152.
434 DN XVIII no. 33. Cf. above Chapter 4, pp. 212–214.
435 *Sturlunga saga*, Old Norse chapter 185, p. 255; English translation I, p. 163; Danish translation I, p. 296.
436 *Hákonar Saga Hákonarsonar*, Old Norse chapter 311, Norwegian translation, p. 333.
437 "Grænlands annal", p. 53 = GHM III, pp. 238–239.
438 DN VII no. 103.
439 IA, V Skálholt, year 1346
440 DN XXI no. 82.
441 IA, VIII Gottskalk, years 1366 and 1367.
442 Cf. Chapter 4, p. 185.
443 Nedkvitne 2014(a), pp. 108–109, cf. index entry word "charter".
444 Nedkvitne 2014(a), chapter 6.

5 Subsistence food production

Thorolv was a chieftain who lived ca. 900 AD in northern Norway at his farm Sandnes.

> Thorolfr exploited well the resources (*fong*) which were in northern Norway (*Hálogaland*). He sent men/servants (*menn*) to places where herring and cod (*skreid*) could be caught. He had access to sufficient places where seal could be caught and eggs gathered. All this he assembled at his manor house. He had never less than hundred free men at his farm.[1]

Thorolv's brother Skallagrim settled as chieftain in western Iceland. He built his manor at Borg where the conditions were best for animal husbandry. He also lived part of the year at a secondary farm where conditions were best for marine resources: cod fisheries, seal hunting, whale hunting and gathering eggs from sea birds. His third farm he called Akrar (*cornfields*) because he sowed grain there; it was also a good place for collecting driftwood. He settled two clients close to rivers where they fished and conserved salmon for the chieftain's consumption and a third was responsible for herding the chieftain's sheep and lived at a farm up in the hills. These men should be seen as servants who were given housing outside the main farm(s). Skallagrim had ten free men on board his ship from Norway to whom he gave land close to his own farm. These farms were operated in the following period as independent economic units, but the ten households were undoubtedly protected judicially by Skallagrim.[2]

Along the Norwegian and Icelandic coasts and even more in Greenland the peasants had to exploit diverse resources over a large area to survive comfortably. Chieftains organised this with the help of servants. Ordinary peasant households had to combine different resources by travelling themselves to where the resources were found, which became a seasonal routine. Combining resources also gave better food security. This economic organisation was adapted to an environment with few and unstable resources.

The historical sources for Norwegian and Icelandic food production are far richer than those from Greenland. This makes it useful to have these two countries as a background or "model" for the development in Norse Greenland.

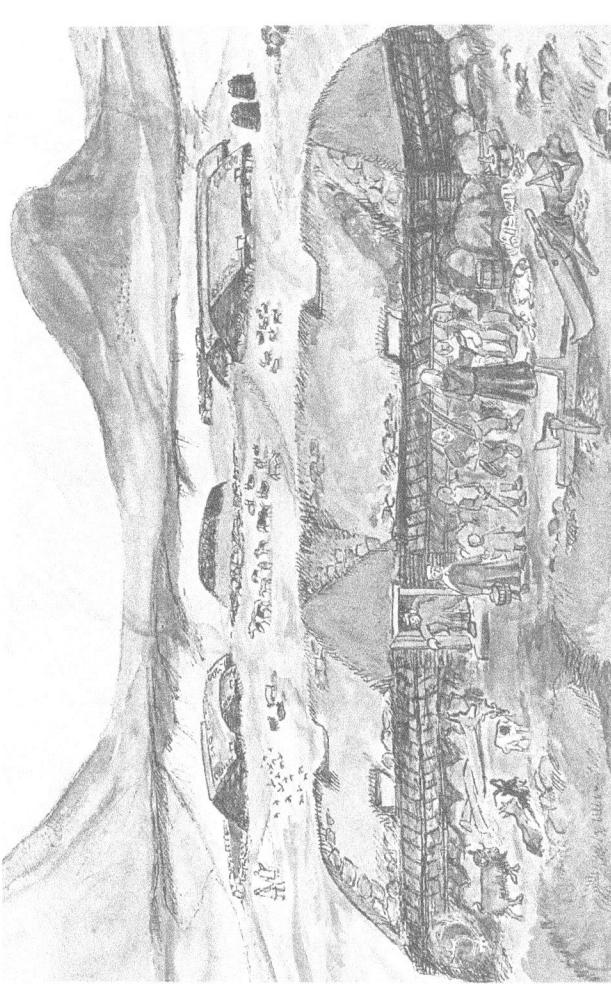

Figure 5.1 W51 Sandnes, watercolour painting by the Danish-Greenlandic illustrator and museum curator Jens Rosing.

Rosing has tried to reconstruct the farm W51 Sandnes on the basis of excavations by Aage Roussell (Roussell 1936, pp. 31–54; Appendix II, map 2).

The house in the front is the dwelling. The outer part of the wall was made of turf, which on the drawing is painted in three layers. Hidden behind it was a thick stonewall. Some 40 cm behind the stonewall was a wooden wainscot, which was the innermost part of the wall and would have been visible to the residents. Both the walls and the air between them gave insulation. The entrance to the corridor is shown on the drawing. To the right of it was the living-room, to the left the sleeping quarters.

The houses at the back are two large combined byres and stables built at the top of a slope. In each of them there is one large byre for the cows, several smaller stables for sheep and goats, and barns for the winter fodder. Rosing has painted domestic animals pasturing between the dwelling and the byres/stables. This is not realistic. There would be the meadow where a significant part of the winter fodder was harvested. No animals were pastured there in the growing season. The meadow was manured from the two byres which were built on higher ground. Far in the background towards the mountains the painter has suggested pasturing animals in the outfield. That is realistic. To the right of the byres turf is shown, which was dried for winter fuel.

Copyright: Jens Rosing/VISDA.dk.

The Nationalmuseum archaeologist Poul Nørlund was the first to call Norway "the motherland" of the Norse Greenlanders.[3]

Scholars today mostly understand changes in Norse Greenland agriculture in an ecological perspective, as described in the Introduction to this book. After ca. 1300 temperatures fell, animal husbandry declined and a hierarchical social structure prevented flexible responses. Hunger crises and the end of the Norse settlements followed.[4] This hypothesis has not been verified,[5] but has won wide acceptance partly because ecological approaches attract great interest in contemporary society. The present chapter is an attempt to discuss the scholarly value of the ecological approach.

1 The basis: animal husbandry

The local resources

In Greenland grain-growing was impossible, and the immigrants lacked the easy access to wood which they were used to. This could to a certain degree be compensated through imports, but the main strategy was to find replacements in Greenland combined with changes in consumer habits. *The King's Mirror* writes that there are good pastures and large farms in Greenland where people keep many cattle, sheep and goats, and they produce a lot of butter and cheese. They also eat a lot of meat from all kinds of wild animals like reindeer, whales, seal and bear.[6] The realistic *Groenlendinga tháttr* from the 12th century mentions a farmer who had in store for the winter 60 slaughtered animals, 500 kg butter and a lot of stockfish.[7] Eirik Raudi called the new land Greenland because he thought it would "encourage people to go there if it had a good name".[8] Green pastures and meadows were important because livestock farming was important. The Norse Greenlanders settled in the fjords, and preferably in the bottom of these fjords, because climate and available land for livestock farming was best here.

Dano-Norwegian colonists who arrived after 1721 preferred the outer coast. They were state officials and merchants for whom shipping from Denmark was all important. The first of them, the Norwegian missionary Hans Egede, noted in his diary that if some of the new settlers who arrived in his own time were to live from cattle farming, they had to settle in the fjords.[9] He sent servants from his dwelling near Nuuk to the fjords to fetch hay, firewood and cabbage, and they also fished and hunted.[10] Egede was the first European to visit the fjords after the Norse had left, and he described in his diary how fertile they were compared to the coast. On 20 August 1723 he visited the Eiriksfjord area in the Eastern Settlement and there he found "beautiful, grassy hillsides where the Norwegians had lived in former times . . . this place was delightful with beautiful, high grass and many pleasing flowers".[11]

The concept of "farm" is ambiguous. In medieval Norway a settlement unit which had its own name was considered as one farm by contemporaries. In the Norwegian scholarly tradition such a farm is called "name farm" (*navnegård*). At one "name farm" there could live one or several households that had their own separate dwelling, byre, stables and domestic animals. In the Norwegian scholarly tradition each of them is called *bruk*, which can best be translated as "household farm". The economic unit was the "household farm" operated by one household.[12]

Archaeologists have to tie their definition of "farm" to visible ruins, a "group of ruins (ruin sites) containing one or more buildings regarded as living quarters".[13] This is what historians would call "name farm". In this book the concept "farm" is used in the sense of "name farm"; if a "household farm" is meant, that concept will be used.

Milk from cows

The best description of how cattle were kept in Norse Greenland is to be found in Daniel Bruun's report of his excavations of the farm E1.[14] One of the houses contained the byre for cows and other cattle at one end, and a barn for hay at the other. The roof was normally ca. 150 cm above the floor, made of timber.[15] The byre was insulated with stones and turf along the walls, and turf on the roof. The cows stood with their heads towards the long walls, which were divided into stalls with the help of flat and large stones raised on end. The cows were tethered to the wall.

Along the northern wall of the byre on E1 there were three stalls, each of them 2.2 m broad.[16] Bruun writes that during his time (he was born 1856) in Iceland one stall was often meant for two cows.[17] The north wall with three stalls would then have room for six cows.

The south wall of the same byre had the same length of 6.6 m, and there were two broad stalls of 2.8 m each, probably for two cows each.[18] The south wall had a third stall of only 0.95 m, which must have been for one cow or heifer.[19] Along the south wall there would then be room for five cattle. In the whole byre there would have been room for 11 (6 + 5) cattle. It was not necessarily full every winter. The byre was situated close to the dwelling, which was convenient since the cows were milked and fed twice a day.

E1 also had another building for domestic animals situated farther from the dwelling. One of its two rooms had stalls, which means that it must have been a stable for horses or a byre for cattle. The internal measurements of this room were 6.3 × 3.2 m. Along the south wall there were three stalls, and along the north wall there were none.[20] Horses were larger than cows, so if this was a stable for horses, it is probable that there was only room for one horse per stall, which means that the farm E1 had room for three horses.[21] The alternative is that this was a separate building for cattle which did not give milk, in other words it had heifers and bulls. Even in this house the stable was in the eastern part, with the western part being a barn for hay.

E1's horse (or horses), were no doubt mostly used as pack horses.[22] Ice made navigation in the Sermilik fjord problematic, and external contact must mostly have gone over land to Brattahlid. The farms between Brattahlid and the Northern Sermilik/Isafjord had sæters, and milk from the sæter and meat from the hunt in the mountains had to be transported. It is possible that E1 needed more horses than most other farms.

E1 is only one of nearly 300 farms in Norse Greenland. In the following pages I shall try to generalise this example by estimating the average number of milk-producing cattle on a Norse Greenland farm.

234 *Subsistence food production*

As a first step Table 5.1 sets out the base measurements in square metres of archaeologically excavated byres. This calculation was possible for 35 byres. Only byres where it is highly likely that all cattle which were accommodated in the byre belonged to the same household, are included in Table 5.1.

Table 5.1 Internal (1) dimensions of excavated byre-rooms

Name farm (2)	Length × breadth (m)	Rows (3)	Source
E1 ruin 3	6.6 × 4.1	2r	Bruun 1896, p. 208
E2 ruin 5, one household	7.5 × 4.1	2r	Bruun 1896, p. 224; Madsen 2014(a), p. 114
ruin 13, one household	9.8 × 3.9	2r	Madsen 2014(a), p. 114
E4 ruin 5	13.9 × 4.1	2r	Bruun 1896, p. 233; Madsen 2014(a), p. 114
E9 ruin 5	3.6 × 3.2		Bruun 1896, p. 241
E18 ruin 4	10.5 × 3.4		Madsen 2014(a), p. 114
E23 ruin 6	9.0 × 3.7		Madsen 2014(a), p. 114
E24 ruin 3	6.1 × 3.5		Madsen 2014(a), p. 114
E29b (Brattahlid) ruin 19	8.8 × 3.5	2r	Nørlund and Stenberger 1934, p. 90
E29a ruin 5 room II	7.5 × 3.5	2r	Nørlund and Stenberger 1934, pp. 83 and 86
ruin 5 room V	4.5 × 3.2	2r	Nørlund and Stenberger 1934, pp. 83 and 86
E39 ruin 8	9.3 × 3.3		Madsen 2014(a), p. 114
E47 (Gardar) ruin 9	31.6 × 4.1		Nørlund and Roussell 1930, pp. 115–117; Bruun 1896, p. 333
ruin 14	24.3 × 4.1		Nørlund and Roussell 1930, pp. 115–117; Bruun 1896, p. 333
E48 ruin 1	8.8 × 3.8		Bruun 1896, p. 344
E63 ruin 4	9.5 × 3.2	2r	Bruun 1896, p. 366
E64a room I (centr.)	5.5 × 1.8		Vebæk 1943, pp. 24, 26
E64c ruin 2 room III	6.0 × (1.5–2.0)	1r	Vebæk 1943, pp. 71–72
E66 (South Igaliku) ruin 3	11.0 × 4.0	2r	Roussell 1941, p. 220
E71 ruin 12, room X one household	12.0 × 2.4		Vebæk 1992, p. 37
ruin 3, one household	7.0 × (2.0–2.5)	1r	Vebæk 1992, pp. 43–44
E80 ruin 2	6.6 × 2.5		Madsen 2014(a), p. 114
E149 ruin 9	8.0 × 3.3		Vebæk 1991(b), p. 55; Madsen 2014(a), p. 114
E167 ruin 7 room X	4.8 × 2.2	1r	Vebæk 1992, pp. 60, 62; Madsen 2014(a), p. 115
ruin 7 room XIII (centr.)	4.6 × 1.8	1r	Vebæk 1992, pp. 60, 62; Madsen 2014(a), p. 115

W7 (Anavik) ruin 7	8.6 × 3.3	2r	Roussell 1941, p. 223; Madsen 2014(a), p. 114
W8 room VIII (centr.)	4.0 × 3.0	1r	Roussell 1941, pp. 168 and 171
W16 room VIII (centr.)	6.0 × 3.0	1r	Roussell 1941, pp. 162–163
W35 room X (centr.)	3.6 × 1.6	1r	Roussell 1941, p. 167; Madsen 2014(a), p. 115
W51 (Sandnes) ruin 5, room I	9.8 × 4.5		Roussell 1936, p. 38
ruin 6 room I	10.5 × 3.9		Roussell 1936, p. 51; Madsen 2014(a), p. 114
W52a room XIII (centr.)	7.4 × 3.2	2r	Roussell 1936, pp. 64, 88; Madsen 2014(a), p. 115
W53c room IX (centr.)	6.2 × 3.2	2r	Roussell 1941, pp. 172, 177–178
W53d room X (centr.)	3.6 × 3.1	2r	Roussell 1941, pp. 180, 188; Madsen 2014(a), p. 115
W54 room II	6.2 × 3.0		Andreasen 1982, pp. 178, 180; Madsen 2014(a), p. 114

1 Where only external measures are known, the byre has not been included in the table.
2 At six "name farms" there were two byres. Where they seem to have belonged to two different "household farms", this is noted. In the other cases they are taken to have belonged to the same household. Some of the farmhouses were "centralised", cf. Chapter 6, Figure 6.1. Byres in such housing complexes have been marked as "centr.".
3 In some of these byres stall-stones were found along both walls, which shows that cattle stood in two rows tail to tail along both walls. In other cases it can be seen that stall-stones only stood along one wall. In that case there must have been only one row of cows along one of the walls. "2r" and "1r" have been used where this can be seen in the excavated ruin. When nothing is written below, there is no indication either way.

In 13 byres it can be shown archaeologically that there were parallel rows of stalls along the two long sides, and the cattle there stood tail to tail. All these byres were between 3.1 and 4.1 m wide. In seven byres it can be shown archaeologically that there was only one row of stalls along one of the long sides, with all the latter byres being 3.0 m wide or less.

In 15 byres no direct evidence exists of whether there were one or two rows of cattle. The evidence presented in Table 5.1 makes it safe to assume that all byres which were 3.1 m wide or more had two rows of cattle, and those which were 3.0 m wide or less had only one row. This method makes it highly likely that in 11 of the 15 byres there were two rows of cattle, and in 4 of them there was only one row. In Table 5.1 35 byres are included, of which 24 (13 + 11) are likely to have contained two rows of cattle and 11 (7 + 4) only one row.

How many cows could be kept in an average byre? In winter the byre was kept warm mainly through the heat from the animals' bodies, but one cannot discount that occasionally the farmer also burnt seal-oil in soapstone lamps there.

236 *Subsistence food production*

The frost made it advisable to make the byre small and make the animals stand close together. But the milkmaid needed room between the cows to milk and feed them. At some Norse Greenland ruins the distance between two stall-stones can be measured (Table 5.2).

Table 5.2 The width occupied by one cow in its stall, where preserved byre-stones on both sides have made this possible to measure. Several stalls with the same width on the same farm have been counted as one width.

E1, ruin 3:   1.4 m, 1.1 m and 0.95 m
   Along the northern wall there were three stalls, each of them 2.2 m wide (Bruun 1896, p. 208: 7 feet wide, each foot 0.316 m). If there were two cows in each stall; each cow would have 1.1 m at its disposal.
   Along the southern wall of the same byre there were two stalls of 2.8 m and one of 0.95 m (Bruun 1896, p. 208: 9 and 3 feet; cf. the description of E1 above). I have assumed that the stalls of 2.8 m were for two cows; one cow would then have 1.4 m at its disposal.
E2, ruin 5:   1.3 m, 1.6 m and 0.95 m
   Holm 1883, p. 93: 1.6 m (5 feet) between the stall-stones; Bruun 1896, p. 224: Along the northern wall four stalls each 1.3 m (4 feet) wide. Along the southern wall three stalls 1.6 m, 1.9 m and 1.6 m wide (5, 6 and 5 feet). I have assumed that the stall of 1.9 m was for two cows.
   ruin 9 (belonging to a different household): 1.3 m
   Holm 1883, p. 94: 5 stalls, each 4.5 feet wide; Bruun 1896, p. 225: 5 stalls each 4 feet wide. Bruun is used here.
E4, ruin 5:   1.6 m
   Bruun 1896, p. 233: 4 stall-stones, the distance between them 5 feet
E9, ruin 5:   0.9 m
   Bruun 1896, p. 241; Internal measures of byre 3.6 x 3.2 m (11.5 x 10 feet). 3 stall-stones separated stalls at northern wall, which means there must have been 4 stalls along a 3.6 m long wall, each stall 0.9 m wide. No drawing is available.
E29b, River farm ruin 19:   1.3 m
   The byre at ruin 19 of Brattahlid's River farm had a length of 8.8 m internally. Along the southern wall there was evidence of six stall-stones, which means there were seven stalls, each 1.3 m wide (Nørlund 1934, pp. 89–91). A bench occupied one stall, which means there was in practice only room for six cows along the southern wall.
E29a, North farm ruin 5, byre II: 1.3 m (+1.6 m?)
   Byre II at ruin 5 had a length of 7.5 m internally. Along the northern wall there were six stalls. This means that each stall was 1.3 m wide (Nørlund 1934, pp. 83 and 86).
   Bruun 1896, p. 293 has registered two stables or byres on the North farm which I was unable to identify with any of the stables or byres described by Nørlund. They may have been removed by owners of the sheep farms. Bruun writes that both byres/stables had stalls which were five feet wide (1.6 m).
E47, Gardar ruins 9 and 14:   0.95 m
   Each stall was 1.9 m wide (Bruun 1896, p. 333: 6 feet). Nørlund assumes that there were two cows in each stall, which means 0.95 m per cow (Nørlund and Roussell 1930, p. 117).

E48, ruin 1:   1.76 m
> On the southern wall there were three stall-stones creating four stalls. The distance between the stall-stones was 5 feet (each foot 0.316 m) and 7 inches (each inch 2.6 cm), that is 1.76 m. There would only be room for one cow in each stall (Bruun 1896, p. 344).

E64c, ruin 2 room III: 1.1 m, 1.0 m and 0.9 m
> "The distance from the west wall to the first stone is 0,9m, and from there to the next one it is 1,1m; finally the distance between this and the third stone is about 2,0m". The 2.0 m wide room must have been for two cows, 1.0 m for each (Vebæk 1943, pp. 71–72).

W51, Sandnes ruin 6:   0.7–1.0 m
> Three stall-stones are standing forming three stalls with unequal distances between them, varying from 0.7 to 1.0 m. Each stall would only give room for one cow or heifer (Roussell 1936, pp. 50–51).

Table 5.3 Width given to one cow in stalls which are measured in Table 5.2, and number of times a particular width is mentioned there

1.76 m	: 1x
1.6 m	: 2x
1.4 m	: 1x
1.3 m	: 4x
1.1 m	: 2x
1.0 m	: 1x
0.95/0.9 m	: 5x
1.0–0.7 m	: 1x

Source: Table 5.2.

The two widths mentioned most often are 0.9 m and 1.3 m. Of the 17 widths that are mentioned, the median value is between 1.1 m and 1.3 m. The figures in Table 5.2 are taken from 11 different household farms, and each of them had an average width per cow as shown in Table 5.4.

Table 5.4 Width given to one cow in stalls which are measured in Table 5.2; average for household farms mentioned there

E1:	1.3 m
E2 first household:	1.3 m
E2 second household:	1.3 m
E4:	1.6 m
E9:	0.9 m
E29a:	1.3 m
E29:	1.3 m
E47:	0.95 m
E47c:	1.0 m
E48:	1.8 m
W51:	0.9 m

Source: Table 5.2.

238 *Subsistence food production*

Five household farms had an average width of 1.3 m and four of 0.9–1.0m. Based on the results from Tables 5.3 and 5.4, an average of 1.2 m will give a realistic picture of how much space one cow normally occupied along the wall.

Table 5.5 Number of cows in one byre

Name farm	Internal length of byre (1)	Stall width for one cow (2)	Double rows? (3)	Number of cows
E1 ruin 3	6.6 m		Double	11
E2 ruin 5, one household	7.5 m		Double	8
ruin 13, one household	9.8 m	1.2 m	Double	16
E4 ruin 5	13.9 m	1.2 m	Double	24
E9 ruin 5	3.6 m		Double	8
E18 ruin 4	10.5 m	1.2 m	Double	18
E23 ruin 6	9.0 m	1.2 m	Double	15
E24 ruin 3	6.1 m	1.2 m	Double	10
E29 (Brattahlid) ruin 19	8.8 m		Double	10
E29a ruin 5 room II	7.5 m		Double	11
ruin 5 room V	4.5 m	1.2 m	Double	7
E39 ruin 8	9.3 m	1.2 m	Double	15
E47 (Gardar) ruin 9	31.6 m	1.0 m	Double	62
ruin 14	24.3 m	1.0 m	Double	48
E48 ruin 1	8.8 m		Double	8
E63 ruin 4	9.5 m	1.2 m	Double	16
E64a room I (centr.)	5.5 m	1.2 m	Single	4
E64c ruin 2 room III	6.0 m		Single	4
E66 (South Igaliku) ruin 3	11.0 m	1.2 m	Double	18
E71 ruin 12, room X, one household	12.0 m	1.2 m	Single	10
ruin 3, one household	7.0 m	1.2 m	Single	6
E80 ruin 2	6.6 m	1.2 m	Single	5
E149 ruin 9	8.0 m	1.2 m	Double	13
E 167 ruin 7 room X	4.8 m	1.2 m	Single	4
ruin 7 room XIII (centr.)	4.6 m	1.2 m	Single	4
W7 (Anavik) ruin 7	8.6 m	1.2 m	Double	14
W8 room VIII (centr.)	4.0 m	1.2 m	Single	3
W16 room VIII (centr.)	6.0 m	1.2 m	Single	5
W35 room X (centr.)	3.6 m	1.2 m	Single	3
W51 (Sandnes) ruin 5 room I	9.8 m	1.2 m	Double	16
ruin 6 rooms I and II	10.5 m	1.2 m	Double	18
W52a room XIII (centr.)	7.4 m	1.2 m	Double	12
W53c room IX (centr.)	6.2 m	1.2 m	Double	10

W53d room X (centr.)	3.6 m	1.2 m	Double	6
W54 room II	6.2 m	1.2 m	Single	5

1 The farm numbers in the first column and the length of byres in the second column are taken from Table 5.1.
2 If no figure is given in the third column, it means that the number of cows in the byre in the final column is taken directly from the text of archaeologists. Source references to them are found in Tables 5.1 and 5.2. If other widths than 1.2 m are used, they are taken from Table 5.2. At E47 the width between two stall-stones was 1.9 m, I have added 0.1 m for the width of the stall-stone which gives 1.0 m per cow. If no width of stalls can be measured for a farm, I have used the average width occupied by a cow calculated in Tables 5.3 and 5.4, which is 1.2 m.
3 The number of rows in the fourth column is taken from Table 5.1.

Table 5.6 Household farms in Table 5.5 enumerated according to the number of cows

Number of cows	Farm identification number
3	W8 room VIII (centralised farm)
3	W35 room X (centralised farm)
4	E64a room I (centralised farm)
4	E64c ruin 2 room III
5	E80 ruin 2
5	W16 room VIII (centralised farm)
5	W54 room II
6	W53d room X (centralised farm)
6	E71 ruin 3, one household
8	E2 ruin 5, one household
8	E9 ruin 5
8	E48 ruin 1
8	E167 ruin 7 rooms X and XIII (centralised farm)
10	E24 ruin 3, one household
10	E71 ruin 12, room X, one household
10	W53c room IX (centralised farm)
11	E1 ruin 3
12	E29 (Brattahlid River farm) ruin 19
12	W52a room XIII (centralised farm)
13	E149 ruin 9
14	W7 (Anavik) ruin 7
15	E23 ruin 6
15	E39 ruin 8
16	E2 ruin 13, one household
16	E63 ruin 4
18	E18 ruin 4
18	E66 (South Igaliku) ruin 3

(continued)

Table 5.6 (continued)

Number of cows	Farm identification number
20	E29a (Brattahlid North farm) ruin 5 rooms II and V
24	E4 ruin 5
34	W51 (Sandnes) ruin 5 room I and ruin 6 room I.
110	E47 (Gardar) ruins 9 and 14

E83 Hvalsey has been left out because it is not clear whether E83 and E83a were one or two household farms (cf. Chapter 2, p. 71). In W51 (Sandnes) the two byres may not have been contemporary.

Table 5.6 includes the livestock from 31 household farms. The farm with the median value is number 16 which had byre-room for 10 cattle. In the corresponding Norwegian figures to be discussed later, the elite farms are excluded. In Table 5.6 two large elite farms should also be excluded: Gardar (110 cattle) and Sandnes (34 cattle). We are then left with 29 farms in Table 5.6. The median farm will then be number 15 which still gives 10 cattle. The average number of cattle is found by summarising all 29 farms and dividing by 29. The resulting figure is also ten cattle. This permits us to estimate that an average household farm had room in its byre (or byres) for ten cattle.

The word "cattle" includes cows, heifers and bulls. On the background of later Norwegian practice I shall assume that the byres included in Tables 5.5 and 5.6 housed cows and heifers, but not bulls. If one assumes that all cattle in the byres were milk-cows, one is likely to exaggerate the milk production.

Statistical information about the number of domestic animals kept by farmers along the Atlantic and North Sea coasts of Norway dates back to 1723. At this time livestock farming had changed little since the Middle Ages, in terms of breed as well as feeding. If the large farms belonging to royal officials and landowners are excluded, the average number of milk-cows per household in the administrative regions along the coast between present day Stavanger and Harstad varied between 4.1 and 6.0, and the average was about five. If bulls and heifers are added, the number of cattle will have to be increased by 50% to an average of about eight.[23] These were "winter-fed animals", that is animals which were kept in byres and stables through the winter. In all regions cattle (milk-cows, heifers and bulls) were kept mainly for milk production, but also for their meat. Where the ambition was to maximise milk production, approximately three-quarters of the winter-fed cattle would be milk-cows, whereas if meat production was more important, only around two-thirds of the winter-fed cattle would be milk-cows.[24]

The figure of ca. ten cattle in byres on Norse Greenland is the number of cattle which were kept in the byre with the milk-cows. That was probably the heifers but not the bulls. Along the Norwegian coast most farmers did not have bulls but borrowed one from a neighbour when his cows were to be made pregnant. If a farm had a bull, it would be kept in a separate room.

Greenland had no town market where farmers could sell their beef, and their possibilities for hunting animals for their own meat consumption were better than in coastal Norway. There can be little doubt that the Norse Greenlanders wanted to get as much milk as possible out of their cattle. The Norwegian background then indicates that three-quarters of the cattle the Greenland peasants owned were milk-cows.

For the Norwegian cadastre from 1723 the numbers of cows, heifers and bulls were counted by government officials. This gave a reliable total number of cattle and reliable percentages of milk-cows. Our statistics for Greenland in Table 5.6 are based on the number of stalls, which may give too high a number of winter-fed cattle because one cannot be sure whether all stalls were in use every year. Another source of error is that some Greenlandic bulls and heifers may have been winter-fed in separate byres. If Norwegian percentages for milk-cows are used in Greenlandic byres, this source of error will make the figure for milk-cows too low. These two sources of error are not serious, as they worked in opposite directions and may cancel one another out. On this background I will assume that ca. 7.5 milk-cows[25] were winter-fed at an average Norse Greenland farm.

The author of *The King's Mirror* claimed in ca. 1250 that "there are good pastures and large farms in Greenland where people keep much cattle, sheep and goats, and they produce much butter and cheese".[26] The size of byres confirms his statement. In 1982 Knud Krogh wrote that "a livestock of 5–10 cows was not unusual at Greenlandic farms, and at the major farms the livestock was surprisingly large".[27] E47 Gardar was an extraordinary farm, with three times as many cattle as the second largest farm in Norse Greenland W51 Sandnes. Brattahlid was at this time divided into three different household farms, and two of them (E29 and E29a) are registered in Table 5.5. Arneborg claims that GUS in the Western Settlement in its final phase had only one or two cows, but her empirical basis for this figure is not clear.[28]

How much milk could a Greenlandic farmer obtain from his cows? The breed of cows in Norse Greenland came from western Norway via Iceland or directly. Norwegian coastal farmers used this breed until ca. 1830, and contemporary officials called it "our small Norwegian breed". In the 18th century officials discussed the productivity of the peasants' cattle, and four of them estimated the annual milk production of a cow on the Norwegian western and northern coasts. Their figures were 640 litres, 720 litres, 960 litres and 800–960 litres. The production was highest while the cows enjoyed the pastures with fresh grass in the summer, which in most regions was for four to five months of the year. If the cows were starved when they were kept in the byre, the milk production per day would decrease significantly in winter. The disparity in the production figures per cow may be explained by the degree of starving or "hunger feeding" in winter and the length of the period when they could eat fresh grass in summer.[29] In this chapter I shall use the lowest figure of 640 litres since the average period of feeding at summer pastures may have been shorter in Greenland than in most of coastal Norway.

242 *Subsistence food production*

This milk was consumed as fresh milk by children, by adults as skimmed sour-milk (*skyr*), butter, different kinds of cheese and sometimes as soup. Butter, cheese and skyr could be conserved for the winter and consumed when the cows produced little or no milk. Skyr was often drunk thinned out with water. In one of the rooms at farm E71 in Vatnahverfi three large tubs were found which the archaeologist Christian Vebæk thought must have been for skyr. At E149 no less than seven similar milk-tubs were found in a single room.[30]

The calorie value of one litre of fresh milk produced by a cow in traditional Norwegian agriculture has been estimated by historians of Norwegian agriculture at 560 kcal.[31] The annual production of one cow would then be 358,400 kcal, and of 7.5 cows 2,688,000 kcal. If the annual calorie production is divided by the year's 364 days, the result of the milk production would be 7,385 kcal per day. For a pre-modern Norwegian peasant household with men, women and children the average daily calorie consumption per person has been estimated to be 2,600 kcal by the Norwegian historian and agronomist Kåre Lunden.[32] This is the level of consumption when the population received what they felt they needed. I see no reason to assume that this was different in Norse Greenland.

How many household members had to share the cow-milk calories? Official, statistical information from Norway is available for the first time from 1701. In the administrative regions along the coast of western Norway the average number of household members varied from 5.0 to 5.9,[33] and in northern Norway there were ca. 6 persons per household.[34] We have no information whatsoever on the size of households in Greenland, but in the present situation the best guide is that it was the same as along the coast of northern Norway at approximately six. If the 7,385 kcal from cow-milk per day is divided between six household members, that would equate to 1,231 kcal each, which is 47% of the daily requirement of 2,600. This confirms that *The King's Mirror* was right when it claimed that milk products were the main source of food for the Norse Greenlanders. All serious historians who have commented on the subject have assumed the same.

The figure of 47% must be seen as a maximum since some byre-stalls may have been empty. Conversely the opposite would be true if the annual milk production per cow was larger than 640 litres. Since bulls and heifers may have been kept in separate byres, the number of milk-cows may have been in excess of 7.5.

The average in Table 5.5 of ten cattle per household hides an important difference between the two settlements. The 21 farms (Gardar excluded) in the Eastern Settlement had on average 12 cattle, corresponding to 9 milk-cows. In the Western Settlement the eight farms (Sandnes excluded) registered in Table 5.5 had on average 7 cattle, corresponding to 5.3 milk-cows. The same calculation as earlier implies that an average household member from the Eastern Settlement received 1,477 kcal per day from cow-milk products, or 57% of his or her daily requirement, whereas a household member from the Western Settlement would receive 870 kcal or 33% of his or her daily requirement.

Needless to say, these are approximate estimates, but the main points should be seen as verified. Milk products from cows satisfied around half of the calorie consumption of the Norse Greenlanders, but was more than that in the Eastern

Settlement, and significantly less in the Western Settlement. The milk production per household in the Western Settlement was approximately the same as along the Norwegian coast, and in the Eastern Settlement it was considerably higher. *The King's Mirror* claimed that the peasants in Greenland produced a lot of butter and cheese, which must be understood as compared to Norway. Statistics based on the size of byres and *The King's Mirror* are independent sources which give the same picture.

Milk from goats and sheep

In Norway goats were milked and so were sheep in some regions. The Norwegian cadastre from 1723 gave combined figures for sheep and goats per household farm, with the average number along the Atlantic and North Sea coasts varying from 8.0 to 11.7, and mostly around 9.0.[35]

To my knowledge archaeologists have only analysed one farm in Norse Greenland with respect to its byres for sheep and goats. Bruun found it likely that at E1 only house no. 6 kept sheep and goats. Internal dimensions for the whole building were 450 "square feet". It was divided into one large and two smaller rooms. The large room occupied about half the length of the building and was probably the hay-barn. This leaves ca. 225 square feet for the animals, and the two smaller rooms were probably for goats and sheep respectively. In Bruun's time Icelandic farmers calculated ca. 12 square feet for each goat or sheep in a winter stable, and a lamb or kid 3–4 square feet.[36] This means that this stable had room for ca. 16 goats or sheep.

Sheep-byres are mostly impossible to identify among extant ruins. Sheep and goats were kept in small buildings with fairly thin walls. They had wool or long hair and could survive in lower temperatures than cattle. Normally the building would not have a separate barn for hay in the same house. But small houses with a single room and fairly thin stone walls could be used for many purposes, and there is no universal method for separating byres for sheep and goats from sheds for storing food. Koch Madsen thought it was likely that 199 houses at the sites he examined were for sheep and goats, but he admits that "the ruins classified as sheep/goat sheds undoubtedly include a number of other outbuilding functions".[37] Identifications of sheep/goat byres have to be done individually for each farm and averages have to be calculated on the basis of verified identifications. This may be a task for future archaeologists.

Thomas McGovern tells his readers in his PhD thesis that in Norse Greenland "it is clear that sheep do not typically outnumber goats by a 4:1 to 10:1 ratio as was common in later medieval Europe".[38] He seems to think that agriculture was the same all over "Europe", in Île de France and along the Norwegian Atlantic coast. Inge Bødker Enghoff identified "slightly" more sheep bones than goat bones at GUS. She finds this a "remarkably" high number of goats, "since goats were not very common in contemporaneous Iceland or Denmark".[39] What I find most remarkable about this statement is that she has not compared scholarly studies from Norway. If she had done so, she would have found a close parallel to her material from Norse Greenland. In the cadastre from 1723 the relationship between sheep and goat in coastal regions was mostly 3 : 2.[40] Five sheep and four goats was the average in many regions. Along the Norwegian coast the proportion of sheep, goats and cows varied, depending on the local natural environment.[41]

In some regions of Norway sheep were milked, in others not. Often the lambs were permitted to follow their mother to the summer pastures and drink her milk, and then sheep were only milked after they had returned to their stables in the autumn. Human consumption of sheep milk must have been negligible.[42] Sheep were kept for their wool and meat, and the Norse Greenlanders made nearly all their clothing from wool.

The household could manage without goats, since goats were mainly kept for their milk, which was also produced by cows. But goats were skilled in climbing hills and mountains which were less accessible to cattle.[43] Norwegian coastal farms often had ca. four goats. At a Greenlandic farm the number of goats is likely to have been higher, since most farms were close to mountainous terrain which goats exploited better than sheep. A guess which is likely to be too low is that an average farm in Greenland had ca. five goats. An average goat milked 100–150 litres per year, five goats ca. 500–750 litres.[44] The goats of an average farm together may have produced as much milk as one cow. This would correspond to 6% of the calorie needs for an average family of six.

According to the estimates above, milk provided ca. 53% of a Norse Greenland household's calories, of which 47% came from cows and 6% from goats. Milk may also have protected the Norse Greenlanders' health. In polar regions scurvy is a serious problem caused by a lack of vitamin C, which is mostly found in fruits and vegetables, among them cochlearia which grows in Greenland.[45] But fresh milk also contains vitamin C, and for children this may have been particularly important.[46]

Meat from domestic animals

Cattle, sheep and goats were partly kept for their meat. The estimates above indicate that an average peasant farm had ca. ten winter-fed cattle. How many kilos of meat did a livestock of this size produce in an average year? This of course depends on how old a cow or a bull was when it was slaughtered, and how large and fat it was. The osteologists have not discussed these questions for Greenland.

In Norway estimates of meat production at farms are possible to date as far back as the decades around 1800 when the traditional breed of small Norwegian cattle was still kept. The weight of an adult cattle when it was slaughtered was then ca. 72 kg, and of this 48 kg could be eaten. But annual meat production per winter-fed cattle also depended on the age of the cattle when it was slaughtered. For each additional winter-fed cattle a Norwegian farmer had in his byre at this time, it has been calculated that he would get an additional 11.5 kg of meat when he slaughtered part of his stock each autumn.[47] If Norse Greenland peasants organised slaughtering of their animals in the same way, a livestock of 10 cattle would give (11.5 kg × 10) = 115 kg of meat at slaughtering time, which traditionally took place at the end of the summer season. This would give 82 kcal per person per day in a household of six persons, or 3% of a daily consumption of 2,600 kcal.[48] The energy value of the cattle's milk was ca. 15 times higher than the energy value of its meat. In this estimate I have calculated that 7.5 cows produced the milk, while 10 cattle of both sexes produced meat at the end of their lives.

The empirical material for estimating the annual meat production from the sheep and goats of an average Greenland farmer is much thinner, almost non-existent. The peasant at E1 seems to have owned 16 sheep/goats.[49] In traditional Norwegian agriculture in the 19th century a slaughtered carcass of a sheep or goat would weigh ca. 12 kg. The annual meat production per winter-fed animal depended on its age when slaughtered. The historian-agronomist Kåre Lunden estimated that a peasant would get an additional annual production of 3 kg of edible meat for each additional winter-fed sheep or goat.[50] If slaughtering practices along the Norwegian west coast were used in Greenland, 16 sheep/goats would give an annual production of 48 kg, and 100 g of meat from sheep or goat gave 155 kcal.[51] The 48 kg divided by 6 persons and 364 days would cover ca. 1% of their daily needs.[52] But how representative is the figure of 16 sheep/goats from E1?

According to the cadastre of 1723 for the Norwegian coast, the average farmer seems to have owned nine sheep/goats.[53] But in some regions male sheep and goats were castrated and left to find their own food even in winter, until they were slaughtered. In Norway they were not registered in the cadastres, and in Greenland they may have been without a stable. No source can tell us of their existence.[54]

Domestic animals may have provided ca. 57% of the Norse Greenlanders' supply of food, 53% from milk and 4% from meat. Of this, 50% came from cattle and 7% from sheep and goats.

Pigs

Since the production of pork is so scarcely attested in Greenland, it is fruitful to start in Finnmark where the environment was similar. Here 15% of the households owned pigs in the period 1686–1707.[55] One of them was a poor widow who owned two cows, three sheep, three goats and one pig.[56] In most other administrative regions in northern Norway between 0% and 13% of the households kept pigs. The exception was Lofoten where 37% of the households had pigs. Lofoten had the richest fisheries, and the pigs' main food was fish.[57] Poor people let their pigs roam freely around the house and there their main fodder would be fish waste. They could eat the fish raw, but some peasants boiled it for both pigs and cattle.[58] Pork from pigs which fed on fish tasted of fish-oil, and this made it unattractive. The elite fed their pigs on grain, which made the meat more palatable. Pork could be food for the elite or for poor people, depending on how the pig was fed.[59]

In Greenland feeding pigs on grain was out of the question, and 13C isotopes confirm that pigs were given mainly marine food. Four measurements of pig bones indicated 49% marine protein in their fodder.[60] Pork must have been unattractive meat in Greenland.

246 *Subsistence food production*

This explains why there were so few pigs in Norse Greenland. Reindeer gave more attractive meat, and they were available for hunting in both settlements. At GUS only one bone from a pig was found,[61] and at Narsaq pigs were few and unimportant for food production.[62] In summer pigs would stray in the open seeking food, or this was at least what they did along the Norwegian coast. In winter they were kept in the same stable as sheep, goats, horses and cattle.[63]

The archaeologists agree that pigs' bones declined and disappeared before AD 1300.[64] Arneborg's explanation is that pork was elite food, and if the Norsemen ceased to keep pigs, this must be indicative of worsening poverty.[65] An alternative explanation is that peasants produced more attractive meat hunting reindeer, and they had more time for that when their *nordrseta* ceased at this time. The pigs' main food was *ammassæt*, which may have disappeared because sea temperatures fell.

Horses

Horse meat was consumed at pre-Christian sacrifices, and after Christianisation it was forbidden by law to eat it. The Gulathing law, which was the model for legislation in the Norse Atlantic islands including Greenland, said: "If a person eats horse meat, he shall pay a fine of three marks to the bishop".[66] In Norway in practice it was only eaten in times of extreme want.[67] One should expect that this was so even in Greenland.

Some transport needs are well documented in Norway and were evidently relevant in Greenland as well. Skyr (skimmed, sour milk), butter and cheese were produced at sæters in both countries, and the skyr in particular was so heavy that it must have saved much work transporting it home on the back of a horse. Hay was often harvested far from the home farm and stored in small barns on the spot until snow made it possible for a horse to pull the hay home to the farm on a sledge.[68] Reindeer carcasses were most easily carried home on the back of a horse, at least in the Western Settlement. Seals may have been towed by a horse over the ice with or without a sledge or on the back of a horse. To be drawn in horse-sledges on the fjord-ice must have been an attractive way of visiting neighbouring farms. The landscape in the two settlements is so mountainous, hilly and full of thickets that it is not well suited for adults riding long distances. But there are exceptions in Vatnahverfi, around Brattahlid and the area between Sandnes and Kapisillit. Bones from domestic animals at 14 farms have been counted, and the three highest percentages of horse bones were found at W52a close to Sandnes, W53d in the Austmannadal where long transports were needed down to the fjord, and at the Brattahlid North farm. At Brattahlid horses were needed for transport to the hills behind the farm and up the Qorlortup valley, and there were many sæters in this area.[69]

Along the Norwegian western and northern coasts small boats were the most relevant means of transport. Households with horse in parishes along the coast and the outer part of fjords in the pre-modern period varied from 0% to 48%.[70] Horsebones excavated in Greenland confirm that only a minority of farms kept a horse. The two farms GUS and Nipaatsoq (W54) were medium inland farms in the Western Settlement a couple of kilometres apart.[71] At W54 only one horse bone was found among 1971 excavated bones, and the author doubts whether even this belonged to a horse which had lived at the farm. The farm seems to have managed without a horse. At GUS 2.3% of the 265 excavated bone fragments were from horses, compared to 11% for cattle. This makes it likely that GUS normally kept a horse.[72]

The pre-modern breed of horse had long hair and was therefore better protected against frost. Along the Norwegian North Sea coast snow covered the soil for only short periods, so horses could graze at pastures for most of the winter. The peasants tarred their bellies to prevent them from freezing to the ground when sleeping outdoors on frosty nights. When snow covered the ground, they were fed indoors.[73] In Greenland snow would cover the ground for most of the winter in the Eastern Settlement, whereas the snow-free periods were longer in the fjords of the Western Settlement.[74] All farms with horses are likely to have had a stable for them.[75]

The horse was the domestic animal which consumed the least marine protein by far. The 13C isotope analyses made of six horse bones excavated at GUS and Gardar (E47) showed the percentages of marine protein in the diet were between 8% and 10%.[76] Cattle were given more marine food: 30 cattle bones from the Western Settlement indicated 15% marine protein, and 22 cattle bones from the Eastern Settlement 18% marine protein, all values between 7% and 29%.[77] The horse was better cared for than other animals.

Conclusions and sources of error

In northern Norway the peasant diet had three mainstays: grain products, milk products and meat from fish and domestic animals. Grain products normally constituted 30–40% of the calorie intake, and domestic animals in many places gave approximately the same percentage.[78] These percentages are from a period when the coastal peasants bought much of their grain in exchange for stockfish, which they started to do after ca. 1100, but they demonstrate a high level of grain consumption even in coastal communities. When the Norse immigrants arrived in Greenland, this had to be replaced. This they did mainly by increasing their livestock to provide their calories.

All elements in the Norse Greenlanders' diet were familiar from Norway, but their relative importance shifted. In Greenland milk products and meat from domestic animals provided 57% of the calorie intake according to the calculations above. There are several sources of error for this figure, but I ended up by estimating that domestic animals provided slightly more than half of the calories and were the basic elements in the diet. How reliable are these quantifications for Greenland?

The first important step was to identify the byres. Strong indications of byre-rooms are stall-stones, a central gutter for cow manure, walls made from a combination of stone and turf, location fairly close to the dwelling and objects which normally belonged to a byre. I have only included rooms which could be

248 *Subsistence food production*

identified with certainty. Normally each household farm had only one byre, and strong arguments were needed when I assigned one household farm two byres (cf. Table 5.1). The sources of error here are minimal.

For calculating the number of cows and heifers in each byre there are fairly good written sources from Iceland which have to be combined with the distance between stall-stones in Greenland and the internal dimensions of byres. Was the byre normally full? Heat in winter came from the bodies of the animals, and it was important that the animals stood close to each other. The peasant would not build a byre which was too large. The byre would normally provide room for the cows and heifers which could be fed on the resources available at the farm under normal circumstances.

Milk and meat production in kilos per cow, goat and sheep and the calorie values of their meat are well documented in pre-modern Norwegian sources, and the breed of cattle in Norse Greenland was the same as in pre-modern Norway before ca. 1800. Bone statistics can give a control material for production estimates based on the size of byres.

The methods used in this section were developed by the Norwegian historian Kåre Lunden (1930–2015). I used them when I analysed the fisherman-peasant economy along the Norwegian Atlantic and North Sea coast during 1500–1730.[79] They are also fruitful when used on the food production of the Norse Greenlanders.

In this section I established the quantitative backbone of the Norse Greenlanders' food production, and it came as no surprise that it was milk and meat from domestic animals. There are sources of error, but they do not alter this basic conclusion. Cows, sheep and goats had all been imported into Greenland from warmer countries. How did the Norse peasants provide fodder for these foreign guests in the Greenland environment?

2 Providing fodder for domestic animals

Danish and American archaeologists and osteologists have assumed that animal husbandry had an established organisation which was brought from Norway to Greenland. The Norse Greenlanders sought to recreate "their homeland's ideal farmyard".[80] Historians with a better knowledge of medieval and pre-modern Norwegian peasant society will know that agricultural organisation along the Norwegian coast varied considerably because the natural environment differed.

Equally important was that it was possible to increase a Norse farm's production by working more at certain times of the year. They could put in longer hours during the day, do productive work at times of the year which until then had been for leisure, and they could exploit resources which were further away from the home farm, or were more labour-intensive.

Did the Norse Greenlanders use methods which they brought with them from their Norwegian motherland, or did they have to invent new methods to adapt to a different environment?

Indoor or outdoor winter feeding?

In the inner fjords of southern Greenland the season for plant growth is today four to five months,[81] and the outdoor pasturing period for modern Inuit farming in the Eastern Settlement is slightly longer, four to six months.[82] One should expect the same time frame in Norse Greenland, so all animals were fed outdoors for around five months of the year. This compares favourably with the northernmost coastal regions of Norway (ca. three months) and further south on the same coast (five to five-and-a-half months) and Iceland (ca. five months).[83] The domestic animals were most productive in this summer season when they were fed outdoors on fresh and nourishing grass. In these months they produced most of their milk and they grew fatter and produced most of their meat.

The summer grass growth was better in the fjords than at the coast because of better soil and higher temperatures. In the former Eastern Settlement the July mean temperature in the fjords today is 10.3–10.7° (Igaliku and Narsarsuaq) and at the coast 5.9–7.0° (Agdluitsup Paa and Nanortalik). In the former Western Settlement the July mean temperature in the fjords is 10.9° (Kapisillit) and at the coast 7.6° (Nuuk).[84]

The winter conditions for outdoor feeding were better in the fjords of the Western Settlement. The annual rainfall, which in winter came as snow, was only 255 mm in Kapisillit. In the Eastern Settlement the fjords had 606–860 mm (Igaliku and Narsarsuaq).[85] When Hans Egede visited Western Settlement fjords on 16–22 April 1723, "the earth was almost free from snow".[86]

Much of the coastal landscape along the Norwegian coast was heather/ling where animals could dig into the snow and reach these and other plants which had a nutritional value even in winter. Milk-cows would lose their milk at low temperatures and were always kept indoors in winter. The peasants fed other animals indoors only when ice or thick snow made it difficult or impossible for the animals to reach their food.[87] They were sheep, rams, goats, billy-goats and horses of the traditional Norwegian breed with long hair. A few domestic animals were never kept indoors and found their food outdoors all year round. In Norway they had a particular name, *uteganger*, literally "outdoor walkers". Some rams and billy-goats were kept exclusively for their meat and at slaughter time they were hunted like wild animals.

Outdoor feeding demanded agricultural insight and power of judgement. When the Inuit started their sheep husbandry ca. 1920, "the sheep were kept outside all year round and had more or less to take care of themselves".[88] Helge Ingstad visited the former Eastern Settlement in 1953, and was told by the Danish official in charge of the sheep breeding project that 80% of all sheep were kept outdoors all winter.[89] This led to periodic crises; for example, in the winter of 1948–49 half of the sheep in the former Eastern Settlement died from starvation, some 10,500 sheep.[90] In the 1980s it became apparent that this kind of sheep-farming was not sustainable. "The conversion to more intensive and secure farming practices involved the establishing of animal housing, barns, roads and new fields for hay production".[91]

250 *Subsistence food production*

The Norse Greenlanders could benefit from five millennia of experience in cattle farming along the Norwegian coast and knew from their motherland how to make the animals survive. Many of the same resources were available. In the Norse fjords in Greenland heather, *revling* (*empetrum nigrum*), willow and other plants stay green and have a nutritional value even in winter, and were available for animals which could dig through the snow.[92] Excavations in the Western Settlement at W53d in the Austmannadal[93] and at GUS[94] documented thick layers of sheep and goat dung in what had evidently been winter stables for these animals. Stables for sheep, rams, goats, billy-goats or horses have been identified on nearly all farms which have been excavated. One should assume that they followed the Norwegian flexible practices when they decided if and when these animals should be fed indoors.

Gathering winter fodder in outfields and common land

The peasants knew how many loads of hay or other fodder an animal needed to survive the winter. A peasant would count how many loads he had brought into his barn, and when the summer was over, he calculated how many animals he could keep in his byre or stable that winter. The redundant ones he would slaughter in the autumn. The unpredictable factor was when the growing season started the following spring. If it came unusually late, the barn could be empty before the grass started to grow outside, and the animals could die from hunger. The need for fodder could be reduced through starvation, and the animals could have their fodder-rations reduced so much that they became emaciated.[95] This was so in Norway and undoubtedly also in Norse Greenland.

The peasants gathered part of their winter fodder in the private outfield (*utmark*) of their farm, and on the common land (*allmenning*) which was open to all peasants. We know how this was organised in pre-modern Norway. It is not mentioned in sources from Greenland, but these practices also suited the Greenland environment.

Norwegian coastal peasants rowed along fjords or to uninhabited islands and sought out grass patches in hills and mountains. Patches of grassland where hay was harvested, were called *utslått* ("distant meadow") along the Norwegian coast. Often a small barn would be built there to protect the dried hay from rain. Hay would be brought back to the main farm on the back of a horse in autumn, on a sledge in winter or in a rowing boat. There would not be a dwelling house there – the stay at the *utslått* was too short for that.[96] Some of the grass was mowed in "steep mountain sides and hillsides", and had to be lowered down to a waiting boat with the help of ropes.[97] Those who have sailed along the Greenland fjords can easily imagine similar situations there.

Ca. 1895 one of the Inuit farmers living at the former Norse farm Narsaq (E17a) told Daniel Bruun that he thought winter fodder for four cows could be found close to his farm. But the farm had nine cows, so fodder for the remaining ones was found on journeys with umiaks along the fjords and in the mountains.[98] The descriptions of these journeys resemble those from northern Norway quoted earlier. Both ethnic groups had to adapt to the natural environment when they organised harvesting of winter fodder.

In the northernmost part of Norway called Finnmark there were large stretches of moss. Four to six people would row or sail in some instances 40–50 km to collect moss along the fjords and elsewhere.[99] According to tables from the Norwegian High School of Agriculture 3 kg of dry moss has the same energy value as 1 kg of barley.[100] Since large parts of ice-free Greenland are also covered by moss, there can be little doubt that such journeys must even have been practised there.[101] Harvesting of grass and other fodder far from the dwelling will be discussed further below under the heading "Sæters".

Trees were also harvested. Several sickles were found in the Western Settlement at Sandnes farm. In Norway they were used among other things as "leaf knives, intended for hewing twigs for winter fodder", and Roussell assumes that this was also their use in Greenland.[102] Dwarf birch is common and could be harvested in the summer months.

Many kinds of fodder were collected as they were needed through the winter, and particularly in early spring when the hay in the barn was running out. In Norway twigs, peeled bark and sprigs of conifer trees were used as such emergency fodder.[103] Juniper and willow are abundant in the settlements and are green all year. The botanist Bent Fredskild points out that juniper, willow and angelica increased in Brattahlid after the Norse peasants disappeared ca. 1410.[104] In the previous period these plants had been kept down by sheep and goats for whom it was an attractive fodder in summer and winter.

In Norway fresh seaweed was cut from boats rowing along the shores, supplemented by fish and fish remains which were not needed for human consumption. In winter fish and seaweed were boiled together and given to the cows.[105]

In May and June a small fish called *ammassæt* arrived in enormous quantities in many fjords in the two Norse settlements to spawn. The same species of fish also arrives to spawn in Finnmark in May and June, where it is called *lodde*.[106] The *ammassæt* spawned at shallow water close to the shore, and a large part of the fish died after spawning. In Finnmark *lodde* was collected with landing-nets or with bare hands and was used to feed domestic animals.[107] One should assume that the same was done in the Greenland fjords. May and June included the final part of the indoor period for the cows, and any hunger crisis for the domestic animals would also have come at this time. The *ammassæt* was a security net for the livestock of the Greenland Norse. The 13C isotope analyses undertaken indicate that cattle, sheep and goats may have received 10–20% of their proteins from marine food, which may be the result of them being fed with *ammassæt* for a short period in spring.[108]

How many days' work did it take to harvest sufficient fodder from outfield and common land to feed one cow? In Finnmark a local parson estimated in the 1820s that 16–24 days' work was needed to harvest sufficient moss for one cow to survive the winter.[109] If ca. 20 days' work per cow is accepted as representative, ca. 200 days' work was needed for an average livestock of 10 cattle, of which ca. 7.5 may have been milk-producing cows. In a household of six persons one should expect four persons to be able to participate in the harvesting. Some 50 days' work per household member who was able to work is then needed to feed a livestock of 10 cattle. The household had to devote their entire time to harvesting work in outfield and on common land for about two months to provide winter fodder for their cows. I see no reason to doubt that collecting fodder in outfields and common land demanded the same amount of time for Norse Greenlanders. The summer season was long enough for them to do it. In the inner fjords of southern Greenland the season for plant growth is four to five months.[110]

On an average Greenland farm around 10–20 sheep and goats also had to be fed for parts of the winter. To compensate for this increased demand, additional food could be collected as it was needed during the winter. More important still, most or all Norse farms in Greenland had a cultivated meadow close to the farmhouses, and the same "food value" of fodder could be harvested with less work from a meadow than from outfields and common land.

Improving the meadow

Norwegian officials who wrote the cadastre in 1723 claimed that the time needed to harvest hay for one cow from a cultivated meadow was only half of what it cost to harvest it from many small grass patches in outfield or common land.[111] Improving the privately owned meadow was a long-term investment. The main methods were fertilisation, irrigation and drainage.

Fertilisation improved the meadows of the Greenland Norse significantly. Land used for agriculture would have an upper layer of decomposed organic material called humus. It contained nutrients which made plants grow and was moist and could give plants water long after the last rainfall. In Greenland this layer was thinner than in more southerly areas. Nutrients were washed away or reduced if the humus layer was thin and the rainfall substantial. Norse Greenland had most rainfall at the outer coast, with the result that the soil there had a low fertility. In the fjords there was less rain and the soil was more fertile.[112] The Norse peasants in the fjords made the humus layer thicker in their meadows and the soil more fertile through manure.

The Danish botanist Bent Fredskild has examined the soil around the houses at Brattahlid and other farms. Before the Norse arrived the upper soil was sandy, and the vegetation was shrub, mainly dwarf birch. The Norse cleared away the shrub either with axe or by fire. The soil of the meadow was improved by adding fertilisers where dung and fresh bog soil were the main elements. A layer of wooden chips from the same period was obviously the remnants of Norse house building. The peasants even fertilised grass patches which were situated 400–500 m from their dwelling and the main meadow.[113]

When the Norsemen withdrew, the shrub often regenerated. At GUS different kinds of herbs replaced the grass after the site was abandoned ca. 1350. A hundred years further on the soil started to dry up and it grew sandy.[114] Is it possible that the soil was dehydrated because it was not given manure? If so the Norse did not move because of environmental problems. It was the other way round – the fact that the Norse disappeared, made the cultural landscape less fertile.[115] The quality of the meadow around the dwelling was better when the Norse disappeared ca. 1350 than it had been ca. 1000 AD when they arrived.[116]

Cow dung was always used as fertiliser. At farm W53d in the Austmannadal the floor of the byre had a gutter for dung 20–25 cm deep running lengthwise.[117] Such gutters or grooves between the two rows of cows are well known from Norwegian byres. Cow dung was shovelled into them and further out of the house into a midden outside. In the byre at ruin 5 at farm Sandnes (W51) there was "a gutter, 30 cm deep [which] runs down through the room", straight and well paved, until it had its outlet through a drain ca. 30 cm wide under the gable wall.[118] Milk-cows could not lie and sleep in their own wet excrements.

Dung from other animals and humans could be carried to the same dungheap or midden just outside the byre gable. The byre was normally built at the top of a slope which would make fluids from the midden slide from the byre wall and fertilise the main meadow which often was just below the byre.[119] In spring manure would be spread on all meadows.

The Norse used cow dung systematically as fertiliser, but the use of sheep dung varied. Dung from sheep and goat was drier, and in Norway it was often left in the stable for the animals to trample or walk on, so in this way the floor level would rise during the winter. The manure was kept indoors which prevented its nutrients from flowing away with the rain. Soil from nearby bogs was dried and mixed with the sheep dung in the stable. When used as fertiliser, seaweed could be added.[120]

Room I in GUS was a stable for sheep and goats. In it was found a 75 cm thick layer of sheep and goat dung which the Norse farmer had mixed with dried turf soil. This indicates that the dung was meant to be used as fertiliser in the spring. At the top was a layer of ashes, wooden coal and burnt turf probably from the roof indicating that the room ended its existence in a fire.[121] How should this be interpreted? One hypothesis is that the dung had accumulated during one winter, but in spring before the manure had been carried out to the meadow, the stable burned down.[122]

The excavation of farm W53d in the Austmannadal confirms that sheep and perhaps goat dung was kept indoors. In the final phase room XVII was a stable for sheep, and even here the floor was "covered by no less than about 75 cm of almost fresh and powerful odorous sheep manure which contained several artefacts". Among the excavated objects was a whale vertebra which apparently was used as a seat, perhaps when the sheep were milked.[123] The larger room XXI on the same farm was also in the last phase "used as a sheep-shed . . . as the floor layers show". It is not clear what the author means, but the floor may even here have been covered with sheep dung.[124] The floors of both sheep stables at Sandnes were "covered with large quantities of sheep and goat excrements".[125]

Sheep dung could also be prepared for use as firewood. In the warm sheep stable during the winter the moisture would evaporate, and when trampled down, the dung would become hard. In spring some of the sheep dung was cut into suitable pieces, dried in the sun, put in piles beside the fireplace, and burned for cooking and heating. A pile of unused, dried pieces of sheep dung was found beside a fireplace in one of the farms in the Austmannadal.[126] In Greenland manure was plentiful and the peasants could afford to use sheep dung as firewood. In Norway manure was scarcer since the cornfield had to be fertilised.

Sometimes peasants may have neglected to even use the cow dung. At farm W52a close to Sandnes the dung accumulated in such large quantities that "we must say with certainty that the farmer has not appreciated its excellent properties in the service of agriculture". Roussell's explanation is that the farm lacked a meadow close to its dwelling because the ground was too wet and boggy.[127] To me it sounds improbable that a Norse farmer had sufficient fertiliser to create a meadow but neglected to do so. Meadows could be created at some distance from the farmhouses.

Today Norse meadows can be identified in the Greenland landscape because of their luxuriant vegetation of grass and other plants. They were manured for centuries and must have grown more fertile as the centuries went by.

Irrigation was the second most important way of improving the meadow in Greenland. In their extensive excavations in Gardar published in 1930, Nørlund and Roussell noticed that stones had been thrown into streams at three spots, and they thought this was done to facilitate communication across the stream with horses and carts. They remarked that at one of the places the "stone bridge" was quite superfluous in 1926.[128] And not only in 1926!

The Norwegian explorer and author Helge Ingstad visited Gardar in 1953 and identified stones in the streams and ditches as remnants of an irrigation system. He had seen similar systems at several locations in western and eastern Norway, and irrigation is mentioned in medieval Icelandic laws and at least one saga. He noticed similar irrigation at other Greenland farms. Ingstad quoted Nørlund and voiced his disagreement with his interpretation.[129] Instead he pointed out how two small rivers or brooks naturally ran from the mountains into Gardar's infield. Across the northern brook the Norse had built a dam, creating a reservoir which was used to irrigate the northern part of the infield in dry periods. The southern river created a natural southern limit to the infield. From it the Norse dug a channel almost 200 m long to a dam which created a reservoir for irrigation of the southern part of the infield. In dry periods the water was made to run through an opening in the dam to a new artificial dam in the middle of the southern part of the infield. When it was opened, it would irrigate the southern part of the infield. In Norway Ingstad had seen movable, wooden gutters (*renne*) being used to spread the water as widely as possible. Even if there is no evidence for it, one could imagine that the bishops' servants used loose, wooden gutters for a similar purpose. Further investigation can give interesting results on the use of irrigation in Norse Greenland, Ingstad says.[130] The addressee was evidently Nationalmuseet. Ingstad's Norwegian background helped him understand what he saw.

Nørlund suggested that the bridge across the imaginary brook had become superfluous because there had been a moister climate in the Norse period when it was thought built. A later Danish archaeologist Skaaning Høegsberg agreed with

Ingstads irrigation-theory but thought the irrigation works should be explained by an increasingly dry climate.[131] For Ingstad the irrigation was part of normal Norse agricultural techniques, no climate change is needed to explain it.

An article on the subject by the Nationalmuseum archaeologist Knut Krogh from 1974 repeats Ingstad's description, but he traces the excavated channels west of the infield up in the hills differently.[132] Krogh does not mention his scholarly debt to Ingstad, which is contrary to academic norms. In 1982 Krogh explicitly claimed the irrigation system to have been his own discovery.[133]

From the small lake Gallium Kær behind Brattahild (E29a) the Norse dug a ditch to irrigate the slope between the lake and the farm, and it may have doubled as a water supply to the farmhouses. "All over Brattahlid . . . systems of irrigation ditches can be seen . . . The effect upon the vegetation downslope of the irrigation is very distinct".[134]

At E59 at the Einarsfjord a "well preserved irrigation system" was found in 1973.[135] The Nordic Archaeological Project 1976–1977 examined farms in the Qorlortup valley in the hills behind Brattahlid. At E36 stones were placed over a stream, perhaps the remains of a dam. At E37 an elongated ditch was found which could have been part of an irrigation system.[136] Another ditch at E31 was probably for irrigation, but may also have been for drainage.[137] The precipitation in the valley is variable, and the irrigation can be seen as a measure to prevent periodic drought.[138] No information is given about the character of the remains of irrigation found at E4, E78a, E79, E149, E172 and W51 (Sandnes).[139]

The irrigation ditches normally led from surrounding hills and mountains and stopped where the infield started. The water may have been spread evenly over the whole infield, but was no doubt conducted above all to the meadow which was only part of the infield. It is in many cases problematic to distinguish between ditches for irrigation, drainage and water supply.[140]

Digging ditches to lead water, and building dams of stone and earth to create artificial pools of water, is so simple that the knowledge probably came to Norse Greenland with the first settlers and was practised when needs arose. Danish archaeologists have suggested that irrigation systems may have been invented independently in Greenland as a response to climatic changes. Some archaeologists have a tendency to give preference to climate when they are in need of an explanation, but in this case it is not the best verified hypothesis![141]

Drainage technologies were well known along the rainy west coast of Norway in the pre-modern period. They were mainly used on cornfields, but also on meadows. The most used technique was to elevate the surface of the soil. The peasant would fetch soil from the neighbourhood and put it on top of the water-soaked land. The soil level would then rise above the surrounding land and leave it drier. I have not come across archaeologists who have discussed this method in a Greenland context.[142]

An alternative method was to dig ditches around or along the meadow to be cultivated so the soil above the water level in the ditch would then become drier.

256 *Subsistence food production*

This leaves traces which are easier for archaeologists to detect. In the Qorlortup valley behind Brattahlid excavations at E34 revealed an 80 cm wide ditch in a bog at the outskirts of the farm. The leader of the excavations thinks it was dug to drain the bog for cultivation. In it was found a cat bone which was radiocarbon dated to AD 1294–1411. The description of the ditch is not clear, but it seems to have been open at the top. In Norway such ditches could be filled with stones, and this seems to have been done also at E34.[143] To my knowledge this is the only ditch in Greenland which the archaeologists agree must have been used for agricultural drainage only. Archaeologists have found evidence of drainage ditches under dwellings at Brattahlid (E29a),[144] Narsaq (E17)[145] and Hvalsey (E83),[146] where they seem to have doubled as water-pipes for the kitchen. Drainage techniques were known but were rarely needed since water-soaked agricultural land was a minor problem in Norse Greenland.

In Norway manure was used mainly for the cornfield. In Greenland it was used for the meadow only, which must have made the work to create a fertile meadow easier. Irrigation seems to have been more common in Greenland for climatic reasons. Drainage ditches were less used in Greenland, again for climatic reasons. The Norse Greenlanders brought with them in their minds Norwegian practices as a model but adapted them flexibly to their new environment. This makes Norwegian agriculture a necessary background for scholars who write about Norse Greenland agriculture.

Summer pastures

In the five months' season for plant growth after the snow had disappeared, potential summer pastures were abundant in Greenland. The farmers' main problem was to keep the grazing animals away from the meadow(s) where he produced hay for the coming winter.

On many farms the domestic animals were kept close to the main farm all summer. They would often build a dyke around the meadow and living quarters that was meant to keep the animals away. They often built one or several smaller pens or folds close to this dyke. In the evening cows, goats and sheep were herded into them to be milked. They stayed there through the night and while they were milked in the morning. Then they left the pen to graze in the vicinity all day. Kids and lambs could be kept in separate pens to prevent them from drinking milk from their mother.[147] The archaeologists have identified one or several such pens at most farms.[148] Some farms were without a dyke around the infield, in which case the domestic animals had to be herded in the daytime.

Sæters

Pastures within short walking distance from the farm would often be insufficient for feeding the animals all summer. The purpose of *sæters* was to give domestic animals pastures which kept them away from the farm and meadow in the four to five months of plant growth. The word *sæter* is not used in written sources dealing with Norse Greenland.

The standard work on *sæters* in Norway is Lars Reinton's *Sæterbruket i Norge*. By the way of definition he wrote:

It is called a sæter when a permanently settled main farm has a summer pasture for its domestic animals at a distance from the main farm, and at this pasture there is a dwelling where a permanent staff lives during the summer season.

Similar definitions of *sæter* are found in dictionaries of Old Norse.[149] In modern Norwegian the spelling is *sæter* or *seter*. The phenomenon does not exist in Denmark, and according to the 28-volume *Ordbog over det danske sprog* "sæter" is a loanword from Norwegian.[150] In the following pages I will use the spelling "sæter" which is common in Norwegian and Danish.[151]

Bruun was the first to describe *sæters* in Greenland in 1896, and he then used this word of Norwegian origin.[152] In his monograph on Greenland from 1918 he replaced it with the word "outfarm", which he seems to have invented himself.[153] Today Danish archaeologists sometimes use "shieling" when they write in English about *sæters*. This word originated in Scotland and means a pasture to which cattle could be driven, or a hut or houses built on such a pasture. In Norwegian a pasture without houses will not be called a *sæter*. Keller recommends the word *sæter* and I see no scholarly reason to replace a Norwegian word which gives the right meaning, social context and associations, with a Scottish one.[154]

At the *sæter* cows and goats, and sometimes even sheep, were milked morning and evening, and this demanded a human presence on the *sæter* every day. One or several of the household's women was given the responsibility for the *sæter*, and

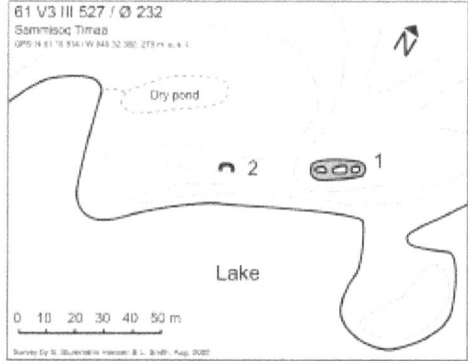

Figure 5.2 E232, example of *sæter*; Appendix II, map 5.

A *sæter*'s function in relation to the farm is described in the text. This *sæter* probably belonged to the nearest farm, E34. It has one building made of stone and turf, ca. 20 × 6 m. The addition of turf meant that the house could be kept so warm that it could be used even if cold spells occurred in the summer season. Even in Norway it was common for the *sæter* house to have three rooms. One was sleeping quarters for the milkmaid, and in the middle room she would produce the dairy products and do other work. The third room may have been for animals who had special needs. Normally the animals were free to find their food where they wanted in daytime but would return or be fetched to the *sæter* in the evening to be milked. If there were beasts of prey around, the animals could be herded by a child in daytime.

Ruin 2 is a small pen, ca. 5 × 3 m, built against a rock wall which functioned as the fourth wall. It may have been for recently born calves and kids, to prevent them from drinking milk from their mother.

Source and copyright: Ole Guldager, Steffen Stummann Hansen and Simon Gleie, Copenhagen 2002, pp. 54–55.

there would be a small dwelling for her and visitors there. Often there would also be a byre where the animals could stay at night or in uncomfortable weather. If the *sæter* was at walking distance from the main farm, she would milk the cows and goats at the *sæter* in the evening, spend the night in the dwelling, milk the animals in the morning, and carry the milk back to the main farm. At the main farm she would participate in the harvesting during the day and return to the *sæter* in the evening. A woman was seen as capable of carrying a maximum of 25 litres of milk in a container on her back and in her hands. If the distance to the *sæter* was so long that walking to and from carrying milk was impracticable, she would live in the *sæter* dwelling all through the summer milking the cattle. Since the fresh milk could not be carried back to the farm every day, she would have to make butter and cheese on the *sæter*. The skimmed, sour milk which remained after butter and cheese had been made, would have to be fetched by farmhands from the main farm on Sundays, often on the back of a horse, and drunk during the week or later by people doing harvest work at the main farm.[155]

The *sæter* could be up in the hills or mountains or on small islands where the animals were brought by rowing-boats. Several ruin groups close to the shore in the Middle Settlement must have been *sæters* because they lacked dwellings and cowsheds of the normal type.[156] A farm which had a good *sæter* could receive domestic animals from other households, and the butter and cheese would then have to be shared.[157] Albrethsen and Arneborg in their publication on the Middle Settlement made a systematic attempt to classify the 38 ruin groups according to function, and estimated that 23 of them were farms and the remainder were *sæters* or buildings for storage of hay or sheds for domestic animals.[158]

The word "sæter" was connected to pasturing and not to hay production.[159] A distant meadow where hay was produced was called *utslått* and could be located at the same place as a *sæter*. If it was, the animals had to be herded during the day to prevent them from eating grass meant for winter fodder.[160]

None of the assumed *sæters* in Norse Greenland have been excavated, and we therefore do not know if the *sæters* were there from the start and if they were in use until the settlement ended. In Norway *sæters* had existed for several centuries when emigration to Greenland started in AD 985.[161]

The Gulathing law was the basis for Greenland law,[162] and it reveals how the local community regulated *sæters* and *utslåtter*. It considered land not actively used by a particular farm as meadow or pasture as common land (*almenning*), and it was free for everybody to hunt and fish there. A farmer was free to build a new *sæter* or move an old one to a new site in the common land if it did not harm an existing *sæter*. If a farm had used a *sæter* for 20 years or more without neighbours objecting to it, it was the private property of the farm's owner. If a farmer produced hay on common land, he was entitled to use this location as *utslått* for the next 12 months, which also included the following summer. If he neglected to do so for one season, he lost the right to it.[163] A farmer who wanted a *sæter* or an *utslått* did not meet serious legal obstacles in the Norwegian tradition.[164]

Sæters and *utslåtter* could create special relations between elite farms and neighbouring smaller farms. The largest farm in Greenland was Gardar, which was excavated by Poul Nørlund in 1926. Its two byres could accommodate ca. 110 cattle when they were full.[165] If three-quarters of them were milk-cows, the bishop would have 83 milk-cows. In 1660–1720 an average peasant living at the Norwegian coast kept around five milk-cows.[166] The Gardar bishop had as many milk-cows as 16 Norwegian coastal peasants.

Medieval Gardar's infield, that is the area within its dyke, measures more than 15 ha today.[167] The sea level has risen during the last millennium, and at Brattahlid the shoreline may have regressed by as much as 100 m.[168] This means that Gardar's infield in 985–1410 must have been more than 15 ha. A reasonable guess might be 20 ha.[169] Along the Norwegian coast the normal size of the infield (*innmark*) at the disposal of a traditional coastal farm may have been ca. 3 ha. This included "all inside the fence", in practice meadow, cornfield, pens and the yard where the farmhouses stood. In Iceland ca. 1930 it was 2–3 ha.[170] Gardar's infield seems to have been 7 times as large and its number of milk-cows 16 times greater than the infield of an average Norwegian coastal farm.

Along the Einarsfjord there are numerous ruin groups which archaeologists have interpreted as farms, but Gardar may have used them as *sæters* for most of their existence. Servants from Gardar may have used other farms as *utslåtter*, transporting the hay back to Gardar in a rowing boat or on a sledge. The uses of these farms may have changed. The first settler chieftain may have been followed by several of his retainers to whom he gave land at favourable locations along the Einarsfjord. The population may have declined in the final century of the Eastern Settlement's existence. In that situation the bishop may have bought or confiscated farms which were without occupants, and instead exploited them as *sæter* or *utslått* for Gardar.

Brattahlid lies in the most fertile agricultural area in Greenland. From the head of the Eiriksfjord (Tunulliarfik) at both sides of the fjord out to today's Sillisit and between this fjord and Isafjord (Northern Sermilik), Danish archaeologists have counted 78 "ruin groups". Of these, 48 were classified as farms where the main criterion is that the ruin group had at least one dwelling and one byre, both of which had size and wall insulation which indicate that they were meant for use by humans or cattle in winter. A further 28 were classified as *sæters* where the main criterion is that there was at least one house where a person could sleep in summertime, and often there would also be a byre for the cows to sleep at night, but this is not a necessary criterion.[171] The registered *sæters* in the Brattahlid region were normally found within walking distance from a farm, that is a couple of kilometres or less. More than half of the farms had a *sæter* at their disposal, if we assume that one *sæter* belonged to only one farm.

The Qorlortup valley is the central part of this area, and here most or all farms had a *sæter* in the hills. Farm E34 was excavated in 1997 and 1998.[172] It is 125 m above sea level, and the nearest *sæter* is E232 ca. 1.3 km away and 275 m above sea level.[173] This *sæter* lies in a grassy area and has one house ca. 20 m long divided into three rooms. The milkmaid or a helping hand from the main farm may have carried the milk products on their backs or in their hands to E34 1.3 km further down the valley. The goods may also have been carried on horseback, as horse bones have been excavated at E34.[174]

In the Brattahlid area *sæters* seem to have been used by many middling farmers to expand their resource base into the neighbouring hills. In the Einarsfjord the *sæter* institution may have been used by one elite farm to strengthen its resource base. The *sæter* is a model which the Norse carried in their minds to Greenland and adapted to the local environment and their own material interests.

Sæters do not exist in Denmark, but Danish archaeologists knew of them from Iceland. The first to hypothesise their existence in Greeenland was Daniel Bruun.[175] Roussell was unsure,[176] while Nørlund rejected it.[177] Helge Ingstad was the first to argue unequivocally that *sæters* in the Norwegian and Icelandic sense existed in the hills behind Brattahlid and possibly elsewhere in Greenland.[178] Scholarly research on the subject started with the so-called Nordic Archaeological Expedition 1974–1977 to the Qorlortup valley and the inner Tunulliarfik fjord. They found ruins which were interpreted as *sæters*. Nationalmuseum archaeologist Krogh in a brief comment declared this to be surprising *(forbausende)*.[179] The project's synthesis was to be written by him, but it never appeared.[180]

In his standard work on Norwegian *sæters*, Lars Reinton used descriptive concepts to classify different types of Norwegian *sæters*. The archaeologists Keller and Albrethsen tried to find *sæters* in Greenland which fitted these concepts. I have found it more fruitful to take my point of departure in functions which the Norse combined differently on individual *sæters*.[181] Keller calculated grass production in the Qorlortup valley partly with the help of satellite pictures. This gives vague results.[182] Quantifications should take their point of departure in the production on individual farms and then add up the number of known farms. Keller also claimed to have estimated the number of cows and sheep at Norse farms on the basis of byre and stable sizes of excavated ruins. Regrettably he did not explain how he made his calculations. This makes them useless as a basis for further studies.

Guldager and his Danish colleagues rightly claim that *sæters* have "added a new element to our understanding of medieval subsistence strategies and hence the character of the settlement and its composition".[183]

Tradition and flexibility

The Norse Greenlanders brought with them from Norway knowledge of how to create a meadow on barren soil and later improve it by using manure and dried soil from neighbouring bogs. Infields which were exposed to drought were irrigated and those which often were soaked by heavy rainfall were drained. It was also important to understand where and when domestic animals could find their own fodder outdoors in the winter season and when they had to be kept indoors. The Norse Greenlanders had to know where patches of grass, moss and other plants for winter fodder could be found, by rowing along fjords or seeking out hills. Most complex to organise were *sæters*.

Subsistence food production 261

All these practices to maximise production from animal husbandry were brought from Norway. Manuring was universal in Norway. Outdoor feeding in winter was most common at islands along the North Sea coast. Moss was an important part of the winter fodder gathered on common land in Finnmark. Irrigation was limited to a few inner fjords in western Norway but may have been used more widely in Greenland for climatic reasons. Different types of drainage were common along the whole Norwegian coast, but it was rare in Greenland. *Sæters* in Norway were most common in the inner parts of the fjords as they were in Greenland. Norse Greenland peasants knew practices from the whole Norwegian coast and adopted those which were most relevant for their new Greenland home. The Norse Greenlanders could make use of the 5,000-year long experience in animal husbandry of their Norwegian forefathers.

3 Animal husbandry in crisis?

Since the 1970s it has been commonly accepted among Danish and American scholars that the animal husbandry of the Norse Greenlanders experienced serious problems and decline from ca. 1300, but there have been several hypotheses about the causes.

Some think they were man-made. Peasants exploited agricultural resources beyond what was sustainable, the result being soil erosion and soil exhaustion. Landowners made demands on their tenants which the latter could not meet, the result being starvation for the poor peasants and crisis for the elite. Others have emphasised natural variations and changes. Temperatures fell and so did agricultural production. The sea level rose and swallowed a significant part of the agricultural land. These hypotheses have created parallels between Norse Greenland and the debate on climate change in our own time.

Historians and archaeologists have always been inclined to claim that problems which are important in their own society were also important in the period they are studying. One reason for this is that it is significantly easier to attract funding for projects if it can be claimed that they are relevant for contemporary social problems.[184] There are strong reasons to submit all claims of lessons to be learnt from history to methodologically correct source criticism.

Landowners exploiting peasants?

In his PhD from 1979 and in an article from 2000 Thomas McGovern claims that landowners controlled a large part of agricultural land in Greenland, and that their conservative outlook prevented flexible responses to the alleged environmental crises after ca. 1250. Their decisions "turned Norse Greenland down its fatal road to extinction".[185] He presents several hypotheses on what these decisions were but lacks methodological judgement and empirical knowledge to verify them. Did a landowning elite capable of making decisions with such far-reaching consequences actually exist?

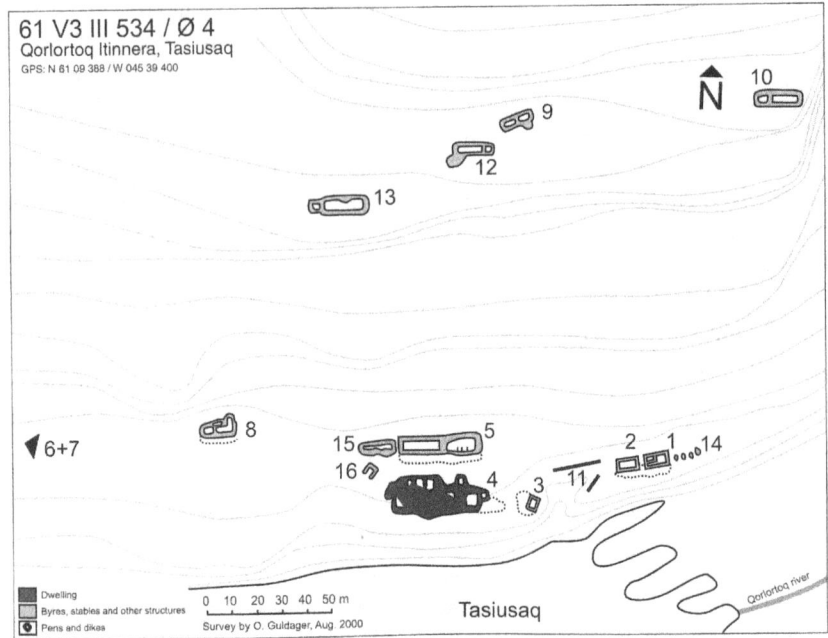

Figure 5.3 E4 was a name farm with only one household (Appendix II, map 5).

In the final century of the settlement's existence, it had the buildings as shown on the map:

4 Dwelling 40 × 10–15 m.

5 A large byre with barn, 34 × 8–10 m. Stall-stones are visible at the eastern end.

6 A very large stone fold, 120 × 40 m.

7 Another fold, ca. 40 × 10 m, built against a rock wall.

8 A stone- and turf-built stable, ca. 10 × 5 m.

9 A stone- and turf-built stable, ca. 14 × 5 m.

10. A stone and turf built stable 20 × 5 m.

11 Remains of a pen which is where the animals were milked.

The farm had the standard housing of a household farm: one dwelling, one byre with barn for cows, several stables, in this case three, which were mostly for sheep and goats, but also for horses. Dwelling and byre were close.

This farm lies where the Qorlortup valley meets the sea. Its hinterland is full of grassy hills and is ideal for summer pastures. It is possible that the unusually large folds were used only in autumn. Then sheep which had been pastured all summer in the hills were assembled in the large pens where they were distributed to their owners.

Some archaeologists have hypothesised that ruin 1 was a church but have won little support for this (Guldager et al. 2000, p. 67). If it was a church, it may have been the churchfarm called Ísafjördur in written sources (cf. Table 3.3 in Chapter 3).

Source and copyright: Ole Guldager, Steffen Stummann Hansen and Simon Gleie, Copenhagen 2002, pp. 66–67.

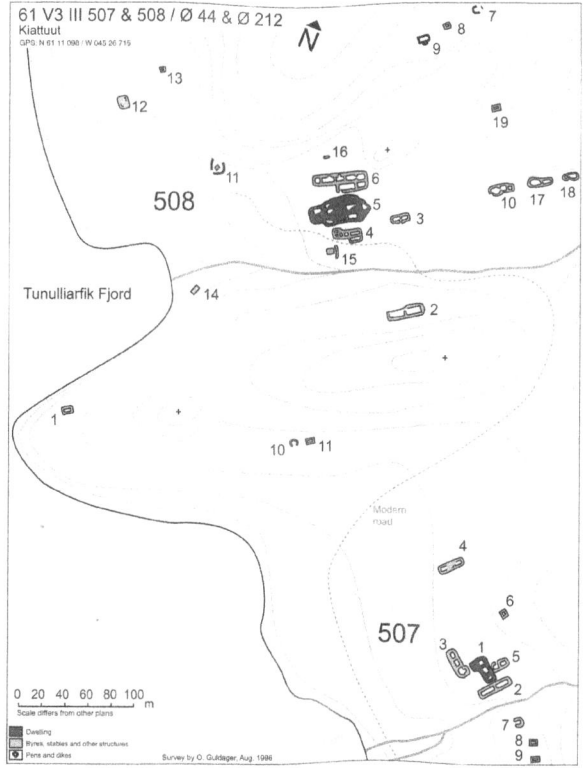

Figure 5.4 E44 (= 508) and E212 (= 507) were no doubt in the Norse period seen as one name farm with two household farms (Appendix II, map 5). On the largest household farm E44 the archaeologists have determined the function of the following houses:

5 Dwelling, ca. 48 × 20 m.
6 A large turf and stone-built byre and barn complex, ca. 42 × 8–12 m.
2 A byre or stable, ca. 29 × 8 m.
10 A turf and stone-built stable, ca. 22 × 9 m.
17 A turf and stone-built stable, ca. 19 × 5 m.

The farm has standard housing with dwelling, byre and three stables for other domestic animals. Unusually it has many smaller houses for which the archaeologists cannot determine the use. The farm is likely to have been Stokkanes, which is mentioned in both Eirik Raudi's saga and *Fosterbroedra saga*. It was situated in Eiriksfjord on the opposite side to Brattahlid. Eirik Raudi let his friend from Iceland Thorbjörn settle there. Later a rich peasant and merchant called Skufr owned the farm. The many unidentified smaller houses may have been storerooms for Skufr's imports and exports.

At the smallest household farm E212 the functions of the following houses have been determined:

1 Dwelling, ca. 20 × 8 m with an extension, 4 × 4 m.
2 A turf-built byre and barn, ca. 20 × 8 m.
3 A stable, ca. 15 × 6 m.
4 A stone and turf-built stable, ca. 15 × 6 m.
5 A small stable, or byre, ca. 10 × 6 m.

This household farm was considerably smaller than the other one. It may have been owned by the rich peasant who lived there.

Source and copyright: Ole Guldager, Steffen Stummann Hansen and Simon Gleie, Copenhagen 2002, pp. 28–29.

Ivar Bárdarson on his visitations ensured that the church's property rights were respected. It is remarkable that the Gardar bishop only owned eight farms on *Langø* (Tugtutoq) plus one farm called *Dalir* in Einarsfjord.[186] There is no reason to believe that Ivar's list was incomplete. He mentions that the nunnery had the right to exploit the warm springs on Uunartoq Island but does not say that the two cloisters owned farms. He describes the tithe rights of each parish church, and if they had owned farms, one would expect him to have listed them. The conclusion must be that the Greenland church possessed surprisingly little land.

Many peasants owned the farms at which they lived. *Fostbroedra saga* was written in Iceland ca. 1220–1250, but the Icelandic author has a good knowledge of Norse Greenland. One should assume that he describes conditions there as he knew them in his own time.[187] Skufr and Bjarni were well-to-do farmers and merchants but did not function as chieftains. They owned in common a farm in Eiriksfjord but wanted to leave Greenland. "That winter Skufr and Bjarni sold their farm (*böinn*) on Stokkanes and other land (*jardar*) which they owned, and also their domestic animals".[188] *Jardar* here probably meant "farm(s)" but could also mean *sæters* or private pastures at some distance from their farm. A woman and head of household called Sigridr decided to do likewise. She visited Skufr and told him that "I want to sell my land and leave Greenland" (*ek vil selja land mitt*). Skufr helped her and sold Sigridr's land (*ok selr land Sigridar*) and she loaded her goods on board Skufr's ship.[189] A widow of middle or modest fortune owned the farm on which she lived.

The black hole in this picture is the landed property of secular chieftains. In Iceland chieftains protected and held judicial and political power over their clients, but normally did not own their farms. In both Iceland and Greenland the first chieftain in an area took (*nam*) large stretches of land. This meant that they decided who should be permitted to live there. The first peasant settlers received a piece of uncultivated land from the chieftain. It would demand much work to build houses for men and animals there.

Eirik Raudi was the chieftain of Eiriksfjord, and a few years later he was visited by an old friend from Iceland and his household who asked to be given land there. "In spring Eirik Raudi gave (*gaf*) Thorbiorn land at Stokkanes, and there was built a proper farm, and Thorbiorn later lived there".[190] Eirik "gave" land, he did not "sell" or "rent it out". He grew politically stronger from having many clients, and it may not have been seen as reasonable to pay for a piece of uncultivated land without houses. Later when the farm had been provided with houses and a meadow, Thorbiorn's descendants such as Skufr and Bjarni mentioned earlier, could sell the farm if they wanted to. The buyer could be a peasant who lived at the farm or a landowner who demanded rents from a tenant.

In 1374 the Bergen merchant Sigurdr Kolbeinssson sailed to Greenland. He was supposed to buy landed property and goods on behalf of the king, making use of the king's right to "first purchase".[191] This presupposes an open market for landed property in Greenland. As mentioned earlier, many members of the local nobility in Bergen had in their possession charters documenting ownership of land in Greenland. They may have bought it from Greenlanders who emigrated to Bergen in the settlement's final years.[192]

Subsistence food production 265

A diminutive part of the land in Norse Greenland belonged to the church, some of it to secular landowners and the remainder to the peasants themselves. McGovern's claim of a dominating landowning class in Norse Greenland is an unverified hypothesis, and so is the claim that they exploited the peasantry economically. The parish churches may have been transferred from secular church-owners to the Gardar diocese shortly before 1300, and the following decades gave churches little time to accumulate landed property. If we are to verify the hypothesis of a man-made crisis in animal husbandry, we have to look elsewhere.

Soil erosion and soil exhaustion

In the 1970s botanists joined the increasing number of scientists who studied Norse Greenland. Botanists had studied the vegetation in Greenland long before that, but it was not focused on soil erosion and exhaustion.

In his PhD from 1973 Bent Fredskild briefly mentioned land erosion in the Norse settlements.[193] In 1982 he published a specialised article on the subject.[194] In the settled areas the first farmers removed thousands of square metres of turf which was used for housebuilding. The soil beneath the turf was then exposed but was after a short time again covered with vegetation, mainly grass and herbs which were better suited as fodder for domestic animals. Removal of turf did not result in widespread soil erosion. There was more sand in the sediments in ponds close to farms, but he thought this was due to people and animals often walking between the farm buildings, destroying the top soil.

The area between Sandnes and Kapisillit in the Western Settlement was used by the Norse as pasture, and there Fredskild examined the sediments at the bottom of a lake which was 3 km from the nearest farm. The arrival of the Norse farmers can be seen because significant quantities of dust from carbonised wood appears in the botanists' diagrams. Along the Norwegian west coast peasants at certain intervals burned the vegetation in their pastures, which would remove old heather, juniper and willow with a low nutritional value and favour fresh heather, grass and herbs with a higher nutritional value. The coal dust from wood may have been the result of this practice. The vegetation changed but was not reduced. The content of sand in the sediments in lakes does not increase significantly in the first period after the *landnám*.[195] The Norse were skilled and experienced peasants and knew where they could remove turf without destroying long-term productivity.

Fredskild's articles on the subject from 1991 and 1992 give a more destructive picture. In a lake near the farm South Igaliku (E66) he found evidence of serious erosion. On dry land near the same farm thick layers of sand loess covered the soil in many places. But the consequences of Inuit sheep-farming in the 20th century were far worse than those from medieval Norsemen. He does not discuss whether the erosion around South Igaliku may have been special to that area, as foehn winds are particularly strong there. Were these winds the main or only cause for the destruction of the topsoil? He also examined sediments from three lakes near Brattahlid, and found increased elements of sand in all of them during the Norse period.[196] His last article on erosion from 1992 summarised his opinion at that time: "sheep and cattle grazing during the era of the Norsemen caused severe erosion and changes in the vegetation cover, undoubtedly among the major factors in the break-down of their community".[197] This contradicted what he wrote in 1973 and 1982. The Danish geographer B. H. Jakobsen voiced similar opinions at this time but lacked the solid empiricism of Fredskild.[198]

Fredskild's opinions should be seen on the background of contemporary developments. In the 1920s the Danish government started a programme of sheep-farming among Inuit, but it met with increasing problems. In 1966 the number of sheep reached a record high of 48,000. During the winter 1966–1967 heavy snow and strong frost saw 60% of the animals starve to death. Similar disasters occurred in the winters of 1971–1972 and 1976–1977.[199] The biggest mistake was that they let the sheep go outdoors and find their own food during the whole winter. Hunger caused the sheep to destroy the plant cover and thereby the turf, causing erosion. In 1983 the authorities appointed a committee which was to give advice on how to make Greenland sheep-farming sustainable.[200] Danish authorities wanted their decisions in the matter to have a sound empirical basis, and in the following period made several analyses which also included animal husbandry in the Norse period.

The area around farm E66 was the main empirical basis for Fredskild's conclusion in 1991 about extensive erosion in Norse Greenland. The Nationalmuseum archaeologist Christian Vebæk already in 1943 and 1992 confirmed that the neighbouring farms E66 and E64c were covered by up to 3 m of sand, and there was extensive erosion in the neighbouring area. He also excavated two other Norse farms E71 and E167 in the same region, but "in neither of these farms could be found any trace of erosion". The erosion was mainly caused by a neighbouring Inuit sheep farm from the 20th century and sand-storms, and Vebæk was uncertain whether the erosion had already started in the Norse period.[201]

Around AD 2000 popular surveys presented it as an established fact that erosion caused by Norse agriculture had been a serious problem. In 1999 Erik Born of the "Greenland Institute of Natural Resources" in Nuuk and Jens Böcher of the Zoological Museum in Copenhagen wrote a textbook for teachers at Greenlandic schools entitled *The Ecology of Greenland*. Here the future teachers could read:

> A dreadful (*afskrækkende*) example of man-made soil erosion can be seen in the Eastern Settlement of the Norse. The seriousness of the situation in medieval South Greenland can be compared to catastrophic soil erosion for example in China, Nepal and several places in Africa in our own time . . . The formerly fertile valleys, where ruins of Norse farms give evidence of extensive agriculture, are today strongly eroded and in certain regions they are desert-like. When the Norse left ca. 1500 much of the landscape was again stabilized . . . As a consequence of modern sheep-farming in the 20th century erosion has again increased strongly.[202]

As evidence the authors use a photo from South Igaliku (E66). They do not mention that other scholars think the erosion there did not start until the 20th century, probably since this would criticise Danish officials and Inuit farmers.

In 2000 a large exhibition was organised in Washington, DC, where Thomas McGovern wrote one of the articles on Norse Greenland, meant for an international readership. "Deforestation followed by overgrazing, followed by irreversible erosion, followed by farm abandonment was the grim sequence of events in much of Iceland in the later Middle Ages, and much evidence suggests a similar chain of events in Greenland".[203] He does not state what this evidence is.

But an understanding which was based on methodologically correct analyses of the empirical material was emerging. In 1991–1995 Nationalmuseet organised an excavation of a Norse farm buried under the sand in the Western Settlement. It was named "The farm under the sand", in short GUS. Close to the farm there was a river which changed its course and flowed directly over the ruin covering it in thick sand. The 14C radiocarbon dating suggests that this started ca. 1450–1500, which is some decades after the Norse had left.[204] The GUS excavation shifted the attention from destructive agrarian practices to natural changes like changing river beds and strong winds.[205] In her survey from 2004 Jette Arneborg claims that erosion in the Eastern Settlement became serious after ca. 1200, but there is insufficient evidence to decide whether it was caused by humans or by stronger and more frequent winds.[206]

Danish authorities wanted to know under what conditions sheep-farming in Greenland could be made sustainable, and in 1998, 1999 and 2000 they sent a research vessel to Greenland. Their main area of interest was again South Igaliku (E66) and its neighbourhood. One hypothesis to be tested was whether "the extensive sand horizons in the area are the result of soil erosion linked to Norse farming activities".[207] The research team combined sediments from the sea floor and from onshore soil. "Preliminary studies of the marine cores and onshore soil profiles indicate that the soil erosion was not a consequence of Norse farming". Sands came with the wind and "are likely to be a result of increased storm activity recorded around A.D. 1300". Stronger winds were created by long-term cooling, which created larger local temperature differences between coast, fjords and the inland ice.[208]

Articles written in the following years by scientists, most of whom worked at Danish institutions, supported this view: "An important conclusion is that enhanced aeolian deposition in the settlement areas could largely be due to regionally intensified atmospheric circulation, and not only due to increased local erosion by Norse land use".[209]

An article by eight scientists from French Universities from 2012 is interesting not because of its conclusions which corresponded to those of the Danish researchers quoted earlier. But instead because they did not work at Danish institutions and so could distance themselves from the political discussion about how sustainable modern Inuit sheep-farming was. In the former Norse settlements "the only substantial eroded area (ca. 10 square kilometers) is situated near South Igaliku".[210] This comes as no surprise, as all who have argued for substantial erosions have taken empirical material from there. "To date there is no reliable quantification of erosion in the Greenland settlements that could support the mass erosion hypothesis . . . nothing definitive can be said as to whether the

Norse agricultural practices caused widespread land degradation".[211] "Our findings question the veracity of the catastrophic scenario of overgrazing and land degradation considered to have been one of the major factors responsible for the demise [of Norse society]".[212]

The Frenchmen measured the thickness of the sediments in the lake in millimetres per century ("mm century").

- Before the *landnám*: 2.5–5 "mm century"
- Norse maximum period 1010–1335: 8 "mm century" (in a period around ca. 1180)
- After the Norse disappeared: ca. 3 "mm century"
- Modern sheep-farming ca. 1960: 21 "mm century".[213]

The sand sediments grew thinner from ca. 1335, but it is not clear whether this was due to special conditions at the South Igaliku farm. The serious erosion was due to Inuit sheep-farming.

What is the picture which scholars present today? Close to the Norse farms there was erosion due mainly to people and animals walking on the turf and in some places destroying it so that the sandy underground was exposed. The Norse removed much turf for house-building, but they seem to have done so in places where it did not create erosion. In a ten square kilometre wide area close to South Igaliku (E66 and E64c) there can be found the only area in the two settlements with substantial and widespread erosion. Most of it took place in the 20th century, a minor part in the Norse period. It is unclear how much of the erosion in the Norse period was due to Norse agriculture and how much to increased wind activity. There is today no evidence that the Norse peasants organised their animal husbandry in a way which created erosion so serious that it limited their livelihood. They belonged to a 5,000-year-old agricultural tradition and knew that the turf which covered the sand had to be preserved if their animals were to have pastures in the future.

There is no evidence of a man-made crisis in Norse animal husbandry. Oppressive landowners did not make peasants impoverished, and soil erosion was not a serious problem. If there was a crisis, it must have been caused by nature, in practice falling temperatures or rising sea levels.

The climate

The best estimates for climate changes in our period AD 985–1410 are from England. According to the standard work of H.H. Lamb, there was a warm period in England and the rest of Europe ca. 900–1200, followed by a gradual cooling[214] which continued at least until ca. 1700. Scandinavian historians have traditionally named the final decades of this cooling period "The Little Ice Age". Some archaeologists use the term differently, calling the whole period ca. 1250–1700 "The Little Ice Age".[215] Scholars analysing the climate in the Alps date their "Little Ice Age" somewhat later to 1350–1850.[216] I find it most fruitful in our context to call 1250–1700 "the medieval cooling period" and reserve the term "The Little Ice Age" for the decades before 1700 when Norse Greenland no longer existed. Hypotheses of falling temperatures in Greenland in the Late Middle Ages were first formulated by the Nationalmuseum archaeologists Nørlund and Roussell.[217]

Ice cores from the inland ice can be used to estimate the surface temperature at the top of the inland ice during the last 2,000 years, but cannot uncritically be used to analyse climatic changes along the Greenland coast.[218] When the Norse arrived AD 985 the average temperatures on the inland ice were higher than today, and ca. 1100 average temperatures started to fall slowly and reached a first low point ca. 1600.[219] For 985–1410 this curve confirms the general North Atlantic trend described by Lamb. There was a warm period before ca. 1250 and afterwards a gradual cooling which continued during the rest of the Norse period.[220]

Kangersuneq Icefjord in the Western Settlement had Norse farms along its shores, and at the head of the fjord a glacier reached the sea. In the warm period before 1250 the glacier stretched as far out along the fjord as it did in 1982. After the Norse had left ca. 1350 the glacier started to expand and ca. 1700 it stretched 20 km further out along the fjord past ruin W16 to W15 (Umivik).[221] The cooling period ca. 1250–1410 did not cause dramatic changes in the glaciers in the Western Settlement. The size of the glaciers in the Eastern Settlement in the Norse period is not known.

In several fjords cores have been taken from the seabed giving profiles of the sediments. This has made it possible to estimate past sea currents, ice conditions and suggest changes in temperature. The scientists express their results with many "may be", "could be" and "perhaps", but the resulting estimates of warm and cold periods at least do not contradict the temperature curve outlined by Lamb.[222]

The strongest indication of a cooling period along the Greenland coast after ca. 1250 comes from Ivar Bárdarson ca. 1360. Traditionally there had been two shipping lanes from Norway to the Eastern Settlement. One went from Bergen westwards across the open Atlantic Ocean directly to Cape Farewell and then along the Greenland west coast to the settlements. The alternative one went via Iceland, from there across the Denmark Strait to the east coast of Greenland, then southwards along the coast to Cape Farewell and finally along the west coast to the settlements. But, says Ivar, "this was old sailing". Ca. 1360 more large ice floes drifted from the North Pole along the east coast of Greenland "so that nobody without endangering their lives can follow this old sea-lane". Those who tried to sail from Iceland through the ice-belt to the east coast of Greenland, and follow it down to Cape Farewell, were likely to have their ship crushed by drift ice.[223]

What had happened? The most evident explanation is that there had been a cooling ca. 1250–1360, more ice floes and icebergs came from the North Pole, and they melted more slowly. But *The King's Mirror* had already described drifting ice along the Greenland coast as a problem for shipping in ca. 1250, depending on the season. An alternative explanation may therefore be that fewer Greenlanders had relatives in Iceland and fewer Icelanders owned ships, therefore fewer ships sailed between Iceland and Greenland. The expertise on how to tackle sea ice was not as readily available as it once was, and people preferred the direct route keeping clear of the Greenland coast for as long as possible. But all these sources combined nevertheless indicate that temperatures fell in the Norse settlements.

The important question in our context is whether this long-term and slow fall in temperature was so serious that it changed the vegetation. The most thorough investigation of vegetation in Norse Greenland has been made by the Danish botanist Bent Fredskild. Important vegetation changes took place in the two settlements when the Norse lived there, but they are unlikely to have been due to climatic changes. No plant species disappeared from Greenland in the Norse period. The changes were due to the Norse introducing new plants and favouring the growth and spread of others. Close to their farms they created a cultural landscape which was meant to favour their animal husbandry, and the influence of man, sheep and cattle on the vegetation was drastic.[224] "The influence of the Norse *landnám* on the vegetation was so radical that the influences of any climatic changes are easily hidden, at least in the lake diagram".[225] From a botanical viewpoint it is an open question of how dramatic the fall in temperature and its consequences really were.

B.G. Hunt makes the interesting point that the climate showed great annual fluctuations. There were always warm years among the cold ones and this made it possible for the farmers and their domestic animals to recuperate. After a cold and dry summer the farmer would have little winter fodder in his barn. He could calculate how many animals it was possible to keep through the winter, and the rest had to be slaughtered. But after warm, moist and fruitful summers his barn would be full, he could feed many cows through the winter and in that way replenish and renew his stock of milk-cows, goats and sheep. In a bad year the family would have to live more on fish and seal than they wanted to, but when the good years returned, they could again have their desired fare of milk products. "The Norse had considerable resilience to short term climatic fluctuations".[226]

Falling temperatures meant that the season when plants grew became shorter, but we do not know by how much. Summer pastures are plentiful in Greenland and cannot have been a problem. But the domestic animals had to be kept indoors longer, therefore more winter fodder was needed. How serious this problem was depended on how much the average temperature sank, and the fall was neither great nor sudden. The peasants could take several counter measures. Part of the hay was produced on the meadow, and fertilisation gradually made the meadow thicker and larger. They could also dry soil from bogs and transport it to the meadow. More time could be spent collecting grass, twigs, moss and seaweed in outfield and on common land. The large number of *sæters* in the Brattahlid region may have been established in the later period to compensate for submerged meadows along the shore. All this meant more work, but since the increasing demand for winter fodder was not dramatic, they may have found the extra workload worth it.

Summing up, 1250–1410 was a cooling period, but it was slow and gradual, giving the Norse farmers time to adapt. It is not clear how serious the fall in temperatures was, and what consequences it had for vegetation and domestic animals. Jon Mathieu concludes for the Alps that climatic variations explain short-term changes in production, but it is a moot point whether they reduced long-term agrarian production.[227]

Rising sea level

In the Norse centuries the sea level in south-west Greenland rose and it has continued to do so until this day. During the more than four centuries of Norse settlement the rise in sea levels may have "exceeded one metre".[228]

In the final period before the Norse disappeared there seems to have been three "household farms" at Brattahlid, which the archaeologist Nørlund called "the North farm", "the River farm" and the "South farm". With today's sea level each of the first two had infields of ca. 8–9 ha., for both 16–18 ha. The infield of the South farm within its dyke is ca. 16 ha., but was of low quality.[229] Compared to the present coastline Brattahlid's shoreline extended ca. 100 m further into the fjord when the Norse arrived there in AD 985.[230] It has been claimed that this led to a loss of 50 ha. for the whole Brattahlid farm during the settlement period, but the authors do not say how much of it may have been infield.[231] Brattahlid's infield may have been halved in the Norse period, but this is only a guess. This does not mean that Brattahlid became uninhabitable, but the owners had to reduce the number of household members, in practice servants. How much land was lost at Gardar has not been estimated.[232]

Conclusion: a sustainable agricultural production

In the period ca. 1250–1410 the temperatures fell in Norse Greenland, but not so seriously that it resulted in important changes in food production. Most sensitive to a colder North European climate were cornfields, and they did not exist in Greenland. Serious man-made soil erosion was limited to an area around farm E66 and did not create problems for animal husbandry elsewhere. A rising sea level submerged agricultural land close to the sea and caused a quantitative reduction in food production, but one cannot discount that better manured meadows and new *sæters* compensated this. On the one hand, the problems were so modest that they did not affect agriculture seriously, and on the other, they appeared so gradually that the peasants could adapt to the situation. Changes in the natural environment caused by man or nature did not necessitate a new approach to animal husbandry.

The farmer had full control of how infield and outfield on his farm were used. It would normally be inherited by the family, and family loyalty was strong. He had the right and interest to prevent over-exploitation of the resources on his farm, and centuries of inherited experience had accumulated knowledge of how to handle the problem.

4 Hunting and fishing as flexible supplements

Hunting walrus and other animals for export to Bergen was discussed in Chapter 4, pp. 174–177. The subject of this section is limited to hunting and fishing for the Greenlanders' own food supply.

The estimates made earlier indicate that animal husbandry satisfied more than half the calorie needs of the inhabitants in the Eastern Settlement, and somewhat less than half in the Western Settlement. From a long-term perspective these proportions seem to have been stable. In years when abnormal quantities of fodder for domestic animals were produced, the alternative food from hunting, fishing and edible plants could be adapted accordingly.

Quantifying hunting and fishing is not possible, but is it likely that these sources could provide the missing calories? Or did the Norse Greenlanders normally live on a subsistence minimum which in lean years could result in hardship?

Hunting and fishing open to all?

The oldest Greenland law has been lost, but it should be assumed that its basic principles were the same as in the west Norwegian Gulathing law. Later, shortly after 1274, a modified version of the Norwegian *Magnus Lagabøte's National Law* was introduced in Greenland.[233] In Norway the norms for hunting and fishing rights did not change from the older Gulathing law to the new *Magnus Lagabøte's National Law*, and there is no reason to think that they did in Greenland. The basic principle for hunting and fishing rights in these Norwegian laws was that if the activity took place on private land or from private shores, it was the private right of the landowner. Fishing and hunting elsewhere, on common land or the open sea, was open to all. This principle was transferred from the Gulathing law to Icelandic law.[234]

The best point of departure for a discussion of the question posed in the heading of the present section is therefore the Gulathing law as practised in western Norway. Along the seashore the border between private land and open sea was drawn where the slowly declining beach below the water surface became much steeper, which point in Norwegian was called *marbakken*. Fastening nets on a private shore was a private right, fishing with nets which floated in the fjord or were not fastened to private ground, was free for all. Fishing with line and hook from a boat was also free.[235]

Seals swimming in the sea or resting on skerries and rocks not belonging to a farm were free for anyone to hunt. Along the coast there were skerries with smooth rocks where seals often rested. Such skerries could be privatised if a peasant built a "seal trap" there.[236]

Fishing char, trout and salmon in rivers and lakes was private if the shore belonged to one or several farms as infield or outfield. Large parts of the land in the two settlements were "common land" (*allmenning*) which was open to all, lakes and rivers included. Certain resources on the common land could be privatised. If a peasant built traps for fish in a river, this was private property. Others were not permitted to do anything which could reduce the capacity of these hunting and fishing gears.

The infield was the area within the fence which surrounded dwelling and meadow. The outfield was an area outside this fence and was traditionally used for pasture by a certain farm. Both were private. The exception was that hunting reindeer and other game was free for all, not only on common land but also in the outfield of other farmers.²³⁷ Making even the outfields free for all must be a consequence of the fact that the game ran across borders. But hunting with dogs was not permitted in other farmers' outfields.

There were also other, more specific rules for the privatisation of hunting and fishing rights, and in many situations it must have been unclear how the rules were to be applied. Claims of private hunting and fishing rights were to be proclaimed and settled at the Thing assembly, and there it is realistic to assume that the most powerful had an advantage.

Summing up, in western Norway the most important fishing and hunting rights were basically open to all, but general norms and specific arrangements made many rights private.

Moving from Norway to Greenland, sources for rights to fishing and hunting are almost non-existent. Ivar Bárdarson informs us ca. 1360 about the private rights of the farm Gardar which belonged to the bishop. This farm is not typical since the bishop in the final centuries of Norse Greenland's existence was the most powerful man in Greenland.

Ivar's task during his stay in Greenland was to register the rights of church institutions administered by the bishop, in practice Gardar cathedral, two cloisters and several parish churches. The bishop received land rents from eight farms on Tugtutoq (*Langø*), and one called *Dalir* in Einarsfjord.²³⁸ He also owned privatised hunting and fishing rights and the right to exploit other non-agricultural resources:

- the right to hunt reindeer on Akia (*Renøe*) and exploit the soapstone on the same island.²³⁹
- the right to catch whales and fish in *Bærefjord* close to Cape Farewell.²⁴⁰
- the right to catch polar bears on *Korsøø* which was even further east.²⁴¹
- the right, in common with the Benedictine nunnery, to exploit the warm springs on Uunartoq island.²⁴²
- "a large wood" in Einarsfjord.²⁴³

Only the right to hunt reindeer on Akia is a hunting or fishing right located within the Norse settlement area. Ivar Bárdarson does not claim that parish churches or the cloisters owned private hunting and fishing rights. Secular chieftains and peasants probably had privatised such rights, but there is no positive evidence for it.

Important game in Greenland were seal, reindeer, whale and cod. The general legal principles practised in the Norse region make it likely that they were mostly open to all. Fishing for char, trout and salmon was more widely privatised. The claims by some archaeologists that the hunting and fishing resources were more or less monopolised by an elite,²⁴⁴ is not supported by the extant sources, and it is contrary to the practices in other parts of the Norse region. Resources which were open to all, benefitted most those of limited means and could function as a security net in years when food production from animal husbandry failed.

Was the hunting and fishing on common land and the open sea sustainable in the Norse period? Niels Egede in 1769 wrote that Danes sold firearms to the Inuit and bought reindeer skins from them. The Inuit skinned the animals, sold the hide to merchants of the Danish state monopoly, and left the meat to foxes and ravens. Firearms combined with market access made the hunt so effective that the number of animals declined.[245] In 1839 37,000 reindeer were shot, and in the period 1838–1855 the total number was officially 462,588. At the end of the century there were no reindeer left to shoot in the Eastern Settlement as they had been exterminated.[246] In the textbook *Greenland Ecology* Erik Born and Jens Böcher blame the disappearance on "natural fluctuations".[247] This liberates the Inuit and Danes from criticism, but it is at most only part of the explanation. In the Norse period reindeer hunters used arrow and lance and with this technology the reindeer hunt must have been sustainable. Before firearms the community could give open access to all kinds of hunting without endangering the sustainable renewal of the species.

Seals: less dominant than assumed?

In the Viking Age (ca. 800–1100) seal seems to have been more important as seafood for Norwegian coastal peasants than it was in the High Middle Ages (ca. 1100–1350) and later. The seal hunt gave more energy for less work with a simpler technology than fishing. How important was seal as a food resource in Norse Greenland?

The King's Mirror states that reindeer, whales, seal and bear were the main wild animals eaten in Greenland.[248] Seals and walruses could not be eaten on days when the church prescribed fast, but whale meat could.[249] The author was evidently not sure that his Norwegian lay readers knew how to categorise seal, which indicates that it was more common to eat seal meat in Greenland than in Norway at the time of writing in ca. 1250.

Archaeologists normally interpret many seal bones at an excavated site as much seal flesh having been eaten. The small household at W48 "clearly relied increasingly on seal flesh".[250] The archaeologist Jette Arneborg and the scientists Niels Lynnerup and Jan Heinemeier write that "The zoo-archaeological record shows that seal was the prime meat supplier for the Norse Greenlandic households".[251] This conclusion is not self evident.

The Nationalmuseum archaeologist Poul Nørlund published the results of his excavations at Brattahlid in 1934, and he interpreted the large number of "seal bones in the middens" as an expression of the need for lamp oil. Several soapstone lamps for burning oil were found. These lamps "correspond to types known in Norway, the Faroes and Iceland".[252] In Norway cod liver oil was called *lysi* meaning "that which gives light", and it was used in lamps far back in time and oil from seal blubber was used for the same purpose.

In Norse Greenland oil lamps have been excavated which were "encrusted with seal oil", according to the Danish scientist Niels Lynnerup who has analysed some of them. "In addition to its use as food . . . marine mammal oil also became the predominant fuel for heating and lightning Norse homes".[253] The Norse Greenlanders brought with them from Norway a tradition where lamp oil made from seal blubber was used in soapstone lamps. The flexible Norsemen must have increased their use of lamp oil from seals in Greenland, since firewood and turf were in short supply.

Seal-oil lamps gave both light and heat. Hans Egede in 1721 and 1722 described how they functioned in the Inuit's large winter houses with room for ca. 30 people. After a visit in 1721 he wrote in his diary: "Their only fire was from oil (*tran*) lamps, but they heated so well that they could sit half naked in their turf house (*gamme*)". The following year in the coldest month January, he paid the Inuit another visit, this time to a house where there lived more than 50 people. "The lamps burned all the time, so it was extremely (*dyktig*) hot".[254]

Experiments have shown that blubber from 12 small seals was needed to keep the inside temperature in an Inuit tent for one household at +8° for two months when the outside temperature was 30° below zero. This test was not realistic since the Inuit lived in large houses made from stone and turf in the winter. The Danish explorer Knud Rasmussen claimed that the "winter hunting score" of one hunter in traditional Inuit society was 10–30 seals, depending on the skills of the hunter. Both Inuit and Norse could keep warm through a cold winter with the help of seal-oil, and the Norse probably combined it with brushwood and turf.[255]

In the Eastern Settlement the elite farms E29a Brattahlid and E149 Vágar slaughtered significantly more seal than the average and small farms.[256] This was not because they ate more seal meat, which was considered low quality meat.[257]

How and where did the Norse Greenlanders produce their seal-oil? If seal blubber is allowed to decompose or rot, oil will come to the surface. It can be skimmed off and used without further processing as lamp oil.

Seal-oil could be prepared further by pouring it into skin bags which are hung on racks in the wind. The oil will then slowly become a thick tar which can be used to preserve wood for example in boats. This production of seal-tar was described by the Icelander Bjørn Jonsson (1574–1655).[258] The saga of Eirik Raudi tells the story of an ocean-going ship which became infested with sea-worms and sank off the coast of Ireland on its way to Greenland. Some of the passengers were saved in the ship's lifeboat "which was treated with seal-tar, because then sea-worms will not infest the wood".[259] In Norway tar was also much used to protect the exterior of wooden buildings; in Greenland they may have obtained the same protection with turf.[260] In Norway tar was made of wood; in Greenland it was replaced with seal blubber.

Bjørn Jonsson, writing more than 200 years after the Norse settlements had disappeared, thought the production of seal-tar took place in the Disco region "because there the seal hunt was better than in the settlements".[261] Bjørn may have got this idea by drawing a parallel to his own time when the Dutch produced their whale- and seal-oil there. The Norse are likely to have produced oil and tar from seal nearer home.

Oil, blubber or meat from seal brought home without bones attached, have left no remains for the archaeologists, but at least some hunters must have pulled seal carcasses on ice and snow or rowed and sailed them back to the farm. At

GUS "the entire skeleton of seal is represented", and the only bone to be entirely absent was the *os penis*, which indicates that the seal was eviscerated before being brought to the farm.[262] E34 also shows "such an even distribution for most of the body parts that it must have been common practice to take whole seal carcasses to the farm".[263] Around 40% of a seal's weight before the viscera are removed, consists of blubber.[264] In the 19th century along parts of the Norwegian coast both blubber and meat from whales were prepared in several ways and eaten, but blubber was seen as less attractive food.[265] The Norse Greenlanders may have valued meat and blubber in a similar way, and they may normally have used the blubber for lamp oil and the seal meat as food for humans or animals.

Seal skins were used to make clothing for special outdoors purposes, probably to make it watertight.[266] Even outside Greenland people may have found sealskins useful for such purposes, as they were exported from Greenland to Bergen and further to England.[267]

Among the seals the walrus occupies a special place. In the Eastern Settlement nearly all excavated bone fragments of walrus are from the skull, tusks and other teeth; the rest of the carcass with its meat was not brought back to the Eastern Settlement.[268] In the Western Settlement the excavated bone fragments represent all main parts of the walrus skeleton. This means that at least some walruses were brought home to the farms, where walrus meat was eaten and blubber used for lamp oil. Walruses went ashore at several places in the Nuuk district in historical times, but this population has been exterminated today.[269]

The assumption that seal was hunted only or mainly because it was needed for food, lacks an empirical basis. This idea has as its underlying premise that the Norse Greenlanders lived at a subsistence level and had to eat all foodstuffs they could get their hands on. That was evidently not the case.

How did the seal hunt fit into the annual work cycle of Norse peasants? Excavated seal bones verify that harp seals (*Grønlandssel, Phoca groenlandica*) dominated among the hunted seal species. At E34 58% of the identified seal bones were from harp seals,[270] and at GUS in the Western Settlement 53%.[271] McGovern's average for five Eastern Settlement farms is 64%, and for eight Western Settlement farms 61%.[272]

Harp seals breed around Newfoundland in March, cross the Davis Strait and arrive into the former Eastern Settlement in May where their presence culminates in June. The migration continues northwards to the former Western Settlement where they also stay during May-June. They enter the fjords in both settlements, although not very far. Households in the fjords must have had seasonal hunting trips to the outer fjord zone in May-June.[273] A store-house of 1.7 × 4 m on an island at the estuary of the Ameralik fjord in the Western Settlement may have been used on such hunting trips.[274] Analyses of teeth of harp seals excavated at farms near Sandnes (W51) in the Ameragdla fjord confirm that most seals were taken in spring.[275] Peasants could make room for trips to the fjord estuaries in May-June before the harvesting started. As mentioned earlier, the growing season for plants along the Greenland fjords normally lasted from May to September, and the vegetation was most productive in the latter part of the period.

In the Eastern Settlement the hooded seal (*klapmyds*, *Cystophora cristata*) was the second most common seal species. Of all identified seal bones at E34, 35% were from hooded seals[276] and at five other farms in the Eastern Settlement 23% of the identified bones were hooded seals.[277] They breed around Newfoundland or on drifting ice in the Davis Strait, then appear at the coast of the former Eastern Settlement at the end of March, and the last ones disappear at the start of June.[278] The most favourable time would be May, but hunting was possible from the end of March until June, approximately the same as for harp seals.

In the Western Settlement common seal (*harbour seal*, *spættet sæl*, *Phoca Vitulina*) was the second most common seal species. At GUS they are represented with 37% (83 of 223) of the identified bone fragments, and at eight other farms in the Western Settlement by 30%.[279] The common seal is a stationary species and the only one in Greenland to breed on land,[280] which makes it vulnerable to hunting. Many bone fragments are from baby seals, so the hunt must have taken place at breeding time when the seals had to stay on the shore.[281] At sand flats close to W51 Sandnes there was a breeding colony of common seals which may have been privatised by Sandnes and other nearby farms. At W51 and the neighbouring farm W59 the percentage of identified bones from common seals is significantly higher than at other Western Settlement farms.[282]

Thomas McGovern claimed that the Norse population starved to death because they insisted on spending their time on animal husbandry instead of seal hunting.[283] The Norsemen's season for seal hunting was some weeks during the months of April-June, before the harvesting of fodder started. Milking and tending the cows was the work of women and old men who always stayed at home. The Norse had the best of both worlds.

How did the Norse catch their seals? The author of *Fostbroedra saga* says that "the Greenlanders always had hunting-weapons on their ships". He describes how the Greenlandic chieftain Thorgrim Trolle arrived in his ship to the Gardar Thing, where the crew moved the weapons from the ship to the shore. There the skald Thormod picked up a "seal-harpoon", but a member of the crew called out to him: "put down the harpoon man, it is no use for you to stand there with it in your hand, you are not able to make the harpoon bite". The hero Thormod answered back that "I am not sure that you can make it bite better than I can". Thormod then composed a poem where the main point was that he had participated bravely in battles, and therefore also was able to make a harpoon bite.[284] The story gives evidence that Greenlanders normally brought a seal-harpoon with them when they sailed along the fjords, and that it gave masculine honour to handle it with skill. The saga author was an Icelander, but he was well informed about conditions in Greenland.

The Gulathing law from Western Norway says that "If a man harpoons a seal, but the seal escapes, then the man who finds the seal shall own it, but the man who harpooned it shall have his harpoon back, if it can be found".[285] People who rowed along the coast and came across a seal in the sea or resting on the shore, were permitted to shoot (*skiota*) it.[286] It is not clear whether the seal was "shot" with harpoon or arrow.

Another instrument mentioned in Norwegian sources is the sealnet (*selnet*). They were stretched from land out into the sea. Along the Norwegian coast there were skerries, rocks or sand beaches where seals often rested. It was attractive to put out nets from there. These places were called *selver*, many of them privatised. The Gulathing law says that:

> [i]f a man finds another man's net in his *selver*, and there is seal in the net, then the owner of the *selver* owns both net and seal. If the owner of the illegal net pays the compensation determined by law, he shall have his net back.[287]

A third method mentioned in Norwegian sources was seal traps (*stilli*). The laws distinguished between *selver* with and without traps.[288] It is not said how these traps functioned, and there may have been several types.

On Iceland medieval sources verify the use of harpooning, sealnets and seal traps, and from the post-Reformation period there is also evidence that seals were clubbed.[289] The only hunting method mentioned in written sources in Norse Greenland is harpooning, but there can be little doubt that the Norse also brought sealnets and seal traps with them from Norway, possibly also clubbing from Iceland and Norway.

Thomas McGovern has claimed that the Norse Greenlanders did not use harpoons, his empirical basis being that "no harpoons or barbed spears have been recovered from any of the excavations of Norse sites in Greenland".[290] The absence of harpoons is repeated in 2012 in an article by Dugmore, McGovern, Vesteinsson, Arneborg, Streeter and Keller.[291] This may be due to the Inuit who removed useful items after the Norse were gone. McGovern has not read relevant sources written in Old Norse, or scholarly literature in modern Scandinavian languages.[292] He thinks seal hunts were "largely" a communal effort, and that they "made full use of communal labour and probably all available boats to carry out mass seal drives".[293] He gives no reference for this. He claims that the Greenland Norse could have survived if they had "increased their efforts to borrow critical arctic technology from the Inuit".[294] He does not state which technology this was. From the diary of Hans Egede from 1723 we can see that the Inuit at that time did not use sealnets,[295] which means that they did not use them in the Norse period either. The Norse used both nets and harpoons and could choose the equipment which was the most effective in the given situation. The Inuit had only harpoons. The Norse seal hunt was technologically superior and more productive.

In the mid 20th century hunters calculated that a fully grown harp seal gave ca. 70 kg blubber, but I do not know how much meat. Six seals giving 70 kg of seal meat or blubber each were needed to cover a quarter of the annual calorie needs of a family of six.[296] As mentioned earlier, the "winter hunting score" of one Inuit hunter was 10–30 seals, depending on the skills of the hunter.[297] This calculation is not realistic since only the meat of young seals was considered to be acceptable food under normal circumstances,[298] and the blubber was considered as unattractive food. But it demonstrates that meat and blubber from seals could prevent people from starving, if that was the only alternative.

A Norse hunter had less time to spend on seal hunting than an Inuit, but he may have been more effective since he used sealnets. The seal hunt functioned as a safety net in lean years and provided a food reserve which in practice was inexhaustible, albeit unattractive.

Reindeer: the most attractive game

The word "rein" comes from Old Norse and "caribou" from Indians living in present day Canada. The Greenland reindeer had emigrated from Canada. Seasonal migrations of reindeer in Greenland "had patterns which varied between regions",[299] and reindeer hunts were therefore organised differently in the two settlements.

In the Western Settlement the reindeer herds stayed in the inner fjords all year; in autumn and winter in the lowlands; and in summer they sought higher ground.[300] In recent centuries the best hunting grounds have been in the inner parts of the Ameragdla and Kapisillit fjords,[301] and there are no indications that this was different in the Norse period. This area was also where the Norse farms were most numerous and largest, and many or most Norse peasants had attractive hunting grounds close to the home farm. They could find time for hunting in between agricultural work in the snow-free summer months. The reindeer would be fleshiest and fattest at the end of the summer season, and most of the hunting probably took place after the harvesting work had ended in the autumn.

The Inuit also saw reindeer as a valuable resource. In Hans Egede's time the Inuit stayed on the coast at the former Western Settlement in winter, but in spring the whole household paddled to the inner fjords where they stayed until autumn. There, hunting reindeer was their main occupation.[302]

The reindeer hunt was less important in the Eastern Settlement. Ivar Bárdarson mentions it briefly ca. 1360:

> The cathedral owns the large island which lies at the estuary of Einar's fjord and is named "Reindeer Island" (*Renø*). It has this name because in autumn numerous (*utallige*) reindeer are running there. The hunt on the island is open to everybody, but they need the bishop's permission.[303]

Today this island is named "Akia". Further north-west there is a larger island which the Norse named "Long island" and the Inuit "Tugtutoq" (Island with reindeer). The name indicates that the Inuit hunted reindeer there. Ivar Bárdarson says in the quotation cited above that this hunt took place in autumn. Peasants would row or sail from their farms in the fjords out to the islands where they remained some days or weeks to obtain reindeer meat for the winter.

Bows, arrows and spears made from Norwegian models were widely used for reindeer hunts in Norse Greenland.[304] At Gardar a mould made of soapstone to cast heads of arrows was found, and the metal used must have been iron.[305] Other arrowheads were made of reindeer antler and indicate that arrows were used by reindeer hunters.

- Narsaq (E17a) is from the early Norse period; one of the excavated arrowheads was made of iron; nearly a dozen were made of reindeer antler.[306]
- At farm E64c in Vatnahverfi an arrow head of iron was excavated. It is long (8.1 cm) and must have been made for a special use.[307]
- At Umiviarsuk (W52) one arrowhead of iron and another of bone were found;[308] from the neighbouring farm of Sandnes (W51) one of flint and another of bone.[309] Three fragments of bows of Norse type were found at Sandnes. They were made of juniper wood and must have been made in Greenland.[310] Four arrow shafts were excavated from Sandnes,[311] and eight other slender sticks of wood from Umiviarsuk and Sandnes may have been arrow shafts.[312]

Spears could be used both for hunting and self-defence, but for the latter purpose axes and swords were the most common.[313] A spear head of iron has been excavated at Brattahlid,[314] and at least seven additional iron objects have been classified as knife blades, some of which may have been used as spear heads.[315] All these iron objects were useful for hunting, but also for other purposes. It is possible that hunting-weapons of iron were more common in real life than among the excavated objects. After the Norse disappeared the Inuit removed iron objects from the sites. These weapons were used for individual hunting but also for collective hunts.

Permanent hunting constructions were built in the Western Settlement where the reindeer hunt was most important, and they had Norwegian models.[316] The Norwegian constructions have been analysed by combining archaeological finds and written laws. One type was a system of walls made of stone or wood and which ended in a funnel. Norwegian laws call these walls *dyrgarda*, which could be translated as "reindeer fences" or "reindeer walls".[317] The walls or cairns often had the form of a half circle, normally 1.5–3.0 m long and 0.6–0.8 m high. They were built of stone close to tracks where herds of reindeer used to pasture or migrate at certain times of the year; 10–15 of them were often built close to each other in a row. The hunters would hide behind them, and when a reindeer came close, it would be killed with an arrow or spear. Often the hunters had helpers who chased the reindeer along the row of cairns.[318] At the end of the funnel other hunters could wait for them. The wall or fence could also lead them to a lake, as swimming reindeer are easier to kill.

Norwegian medieval laws often name permanent constructions for hunting without describing how they functioned. One of them is named *spjotgardr*.[319] This may have been a wall or cairn behind which an individual hunter hid, with his spear ready. In the 17th and 18th centuries firearms made collective hunting less relevant in Norway and Greenland.

Fences of wood can be dated, and in Norway the oldest were built many centuries before AD 985.[320] The Hardanger plateau (*Hardangervidda*) and other mountain plateaux with large reindeer herds were accessible for coastal or fjord peasants through long fjords.

Greenland had permanent hunting constructions which have been analysed by comparing them to the Norwegian ones described earlier, and to Inuit constructions from a later period. The Norwegian archaeologist Otto Blehr participated in the Inuit–Nordbo project in 1976–1977. He found constructions for reindeer hunting between the Ameragdla fjord and the inland ice close to the Norse farms W63, W54 and W55, and which had parallels in the Norwegian reindeer fences just described. They had cairns built in rows which would lead herds of reindeer to run along a certain track. Sometimes this led to a precipice where the animals would fall and be seriously injured or killed. Elsewhere reindeer were led to a lake where the swimming animals were an easy prey. The cairns could also hide hunters with arrows or spears. Blehr argued that these constructions were Norse and not Inuit because they were built close to the three Norse farms and had Norwegian models.[321]

The role of the Norse is sometimes debatable. Danish archaeologist Karen Christensen claimed to have found similar constructions in the mountains between the Norse farms W35 and W33. She does not state exactly where she found them, neither does she provide photographic evidence.[322] In Itinnera at the Kapisillit fjord in the Western Settlement there is a system of cairns which was probably used in collective reindeer hunts, but it is not clear by whom.[323] Far north of the Norse settlements similar constructions have been identified at Aasivissuit. They were probably built by the Inuit after the Norse had disappeared from Greenland.[324]

Reindeer hunters in Norway dug graves or pitfalls where reindeer had their seasonal tracks.[325] They have not been found in Norse Greenland, probably because the layer of soil is mostly too thin to dig them. Helge Ingstad, who was an experienced hunter and knew the Norwegian tradition, looked for them during his stay in Norse Greenland in 1953, but did not find any.[326]

In the Eastern Settlement collective hunts may have been organised when the reindeer swam from the islands to the mainland in autumn.[327] Constructions for collective hunts have not been found. The reindeer's main winter food is lichen, which they dig from under the snow, and in the Eastern Settlement lichens are most common in the mid parts of the fjords.[328] It is possible that this was where the reindeer of the Eastern Settlement stayed in winter.

The Western Settlement gave easier access to the attractive reindeer meat and to the hunt for walrus tusks in the north.[329] This must to some extent have compensated for the poorer agricultural conditions compared to the Eastern Settlement.[330]

In the Norse tradition seal meat had a low status, and reindeer meat was thought to have a high status and quality.[331] The Norwegian author of *The King's Mirror* described ca. 1250 in detail different types of seals to be found in Greenland, but there are indications that he normally did not eat seal meat himself. He says that seal meat "may well be eaten by humans" (*ero their mannum væl ætir*), but this would have been superfluous information if it was normal fare for himself and his readership in Norway.[332]

The highest government official in Norwegian Finnmark wrote ca. 1700 that there was no lack of seals at the coast and in the fjords, and they were caught with nets. The blubber was eaten by peasants, and lamp oil was produced with some of it. The meat was eaten fresh. His way of describing seal meat indicates that he did not eat it himself.[333]

From Greenland *Fostbroedra saga* describes a poor old couple living by themselves in Eiriksfjord. One day they received unexpected visitors while the wife sat by the fire boiling seal. The author sees seal as appropriate food to characterise poor people.[334]

Reindeer meat was valued more highly. In 1770 the Danish merchant Niels Egede upbraided the Inuit for shooting a large number of reindeer just for the sake of the hide. They left the "delicate (*delekate*) meat in the field for ravens and foxes to eat".[335] Daniel Bruun in 1918 likewise condemned the Inuit for shooting reindeer just for sport. He praised the authorities for having permitted the hunt only if the hunters were able to carry the meat home.[336] They did not issue similar prohibitions against letting seal meat rot. The high food value given to reindeer meat is still shared by today's Norwegians.

High quality meat for the Greenland Norse was not only reindeer but also mutton and beef. All Norse peasants produced some of it, but how important was it really for them to get as much of it as possible? Table 5.7 includes elite farms (Sandnes, Vágar, Brattahlid) and medium-sized and small farms from both settlements.

Reindeer consumption at the elite farm Sandnes was only marginally larger than at the average farms of the Western Settlement. In the Eastern Settlement the reindeer consumption at the elite farms E29a Brattahlid and E149 Vágar was not higher than at the other farms. Elite households do not seem to have made great efforts to obtain as much high quality meat as possible.

But the shorter the distance from the farm to the relevant hunting grounds, the greater the consumption. The percentage of reindeer bones was three to four times higher in the Western Settlement where the distance to the hunting grounds was shorter. Within the Western Settlement Sandnes, Nipaatsoq and GUS were close to the best hunting ground for reindeer, Niaquusat was further out along the fjord. In the Eastern Settlement both rich and poor peasants lived in the fjords and had a longer distance to travel to the hunting grounds at the coast. The farmers in the

Table 5.7 Bone fragments from main meat-bearing animals by percentage

	Seal	Reindeer	Sheep/goat	Cattle	Total
W54 Nipaatsoq	42%	20%	29%	9%	100%
GUS	44%	17%	30%	9%	100%
W51 Sandnes	48%	23%	17%	12%	100%
W59	64%	18%	13%	4%	99%
W48 Niaquusat	82%	5%	11%	2%	100%
E34 in Qorlortup valley	39%	6%	36%	16%	97%
Vatnahverfi	43%	2%	38%	17%	100%
E17a Narsaq	49%	8%	27%	16%	100%
E149 Vágar?	63%	4%	16%	17%	100%
E29a Brattahlid	71%	4%	16%	10%	101%

Sources: Empirical material with references in Appendix I.

Eastern Settlement had also less time to spend on hunting since they had a larger livestock which demanded more work in the snow-free summer months.

Seal was used both for lamp oil and food, and the figures are therefore difficult to interpret. The high figures at the elite farms E29a Brattahlid and E149 Vágar are probably due to large farms needing more heating and light than small ones. The high figures at W59 and W48 may be due to needs for both lamp oil and food. The difference between the two settlements in seal consumption was insignificant: lamp oil was needed along all fjords.

The written laws gave rich and poor the same open access to reindeer and other game on outfield and common land. Archaeological evidence indicates that the law was practised, and geography determined how much use the households made of their hunting rights. Contrary to what many archaeologists have claimed, the landowning elite did not monopolise or dominate access to hunting.

Is it possible to estimate how important reindeer meat was in the diet at an average farm in the two settlements? Reindeer and cattle had approximately the same number of bones in their bodies. If the number of bones from cattle and reindeer is at the same level at two sites or areas, it is likely that the number of reindeer and cattle slaughtered there was also at the same level. If the number of reindeer bones was double that of cattle bones, it is an indication that the number of slaughtered reindeer was also double (Table 5.8).

In Table 5.8 seal bones have been left out since seal on many farms were mainly hunted for lamp oil.

In pre-modern Norwegian coastal agriculture, "winter-fed cattle", that is cattle which had been fed in the byre for at least one winter, were slaughtered when they were four or five years old on average. This means that somewhat less than a quarter of the cattle livestock was slaughtered each year.[337]

Table 5.8 Bone fragments from main domestic animals and reindeer in percent

	Reindeer	Sheep/goat	Cattle	Total
W54 Nipaatsoq	34%	50%	16%	100%
GUS	30%	54%	16%	100%
W51 Sandnes	44%	33%	23%	100%
W59	52%	38%	11%	101%
W48 Niaquusat	28%	61%	11%	100%
E34 Qorlortup valley	10%	59%	26%	95%
Vatnahverfi	4%	67%	30%	101%
E17a Narsaq	16%	53%	31%	100%
E149 Vágar?	11%	43%	46%	100%
E29a Brattahlid	14%	55%	34%	103%

Source: Table 5.7. In the present table, seal has been excluded.

284 *Subsistence food production*

The 8 households (Sandnes excluded) registered from the Western Settlement in Table 5.6 had on average 7 winter-fed milk-cows and heifers; roughly 1.5 of them may have been slaughtered each autumn. Of the 7, 5.3 may have been milk-cows, and each milk-cow gave birth to at least one calf each spring. At an average farm in the Western Settlement this would have meant 5.3 calves. The farmer would only keep the 1.5 calves which were necessary to replace the adult cattle which he slaughtered that year, and the remaining 3.8 calves were slaughtered in the autumn. This means that an average Western Settlement household slaughtered annually around 1.5 adult cattle and 3.5 calves, in all around 5 cattle.

At Western Settlement farms there were about twice as many reindeer bones as cattle bones, according to Table 5.8. This suggests that the number of reindeer slaughtered was twice the number of cattle slaughtered, which is ten reindeer per household. Domesticated reindeer in Finnmark in the 1970s gave ca. 30 kg of meat per slaughtered animal, which was an average where animals of both sexes were included.[338] Wild reindeer when hunted on the Hardanger plateau today give between 40 and 60 kg of pure meat per reindeer buck and for female reindeer between 25 and 28 kg. Archaeologists have compared excavated medieval reindeer bones to bones from today's reindeer and have found no major difference in size. They assume ca. 35 kg edible meat per slaughtered animal on average at the Hadanger plateau.[339] Ten slaughtered reindeer will then give 350 kg reindeer meat per household per year. Since 100 g of reindeer meat gives ca. 120 kcal,[340] 350 kg gives 192 kcal per person per day or 7% of normal daily consumption in a household of six.[341]

The 21 households (Gardar excluded) from the Eastern Settlement in Table 5.6 had on average 12 winter-fed cows and heifers, and around 2.5 of them may have been slaughtered each autumn. In addition, each of the 9 milk-cows gave birth to at least one calf each spring, which may have given 9 calves, of which 2.5 were kept through the coming winter to replace the slaughtered cows and 6.5 calves were slaughtered in the autumn. This means that an average Eastern Settlement household slaughtered annually 2.5 adult cattle and 6.5 calves, in all 9 cattle. The number of reindeer bones was roughly one-third of the number of cattle bones according to Table 5.8. This indicates that each farmer slaughtered around three reindeer annually. As each animal gave 35 kg of edible meat, this gives ca. 105 kg of edible meat per household per year. Since 100 g reindeer meat gives 120 kcal, 105 kg gives 58 kcal per person per day, or 2% of normal daily consumption.[342]

High quality meat must for the Norse have been cattle, sheep/goat and reindeer. In the Eastern Settlement cattle gave ca. 3%, sheep/goats ca. 1% and reindeer ca. 2%, in all ca. 6% of daily calorie needs. In the Western Settlement cattle gave ca. 2%, sheep/goats ca. 1% and reindeer ca. 7%, in all ca. 10% of daily calorie needs. High quality meat must have been a desirable part of the diet, but it was not essential for survival and the elite did not make great efforts to obtain as much of it as possible. In an average household it may have been eaten at their Sunday dinner but hardly more than that.

Measured in calories, meat from the animals mentioned in Table 5.8 was in normal years not essential for survival, but it was more important in the Western Settlement than in the Eastern Settlement. Meat from cattle, sheep/goats and reindeer was considered as quality food, which means that people in the Western

Settlement were considered to have a higher food standard on this point. But as always it must also have been important to have a varied diet, and the Norse Greenlanders were used to a balanced diet of grain products, milk products, meat and fish. In Greenland they must have missed the bread and not least the beer.

Whales

In the period 985–1410 whales were far more numerous than today in the North Atlantic, the coasts of western Greenland included. The Dutch hunted whales at Spitzbergen, Jan Mayen and in the Davis Strait from the 17th century. The whale population was decimated and is today only a fraction of what it was in the Greenland Norse period. The account in *The King's Mirror* of large numbers of whales in northern waters is not necessarily exaggerated. The archaeologists' osteological material underestimates the importance of whaling, because blubber and meat were brought to the farm without the heavy whale bones attached.

Norse norms on hunting rights also applied to whaling. According to the Norwegian Gulathing law, whaling was in principle free for all if it took place on the open sea. If a whale was found on, caught from, or butchered on private land, the landowner acquired property rights.[343]

The hunt for small and large whales was organised differently. Many fragments of whalebones have been excavated at Norse sites, but osteologists find it difficult to determine to which species the whale belonged. Most of the identified ones were small whales.

- At GUS in the Western Settlement 31 bone fragments were from whales, two of them identified as small whales: long-finned pilot whale[344] and white whale.[345]
- At E34 80 fragments of whales were found, of these the species of only two could be determined, both from white whale.[346]
- At E17a the species of three bone fragments could be determined, all from white whale.[347]
- At E167 in the Vatnahverfi nine bone fragments from whales were found, one identified as white whale, another as porpoise.[348]

The author of *The King's Mirror* confirms that the most numerous whale type is small, only 5–10 m and called *nydingr*. Hundreds of them could be chased ashore at the same time, and they provided plenty of food (*mikil foedsla*).[349] There can be little doubt that the author means what today is called a pilot whale. It is 6–8 m and normally stays far out at sea, but in warm periods it draws close to the Greenland west coast and sometimes swims into the fjords. The white whale is smaller, only 4–5 m long, and it stays all year along the west coast, mostly north of the two settlements. Both white and pilot whales swim in shoals which could be chased into bays and killed in large numbers.[350] Among the small whales, pilot whale, white whale and porpoise were actively hunted for food.

Ivar Bárdarson says ca. 1360 that whales were hunted close to Cape Farewell in *Bærefiord*. When there was a strong current into the fjord, numerous whales swam

286 *Subsistence food production*

with the current. When the water level sank again, many whales could be trapped in a deep hole in the fjord called "the whale-hole" (*hvalshøøll*). They could be killed, probably with lances and spears. This whale fishery was privately owned by the bishop.[351]

Bays into which small whales were chased or where they were trapped for natural reasons were often called "whale bays" (*kvalvåg* or *kvalvik*) in Norway. The Norwegian Gulathing law regulated briefly the economic rights of hunters and landowner when small whales were chased into "whale bays" which often were privatised.[352] This hunting method was in recent centuries best known in the Faroes, where the prey was also pilot whales. It was also known from western Norway, but on a smaller scale.[353]

Sometime before he died in AD 899, king Alfred of England was visited by a chieftain who had his farm in northern Norway near the present town of Harstad. He related among other things that in his country there was good hunting for whales which were around 24 m long.[354] If this is correct, the Norse at the time when Norse Greenland was settled hunted the largest whales in the North Atlantic.

At GUS 4 of 31 bone fragments of whale could be identified as "The Greenland right whale" also called "the Bowhead whale".[355] It was 15–20 m long, and was numerous in the Norse period along the Greenland west coast, but is today almost extinct.[356] A Dutch narrative from the 17th century tells how it was easy to hunt because it swam slowly. It did not sink when it was killed, which made it easy to tow it to a nearby ship where it could be slaughtered floating alongside the ship or landed on a shore. It was the main prey of Dutch whalers.[357]

The King's Mirror describes several large whale species, but the author does not classify them in the same way as modern biology, and it is a challenge to find which species are meant. A species called *reydr* is said to give better food than any other whale. It was a preferred prey for Norse hunters[358] because it was so mild and peaceful (*hoegværi* and *spektr*) as well.[359] This resembles the Dutch description of the Greenland right whale just quoted. It seems that this was the only large whale species which was actively hunted for food by the Norse Greenlanders. The others could be killed and eaten if they were stranded or the opportunity arose for other reasons. *The King's Mirror* claims that the largest *reydr* which has been caught and measured was 60m long.[360] This is exaggerated because the largest whale on earth is the blue whale which has a maximum length of 33m.[361] The author's knowledge about the large whales was less accurate.

A bone fragment from a second large whale species has been found at a site in Austmannadalen in the Western Settlement. It is the "Humpback whale" which can still be seen close to Nuuk.[362]

The west Norwegian Gulathing law confirms that the Norse caught large whales on the open sea:

> People have the right to chase whales wherever they can. If a whale is hunted and dies on deep water, the hunter owns the whale, irrespective of whether it is small or large. Now a man shoots at a whale and hits (*Nu skytr madr hval oc hoever*), and the whale swims ashore, then the hunter owns half and the landowner half of the whale.[363]

Were the whales swimming in deep waters "shot" with an arrow or a harpoon? The lawmaker keeps open the possibility that the hunter could miss a large whale, which was more likely to happen if an arrow was shot from a long distance.

This points to whale hunting using poisoned arrows, which was still being practised along the west coast of Norway in the 19th century. The arrows were made poisonous by standing them with their pointed end in a bucket of rotten meat. The arrow was shot with a crossbow from a rowing-boat. The peasants were not good marksmen, and the arrow often missed. But the shaft was made of wood, which made the arrow float and so it could be retrieved if it did not hit the whale. If such an arrow penetrated the whale's hide and stood fixed in its flesh, there was a chance that the whale would develop an infection from which it would die within a few days. The poisoned pointed end was made to separate itself from the shaft, and there was no line between the pointed end in the whale's flesh and the hunter's boat. The hunter had to wait some days looking for a dead or half-dead poisoned whale nearby. In its reduced state the whale was less dangerous for hunters, and lances or a harpoon could be thrust into it.[364] Many poisoned whales were never found. Along the Norwegian coast it was labour-intensive to hunt large whales, and often a great deal of work resulted in no catch. It was practised by a few peasants in particular regions. The situation may have been similar in Norse Greenland.

Other sources confirm that the Norse Greenlanders actively hunted whales. In his narrative about the men who sailed north of Disco in the 1260s, the priest Halldor writes that they there saw "many kinds of game for hunting (*veidiskap*): seals, whales and a lot of polar bears".[365]

How did the Norse Greenlanders use their whales? The blubber is a layer of fat between the skin and the flesh. If a drifting whale was found at sea, it belonged to the hunter who had shot it, but the finder had the right to "finder's blubber",[366] which was a rowing-boat of specified size fully loaded with blubber.[367] *The King's Mirror* points out that some whale species were fat and so had a lot of blubber.[368]

The King's Mirror classifies whale species in the North Atlantic as "well edible", "edible" or "not edible". In the 19th century along parts of the Norwegian coast both blubber and meat were prepared in several ways and eaten.[369] Whale blubber is said to taste of fish-oil (*tran*) and was considered by many as second-rate food.[370] The meat was valued more highly and is still eaten along the Norwegian coast.

The King's Mirror remarks that the blubber of one of the whale species was inedible for both humans and animals, and the wording implies that blubber from other species could be given to domestic animals.[371]

It is not known how long whale blubber and meat could remain edible in Norse Greenland. Most months were so cold that no salt was needed, and "refrigerators" could be dug into the permafrost to keep the meat edible even in summer.

In Norway and Iceland a large part of the blubber was used to extract oil for lamps and for frying.[372] A stranded whale could be a bonanza. An average Greenland right whale weighs ca. 40 tons,[373] of which about 40% is blubber,[374] that is 16 tons. One fully grown harp seal[375] weighs ca. 200 kg, of which ca. 70 kg is blubber.[376] This means that one Greenland right whale gave the same quantity of lamp oil as 230 harp seals. The very size of the catch made it natural to divide it between several households. In many cases the Gulathing law stipulated that the right to the whale was to be divided between finder, hunter, landowner and others according to complex rules.[377]

Remnants of what Niels Lynnerup calls "marine-mammal oil" has been found encrusted in soapstone lamps excavated at Norse sites in Greenland, and the identification was done by scientific methods.[378] Marine mammals include both seal and whale. Lynnerup and Jette Arneborg confirm that the methods used in this case do not permit the distinction between seal and whale oil.[379] In the future it will probably be possible to verify that whale blubber was used to produce lamp oil in Norse Greenland.

Whale teeth provided raw materials for knife-handles and game pieces.[380] Whale bones were also used for game pieces, and many have been excavated at Sandnes[381] and another two at Gardar.[382] They were also used as sword-sticks in weaving,[383] ladles,[384] sledge shoes[385] and axes.[386] In Norway spades were made of wood, often with a shoeing of iron, but in a country where both large pieces of wood and iron were hard to come by, bones of large whales were an alternative.[387] At Sandnes small chips and flakes of whalebone were excavated suggesting that the objects were made indoors.[388] At one of the farms in the Austmannadal in the Western Settlement a large vertebra from the spine of a Humpback whale had been used as a chopping-block.[389] Baleen were used as hoops around barrels,[390] and even to sew the planks of a ship's hull.[391] But for all these purposes whale bones, whale teeth and baleen could be replaced with other available material.

Whaling could be perilous and needed a lot of work, with uncertain returns. It demanded the cooperation of many, and legislation complicated the hunt. Whales provided large quantities of meat and blubber in one go, which complicated preservation and distribution. Whales appeared at irregular times, normally in summer when there was much agricultural work to be done. Whale hunts gave nothing which could not also be obtained from seal, that is oil, meat and skins. Seal hunts took place at the same time each year in spring before agricultural work started. Seals could be hunted by individuals with harpoons, nets, traps and possibly arrows. From the hunter's point of view, the seal hunt was simpler to organise and gave more predictable results. The Greenland Norse may therefore have given a low priority to whaling.

Hunting expeditions to the east coast

Hunting for reindeer, seal and whale took place in the settlements and the prey was used in the Norsemen's subsistence economy. This seems to have continued as long as Norse Greenland existed. In the 11th to 13th centuries the Norsemen also travelled north to the Disco region to produce walrus products for export. This ended ca. 1340 at the latest because the Inuit made the journeys hazardous and the market for walrus tusk declined. What about the hunting expeditions east of Cape Farewell?

Ivar Bárdarson ca 1360 does not mention the walrus hunts in the Disco region, but he is acquainted with the hunting along the uninhabited eastern coast. In *Bærefiord* whales were hunted, the fisheries were rich and the bishop had privatised the fjord. Further east was another fjord called *Allumlenger* which was rich in birds and eggs. Ivar writes that further east "towards the icebergs" were "Finn's booths" and "Cross-Island". This was the central hunting station. Ivar presents *Korsøø* (Cross-Island) as the easternmost location in Greenland which he knew. Both Greenlanders and Icelanders seem to have hunted there.[392] "Finn's booths" was a hunting station with booths for hunters. A ship with one of King Olav Haraldsson's servants on board was wrecked there, and stone crosses were erected which could still be seen in Ivar Bárdarson's time more than three centuries later.[393] Finn's booths and these crosses seem to have been built on the same island, which was named "Cross-Island" (*Kaarsø*) and situated just east of Cape Farewell. The main prey hunted there was polar bears.[394] Asmundr Kastandratzi hunted there in 1189 with 13 men on his ship.[395] "Further east there is nothing but ice and snow on land and sea as far as one can see". He explicitly says that the bishop had privatised the hunt for polar bears on Cross Island.[396] It may seem that Ivar had sailed as far up the eastern coast as the bishop had property interests.

How far up the east coast did the Norse travel on their hunting expeditions? In 1942 no archaeological remains of Norsemen had been found north of Lindenow fjord.[397] Cross Island and the property interests of the bishop may have ended in the same area. But this is not evident, and the description of the hunting expedition in the 1120s gives the impression that they voyaged further up the coast.[398]

No walruses are mentioned. They are today only found along the northernmost part of the east coast north of Tasiliaq,[399] but it cannot be ruled out that they lived further south before the Hollanders reduced the stock in the 17th century. The polar bears had a market in foreign countries, either alive or as bearskin. Asmundr Kastandratzi sailed from Cross Island via Iceland towards Norway, and one of his commodities may have been polar bears. Whales, fish, birds and eggs[400] must have been for home consumption and supplemented the catches taken in the settlements.

The Greenlander Sigurdr Njálsson in the 1120s "went often in autumn for hunting expeditions to the east coast". On one occasion in the late 1120s he had 15 men on his ship.[401] Hunting in the Disco region was undertaken in spring before the main agricultural work, and on the east coast it was in autumn when the work load in agriculture had passed its peak. But the hunt in the Disco region was much richer and the expeditions along the east coast could not replace them.

Cod and other sea fish

The fish resources along the Atlantic and North Sea coasts of Norway were in the pre-industrial period one of the world's richest. They were so close to the shore that ordinary peasants could participate with small boats and inexpensive fishing gear. The fish resources were so abundant that coastal households always had as much fish as they needed for their own consumption. The Norse Greenlanders came to a country where fish resources were scarcer and demanded more work to exploit. Did they react by reducing their consumption of fish or by spending more time on fishing to keep up their traditional consumption?

The number of fish bones found at Norse sites is small indeed, but this does not necessarily mean that little fishing took place. Fish bones are small, fragile and rot easily. The excavated soil has to be sieved with small-meshed nets to extract fish bones, and this was not done until recently.[402] Norsemen often gave fish remains, bones included, to domestic animals, and foxes and other wild animals ate from farm middens at night. It is difficult to determine to which species a particular fishbone belongs. These sources of error make it impossible to use tables of fishbones quantitatively in comparisons of different sites or in discussions of chronological changes. But the figures can be used to compare different fish species at the same site.[403] Fishbones can also be used qualitatively as evidence that a fish species was consumed at a particular farm (Table 5.9).

From Table 5.9 it can be concluded that cod dominated among the sea fish and char among the freshwater fish. Table 5.9 gives qualitative evidence that halibut, eelpout and sculpin among the sea fish and salmon among the freshwater fish were also used in the household. It must remain an open question whether the capelin was food for the Norse Greenlanders, because the capelin bones may have found their way to Norse middens through the stomachs of slaughtered cod.

Table 5.9 Number of fishbones from identified species found at Norse farms

Farm	Cod	Halibut	Eelpout	Capelin	Sculpin	Char	Salmon	Source
E47	1							Vesteinsson 2014, p. 84
E172						1		Smiarowski 2007, p. 12
E34	5	2	1					Nyegaard 2014[404]
W48	1				1	7	1	McGovern 1979, pp. 371–373
W54		4				6		McGovern 1979, p. 374
W59	3					2		McGovern 1979, p. 375
GUS	31	2		29	1	69		Enghoff 2003, p. 24

Cod = Latin: gadus morhua; Norwegian: torsk
Halibut = Latin: hippoglossus hippoglossus; Norwegian: kveite
Eelpout = Latin: lycodes; Norwegian and Danish: Ålebrosme
Capelin = Latin: mallotus villosus; Greenlandic: ammassæt; Norwegian: lodde
Sculpin = Latin: cottidae; Norwegian: ulke; Danish: ulk
Char = Latin: salvenius alpinus; Norwegian: røye; Danish: Fjeldørred
Salmon = Latin: salmo salar; Norwegian: laks

The fishing gear used in Norwegian cod fisheries at that time was handlines ending in a sinker of soapstone and a hook made of iron. Cod is a "species" (*gadus morhua*) which belongs to a larger "family" of "cod fish". Other species in this family are haddock,[405] saithe and ling, and the same equipment can be used to fish for all these species and all are considered good for eating.

Norwegian handlines for cod fisheries were normally ca. 120–160 m long, but when fishing at over ca. 100 m they were heavy to draw. The line was made of hemp and would be soaked in water, and the sinker and cod could also be heavy.[406] When they were feeding, local cod in the Greenland fjords mostly swam near to the bottom at more than 100 m and were therefore out of the reach of Norse handlines.[407] But they spawned at shallow waters, and then they were accessible.

Sinkers have been excavated at several sites:

Narsaq (E17a) belonged to the first Norse farms from AD 985 or shortly thereafter, and three sinkers found there are of a type well known in Norway. They are symmetrical, polished and streamlined so that they will sink vertically and rapidly through the water down towards the bottom. Their height was ca. 6 cm, which means that they were rather light and for moderate depths. When in use the sinker had to be tied to a wooden stick. The line to the fisherman was bound to the top of the wooden stick, the line to the hook was bound to the bottom of the stick.[408]

At E149 Vágar a sinker was found which was almost round like a ball but with a groove round it. If it had been used in Norway the groove would have been for a line made of hemp. In Greenland the line may have been made of sealskin or baleen. Vebæk suggests that the sinker was for a fishnet, but it is unlikely that they would have spent so much time on polishing a sinker which was only meant for keeping a net at the bottom. A stone of any form would have served that purpose.[409] It is more likely to have been for a handline. Vebæk points out that no fishbones were found at Vágar, but "there undoubtedly are fishbones at the site; it is quite unbelievable that the Norsemen of this locality would not have fished".[410] The sinker provides evidence that they did.

At the Hvalsey ruin site E83a a sinker of soapstone was found. It had a similar ball-like form and was 13.9 cm high.[411] Another similar sinker for a handline was found in the living quarters of the Brattahlid North farm (E29a).[412]

At E167 in the inland district of Vatnahverfi a soapstone object formed like a ball was found with a hole which penetrates the whole object. They must have put a stick through this hole. Vebæk assumed that it was a spindle whorl but admits that it is "very large" for that purpose being 8 cm high. An alternative hypothesis is that it may have been a sinker for fishing, perhaps for char in a nearby lake. The stick would then serve to fasten lines from the sinker upwards to the fisherman and downwards to the hook.[413] An argument against the fish-sinker hypothesis is that the sinker has decorative grooves, and fish sinkers are often lost when used. It is more likely that spindle whorls were decorated.[414]

292 Subsistence food production

A sinker is normally used until it is lost and only exceptionally ends its life in the midden. It is therefore not surprising that few sinkers have been excavated at Norse sites.

Fish hooks were in the Norse medieval tradition made of iron, but remarkably few remnants of them have been found in Norse Greenland. At E74 in Vatnahverfi a hook was found "which possibly could be a fish hook",[415] and at E167 in Vatnahverfi a "fragment of an object of iron, possibly the point of a fish hook".[416] The Inuit in the period after the Norse disappeared searched their houses for useful objects, particularly of iron and bronze, and this may explain why so few fish hooks have been found. But even in the Faroes "the amount and variety of metalwork is rather poor in general . . . metalwork occurs only in small quantities on settlement sites".[417] Few extant iron objects may be due to rust in a wet climate. An alternative hypothesis is that the lack of iron and forging skills made it difficult to forge fish hooks in Norse Greenland, and after the walrus trade ceased they may have lacked money to buy them in Bergen. A lack of iron for fish hooks may have become a serious problem and obstacle in the Norse Greenlanders' cod fisheries.

Many, perhaps most, Norse farms owned a rowing boat which could be used for fishing in the fjords.[418] The common type was the *sexæringr* which normally was manned by three men. One man would then sit at the oars and keep the boat in the right position above the fishing ground. Another would sit at a seat (thwart) near the bow with his handline, and another near the rear end of the boat with another handline. If the two sat too close to each other, their lines could become entangled. If they sat at each end of a *sexæringr* with a sufficiently heavy sinker which made the handline go down perpendicularly, this would normally have been prevented. The victims of Thormod Kolbrunarskald's last murders in Greenland were four men who sat in a boat fishing on the fjord. The saga author wrote 200 years after the event, and it is fruitless to speculate on why the saga author ca. 1220–1250 put four and not three men in the boat.[419]

There were two kinds of cod: stationary fjord cod and bank cod which arrived from the Davis Strait. In May-June large shoals of capelin entered the fjords of the two settlements to spawn.[420] They were important food for both fjord cod and bank cod. Bank cod followed the capelin from the banks in the Davis Strait. The capelin stayed in the fjords in shallow waters and this made the cod which ate them accessible to Norse handlines.[421] The stationary fjord cod spawned where the sea temperature was highest, which was in the inner parts of the fjords.

Warm fjords favour production of food for cod, but sea temperatures not only depend on air temperatures, but also on ocean currents from the Atlantic along the Greenland west coast. In winter cold ocean currents from the Atlantic reach south-west Greenland fjords and make them cold. In summer warm currents deep under the surface will reach the same fjords. Some Greenland fjords have at their estuary a high threshold which keeps these deep warm summer currents out of the fjords. Such "threshold fjords" will stay cold even in summer, and because of the temperature food production is lower and fish stocks smaller. Other fjords have an estuary which is open to these warm summer currents, and here the production of food for fish will be higher in summer and the stocks of cod and other fish larger.[422] Large fjords which have such favourable conditions for fish are the Nup Kangerdlua/Godthåbsfjord in the Western Settlement, the Kapisillit fjord included. In the Eastern Settlement the large fjords are Tunulliarfik/Eiriksfjord, Igalikup Kangerlua/Einarsfjord and Agdluitsup fjord/Lichtenau fjord. "Threshold fjords" with poor fishing in the Western Settlement are Ameralik/Lysufjord and in the Eastern Settlement Tasermiut/Ketilsfjord.[423] There is no automatic causality from declining air temperatures, to declining sea temperatures, to declining food production in the sea and finally to diminishing stocks of cod.

Helge Ingstad visited some of the fjords with "open" estuaries with his motorboat in 1953, which was in the middle of a period with warm sea temperatures. In the fjord called Alluitsup or Lichtenau the fishing was excellent, mostly char which fed on capelin, and large cod.[424] Ingstad also tested the fish resources at the head of the Eiriksfjord, and soon found his boat surrounded by a shoal of large cod.[425] Cod and salmon were important for the Inuit in Einarsfjord.[426]

In good fishing-fjords Norse peasants could stay at their home farm, row out in the morning, spend the day fishing cod and other types of cod fish in the fjord, and return in the evening.[427] Peasants in poor fishing-fjords could sail to a neighbouring fjord with good fishing grounds and stay there for a limited period with local peasants. Such arrangements were well known along the Norwegian coast and are so evidently convenient that it should be assumed that they were practised in Norse Greenland. Peasants from Vatnahverfi, Hvalseyfjord and the rest of the Eastern Settlement could participate in cod fisheries in Eiriksfjord, Einarsfjord and the Agdluitsup fjord if they had the equipment for it. The Western Settlement's best cod fisheries were normally in the Kapisillit fjord, but when sea temperatures were favourable there would also be cod in Lysufjord/Ameralik. The church farms W51 Sandnes and W7 Anavik were in rowing or walking distance of good fisheries in the Nup or Kapisillit fjords. Two church farms in the Eastern Settlement, Herjolvsnes (E111) and Vágar (E149), both lie a short distance from the coast. The most densely populated fjords and all main farms had access to the important seasonal cod fisheries.

Natural scientists assume that summer sea temperatures in the Greenland fjords and the banks in the Davis Strait were relatively high when the Norse arrived in AD 985. Cod fisheries which took place in April to June,[428] must have been good ca. 985–1250.[429] In the following centuries there was a gradual fall in air temperatures, but did this influence sea temperatures so seriously that the cod population declined?

The Norwegian missionary Hans Egede visited the Ameralik fjord in April 1723 followed by a local Inuit and he interviewed the Inuit living in the fjord. At that time air temperatures were even lower than at the end of the Norse period, but capelin still arrived in May and with it bank cod which fed on it. This fish stayed there all summer until autumn. The fishing was best in the neighbouring Kapisillit fjord, which was an "open" fjord, and "many Inuit stayed there to fish cod, salmon and capelin and shoot seal and reindeer". A stationary, local stock of "small cod" spawned in the Kapisillit fjord, and could be fished even in winter.[430] The fall in temperatures ca. 1250–1720 was not so serious that the annual migrations of capelin and bank cod to the cold threshold fjord Ameralik ceased, and fishing for cod in the warm "open" Kapisillit fjord was still good. The shoals of cod may have become smaller, but that is impossible to verify.

In the Western Settlement the Kapisillit fjord was a far better fjord for fishing than the Ameralik/Ameragdla, which was a "threshold fjord". Both fjords had many farms. The main factor which attracted Norse settlers was favourable conditions for agriculture; fishing was of marginal importance.

In addition to cod there is evidence of halibut fishing. There are two species of this fish. "Greenland halibut"[431] is today one of the commercially most important fish species in Greenland.[432] It is normally found at 200–1500 m,[433] which was too deep for Norse handlines of hemp, but it happens that Greenland halibut swims nearer the surface.

Along the south Greenland coast there is another species in the halibut family, which in English is just called "halibut".[434] It lives in shallower waters of 100–1500 m at banks in the Davis Strait and in the outer part of the west Greenland fjords.[435] At this depth Norse handlines could have reached it. The Norse rarely visited the outer coast, and in Table 5.9 halibut bones appear in modest quantities at three of the seven sites.

At this time the Norse fished halibut exclusively with handlines, but since the halibut is heavier, the hook had to be large and the line stronger.[436] In 1741 the Inuit fished halibut with handlines cut from sealskin and of hemp which they bought from merchants.[437] Norse Greenland fishermen may have used the same equipment. Halibut meat was cut into strips, and drying it was unproblematic in cold and dry weather. In Norway it was considered a delicacy.

Eelpout are common in the fjords of south-west Greenland, where they are found at great depths. Together with the bones of halibut, this suggests that some Norsemen fished at the maximum depths permitted by their fishing lines.[438]

Redfish[439] was seen as good for eating in Norse tradition. It lives at depths of 100–500 m in the Davis Strait and in the fjords where they can be fished with handlines.[440] Egede sent some of his servants from Nuuk to fish redfish in the fjords on 7 February 1724 where they could be caught even in winter. They probably needed fresh food.[441] There is no written or archaeological evidence that the Norse fished for them, but they must at least have caught some by accident when they fished for cod.

Herring is particularly sensitive to changes in sea temperatures, and southern Greenland is at the border of where it is possible for herring to live, which made its appearance irregular. The herring in Greenland and Iceland belong to the same stock, and spawns on the south-west Greenland coast in periods with high sea temperatures.[442] It withdraws to Iceland when ocean temperatures fall. Archaeologists have not excavated herring bones, but bones of fat fish have a low survival rate in moist soil.[443] Hans Egede's 15-year stay in Greenland during 1721–1736 coincided with the "Little Ice Age" and he only saw "a few individuals" of herring.[444] The first firm evidence of herring shoals on the Greenland coast is from ca. 1780 at a time of rising temperatures in the whole North Atlantic region. They may have been there even earlier, but it is also possible that they now extended their feeding and spawning to Greenland for the first time. Later, small quantities existed in Greenlandic waters, and some even spawned there.

Even if herring were in Greenland waters in the Norse period, it is not certain that the Norsemen fished for them. Herring is caught with herring-nets or seine-nets which were specifically made for the purpose. If the herring shoals were irregular and the catches small, it is improbable that the Norsemen would care to bind such nets. The knowledge available at present makes it safest to assume that the Norse did not fish for herring.[445]

In Greenland as well as Norway the small sculpin is abundant along the shores in shallow waters.[446] Hans Egede with his Norwegian background remarks that the Inuit have sculpin "as their most important daily fish". The Danish biologist Muus confirms that sculpin "always has played a role in Greenland" because it is so easily available.[447] The Greenland Inuit, as far back as the source material goes, dried it and used it as winter provisions for humans.[448] In Norway many fish species were not eaten because the peasants felt other species tasted better. Sculpin was never eaten by humans; if caught by accident they could be given to cats. Capelin (*ammassæt*) arrived on the northern coast of Norway in large quantities each spring, but was not seen as food for humans. It was only used as fertiliser for cornfields and meadows in Norway, and also as bait in the cod fisheries or fodder for domestic animals. There is no evidence that capelin was food for the Norse Greenlanders either.

The Norse had better equipment for sea fishing and made better catches. They could therefore be choosy about their fish consumption.

Char and other fish in lakes and rivers

Two freshwater fish are represented in Table 5.9 of excavated fishbones: Arctic char and salmon. Char was found at five of the seven sites, salmon at one. Some 85 bones of char have been found but only one of salmon. Table 5.9 indicates that char was by far the most common freshwater fish for the Norse. Salmon was caught and eaten but was of limited importance, and other freshwater fish were not used. Does this picture correspond to what is known about fish resources in Greenland?

Arctic char is found in most lakes and rivers in both settlements. The first four to six years of its existence is spent in freshwater. When it has attained a certain length, it swims with older fish along the river down to the fjord. Many char assemble in May-June at the river estuary. At this time large quantities of capelin arrive in the fjords, and they are the char's main food for a couple of months while they stay in the fjord. Char normally keep to within ca. 20 km of the estuary of their "river of birth" and do not visit the outer coast. In the inner fjords they were close to where most Norsemen lived. When the capelin disappear in late summer, the char return to the estuary of their river, and large numbers of them again assemble there. This happens from mid-August to September. They then swim upstream, but unlike the salmon they are not able to swim and jump through high waterfalls. When they meet such a waterfall, they will stop and remain below it in the river all winter and spawn there. In some rivers it is possible for them to reach a lake where they stay for the winter. Some char do not take this annual trip to the fjord to feed, but stay all year in their river or lake of birth. No char stay in the fjord throughout the winter.[449] Char must have been rather easy to catch for the Norse both when they assembled at the river estuaries in spring and autumn, and when they swam along the rivers. It must have been most attractive in autumn when it was well fed.

Ivar Bárdarson describes ecological crises which sometimes happened at the head of the Amitsuarsuk fjord near E91. His story is far from clear, but seems to describe char which in the autumn followed a river from the fjord up to a small lake close to the farm E91 and assembled there.[450] The char, in Ivar's text called "large fish", would most likely have remained in the lake all winter because further upstream there was a steep waterfall ca. 60 m long which the char would have had great problems navigating.[451] There were a large number of char in the lake in autumn. If there was then heavy rain, much water flowed down the river from Vatnahverfi and the water level in the lake rose. When the water level later subsided to normal levels, "innumerable fish" could lie stranded on dry land on the sand along the shores.[452]

More than 99% of the salmon which feed along the coasts of Greenland spawn in Europe and North America, and do not enter the Greenland fjords. They were not available to the Norse Greenlanders who lived and fished in the fjords. But in the southern part of the Eastern Settlement in the Nanortalik region, many farms were close to the Davis Strait and the salmon which fed there. Here it must have been possible for the Norse to fish for salmon, but so far evidence is lacking to support this.[453]

Salmon spawn in a single river in Greenland, the Kapisillit. The fry stay there for the first four to six years of their life, then swim out through river and fjords to the ocean where they stay for one to three years. When they are mature for spawning, they return to the Kapisillit river. After spawning there, the survivors return to the ocean.[454]

Excavated fishbones and biological knowledge of fish species in Greenland both make it likely that char was the main fresh water fish consumed by the Norse Greenlanders, and salmon was of secondary importance.

The main equipment in the freshwater fisheries was handlines. Nets were probably used but this is difficult to verify. Perforated pieces of soapstone have been excavated at almost every Norse site, but it is in most cases not possible to distinguish between net-sinkers and loom-weights. They were both made to keep threads in a straight, vertical position. Nipaatsoq (W54) is an inland farm and a floater of wood was found there which was probably made for a fishnet.[455] Char appeared every year and were predictable, which may have motivated many Norse to acquire nets which were used in the fjords.

Lakes in the settlements were mostly small, but there were exceptions. Ivar Bárdarson points out that Lake Tasersuaq in Ketilsfjord is ca. 15–20 km long and "full of fish".[456] A lake rich in fish was a valuable resource worth remembering even if the church did not own it. If local farmers had a boat in the lake, seine-nets could be lowered into the lake at some distance from the shore, and then drawn ashore. Ordinary nets could be stretched out from the shore, set in shallow waters further out, or made to float near the surface in deeper waters. Where the fishermen lacked a boat, nets could be stretched across estuaries or bays.

In rivers the cheapest fishing gear was the fishing rod. They could also walk along the river banks looking for a large char or salmon and stick it with a fishing-spear.[457] Nets could be used if the river was slow and broad. Permanent fish traps made of stone and wood were also known.

For char the most rewarding fishing period was when shoals of them assembled at the river estuaries on their way to feed in the fjords in May-June, and particularly when they returned there fatter and heavier in mid August-September.[458] The Kapisillit salmon was accessible when it assembled at the river estuary, and when it swam up the Kapisillit river to spawn.

Kapisillit was in an area with many Norse farms. Char, cod and salmon were all fished in the fjords close to the farms, which means that fishing could take place in between other tasks. But it must have been a problem that so much agricultural work, hunting and fishing were concentrated in the summer months. Along the Norwegian coast the most important fisheries were for spawning cod and herring, and both took place in January-March when no outdoor agricultural work was possible. Food production was more stretched out over the whole year.

Fish decays more rapidly than most foods. In Greenland salt was not available, and smoking required firewood which was scarce, so drying without salt was the main method for preserving fish. The reliable *Groenlendinga tháttr* tells that a Norse peasant in Einarsfjord had stored "much dried cod" (*skreið mikla*).[459] In Norway the cod was hung drying on a scaffolding of wood. In treeless Finnmark it was sometimes laid on rocks to dry. In Iceland this method was used more extensively and so it was by the Inuit who until recently dried capelin on rocks.[460]

Dried fish and meat often needed to be stored, sometimes for years as reserve food in case of crop failures or poor fishing and hunting. Most Greenland farms seem to have had small store houses where the stone walls had not been made tight with soil or clay, which made it possible for the wind to blow through it. Dried fish, meat, butter and other foodstuffs must have been kept in some of these houses. Sheds for this purpose are known in coastal Norway, but there are made of wood.

The Norse Greenlanders also invented a method for preserving food which was unknown in Norway. They dug a storeroom in the soil close to their farmhouses, probably into the permafrost. It then functioned as a freezer. The dried cod mentioned above was stored in such a subterranean freezer, with meat and butter. If cod and meat were first dried and then kept in a freezer, it must have been edible for many years. Effective long-time storage protected against hunger in lean years, and it was an insurance against starvation.

How important was fish for the Norse Greenlanders?

The written sources describe peasants fishing for cod in the Eastern Settlement fjords. They used *sexærings* which were well adapted to fishing of this type.[461] The archaeological sources are more problematic. Few examples of fishing gear have been excavated. Sinkers tend to be used until they are lost at sea. Lines and nets made of hemp or other material will rot. Iron hooks have rusted or were later removed by Inuit scavengers. Boathouses have been submerged by the sea. Archaeologists have given credible reasons for why so few fish bones have survived: they rot easily, sieving is needed to find them and until recently this was rarely done.

Was fishing important? The immigrants from Norway had a long tradition behind them in cod fishing reaching back several centuries, and in their Norwegian homeland fish in coastal districts normally provided ca. 25% of the peasants' calorie needs.[462] In Greenland food resources from agriculture, hunting and fishing were unstable, therefore it was important to combine food from many sources. Cod which was first dried without salt and then stored in a "freezer", could be kept as reserve food for years.

The Norse immigrants brought with them technologies which made it possible to exploit fish resources in the Greenland fjords. By far the most important in sea fisheries was the handline. In lakes and rivers nets, seine-nets, fish-spears and permanent fish traps were probably used. Against the background of the better-known situation in later centuries, there can be little doubt that substantial quantities of cod and char existed and could be caught using these types of fishing tackle.

The environment made conditions for fishing less favourable in Greenland than in Norway. The sea was colder, which meant that cod in particular normally stayed in deeper waters, and Norse handlines could not fish deeper than 100–140 m. Much of the seafood which is caught today by the Greenlandic fishing fleet would have been unavailable to the Norse with their fishing gear. In the last part of Norse Greenland's existence, iron for fish hooks may have been difficult to get hold of.

The best verified hypothesis is that fjord fishing for cod and other sea fish, and fishing for char which was caught in both sea and freshwater, was important to the Norse Greenlanders. Regrettably the empirical material makes it impossible to say how important.

Edible plants

Were plants which had been harvested or gathered in Greenland part of the Norse diet? The well-informed author of *The King's Mirror* wrote:

> You asked whether cereals are sown there or not, but I think the country is little improved by that. But there are some men, mostly those who are called the most respected and richest, who make an effort, just to have tried. But most people in that country do not know what bread[463] is, and have never seen bread.[464]

The text is not clear, but the best interpretation is that the seed mostly did not ripen, but it must have succeeded in some years, otherwise the rich and respected would not have tried growing it. The author can also be interpreted as saying that it never ripened.

Hans Egede gives similar information in his diary. On 18 May 1724 he sowed grain, probably barley, in the Ameralik (*Amaralich*) fjord.

> I journeyed into the Ameralik fjord to sow some grain in the soil close to one of the farms where the Norwegians (*de gamle norske*) had formerly lived, as an experiment, to see how the seed would develop . . . I arranged for the old, withered grass to be burnt, and then I sowed a little grain and turnip . . . I firmly believe that it will sprout and grow.[465]

He returned on 13 September, but the plants were "green and the grains small. One understands that grain in this country hardly will ripen, because the frosty nights start too early".[466] Like most parsons from northern Norway in the 18th century Egede was highly competent in agriculture, and his judgement should be trusted. But it should be borne in mind that in 1724 the chance to succeed was poorer than in the 13th century because the temperatures were probably lower.

Inuit sheep farmers planted barley, oats and rye in the middle of the 20th century, but it rarely grew ripe, and unripe grain was used as fodder.[467] Experiments conducted in 1997 by a local agricultural consultant in Greenland showed that it is possible for Norwegian and Icelandic grain to ripen in the inner, warmest regions of the Eastern Settlement.[468] Was this also the case before the medieval cooling period started ca. 1250? Then temperatures would have been at approximately the same level as those of today.

Pollen from oats was found in the turf wall of Brattahlid's first church from ca. AD 1000, the so-called Tjodhild's church.[469] The Scottish scholar Kevin Edwards examined pollen at the E2 site and found "Hordeum-type pollen"[470] there. It has also been found at eight other Norse sites. The problem is that the botanists cannot determine whether such pollen derives from barley or from lyme grass which grows wild and existed in Greenland before the Norse. Pollen analyses cannot be used to verify the cultivation of barley or oats in Norse Greenland.[471]

Grains are better suited for this purpose than pollen. Grains of barley were found in a midden at E47 Gardar, at the nearby farm of E49 and at E3 which is in the Qorlortup valley.[472] But it is an open question as to whether these grains had been cultivated in Greenland or imported from Norway.[473] "Two rachis of barley" were found at E35, also in the Qorlortup valley. "Rachis" are the leaves which surround the grain at the top of the straw, but which are removed during threshing. Cereals were threshed before longer transports, and unthreshed barley was "a very strong indication that there was local cultivation of cereals" in Greenland.[474] But an alternative hypothesis is that the threshing in Norway had not been done properly and did not remove the "rachis" from all grains.

Millstones turned by hand have been seen as indirect archaeological evidence for bread-making from imported grain. One millstone has been found at each of the farms Brattahlid,[475] E66 South Igaliku and Hvalsey,[476] and at least four at Gardar.[477] GUS was first settled ca. AD 1000, and in the second oldest archaeological level a millstone was found.[478] Helge Ingstad points out that millstones (quernstones) turned by hand in Norway were also used to mill different kinds of wild plants, mosses, roots and fishbones which were used in bread or porridge. Not all quernstones were meant for imported grain.[479] Discs made of soapstone for frying crisp bread have been found at several of the same sites.

The King's Mirror claims that only the richest and most honorable of the Norse farmers sowed cereals or could afford to buy imports. Archaeological sources have confirmed this. Grains and rachis of barley have so far been excavated at E47 Gardar and at the neighbouring farm E49, which probably belonged to Gardar, and at E3 and E35 in the Qorlortup valley, both within walking distance of Brattahlid.[480] The written sources can tell that imported cereals in Greenland were used to brew beer and make bread.[481] In Norway they were also used for porridge, but in Greenland they were probably too expensive for that.

Wild, edible plants were gathered and eaten:

Pollen from *Angelica* was found in the midden at W48 Niaquusat. It was the palatable type *Angelica archangelica* or *Norvegica* which grew there. It was widely eaten in pre-modern Norway and was until recently eaten by the Inuit in Greenland. The *Angelica* on Iceland was of a different type, *Angelica Litoralis*, which is less palatable. *Angelica* had evidently been imported to Greenland from Norway and not from Iceland.[482] It was eaten in the Norse area as a vegetable.

Linen cloth was made from flax (*Linum*), but seeds of flax were also eaten and are rich in energy. For ground flax seeds, 100 g contains 42 g of fat, 29 g of carbohydrate and 18 g of protein, which gives 534 kcal.[483] By comparison 100 g of sheep or cattle meat gave 155 kcal. Since both seeds and pollen have been found in middens, it is "most probable" that the flax was grown in Greenland.[484] It may have been cultivated as a garden plant, to be used as food for humans or animals, or/and for making linen cloth.[485]

The edible plant which grows most widely in Greenland is lyme-grass.[486] It grows on sandy soil along the coast of western Norway and in Greenland.[487] In 1918 Daniel Bruun described the rich vegetation of lyme-grass which grew around the Norse ruins along the Ameralik fjord in the Western Settlement.[488] Norse peasants may have cultivated it.[489] In recent centuries lyme-grass has been used as "poor men's cereal" in Iceland.[490] The caloric yield of lyme-grass was measured at the Department of Nutritional Science, King's College, London, and proved to be 419 kcal per 100 g.[491] Barley flour produced in Norway gave 350 kcal per 100 g,[492] but it seems that lyme-grass seeds need more work to produce per weight unit.[493] Lyme-grass ground to flour was normally mixed with milk and consumed as porridge or soup. It could also be made into a dough and consumed as cake.[494]

Cochlearia or "scurvy grass" was traditionally eaten along the coast of northern Norway[495] and by Greenland Inuit as a remedy against scurvy. In his diary from 1728 Hans Egede wrote that in February-March many members of the Danish colony at Nuuk used to become sick with scurvy, but they were cured by eating cochlearia (*Cochleare-Græs*) which they found under the snow.[496]

Among the berries which the humans at Sandnes (W51) and Niaquusat (W48) digested were crowberries[497] and mountain cranberries.[498] The seeds were found in human faeces at the middens of these farms.

Knotgrass[499] was also found in the middens at Sandnes (W51) and Niaquusat (W48), the variety *polygonum cognatum* is today regularly eaten in central parts of Turkey.[500]

Seaweed is abundant along the North Atlantic coasts, and some species are edible for humans and domestic animals. In his "Description of Norway" the bishop of Bergen wrote ca. 1750 that seaweed in Iceland was dried, milled to flour, mixed into porridge and eaten by humans. In northern Norway seaweed was winter fodder for animals, and in western Norway it was used as fertiliser in the cornfield.[501] The bishop's information on the use of seaweed along the Norwegian coast is confirmed by other sources from pre-modern Norway.[502] There is no positive evidence that seaweed was eaten by humans in Norse Greenland. If they followed Norwegian practice there is no reason to think that they did, but if they followed the practice in Iceland they may have done so.[503] Greenland and Iceland both needed replacements for the missing grain harvest.

The peasants used their most fertile grassland to produce winter fodder for their animals but seem to have used soil which was not suitable for that purpose near their farm to plant lyme-grass and flax. Other edible plants were collected in the outfield. Danish and American scientists have chosen to disregard plant food in the Norse Greenlanders' diet.[504] This creates an unknown but probably small source of error.

Peasants and hunters

The Norse Greenlanders were primarily peasants. My estimates of an average Norse peasant household's food consumption measured in calories was that in the Eastern Settlement ca. 57% came from cow milk, ca. 6% from goat milk, ca. 3% from cattle meat, ca. 1% from sheep and goat meat. In total some 67% of a household's calorie needs came from domestic animals. In the Western Settlement ca. 33% came from cow milk, ca. 6% from goat milk, ca. 2% from cattle meat, ca. 1% from sheep and goat meat. In all 42% of a person's and household's calorie needs came from domestic animals.[505]

Is it realistic to think that hunting, fishing and collecting edible plants could produce the rest of the food? In the Western Settlement ca. 7% may have come from reindeer meat. The main non-quantifiable food sources were seal, cod and char, and qualitative sources verify that all three were important. Hunters may have brought back walrus meat from their *nordseta* to the Western Settlement. Whale, salmon and wild plants were of minor importance.

In the Eastern Settlement ca. 2% of the diet may have come from reindeer, and the non-quantifiable food sources were the same as for the Western Settlement.[506] It cannot have been insurmountable to provide it.

302 *Subsistence food production*

All these activities were limited to particular seasons and none of them needed to coincide with the important harvesting of winter fodder. Seal hunts took place in the spring before, and reindeer hunts in the autumn after, the harvesting work. Cod and char could be fished both before and after the harvest, char preferably after when it was well fed. Whale hunts took place whenever suitable whales appeared, but in the fjords this may have been a rare event. In the Western Settlement hunting and fishing for seal, reindeer, cod, char and salmon took place close to the farms and some of it could therefore be fitted in between other activities in the busy summer months. In the Eastern Settlement the fjord peasants had to travel longer distances for the reindeer and seal hunts, which in practice must have meant that it had to be limited to the seasons before and after the harvest.

5 Did the quality of the diet decline?

It is today generally accepted that Greenland grew colder from ca. 1250 to the end of the Norse settlement's existence. But the analyses in the present chapter have not verified that this cooling was so serious that it created problems for the Norse Greenlanders' subsistence food production. Falling temperatures and a shorter growth season will first and foremost create problems for grain harvests, and animal husbandry will be less affected. The sea level rose and reduced meadows and pastures, but this was a limited quantitative reduction which could be compensated by establishing *sæters* and extending the farms' meadows. There is no evidence that hunting and fishing were reduced because of falling temperatures. The analyses in the first four sections of this chapter have not confirmed that man-made or natural environmental problems reduced the Norse Greenlanders' food supply.

But "ecologist" scholars have not only claimed that each household found it increasingly hard to satisfy their need for food, but that the quality of their diet also deteriorated. The general trend was a transition from "terrestrial" to "marine" food. Norsemen ate less meat from cattle and replaced it with mutton and goat meat, but above all with unattractive seal meat and other food from the sea. This development struck social groups differently. Large farms consumed as much cattle meat as before. Small households ate less cattle meat, sheep and goat meat was more stable, and seal was increasingly important. None of the "ecologist" scholars have discussed the role of milk products in this development, probably because they have not realised how important they were. The "ecologist" scholars' claims have to be examined critically, and new methods have made this possible.

From terrestrial to marine food in the diet

"Marine food" is in our context fish,[507] seal, walrus and whales. Isotope analyses examine excavated skeletons and bones, measuring how many percent of the person's or animal's protein consumption had come from marine food.

In 1998 Niels Lynnerup published his PhD in medicine, and one chapter was co-authored with the Danish physicists Jan Heinemeier and Niels Rud. Here isotopes were used in a study of Norse Greenlanders for the first time.[508] Since then the three have published numerous articles on the Norsemen and the isotopes in their bones.

Isotopes are atoms which have the same number of electrons and protons, but where the number of neutrons can vary. The most interesting type of atom in our context is the carbon atom which always has a nucleus of six protons, but neutrons vary from six to eight. This gives the carbon atoms nuclei which consist of 12, 13 or 14 particles. They are all carbon atoms, but are specified as 12C, 13C and 14C isotopes. Such carbon atoms exist in bones from humans and animals even after they are dead. The proportion of different types of carbon isotopes in the bones of buried Norsemen makes it possible to analyse the proteins in their diet. Heinemeier and Lynnerup explain:

> The method exploits the fact that organisms absorb carbon differently in the sea and on dry land. The proportion between the stable carbon isotopes 12C and 13C in plants and animals depend[s] on whether they are part of the marine or a terrestrial food chain. The proportion between the two carbon isotopes in dead people's bones can be measured, and this can be used to estimate the proportion between protein from the sea and protein produced on land in the dead person's diet.[509]

A key element in the quantification of marine and terrestrial protein in the diet is what Heinemeier and his colleagues call "endpoint values".[510] The quantity of 13C isotopes in bone is measured in units of one thousandth or "per-mil". Heinemeier and Lynnerup estimated that the bones of a person who had lived only on marine food would contain −12.5 per-mil of 13C isotopes, a person who had "mainly eaten terrestrial food" would have −21 per-mil.[511] In 2000 the archaeologist James Barrett adopted as his "working estimate" for Northern Europe "endpoints for marine and terrestrial diets of −12 per-mil and −20.6 per-mil respectively".[512] The Norwegian archaeologist Elise Naumann wrote a PhD on how isotopes can be used on objects in Norwegian archaeology dating to AD 400–1050, and she says that "In Northern Europe it is often assumed that 13C ratios range from approximately −22 per-mil for a purely land based nutrition to −12 per-mil for an exclusively marine diet".[513] From 1998 to 2014 archaeologists have extended the "endpoint values" at both ends.

The woman with the most marine isotope value among the analysed Norse had a 13C value of −14.1 per-mil.[514] With Heinemeier's endpoints −12.5 and −21 per-mil, she would have had 81% marine proteins in her diet, with Naumann's endpoints −12 per-mil and −22 per-mil she would have had 79% marine proteins. The difference is not great. As of today, the Danish scientists are confident that their endpoints are valid for Norse Greenland.[515]

Endpoint values are fixed by analysing 13C isotope values in the bones of Eskimos who are assumed to have lived almost exclusively on marine food, or pre-modern farmers in Norwegian inland valleys who are assumed to have lived almost exclusively on terrestrial food.[516] But it is possible that those individuals had a more mixed intake of proteins than the European scholars imagined.[517] All

304 *Subsistence food production*

Eskimos must have consumed some meat from land animals like reindeer, and edible plants. All inland districts had lakes and rivers with fish. In the future new information may be obtained about individuals or groups who had even more purely maritime or terrestrial protein intakes than those known so far.

A human bone which had a 13C value identical to the terrestrial endpoint is assumed to belong to a person who had lived 100% on terrestrial proteins and a person with a value at the other endpoint is assumed to have lived on 100% marine proteins. The next step is to assume that there was "a strict linear relationship" between increasing figures for per-mil of 13C isotopes and increasing percentages of marine proteins in the dead person's diet. This makes it possible to calculate from per-mil of 13C isotopes to the rate or percentage of marine and terrestrial proteins in the diet of the dead Norseman.[518] According to James Barrett, it has been demonstrated that this relationship "is not strictly linear". He does not explain how serious this source of error is.[519]

Another source of error is that reindeer in the Norse region consumed lichen which pushed the 13C isotope value in reindeer bones nearer to the marine endpoint.[520] Norse Greenlanders who consumed much reindeer meat would as a consequence have their 13C isotope values shifted towards the marine endpoint.[521] They did not consume as much marine protein as the measurements indicate.[522]

Uncertain endpoints, uncertainty about linearity between the endpoints and reindeer bones with 13C isotope values closer to the marine endpoint because of lichen, give the percentages sources of error.[523] Naumann in her article and PhD thesis from 2014 does not translate "per-mil" of 13C isotopes into percentages of marine proteins in the dead person's diet. She limits herself to verifying that one individual or social group consumed more marine proteins than another. "To address these issues, focus will be on the relative amount of marine versus terrestrial protein food sources, and avoiding exact estimates of exact amounts [that is percentages] of the different subsistence sources".[524] I find percentages of proteins consumed a useful pedagogical tool, and have chosen to follow James Barrett and Jan Heinemeier who use them.[525] The resulting source of error has to be taken into account.

What evidence can isotopes provide about the importance of marine food in the Norsemen's diet? In an article from 2008 Arneborg, Heinemeier and Lynnerup analysed the isotopes of 57 dated bones from humans. They covered all chronological stages in the period AD 985–1410. Two were excluded because the excavation circumstances were special and the measured values atypical. This left them with 55 dated 13C values.[526]

From the period before 1250 there were 19 bones, all of them with 13C isotope values between -16,5 and −20 per-mil. On the background of the methodological discussion presented above I find it most realistic to use the endpoint values −12 and −22. This means that the 19 persons had received between 20% and 55% of their protein by eating food from the sea. The average was −18 per-mil indicating that 40% of the protein came from the sea.[527]

From the final period ca. 1250–1410 36 bone fragments were analysed and all of them had 13C isotope values between −14 per-mil and −17.5 per-mil. This means that the 36 persons had received between 45% and 80% of their proteins by eating food from the sea. The average was −16.2, indicating that 58% of the proteins came from the sea. If these figures are taken to express a chronological development between the two periods, there was an important increase in the average consumption of marine protein from ca. 40% to ca. 58%, the great change coming ca. 1250–1300.

But the difference between the two periods may partly express differences in geographic position of and social status in the churchyards from where the bones were excavated. In the first period the following churchyards are represented with the following number of analysed skeletons:

- 9×   E29 Brattahlid church farm
- 4×   E35 church farm close to Brattahlid
- 1×   E47 Gardar episcopal see
- 2×   E48 church farm close to Gardar
- 2×   W51 Sandnes church farm
- 1×   W7 Anavik church farm

Brattahlid and Gardar were the two largest farms in Norse Greenland, located at the head of the warmest fjords in the Eastern Settlement, Eiriksfjord and Einarsfjord, where the conditions for animal husbandry were exceptionally good by Greenlandic standards. The temperatures and the quality of the soil were more favourable than elsewhere. E35 and E48 were situated close to these farms. Sandnes belonged to the Brattahlid clan and had the richest resources for animal husbandry in the Western Settlement. Households living at these farms had access to milk and meat from domestic animals in quantities above the Greenland average.

Moreover, in the earliest period churches and churchyards were privately owned by chieftains. They probably only permitted members of their own clan to be buried there, and it is not clear if this opportunity was given only to the most prominent members or if they also admitted poor peasants belonging to the clan. The alternative for low status people was to be buried close to their home farm and have the grave blessed later by a visiting priest. This is likely to have been practised to some extent until the Greenland diocese was established in 1126, some places even longer.[528] The churchyards at E35 and E48 may have belonged to members of the Brattahlid and Gardar clans. The bones analysed from the first period may have belonged to people who had lived on larger farms with more fertile soil than the average Norse Greenlander.

The 36 bones from the final period (1250–1410) were excavated at the following churchyards:

- 9×   W51 Sandnes church farm
- 8×   E111 Herjolvsnes church farm

8× E149 Vágar church farm

3× W7 Anavik church farm

3× E23 Undir Solarfjöllum, church farm

2× E66 church farm

2× E1 church farm

1× E47 Gardar episcopal see

All churchyards now belonged to parish churches where rich and poor from the whole parish were buried. It is not known when these churches ceased to be private and came into the possession of the bishop's organisation, but it must have happened in the 13th century and probably was a reality at the end of that century.[529] Those buried at a parish churchyard were from that time representative of the parish population as a whole. Only Gardar churchyard represented by one burial in this late period was situated at the head of the two warm and fertile fjords mentioned above. In the first period 16 of the 19 burials were from churchyards in this area.

The reason for the difference between the two chronological groups in the consumption of marine proteins is most likely to have been social. In coastal Norway lower class people also consumed more marine food than the elite, and undoubtedly did so even in Norse Greenland. Socially differentiated diets are known from most pre-modern societies. But this does not exclude that there may also have been a chronological development from the early to the late period.

Quantifications based on 13C isotopes give percentages of marine and terrestrial *proteins*. To compare them one has to measure in the same unit. Is it possible to convert percentages of proteins into percentages of *calories*, and how relevant and reliable would such conversions be? Archaeologists have not provided methodological discussions of the relationship between percentages of marine protein and percentages of marine calories. This can be a problem for readers. Authors name and enumerate animals which they correctly say were eaten, and then give percentages of terrestrial and marine proteins in the diet.[530] In such contexts the reader should be told explicitly that percentages in proteins are different from percentages in calories.

The 13C isotopes were first used to analyse the Greenland diet in 1998 and 1999.[531] Arneborg, Heinemeier and Lynnerup in 1999 assumed without discussion that percentages of marine proteins were the same as percentages of energy measured in calories. The 13C isotope values "reveal" that the "average diet of the Norse people" "changed from 20% marine to 80% marine during the approximately 500 years that the settlement lasted". In 2012 the same authors repeat that "between 20% and 30% of the diet of the early 11th century settlers was marine in origin", but "in the late settlement period in the first half of the 15th century up to about 80% of the food of some Norse Greenlanders was of marine origin".[532]

Table 5.10 Nutritional value of foods which were important in Norse Greenland, per 100 g edible goods

	Protein	Fat	Carbohydrate	Energy	Kcal/protein
Fresh milk	3.2 g	4.9 g	3.7 g	65 kcal	20x
Fresh meat cattle	21.1 g	7.7 g	0	155 kcal	7x
Fresh meat sheep	18.5 g	9.0 g	0	155 kcal	8x
Meat of reindeer	20.4 g	4.5 g	0	120 kcal	6x
Fresh cod	17.1 g	0.3 g	0	70 kcal	4x
Ore/arctic char	21.6 g	3.0 g	0	110 kcal	5x
Meat of seal	26.0 g	6.7 g	0	165 kcal	6x

Source: Schulerud 1945.

The energy value of milk was lower before the improvement of the breed of cattle started in the 19th century, Norwegian historians estimate it to have been ca. 65 kcal per 100 g (Nedkvitne 1988, p. 189).

The values for fresh meat of cattle and sheep are said to be from "middle fat" animals.

The last column is energy measured in kcal as registered in the fourth column divided by protein measured in grams as registered in the first column.

They do not define what they mean by percentages of "food" and "diet", but it must be assumed that it is percentages of the daily energy need. Can percentages of proteins be used as if they were percentages of energy measured in calories?

The human body receives energy by eating food which contains proteins, fat and carbohydrates. The proportion between the three sources of energy varies in different types of food. Figures for nutritional values of foods produced in Norway were published in tables in 1945 in a book called "Norwegian Nutrients" (Table 5.10).[533]

A measure of 100 g of fresh milk contains 3.2 g protein, 4.9 g fat and 3.7 g carbohydrates, and consumed in the human body it will give 65 kcal.[534] This means that the protein value measured in grams has to be multiplied by 20 to arrive at the energy measured in kcal. For "Meat of seal" protein measured in grams has to be multiplied by only six to arrive at the energy measured in kcal. If one person drinks milk giving a certain weight of protein, and another person eats seal meat giving the same weight of protein, the person drinking milk will get three times as much energy measured in calories.

The additional energy is due to relatively more fat and carbohydrates in terrestrial food. The translation from protein to energy therefore has to be made separately for each food species. Since each person has his or her individual diet, the percentage of marine proteins also has to be multiplied by a different figure for each person/skeleton analysed to arrive at the percentage of kcal from marine food. The empirical material to do this does not exist.

But the evidence in Table 5.10 makes clear that the percentage of marine energy in kcal which a Norse Greenlander received through his or her food in a certain period, was significantly lower than the percentage of marine protein which he or she received as part of his or her total protein consumption in grams. The Danish scholars mentioned earlier are mistaken when they assume that the percentage of marine energy consumed is identical to the percentage of marine protein consumed.

Danish scholars have claimed that "in the late settlement period in the first half of the 15th century AD up to about 80% of the food of some Norse Greenlanders was of marine origin".[535] This percentage is the result of the analysis of 13C isotopes in the bones of two women. A 20- to 25-year-old woman was buried at Herjolvsnes at the end of the farm's existence, which was shortly after 1410. Her bones had 13C values which indicate that she had consumed 78% marine proteins. The authors assume that the percentage reflects her diet in the last ten years before she died.[536] A woman of the same age was buried at Sandnes at the end of that farm's existence, which was before ca. 1360. Some 81% of her protein consumption had been marine.[537] These women undoubtedly had also consumed many milk products. If it had been possible to calculate the two women's energy consumption, the marine percentage of their consumption would have diminished towards 50%. They still may have been poor with a lot of marine food in their diet, but contemporaries did not necessarily consider their condition as unacceptable.

The average marine 13C protein value of 58% for Norse Greenland ca. 1250–1410 cannot be translated into an energy value for the reasons explained earlier. But a comparison between terrestrial food (milk, cattle meat, mutton and reindeer meat) and marine food (seal, cod and char) in Table 5.10 indicates that the percentage of marine calories must have crept well below 58%, perhaps half the percentage of marine proteins, in practice half of 58%.

This indicates that the consumption of marine calories in Norse Greenland may have approached the levels along the North Sea and Atlantic coast of Norway. In the 18th century the households of peasant-fishermen normally consumed fish at two meals on workdays. Part of the fish would be replaced by meat on Sundays, but even at wedding feasts fish was served, but then prepared differently.[538] It is not said how much fish was consumed at each meal, but ca. 200 g per person would be normal. The fish consumed along the Norwegian coast was mostly herring and saithe, which had a higher calorie value than cod, and would give ca. 700 kcal per person per day, or ca. 25% of a daily consumption of 2,600 kcal.[539] These percentages should not be taken literally. The main point is that correctly interpreted 13C isotopes cannot support a hypothesis of a dependence on marine food which Norsemen saw as unacceptable, resulting in malnutrition or an unwanted diet.

A comparison with Norse Orkney brings out the geographic flexibility of Norse food production in the North Atlantic (Table 5.11).

Orkney is rich in cornfields, and grain contains little protein but a lot of carbohydrates. The percentages of marine proteins in Table 5.11 should have been converted into percentages of energy, but this cannot be done for the reasons explained earlier. The percentage of marine calories must have been well below 33%; perhaps this figure should even be halved.

Was there a transition from terrestrial to marine food in the diet of the Norse Greenlanders after ca. 1250? The discussion in this section has not confirmed this

Table 5.11 Marine proteins in the human diet on Norse Greenland and Norse Orkney

	Greenland before 1250	Greenland after 1250	Norse Orkney
Average 13C isotope value in per-mil	−18.0	−16.2	−18.7
Marine protein in % of total protein in diet	40%	58%	33%
Number of bones analysed	19	36	15

Figures from Greenland: Chapter 5, pp. 304–305.

Figures from Orkney: Barrett and others 2000, p. 541. Human bones from the site at Newark Bay. Barrett analysed 20 bones. I have assumed that the 5 oldest were Pictish, the 15 youngest Norse.

Terrestrial endpoint value: −22.0; Marine endpoint value: −12.0.

hypothesis. If there was an increase in the consumption of marine energy, it did not reach crisis level and should not be seen as a symptom of a Norse Greenland in decline. Many Greenlanders may have received a quarter of their energy from marine sources, but this was on a level with the Atlantic and North Sea coast of Norway.

Was the Norsemen's "marine food" fish or seal?

The Scottish geoscientist Andrew Dugmore thinks that "the most striking Norse adaptation of all seems to have been the immediate switch in emphasis in Greenland from sea fishing to the large-scale harvesting of migrating seals".[540] Arneborg, Lynnerup and Heinemeier wrote the same year that the "marine food" of the Norse Greenlanders was "marine mammals", in practice seals.[541]

Isotopes of nitrogen, "15N isotopes", can in theory distinguish between fish and seal. Fish may eat seaweed, seal may eat fish, a polar bear may eat the seal and a human may eat the polar bear. For each step the 15N value in the bones of the consumer will increase by 3–5 per-mil.[542] Humans who eat a lot of meat from animals which are high up in the nutrition chain, will have bones with a high 15N isotope value. If a Norse Greenlander has a 13C value which gives evidence of a lot of marine food and a high 15N value, the marine food is likely to have been mainly seal.

There is, however, a serious source of error to this. If a meadow is fertilised with manure, the level of 15N in the soil and plants will increase.[543] The winter fodder for domestic animals was partly produced from meadows which had been manured.[544] This increased 15N was transferred to sheep, goats and cattle who ate the hay and further to humans who ate meat, butter, cheese or other milk products from these animals. Since the Norse Greenlanders had no cornfields, they are likely to have used all or most of their manure on the meadow. Manure may have been the main cause of the high 15N values. Scholars are reluctant to use 15N values to distinguish between fish and seal in the diet.[545]

An alternative method to compare seal and fish is to quantify seal bones as a percentage of all mammal bones in finds. 13C values in human bones which indicate a marine diet, combined with a high percentage of excavated seal bones at the same site, may be seen as evidence that the marine food was mainly seal.

The percentage of seal bones has been calculated at the following ten[546] farms:

- At the medium-sized Nipaatsoq (W54) there were 39% seal bones for the entire period.[547]
- Georg Nyegaard has analysed the farm E34 in the Qorlortup valley above Brattahlid. "Collectively, seals constitute the largest animal group in the assemblage, with a total of 6,056 fragments corresponding to 39 % of all the identified mammal bones, i.e. a slightly higher proportion than the sum of sheep and goat (36 %)".[548]
- At the two farms E71 and E167, 40% of all mammal bones were seal.[549]
- At E149, 61% of 610 mammal bones were seal.[550]
- At the small farm of Niaquusat (W48), 82% of bones were seal.[551]
- At the medium-sized GUS the percentage of seal bones increased: 28% (AD 1000–1150), 36% (1150–1300) and 41% (AD 1300–1400).[552]
- At the chieftain's farm of Sandnes (W51) the percentage of seal bones varied from 43% (AD 1025–1150) via 23% (AD 1150–1200) and 30% (AD 1200–1250) to 30% (AD 1250–1325).[553]
- At E17a seal constituted 50% of bone material in both upper and lower layers.[554]
- At Gardar (E47) seal constituted 70% of the bones in the first period around 1200 compared to 60% in the second period around 1300.[555]

The bone counts have resulted in high percentages of seal bones at all farms in both settlements in the whole Norse period. The median value for the individual farms varied between 30% and 82% and the median value for all nine is 40%.[556] These percentages of bones exaggerate the importance of seal in the diet. Many seals were hunted for their blubber to be made into lamp oil. Secondly, a seal produced food only in the form of meat, whereas other mammals included in the bone statistics like cow and goat produced far more calories by way of milk than as meat in their lifetime.[557]

Animal bone statistics have been cited to verify a hypothesis that "by 1300 seal meat probably played a critical role in Norse subsistence".[558] With an empirical basis in animal bones the Danish scientists Lynnerup and Heinemeier and the archaeologist Arneborg claimed that "the final generations of Norse Greenlanders consumed far more seal meat than their ancestors had done".[559] Or perhaps they consumed more lamp oil for heating because other fuel had grown scarcer? This could be an interesting discussion, but the empirical material for it does not exist.

Neither the osteological material nor isotope analyses can quantify the importance of seal meat in the Norse diet; neither can it be verified that the Norse Greenlanders included more seal in their diet towards the settlement's end. Contemporaries would doubtless have seen a transition from products of animal husbandry to seal in the final part of the settlement's existence as a decline in quality, but there are no indications that this happened.

From cattle to sheep and goats?

GUS was a middle-sized or small farm[560] and is the best documented farm in Norse Greenland. In the oldest phase (AD 1000–1150) there were around twice as many bones from sheep and goats as from cattle. In the second period 1150–1300 there were three times as many, and in the final period 1300–1400 five times as many. "The role of cattle seems to have decreased through time".[561] Scholars have generalised this trend, "in Greenland, on medium- and small-sized farms, goats and sheep replaced cattle over time".[562]

Another "smallish" farm E34 in the Qorlortup valley developed differently:

> It is possible to draw the significant conclusion that the importance of cattle was not reduced through time . . . The differences revealed in the species compositions are relatively modest and an overall picture seems to emerge of a very conservative economic system with no dramatic changes through the lifetime of the settlement.[563]

At the elite farm Sandnes a larger number of cattle bones were found. The ratio between sheep/goats and cattle varied unsystematically but within such narrow limits that it must be considered as stable.[564] Scholars have generalised this to be valid for all elite farms: "cattle and sheep/goats are represented in almost equal numbers . . . There do not seem to be any changes through time".[565] At Gardar (E47) development over time could not be quantified but according to the archaeologist "it does not appear that cattle keeping was reduced at Gardar in the late time period".[566]

The elite farm of Sandnes and possibly Gardar, and the "smallish" farm E34 all show a stable ratio. Only at the small farm GUS can a decreasing percentage of cattle bones compared to sheep/goats be verified. Besides, a sample of four farms is insufficient for a generalisation which includes ca. 300 Norse farms. The hypothesis that smallholders reduced the number of cattle and replaced them with sheep and goats has not been verified.

The Norwegian model

In the introduction to this book I proposed that the methods used in research on Norse Greenland could be improved by using the Norwegian background and the written sources more actively. This has been particularly fruitful in this chapter on subsistence food production.

Agricultural practices along the long and changeable coast of western and northern Norway with varying climatic conditions gave patterns for how similar resources in Greenland could be exploited successfully. There is no evidence that the fall in temperatures was so important that it created insurmountable problems for animal husbandry, hunting or fishing. The immigrants carried in their tradition knowledge of how they should make use of the Greenland agricultural resources and environment without reducing or damaging future productivity. The Norse Greenlanders did not make original inventions and did not learn anything from the Inuit.

312 *Subsistence food production*

It was part of the Norwegian coastal tradition to combine several industries and adapt them to the local environment. The long coast had a variable geography and gave a peasant several alternative models. Some American scholars have imagined that the "European" peasants arrived in Greenland with fixed ideas which they were unable to adapt to the realities they met in their new homeland. Inflexibility doomed Norse Greenland to ruin. This hypothesis has no root in historical realities. The Norse immigrants possessed a flexibility which enabled them to expand the practices which functioned well and curtail or marginalise practices which did not suit their new environment.

The Norse peasants brought hunting and fishing technologies with them from the Norwegian Atlantic and North Sea coast. Seal was killed with harpoon, sealnet and seal traps. Reindeer were caught with bow and arrow, spears and permanent installations with fences and cairns. Small whales were killed in "whale bays", larger whales probably with poisoned arrows from a crossbow. Cod was fished by handline with sinker and iron fish hook in a rowing boat. Char was taken with handlines, nets, seine-nets and possibly permanent fish traps. They had learnt their hunting and fishing practices from their Norwegian forefathers and foremothers, so no long learning process with experimenting was needed. I did not find a single fishing or hunting method which may have been invented in Norse Greenland or copied from the Inuit, nor a single practice in subsistence food production which did not have parallels in coastal Norway.

All hunting and fishing on common land and at sea was in principle free and open to all; privatisation was the exception. Most free was cod fishing which always took place on the open sea. Least free were fisheries for char which took place along rivers and in lakes where the shores were privately owned. But the main part of char fishing seems to have taken place in the fjords. The reindeer hunt was free on common land and outfields, the exception being the hunt on Akia and possibly other privatised locations.[567] Seal hunts were free on the ice or on the open sea, but they were private when they took place on private land or permanent traps were built.

Greenland was governed by chieftains and peasants at the Thing assembly, and they created a framework which made it possible for all peasants to supplement their animal husbandry with hunting and fishing in a flexible manner. The outcome is likely to have been a society where all households normally had a secure food supply, and where the years of famine were rare or non-existent.

Notes

1. *Egils saga* IF II chapter 10, p. 28; English translation: CSI and Penguin same chapter division as IF; Norwegian translation: Norrøn saga I, p. 41.
2. *Egils saga* IF II chapters 28 and 29, pp. 73–74; English translation: CSI and Penguin same chapter division as IF; Norwegian translation: Norrøn saga I, pp. 73–74.
3. Nørlund 1942, p. 67; English translation, p. 72.
4. Cf. the "Introduction" to the present book; the hypothesis was first and most forcefully presented in McGovern 1979, in concentrated form pp. 261–264.
5. Cf. McGovern 1979, pp. 245–281, and the way the thesis is argued there. Later authors have not confronted his hypotheses and arguments with counter-hypotheses.

6 *Konungs skuggsiá*, Old Norse, p. 30; English translation, p. 145; Norwegian translation, p. 69.
7 *Groenlendinga tháttr* IF IV chapter 6, pp. 289–290; English translation: CSI chapter 6, p. 381.
8 *Islendingabok* authored by Ari Frodi, IF I, chapter 6, pp. 13–14; English translation: chapter 6, p. 7; Norwegian translation, p. 54.
9 Egede/Bobé, p. 105, 5 October 1723.
10 Egede/Bobé, pp. 253 and 326.
11 Egede/Bobé, p. 96.
12 A terminology which is imprecise can make discussions unclear. Cf. Albrethsen and Arneborg 2004, p. 11.
13 Arneborg et al. 2012(a), p. 6.
14 Bruun 1896, pp. 206–215.
15 The byre at E1 is ruin no. 3. 150 cm is taken from W51 Sandnes (Roussell 1936, pp. 40–41).
16 Bruun wrote 7 feet broad, each foot = 0.316m.
17 Bruun 1896, pp. 214–215.
18 Bruun wrote 9 feet broad, each foot = 0.316m. One of them was possibly divided by a stall-stone creating two stalls which were 1.6m and 1.3m wide. Cf. Table 5.2.
19 Bruun 1896, pp. 214–215.
20 Bruun 1896, pp. 211–212; the ruin is number 5.
21 Bruun 1896, p. 215.
22 In Norwegian *kløvhest*.
23 Nedkvitne 1988, pp. 416 and 653–654.
24 Nedkvitne 1988, pp. 415–423.
25 Three-quarters of ten cattle.
26 *Konungs skuggsiá*, Old Norse, p. 30; English translation, p. 145; Norwegian translation, p. 69.
27 Krogh 1982, pp. 91 and 95.
28 Arneborg 2004, p. 265.
29 Nedkvitne 1988, pp. 425–427.
30 Vebæk 1992, p. 34.
31 Nedkvitne 1988, pp. 189; his source is Kåre Lunden who was an agronomist and historian, and Arne Schulerud who was a nutritional engineer.
32 Lunden 1975, p. 289.
33 Nedkvitne 1988, p. 423.
34 Nedkvitne 1988, pp. 310 and 365.
35 Nedkvitne 1988, pp. 653–662 and 322.
36 Bruun 1896, pp. 212 and 215.
37 Madsen 2014(a), pp. 130–138, here p. 131. His table 6.4 has average measures for these 199 sheep-sheds, but his measures are external. The median is externally 7.5 × 4.1 m, the walls were on average 0.9 m thick, which means that the rooms internally were 5.7 × 2.3 m or 13 m². As mentioned earlier each sheep/goat needed ca. 12 square feet or 1.2 m². Koch Madsen's median sheep/goat byre would then have room for 11 sheep/goats.
38 McGovern 1979, p. 133.
39 Enghoff 2003, pp. 67, 69 and 89.
40 Nedkvitne 1988, pp. 653–662 and 322.
41 Nedkvitne 1988, pp. 322 and 326, cf. p. 558.
42 Nedkvitne 1988, pp. 427–428.
43 Nedkvitne 1988, pp. 322 and 326, cf. p. 558.
44 Nedkvitne 1988, p. 427; cf. Borgedal 1966–68, volume 2, pp. 102 and 276.
45 Gensbøl 1999, p. 374; cf. Chapter 5, p. 300.
46 Nedkvitne 1988, pp. 132–133.

314 *Subsistence food production*

47 Lunden 1975, p. 304. This included the weight of the adult cattle and the weight of the calves which were slaughtered in the autumn after having lived their first and only summer.
48 Meat gave 155 kcal per 100 g or 178,250 kcal for 115 kg. If these calories were consumed equally in the year's 364 days, the household would have 490 kcal per day for consumption or 82 kcal per person per day in a household of six persons. 82 kcal is 3% of an estimated daily need of 2,600 kcal.
49 Bruun 1896, pp. 212 and 215.
50 Lunden 1975, p. 308; Nedkvitne 1988, pp. 189, cf. p. 139. This included the weight of the meat from slaughtered adult sheep and goats, and the weight of lambs and kids which were slaughtered in the autumn after having lived their first and only summer.
51 Cf. Table 5.10.
52 Meat from cattle, sheep and goats gives 155 kcal per 100 g, (Nedkvitne 1988, p. 189). 48 kg will give 74,400 calories per year and 34 kcal per day per person in a family of six. This is ca. 1% of a daily requirement of 2,600 kcal.
53 Nedkvitne 1988, pp. 651–652.
54 Nedkvitne 1988, pp. 411, 412 and 418.
55 Nedkvitne 1988, p. 138.
56 Nedkvitne 1988, pp. 114 and 139.
57 Nedkvitne 1988, p. 322.
58 Nedkvitne 1988, p. 246.
59 Nedkvitne 1988, p. 322.
60 Nelson et al. 2012(b), p. 85.
61 Enghoff 2003, p. 79.
62 Vebæk 1993, pp. 63–64.
63 Nørlund and Roussell 1930, p. 117; Roussell 1936, pp. 36–56, here p. 43.
64 Arneborg et al. 2008, p. 151; McGovern 1985, p. 86; Vebæk 1993, pp. 63–64.
65 Arneborg et al. 2012(b), here pp. 128 and 130–131.
66 Gulathings-lov § 20, printed NGL I, p. 11.
67 *Sverris saga*, Old Norse, p. 27; Norwegian translation p. 40.
68 Cf. Chapter 5, pp. 250, 259.
69 McGovern 1985, p. 88.
70 Nedkvitne 1988, pp. 395–396. The figures are from the 18th century.
71 Enghoff 2003, p. 95.
72 Unpublished table of animal bones from GUS written in 1991, author unknown. Journal number KNK 1950.
73 Nedkvitne 1988, pp. 410–412.
74 Cf. Chapter 5, p. 249.
75 Cf. Chapter 5, p. 233, on E1.
76 Nelson et al. 2012(b), p. 85.
77 Nelson et al. 2012(b), p. 82.
78 Nedkvitne 1988, pp. 328 and 324 and tables III.39, III.40 and III.41. The percentages are estimates with sources of error.
79 Nedkvitne 1988.
80 McGovern 2000, p. 331.
81 Born and Böcher 1999, p. 239.
82 Bruun 1896, p. 322; Ingstad, H. 1959, p. 103; reprint 2004, p. 83; English translation, pp. 60–61.
83 Nørlund 1942, p. 65; English translation, p. 69.
84 Böcher and Jens 2000, pp. 40–41; cf. Fredskild 1973, p. 137.
85 Böcher and Jens 2000, pp. 40–41.
86 Egede/Bobé, p. 75; in Nuuk at the coast where Egede lived, the annual rainfall is today normally 515 mm.
87 Nedkvitne 1988, pp. 321, 326 and 410–412.

88 Nyegaard 2014; section 1, Introduction.
89 Ingstad, H. 1959, p. 561 endnote 71, cf. p. 105; reprint 2004, p. 443 endnote 71; English translation, p. 65.
90 Ingstad, H. 1959, pp. 113–114; reprint 2004, p. 92; English translation, p. 65; cf. Krogh 1982, pp. 82–90.
91 Nyegaard 2014; section 1, Introduction.
92 Gensbøl 1999, pp. 382–383, 400–401 and 405; Born and Böcher 1999, pp. 237–257, particularly 240 and 251.
93 Roussell 1941, pp. 184–185 and 188.
94 Malmros 1992.
95 Nedkvitne 1988, pp. 326 and 137.
96 Nedkvitne 1988, pp. 324–325.
97 Nedkvitne 1988, p. 324.
98 Bruun 1896, pp. 252–254.
99 Nedkvitne 1988, p. 137.
100 Ingstad, H. 1959, pp. 111–112; reprint 2004, p. 90; English translation, p. 64.
101 Mogensen 1999(a), "Mosser", pp. 258–263.
102 Roussell 1936, p. 111.
103 Nedkvitne 1988, p. 413.
104 Fredskild 1973, p. 123; He dates this change in vegetation to "560 years before present", that is before 1973. This gives AD 1413. His margin of error is plus or minus 100 years.
105 Nedkvitne 1988, p. 137.
106 Mogensen 1999(b), "Ammassæt", p. 164; Gensbøl 1999, p. 324; Nedkvitne 1988, p. 141.
107 Nedkvitne 1988, p. 72.
108 Nelson et al. 2012(b), pp. 80–92.
109 Nedkvitne 1988, pp. 136–137.
110 Born and Böcher 1999, p. 239.
111 Nedkvitne 1988, p. 414.
112 Born and Böcher 1999, pp. 212–214.
113 Fredskild 1973, pp. 122, 128 and 148; Fredskild 1978/9, p. 38; Arneborg 2004, p. 277.
114 Malmros 1992.
115 The same point has been made by Knud Krogh 1982, p. 74.
116 Cf. Chapter 1, Figures 1.1 and 1.2.
117 Roussell 1941, p. 188. The byre was room X.
118 Roussell 1936, p. 38, cf. p. 12.
119 Cf. maps in Guldager et al. 2002.
120 Nedkvitne 1988, pp. 381–387 and 399.
121 Malmros 1992.
122 Cf. Chapter 6, p. 354.
123 Roussell 1941, pp. 185–186.
124 Roussell 1941, p. 188. Were the archaeologists competent to distinguish between sheep and goat dung?
125 Roussell 1936, pp. 47 and 51: ruin 5 room IV and ruin 6 room III.
126 Arneborg 2004, p. 245; according to Nørlund Icelandic peasants continued to use sheep dung in this way as late as the 1930s (Nørlund 1942, p. 64, English translation, pp. 68–69).
127 Roussell 1936, p. 68.
128 "In the home-field they may also have been built for carts, for instance manure carts, or perhaps ploughs". Nørlund and Roussell 1930, p.109, relevant map p. 9, fig. 2.
129 Ingstad, H. 1959, pp. 297 and 307–309; reprint 2004, pp. 233 and 241–242; English translation, pp. 184 and 190.
130 Ingstad, H. 1959, pp. 109–110 and 307–309; reprint 2004, pp. 88–89 and 241–242; English translation, pp. 62–62 and 190.

131 Skaaning Høegsberg 2005, p. 93.
132 Krogh 1974, p. 72; Krogh 1982, p. 92. Ingstad thought that the northern dam got its water from a separate brook from the hills. Krogh claimed to have found a ditch or channel from the main dam along the hillside to this northern dam which he gave the number 43. If Krogh is right, the irrigation system was even more complex.
133 Krogh 1982, pp. 92 and 96.
134 Fredskild 1973, p. 123.
135 Krogh 1974, p. 79.
136 Guldager et al. 2002, pp. 60–62.
137 Arneborg 2005, pp. 141–142.; Skaaning Høegsberg 2005, p. 93.
138 Albrethsen and Keller 1986, p. 99.
139 Arneborg 2005, pp. 140 and 143–144.; Skaaning Høegsberg 2005, p. 93.
140 Arneborg 2005, pp. 140–141; Arneborg 2004, pp. 237–238.
141 Skaaning Høegsberg 2005, p. 93; Cf. Chapter 5, pp. 254–255; On climate, cf. Chapter 5, pp. 268–271.
142 Nedkvitne 1988, pp. 387–391.
143 Nyegaard 2014, section 4.2. The mire stratigraphy.
144 Nørlund and Stenberger 1934, pp. 50ff.
145 Vebæk 1993, pp. 25 and 29.
146 Roussell 1941, pp. 146–147.
147 Bruun 1918(b), p. 164; Krogh 1982, p. 74.
148 Guldager et al. 2002.
149 Heggstad et al. 2008, entry word "sætr".
150 *Ordbog over det danske sprog*, volume 23, Copenhagen 1946, entry word "sæter".
151 Reinton 1955 I, p. 2.
152 Bruun 1896, p. 302.
153 Bruun 1918(b), p. 166.
154 Keller 1989, p. 139; *Oxford English Dictionary*, reference word "shieling".
155 Reinton 1955, I, pp. 18–50.
156 Cf. M2a, M29, M3 and M28; Albrethsen and Arneborg 2004, pp. 14–15.
157 Nedkvitne 1988, pp. 414–415.
158 Albrethsen and Arneborg 2004, pp. 12–17 and catalogue, pp. 20 ff.
159 Reinton 1955 I, p. 25.
160 Reinton 1957 II, pp. 7–204.
161 Mahler 1993, p. 488.
162 Cf. Chapter 2, pp. 50–51.
163 Gulathings-lov V.81, V.84 and V.86; cf. *Frostatingslova* XIV.8 and *Magnus Lagabøte's National Law* VII.40, VII.41, VII.43, VII.62; KLNM entry word "sæter".
164 Madsen 2014(a), p. 20 gives his own definition which does not correspond to the way the word was used in Old Norse and later in Norwegian. I find the traditional usage which is based on how the *sæter* in fact was organised in the Norse period more useful as analytical concept.
165 An average Greenlandic peasant had 10 cattle; Nørlund and Roussell 1930, pp. 115–117.
166 Cf. Chapter 5, p. 240; Nedkvitne 1988, pp. 653–656.
167 Nørlund and Roussell 1930, p. 106.
168 Nørlund and Stenberger 1934, p. 24; Kuijpers et al. 1998, p. 64.
169 Nørlund and Roussell 1930, pp. 9 and 105–107.
170 Nørlund and Roussell 1930, p. 106.
171 Guldager et al. 2002, the previous figures are calculated on the basis of identifications in this report, particularly pp. 3–4.
172 Nyegaard 2014, section 3.2.
173 Nyegaard 2014, section 2.3; Guldager et al. 2002, pp. 23 and 53–55.
174 Nyegaard 2014, section 7.3; Figure 5.2.
175 Bruun 1896, p. 302; Bruun 1918(b), p. 166.

Subsistence food production   317

176 Roussell 1936, p. 30; Roussell 1941, p. 230.
177 Nørlund 1942, p. 65; English translation, p. 70.
178 Ingstad, H. 1959, pp. 106–108; reprint 2004, pp. 86–87; English translation, p. 62. His visit there was in 1953.
179 Krogh 1982, pp. 101 and 103.
180 Keller 1983, pp. 59–66, here p. 59.
181 Keller 1983, p. 66.
182 Keller 1983, pp. 60 and 64–65.
183 Guldager et al. 2002, p. 15.
184 Cf. Introduction to this book, p. 9.
185 McGovern 2000, p. 338, cf. McGovern 1979, pp. 264–279.
186 *Det gamle Grønlands beskrivelse af Ivar Bárdarson*, pp. 25 and 26.
187 Cf. Chapter 1, p. 20.
188 *Fostbroedra saga* IF VI chapter 24, p. 248; English translation: CSI chapter 24, p. 386.
189 *Fostbroedra saga* IF VI chapter 24, p. 251; English translation: CSI chapter 24, p. 387.
190 *Eiriks saga Rauda* IF IV chapter 4, p. 209; English translation: CSI chapter 4, p. 7 and Penguin chapter 4, p. 33.
191 DN XV no. 29.
192 Cf. Chapter 4, p. 207; *Om Norgis Rige*, edition from 1968, p. 50; GHM III, pp. 226–233.
193 Fredskild 1973, pp. 122 and 148.
194 Fredskild 1982, pp. 189–196.
195 Fredskild 1982, pp. 189–196.
196 Sandgren and Fredskild 1991, pp. 318 and 326.
197 Fredskild 1992, p. 14.
198 Jakobsen 1991, p. 67; "Since, for the most part, any large-scale agricultural land use will be destructive to vital resources in this low arctic landscape, it was impossible for the Norsemen to respond appropriately to environmental feedback". These are unverified hypotheses.
199 Massa et al. 2012, p. 121; Greenland Agriculture Advisory Board, 2009.
200 Fredskild 1992, p. 14.
201 Vebæk 1992, p. 108.
202 Born and Böcher 1999, pp. 217–218.
203 McGovern 2000, pp. 327–339.
204 Malmros 1992, p. 30; Arneborg 2003(c), p. 10.
205 Løvberg 1991; Vebæk 1943, p.108
206 Arneborg 2004, p. 276.
207 Mikkelsen et al. 2001, p. 67.
208 Mikkelsen et al. 2001, pp. 67–68.
209 Lassen et al. 2004, p. 170. The same conclusion is in Jensen et al. 2004, p. 161. Same conclusions are also in Kuijpers et al. 2014, pp. 1–13.
210 Massa et al. 2012, p. 120.
211 Massa et al. 2012, p. 120.
212 Massa et al. 2012, p. 128.
213 Massa et al. 2012, pp. 125–128.
214 Lamb 1995, pp. 84 and 171.
215 Lamb 1995, p. 318; Dahl-Jensen et al. 1998, p. 270; Kuijpers et al. 1998, pp. 62 and 66.
216 Baetzing 2015 (orig. 1984), p. 43; Mathieu 2015, p. 84.
217 Nørlund 1924, pp. 228–244; Roussell 1941, p. 9.
218 Kuijpers et al. 1998, pp. 61–67.
219 Dahl-Jensen et al. 1998, p. 270. Fredskild claimed in 1982 that cores from the inland ice show that temperatures were at the same level in AD 985 and in the first part of the 20th century (Fredskild 1982, p. 189).
220 Arneborg et al. 2012(a), p. 4.
221 Weidick 1982, pp. 241 and 251.

318 Subsistence food production

222 Kuijpers et al. 1998, pp. 61–67; Kuijpers et al. 2014, pp. 1–13.
223 *Det gamle Grønlands beskrivelse af Ivar Bárdarson*, pp. 16–17.
224 Fredskild 1973, p. 122.
225 Fredskild 1973, p. 132. Fredskild's main source was diagrams of pollen in lakes and bogs.
226 Hunt 2009, pp. 398–401 and 405.
227 Mathieu 1998, pp. 50 and 52.
228 Mikkelsen et al. 2008, p. 47. The scientists measure the rise in sea levels by metres per 1,000 years. The estimates recorded by the Danish geologist Naja Mikkelsen suggest rises at different locations of one to three metres during the last millennium. The sea level rise during the ca. 430 years Norse Greenland existed may have been half of this.
229 Nørlund and Stenberger 1934, pp. 79–80 cf. pp. 24–25.
230 Nørlund and Stenberger 1934, p. 24; Kuijpers et al. 1998, p. 64.
231 Mikkelsen et al. 2008, p. 48.
232 Skaaning Høegsberg 2005, p. 34.
233 Cf. Chapter 2, pp. 52–53.
234 Nedkvitne 1988, pp. 506–509; KLNM volume XVII, entry word "Säljakt. Island".
235 Nedkvitne 1988, pp. 506–509.
236 Gulathings-lov §91.
237 Gulathings-lov §91 and §95.
238 *Det gamle Grønlands beskrivelse af Ivar Bárdarson*, pp. 25 and 26.
239 *Det gamle Grønlands beskrivelse af Ivar Bárdarson*, p. 26; Ingstad, H. 1959, pp. 138–139, cf. p. 72; reprint 2004, pp. 111 and 60; English translation, pp. 78–79.
240 *Det gamle Grønlands beskrivelse af Ivar Bárdarson*, p. 20.
241 *Det gamle Grønlands beskrivelse af Ivar Bárdarson*, p. 22; Ivar Bárdarson presents *Korsøø* (Cross Island) as the easternmost location on Greenland which he knew.
242 *Det gamle Grønlands beskrivelse af Ivar Bárdarson*, p. 24.
243 *Det gamle Grønlands beskrivelse af Ivar Bárdarson*, p. 25.
244 McGovern 1979, pp. 264–279.
245 Egede, Niels: Description of Greenland, pp. 254–255.
246 Ingstad, H. 1959 p. 138; reprint 2004, pp. 110–11; English translation, p. 77.
247 Born and Böcher 1999, pp. 328–329.
248 *Konungs skuggsiá*, Old Norse, p. 30; English translation, p. 145; Norwegian translation, p. 69.
249 *Konungs skuggsiá*, Old Norse, pp. 28–29; English translation, p. 140–141; Norwegian translation, pp. 65–67.
250 McGovern 2000, p. 333.
251 Arneborg et al. 2012(b), p. 128.
252 Nørlund and Stenberger 1934, pp. 126–128.
253 Lynnerup 2000, p. 292.
254 Egede/Bobé, pp. 20–21 and 23.
255 Grønnow et al. 2014, p. 408.
256 Table 5.7.
257 Cf. Chapter 5, pp. 281–285.
258 "Grænlands annal", p. 55 = GHM III, pp. 242–243.
259 *Eiriks saga Rauda* IF IV chapter 13, pp. 234–235 (*bræddr var med seltjoru, thvi at thar fær eigi sjomadkr á*). English translation: CSI chapter 13, p. 18 and Penguin chapter 13, p. 48.
260 On the uses of seal-oil in the northern Baltic, see Gustavsson 1997, p. 114.
261 "Grænlands annal", p. 55 = GHM III, pp. 242–243.
262 Enghoff 2003, p. 34.
263 Nyegaard 2014, section 8.1.2.
264 Born and Böcher 1999, p. 199.
265 Kalland 2014, p. 69.

Subsistence food production   319

266 *Fostbroedra saga* IF VI chapter 22, p. 227; English translation: CSI chapter 22, p. 375.
267 Cf. Chapter 4, p. 179. The sealskins exported from Bergen to England may have been produced in Norway.
268 Cf. Chapter 4, pp. 175–177.
269 Enghoff 2003, pp. 39–40.
270 Nyegaard 2014; section 9.6, Seal hunting.
271 Enghoff 2003, p. 34.
272 McGovern 1985, p. 89.
273 Enghoff 2003, p. 34; Nyegaard 2014, section 9.6, Seal hunting; McGovern 1979, p. 111; www.greenland.com/en/about-greenland/nature-climate/fauna-of-greenland/seals/.
274 Berglund 1973/4, pp. 11–13.
275 McGovern et al. 1996, p. 112.
276 Nyegaard 2014, section 9.6, Seal hunting.
277 McGovern 1985, p. 89.
278 Born and Böcher 1999, pp. 186 and 335–336; Nyegaard 2014, section 9.6, Seal hunting.
279 McGovern 1985, p. 89.
280 Born and Böcher 1999, p. 186.
281 Enghoff 2003, pp. 28–29.
282 McGovern et al. 1996, pp. 106 and 112–113.
283 McGovern 2000, pp. 338–339.
284 *Fostbroedra saga* IF VI chapter 23, p. 230; English translation: CSI chapter 23, p. 376.
285 Gulathings-lov §91; Magnus Lagabøte's National Law VII.65.
286 Gulathings-lov §91; Magnus Lagabøte's National Law VII.65.
287 Gulathings-lov §91; Magnus Lagabøte's National Law VII.65.
288 Gulathings-lov §91; Magnus Lagabøte's National Law VII.65.
289 KLNM entry word "Säljakt. Island".
290 McGovern 1985, p. 101.
291 Dugmore et al. 2012, pp. 3659–3660.
292 McGovern 1985, p. 101; McGovern 2000, p. 336.
293 McGovern 1985, p. 101; McGovern 2011, p. 297.
294 McGovern 2000, p. 338.
295 Egede/Bobé, p. 76.
296 For the calorie values of seal meat, cf. Schulerud 1945, p. 62; 100 g seal meat gives 165 kcal. I have assumed that seal blubber had the same calorie value as seal meat.
297 Grønnow et al. 2014, p. 408.
298 Born and Böcher 1999, p. 199; Sivertsen 1947, pp. 188–189 and 193.
299 Vibe 1990, p. 395; Vibe 1981, pp. 482–486.
300 Vibe 1990, pp. 394–395.
301 Bruun 1918 (a), pp. 67–68.
302 Egede/Bobé, p. 335.
303 *Det gamle Grønlands beskrivelse af Ivar Bárdarson*, p. 26.
304 Vebæk 1993 (Narsaq), p. 32; Roussell 1936 (Sandnes), pp. 106–107.
305 Nørlund and Roussell 1930 (Gardar), p. 146; the blade was 2.1 cm wide and 2.3 cm long.
306 Vebæk 1993, pp. 31–32 and p. 76 nos. 92–99.
307 Vebæk 1943, figure 63, pp. 92 and 100.
308 Roussell 1936 (Sandnes), figures 80, pp. 107–108 and p. 179.
309 Roussell 1936 (Sandnes), pp. 179–180.
310 Roussell 1936 (Sandnes), figures 76 and 77, pp. 105–106.
311 Roussell 1936 (Sandnes), pp. 179–180.
312 Roussell 1936 (Sandnes), pp. 108 and p. 180 (S. 220 and U. 221).
313 Spear as weapon used against humans is mentioned once in Greenland, *Fostbroedra saga* IF VI chapter 24, pp. 254–256; English translation: CSI chapter 24, p. 389.

320 *Subsistence food production*

314 Nørlund and Stenberger 1934, p. 133.
315 Nørlund and Stenberger 1934, p. 133, figure 99.
316 Gulathings-lov §93; Frostatingslova XIV.9; Magnus Lagabøte's National Law VII.63.
317 Frostatingslova XIV.9.
318 Barth 1982, pp. 40–41.
319 Frostatingslova XIV.9; Magnus Lagabøte's National Law VII.63.
320 Barth 1982, pp. 39–40 and 46.
321 Blehr 1982, pp. 15–18.
322 K. M. B. Christensen 1989, pp. 20–22.
323 Rosing 1988, pp. 69–79.
324 Grønnow et al. 1983, pp. 45–46, pp. 68–69, p. 63, p. 53 and p. 82, cf. p. 89, note 18.
325 Indrelid 2015, pp. 29–36
326 Ingstad, H. 1959, p. 140; reprint 2004, p. 112; English translation 1966, p. 78. 1966.
327 Ingstad, H. 1959, p. 139; reprint 2004, pp. 111–112; cf. English translation, p. 78.
328 Born and Böcher 1999, pp. 272–273 and 303.
329 Cf. Chapter 4, pp. 174–179; Chapter 5, pp. 279–285.
330 Cf. Chapter 5, pp. 242 and 301.
331 KLNM volume 14, Copenhagen 1982, entry word "Ren", column 66.
332 *Konungs skuggsiá*, Old Norse, p. 29; English translation, p. 141; Norwegian translation, pp. 66–67.
333 Nedkvitne 1988, p. 144.
334 *Fostbroedra saga* IF VI chapter 23, p. 245–246; English translation: CSI chapter 23, p. 384.
335 Egede, Niels: Description of Greenland, pp. 254–255.
336 Bruun 1918 (a), pp. 68–69.
337 Lunden 1975, p. 304.
338 Sara 1979, p. 365.
339 Indrelid 2015, p. 33.
340 Schulerud 1945, p. 62.
341 Six persons per household, daily need 2,600 kcal.
342 Cf. the method used in the calculations for the Western Settlement.
343 Cf. the introduction to the present chapter.
344 Latin: Globicephala melas, Norwegian and Danish: grindehval. 6–8 m long.
345 4–5 m long. Also in English: White dolphin, beluga; Latin: delphinapterus leucas; Danish and Norwegian: hvidhval; Enghoff 2003, pp. 22, 26–27 and 40–41; Her figures are based on an unpublished report by Georg Nyegaard from 1992 to the Zoological museum in Copenhagen.
346 Nyegaard 2014; section 8.3, Whales.
347 Vebæk 1993, p. 59.
348 McGovern 1992, p. 95.
349 *Konungs skuggsiá*, Old Norse, p. 15; English translation, p. 119; Norwegian translation, p. 42.
350 Born and Böcher 1999, pp. 191–193; Gensbøl 1999, pp. 312–321.
351 *Det gamle Grønlands beskrivelse af Ivar Bárdarson*, pp. 19–20.
352 Gulathings-lov §150.
353 Kalland 2014, pp. 97–156.
354 Ottar og Wulfstan 1983, p. 22.
355 Latin: balaena mysticus, Norwegian and Danish: grønlandshval; Enghoff 2003, p. 22 and pp. 40–41 objects no. 561 and 631; cf. pp. 26–27; Enghoff's figures are based on an unpublished report by Georg Nyegaard from 1992 to the Zoological museum in Copenhagen. She keeps the possibility open that two of the identified bones may be from the North Atlantic right whale, Latin: Balaena glacialis, Norwegian and Danish: Nordkaper.
356 Born and Böcher 1999, pp. 191–193; Gensbøl 1999, pp. 312–321.

357 Hacquebord 2014, pp. 87–89.
358 verdur han opt veiddur af veidi monnum.
359 *Konungs skuggsiá*, Old Norse, p. 17; English translation, p.124, Norwegian translation, pp. 45–46. "An active, open pursuit of great whales is probably an early 16th century innovation in the Scandinavian North Atlantic" (McGovern 1992, p. 96). This is yet another example that McGovern draws conclusions without having read the written sources.
360 *Konungs skuggsiá*, Old Norse, pp. 17; English translation, p. 124; Norwegian translation, pp. 45–46; 130 ells (*alen*), each ell 47 cm.
361 Gensbøl 1999, pp. 318–321.
362 Degerbøl 1941, p. 346; cf. McGovern 1992, p. 96 for a similar find at E71; normal length 12–14 m, cf. Gensbøl 1999. Latin: Megaptera nodosa or Megaptera novaeangliae; Danish: Pukkelhval; Norwegian: Knølhval.
363 Gulathings-lov §149.
364 Kalland 2014, pp. 19–21 and 49–50.
365 "Grænlands annal", pp. 53–54.
366 Gulathings-lov §150; *finnanda spic*.
367 Frostatingslova XIV.10.
368 *Konungs skuggsiá,* Old Norse, p. 17; English translation, p. 124; Norwegian translationn, p. 45.
369 Kalland 2014, p. 69.
370 Kalland 2014, p. 70.
371 *Konungs skuggsiá*, Old Norse, p. 15; English translation, p. 120; Norwegian translation, p. 42; "*tha meiga menn eigi mellta med sier sialfum og ecki annat kvikindi*".
372 KLNM entry word "Spekk".
373 Born and Böcher 1999, p. 202.
374 Born and Böcher 1999, p. 199.
375 Latin: Phoca groenlandica or Pagophilus groenlandicus; Norwegian and Danish: Grønlandssel; cf. Chapter 5, p. 276.
376 Internet search homepage of "Havforskningsinstituttet", and "Grønlandssel"; Sivertsen 1947, pp. 188–189 and 193.
377 Gulathings-lov §149 and §150.
378 Lynnerup 2000, p. 292.
379 In emails dated 3 July 2015 and 6 July 2015.
380 *Konungs skuggsiá*.
381 Roussell 1936, pp. 125–128 and 286–290.
382 Nørlund and Roussell 1930, p. 163.
383 Vebæk 1993 (Narsaq), p. 35.
384 Vebæk 1993, p. 37.
385 Roussell 1936, p. 172.
386 Roussell 1936, p. 180, cf. figure 74.
387 Roussell 1936 (Sandnes), pp. 114–116; Vebæk 1991(b), p. 78 object no. 152, in "List of the finds"; shaft of whalebone, undoubtedly for a spade, with runic inscription: "Gunnar owns" (Vebæk 1992, p. 119, figure 129); spade of whalebone (Vebæk 1992, p. 119. object no. 226; Vebæk 1993, p. 37).
388 McGovern et al. 1996, p. 113.
389 Degerbøl 1941, p. 346; cf. McGovern 1992, p. 96 for a similar find at E71.
390 Roussell 1936, p. 192; Vebæk 1991(b), pp. 71–72.
391 Pilgrim 2004, pp. 33–34.
392 The island is mentioned several times in the Icelandic Annals. IA, I Resiniani years 1189 and 1190; III Høyer 1189 and 1190; IV Regii 1189 and 1190; V Skálholt 1190; *Oddaannalar og Oddverjaannall* 2003, p.136 (AD 1189 and 1190); Cf. "Grænlands annal", pp. 61–64 and GHM I, pp. 135–149.
393 *Det gamle Grønlands beskrivelse af Ivar Bárdarson*, pp. 20–22.

322 Subsistence food production

394 *Det gamle Grønlands beskrivelse af Ivar Bárdarson*, pp. 20–22.
395 Cf. Chapter 4, p. 191; IA, IV Regii; *Oddaannalar og Oddverjaannall* 2003, p.136 (AD 1189 and 1190); *Sturlunga saga*, Old Norse chapters 95 and 96, p. 122; English translation II, chapter 13, pp. 118 and 119; Danish translation I, pp. 141 and 142.
396 *Det gamle Grønlands beskrivelse af Ivar Bárdarson*, pp. 20–22.
397 Nørlund 1942, p. 88; English translation, p. 93.
398 *Groenlendinga tháttr* IF IV chapter 2, p. 276; English translation: CSI chapter 2, p. 374; Norwegian translation: Norrøn saga V, p. 249.
399 Born 2005, p. 16; Ingstad, H. 1959, pp. 179–180; reprint 2004, p. 144; English translation, p. 180.
400 *Det gamle Grønlands beskrivelse af Ivar Bárdarson*, pp. 20–22.
401 "*Han for opt á haustum til fangs i obyggdir*"; *Groenlendinga tháttr* IF IV chapter 2, pp. 276–277; English translation: CSI chapter 2, p. 374; Norwegian translation: Norrøn saga V, pp. 249–251.
402 Nyegaard 2014, section 8.10, Fish: "The small assemblage of eight fish bones does not reflect the actual significance of fishing at the site. Systematic wet sieving might have given a different result, although the fish bones from the mire would have been further fragmented as a result, due to their poor state of preservation". Nyegaard writes about the fishbones at E34: "Given that today it is possible to catch large numbers of arctic char in the late summer, in small pools below the waterfall at the foot of the valley where it meets Tunulliarfik Fjord, it is also very strange that not a single bone of this fish has been demonstrated at the site". Cf. McGovern 1985, p. 75; Enghoff 2003, p. 7.
403 Even here there is a caveat, bones from fat fish rot more easily than other fish.
404 Nyegaard 2014, section 8.10 Fish: "Four fragmented vertebrae and a cleithrum are of cod". "A fragmented vertebra and a spiny process from a vertebra are of flatfish". Nyegaard thinks it is likely that the flatfish is halibut.
405 Latin *Melanogrammus aeglefinus*; Danish kuller, Norwegian hyse.
406 Nedkvitne 1988, pp. 70–72.
407 The Eiriksfjord was ca. 10 m deep at its head, midfjord outside Brattahlid ca. 130 m, outside Sillisit 200–250 m and further out at Narsaq ca. 300 m. Einarsfjord was midfjord outside Gardar ca. 50 m, between the Kujalleq and Eqaluit side fjords 300–400 m. The inner Amitsuarsuk fjord near Foss is ca. 120 m midfjord, its continuation the outer Agdluitsup fjord is 300–400 m all the way (Vandrekort Sydgrønland, ed. Greenland Tourism. Hiking Map South Greenland, Scale 1:100.000, three map sheets Narsarsuaq/Narsaq/Qaqortoq, first edition, Copenhagen 1994. The depths of the fjords are included on these maps.)
408 Vebæk 1993(b), p. 44, cf. p. 77.
409 Vebæk 1991(a), p. 13, figure 4; cf. Vebæk 1993, p. 79, no. 179.
410 Vebæk 1991(b), p. 71 (E149).
411 Arneborg et al. 2009, pp. 24–29, figure 4.
412 Arneborg et al. 2009 found this information in the "Danish Nationalmuseum register".
413 Vebæk 1992, p. 81, figure 109 and p. 123 no. 51.
414 Vebæk 1992, pp. 80–81 and 122–123.
415 Edvardsson 2006, pp. 28 and 53.
416 Vebæk 1992, p. 127 no. 154. Enghoff 2003, p. 50 writes that "a large iron hook which would have been suited for catching large fish" was found at W54 Nipaatsoq. The source for this is "Hans Kapel, personal communication". This is not sufficient to verify the claim.
417 Struman-Hansen 2003, p. 48.
418 Cf. Chapter 4, pp. 174–175 and 186–187.
419 *Fostbroedra saga* IF VI chapter 24, p, 257; English translation: CSI chapter 24, p. 390.
420 Anker Pedersen 1999, p. 164.
421 Born and Böcher 1999, pp. 160–161; Muus et al. 1990, pp. 67–69.
422 Born and Böcher 1999, p. 130; Muus et al. 1990, pp. 25–26.

423 Muus et al. 1990, p. 25.
424 Ingstad, H. 1959, p. 403; reprint 2004, p. 319; English translation, pp. 248–249.Petersen 1896, pp. 415–418; Bruun 1918(b), p. 181; cf. informative photo Madsen 2014(a), p. 48; Holm 1883, p. 129 says he did not visit E91 on his journey in 1880, only E73.
425 Ingstad, H. 1959, pp. 49–50; reprint 2004, p. 42; English translation, p. 32.
426 Ingstad, H. 1959, p. 298; reprint 2004, p. 232; English translation, p. 183.
427 Cf. Chapter 5, pp. 291–294.
428 Muus et al. 1990, p. 68.
429 Kuijpers et al. 2014, pp. 8–9; Lassen et al. 2004, p. 170.
430 Egede/Bobé, p. 75; dates 15–19. April.
431 Latin: Reinhardtius hippoglossides; Danish: hellefisk; Norwegian: blåkveite.
432 Born and Böcher 1999, p. 159.
433 Born and Böcher 1999, p. 165; Muus et al. 1990, p. 145.
434 Latin: Hippoglossus hippoglossus; Danish: helleflynder; Norwegian: kveite.
435 Muus et al. 1990, pp. 148–149; Born and Böcher 1999, p. 159.
436 Nedkvitne 1988, pp. 237–238.
437 Egede, Hans 1741, p. 358.
438 Table 5.9; Nyegaard 2014, section 8.10, Fish.
439 Latin: Sebastes marinus; Danish: Rødfisk; Norwegian: Uer.
440 Muus et al. 1990, pp. 110–112; Born and Böcher 1999, pp. 159 and 166.
441 Egede/Bobé, pp. 76 and 111, cf. p. 257.
442 Muus et al. 1990, pp. 45–46.
443 Cf. Table 5.9.
444 Egede, Hans 1741, p. 351.
445 Muus et al. 1990, pp. 45–46; Born and Böcher 1999, p. 336.
446 Muus et al. 1990, pp. 113–131.
447 Egede/Bobé, p. 351; Muus et al. 1990, p. 121; Born and Böcher 1999, p. 325.
448 Egede/Bobé, pp. 228 and 361; Born and Böcher 1999, p. 325.
449 Muus et al. 1990, pp. 49–50; Born and Böcher 1999, p. 231.
450 There is an informative photo of the site in Madsen 2014(a), p. 48, but he wrongly calls the "Amitsuarsuk fjord" the "Ameralik fjord".
451 Petersen 1896, p. 416; Petersen writes 200 feet, each foot = 32 cm.
452 *Det gamle Grønlands beskrivelse af Ivar Bárdarson*, pp. 24–25.
453 Cf. Born and Böcher 1999, pp. 336–337 about the Inuit fishing salmon there today.
454 Muus et al. 1990, pp. 47–49.
455 Arneborg 2004, p. 269.
456 *Det gamle Grønlands beskrivelse af Ivar Bárdarson*, p. 23; The length is "ij uge søes".
457 Vebæk 1991(a), p. 12.
458 Muus et al. 1990, pp. 49–50; Born and Böcher 1999, pp. 320–321.
459 *Groenlendinga tháttr* IF IV chapter 6, pp. 289–290; English translation: CSI chapter 6, p. 381.
460 Born and Böcher 1999, p. 325.
461 Cf. Chapter 4, pp. 186–188 and Chapter 5, pp. 289–295.
462 Nedkvitne 1988, pp. 532 and 584.
463 "Bread" is here flat, thin, crisp bread without yeast.
464 *Konungs skuggsiá*, Old Norse, pp. 29–30; English translation, p. 142; Norwegian translation, p. 68.
465 Egede/Bobé, p. 124.
466 Egede/Bobé, p. 147.
467 Krogh 1982, p. 104.
468 Henriksen 2014, p. 429.
469 Krogh 1982, p. 103.
470 "hordeum" = "barley".
471 Edwards 2014, p. 196; Henriksen 2014, p. 429.

472 Henriksen 2014, p. 428, table 1; cf. Nørlund and Roussell 1930, pp. 133–135, 141 and 142.
473 Henriksen 2014, pp. 428–229.
474 Henriksen 2014, pp. 429.
475 Nørlund and Stenberger 1934, pp. 131–132.
476 Nørlund and Roussell 1930, p. 141 note 4.
477 Nørlund and Roussell 1930, here p. 141.
478 Arneborg and Berglund 2007. Report in Greenland National Museum and Archive, p. 4. The levels have not been dated.
479 Ingstad, H. 1959, pp. 118–123, particularly p. 119; reprint 2004, pp. 95–98, particularly p. 95; English translation, pp. 68–69. Nørlund 1942, pp. 66–67; English translation, pp. 70–72.
480 Henriksen 2014, p. 428, table 1.
481 Cf. Chapter 4, pp. 161, 166, 169 and 183; Chapter 5, pp. 285 and 300.
482 Sørensen 1982, pp. 297 and 300; Gensbøl 1999, pp. 380–381.
483 Wikipedia "Flax"; The Norwegian www.matvaretabellen.no says 513 kcal.
484 Arneborg et al. 2012(a), p. 7; Sørensen 1982, pp. 300–301.
485 Arneborg et al. 2012(a), pp. 7–8.
486 Arneborg et al. 2012(a), p. 7; in Latin: elymus arenarius, Danish: sand-hjælme, Norwegian: marehalm.
487 Wikipedia "Lyme grass" and "Elymus arenarius".
488 Bruun 1918(a), pp. 62–63.
489 Vebæk 1941, p. 41; the English version of Wikipedia states in general terms that seeds of lyme-grass have provided food in the past (Wikipedia English version "Lyme grass").
490 Nørlund 1942, p. 66; English translation 1936, p. 71; Gudmundsson 1966, pp. 13–23.
491 Gudmundsson 1966, p. 20.
492 Schulerud 1945, p. 48; Nedkvitne 1988, p. 187.
493 Ingstad, H. 1959, p. 121; reprint 2004, p. 97; English translation, p. 69.
494 Gudmundsson 1966, p. 20.
495 Fægri I 1958, pp. 204–205.
496 Egede/Bobé, p. 214; 30 December 1728.
497 Latin: empetrum; Norwegian: krekling; Danish: revling.
498 Latin: vaccinium; Norwegian and Danish: tranebær.
499 Latin: polygonum; Norwegian: slirekne; Danish pileurt.
500 Arneborg et al. 2012(a), p. 7; Wikipedia "Polygonum".
501 Pontoppidan 1752–53, volume 1, p. 245; Nedkvitne 1988, p. 413.
502 Nedkvitne 1988, index, entry word "tare".
503 Cf. Henriksen 2014, p. 427.
504 Nelson et al. 2012(c), p. 94. "As grain agriculture was not possible and as there were no wild plant food that could play a primary role in human diet, the Norse diet was based on meat and fat from the terrestrial and marine reservoirs. A little carbohydrate would have come from the milk products of their domestic animals and perhaps a very little more from wild berries and a few plants, but animal protein and fat provided essentially all human dietary energy requirements".
505 Cf. Chapter 5, p. 301.
506 Cf. Chapter 5, pp. 301–302.
507 I have assumed that the term "marine food" included fresh water fish.
508 Lynnerup printed edition 1998, cf. pp. 7 and 129.
509 Arneborg et al. 2008, pp. 153–154.
510 Arneborg et al. 1999, p. 158; Arneborg et al. 2008, p. 155; Naumann 2014, p. 40.
511 Lynnerup 1998, pp. 47–48; Arneborg et al. 1999, p. 158; Arneborg et al. 2008, p. 155.
512 Barrett et al. 2000, p. 539.
513 Naumann et al. 2014(a), p. 535; Naumann 2014, p. 18.
514 Arneborg et al. 1999, p. 161.
515 Nelson et al. 2012(c), p. 110.

Subsistence food production 325

516 Arneborg et al. 1999, p. 158; Barrett et al. 2000, p. 539.
517 Lynnerup 1998, pp. 49–50; Arneborg et al. 1999, p. 158.
518 Lynnerup 1998, p. 48; The figures are given in negative values, which means that larger figures mean fewer 13C isotopes.
519 Barrett et al. 2000, p. 540.
520 Nelson et al. 2012(a), pp. 44–45.
521 Nelson et al. 2012(c), pp. 112–113.
522 The reindeer bones in the Norse region had a 13C value closer to the marine endpoint than reindeer bones from north-east Greenland; 21 reindeer bones excavated from Norse sites in Greenland had an average 13C value of −18.2 per-mil (between −17.3 and −18.6 per-mil). Six reindeer bones from north-east Greenland had an average 13C value of −19.3 per-mil (19.1–19.6 per-mil) (Nelson et al. 2012(a), p. 45). Did the reindeer in the Norse region eat more lichen?
523 Nelson does not explain whether it is possible to identify or compensate for a large intake of reindeer meat in the isotope analyses of a human bone (Nelson and others 2012(a), p. 44).
524 Naumann et al. 2014(b), p. 324.
525 Arneborg et al. 1999, p. 158.
526 Arneborg et al. 2008, pp. 154–159; the same authors presented the same results in Arneborg et al. 2012(b), pp. 121–130.
527 Arneborg et al. 2008, pp. 156–157.
528 Cf. above Chapter 3, pp. 89–90.
529 Cf. Chapter 3, pp. 102–103.
530 See for example Enghoff 2003, p. 87.
531 Lynnerup 1998; Arneborg et al. 1999.
532 Arneborg et al. 1999, pp. 161 and 165; Arneborg et al. 2012(a), p. 1.
533 Schulerud 1945.
534 Schulerud 1945, p. 58.
535 Arneborg et al. 1999, p. 161; Arneborg et al. 2012(a), p. 1.
536 Arneborg et al. 1999, p. 157.
537 Arneborg et al. 1999, p. 161.
538 Table 5.11; Nedkvitne 1988, pp. 141, 143–145, 531–534, cf. p. 429.
539 Nedkvitne 1988, pp. 532 and 584. Fresh saithe: 120 kcal per 100g; salted herring: 230 kcal per 100g.
540 Dugmore et al. 2012, p. 3659.
541 Arneborg et al. 2012(b), pp. 128–129.
542 Nelson et al. 2012(c), p. 110; Naumann et al. 2014(b), p. 324.
543 Nelson et al. 2012(c), p. 110.
544 Cf. Chapter 5, pp. 253–254.
545 Nelson et al. 2012(c), pp. 110 and 115.
546 E71 and E167 have been counted together, which gives nine items in the list below.
547 Enghoff 2003, pp. 36 and 94–95.
548 Nyegaard 2014; section 8.1.1, Representation of seal species.
549 Arneborg et al. 2012(a), p. 20; Vebæk 1992, p. 95.
550 Arneborg et al. 2012(a), p. 24.
551 Enghoff 2003, pp. 36 and 94–95.
552 Enghoff 2003, pp. 36 and 94–95.
553 Enghoff 2003, pp. 36 and 94–95.
554 McGovern et al. 1993, p. 64.
555 Smiarowski 2012.
556 30%, 36%, 39%, 39%, 40%, 50%, 60%, 61% and 82%.
557 On seal as food, cf. Chapter 5, pp. 281–283.
558 McGovern 2000, p. 336. McGovern 1985, pp. 101–102.
559 Arneborg et al. 2008, p. 151.

326 *Subsistence food production*

560 Arneborg 2003(c), p. 10.
561 Enghoff 2003, pp. 89 and 36.
562 Arneborg et al. 2012(b), p. 128.
563 Nyegaard 2014, section 9.2, The general picture.
564 McGovern et al. 1996, p. 106; 1.0× as many bones from goats and sheep as from cattle (1025–1150), 1.6× (1150–1200), 1.3× (1200–1250) and 1.2× (1250–1325).
565 Arneborg et al. 2012(a), p. 29; Arneborg et al. 2008, p. 151.
566 Smiarowski 2012, p. 11; Degerbøl 1930, pp. 183–192.
567 *Det gamle Grønlands beskrivelse af Ivar Bárdarson*, p. 26.

6   One land – two societies

In the decades prior to ca. AD 1410 the Inuit settled increasingly close to where the Norse lived. In this final chapter an attempt will be made to describe the resulting interaction and discuss how it ended.

1   Inuit attitude to violence

Despite persistent efforts in the last 30–40 years the hypothesis that the Norse settlement ended its existence in an ecological crisis has not been verified. This makes it necessary to submit the alternative hypotheses to more serious analysis. Conflicts with the Inuit are today normally seen as a secondary cause for the ruination of the Norse community. Is it possible that this conflict should be raised to the primary cause?

Who exploited Greenland's resources most efficiently?

The Norsemen and the Inuit both produced their food and other daily necessities within the framework of a subsistence economy. The prevailing hypothesis in the last decades has been that the Inuit had knowledge of food resources in Greenland and technologies to exploit them which the Norse with their European background lacked. This made it possible for the Inuit to survive better in the Arctic environment than Norse households.

Norse and Inuit food production has to be discussed in a long chronological perspective. Humans started to settle along the Norwegian coast ca. 11000 BC, and in the following 7000 years people there learnt how to survive by combining terrestrial and marine hunting, supplemented with the gathering of plants. From ca. 4000 BC agriculture was gradually introduced. This did not mean that they abandoned hunting, but they now had to learn how to combine hunting and fishing with agriculture. When Norwegians settled in the North Atlantic islands they had 12,000 years of experience of how to combine terrestrial and marine hunting, and they had 5,000 years of experience of how to combine marine hunting, terrestrial hunting and agriculture. Agriculture grew increasingly important, but in AD 985 fishing and hunting were still an important part of their food production.

Some non-Scandinavian scholars lack this background knowledge and think that the Norse in their motherland lived from agriculture only, while the Inuit lived from hunting only. In reality the Norwegian immigrants brought expertise in hunting and fishing with them to Greenland, and when Norse met Inuit after ca. AD 1250, the Norse had been adapting this expertise to the Greenland environment for nearly 300 years. The Norse exploited agricultural, hunting and fish resources; the Inuit practised hunting and to a limited degree fishing.

The Norse had iron to make tools. The Inuit realised that metals were useful, and after the Norse had disappeared, the Inuit dug for valuables at abandoned farms, and they were most interested in metal. But there are no indications that the Inuit during 1250–1410 bought iron from the Norse or tried to learn how to operate a smithy. Numerous Inuit objects have been found at Norse sites, but practically all of them may have been brought there by the Inuit after the former Norse inhabitants had disappeared.[1] Numerous Norse objects have been found at Eskimo sites, but they seem to be the result of Eskimo treasure hunts at abandoned Norse sites. Neither archaeological nor written sources give "unambiguous evidence that the two peoples lived side by side in the two Norse Settlements".[2] The two peoples lived isolated from each other and there was no room for trade and learning.

Arneborg claims that the Norse closed themselves off from impulses from the Inuit because they saw their own culture as superior. This was dangerous complacency which prevented them from adapting to the Greenland environment effectively. The real reason may be that the Norse in their centuries-old tradition found answers to the ecological challenges they met in south-west Greenland.[3]

Seal hunting is often presented as a field where the Inuit had special skills. The Norse used both harpoons and sealnets. The Inuit used harpoons, but did they also use sealnets in the period before ca. 1410?[4]

In 1934 the Danish archaeologist Therkel Mathiassen published an excavation he had made in Disco Bay. There he found what he identified as a sealnet made of baleen, evidently made by the Inuit.[5] He dated the net with traditional methods to before AD 1500.[6] In his PhD from 1997 the Nationalmuseum archaeologist Hans Christian Gulløv radiocarbon dated the same sealnet to the 16th century.[7] Mathiassen thought that "the obvious thing to do is to place it among the elements which the Eskimos learnt from the Norsemen".[8] Gulløv is a specialist in Greenland Inuit history, and he commented in 2004:

> Seals seem to have been caught with nets around Disco Bay from the 16th century. This method was probably introduced by the Norse settlers (*nordboer*). It has so far not been possible to verify that catching seals with nets was practiced by Eskimos elsewhere in the Arctic, but it is still a moot point where the technique came from.[9]

The Hollanders started their whale hunts in Disco Bay in 1614, which means that the Inuit cannot have learnt to use sealnets from them.[10] Mathiassen and Gulløv defended the "politically incorrect" view that the Inuit learnt from the Norse how to become more effective seal hunters.

In his diary from 1723 Hans Egede wrote that he let one of his servants make a couple of sealnets because he wanted to experiment with them. This indicates that the Inuit did not use them, at least not in the Nuuk region.[11] The Inuit's use of sealnets needs further investigation.

The Inuit at first only used fish-spears in their fishing for char and salmon in south-west Greenland, and this fishing gear can only be used in shallow waters. "Arctic peoples" in Canada built dam-like constructions made of rocks across streams to stop or trap migrating fish, and they speared fish which concentrated in front of the dam. Similar technologies may have been used by the Greenland Inuit.[12] The Norse in addition to fish-spears used handlines with sinkers and hooks which could be used in deeper waters. They knew how to use, and may have used, nets and seine-nets for freshwater fish. Fishing increased in importance for the Inuit as they moved southwards along the west coast, but Gulløv does not discuss whether this may be due to more effective fishing gear which they copied from the Norse.[13]

The Inuit did not change the Greenland environment, they only skimmed the cream off the milk by hunting reindeer, seal and other prey which lived in Greenland before the Inuit arrived. The Norse altered the Greenland environment to make it more productive for humans. They imported animals which did not belong in the original Greenlandic fauna: cattle, sheep, goats, pigs, dogs and horses.

They also imported new plant species to feed these animals, and it has been estimated that ca. 13% of all plant species growing in Greenland today were imported by the Norse. Some of the imports may have been planned, and the peasants could burn the original vegetation in a certain area and sow seeds for plants suitable for fodder. Other plants may have come as fodder for domestic animals on the voyage across the Atlantic, and the later diffusion in Greenland was not necessarily planned. Near their dwelling they cultivated meadows which can still be identified in the landscape. Norse "infields" were more fertile when the Norse disappeared than when they arrived, and still are today.[14]

Norse technology and expertise made it possible for the Greenlandic environment to support more people than it did when only Inuit technology was used. The Norse created an ecology which in modern terminology could "sustain" a larger population.

The 21 farms from the Eastern Settlement in Table 5.5 in Chapter 5 had on average 12 cattle. My estimates of the Norse peasants' food consumption in the Eastern Settlement were 57% milk products from cows, 6% from goat milk, ca. 3% cattle meat, ca. 1% sheep and goat meat; in total 67% of a household's calorie needs came from domestic animals. The remaining 33% came from reindeer (ca. 2%), seal, cod, char and plants which cannot be quantified. The quantifiable sources of food in the Western Settlement were ca. 33% from cow milk, ca. 6% from goat milk, ca. 2% from cattle meat, ca. 1% from sheep and goat meat; in all 42% of an average household's calorie needs came from animal husbandry. The remaining 58% came from reindeer meat (ca. 7%), seal, cod, char and plants and possibly walrus meat from their *nordrseta*, for which no quantification is possible.

The Norse skimmed the cream off the milk through their hunting and fishing just as the Inuit did, but more than half of their subsistence food production came from their cultivation of the environment.[15]

The Norse belonged to an agricultural tradition where a large part of the food production took place on private land. It was the farmer's ambition to make his land more productive than it had been when he received it, and he knew from his forefathers how to do it. Part of the production also took place on common land and in fjords and lakes open to all. In Norse Greenland "the commons" were so large that it in practice could not be exploited in a manner which was unsustainable. This combination of private resources, which were intensely cultivated and protected, and common resources, which functioned as a food buffer open to all who had the manpower to exploit it, favoured productivity, that is production per household.

Norse technologies and methods for food production gave a higher production per household and a wider range of products. The Norse could therefore be more choosy in the foods they consumed. The Inuit's main fare was seal meat. In Norse eyes this was second rate food and they consumed it in larger quantities only when more attractive food was unavailable.[16] Seaweed was eaten by the Inuit all year and was in fact nourishing.[17] The Inuit dried capelin/*ammassæt* on the cliffs and used it as winter food for humans,[18] but the Norse carried it to the meadow as fertiliser or used it as fodder for animals. Only the Inuit ate sculpins. When the Inuit gradually moved to villages and small towns established by Danish colonial authorities after 1721, they also started to eat more food produced in agriculture, and these products evidently satisfied them better.

Modern industrialised societies can transform the natural environment to make production for human needs more effective and daily life more comfortable and predictable. Western societies have in the last centuries developed from being forced to adapt to the natural environment, to being manipulators of the same environment. Today's ecological situation has been given a name, "the Anthropocene". The first example of the word "Anthropocene" in *The Oxford English Dictionary* is from 2000, and the word's definition is "the time during which human activity is considered to be the dominant influence on the environment, climate, and ecology of the earth".[19] In the period 985–1410 the human capacity to transform the environment was in its initial phase. The Norse transformed the Greenland nature and fauna from the moment they settled there, but it has not been verified that the Norse exploited natural resources in Greenland in a way which was not sustainable.

The Inuit and Norse Greenlanders were on different stages in a development towards "the Anthropocene" of the present time. The Inuit hunters had no ambition to change the natural environment in Greenland. Their food production did not require it. The Norse intervention in the natural conditions was not profound, and their productive work was more adaptation based on experience rather than transformation. They knew which problems could arise when they used pastures and meadows which had a thin humus layer, but they also knew that by manuring with dung and bog soil and spreading their pasturing animals over a larger area, they could compensate for it and protect and increase fertility. It was still a long way to "the Anthropocene" with man-made changes which had deep and unpredictable consequences.

How exposed were the Inuit to starvation?

In the Norse period ca. 985–1410 no contemporary written or archaeological source informs us about social conditions among the Greenland Inuit. But in 1721 the Norwegian missionary Hans Egede settled for 15 years near today's Nuuk, and he wrote a detailed diary where daily life and the mentalities of the Inuit are described. He also wrote a description of Greenland which was later continued by his sons Poul and Niels. In 1721 direct European influence on Inuit daily life had not yet started.

At the east coast between Cape Farewell and Ammassalik the hunter communities retained much of their original character until the end of the 19th century. From 1904 Knud Rasmussen (1879–1933) and others collected information from the Inuit who had lived there until 1900. At this time ethnography was emerging as a scholarly discipline, and Knud Rasmussen was its most prominent representative in Greenland. He was born and grew up in Ilulissat where his father was a parson. His great strength was that he spoke fluent Greenlandic and could talk to the Inuit about any subject. His weakness was that he lacked the methodological training which is necessary in scholarly ethnography. He wrote down stories told by the Inuit without subjecting them to source criticism and analysing them in relation to social questions.

Rasmussen made notes of his conversations with the east coast Inuit shortly after they had taken place. These notes still exist and show that in his book from 1906 "Under the whip of the northern wind" (*Under nordenvindens svøbe*) he followed them closely. He did not use the narratives to argue for a hypothesis, which makes the narratives descriptive and more useful for later scholars. And finally, his book was published two years after the interviews had taken place in 1904, and at that time the informants were still alive and could check the content.

Rasmussen's book from 1906 contains stories which the Inuit informants meant to be factual, but also stories which they meant to be fiction. The same goes for Rasmussen's *Notes on the Life and Doings of the East Greenlanders in Olden Times* which were edited and published after Rasmussen's death.[20] Each story has to be subjected to individual source criticism. In most cases it is evident to which category a story belongs. Rasmussen sometimes gives the name of the person who told the story and writes that he or she was present when the events took place. The informant had what a historian would call first-hand knowledge. I will consider such events as having taken place, unless special circumstances make me conclude otherwise. In other cases the informant is not named, or the story is said to have been transmitted through several people. In such cases I shall only accept the event as real if it is confirmed by other independent sources.

Egede and Rasmussen had a positive attitude to the Inuit as individuals, but they were critical about their attitude to violence. Egede was a missionary and made great efforts to make the Inuit accept and practise Christian ethics. Rasmussen was a nationalist and thought the Inuit would have a better life if they adopted Danish social norms. Both shared the values of the time in which they lived. Egede and Rasmussen understood Inuit attitudes to violence as created by the society in which they lived. Their interest in relations between social environment and mentalities makes their writings useful as sources for modern historians and social anthropologists. Both interviewed people who were little influenced by European values and practices. In this section Egede's and Rasmussen's narratives will be used as sources in an anthropological discussion of starvation and violence among the Inuit.

The Inuit's dependence on seal and reindeer hunting made them vulnerable. Their seal hunt could fail, resulting in "a distress sometimes so severe that people died of starvation". The parson in Ammassalik Christian Rosing told Knud Rasmussen that there was periodically hunger in the surrounding area.[21] Winter ice could become thick and covered by deep snow, which made winter hunting of seal through blow-holes in the ice impossible. If the wind did not blow the ice from the east or west coast in spring, the winter ice remained longer there than usual and could make the seal hunt poor.[22] If they could not get hold of nourishing food, they would start eating food without nutritional value, but which could remove the feeling of being hungry. They ate skin by cutting pieces from their skin clothes, skin kayaks and skin umiaks.[23] But Rasmussen does not provide any evidence of general starvation which resulted in collective deaths, where he verifies his claims by giving precise information about time, place and names. His claims of this happening are unspecified and general and cannot be accepted as verified.

The basic social unit in traditional Inuit society was the nuclear family, and the head of the family was hunter and breadwinner. Several nuclear families formed one hunting group. In winter the group lived in a large stone and turf house which normally had room for around 30 people but could have as many as 50.[24] In summer each nuclear family would live in its own tent and move to where hunting was best. The breadwinner was responsible for providing food for his own nuclear family, and helping other members of the hunting group was more or less voluntary. If the family's hunter no longer functioned or the nuclear family was expelled from the hunting group, it could be difficult for them to survive.

The hunters chased seal in their kayaks, and there was a high mortality rate among them. If the breadwinner died and nobody else was willing to feed his widow and orphaned children, the situation of the latter was precarious.

Age pyramids from the east coast in the 19th century reveal that a significant number of newborn girls were killed. These murders were meant to secure a balance between the number of breadwinners and persons to be fed.[25] Egede had met the same attitude 150 years earlier on the west coast. He wanted to educate some Inuit boys as preachers at the colony, but their parents often refused to let them go because they needed them as hunters. Girls were no problem.²⁶ In 1379 the Inuit attacked and killed 18 Norse people (*menn*), and made 2 boys (*sveina*) slaves.²⁷ They may have abducted the boys because they wanted to train them as hunters.

There was a lack of food at regular intervals. "In such situations there was a high risk that widows and orphans might be killed or left behind at a site when the hunting group made its seasonal itinerary, to die from hunger".²⁸ Rasmussen had a positive attitude to Inuit society, but this did not make him suppress stories which clearly disturbed him because they told of the callous deprivation of food to kill people. One of Rasmussen's informants was the Inuit "Susanne" who arrived from the east coast ca. 1885 and was interviewed by Rasmussen in 1904.

> The people from the Ammassalik region showed no mercy towards those who had lost their parents or breadwinner. They left children and half-grown youths on the uninhabited coast because they did not want to be burdened with nourishing them. When the young ones tried to enter the umiaks, they were thrown ashore and there were fights each time they left a camp. Those which the leader of the group had decided should remain behind, threw themselves at the umiaks when these were pushed into the water. But the crew of the umiaks beat them unconscious with their oars and left them to die from famine, if they had not thrown themselves into the sea before it got that far.²⁹

When Susanne lived at the east coast, umiaks from the Ammassalik district passed her home region. She therefore had some knowledge of them, but she does not say that she had seen what she described. It must have been general knowledge in her region.

In 1824 German missionaries founded a colony at Fredriksdal a short distance west of Cape Farewell.³⁰ East coast Inuit at that time sometimes paddled westwards to trade in Nanortalik, and when they passed Fredriksdal they could leave unwanted members of the group there. The church register from Fredriksdal mentions widows, orphans, stepchildren and seriously ill people. The missionaries gave them economic support. This was known in east Greenland, and created the possibility for unwanted members of a group to survive.³¹ Some also settled in the earliest Danish colony on the east coast called Ammassalik founded in 1886. Food security and a pacified society made Danish colonies a safe place.³²

Knud Rasmussen was told numerous stories of cannibalism, but none of them can be verified using accepted methods of source criticism. Referring to general knowledge, he claims that in times of famine the Inuit ate humans who had died. "The survivors then ate the bodies of their fellow villagers to avoid suffering the same fate. Undoubtedly there are people still living today who have had to resort to cannibalism".³³ But the fact that the stories were told to Rasmussen and claimed to be true, says something about mentalities. Fictional stories about cannibalism were popular,³⁴ and they should be seen as horror stories disclosing deep fears about what could happen if they were left alone without food and lamp oil in a dark and cold house. In 1723 Hans Egede wanted to row around Cape Farewell to the east coast, but his Inuit rowers refused because they claimed that people there killed foreigners and ate them. Egede comments that he did not believe it, and he thought it was a fabrication because they wanted to return home.[35] He was probably right, but such stories were part of Inuit folklore.

Expulsion motivated by a wish to get rid of members whom the hunting group did not want to feed, was also practised on the west coast two centuries earlier. In March 1724 Hans Egede visited a family of husband, wife and children who had been told by the leader (*angekok*) of their hunting group that the husband would die the following summer. This was probably to be understood as an order to leave the group and possibly a threat. The family had to leave the hunting group's common house, which was made of stone and turf, and live separately in a tent during the cold winter and spring months.[36]

In March 1726 Egede learnt about a mother who died shortly after having given birth to a baby. None of the other women in the hunting group who could breast-feed and foster the baby, accepted to do so. The father then put the baby in the same grave as its mother, where it died. He claimed to have no choice because he lacked milk or other food for the baby. Egede gave the community a scolding when he learnt about this.[37]

Even solidarity within the nuclear family had its limits. Poul Egede in his diary tells of a leprous woman who was left by her family on an islet to die from starvation, but another family found her and brought her ashore and gave her food.[38] These are not examples of starvation for lack of food but rather starvation caused by exclusion. In Poul Egede's diary 1734–1740, Niels Egede's diary 1739–1743 and Niels Egede's description of Greenland from 1769 there is no mention of starvation for general lack of food.[39] But exclusions may have a background in the excluded person's reduced ability to do productive work.

Hans Egede gives numerous examples in his diary (1721–1736) that individuals or families who suffered hardship came to the colony[40] and received food and in some cases lodging there.[41] It is possible that people who earlier were excluded from their hunting group, which did not want to be responsible for feeding them, now received help which enabled them to survive.

Niels Egede describes how west Greenland society had changed in the 48 years since his father arrived there in 1721. An increasing number of the Inuit had settled in or close to the Danish colonies. This was partly because the missionaries encouraged them, since this made it easier to organise preaching, religious education and divine service. But the Inuit also moved to the colonies because there the authorities would give them food in situations where they were threatened by famine. According to Niels Egede, the colonies gradually came to function like social security offices.[42] Hans Egede started a development in 1721 which increased food security among the Inuit on the west coast.

From the Norse period before 1410 there is one source which demonstrates that the Inuit even then reduced the size of their hunting groups through exclusion and death by starvation. The Icelander Bjørn Einarsson wrote a diary and excerpts from it have been preserved. When he sailed along the Greenland coast in 1385, he found a brother and a sister, both young, on a reef which was submerged at high tide. It is not said where Bjørn picked them up, but it is likely to have been between Cape Farewell and Eiriksfjord where we know that Bjørn sailed and lived during his two years' stay. Bjørn calls the boy and girl "trolls" in his diary, which word was used in Old Norse about humans who did not live in society but out in nature and were not Christian. There can be no doubt that they were Inuit. In fiction written in Iceland "trolls" sometimes appear on the east coast of Greenland, and they must also have been Inuit.[43]

The brother and sister swore an oath of loyalty to Bjørn. They were good hunters and provided their master with all kinds of prey. The girl was a good nurse for Bjørn's child. Both committed suicide by throwing themselves from a rock into the sea when Bjørn left for Iceland and did not permit them to go with him.[44] It is possible that Bjørn did not understand their situation. They had probably first lost their parents, then they were excluded from their hunting group which tried to drown them, and finally they were rejected by Bjørn and his wife.

The availability of resources may have been better for the Inuit in the Norse period before 1410, and may have deteriorated in the following period. From 1614 Hollanders started a large-scale whale hunt on the west coast of Greenland. At the end of the 18th century Inuit started to buy firearms, and in the following century the reindeer stock was exterminated in the most populated parts of Greenland.

Summing up, "death through exclusion and starvation" was being practised before 1410. After 1721 the Danish colonies provided a security net which made it less practised on the west coast, but reduced resources may have made it more practised on the conservative east coast.

Only one hunger crisis in a Norse Greenland community is described in an extant source. "At this time it was a very bad year in Greenland, the hunters who had gone on hunting expeditions had caught little, and some had not returned". At Herjolvsnes a magician predicted that "this bad year will only last this winter, and in spring the harvests will improve ... The contagious disease will also end before you expected it". The author adds that "the weather soon improved as the magician had predicted".[45] This episode is found in an *Islendingasaga*, it is peripheral to the main story and is likely to be fiction inserted to make the saga exciting. The Icelandic author does not say that people died from starvation.

Reasons for temporary declines in Norse food production were discussed earlier:

- The quantity of winter fodder of hay which was harvested depended on the length of the growing season for plants and summer temperatures.
- If spring arrived later than usual, the fodder could run short, domestic animals died, humans became undernourished and vulnerable to contagious diseases.
- The reindeer hunts depended on the animals' chances of finding food under snow and ice to survive in winter.
- Fishing depended on sea temperatures which were determined by air temperatures and ocean currents. If sea temperatures sank near the surface, fish could spawn or feed in such deep waters that they were out of reach of Norse handlines.
- The seal hunt depended on ice conditions in the fjords.

The peasants avoided famine by relying on many food resources, and it was highly unlikely that all of them failed in the same year. The Norse were sedentary, and this made it possible for them to store large quantities of dried fish, meat and butter as a reserve for lean years.

Both the Norse and the Inuit had to create a balance between population size and food production, but they did so differently. The Norse had a reservoir of technologies, resources and working time which enabled them to increase food production when the population increased. Traditional Inuit hunting society obtained the same balance by limiting or reducing the size of their hunting group to what the breadwinners could feed.

Violence to demonstrate power

A commonly used definition of "violence" is "use of physical force which has not been authorised by the state", but this definition does not function in a stateless society. In this book I have found it most fruitful to use "violence" in the sense "use of physical force by one or several individuals after a decision which the perpetrators made themselves".

Both Inuit and the Norse Greenlanders lived in societies without a state. Each nuclear family and hunting group had to defend its interests with violence if necessary.[46] These groups had one or several leaders who created internal discipline by using force. The oldest evidence of this is an entry in Hans Egede's diary from June 1725. At his colony near present day Nuuk they were visited by some "evildoers and murderers" who were feared by members of their own group and by the Inuit living in the colony. Egede was warned against them but declared that he would punish them if they harmed anybody while they stayed at the colony. The following day they left in their umiaks.[47]

Leaders punished offenders in their own group. In 1732 a woman near Nuuk was accused of having killed several persons by magic. Some local people stung her to death, cut off her limbs, removed her heart and threw it all into the sea. They had also done this to another woman a couple of years earlier.[48] Hans Egede's son Poul was the missionary priest in Disco Bay. He wrote in his diary 19 January 1739 that an angekok (shaman) in present day Ilulissat had accused an old woman of sorcery, and helped by others he killed her with knives between her ribs. Next they cut her limbs from her body to prevent her reviving.[49] Another woman at the same place was also accused of sorcery. Some of those present told Poul that she was drawn naked out of her bed where she slept at her husband's side at night.

> They killed her with stones to her head and stung her with knives. They wanted to cut her in pieces, but to prevent it her husband threw himself over her. But they threatened to kill him if he did not leave her, and he had to leave her and dared not even weep.[50]

The most common motive for a killing seems to have been revenge for harmful magic. People who believe that magic can kill will think such murders should be

One land – two societies 337

punished like any other murder. But magic is impossible to prove, and one could therefore suspect that the real motive was something else. Leaders demonstrated their power by killing members of their own group.

Some murders were revenge for an offence which even today would be punishable. A woman killed her husband to marry another man, but afterwards she dared not leave her house because she feared a revenge killing.[51]

The last traditional hunting group consisting of 38 persons arrived in Fredriksdal from the east coast in 1900. As mentioned earlier, Rasmussen interviewed several of them in 1904. Their leader had earlier had a rival for leadership called Kunigsarfik. In 1895 the leader's brothers and sisters died and the leader accused Kunigsarfik of having killed them by magic and had him expelled from the hunting group. Kunigsarfik and his nuclear family fled northwards, and nobody saw them again. Rasmussen's informants about this were ordinary members of the group which arrived in 1900.[52] They were the last representatives of the traditional Greenland hunter culture.

Sadism

Niels Egede tells a story of 16- to 17-year-old boys who played together. One of them behaved in a way which the others found silly, and they started hitting him with stones until he died. When the children told their parents how silly the dead boy had behaved, the parents laughed and did not chastise their children.[53] They educated their children not to feel empathy.

Knud Rasmussen was also told murder stories which express lack of empathy and even sadism. Some of them were told by named individuals who had arrived from the east coast in 1900 and who told their stories to Rasmussen in 1904 and later. This makes them credible, and Rasmussen insisted that they were realistic.

> No people have been given a history more sinister than the memories of the Eskimos. They have been made so by the bitter struggle for survival. Earlier authors have always emphasised that their good-natured and peace-loving nature is what characterises them most. They were so good and decent! Yes, they are good-natured and they thirst for peace – after all. That is admirable. But don't forget that they are above all humans who are shaped by the nature in which they live.[54]

The Greenland nature was brutal and could make its people brutal. This way of thinking was part of the nationalist understanding of human nature. The following stories were told by "Besuk" to Knud Rasmussen in 1904. She was one of the members of the last hunting group which arrived from the east coast in 1900.

> Christian was the leader of the hunting group and he ruled by terror. He shot his wife half dead after a quarrel, then asked a small boy who played near by to give him his arrow and finished her off by pushing it though her throat. Next he skinned her, cut off her limbs and threw the corpse into the sea. After

having murdered another woman he ate her heart raw. He was not the only one to use brute force. The woman Katiaja seriously wounded a widow and left her half dead and suffering in the snow until another woman finally killed her with a large stone. After her mother had been killed before her eyes, the four year old daughter of the dead widow was killed by being crushed against a stone.[55] Christian finally killed Katiaja.

When Katiaja had been killed, everybody thanked the murderer: "Thank you, thank you, now she is out of our thoughts". They said this to flatter Christian, because they all feared him.[56]

This final comment from "Besuk" shows that she did not accept the violence of Katiaja and Christian, at least not after she had moved west to the Danish colony Fredriksdal and been baptised.

When Christian planned to kill a member of his group, he told the victim a couple of days beforehand to prolong its anguish.[57]

Rasmussen quotes three old women he had talked to and who regretted that a quarrel one of them had witnessed at Umivík did not escalate into a revenge murder. That would have made an exciting story which the old woman who was there, could have told as entertainment at future get-togethers.[58] Niels Egede accused them of having "a hard heart against all creatures, and they can with pleasure and delight cut up animals which are still alive".[59]

The Inuit were educated to become hunters. Animals were there to be killed, and the hunter ought to feel a satisfaction in killing. This attitude also had a religious dimension. According to Rasmussen, the central point of pre-Christian Eskimo religion was that the world was full of evil forces. Struggling against these forces and uncovering sorcerers were part of the angekok's tasks.[60]

Fear of being killed

According to "Besuk" fear prevented members of her former hunting group from expressing their disapproval of their leader's violence.[61] Another member of Christian's and "Besuk"'s hunting group was 15 years old when he arrived from the east in 1900. He was interviewed by Rasmussen in 1904. He had just been baptised and said that "One feels so safe here among Christians, because here one is not constantly anxious to be killed. I never felt safe on the east coast because my father was dead".[62] He said "among Christians" but what really protected him was the Danish state. Parson Rosing in Ammassalik on the east coast confirmed this to Rasmussen: "they lived in a constant state of suspicion that someone would murder them".[63] Rasmussen himself ends his chapter on the east coast homicides with the following words:

> Now there is peace, and people's minds have calmed down. And it is a blessed feeling, the feeling of security when one is out in a kayak, with no thought – and no need to think – of anything but seals and the other game to be caught.[64]

The Dutch hunted whales in the Disco region from 1614, but they rarely sailed inside the outer islands, because they feared being attacked by the Inuit, and they did not sell firearms to the Inuit.[65] The Inuit reciprocated; they did not trust Europeans. When the ship of Captain Ross visited the settlement at Thule in 1818, the Inuit sent their women up in the mountains. In 1823 the English captain Clavering visited the island which today bears his name on the east coast. They met 12 Inuit who stayed there four days. On the morning of the fifth day the Inuit had disappeared without warning, perhaps because they feared the visitors.[66] And not without reason, earlier Inuit had been abducted and sent to west European cities to be exhibited. In Inuit hunter society, people seem to have lived in an atmosphere of fear.

The social background

Both Inuit and Norse society were stateless, which means that households and larger networks had to use violence to defend themselves in internal disputes. But there was an important difference: the Norse had institutions for peacemaking. Most important were the Gardar Thing and in normal circumstances the Brattahlid chieftain, who later became the king's lawman. The Inuit lacked such institutions. The blood feud between the Brattahlid chieftain and the visiting merchants in the 1130s ended when peasants present at the Gardar Thing decided that peace should be concluded with the payment of fines.[67] A Thing assembly which imposed peace and afterwards protected the weaker household, made it possible for the losing party in a feud to survive at his farm. A blood feud between the Inuit was more difficult to stop because individuals or networks external to the conflict and with power to impose their will, felt less obliged to interfere.

The other conspicuous difference between Inuit and Norse violence is the sadism in Inuit society and which is only comprehensible if seen against the background of the Inuit's training as hunters. They transferred their handling of animal prey to human victims. The attitude of Norse households to animals was different. Their main task was to take care of their domestic animals and make them thrive.

Internal violence in Inuit hunting groups often had its origins in fear of not having sufficient food for all members of the group. This could make them reduce the number of mouths to be fed by removing them from the hunting group. The Norse combined more independent sources of food, which made them better prepared to survive a crisis in one of these sources. Fear of famine is not known to have been a cause of violence in Norse Greenland or other Norse societies in the North Atlantic.

For these reasons violence seems to have been more accepted in Inuit society than in Norse society in the relevant period ca. AD 985–1418.

2 Norse encounters with the Inuit from beginning to end

The most prominent Norse Greenland archaeologist of the last decades has been Jette Arneborg. According to her, "The idea that the Eskimos devastated the Norse settlements in south western Greenland must be abandoned on the basis of the sources used [in my PhD]".⁶⁸ "In time the discussion has become subtler, and today there is no one who believes Inuit attacks were crucial".⁶⁹ The argument "no one believes it" is not valid in a scholarly discussion. If "subtler" means that the number of unverified hypotheses has increased, this makes the work of falsifying or verifying them more laborious, but it does not favour any of the hypotheses. The only scientifically valid criticism of a hypothesis is that it has less support in the empirical material than alternative hypotheses. For Arneborg conflicts with the Inuit were a reality but a secondary problem. This is at present the commonly held position. Archaeologists make little or no use of written sources. They have created a discourse based mainly on archaeological sources which in practice cannot be used to verify ethnic violence.⁷⁰

By giving a harmonious picture of the past, the Nationalmuseum archaeologists may also hope to contribute to harmonious relations between the Inuit and the Danes in today's Greenland. From the 1970s American scholars have participated in the debate, and in America it has become politically incorrect to conclude that "native Americans" behaved aggressively. In a university tradition it is an ideal that scholarly research should be free from political influence.

Did the Inuit exterminate the Dorset?

The Inuit arrived in North Canada in the 11th century. The Eskimos who lived there already have been named the "Dorset" by scholars. They disappeared and were replaced by the Inuit ca. AD 1000–1200.⁷¹ DNA analyses verify that the two ethnic groups were genetically different.⁷² American scholars from the Smithsonian Museum comment that "The nature of contact between these peoples remains an unresolved question in the archaeology of the region".⁷³ When a common name for Dorset and Inuit is needed in this book, "Eskimo" will be used.

The Inuit settled on the Greenland side of Smith Sound in the 13th century and met Dorset hunters who had lived there since ca. AD 800. The Dorset disappeared from archaeological sources ca. AD 1300.⁷⁴ The archaeological material cannot tell why the Dorset disappeared from Greenland. Alternative, unverified hypotheses for both Canada and Greenland are that climatic changes favoured the Inuit, or that the Inuit pushed the Dorset into less favourable regions where they starved to death, or that the Dorset were killed in violent confrontations with the Inuit.

In Canada there was an Inuit tradition which said that the land was originally occupied by a people called Tunit. It was written down by the American anthropologist Franz Boas in 1888. Scholars have assumed that this was a distant memory of the Dorset. The essence of the narrative was that the Inuit took the Tunit's women and houses and forced the Tunit to leave the country.⁷⁵ The tradition states that the Inuit used violence against the Tunit, but does not say that the Inuit killed them.⁷⁶

The Dorset people lived in skin tents in summer and houses of turf or snow in winter. "Dorset settlements of the Viking period were generally limited to one or two houses of perhaps 8–10 people each", that is 8–20 men, women and children in each settlement. The early Inuit needed more manpower because of their whale hunts. Their settlements "consisted of several houses and were probably occupied by thirty to forty or more people".⁷⁷ In violent conflicts the Inuit would in most situations be able to mobilise more armed men than their Dorset opponents. On a small or middle Norse farm there would normally be households of ca. six people, more at the farms of chieftains, rich farmers or on name farms with several households. In confrontations with both ethnic groups the Inuit would be numerically superior.

The Norse and the Inuit AD *985–1341*

The Icelandic clergyman Ari Frodi (1067–1148) wrote his *Islendingabok* ca. 1130, and he is the first to mention the Greenland Eskimos. He claims that Eirik Raudi and his followers ca. AD 985:

> [f]ound remnants of dwellings for humans in both the Eastern and Western Settlements and fragments of skin boats and objects made of stone. This made them understand that there had formerly lived the same kind of people (*thess konar thjod*) as those who live in Vinland and whom the Greenlanders call *skrælinga*.⁷⁸

Ari got his information about Greenland from his uncle Thorkell Gellison who visited Greenland some time in the period 1050–1090. Thorkell evidently had not told Ari about meetings with living *skrælinga* in Greenland. If the Norse had met them, Ari would certainly have mentioned it. From this it must be concluded that at the time of Thorkell's visit no meeting had taken place between the Norse and the Dorset. The first meeting between the Norse and the Eskimos must have taken place after ca. 1050.⁷⁹

The next source to mention Greenlandic Eskimos is the *Historia Norwegie*, which was written ca. 1150 or shortly afterwards at a Norwegian cathedral, probably Nidaros.

> North of the Greenlanders, hunters have come across "small men" (*homunciones*) whom they call *Scrælinga*. If they are stung with weapons and survive, their wounds grow white without bleeding, but if the wound is fatal the blood scarcely stops flowing. They are totally without iron and employ walrus teeth as missiles, sharp stones as knives.⁸⁰

"North of the Greenlanders" means "north of the Western Settlement". Archaeologists claim that Eskimos at this time only lived north of Melville Bay, which means that Norse explorers had sailed far north. This would not have been a problem with ocean-going Viking ships, but it may have been more problematic but not impossible with a *sexæringr*.⁸¹

When did this encounter take place? It must have been before ca. 1150. The story about how the Eskimos bled is not realistic and may have been retold and "improved" through several narrators. It may be a distant memory of voyages of discovery which had taken place at the end of the 11th century. A safe assumption is that the first meeting between the Norse and the Eskimo in Greenland took place sometime during 1050–1150.

The Eskimos are called *homunciones*. *Homuncio* may mean a physically small man, or a person of inferior value mentally. In the first case the word emphasised that the Eskimos were different from the Norse and in the second case that they were inferior. Since physical strength was an important quality to the Norse, it is possible that both meanings are relevant. The information that the Norse stung the Eskimos with weapons, indicates that the early encounters were not always peaceful.

Ari, *Historia Norwegie* and the Vinland sagas should be seen in context. The Greenland Norse in the 11th century made voyages of exploration to distant destinations northwards to Melville Bay and south-westwards to Vinland in search of new resources. But the results were poor, partly because of enmity from the natives. They withdrew and contented themselves with the Western and Eastern Settlements and the *nordrseta* for hunting.

The King's Mirror written ca. 1250 has a long section on contemporary Greenland. Most attention is given to the voyage, and it was a manly feat to have crossed the Greenland Ocean. No mention is made of Eskimos. If the Norse had traded peacefully with them or struggled against them, it would certainly have been mentioned. This must mean that the Inuit had not yet started their push southwards from Smith Sound past Melville Bay, and that the Norse had ceased their voyages of exploration to this area.

During the 13th century the Dorset disappeared from the western half of Greenland, and the Inuit became the only Eskimo people there. The Inuit had umiaks and kayaks which the Dorset lacked, and could therefore cross Melville Bay and move southwards towards the Norse hunting grounds around Disco Island. In 1266 the clergy at Gardar received information from hunters that the Inuit had reached the Nuussuaq peninsula in the northern part of the Disco region. In 1267 the clergy allied themselves with hunters to find out more about the Inuit's whereabouts. They sailed and rowed a *sexæringr* northwards from Nuussuaq and at some islands a short distance to the north of Disco, they found Inuit housing which was still in use. The Norse had found proof that the Inuit now lived between Melville Bay and the Nuussuaq peninsula. Arneborg suggests that the Norse searched for the Inuit because they wanted to trade with them.[82] The impression is rather that their aim was to find out whether it was still safe to continue the traditional *nordrseta* in the Disco region. They were worried – and with good reason.[83]

After 1267 the Inuit must have pushed further southwards, and archaeological excavations have verified that at the end of the 13th century they lived in Disco Bay near Ilulissat.[84] No written source mentions the Inuit between 1267 and 1341, but it may have become increasingly problematic for the Norse to continue their traditional walrus hunt in the Disco region between Nuussuaq and Sisimiut.

Ivar Bárdarson's account 1341–1363

The best single source about the ruination of the Western Settlement ca. 1341 or shortly afterwards is an account written by a priest called Ivar Bárdarson *Det gamle Grønlands beskrivelse af Ivar Bárdarson*. The text presents scholars with methodological challenges which archaeologists have not been competent to handle, and in the last decades there has been consensus among them to discard this source as too difficult. If the ecological hypothesis of the ruination of the Western Settlement is to be accepted, it has to be verified that Ivar's account is unreliable. Ecologist scholars have dismissed it without a methodologically correct source criticism. In an article from 2000, Thomas McGovern discusses "The demise of Norse Greenland" without using Ivar Bárdarson's account. His mention of Ivar Bárdarson at pages 336–338 is name-dropping without analysis. In this case it is evidently a problem that Ivar's account has not been translated into English.[85] Arneborg and others in 2012 implicitly dismissed Ivar's account when they claimed that the Western Settlement was not abandoned until "around 1400", due to environmental and climatic problems.[86] This will be the first attempt to subject it to a thorough source criticism.

On 8 August 1341 the Bishop of Bergen issued a letter of protection for a priest in Bergen diocese named Ivar Bárdarson. He was to sail from Bergen to Greenland to execute some business for the bishop and cathedral in Bergen. The cathedral in Bergen seems to have had a special responsibility for contacts with the Greenlandic, Faroese and Orcadian churches on behalf of the archbishop. The letter is written in Latin and was clearly meant to be read by members of the Greenlandic clergy. The bishop asks the recipients to give Ivar necessary help with his voyage to Greenland, with his business there and with his return voyage. Ice conditions made August the most advantageous season for voyages to Greenland, and we can assume that he set off immediately.[87] If wind and ice were favourable, he probably reached the cathedral at Gardar a month or so later.[88] His business may have required some travelling, and if so he is most likely to have executed it during the following summer of 1342. He may have returned to Bergen in late summer 1342 or alternatively in the sailing season of 1343. We are not told what his business was in Greenland.

Ivar Bárdarson seems to have been a young priest without a permanent position, and he used the following winter of 1343–1344 to travel south to the papal court in Avignon. At this time the popes had developed a practice which made it possible for job-seekers to buy a "letter of provision" there. In such letters the pope asked the church authorities in the job-seeker's home diocese to provide a job for him. A priest named Ivar Bárdarson from Bergen diocese was at the papal court in Avignon on 18 March 1344, and it undoubtedly was our man. He bought a letter which ordered the leader of the king's chapel in Bergen and a named canon of Bergen cathedral to take responsibility for Ivar Bárdarson and see to it that he was given an ecclesiastical office with a stipulated maximum wage in Bergen diocese.[89] He must have returned to Bergen with the letter in his pocket. We should assume that he was given a permanent post in the Bergen diocese, as stipulated in the letter. This may have been either at the king's chapel in Bergen or at a church administered by the bishop.

There are two main hypotheses about Ivar Bárdarson's task in Greenland in 1342. The Norwegian bishops had a legal duty to visit the churches in their diocese, and the norm was that this should be done every third year. Visitations took place at two levels: local bishops had to visit parish churches in their diocese, and the archbishop had to visit cathedrals in his church province if this was feasible.[90] The Norwegian archaeologist Christian Keller has pointed out that Archbishop Pål Bárdarson (1333–1346) was particularly eager to strengthen the organisation in his church province through visitations.[91] On 31 July 1341 the Bishop of Bergen received an order from his archbishop to attend a synod in Nidaros later the same year,[92] and we should assume that the same messenger ordered him to send Ivar Bárdarson to Greenland. This resulted in the letter of protection dated 8 August mentioned above. The same year the archbishop sent a canon from Nidaros as his representative on a visitation to Iceland.[93] Ivar Bárdarson was sent by the bishop of Bergen and sailed from Bergen because he was a priest in that diocese and most ships to Greenland left from Bergen. This hypothesis makes Ivar's mission part of normal church administration at this time.

The alternative hypothesis is that information or rumours had reached Bergen about problems in the Greenland church, and that Ivar was sent to Greenland to verify them.

An independent source confirms that the Norse settlement in Greenland may have had serious problems in 1342. Gisli Oddson was bishop in Skálholt during 1630–1638 and the author of "Annals" which he finalised in 1637. Under 1342 he wrote the following entry:

> The [Norse] inhabitants of Greenland abandoned of their own free will (*sponte*) the true faith and Christian religion, after they had repudiated all honest customs and true virtues, and they turned to the peoples of America (*Americae populos*).[94]

What was Bishop Gisli's source for this information? Most of the information in his "Annals" can be traced back to older annals which exist today, but this information from 1342 is not among them. Many documents belonging to Skálholt cathedral were destroyed by fire some years earlier in 1630. Gisli Oddson worked at the cathedral before that fire and had no doubt read documents which were consumed by fire in 1630. He used written material but also his own memory in his "Annals".[95] It is possible that in 1637 he remembered vaguely a document which had been destroyed in 1630. The term "peoples of America" was used in 1637 but not in 1342. The term used in the burned document must have been *skrælingar*. The Norse used *skræling* about Eskimos, but also about native Americans. Literally the word meant "small people", in Latin sources the word *pygmæi* is used.[96]

It is impossible for us to reconstruct what Gisli had read in that half-forgotten document or piece of writing. But it is likely to have said that at least some Norse Greenlanders in 1342 had problems, and that this had something to do with the *skrælingar*. The year 1342 was when Ivar Bárdarson stayed in Greenland, and the information may have come from him to Skálholt via intermediaries. Gisli evidently did not remember what the lost annals had said more precisely about *skrælingar*. He of course knew that the Norse Greenlanders had disappeared. He

One land – two societies 345

confused the *skrælingar* in Vinland and the *skrælingar* in Greenland and invented the story about emigration to America himself.

None of the two hypotheses about Ivar's voyage have been verified or can be verified. My guess would be that he was sent to Greenland on a visitation, and during his stay he learnt that Norsemen in the Western Settlement had problems with the Inuit. He gave this information to the relevant bishops in Norway as was his duty, and from there it was transmitted to Skálholt cathedral where a note was made of it.

Ten years later Ivar Bárdarson seems to have made a second journey to Greenland. Orm Eysteinsson, who was regent of Norway and leader of the "council of nobles" (*riksrådet*), visited Bergen on 3 November 1354. Also present in Bergen was Paul Knutsson who had been the "lawman in Gulathing" during 1347–1351[97]. This had made him the highest judge in western Norway. On this day Orm ordered Paul to organise a voyage to Greenland on a ship manned by armed warriors,[98] and for this purpose he gave Paul the command over a vessel of a type called *knarri* in Old Norse. The warriors could be the king's retainers, or the retainers of "other men". Paul was authorised to appoint the men who were best suited to the task, but also men who volunteered to participate.

On behalf of the king Orm stated that earlier kings of Norway "have maintained Christianity in Greenland until this day, and we will not let it decline in our days". He uses crusading ideology when he says that he does this "to honour God and for the good of our soul".[99] The background for this expedition must have been some kind of military threat, otherwise a ship full of armed warriors would have been meaningless. The threat also must have come from pagans, otherwise claiming that Christianity in Greenland was threatened would have been meaningless. The only pagans who threatened Christianity in Greenland at this time were the Inuit. The letter was issued in 1354, five years after the Black Death had hit Norway and the expedition must have made heavily felt inroads into the king's coffers.

Ivar must have left for Greenland the same or the following year in 1354 or 1355. A scribe in Bergen after his return ca. 1363 claimed that Ivar was one of those who were "appointed" by the *lagmann* to voyage to the Western Settlement against the *skrellinge*, to force them out of the Western Settlement.[100] It is not said which lawman, and the scribe evidently assumes that potential readers would know. Theoretically it could be the lawman in Greenland, but on the background of Ivar's account being written in Bergen and the order given to the former Gulathing lawman Paul Knutsson in Bergen in 1354, it is more likely that the Bergen scribe referred to him. Paul Knutsson on behalf of the Norwegian crown in 1354–1355 probably ordered Ivar to participate in the planned voyage to Greenland. Ivar at this time probably held a position at the king's chapel in Bergen,[101] and it would be within Lawman Paul's authority to mobilise Ivar Bárdarson for the Greenland expedition. Ivar's previous experience in Greenland was an evident reason for nominating a priest who would be a non-combatant.

Our next information about Ivar is that he was witness to a charter issued in Bergen on 25 June 1364.[102] This is early in the sailing season, and he is likely to have returned to Bergen from Greenland the previous year in 1363 or earlier. After Ivar's return a scribe in Bergen recorded Ivar's oral account about

Greenland. After having written the account the scribe in Bergen added some final comments of his own. Here he calls Ivar "Greenlander". Finnur Jonsson guesses that the scribe gave Ivar this byname because he had lived for a long time in Greenland.[103] He may be right, but it is more likely that this meant that Ivar was born in Greenland. In the realistic and well-informed *Groenlendinga tháttr* two Greenlandic peasants living in Greenland are given the byname "Greenlander": Thorfinn Greenlander and Bjarni Greenlander.[104] Birthplace in Greenland would explain why the bishop found him to be the right person for a mission there in the service of the church in 1341, and why Lawman Paul saw him as a useful local guide in the king's service in 1355.

The scribe in Bergen who wrote down Ivar's account ca. 1364 states that Ivar in fact had followed the lawman to Greenland, probably in 1355. Their task was to chase the Inuit from the Western Settlement. The scribe writes that they reached their destination. It must have been possible for them to sail outside the polar ice and arrive directly in the Western Settlement in the summer of 1355. They could also have made a stop at Gardar before they sailed on. But when they arrived in the Western Settlement they found "neither Christians nor pagans". They found cattle and sheep alive there, which may have survived several winters. They slaughtered "as many as the ships (plural) could carry and sailed home with it, and Ivar was on board".[105] For Ivar, "home" must have been Gardar. It is uncertain how "ships" in plural should be interpreted. If Ivar Bárdarson's account is to be taken literally, the ruin of the Western Settlement was known in Bergen in 1354 when the "crusade" was prepared, and Ivar saw the ruin with his own eyes the following year in 1355.

Ivar Bárdarson seems to have remained in Greenland for some time after 1355, as the church needed his services there. Old bishop Arni of Greenland was alive in 1343 and died in 1349.[106] A new bishop was not consecrated until 1365.[107] The office of Greenland bishop must have been without an officeholder for 16 years during 1349–1365.[108] The new bishop arrived in Greenland in 1368, three years later.[109] In the account dictated by Ivar Bárdarson after his return to Bergen, it is said that he had been the leader of the bishop's residence (*forstander paa biscopsgaarden*) at Gardar in Greenland for many years.[110] This was probably after 1355 when Ivar seems to have arrived in Greenland for the second time, as at that time there was no bishop present there. In 1364 he was back in Bergen and functioned as canon at the king's chapel (*Apostelkirken*). That year he was witness to the charter mentioned earlier and he oversaw the collection of papal taxes in Stavanger diocese south of Bergen.[111] Economic administration had been among his tasks when he led the bishop's residence in Greenland. The most likely hypothesis is that he led the bishop's residence from 1355 and possibly until 1363. He is likely to have born the title *officialis*. When Ivar administered Gardar is not important in our context, but itABC is long enough to give him competent knowledge.

Next to sagas and annals, Ivar's account is our main written source of the history of Norse Greenland. How reliable is it? Ivar Bárdarson dictated his account around 1364, and he must have returned to Bergen from Greenland shortly before. His account has to be subjected to the usual tests of source criticism.

Did Ivar know what he was talking about? After what has been said here, there is no doubt that he did.

Had Ivar motives for lying or speaking the truth? Ivar gave an oral account about the situation of the Greenland church to a scribe who evidently worked at Bergen cathedral. Ivar at this time worked for the king's chapels (*Kongelige kapellgeistlighet*), but he had formerly worked for the cathedral of Gardar. He must have wanted to give correct information so that the right measures could be taken to support church and state interests in Greenland.

The basic principle in historic source criticism is to compare the relevant source to other independent sources. Such sources are the topography of Norse Greenland as experienced today, and as described in other extant sources. Ivar knew the Greenland topography.[112]

Elements in Ivar's account are confirmed by independent, extant documents mentioned earlier. An extant, independent charter (*diplom*) verifies that he was sent to Greenland on a mission for the church in 1341; another independent document which dates itself to 1342 indicates problems in Greenland in that year; and a document from 1354 confirms that the Norwegian king's lawman sent an armed expedition against the Inuit. Documents from 1344 and 1364 mentioned earlier confirm that Ivar had double ties to cathedral clergy and the Royal chapels. No independent document contradicts Ivar's information.

Those who want to put Ivar's account aside and concentrate on the archaeological material, point out that Ivar's account, which he could check and control, was transcribed later after his death, and this leaves open a possibility for misunderstanding. Only transcribed versions are extant today. But this is the situation for most medieval narratives, sagas included. The test for disregarding a source or a transcript of it must be that the manuscript is incoherent, demonstrating that the scribe has not understood the meaning. This is not the case here.

The scribe goes out of his way to convince readers that Ivar is reliable. He gives some short information about the person, as reported earlier. The most incredible part of the narrative and that which the scribe anticipates his readers may be reluctant to believe, is that the Western Settlement is now without Norse inhabitants. The scribe repeats Ivar's words: this is really the case! He feels obliged to give arguments that Ivar is credible on this point. First Ivar lived at Gardar as the manager of the bishop's residence for many years. This enabled him to see with his own eyes the churches and fjords which he describes in the Eastern Settlement and the deserted Western Settlement. Secondly the lawman had appointed him to be one of his followers to the Western Settlement in 1354. This proves that both state and church had shown confidence in him, so he must be a reliable man.[113]

The manuscript ends with some meaningless information about Greenland which clearly does not come from Ivar, must have been added much later and has no source value whatsoever. It looks like an exercise in handwriting written by a schoolboy. This final part cannot be used to detract from the reliability of Ivar and his scribe.[114]

A modern historian using methodologically correct source criticism must agree with the scribe that Ivar Bárdarson's account is a reliable source! It is a serious methodological mistake and demonstrates methodological incompetence to neglect this highly relevant source in a discussion of the ruination of the Western Settlement.

The most important question in the present context is what Ivar saw when he arrived in the Western Settlement. The story of the Inuit occupation of the Western Settlement was well known among the Bergen clergy around 1364 and was evidently seen as permanent. Long descriptions of it would be a waste of parchment, and Ivar's story is therefore brief. The scribe in Bergen wrote:

> Now Inuit (*skrelinge*) have the whole Western Settlement. There are enough horses, goats, cattle and sheep, all are wild, but no people, neither Christian nor pagan. This was told us by Ivar Bárdarson Greenlander, who was leader at the episcopal residence at Gardar in Greenland for many years. He had seen all this, and he was one of those who were appointed by the lawman to go to the Western Settlement against (*emod*) the *skrelinge*, to chase (*drive*) them out of the Western Settlement. When they arrived there, they found no man neither Christian nor pagan, only some wild cattle. They took provisions of wild cattle and sheep as much as they could carry, and they sailed home with it, and the aforementioned Ivar was one of them.[115]

Ivar and his Norse companions did not see any Inuit. This was summer time, and they must have been somewhere in the fjords hunting reindeer and where it would be possible for them to hide if a Norse expedition arrived.

Neither did they see Norse peasants. There were always people at Norse farms summer and winter. The fact that the farms were depopulated told Ivar and his companions that something was wrong. It is said that the domestic animals were wild. This means that nobody had milked them, and summer was the time when the major part of the milk production took place on Norse farms. Neither had anybody collected winter fodder or cared for the cows. The cattle were not herded, they were free to eat the winter fodder in the meadow. Entire Norse households with all their family members could not have moved to the *sæters*, leaving the domestic animals behind. Nobody lived at the farms any more. Where had they gone? They could not have starved to death, as the wild cattle, sheep and goats provided sufficient and good food. Everybody from every farm would not have gone on a temporary journey somewhere neglecting to milk their cows and goats. This would be unimaginable for peasant households. If they had fled when they saw the hostile Inuit coming, they would have rowed or sailed to the Eastern Settlement and related what had happened. The "wild" domestic animals and their disappointment not to find the peasants they were supposed to defend cannot be combined with an orderly migration. Ivar does not say what had been their destiny, evidently because the readers knew the answer. They were all dead.

Who had killed them? Ivar and his companions had been "appointed by the lawman to go to the Western Settlement against (*emod*) the *skrelinge*, to chase them out of the Western Settlement". There is no doubt that the enemy was the Inuit. But the effort failed, "Now the Inuit have the whole Western Settlement". Only one interpretation of the text is possible: an unknown number of Norse peasants had been killed by the Inuit. There were many people on the lawman's expedition to the Western Settlement, and they could control his information.

This was the traditional interpretation of Ivar's text. Why is it not accepted in the archaeological community today? Firstly, Danish archaeological institutions have felt obliged to ideologically support the Danish state's efforts to create harmony between the Inuit and the Europeans. In America it is politically incorrect to present "native Americans" as aggressive. Secondly, archaeologists prefer archaeological sources where they know the methods, and they want to marginalise or exclude written sources where they often lack methodological competence. A scholar who limits him or herself to archaeological sources can verify that the Western Settlement was depopulated in the 14th century, but cannot tell more precisely when and why it happened. In this case the written sources are indispensable.

How did the Norse defend themselves?

"Legitimate violence" organised in Norse Greenland aimed to enforce verdicts and agreements made at the Gardar Thing where both parties were Norse.[116] Until the 1260s no external threats existed. At that time the Inuit came close to the Disco Bay hunting ground and later to the Western Settlement. This added an important new dimension to the Norse society's need for protection against violence. At the same time in 1261 Greenland became part of the Norwegian realm.

There are no traces of organised defence against external enemies either before or after this date. The farms were scattered, and it is not clear whether the king had officials with military duties in Greenland after 1261. Warships did not exist. Large-scale mobilisation was hardly practicable against hit-and-run Inuit raids. Help from Norway would arrive years later, if at all. Thormod Kolbrunarskald's murders in Greenland are described in *Fostbroedra saga* and demonstrate how easy it was to attack isolated farms, one by one. Normally each farm must have been left to its own devices.

One defence measure was the "centralised house" where all or most functions were given rooms in one building complex.[117] An alternative was to move under the protective wings of the largest and most central farms of Gardar and Brattahlid.[118]

The 1662 m high Burfeld (Itlerfissalik) has free view to both Eiriksfjord and Einarsfjord and the two major farms Brattahlid and Gardar. The Danish archaeologist Daniel Bruun mounted it in 1895, and found ruins of two square huts, which he assumed were for watchmen.[119] What were they looking for? It may have been for drifting ice or the Inuit, or both. They may have lit bonfires as signals, as was done in Norway.[120]

In the Western Settlement at the estuary of the Kapisillit fjord there is a small island called Quequertannguaq where a rune inscription has been found, but not interpreted.[121] A watchman on this island would have control of all boats approaching the entrance to this fjord, which is the second most populated in the

Western Settlement after Ameragdla/Lysufjord. He would also have free view to other less-populated fjords. This may have been one of several observation posts in the Western Settlement.

Watch posts as early warning systems and centralised houses which were easier to defend may have been of some help, but it may not have been sufficient if the Inuit organised surprise attacks with a superior number of armed men. This is a situation well known to historians. Peasants have a farm with living quarters, domestic animals and stores of food, and they have to defend it if attacked. If they flee from their farm, they may die from hunger or cold. The means of production for hunter groups were their weapons which were easy to carry, and they lived in tents and other improvised housing. It was easier for them to organise surprise attacks and flee from an enemy who had superior forces. Even if farmers in peacetime had a higher standard of living and were more numerous, they were inferior in armed conflicts.

The situation in northern Norway throws some light on the Norwegian state's methods for defending peripheral parts of the kingdom. Between 1250 and ca. 1450 Carelians and Russians repeatedly raided the northernmost Norwegian administrative regions of Finnmark and Troms. They arrived from the east partly over land, partly by ship and plundered and burned churches and farms belonging to Norwegian chieftains and peasants. In the 10th century before the raids started, the state imposed a duty on peasants along the whole coast to build and man warships (*leidang*). After 1250 they were used against the raiders in the northernmost regions. The ships are likely to have also been used in counter-attacks against the raiders' home bases in the White Sea area. State authorities organised a signalling system by bonfires on mountain tops to warn of approaching enemy ships.[122] It is not clear how effective these measures were. They were organised by local chieftains and state representatives.

When did the Western Settlement cease to exist?

According to the written sources, Ivar Bárdarson saw the deserted Western Settlement in 1355, but possibly as early as 1342. The Western Settlement is most likely to have been deserted by its Norse inhabitants a few years before 1355. How does this correspond with the archaeological material?

Radiocarbon dates are normally given with one "most likely" date, and a margin of error. If a radiocarbon date is to be used to correct a date from a written source (for example 1355), the margin of error has to be included. Is there evidence that Norsemen lived in the Western Settlement after 1355?

- From GUS are five radiocarbon dates of bones from domestic animals; all of them have margins which include the period before AD 1340.[123]
- From W7 Anavik there are also five radiocarbon dates; four of them have margins which include the period before AD 1340. One has a margin of error which is entirely after 1355 (AD 1535–1618). This date is so late that there must be something wrong with the sample.[124]

- From W51 Sandnes there are 11 radiocarbon dates; all 11 objects are bones of Norse humans taken from the churchyard. Of the dates ten have margins which include the period before 1330, and one has a margin of error which is entirely after 1355 (AD 1390–1428). I have learnt that one diverging radiocarbon date is not enough to change established chronologies. The authors are careful in choosing their words; the diverging date "challenges" the "traditional" date of ca. 1350 and "indicates" that the Norsemen's life in the Western Settlement may have continued until about 1400.[125]
- McGovern in his analysis from 1996 of the osteological material from Sandnes uses 1325 as the end date in his tables.[126]
- From W48 Niaquusat the most recent of two radiocarbon dates is 1345–1445.[127] Both margins include dates from before 1355.
- From W54 Nipaitsoq the most recent of two radiocarbon dates is 1340–1470. Both include dates from before 1355.[128]
- From M15 and M21 in the Middle Settlement three cattle bones and two sheep/goat bones have been dated from the period before 1500. All include dates from before 1300.[129]

It cannot be verified either by written or by archaeological sources that Norsemen lived in the Western Settlement after 1355. Archaeological evidence is lacking for Norse inhabitants in the Middle Settlement after ca. 1300. This confirms Ivar Bárdarson's account which claims that the Norse no longer lived either in the Western or in the Middle Settlement when he administered the diocese, which seems to have been sometime between 1355 and 1363.

Did the Western Settlement meet a sudden end shortly before 1355, or was this the endpoint of a long and gradual decline? In the Eastern Settlement shards of broken church bells have been found at several Norse church farms and other farms.[130] In the Western Settlement two church sites have been identified archaeologically, W51 Sandnes and W7 Anavik. At neither were pieces of bronze from broken church bells found, nor has bell metal been found at other Norse sites in the Western Settlement.[131] The Norse may have had time to transport their church bells to the Eastern Settlement;[132] if so the evacuation of these church farms took place in an orderly manner.

The hunt for walrus tusks took place in the region between Sisimiut and the Nuussuaq peninsula. The Inuit started to penetrate this region from the 1260s, and at the end of the century they had a settlement near Ilulissat in Disco Bay.[133] At the same time walrus tusks fell in price at European markets. This may have resulted in fewer Norse hunting expeditions which normally started from the Western Settlement.[134] Most peasants along the fjords in this settlement would own a *sexæringr* which made it possible to evacuate southwards.[135] There may have been deserted farms along the fjords in the last decades before 1355.

Several inland farms existed within walking distance of W51 Sandnes. They were situated eastwards from Sandnes up the Austmannadal and northwards to Kapisillit.[136] Normally Norse farms had separate houses for separate functions, but at the inland farms in the Austmannadal all or most functions were in many cases given rooms in one building complex; they were "centralised". They include the farms W52a, W53c and W53d.[137] Northwards towards Kapisillit there was another centralised farm (W35),[138] southwards W54 Nipaitsoq[139] and GUS. The northernmost farm in the Western Settlement is W8, which is centralised and lies close to an arm of the Inland Ice.[140] The eighth centralised farm in the Western Settlement is W16 Sarqarssuaq situated at the Kangersuneq icefjord. The fjord ends at an arm of the inland ice. The sea close to the farm is normally covered in ice even in late summer.[141]

All eight known centralised farms were difficult to access from the main traffic arteries, which were the fjords, six of them because they were inland farms and two others because they were close to the head of icefjords. Poul Nørlund pointed out that many rooms under one roof saved fuel, but he also thought centralised houses could have been a defensive measure: "feuds with the Eskimos made daily life unsafe. They had to prevent Eskimos from igniting stables and byres, burning the cattle to death. Keeping watch was easier when all rooms were in one complex".[142] Aage Roussell excavated several farms in the Austmannadal. "Did the Norsemen retire to these more out-of-the-way parts, after the Eskimos had begun to embitter their lives on the banks of the fjords?"[143]

At least two (W35 and W53d) and possibly three (GUS) of the eight excavated centralised farms ended their life in a fire. Both were inland farms in the hinterland of Sandnes. The fires cannot be dated but may have been in the final phase.

At W35 there is a corridor from the house entrance up to the living-room. In this corridor there was a fire which included the part of the living-room (room IV) closest to its door. It is possible that someone went through the outer door and into the corridor, starting a fire outside the door to the living-room. This may have suffocated the people who were there. This is only one of the hypotheses which could explain the empirical evidence.[144]

W53d is the innermost farm in the Austmannadal and also the largest centralised house in the Western Settlement. Its fire in the final phase resembles that in W35. Persons may have gone through the main entrance into the corridor (room XVIII).[145] Here they may have started a fire which spread into the living-room (room XXI). The fire did not spread into the three other rooms for humans (rooms XVI, XVII and XIX) which also had exits to the corridor. Room XIX is likely to have been the sleeping quarters. The fire must have incapacitated people who were in the living-room and sleeping quarters. Many objects were found in the living-room (XXI), among them a handsomely carved crucifix, made in Greenland from driftwood, hidden in a bench. A religious rune inscription was also found in addition to 98 loom-weights.[146] In the sleeping quarters (room XIX) "a surprisingly large number of artefacts were found ... in all 147 in addition to 240 steatite shard pieces with a hole", the latter evidently loom-weights.[147] The farm was not evacuated in an orderly manner, if so they would at least have taken the crucifix with them. But the fire was not necessarily started by people coming from outside. An alternative hypothesis is that it started in the living-room (room XXI) and spread into the corridor.

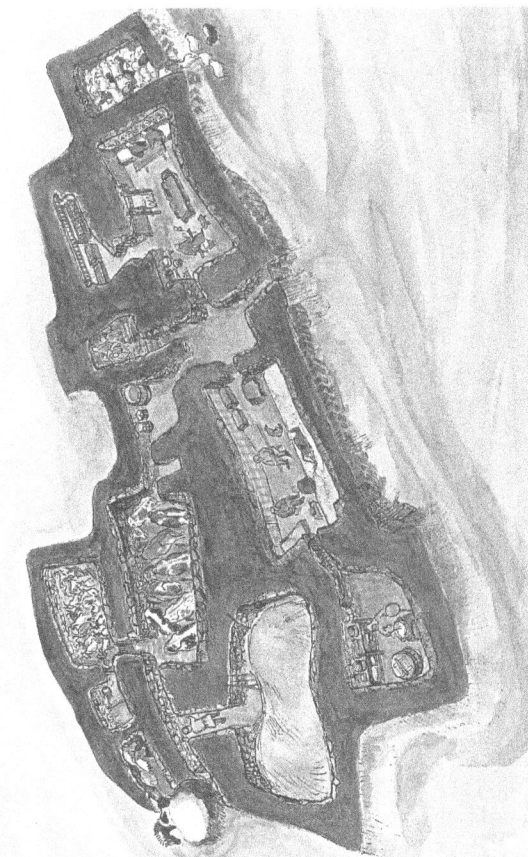

Figure 6.1 W53c in the Austmannadal is an example of a "centralised farm". In this watercolour painting the Danish-Greenlandic illustrator and museum curator Jens Rosing has tried to reconstruct it on the basis of excavations by Aage Roussel (Roussell 1941, pp. 171–179). The farm is 12 km from the inland ice, which is second nearest the inland ice in the Austmannadal (Appendix II, map 2).

Farm W53c had a centralised farmhouse. Eight such farmhouses are known to have been built in the final phase of the Western Settlement's existence. The social background is discussed in the main text.

The dwelling rooms for humans were at the front of the house and for animals mainly at the rear. Walking through the main front entrance one would enter a corridor. Turning to the left from there one would arrive in the main sleeping room. Along one wall there was a 6 m long bench meant for sleeping. Continuing to the next room one would arrive in the "fire-room" (*eldhus*) which was a forerunner for the later kitchen and where cooking and laundry were done. Turning from the corridor to the right, one would arrive in the living-room with a central fireplace. From there one would have access to a small room of uncertain use. Roussell suggested that it may have been the bed chamber for the farmer and his wife. The room to the extreme right also had an uncertain function. Rosing painted it as a stable for sheep. Roussell thought it was a pantry, a store room for winter food for humans. I find the last alternative most likely.

In the section for animals the central room was a byre for cows. They had to be kept warm or they would stop producing milk. It lies snuggly surrounded by the other rooms and had almost no outer wall. The barn was always close to the byre. The other smaller rooms in the animal section must have been for sheep and goats, and possibly a horse.

Copyright: Jens Rosing/VISDA.dk.

354 *One land – two societies*

GUS was also of a centralised type in its last phase.[148] All excavators agree that the domestic animals continued to live at and around the farm after the Norse had left,[149] which confirms Ivar Bárdarson's description of what he saw. In the stable for sheep and goats a 75 cm thick layer of sheep and goat dung was found which the Norse farmer had mixed with turf soil. This indicates that the dung was meant to be used as fertiliser in the spring. At the top was a layer of ashes, wooden coal and burnt turf probably from the roof.[150] In spring before the dung had been carried out onto the meadow, the stable burned down. The whole building has traces of a fire in the final phase. Some excavators suggest that this fire may have been started by accident by Inuit reindeer hunters after the Norse had left.[151] W35, W53d and possibly GUS were the victims of fires in the last phase, but archaeological sources cannot verify how they started.

Figure 6.2 Crucifix excavated at farm W53d in the Austmannadal (Appendix II, map 2). The context in which it was found is described in the text (cf. pp. 113, 145 and 352).

Photo: CC-BY-SA Niels Elswing, Nationalmuseet.

Copyright: The Nationalmuseum in Copenhagen.

Declining profits from the walrus hunt and Inuit threats against their farms may have motivated Norse households to evacuate south to the Eastern Settlement in an orderly manner even taking with them their church bells. But a significant number of Norse peasants must have remained to the end, otherwise it would be difficult to explain Ivar Bárdarson's description of "wild" domestic animals and his reaction when he did not find any Norsemen there.

The Inuit close in on the Eastern Settlement 1379–1406

The Inuit continued their expansion southwards. In 1346 the Skálholt Annals wrote that "the knarri came safely from Greenland with much merchandise".[152] The final destination for the merchandise must have been Bergen, but the knarri may have sailed via Iceland. This is the first time that the annals register a normal journey to Greenland, indicating that at this time it was not a matter of course that a winter stay in the Greenland fjords should run smoothly.

The following year in 1347 the annals reported that a ship with a crew of 18 or 17 had sailed from Greenland to Markland (Labrador), but on the way back they had been driven by unfavourable winds or currents to Straumfjord in Iceland. The ship was smaller than the smallest ships which sailed between Iceland and Norway, and it lacked an anchor.[153] This is the only information in the annals about a voyage to Markland. Why did Greenlanders sail there just then with a ship which may not have been fit for purpose? One hypothesis is that it had now become too dangerous to visit the Disco region, and Norse Greenlanders explored new hunting grounds across the Davis Strait for skins, furs and possibly ivory, using *skutur* and *ferjur* which earlier had sailed inshore up to the Disco region.

In 1379 annals written in Iceland have the following entry: "Inuit attacked violently the Greenlanders killing 18 men, and captured two boys who were made slaves".[154] The Western Settlement had been devastated, Ivar Bárdarson's account shows that the Middle Settlement did not exist when he administered Gardar ca. 1360, so this must have been an attack on the Eastern Settlement. It is the first evidence that the Inuit had reached that far south. "Men" (*menn*) had in Old Norse a restricted meaning of "males" and a wider meaning of "humans". If "humans" is meant, 20 people may have corresponded to three households of middle size.

The following year in 1380 two ships called *Thorlaks-sudinne* and *Olavs-sudinne* left Norway. The first belonged to Skálholt cathedral, the owner of the other is unknown. They ran into bad weather, and *Thorlaks-sudinne* perished on the open sea but some survivors reached Greenland in a lifeboat. *Olavs-sudinne* reached Greenland safely. It is not said whether their original destination was Greenland, or if it was Iceland and stormy weather drove them to Greenland. The travellers stayed in Greenland for two winters, and both crews returned to Norway on board *Olavs-sudinne* in 1382.[155]

The Icelandic farmer Bjørn Einarsson sailed from Norway to Iceland in 1385, but his and three other Icelandic ships were driven off course to Greenland. All four ships stayed there for two winters. An unknown number of Greenlanders emigrated on the unexpected Icelandic ships,[156] and they may have needed time to organise their final departure. The four ships continued in the summer of 1387 to Iceland, where they must have sold the goods they had bought in Bergen, as originally planned.[157] In the summer of 1388 they sailed from Iceland to Bergen,[158] sold their Greenlandic goods,[159] and stayed there during the winter of 1388–1389.

But in May 1389 they were accused in Bergen of trading illegally in Greenland.[160] Bjørn Einarsson then produced two witnesses who told the court that they had lived in Greenland before Bjørn and his companions arrived in 1385. They were probably Greenlanders who had followed Bjørn's ships from Greenland via Iceland to Bergen. Other Greenlanders may have emigrated to Norway or Iceland on the same four ships.

In the 1370s and 1380s Inuit paddled and sailed in their umiaks along the coast of the Eastern Settlement. Evidence for this is the manslaughters in 1379 and the notice in Bjørn Einarsson's diary that he picked up two Inuit youths on the Greenland west coast.[161] The manslaughters in 1379 may have motivated many Greenlanders to leave the island, but they lacked ocean ships. The two ocean ships in 1380–1382 may have been sent for by Greenlanders who wanted to emigrate, and the four ships in 1385–1387 arrived there by accident. Other emigration ships may have arrived without Icelandic annalists – and modern historians – knowing it.

The Nationalmuseum archaeologist Hans Christian Gulløv has argued that the Norse and the Inuit lived harmoniously together. In Sandhavn close to the Norse farm Herjolvsnes he has excavated an Inuit house (house 6) and radiocarbon dated it to 1235–1370. He thinks it was used as a summer settlement. Today's archaeologists agree that house 6 was Inuit, but Gulløv's dating is controversial, and the house may have been from a later period after the Norse were no longer there.[162] He has also argued that there were lively commercial exchanges between the two ethnic groups from the 13th century in the Disco region and later further south, but his sources do not verify this hypothesis.[163] So far there is no evidence that they lived close to each other or exchanged goods. They seem to have kept each other at a distance.

The last ship

The last events in Norse Greenland for which contemporary written evidence has survived, took place 1406–1410. The sources are three charters written in Greenland and Iceland, and four notices in the Icelandic Lögmann Annals.[164] To interpret these sources correctly, it is necessary to know why they were written.[165]

The Lögmann Annals was written at Skálholt cathedral. It is contemporary to the events it describes. It has not been copied from another annal and is therefore considered to be reliable.[166] Notices were entered in Icelandic Annals either because the events they describe were unusual and important, or because they somehow were relevant for the Icelandic church or individual members of its clergy. In this case they describe problems concerning the validity of a marriage and a death penalty for magic. The four relevant entries were also entered in the annals because they describe a visit to Greenland which by now was unusual.[167]

One land – two societies 357

The three charters were preserved because they were evidence in an Icelandic court of justice that a marriage contracted in Greenland was valid. None of the seven relevant sources had as their purpose to describe the situation in Norse Greenland in its final phase.

The sources give short, factual information about details from which it is difficult to draw wider social conclusions. They make it possible to argue that everything was normal, since nothing to the contrary is said explicitly. But it is also possible to argue that there may have been great problems which are not mentioned because they were irrelevant to the Icelandic owners of the documents.

In 1406 an Icelandic ship left Norway, probably from Bergen, and its destination was Iceland. But unfavourable weather conditions forced them to seek harbour in Greenland.[168] One of the Icelanders on board was Thorstein Olafsson. He owned the farm Ökrum in Skagafjord in north Iceland. It should be assumed that the ship was on its way to Skagafjord.[169] Later in 1414 and 1424 two letters were issued where people who had been aboard the ship witnessed events which had taken place during their involuntary stay in Greenland. Both letters were issued at the farm Ökrum. These two extant letters were written and kept because it was in Thorstein Olafsson's interest.

The ship had probably sailed from Bergen to Langanes in north-east Iceland and from there continued along the north coast until they were at the same longitude as Skagafjord.[170] The plan had been to turn south into Skagafjord, but the weather must have made this impossible. They had to continue to the Greenland east coast where they must have turned south to Cape Farewell, finally reaching the Eastern Settlement.

The Icelanders seem to have been accommodated at Hvalsey, which in this late period was probably the king's farm.[171] Two independent charters confirm that one of the Icelandic women on board the ship, Sigridur Bjørnsdottir, was married at this farm on 14 September 1408. The reason must be that Sigridur, and perhaps the whole Icelandic crew, lodged at Hvalsey.[172] The king's representative may have imposed taxes on the Greenlanders to feed the unexpected visitors from Iceland.

One of the Icelanders on the ship was Thorgrimur Solvason who brought his wife Stenum/Sigridur with him.[173] Her father was the lawman Hrafn who had been the supreme judge in Iceland and had died in 1390. This means that she belonged to the Icelandic elite. She went to bed with a man called Kolgrimr, which was a rare name in Iceland, so he was most likely to have been born in Greenland.[174] The annalist writing at Skálholt cathedral claims that Kolgrimr used black magic to control her will. For this he received the death penalty and was burned in 1407.[175]

At this time the law in force in Greenland was a modified version of *Magnus Lagabøte's National Law* issued in 1274. In section IV.3 it says that "a man who runs away with another man's spouse, has committed a crime which can't be settled with a fine [to the king] or indemnity [to the husband]. The king or any man may kill him wherever they meet him".[176] In practice this was a legal permission for the offended husband to kill the seducer. At the same time the law said that if a man who has committed an offence which makes him the potential victim of an honour killing offers to pay a compensation to the offended person, the latter cannot refuse to accept this peaceful settlement.[177] In practice this meant that an honour killing or a public execution could no longer be done legally in such cases. The guilty man paid a fine to the king and the bishop and compensation to the offended person.[178] The reaction against Kolgrimr may have been unusually harsh because he could not afford to pay an appropriate compensation to the husband. Stenum/Sigridur belonged to the elite and her husband was present and no doubt wanted his honour to be restored. Kolgrimr may have been a low-class Greenlander. To make the death penalty agree with the law, the judges may have felt it was necessary to add an accusation of sorcery. Sorcery took the case out of the sphere of offence and revenge, and into the sphere of a crime to be punished by church and state in cooperation. The penalty was death. The verdict was based on the law, and the case cannot be used as evidence that the courts of justice and legality had collapsed in Greenland in 1407.

"Stenum/Sigridur lost her reason, was never her former self, and died shortly afterwards".[179] Her husband returned to Iceland in 1410, and there later sealed a charter which concerned his stay in Greenland.[180]

The following year on 14 September 1408 a marriage took place at Hvalsey between another Sigridur, Sigridur Björnsdottir, and Thorstein Olafsson. The bridegroom Thorstein was the owner of the farm Ökrum in Skagafjördr, as mentioned earlier.[181] He later became a prominent member of the Icelandic elite, and was the highest judge over southern and eastern Iceland from ca. 1421 until he died after 1432.[182] His bride Sigridur must have arrived in Greenland on the same ship, even if this is not said explicitly.

Her legal guardian was a relative of hers called Sæmundr Oddsson. He was also present at Hvalsey when the marriage took place. Like Sigridur he normally lived in Iceland and was present at Ökrum in Skagafjord in 1424. Sigridur and her guardian had probably travelled together from Iceland to Norway and then to Greenland on the same ship.[183]

After they were married Sigridur and Thorstein had a daughter Christine who could expect a large inheritance from her parents. The law said that she could receive this inheritance only if her parents were legally married, and this often created problems. Distant relatives claimed that the marriage of the child's parents was not lawful, and in this way tried to disinherit the child. This was a common type of court case in Norway. Thorstein must have foreseen that such problems could arise when they returned to Iceland. On 19 April 1409, seven months after the marriage, Gardar cathedral's "officialis" Eindride Andersson issued a charter witnessing that he on three Sundays had announced the marriage of Sigridur and Thorstein "in the Holy Church". "There were many respectable people (*mörgum dannamend*) present, both foreigners and natives (*utlendskum oc innlendskum*) but none of them had raised legal obstacles to the marriage taking place". In this case "foreigners and natives" must have meant "Icelanders and Greenlanders".[184] This threefold announcement in church was a procedure required by law for a marriage to be legal. It is not said whether it had been made in Hvalsey or Gardar church, but since the officialis had made it, it was probably in the cathedral.[185] He was the substitute for the absent bishop. This announcement was the only mandatory procedure which had to take place in a church and therefore Thorstein made a priest write the relevant charter. The other marriage ceremonies were secular and could take place in a secular hall or room, in this case at Hvalsey.

In 1410 the ship left Greenland for Norway.[186] It is not said why they did not go directly home to Iceland. In 1414 Thorstein Olafsson had returned to Iceland and took one further precaution to ensure that his daughter Christine received her inheritance. He invited four of the Icelanders who had voyaged with him to Greenland to his farm Ökrum and they issued a charter which said that they had "seen and heard" both the betrothal ceremony and the marriage ceremony which took place on the same day at Hvalsey in 1408. They witnessed that the ritual was performed according to the laws of God and the Holy Church. Sigridur's legal guardian Sæmundr Oddsson had been present and advised her and consented to the marriage, as the law prescribed.[187]

In 1424, 16 years after his marriage, Thorstein Olafsson took his last step to protect his daughter's interests. He invited his wife's legal guardian in 1408, Sæmundr Oddsson, to Ökrum and made him issue a charter where he confirmed that he had advised her (Sigridur) and consented to the marriage as the law prescribed. Sigridur had shaken Thorstein's hand and said "yes" to marrying him, the woman's consent was at this time a condition for a marriage to be valid. Four witnesses who had been present at Hvalsey confirmed this.[188]

The letters verified that all conditions for a valid marriage had been met. The marriage announced in church on three Sundays, the betrothal, the marriage with a handshake where the conditions of the marriage contract were recited, and consent from the legal guardian of the bride and from the bride herself. Thorstein's efforts on behalf of his daughter succeeded. Christine was later married to the Danish king's supreme official in Iceland.[189] To obtain this she must have brought a rich dowry from her parents.

In this period 1406–1410 the farms and churches of Gardar and Hvalsey still functioned, and so did communications along the fjords between them. The Greenlanders were able to provide extra food for perhaps 30 unexpected Icelanders for four years. They probably did not have sufficiently large stores, which means that they organised extra large harvests during these years. Hvalsey and Gardar belonged to the central part of the Eastern Settlement, and it is an open question whether conditions were equally normal in more peripheral regions. The margins of error of radiocarbon dating are too large to be of any help.[190]

There are nevertheless indications of extraordinary circumstances during the Icelanders' stay in Greenland. They stayed there for four winters, whereas earlier Icelandic ships which had involuntary stays in Greenland remained in one case for three winters,[191] and in four cases for two winters.[192] It is also striking that an elite couple from Iceland chose to marry during an involuntary stay in Greenland. Would it not be more natural to wait until they returned to their relatives in Iceland?

One hypothesis is that Thorstein and Sigridur had decided to marry before they arrived in Greenland. Then Sigridur became pregnant, and they had to act rapidly. If the coming child was declared illegitimate, it was given a low position in the inheritance line for her parents' goods. Christine may have been conceived a couple of months before her mother was married to her father. *Magnus Lagabøte's National Law* said that in such cases the child had full inheritance rights from its parents.[193] But the circumstances may have made it particularly important for Thorstein to have evidence that Christine's parents were legally married when she was born. This could also explain the energetic efforts of Thorstein which started seven months after his marriage. Christine was to be his only child. His wife Sigridur is not mentioned in the sources after her marriage, and it cannot be ruled out that she died in Greenland before the ship left, during or shortly after childbirth.[194] Thorstein was the most prominent and powerful of the Icelanders who were stranded in Greenland, and it is possible that he owned or had hired the ship. He may have delayed its departure from Greenland because he did not want to expose his wife and/or child to a strenuous voyage across the North Atlantic. This hypothesis describes an extraordinary situation for Thorstein and Sigridur but suggests normal life in Greenland society.

There is however an alternative hypothesis which gives a more sinister picture of Greenland society in its last phase. The Icelanders may have brought the Black Death to Norse Greenland. Earlier it was thought that the Black Death was spread by bacteria which lived on fleas which again lived on rats. Today it is recognised that the plague-bacteria had two main forms. The abscess-plague could be spread by fleas which did not necessarily live on rats, but found their way to humans and between humans in other ways. The other form was the pneumonic plague where bacteria could spread directly from one human to another. The Black Death could be brought to Greenland even if no rats lived on the ship or in Greenland.[195] Stenum/Sigridur Rafnsdottir died and Sigridur Bjørnsdottir may have died in Greenland. So may other people present in Greenland during 1406–1410 without being mentioned because the annalist and Thorstein Olafsson who dictated the charters saw it as irrelevant. The Icelanders may have stayed for four winters in Greenland because they were waiting for the epidemic to subside.

A strong argument against an epidemic plague in Greenland is that it is not mentioned in the Lögmann Annals. If the Black Death had killed a large number of Icelanders and Greenlanders during 1406–1410, this would have been a dramatic event of the type which is normally included in the Lögmann Annals. These annals are detailed in the years 1400–1430, and were written shortly after the events. The Icelandic annalists were well informed about events in Greenland because of the ship which had stayed there during 1406–1410 and its passengers who returned to Iceland shortly afterwards.[196] The arrival and effects of the Black Death in Bergen in 1349 and in Iceland in 1402–1403 are given extensive coverage.[197] The hypothesis focusing on the Black Death is unverified and so far no empirical material supports it. At present the hypothesis focusing on Christine's birth is better verified. But a methodologically correct analysis has to conclude that we do not know why the Icelanders stayed for four winters in Greenland.

When the last ship left Norse Greenland in 1410 the situation is likely to have been normal in the central area of the Eastern Settlement between Gardar and Hvalsey. The last ship sailed to Norway, probably Bergen. This may have been because they had Greenlanders on board who wanted to emigrate to the "motherland", but the ship may also have returned there because they had on board Greenlandic merchandise which had been produced by Greenlanders who remained at their home farm. These Greenlanders still had much to defend.

When did the Eastern Settlement cease to exist?

The next written source with information on the Norse Greenlanders is from 1448. The letter was written in Rome by pope Nikolas V to the Icelandic bishops of Skálholt and Hólar.[198] The background was that the two bishops had applied for permission to appoint a new bishop and parish priests in Greenland. The last bishop who resided at Gardar died in 1378, and since that time a row of new bishops had been appointed and there was a bishop of Gardar in 1448. None of them visited Greenland. The Catholic Church was at this time corrupt, and the bishop of Skálholt was a disreputable German swindler who never visited Iceland.[199] The intention of the two applicants was probably to sell the title of bishop of Gardar to the highest bidder.

The pope in his letter paraphrases the content of the bishops' application, which included a description of the situation in Greenland. Most of it served to support the application of the two swindlers and cannot be trusted. We are told that many Greenlanders had been killed in an attack, but some survived and now lived in nine parishes. The two Icelandic bishops claimed to have been asked by these survivors to make the application because the Greenlanders wanted to keep up contacts with the Roman church. In practice the two Germans asked for permission to appoint one bishop and nine parish priests.

Only one sentence deserves to be examined closely because it can be reconciled with other independent sources:

> From the close-lying coasts of pagans, more than 30 years ago, a fleet of barbarian ships appeared and attacked cruelly all inhabitants of the previously mentioned people [the Norse Greenlanders], and destroyed the fatherland and its holy buildings with fire and sword.[200]

The sentence makes the following claims about the attack:

- The attack took place more than 30 years ago (*ante annos triginta*). Taken literally this means that the attack took place between 1410 and 1418 or shortly after the last Icelanders had left in 1410.
- The attackers were pagans who lived close to the Norse. This description only suits the Inuit; English fishermen did not live close by, neither were they pagans.
- Parts of the Norse settlement were destroyed with "fire and sword". This is a standard expression; the two German bishops could not know that the Inuit did not have swords! The meaning is evidently that the attackers burned houses and killed people. Among the burned houses were churches.

An independent source here is the Icelandic Lögmann Annals which continued to be written until 1430 and was detailed and contemporary with the events in this period. If dramatic news had arrived from Greenland during 1410–1430, Lögmann Annals would have noted it. But what about the period 1430–1448? The two German bishops of Iceland must have been in contact with some Icelanders even if they had never visited their dioceses. It is not likely that they would tell lies which were contradicted by factual information known in Iceland. The best verified hypothesis is that no news about the fate of the Norse Greenlanders reached Iceland during 1430–1448 either. The two swindler bishops were free to tell lies about the situation during 1410–1448 because no factual information existed to contradict it.

It is not surprising that no Icelanders visited Greenland during 1410–1448. The Icelanders did not sail to Greenland before 1410 either, since there was no exchange of goods between the two countries.[201] All known Icelandic visits to Greenland in the previous century had been due to ships being driven off their correct course on their way from Norway to Iceland. After ca. 1412 English merchants started to visit Iceland, and trade from Bergen to Iceland declined. There was less chance of ships being drive off course to Greenland on their way between Bergen and Iceland.[202]

But the story which the two Germans told at the curia in 1448 has elements which show that they must have talked to Icelanders. The story can therefore be used as a source to the ideas in Iceland about the destiny of the Norse settlements. The Icelanders seem to have thought that the Norse had been the victims of a violent attack by the Inuit, and that houses had been burnt and people killed. From where had they got this idea if no Icelander had been to Greenland and seen it? The most likely explanation is that Icelanders knew there had been violent conflicts between the Inuit and the Norse before 1410, and that the Norse Greenlanders felt the Inuit presence as a threat. They had not received news from Greenland after 1410. From this the Icelanders formulated the explanation which they found most likely.

Can archaeological material verify that the Eastern Settlement had a Norse population after ca. 1418?

> The first attempt to date archaeologically the final abandonment of the Eastern Settlement was made by Nørlund in 1924. He dated what he believed to be a "Burgundian cap" from Herjolvsnes (E111) to the end of the 15th century. Radiocarbon dating was a significant step forward and gave more reliable results. In 1996 Arneborg used the method to date the same cap to 1250–1400.[203]
>
> Radiocarbon dates have wide margins of error. At E47 Gardar there are two late dates (1256–1392 and 1290–1400),[204] and the margins of error are 136 and 110 years. Gardar is known from written sources to have existed in 1410, that is after the last 14C date.
>
> The most comprehensive attempt to date the end of the Eastern Settlement has been done by Koch Madsen, and the main part of his empirical material is from Vatnahverfi. He thinks the Norse started to withdraw from

Vatnahverfi ca. 1250, and the population had contracted markedly "already some time before AD 1400".[205] Ca. 1400 only a few sites were still farmed in Vatnahverfi.[206] Madsen has 52 radiocarbon dates for "the central Eastern Settlement", mostly Vatnahverfi, 50 of them having a start date for their margin of error before 1418 and only two after 1418. These two last starting dates are unpublished and have so far not been subjected to source criticism and therefore have to be left out.[207] Madsen hypothesises that there was a decline until ca. AD 1450, when he thinks the settlement ended. The year 1450 has a weak empirical basis.[208] If written and archaeological sources are seen in context, the verified end date for Vatnahverfi is today ca. 1418.

Arneborg and others analysed 23 human bones from churchyards in the Eastern Settlement in 1999. It could not be shown that any of the 23 was buried after ca. 1410–1418.[209]

Dates from individual farms confirm this general picture. In 2003 Else Østergård dated 12 textiles from burials at Herjolvsnes. None of them has an initial date after 1410. The two youngest were dated 1390–1450 and 1390–1490. She gave the four textiles which have been claimed to be the youngest a thorough analysis and concluded that none of them "with certainty can be dated to after 1400".[210]

Georg Nyegaard has dated the end of Norse settlement at E34 in the Qorlortup valley to "ca. AD 1400" on the basis of pollen data.[211]

The botanist Bent Fredskild points out that juniper, willow and angelica increased in Brattahlid after the Norse peasants disappeared ca. 1410.[212] In the previous period these plants had been kept down by sheep and goats for whom it was attractive fodder.

Arneborg and her co-authors claimed as late as 2012 that "life in the Eastern Settlement continued at least until the middle of the 15th century". This is not supported by their own archaeological material. So far the archaeologists have not falsified the end date suggested by the written sources, which is ca. 1410–1418.[213] A combination of written and archaeological sources suggest that the last Norsemen disappeared from the Eastern Settlement around 1410–1418.

Inuit memories of a vanished society

Memories of a vanished society existed among the Inuit when Europeans returned to Greenland three centuries later. The first to write down Inuit traditions about the Norse was Hans Egede who arrived in Greenland in July 1721. One of his tasks was to find out whether descendants of the Norse population still lived somewhere in Greenland. Egede wrote a detailed diary which he published in 1738.

On 5 March 1722, eight months after his arrival, Egede visited a community of the Inuit who lived in their winter houses not far from Nuuk. They permitted him to stay overnight there and he slept in their large common room. The first evening he had an unexpected experience. After he had fallen asleep:

I heard in my sleep a strange song, screams and noise and which woke me up. But they had put out all their lamps, and it was quite dark. It was terrible to hear how one of their Angekoks or sorcerers sat on the floor and played a drum, screamed and talked now with a coarse, now with a thin voice, now he whistled, now he had a trembling voice like a man who was afraid or frozen and hardly could speak. When he stopped speaking, all the women in the house started speaking in a low and fearful voice, sometimes they started singing. They kept on doing this for a couple of hours, and they half scared me, because I did not know what it meant. None of my people slept in the same house, they were in another house. I could not leave the house because it was quite dark, so I lay quite still and pretended not to hear what they did.

What this monkey business meant I got to know much later when we had learnt some of their language. Then I spoke to some of the people who had been present at that time. The reason was that the Greenlanders feared us, and could not understand why we had come to their country. Then the so called Angekoks, who are their wise men and prophets/soothsayers, had to ask their Tongarsuk (protecting spirit) what we planned to do against them. Had we come to take revenge for what their ancestors in former times had done against our people, who had lived in the country, and whom they had killed? The art of the Angekok and the help of the Tongarsuk should prevent us from carrying out our plans, and somehow bring us misfortune and ruin, since they did not dare to attack us on their own.[214]

This is the first evidence that the Inuit had a tradition that the Norse had been killed by their Inuit forefathers in the distant past. They understood this in a context of manslaughter and revenge, which is a universal way of thinking in pre-state societies. They had no problems accepting that their forefathers had killed people belonging to another group. They also thought it was a natural thing that the Norse sought revenge. Egede was brought up in a state society, and such ideas never entered his mind.

Some scholars have claimed that the idea that the Norse Greenlanders were killed in a conflict with the Inuit came from the Danes who repeated it to the Inuit so often that the Inuit started to believe it.[215] Arneborg writes that "it is worth noting that what the Greenlanders confirm is Egede's own preconceived opinion of the course of events".[216] This was definitely not the case, and only demonstrates that Arneborg has not analysed, perhaps not even read, the written sources which she claims as empirical basis for her hypothesis. There are no indications in Egede's diary that he had mentioned the matter to the Inuit before the event described above. Eight months after Egede had arrived, the Inuit believed so firmly that they now might have to face the consequences of what their ancestors had done, that they organised a séance to protect themselves. Egede definitely had not threatened revenge killings, but the Inuit immediately interpreted his arrival within their own understanding of legitimate responses to manslaughter. It should be seen as verified that there was a tradition among the Inuit before Egede's arrival which said that the Inuit's forefathers had killed the people who had lived in the ruins which still existed, and which the Inuit identified as European.

The following year on 17 February 1723 Egede was visited by two Inuit from the inner fjords of the former Western Settlement and he asked them about Norse ruins there.

> Concerning the ruin of the Norwegian[217] west coast settlements, the Greenlanders tell that the Norwegians were taken by surprise and killed by Inuit's forefathers. Still they can point out a place of memory where they fought, it has been given the name *Pisiktarbik*, that is the place where one shoots with bows. This is in accordance with what is said in old Icelandic and Greenlandic written narratives, that the Norwegian inhabitants of the Western Settlement were overpowered and killed in the 14th century by the *skrælinge*. The latter were wild people which the Norse met in the country and who came from the north.
>
> This narrative was told by a young Greenlander impulsively (*uforvarende*). The old men did not appreciate it, and reproached him, fearing that we would take revenge on Inuit. We let them understand that we knew this beforehand and how it happened, but because it was so long ago we did not care about it any longer. They need not fear that we would harm them in any way, if they themselves did not behave offensively. They accepted this, and told us everything.[218]

The Inuit knew a tradition which said that their ancestors had killed the Norse before Egede had the occasion to tell them that this was so. Again they automatically thought it likely that this would provoke revenge.

Egede's housing was near today's Nuuk in the former Western Settlement, and when the two incidents mentioned above took place, he still had not visited the former Eastern Settlement. After his return to Copenhagen in 1741 he published a "Natural history of Greenland" where he among other things summarised what he had learnt from the Inuit about the fate of "the Norwegians". Here he wrote without distinguishing between the two settlements that the Inuit knew that the extant ruins and their meadows, "had formerly been inhabited by another people than themselves. They confirm that their ancestors had waged war on them and killed them, which confirms what can be read in old narratives".[219] There are no indications that the Inuit distinguished between how the Western and Eastern Settlements had been depopulated.

Scholars have claimed that it is unimaginable that the memory of such manslaughters could survive three centuries in an illiterate society.[220] The durability of memory depends on what supports there are for it. Inuit had before their eyes hundreds of ruins, and the story about the Norse explained how the ruins had been created. Stories connected to material objects which demand an explanation can survive for centuries, but stories about individual Norsemen and Inuit in conflict and friendship are likely to be fiction. It is perfectly possible that the memory of the killing of people who had lived in the ruins could survive three centuries.

Egede's two stories above are taken from the printed edition of his diary which he published himself in 1738 immediately after his return from Greenland to Copenhagen. Today the standard edition is Louis Bobé's from 1925. Here the two stories above were omitted,[221] evidently because they gave a negative picture of Inuit society, and show Egede's prejudices against traditional Inuit religion. In the 1920s it was important to provide historical evidence of harmonious relations between Danish authorities and Inuit communities. The conflict between Denmark and Norway over the uninhabited part of east Greenland lasted from 1921 to 1933. Today's historians should use Egede's original printed diary from 1738 and not Bobés "politically correct" and purified edition from 1925.

Was the end of the Eastern Settlement violent?

Inuit tradition claimed that the end of the Eastern and Western Settlements was violent. Ivar *Bárdarson* claimed the same for the Western Settlement. Archaeological sources can tell whether a church or farm ended its existence in a fire, but it only exceptionally can tell whether the fire started by accident or was started on purpose, and in the latter case by whom.

The largest building with the greatest symbolic value was Gardar cathedral. All medieval cathedrals had an archive of received letters and copies of sent letters. From Norwegian and Icelandic cathedrals numerous written documents have been preserved from the period before 1410. Nothing has survived from Gardar's archive, but one piece of writing, written by the cathedral's officialis, has survived in a transcript which was kept in Iceland.[222] This may indicate that there was no orderly retreat where the staff brought with them the cathedral's valuable objects from Greenland to Iceland or Norway. But that is not the only possible explanation since no documents have survived from the archive of the Faroese cathedral either. The Faroes and Greenland were the smallest dioceses in the Nidaros province.

There is archaeological evidence for church fires in the final phase:

> At Gardar a final fire is well documented. Daniel Bruun reported in 1895: "The church is likely to have been destroyed by fire, since much charcoal has been found in layers over the whole floor . . . A small piece of bell metal was found".[223] Many pieces of bell metal at Gardar were more or less melted, verifying that they had been exposed to strong heat. The Nationalmuseum archaeologists Nørlund and Roussell in 1929 thought this was because attempts had been made to use the metal for casting.[224] But the most obvious explanation is that the bells broke into pieces when they fell down in the final fire, and then partly melted in the flames. Before Nørlund started his excavations both the Inuit and the Europeans, Bruun included, had been digging in the ruins, disturbing the layers. Norwegian archaeologist Schirmer has calculated the height of one of the best preserved bells at Gardar to be ca. 40 cm, which is a bell of moderate size.[225] The church bells had evidently been broken into pieces when the towers collapsed. Nørlund who led the excavations at

Gardar, claims that more than 50 fragments of bronze bells were found, and "hardly a day passed when we did not find one or more pieces of bell-metal, and the Greenlanders often find fragments here and there in the fields when digging or removing stones".[226]

Holm in 1883 wrote that he had excavated part of the Brattahlid church, but the ruin had been badly destroyed by earlier excavations. He found some small shards of metal. He did not identify them as bell metal of bronze, probably because he lacked the competence to do so. Nørlund later identified three pieces as bell metal.[227] The Inuit had evidently searched for and removed other pieces of metal. Holm and Nørlund say nothing about a fire.[228] In the dwelling house of the Brattahlid river farm Bruun found a thin layer of charcoal and many burned bones. He thought it came from fireplaces and shuffled away the coal without first discussing the alternative that it might have come from a final fire.[229]

Hans Egede visited Hvalsey on 29 August 1723. He seems to have dug in the church, but it may also have been in the house beside it. He found some coal and small bones.[230] W.A. Graah in 1828 found charcoal and bones in the church. He hired 21 men for 12 hours to turn over the soil inside the church,[231] and after this treatment the value of the church floor as an archaeological site must have been destroyed. Loose ashes could have been washed away by rain in the following days. The bones were evidently remnants of burials, the charcoal may have been the result of a final fire, or Inuit visitors making a cooking fire. Later bell metal was found at the site.[232]

Bell metal was also found at the church farms of E66 (South Igaliku)[233] and E149 (Vágar?),[234] and at a farm without a church (E64c).[235] E34 was a farm of middle size in the Qorlortup valley behind Brattahlid. It was not a church farm. The uppermost layer had a large content of charcoal. "This could possibly be due to the fact that the farm was burned down when it was abandoned".[236]

Bell metal, some of it melted, has only been found in the Eastern Settlement and not in the Western Settlement. This indicates that the church farms in the Eastern Settlement were not evacuated in an orderly manner. They did not have time to remove their church bells or their archives.[237] Gardar, Hvalsey and probably Brattahlid survived until the end, but the two first and possibly all three, burned in the last phase. These are the three politically most important farms belonging to bishop, king and lawman. E34 close to Brattahlid is also likely to have been destroyed by fire in the final phase.

In the post-Reformation period there were three independent traditions on the fate of the Norse Greenlanders. In Bergen Ivar Bárdarson's description of Greenland was kept in the archives of Bergen cathedral. The account said that the Western Settlement ended in a violent and deadly confrontation with the Inuit but kept open the possibility that the Eastern Settlement still existed. This was the tradition which the Danish administration in Copenhagen and Hans Egede knew.

There was an oral tradition in the Inuit community which said that the people who had lived in the ruined Norse houses had been killed by the Inuit's forefathers in the distant past.

The Icelanders thought that the Norse Greenlanders had been attacked by the Inuit and many of them killed, but this may have been little more than guesswork. It seems that no Icelanders visited Greenland after 1410. All known Icelandic visits to Greenland in the previous decades had been due to ships being driven off course on their way from Norway to Iceland. After ca. 1412 English merchants started to visit Iceland, and trade from Bergen to Iceland declined. There was less chance of ships being driven off course to Greenland.[238]

Archaeological sources are not well suited for a discussion of a possible violent end, but indications exist of a violent end even in these sources. Neither written, nor oral nor archaeological sources confirm claims of a peaceful coexistence followed by an orderly emigration of the Norse from Greenland. The best verified hypothesis is at the present time that the end was violent.

The cause and development of a final confrontation is not known, and hypotheses about it cannot be verified or falsified. But it is possible to point out social mechanisms which may have fuelled a conflict. The Inuit and the Norse both lived in stateless societies where serious conflicts easily escalated into blood feuds. In 1721 the Inuit thought Egede had come to take revenge for killed Norsemen.[239] A blood feud could rapidly become a question of killing your enemy before he kills you. This explains why Thormod killed so many of Thorgrim Trolles male relatives.[240] The Norse peasants living at their isolated farms were not mobile because they had to take care of their cattle, at least as long as the snow covered the ground. In the Eastern Settlement the coast and fjords were normally blocked by polar ice and fjord ice until the end of July. If the Norse saw that their situation was becoming hopeless, ice may have prevented them from trying to escape in their small boats to Iceland. These circumstances make it perfectly possible that the Norse peasants succumbed to a numerically inferior Inuit population.

The sequence of events suggested here will always remain a hypothesis which we lack sources to verify or falsify. But on a more general level, the hypothesis of an ethnic confrontation is today significantly better verified than the alternative hypothesis of an ecological crisis.

Was the end preceded by a slow decline in population?

The archaeologist Koch Madsen has argued that the population in the peripheral area Vatnahverfi in the Eastern Settlement started to decline ca. 1250, when temperatures started to fall. The Norse had almost disappeared from Vatnahverfi by AD 1400.[241]

Population declines are difficult to verify archaeologically. From most farms there will only be one or two dated objects which can only tell the age of the object examined. Close by there may be an undated object with a different age.[242] The large margins of error of radiocarbon dating also make it a challenge to use the method to verify a gradual decline. According to Koch Madsen "interpreting the timing of settlement abandonment is far more difficult than interpreting the evidence for *landnám*".[243] Koch Madsen's lack of empirical evidence for his hypothesis of a slow population decline in Vatnhverfi does not demonstrate that it did not happen, only that the methods existing today are useless for verification purposes.

But if future research should verify that there was a long-term decline in population, it is not difficult to find reasons why. Emigrating to Norway became more attractive. The Black Death hit Norway in 1349, which resulted in deserted farms, and surviving peasants moved to the best farms in central areas. Farms without tenants in Norway may have tempted Greenlanders who lived on peripheral and small farms in Greenland to emigrate. But many may not have wanted to leave the farm and environment they knew, and they did not starve in Greenland. Ship room to Bergen may also have become increasingly difficult to find, particularly if they wanted to take their valuables.

Declining incomes from walrus tusks after ca. 1300 had a larger impact in the Western Settlement, but it must have reduced the standard of living even in the Eastern Settlement. At the other side of the North Atlantic the Norwegian stockfish production and stockfish trade was at its most profitable in the century after ca. 1350.

In the final period of its existence Norse Greenland was short of iron and this complicated their subsistence food production and daily lives. Lack of wood and iron made it impossible for them to build and own ships which would give them control over their contacts with overseas destinations.

The Inuit represented an unpredictable menace and may have motivated the Norse to move closer to large elite farms like Gardar with its 100 cattle, or to the mountains and valleys behind Brattahlid where ruins of numerous small and medium-sized farms can be found. The king's farm Hvalsey may have played a similar protective and centralising role.

The most widely held hypothesis has in the last decades been that the Norse started to leave the Eastern Settlement long before the end because climatic and ecological problems made conditions for agriculture worse.[244]

It has not been verified that there was a gradual population decline preceding the final ruin of Norse Greenland. But there is nothing in the extant sources which contradicts or falsifies that such a decline took place. A slow population decline before ca. 1410 is reconcilable with both the "ecological" and the "ethnic" hypotheses.

Four new methods and four new conclusions

In the Introduction to this book I emphasised four methods which so far have not been exploited as much as their potential permits.

The first was a systematic comparison with the food production along the Norwegian Atlantic and North Sea coast. This has shown that the Norse were skilled peasants who were well prepared to tackle the challenging ecology and falling temperatures.

370 *One land – two societies*

The second was an analysis of the written sources using modern saga criticism, general source criticism and new methods available to schooled historians. The analysis of the written sources made it possible to describe how problematic the relationship was between the Norse and the Inuit and quantify the Norse food production.

Sociological analyses where different social fields were seen in context, demonstrated that the Norse mastered the important subsistence food production, and they made their religious practices and jurisdiction function until the end. What they did not master and control were relations with external military and political powers, in practice a distant state and the Inuit, and this created fatal problems after ca. 1260.

The fourth method was to subject both the dominant "ecological" hypothesis and the alternative "ethnic conflict" hypothesis to methodologically correct verification and falsification. Opposing hypotheses and counter hypotheses have made it possible to conclude that the ethnic hypothesis today is better verified than the ecological one.

3 "We found a rich land, but are not destined to enjoy it"

Eirik Raudi's son Thorvaldr participated in the attempt to establish a Norse settlement in Vinland but was killed by an arrow from a native. Before he died he is reputed to have said: "We found a rich land, but are not destined to enjoy it".[245] The Newfoundland settlement was abandoned shortly afterwards. The leader of the expedition the Icelander Thorfinn Karlsefni and his men "realized that although the land was good, they would always have to fear and live in enmity with those who had settled there before them".[246] Four centuries later Thorvaldr's prediction proved true even for his father's settlement in Greenland.

If the final confrontation with the Inuit had been avoided, could the Norse settlements have survived? The subsistence food production still functioned, that was so for animal husbandry, hunting of reindeer and seal, and fishing for cod, char and salmon. For light and heating they obtained lamp oil from seal and whale, and they could build small boats for communications in the fjords and close to the coast. At the Gardar Thing they could settle disputes and keep their society pacified. They practised their religion as they had been in the habit of doing for centuries, which confirmed their identity as Norse and Europeans. They seem to have organised this basic economic, social and cultural framework on their own until their settlement ended.

But the Greenlanders in the final century gradually lost control of the political and military framework of their society. Norse Greenland was founded in AD 985 as a pre-state society and it remained so to its end. Norway was also a pre-state society in AD 985 but developed in the following centuries into a state society. For the Greenlanders it was not practicable to organise a state of their own, and their alternative was integration into the new Norwegian state. Norway was unable to administer Greenland as a province, partly because the communications were so problematic and partly because population and taxes there were so small that they could not finance a provincial administration. Greenland was part of the

Norwegian state, after 1380 of the Danish state, but did not receive state services. The Inuit challenge demanded military support from a state, but the Greenlanders never received it.

Ecologist scholars think the Norse Greenlander lost a struggle against the environment. Those who focus on ethnic conflicts think they lost a struggle against a competing ethnic group. Both alternatives have their basis in social and political models which are relevant today. But this does not necessarily mean that the scholars' conclusions are determined by their political preferences. In this book both models have been used as hypotheses which have been tested against all relevant empirical material which is available today. Verification according to the scholarly methods of history and archaeology showed that the "ethnic conflict" model explained what actually happened better than the "ecological" model. This may change in the future.

Notes

1 Arneborg 1991(a), p. 149.
2 Arneborg 1991(a), pp. 155–156.
3 Arneborg 2004, pp. 274–275.
4 Cf. Chapter 5, pp. 277–279.
5 Mathiassen 1934, pp. 95–96, figure 44.
6 Mathiassen 1934, pp. 86, 96 and 177–178.
7 Gulløv 1997, p. 439.
8 Mathiassen 1934, p. 97.
9 Gulløv 2004(b), p. 329.
10 Gulløv 1997, p. 439.
11 Egede/Bobé, p. 76.
12 McGhee 1990, p. 124. Photograph of how Canadian Inuit practiced it in *Handbook of North American Indians*, volume 5 Arctic, pp. 399 and 421; Gulløv 2004(b), p. 318.
13 Gulløv 2004(b), pp. 296 and 328–329; cf. Porsild 1919, pp. 9–16.
14 Ostenfeld 1926; cf. Chapter 5, pp. 252–254.
15 Figures from Chapter 5, conclusion, pp. 301–302.
16 Cf. Chapter 5, pp. 281–283.
17 Rasmussen 1938, pp. 131–132.
18 Egede/Bobé, p. 228, dated 12 July 1729; Egede Bobé, p. 361.
19 Oxford English Dictionary, "oed.com". The word was entered in the "oed.com" in 2014, and OED's first example is from AD 2000.
20 Rasmussen 1938, pp. 1–215.
21 Rasmussen 1938, pp. 63–64.
22 Rasmussen 1938, pp. 63–64 and 50, cf. Rasmussen 1906, p. 131.
23 Rasmussen 1906, pp. 131, 187.
24 Rasmussen 1938, p. 48.
25 Lund Jensen 2014, pp. 115–125. His empirical material is from eastern Greenland in the 19th century.
26 Egede/Bobé, p. 231.
27 IA, VIII Gottskalk, year 1379.
28 Lund Jensen 2014, pp. 100, 116 and 120.
29 Rasmussen 1906, pp. 178–179.
30 Lund Jensen 2014, pp. 50–51.
31 Lund Jensen 2014, pp. 67–68, 120–121 and 124–125.
32 Lund Jensen 2014, pp. 53–71.

33 Rasmussen 1938, p. 64.
34 Rasmussen 1938, pp. 65–67, cf. pp. 186–188.
35 Egede/Bobé, p. 45, date 26 August 1723.
36 Egede/Bobé, pp. 118–119; 12 March 1724 and 14 March 1724.
37 Egede/Bobé, p. 182.
38 Egede, Poul Diary 1734–1740, p. 81; 15 August 1739.
39 Egede, Poul Diary 1734–1740; Egede, Niels, Diary 1739–1743; Egede, Niels, Description of Greenland.
40 A locality where there was a missionary or representatives for the Danish state, was called a "colony".
41 Egede/Bobé, pp. 191–304.
42 Egede, Niels, Description of Greenland, pp. 236–237 and 243.
43 *Jökul tháttr Buasonar* IF XIV; *Flomanna saga* IF XIII, p. 290. Cf. index of this book, entry words "troll" and "wild people".
44 "Grænlands annal", p. 45; GHM III, pp. 438–439.
45 *Eiriks saga Rauda* IF IV chapter 4, pp. 206, 208–209; English translation: CSI chapter 4, pp. 5 and 7 and Penguin chapter 4, p. 33.
46 Cf. Chapter 2, pp. 49–50.
47 Egede/Bobé, p. 169.
48 Egede/Bobé, p. 256.
49 Egede, Poul Diary 1734–1740, p. 69.
50 Egede, Poul Diary 1734–1740, p. 81 .
51 Egede, Poul Diary 1734–1740, pp. 81–82.
52 Rasmussen 1906, pp. 114–115.
53 Egede, Niels: Description of Greenland, p. 245.
54 Rasmussen 1906, p. 117.
55 Rasmussen 1906, pp. 121–132.
56 Rasmussen 1906, p. 128.
57 Rasmussen 1906, p. 126.
58 Rasmussen 1906, pp. 180–181.
59 Egede, Niels: Description of Greenland, p. 245.
60 Rasmussen 1938, pp. 70–71.
61 Rasmussen 1906, p. 128.
62 Rasmussen 1906, p. 130.
63 Rasmussen 1938, p. 75.
64 Rasmussen 1938, p. 89.
65 Gad 1984, p. 146.
66 Gulløv 2004(b), p. 307.
67 *Groenlendinga tháttr* IF IV chapter 6, pp. 288–289; English translation: CSI chapter 6, p. 381.
68 Arneborg 1991(a), p. 156.
69 Arneborg 2003(b), p. 117; cf. Arneborg and Seaver 2000, p. 282.
70 Gulløv 2000, pp. 321–322; Arneborg 2004, pp. 274–276; McGovern 2000, pp. 327–339. His mention of Ivar Bárdarson at pp. 336–338 is name-dropping without analysis.
71 McGhee 1990, p. 73.
72 Appelt 2004, p. 200.
73 Odess et al. 2000, pp. 198–199.
74 Gulløv 2004(a), p. 216.
75 Gulløv 2004(b), p. 297.
76 "Inuit" is the name used about the ethnic group, in its early phase also called "proto-Inuit". "Thule culture" is the name used by archaeologists about this ethnic group's culture in the period ca. AD 900–1500. I have chosen to use the name "Inuit" about them from their first appearance until the present time since it is the same ethnic

group with a continuity which is biological, cultural and linguistic ("Thule culture" in Wikipedia; "Thule culture" in britannica.com).
77 Odess et al. 2000, p. 199.
78 *Islendingabok* IF I, chapter 6, pp. 13–14; English translation: chapter 6, p. 7; Norwegian translation, p. 54.
79 For relevant information on *Islendingabok*, cf. Chapter 1, pp. 14–15.
80 *Historia Norwegie*, p. 55.
81 Chapter 3, pp. 136–138; Chapter 4, pp. 186–188; Chapter 6, pp. 342–341.
82 Arneborg 2004, p. 274.
83 A detailed description of the expeditions is found in Chapter 3, pp. 137–139. Cf. GHM III, pp. 238–243; "Grænlands annal", pp. 53–54.
84 Meldgaard 1995, pp. 207–209 and Gulløv 2004(a), p. 217.
85 Gulløv 2000, pp. 321–322; Arneborg 2004, pp. 274–276; McGovern 2000, pp. 327–339.
86 Arneborg et al. 2012(a), p. 4.
87 DN V no. 152.
88 Chapter 4, pp. 194 and 198.
89 DN XVII nos. 59a and 59b = RN V nos. 688–689.
90 KLNM entry word "Visitation".
91 Keller 1989, p. 267.
92 DN VII nos. 182, 185 and 186 = RN V nos. 463, 479 and 480.
93 IA, VII Lögmann, 1341, p. 273.
94 GHM III, p. 459.
95 Storm 1890, pp. 351–357.
96 GHM III, p. 459; Storm 1890, p. 357; Keller 1989, p. 268.
97 Cf. RN V, index; DN XII no. 98; DN II no. 295.
98 The titles of the men on the ship shows that they were military personnel: in Norwegian *håndgangne menn, svenner, høvidsmann, mestermenn*.
99 DN XXI no. 83.
100 *Det gamle Grønlands beskrivelse af Ivar Bárdarson*, p. 30; hand vor en aff thennom, som vor udneffnder aff laugmader ath fare till Vesterbijgdt emod the Skrellinge, at udedrifve the Skrellinge udaff Vesterbijgd.
101 DN IV no. 442.
102 DN IV no. 442.
103 Jonsson 1930, p. 7.
104 *Groenlendinga tháttr* IF IV chapter 6, p. 290; English translation: CSI chapter 6, p. 382.
105 *Det gamle Grønlands beskrivelse af Ivar Bárdarson*, p. 30.
106 IA, VI Skálholt, year 1368, p. 228; in 1368 a new bishop called Alfr arrived in Greenland, and then Greenland had been without a bishop for 19 years, "*Herra Alfr byskups kom til Grænlands hafde dar verid biskupslaust i 19 ár*". This means that Alfr's predecessor Arni died in Greenland in 1349, the year of the Great Plague in Bergen, but not necessarily from the plague.
107 IA, VI Skálholt, year 1365, p. 227.
108 DN XVII, no. 900. A successor to the deceased bishop Arni of the Faroes received a letter of provision at the papal curia in Avignon on 19 December 1348. It is not clear whether this deceased Arni of the Faroes was the same as the old bishop Arni of Greenland. He must then have been transferred from Greenland to the Faroes without this being registered in extant sources. This is perfectly possible. Kolsrud assumed that the two Arnis mentioned above were the same person (DN XVII no. 900), but Arni was a common name at this time. The successor to Arni of the Faroes mentioned above was also called Arni!
109 IA, VI Skálholt, year 1368, p. 228.
110 *Det gamle Grønlands beskrivelse af Ivar Bárdarson*, pp. 29–30.
111 DN IV no. 442.

112 Cf. Chapter 3, pp. 96–99; Jonsson 1899, 1930.
113 *Det gamle Grønlands beskrivelse af Ivar Bárdarson*, pp. 29–30; DN IV, no. 442; DN XVII no. 59a and 59b.
114 *Det gamle Grønlands beskrivelse af Ivar Bárdarson*, pp. 30–32.
115 *Det gamle Grønlands beskrivelse af Ivar Bárdarson*, pp. 29–30.
116 Cf. Chapter 2, pp. 53–56.
117 Cf. Chapter 6, pp. 351–353; Figure VI.1.
118 Cf. Chapter 5, pp. 258–261 and 270.
119 Bruun 1896, p. 189.
120 Ingstad, H. 1959, p. 47; reprint 2004, p. 40; English translation, p. 31.
121 Nationalmuseet Copenhagen, Korrespondancearkivet, Journalsag 541/68 (p. 6). Rune inscription at Quequertannguaq, Godthåbsfjorden, report written by Ilkjær and Gulløv with photographs.
122 Bratrein 1989, pp. 234–238.
123 Arneborg et al. 2012(a), table 14, p. 34.
124 Arneborg et al. 2012(a), table 15, p. 36.
125 Arneborg et al. 2012(a), table 12, p. 30, cf. p. 4.
126 McGovern et al. 1996.
127 Andreasen 1982, p. 187.
128 Andreasen 1982, p. 187.
129 Edwards et al. 2013, table 1, p. 8.
130 Cf. Chapter 6, pp. 366–367.
131 Bell metal has been found at Inuit sites in the Western Settlement, but they must have come from the Inuit who had excavated them at Norse sites in the Eastern Settlement; Arneborg 1991(a), pp. 105–106.
132 Arneborg 2004, p. 253; Arneborg 1991(a), p. 125.
133 Cf. Chapter 6, p. 342.
134 Cf. Chapter 4, p. 174.
135 Cf. Chapter 4, pp. 186–187.
136 Cf. Appendix II, map 2.
137 Roussell 1941, pp. 159–190; Roussell 1938, pp. 55–64; Figure VI.1.
138 Roussell 1941, pp. 164–167.
139 Andreasen 1982, p. 178.
140 Cf. Appendix II, map 1; Roussell 1941, pp. 167–171.
141 Roussell 1941, pp. 162–164.
142 Nørlund 1942, p. 75; in the English translation it is mentioned that the centralised house type saved fuel, but not that it made defence against the Inuit more effective (English translation, p. 79).
143 Roussell 1936, p. 61; Roussell 1938, p. 56.
144 Roussell 1941, p. 166.
145 Map of W53d in Roussell 1941, p. 180.
146 Figure 6.2; Roussell 1941, pp. 247 and 179–190.
147 Roussell 1941, p. 184.
148 Berglund 1998, pp. 9–10; Arneborg and Berglund 1994, p. 2; GUS was excavated in the 1990s.
149 Arneborg and Berglund 1994, p. 5; Berglund 1993, p. 18.
150 Malmros 1992.
151 Arneborg and Berglund 1994, p. 5; Berglund: *GUS-journal* 1995, 19 June–17 July, p. 7 and 1993, 18 June–17 July, p. 10; Berglund 1998, p. 10.
152 IA, V Skálholt, year 1346.
153 IA, V Skálholt; IX Flatø, year 1347.
154 IA, VIII Gottskalk, year 1379, p. 364.
155 IA, VII Lögmann, year 1282; The chronology in the different annals is confusing. I have chosen to rely on the Lögmann Annals because they were at this time written at

Skálholt cathedral and they should be well informed since they owned the wrecked ship. This means that the two ships must have left Norway in 1380, the survivors stayed in Greenland the winters 1380–1381 and 1381–1382, and returned to Bergen the summer of 1382. The relevant annals are: *Oddaannalar og Oddverjaannall*, p. 180, years 1380 and 1381; IA, VII Lögmann year 1381; IX Flatø year 1382; VIII Gottskalk year 1382; VII Lögmann 1382; IX Flatø 1383.
156 GHM III, pp. 135–142; DN XVIII no. 33.
157 IA, VII Lögmann, years 1384 and 1386; VIII Gottskalk, years 1385 and 1387; IX Flatø, years 1385 and 1387.
158 IA, IX Flatø, year 1389 says that Bjørn Einarsson continued to Norway in 1389. This must be wrong for 1388. The annals often give incorrect dates to real events.
159 GHM III, pp. 135–142; DN XVIII no. 33.
160 Cf. Chapter 4, pp. 212–214; GHM III, pp. 135–142; DN XVIII no. 33.
161 "*Grœnlands annal*", the excerpt from Bjørn Einarsson's diary is printed on pp. 44–46; Chapter 6, pp. 334–335.
162 Raahauge et al. 2003, pp. 51–52 and p. 65; Gulløv 2004(b), p. 316; Gulløv 2008, p. 21.
163 Gulløv 2008, p. 20.
164 Two notices in the Icelandic Oddverja Annals from 1405 and 1408 are word for word identical to entries in the Lögmanns annal which date them differently, to 1406 and 1410. A charter confirming the legality of the marriage of a visiting Icelander was issued in Greenland on 19 April 1409 (DI III no. 597). This verifies that at that time the Icelandic ship was still in Greenland. The Lögmann Annals says that the Icelandic ship left the following year in 1410, which is in harmony with the charter. Oddverja annal says the ship left in 1408, which is contradicted by the charter. The dating in Lögmann Annals has to be trusted.
165 When the extant Icelandic Annals started and stopped being written is discussed in connection with Table 4.1 in Chapter 4.
166 KLNM entry word "Nýi annall".
167 IA, VII Lögmann, years 1406, 1407, 1410 and 1413.
168 IA, VII Lögmann, year 1406.
169 DI III no. 632 = GHM III, pp. 152–154; DI IV no. 376 = GHM III, pp. 155–156.
170 Cf. Chapter 4, p. 195.
171 Cf. Chapter 2, pp. 69–73.
172 DI III no. 632 = GHM III, pp. 152–154; DI IV no. 376 = GHM III, pp. 155–156.
173 Her first name is unclear, but this is not important here; IA, VII Lögmann, p. 288 footnote 2.
174 GHM III, p. 65.
175 IA, VII Lögmann, years 1406 and 1407.
176 *Magnus Lagabøte's National Law* IV.3.
177 NGL I, pp. 121–123 = Norske Middelalderdokumenter, no. 23, pp. 98–101.
178 Nedkvitne 2011, pp. 99 and 227.
179 IA, VII Lögmann, years 1406 and 1407.
180 IA, VII Lögmann, year 1410; DI IV no. 376 = GHM III, pp. 155–156, year 1424.
181 DI III no. 632 = GMH III, pp. 152–154; DI IV no. 376 = GMH III, pp. 155–156.
182 GHM III, pp. 146–147.
183 DI III no. 632 = GMH III, pp. 152–154; DI IV no. 376 = GMH III, pp. 155–156.
184 Cf. Chapter 2, pp. 42–43.
185 DI III no. 597 = GMH III, pp. 148–150.
186 IA, VII Lögmann, year 1410.
187 DI III no. 632 = GMH III, pp. 152–154.
188 DI IV no. 376 = GMH III, pp. 156–157.
189 GHM III, p. 147.
190 Cf. Chapter 6, p. 350.
191 IA, IV Regii, from AD 1209 to AD 1212.

192 *Oddaannalar og Oddverjaannall* year 1381, p. 180; IA, VII Lögmann 1382, 1384 and 1386.
193 *Magnus Lagabøte's National Law* V.7.10; KLNM entry word "arveret", column 265; after the Reformation numerous cases show that the inheritance right of a child which had been conceived by unmarried parents could be disputed, even if they married before the child was born (Nedkvitne 2011, pp. 195–200).
194 Krisitin Seaver in her book *The Frozen Echo* from 1992 assumes that Sigridur followed her husband back to Iceland and describes her new life there. This is an unverified hypothesis, and she does not give a single source in support of it.
195 Karlsson 2000, pp. 111–117.
196 IA, VII Lögmann 1413.
197 IA, VII Lögmann 1349 and 1402.
198 GHM III, pp. 168–175; DN VI no. 527.
199 Johnsen 1940.
200 GHM III, pp, 168–175; DN VI no. 527.
201 Chapter 4, p. 204.
202 Nedkvitne 2014(a), pp. 525–529.
203 Arneborg 1996, pp. 80–81.
204 Madsen 2014(a), table 8.2, p. 232.
205 Madsen 2014(a), figure 8.9, p. 234.
206 Madsen 2014(a), p. 3.
207 Madsen 2014(a), pp. 232–233, table 8.2. From the farm *Undir solarfiöllum*/Sillisit (E23) an object dated 1436–1469 has been excavated, and from a midden at E168 in Vatnahverfi an object was dated to 1454–1618.
208 "The final abandonment of the Eastern Settlement is traditionally dated to around AD 1450, and there is nothing in table 8.2 to oppose this. However, it is clear from table 8.2 that relatively few of the 'terminal' dates extend that far up in time. In fact the majority seems to fall already in the late 13th to 14th centuries"; Madsen 2014(a), p. 233.
209 Of the 23 human bones the most recent was dated by 14C to 1413–1467, which overlaps with the written date. Arneborg et al. 1999, pp. 160–161, table 2.
210 Østergård 2003, pp. 143 and 253.
211 Nyegaard 2014, section 4.3, Vegetation history.
212 Fredskild 1973, p. 123; he dates this change in vegetation to "560 years before present", that is before 1973, which gives AD 1413. His margin of error is plus or minus 100 years.
213 Arneborg et al. 2012(a), p. 4.
214 Egede, Hans 1738, p. 44.
215 Arneborg 1991(a), pp. 96 and 150.
216 Arneborg 2003(b), p. 118.
217 Hans Egede calls the former inhabitants of the ruins "Norwegians", never "Nordic" (nordbo) as is done by Danish Nationalmuseum archaeologists today.
218 Egede, Hans 1738, pp. 80–91, cf. Egede/Bobé, p. 65.
219 Egede, Hans 1741, p. 316.
220 Arneborg 1991(a), p. 50.
221 Egede/Bobé, pp 17–18.
222 DI III no. 597.
223 Bruun 1896, p. 329.
224 Nørlund and Roussell 1930, p. 149.
225 Nørlund and Roussell 1930, p. 145.
226 Nørlund and Roussell 1930, p. 145.
227 Nørlund and Stenberger 1934, p. 135.
228 Holm 1883, p. 79.
229 Nørlund and Stenberger 1934, pp. 74–75.

230 Egede/Bobé, p. 99, date 20 August 1723.
231 Nyegaard 2009.
232 Roussell 1941, p. 260.
233 Arneborg 1991(a), p. 125.
234 Vebæk 1991(b), p. 75.
235 Arneborg 1991(a), p. 125.
236 Nyegaard 2014, section 4.2, The mire stratigraphy.
237 Cf. Chapter 6, pp. 351, 355 and 366–367; Arneborg 2004, p. 253; Arneborg 1991(a), p. 125.
238 Nedkvitne 2014, pp. 525–529.
239 Cf. Chapter 6, pp. 363 and 366.
240 Cf. Chapter 2, pp. 62–63.
241 Madsen 2014(a), figure 8.9, p. 234, cf. p. 3.
242 Madsen 2014(a), table 8.2.
243 Madsen 2014(a), p. 231.
244 Cf. for example Arneborg 2004, p. 276–278.
245 "*Gott land hofu ver fengit kostum, en tho megu ver varla njota*"; *Eiriks saga Rauda* IF IV chapter 12, pp. 231–232; English translation: CSI chapter 12, p. 17 and Penguin chapter 12, p. 47; Norwegian translation: Norrøn saga V, p. 219.
246 *Eiriks saga Rauda* IF IV chapter 11, p. 230; English translation: CSI chapter 11, p. 16 and Penguin, p. 100; Norwegian translation Norrøn saga V, p. 219.

Bibliography

A large part of sources and scholarly literature on Norse Greenlannd was until the 1990s published in the series "Meddelelser om Grønland". The following abbreviations were used in the bibliographies and references:

MoG = *Meddelelser om Grønland*, ed. Kommissionen for Videnskabelige Undersøgelser i Grønland, volume 1, Copenhagen 1879–volume 205, Copenhagen 1975/77.

MoG, Man and Society = The preceding series in 1980 was split up into several series. Subjects which are relevant in our context were mostly included in *Meddelelser om Grønland, Man and Society*, volume 1, Copenhagen 1980 and following annual volumes.

I have chosen to list sources and literature separately. This is partly because more comprehensive and individual information has to be given for sources, translations to modern languages included, and partly because sources have to be listed according to their title, since the name of the author often is not known.

Sources

Two multi-volume saga editions are used:

IF = *Islenzk Fornrit*. I have chosen to refer to the series Islenzk Fornrit because practically all Old Norse sagas are published there, and because the series is available at most relevant libraries. The references in the footnotes were so numerous that an abbreviation was necessary. My analyses are based on the Old Norse texts in IF.

CSI = *The Complete Sagas of Icelanders* volumes I-V, edited by Vidar Hreinsson, Reykjavik 1997. All "Sagas of Icelanders" (*Islendingasögur*) used as sources in the present book are translated to English in this series. Some of the relevant translations in CSI have mistakes, but it is not my task to correct them. Many university libraries do not have this series, so I have also referred to other English translations when these are commonly used.

Adam of Bremen. The Latin text is edited as *Hamburgische Kirchengeschichte*. Original title: *Magistri Adam Bremensis Gesta Hammaburgensis ecclesiae pontificum*. Series: Scriptores rerum Germanicarum in usum scholarum vol. 2; Edited by Bernhard Schmeidler, Hannover 1917.

   English translation: *History of the Archbishops of Hamburg-Bremen*; Series: Records of western civilization, sources and studies no. 53; Translated with an introduction by Francis J. Tschan, New York 2002, 257 pages.

Norwegian translation: *Adam av Bremen* by Bjørg Tosterud Danielsen and Anne Katrine Frihagen, Oslo 1993. All have the same division into books and chapters.

Ældre Bjarkø-Ræt, Old Norse in: NGL I, pp. 301–336; Norwegian translation by Jan Ragnar Hagland and Jørn Sandnes, in: *Bjarkøyretten*, Oslo 1997.

Alfrædi Islenzk, From a vellum AM 194, 8vo written 1387; printed in: *Islandsk encyclopedisk litteratur*, ed. Kr. Kålund, Copenhagen 1908, volumes 1–3.

Arna saga biskups, in: IF XVII, ed. Gudrun Ása Grimsdottir, pp. 1–207; also incorporated in *Sturlunga saga* II, ed. Örnolfur Þórsson, Reykjavík 1988, pp. 771–882; Norwegian translation, *Biskop Arnes saga* by Gunhild and Magnus Stafansson, Oslo 2007.

Audunar tháttr vestfirzka, in: IF VI, ed. Björn Thorolfsson and Gudni Jonsson, Reykjavik 1943, pp. 361–368; English translation by Anthony Maxwell, in: CSI volume 1, pp. 369–374.

Bárdar saga Snæfellsáss, in: IF XIII, ed. Torhallur Vilmundarson and Bjarni Vilhjalmsson, Reykjavík 1991, pp. 99–172; English translation by Sarah Anderson, in: CSI volume 2, pp. 237–266.

Calendar of the Liberate Rolls, Henry III 1226–1272 volumes 1–6, London 1916–1964.

Chronica Majora authored by Matheus Parisiensis, volume 4 (1240–1247). Edited with an introduction by Henry Richards Luard. In series: *Rerum Britannicarum Medii Aevi Scriptores* 57.4, London 1877.

Clément VI, Lettres closes, patentes et curiales, interessant les pays autres que la France, eds. Déprez, J. and Mollat, G., Paris 1960/1.

Danish Arctic Expeditions 1605 to 1620 volumes I-II, Gosch, C. C. A. ed.; published by the Hakluyt Society, First series, volumes 96–97, London 1897. Reprint Cambridge University Press 2010.

Den norsk-islandske skjaldedigtning, ed. F. Jonsson, volumes A1, A2, B1 and B2. Copenhagen 1912–1915.

Det gamle Grønlands beskrivelse af Ivar Bárdarson, ed. Finnur Jonsson, Copenhagen 1930, pp. 17–32.

DI = *Diplomatarium Islandicum I-XVI*, Copenhagen 1857–Reykjavík 1972.

Diplomatarium Danicum, 1.række, 1.volume–4.række, 4.volume, Copenhagen 1938–1994. Translated into Danish in: *Danmarks riges breve*, 1.række, 1.volume–4.række 5.volume, Copenhagen 1957–1998.

DN = *Diplomatarium Norvegicum I–XXIII*, ed. C. C. A. Lange and others, Christiania 1849–Oslo 2011.

(The) Ecclesiastical History of Ordericus Vitalis I-VI edited and translated by M. Chibnall, Oxford 1972–1980, in this book volume VI is used. Series: Oxford Medieval Texsts.

Egede, Hans 1738 = Egede, Hans: *Omstændelig og udførlig Relation, angaaende den Grønlandske Missions Begyndelse og Fortsettelse: Samt hvad ellers mere der ved Landets Recognosering, dets Beskaffenhed og Indbyggernes Væsen og Leve-Maade vekommende er befunden*. This is Egede's diary from his years on Greenland 1721–36, edited by the author, Copenhagen 1738, 408 pages.

Egede, Hans 1741 = Egede, Hans: *Det gamle Grønlands nye Perlustration eller Naturelhistorie, og Beskrivelse over det gamle Grønlands Situation, luft, temperatur og Beskaffenhed; De gamle norske Coloniers Begyndesle og Undergang der samme-steds*. This is Hans Egede's description of Greenland edited by the author, Copenhagen 1741, 131 pages.

Egede/Bobé = Egede, Hans: *Relationer fra Grønland 1721–36 og Det gamle Grønlands Perlustration 1741*, ed. Louis Bobé, in MoG volume 54, Copenhagen 1925. This is an edition of Egede's diary from Greenland 1721–36 first published by Egede himself in

1738, and the description of Greenland first published by Egede himself in 1741. Cf. the two previous entries. Both were "censored" or "purified" by Bobé in this edition from 1925.

Egede, Niels: Diary 1739–1743 = Egede, Niels: "Tredie continuation af relationerne betreffende den grønlandske missions tilstand og beskaffenhed," in: *Poul og Niels Egede: Continuation af Hans Egedes relationer fra Grønland, samt Niels Egede: Beskrivelse over Grønland,* ed. H. Ostermann, printed in MoG volume 120, Copenhagen 1939, pp. 123–206. Notes and appendices, pp. 273–380. This is Niels Egede's diary from Greenland 1739 to 1743.

Egede, Niels: Description of Greenland = Egede, Niels:"Beskrivelse over Grønland" with an end date 01.01.1770, in: *Poul og Niels Egede: Continuation af Hans Egedes relationer fra Grønland, samt Niels Egede: Beskrivelse over Grønland,* ed. H. Ostermann, printed in MoG volume 120, Copenhagen 1939, pp. 233–269. Notes and appendices, pp. 273–380. Copenhagen 1930, 380 pages. This is Niels Egedes description of Greenland.

Egede, Poul: Diary 1734–1740 = Egede, Poul: "Continuation af relationerne betreffende den Grønlandske Missions Tilstand og Beskaffenhed, forfattet i form af en Journal fra Anno 1734 til 1740", ed. H. Ostermann; in: *Poul og Niels Egede: Continuation af Hans Egedes relationer fra Grønland, samt Niels Egede: Beskrivelse over Grønland,* printed in MoG volume 120, Copenhagen 1939, pp. 1–122. Notes and appendices, pp. 273–380. This is Poul Egedes diary from Greenland 1734–1740.

Egils saga Skallagrímssonar, in: ÍF II, ed. Einar Ól. Sveinsson, Reykjavík 1954; English translation by Bernard Scudder, in: CSI volume 1, pp. 33–177, same translation in: *Egil's saga,* Penguin Books, London 2004; Norwegian translation by Hallvard Lie, in: *Norrøn saga* I, Oslo 1992, pp. 25–224.

Eiriks saga Rauda, in: ÍF IV, ed. Einar Ól. Sveinsson and Mathias Þórðarson, Reykjavík 1935, pp. 193–237; English translation by Keneva Kunz, in: CSI volume 1, pp. 1–18, the same translation, in: *The Vinland Sagas,* Penguin Classics, London 2008, pp. 25–50; Norwegian translation *Eirik Raudes saga* by Anne Holtsmark, in: *Norrøn saga* V, Oslo 1992, pp. 197–222. Old Norse text and English translations have same chapter numbers.

Eyrbyggja saga, in: ÍF IV, ed. Einar Ól. Sveinsson and Mathias Þórðarson, Reykjavík 1935, pp. 1–184; English translation by Judy Quinn, in: CSI volume 5, pp. 131–218, alternative English translation by Hermann Pálsson and Paul Edwards in: *Eyrbyggja saga,* Penguin Classics 1989; Norwegian translation *Øyrbyggja saga* by Sigurd Angell Wiik, in: *Norrøn saga* III, Oslo 1992, pp. 7–123. Old Norse edition and Norwegian translation have same chapter numbers.

Fagrskinna, ed. Finnur Jonsson, Copenhagen 1902–1903. English translation by Alison Finlay, Brill Publishers, Leiden 2004

Flateyjarbok I-IV, ed. Sigurdur Nordal, Reykjavík 1944–1945.

Flomanna saga, in: IF XIII, ed. Torhallur Vilmundarson and Bjarni Vilhjalmsson, Reykjavík 1991, pp. 229–327; English translation by Paul Acker, in: CSI volume 3, pp. 271–304; alternative English translation: "The Story of Thorgils", in: *Origines Islandicae* volume 2, edited and translated by Gudbrand Vigfusson and F. York Powell, Oxford 1905, pp. 629–672.

Fostbroedra saga, in: IF VI, ed. Björn Thorolfsson and Gudni Jonsson, Reykjavik 1943, pp. 119–276; English translation by Martin Regal, in: CSI volume 2, pp. 329–402; Alternative English translation in: *Origines Islandicae* volume 2, edited and translated by Gudbrand Vigfusson and F. York Powell, Oxford 1905, pp. 673–747; Norwegian translation in *Norrøn saga* II by Anne Holtsmark, Oslo 1989, pp. 179–254.

Frostatingslova, Old Norse edition in NGL I, pp. 119–258; English translation by Lawrence M. Larson, *The Earliest Norwegian laws: being the Gulathing law and the Frostathing law*, New York 1935, pp. 213–405; Norwegian translation: *Frostatingslova* by Jan Ragnar Hagland and Jørn Sandnes, Oslo 1994.

GHM = *Grønlands historiske mindesmærker* (*Remnants from Greenland's history*), volumes I-III, Copenhagen 1838–1845. The volumes include Old Norse and Latin texts and Danish translations of all written sources to Greenland's history which at that time were known. References to Danish translations are normally not given in the footnotes because reliable translations to Danish are easily accessible in GHM I-III.

Gisla saga Surssonar, in: IF VI, ed. Björn Thorolfsson and Gudni Jonsson, Reykjavik 1943, pp. 1–118; English translation by Martin Regal, in: CSI volume 2, pp. 1–48; Alternative English translation, in: *Origines Islandicae* vol. 1, edited and translated by Gudbrand Vigfusson and F. York Powell, Oxford 1905, pp. 188–337; Norwegian translation *Gisle Surssons saga* by Vera Henriksen, in: *Norrøn saga* III, Oslo 1990, pp. 259–329.

"Grænlands annal", written by the Icelander Bjørn Jonsson (1574–1655). It is printed in *Grænland i midaldaritum*, ed. Olafur Halldorsson, published by *Sögufelag*, Reykjavik 1978, pp. 1–73.

Grágás, ed. Gunnar Karlsson, Kristján Sveinsson and Mörður Árnason, Reykjavík 1992; English translation: *Laws of Early Iceland, Grágás. The Codex Regius of Grágás*, by Andrew Dennis, Peter Foote and Richard Perkins, Winnipeg 1980; Danish translation *Grágás. Islændernes Lovbog i Fristatens Tid*, 4 vols, edited and translated by Vilhjalmur Finsen, Copenhagen 1852–1870.

Groenlendinga saga, in: IF IV, ed. Einar Ól. Sveinsson and Mathias Þorðarson, Reykjavík 1935, pp. 241–269; English translation by Keneva Kunz, in: CSI volume 1, pp. 19–32, same translation in: *The Vinland Sagas*, Penguin Classics 2008; Norwegian translation by Anne Holtsmark, in: *Norrøn Saga* V, Oslo 1994, pp. 223–241.

Groenlendinga tháttr, in: IF IV, ed. Einar Ól. Sveinsson and Mathias Þorðarson, Reykjavík 1935, pp. 273–292; English translation by John Porter, in: CSI volume 5, pp. 372–382; Norwegian translation by Anne Holtsmark, in: *Norrøn saga* V, Oslo 1953, pp. 245–259 and by Erik Simensen, in: *Islendingesagaene* V, Reykjavík 2014, pp. 358–366. Old Norse edition and English translation have the same chapter division.

"Gulathings-lov", Old Norse edition, in: NGL I, pp. 1–118; English translation *The Earliest Norwegian laws: being the Gulathing law and the Frostathing law*, by Lawrence M. Larson, New York 1935, pp. 35–210; Norwegian translation *Gulatingslovi*, by Knut Robberstad, Oslo 1981.

Hákonar saga Hákonarsonar, Old Norse text in: *Rerum Britannicarum medii ævi scriptores* volume 88, part 2: *Icelandic sagas and other historical documents relating to the settlements and descents of the Northmen on the British Isles*, edited by Gudbrand Vigfusson, London 1887.

English translation: *The saga of Hacon* by Sir George W. Dasent, in: *Icelandic sagas and other historical documents relating to the settlements and descents of the Northmen on the British Isles* vol. 4, London 1894, pp. 1–373.

Norwegian translation: *Håkon Håkonssons saga* by Kr. Audne, Oslo 1963. In these three editions and translations chapter divisions are the same.

Hamburgisches Urkundenbuch I-III, ed. J. M.Lappenberg and others, Hamburg 1842, 1939 and 1953.

"Hávamál", Old Norse in: *Eddadigte* vol. 1, ed. Jon Helgason, Copenhagen 1971, pp. 16–39; English translation by Carolyne Larrington, in: *The Poetic Edda* in Oxford

World Classics, pp. 14–38; Norwegian translation by Ludvig Holm-Olsen, in: *Eddadikt*, Oslo 1975, pp. 30–60. The edition and the translations have the same stanza numbers.

Heimskringla authored by Snorri Sturluson, IF volumes 26, 27, 28, ed. Bjarni Aðalbjarnarson, Reykjavík 1979. English translation by Lee M. Hollander, *Heimskringla: History of the Kings of Norway*, University of Texas Press, 1964 and 1995. Numerous translations into Scandinavian languages. All editions and translations have identical chapter divisions.

"Hirdskrá from 1273", in: NGL II, pp. 387–450; *Hirdloven til Norges konge og hans håndgangne menn etter AM 322*, ed. Steinar Imsen, in Old Norse and Norwegian translation, Oslo 2000.

Historia Norwegie, Latin text and English translation, ed. Inger Ekrem and Lars Boje Mortensen, translated by Peter Fisher, Copenhagen 2003.

Hungrvaka, Old Norse text in: IF XVI, ed. Ásdis Egilsdottir, Reykjavik 2002, pp. 1–43; Old Norse text and English translation, in: *Origines Islandicae* vol. 1, edited and translated by Gudbrand Vigfusson and F. York Powell, Oxford 1905, pp. 425–458; Old Norse text in: *Biskupa sögur* vol. 1, ed. Jón Sigurðsson and Gudbrand Vigfusson, Copenhagen 1858, pp. 57–86; Danish translation in: *To islandske bispekrøniker* by Agnete Loth, Odense 1989, pp. 31–58.

IA = *Islandske Annaler*, ed. Gustav Storm, Christiania (Oslo) 1888. In the notes the annals are referred to with their number and name in Storm's edition. The year of the relevant entry will appear from the main text or be given in the note.

Islendingabok authored by Ari Frodi. Printed in Old Norse, in: ÍF volume 1, ed. Jakob Benediktsson, Reykjavík 1986, pp. 1–28; English translation, in: *Islendingabok, Kristni saga*, translated by Sian Grønlie, published by The Viking Society for Northern Research, University College London, London 2006, pp. 3–14; Norwegian translation by Hallvard Magerøy, in: *Den norrøne litteraturen* VI, Oslo 1963, pp. 49–62.

Jökuls tháttr Buasonar, in: IF XIV, ed. Johannes Halldorsson, Reykjavik 1959, pp. 47–59; English translation in CSI volume 3 by John Porter, pp. 328–334; Alternative English translation: "The story of Jokul Buason", in: *Forty Old Icelandic Tales*, translated with an introduction by W. Bryant Bachman, Jr. University Press of America, Lanham (Maryland) 1992, pp. 283–291.

Jons biskups saga hin elzta, Old Norse text and English translation in *Origines Islandicae* vol. 1, edited and translated by Gudbrand Vigfusson and F. York Powell, Oxford 1905, pp. 534–567. The first Old Norse edition in: *Biskupa sögur* I, ed. Jón Sigurdsson and Gudbrand Vigfusson, Copenhagen 1858, pp. 149–202; These editions and translations of the saga of Bishop Jon is based on a short version with a different chapter division.

Jons saga helga eptir Gunnlaug munk, in: *Biskupa sögur* I, ed. Jón Sigurðsson and Gudbrand Vigfusson, Copenhagen 1858, pp. 213–260; Norwegian translation "Soga om Jon den heilage" by Kjell Venås, in: *Den norrøne litteraturen* VI, Oslo 1963, pp. 72–110. Edition and translation have the same chapter division. This version of the saga of Bishop Jon has not been translated into English.

Konungs skuggsiá, ed. Ludvig Holm-Olsen, Oslo 1983; English translation by Laurence Marcellus Larson: *The King's Mirror*, New York 1917, reprint 1973; Norwegian translation by Alf Hellevik, *Kongespegelen* in the series Norrøne bokverk XIV, Oslo 1965/1976.

Kristni saga, Old Norse text and English translation by Gudbrand Vigfusson and F. York Powell, in: *Origines Islandicae* I, Oxford 1905, pp. 376–406. The first Old Norse edition: *Biskupa sögur* I, ed. Jón Sigurðsson and Gudbrand Vigfusson, Copenhagen 1858, pp. 1–32. English translation by Sian Grønlie: *Islendingabok, Kristni saga*, published by Viking Society for Northern Research, University College London, London 2006, pp. 35–55.

Kroka-Refs saga, in: IF XIV, ed. Johannes Halldorsson, Reykjavik 1959, pp. 117–160. English translation in CSI volume 3, by George Clark, pp. 397–420; Alternative English translation by W. Bryant Bachman, "The saga of Clever Ref", in: *Four Old Icelandic sagas and other tales*, Lanham University Press of America 1985, pp. 1–37.

Landnámabok, in: ÍF volume 1, ed. Jakob Benediktsson, Reykjavík 1986, pp. 29–397; "S" is an abbreviation for "Sturlubok version" and "H" for "Hauksbok version". English translation of the "Sturlubok version" in *The Book of Settlements* by Hermann Pálsson and Paul Edwards, Winnipeg 1972. The English translation has the same chapter division as the Sturlubok version of the ÍF. In Norwegian there is one separate translation of the "Sturlubok" version, Liv Kjørsvik Schei: *Landnåmsboken*, Oslo 1997, which is referred to in the footnotes of this book. This translation follows the chapter division of Sturlubok in the ÍF. There is another separate translation of the Hauksbok version, Jan Ragnar Hagland: *Landnåmabok*, Stavanger 2002.

Laurentius saga authored by Einar Haflidason, Old Norse in: *Biskupa sögur* I, ed. Jón Sigurðsson and Gudbrand Vigfusson, Copenhagen 1858, pp. 787–877; English translation: *The Life of Laurence, Bishop of Holar in Iceland* by Oliver Elton, London 1890; Norwegian translation: *Soga om biskop Laurentius* by Kjell Venås, in the series *Den norrøne litteraturen* VI, Oslo 1963, pp. 111–180. Danish translation: *Historien om biskop Laurentius på Holar*, by Jørgen Højgaard Jørgensen, Odense University Press 1982.

Magnus Lagabøte's National Law from 1274. Old Norse text, in: NGL II, pp. 1–178; Norwegian translation *Magnus Lagabøtes landslov*. Edited by Absalon Taranger and translated by Knut Robberstad, Kristiania 1915, reprint Oslo 1979.

Magnus Lagabøte's Urban Law from 1276. Old Norse text, in: NGL II, pp. 185–290; Norwegian translation *Magnus Lagabøtes bylov*, edited by Absalon Taranger and translated by Knut Robberstad, Kristiania (Oslo) 1923.

Morkinskinna, ed. C. R. Unger, Christiania (Oslo) 1867; English translation Andersson, T. and Gade, K. E., Ithaca and London 2000.

NGL = *Norges Gamle Love* (Norway's Ancient Laws), 5 volumes, which cover the period until 1388, Christiania (Oslo) 1846–1895.

"Norrigis Bescrivelse", authored by Peder Clausson Friis who lived 1545–1614. Printed in *Samlede skrifter* ed. Gustav Storm, Christiania 1881.

Norrön Fornkvædi, ed. Sophus Bugge, Oslo 1965; first edition 1867.

Norske middelalderdokumenter, ed. Sverre Bagge, Synnøve Smedsdal and Knut Helle. Old Norse text and Norwegian translation, Oslo 1973.

Odda-annalar og Oddverja-annall, eds. E. Thormodsson and G. Á Grimsdottir, Reykjavík 2003.

"Om Norgis Rige" written by Absalon Pederssøn Beyer ca. 1567, printed in: Gustav Storm ed. *To norske Historisk-Topografiske Skrifter fra 1500-tallet*, Christiania 1895, reprint Oslo 1968, pp. 1–116.

Othere's account to King Alfred – Old English text: *The Old English Orosius*, ed. Janet Bateley; Published for "The early English Text Society" by the Oxford University Press, London 1980. Othere's account to King Alfred is printed on pp. 13–16.

Danish translation and Old English text: *Ottar og Wulfstan. To rejsebeskrivelser fra vikingetiden*, translated by Niels Lund, Roskilde 1983.

Several English translations exist on the internet. One alternative is: https://classesv2.yale.edu/access/content/user/haw6/Vikings/voyagers.html.

Páls saga byskups, in: IF XVI, ed. Ásdis Egilsdottir, Reykjavik 2002, pp. 295–332; Old Norse text and English translation by Gudbrand Vigfusson and F. York Powell, in: *Origines Islandicae* volume 1, Oxford 1905, pp. 502–534.

Pipe Rolls [= *Magnum Rotulum Scaccari* or *Magnum Rotulum Pipæ*], *31 Henry I*, Lincolnshire, ed. Joseph Hunter, published by "Commissioners of the public records of the Kingdom", London 1833, p. 111.

Now superseded by: *The Great Roll of the Pipe for the Thirty-First Year of the Reign of King Henry I: Michaelmas 1130 (Pipe roll 1): A New Edition with a Translation and Images from the Original in the Public Record Office/the National Archives*, ed. Judith Green. Published by The Pipe Roll Society, volume 95. London 2012, p. 88. Original in the Public Record Office in London–Pipe Rolls 31 Henry I. Norwegian summary, in: RN I no. 73.

Profectio Danorum in Hierosolymam, printed in: *Scriptores minores historia Danica medii aevi* II, ed. M.C. Gertz, Copenhagen 1922; Norwegian translation: "Historien om danenes ferd til Jerusalem" by Astrid Salvesen, in: *Norges historie, Historien om de gamle norske kongene, Historien om danenes ferd til Jerusalem*, Oslo 1969, pp. 97–136.

Rimnasafn volume 1, samling af de ældste islandske rimer, ed. Fnnur Jonsson, Copenhagen 1905–1912.

RN = *Regesta Norvegica*, 10 volumes, Oslo 1978–2015. Charters and other letters concerning Norway until 1430.

Saga Óláfs Tryggvasonar af Oddr Snorrason munk, ed. Finnur Jónsson, Copenhagen 1932; English translation by Theodore Andersson, *The Saga of Olaf Tryggvason by Oddr Snorrason*, Ithaca 2003; Norwegian translation by M. Rindal, *Soga om Olav Trygvason etter Oddr munk Snorrason*, Oslo 1977. The Old Norse and the English publications have the same chapter divisions.

Skaldic Poetry of the Scandinavian Middle Ages, volume II, Poetry from the Kings' sagas, ed. Kari Ellen Gade, Brepols publishers 2009.

Sturlunga saga volumes 1–3 in Old Norse, ed. Örnolfur Þórsson, Reykjavík 1988; English translation *Sturlunga Saga* volumes 1–2 by Julia McGrew and R. George Thomas, New York 1970–1974; Danish translation *Sturlunga saga* volumes 1–2 by Kr. Kålund, Copenhagen 1904.

Sverris saga, ed. Gustav Indrebø, Kristiania (Oslo) 1920; English translation by John Sephton: *Sverrissaga. The Saga of King Sverri of Norway*, London 1899, reprint 1994; Norwegian translation by Halvdan Koht: *Den norrøne litteraturen* vol. IV, Oslo 1962. All these have the same chapter divisions.

"Talen mot biskopane", several Old Norse editions are listed in KLNM volume 18, columns 98–102. Norwegian translation by Erik Eggen, in: *Den norrøne litteraturen* V, Oslo 1963, pp. 207–232.

Tristrams saga ok Isöndar, ed. Vesteinn Olason, Reykjavik 1987; English translation by Paul Schach: *The saga of Tristram and Isönd*, a Bison book 608, University of Nebraska Press 1973.

Urkundenbuch der Stadt Lübeck I-XI, Lübeck 1843–1905; *Wort- und Sachregister*, Lübeck 1932.

Vatnsdoela saga, in: ÍF VIII, ed. Einar Ól. Sveinsson, Reykjavík 1939, pp. 1–131; English translation by Andrew Wawn: CSI IV, pp. 1–66; Alternative English translation Gwyn Jones: *The Vatnsdalers' saga*, Millwood N.Y. 1973 (1st edition 1944); Norwegian translation by Sigurd Angell Wiik, in: *Norrøn saga* II, Oslo 1989, pp. 255–335.

Literature, reference books and abbreviations

Albrethsen, S. 1970. Unprinted report dated 1970 in "Nordboarkivet", Nationalmuseet in Copenhagen, on E105 (The Augustinian monastery). Cf. Nørlund 1926.

Albrethsen, S. 1972. "Nordbonytt", in: *Skalk* 1972/4, Århus, pp. 11–15.

Albrethsen, S. 1982. "Træk af den norrøne gårds udvikling på Grønland, vestnordisk byggeskik gennem to tusen år", in: *Arkeologisk Museum Stavanger skrifter* 7, Stavanger, pp. 269–287.

Albrethsen, S. and Arneborg, J. 2004. *Norse ruins of the southern Paamiut and Ivittuut region*, published by SILA–The Greenland Research Centre at the Nationalmuseum of Denmark and the Danish Polar Centre; Danish Polar Center Publication no. 13, Copenhagen.

Albrethsen, S. and Keller, C. 1986. "The use of Sæter in Medieval Norse Farming in Greenland", in: *Arctic Anthropology* 23, Madison, pp. 91–108.

Albrethsen, S. and Ólafsson, G. 1998. "A Viking age hall", in: Arneborg, J. and Gulløv, H. C. eds. *Man, Culture and Environment in Ancient Greenland–Report on a Research Program*, pp. 19–26.

Andersen, E. and Malmros, C. 1992. "Skibsdele fra nordbobygderne i Grønland. Foreløpig vurdering og vedbestemmelse", in: Claussen, I.B.I. ed. *Vikingernes sejlads til Nordamerika*, Roskilde, pp. 118–122.

Andersen, P. S. 1977. *Samlingen av Norge og kristningen av landet* 800–1130, Oslo.

Andreasen, C. 1982. "Nipaitsoq og Vesterbygden", in: *Tidsskriftet Grønland* 1982(5), pp. 177–188.

Anglo-Saxon Dictionary, ed. Joseph Bosworth, Oxford 1976 (first edition 1898).

Anker Pedersen, S. 1999. "Ammassæt", in: Born, E. W. and Böcher, J. eds. *Grønlands økologi–en grundbog*, Atuakkiorfik Undervisning, Nuuk, p. 164.

Antonsson, H. 2005. "The minsters. A brief review of the "Minster hypothesis" in England and some general observations on its relevance to Scandinavia and Iceland," in: Thorlaksson, H. ed. *Church centres*, Reykholt, pp. 175–186.

Appelt, M. 2004. "De sidste Dorsetfolk", in: Gulløv, H. C. ed. *Grønlands forhistorie*, Copenhagen, pp. 177–200.

(a) Arneborg, J. 1991. Kulturmødet mellem Nordboer og Eskimoer, unpublished PhD thesis, University of Copenhagen.

(b) Arneborg, J. 1991. "The Roman Church in Norse Greenland", in: *Acta Archaeologica*, 61. Copenhagen, pp. 142–150.

Arneborg, J. 1996. "Burgunderhuer, baskere og døde nordboer i Herjolfsnæs, Grønland", in: *Nationalmuseets arbejdsmark*, Copenhagen, pp. 75–83.

Arneborg, J. 2000. "Greenland and Europe", in: Fitzhugh, W. ed. *Vikings. The North Atlantic Saga*, Washington, pp. 304–317.

(a) Arneborg, J. 2003. "Norse Greenland: Reflections on Settlement and Depopulation", in: Barrett, J. ed., *Contact, Continuity and Collapse*, Brepols Publishers, pp. 63–181.

(b) Arneborg, J. 2003. "Norse Greenland Archaeology: The Dialogue between the written and the Archaeological Records", in: Lewis-Simpson, S. ed. *Vinland Revisited: the Norse World at the turn of the First Millennium* published by "Historic sites Association of Newfoundland and Labrador, Inc.", St. John's Newfoundland, pp. 111–122.

(c) Arneborg, J. 2003. "The Archaeological background", in: Enghoff, I. B. ed., *Hunting, fishing and animal husbandry at the Farm Beneath the Sand, Western Greenland*, MoG, Man and Society volume 28, Copenhagen, pp. 9–17.

Arneborg, J. 2004. "Det europeiske landnám–nordboerne i Grønland", in: Gulløv, H. C. ed. *Grønlands forhistorie*, Copenhagen, pp. 221–278.

Arneborg, J. 2005. "Greenland irrigation systems on a West Nordic background. An overview of the evidence of irrigation systems in Norse Greenland c. 980–1450 AD", in: *Proceedings from Ruralia* 5, Prague, pp. 137–145.

Arneborg, J. 2006. *Saga trails–A visitor's guidebook*, published by The Nationalmuseum of Denmark, Copenhagen.

Arneborg, J. and Berglund, J. 1994. *Gården under sandet. Status Januar 1994.* Greenland's National Museum and Archive, Nuuk.

Arneborg, J. and Berglund, J. 2007. *Gården under sandet. Arkeologisk undersøgelse af nordbogård i Grønlands Vesterbygd, Nuup kommunea. Status Januar 2007.* Report in Greenland's National Museum and Archive.

Arneborg, J., Heinemeier, J. and Lynnerup, N. 2008. ". . . Husk at folk lever af flere ting end bare af brød. De norrøne grønlenderes kost", in: *Nationalmuseets arbejdsmark 2008*, Copenhagen, pp. 149–160.

Arneborg, J., Heinemeyer J., Lynnerup, N., Nielsen, H. L., Rud, N., Sveinbjörnsdóttir, Á. E. 1999. "Change of Diet of the Greenland Vikings determined from stable carbon isotope analysis and 14C datings of their bones", in: *Radiocarbon*, 41(2), pp. 157–168.

Arneborg, J., Larsen, F. and Clemmensen, N. C. 2009. "The Dairy Farm of the Hvalsey fjord farm", in: *Journal of the North Atlantic* 2009, special volume 2, papers from the Hvalsey conference 2008, pp. 24–29.

(a) Arneborg, J., Lynnerup, N., Heinemeier, J., Møhl, J., Rud, N and Sveinbjörnsdóttir, Á.E. 2012. "Norse Greenland Dietary Economy AD c.980–AD c.1450: Introduction", in: *Journal of the North Atlantic*, special volume 3, 2012, Copenhagen, pp. 1–39.

(b) Arneborg, J., Lynnerup, N. and Heinemeier, J. 2012. "Human Diet and Subsistence Patterns in Norse Greenland AD c.980–AD c.1450: Archaeological interpretations", in: *Journal of the North Atlantic*, special volume 3, 2012, pp. 119–133.

Arneborg, J. and Seaver, K.A. 2000. "From Vikings to Norsemen", in: Fitzhugh, W. ed. *Vikings. The North Atlantic Saga*, Washington, pp. 281–284.

Baetzing, W. 2015. *Die Alpen. Geschichte und Zukunft einer europäischen Kulturlandschaft*, München (first edition 1984).

Barrett, J. and others 2000. "Radiocarbon dating and marine reservoir correction of Viking Age Christian burials from Orkney", in: *Antiquity* volume 74, number 285, September 2000, pp. 537–542.

Barth, E. 1982. "Metoder for fangst av villrein i Sør-Norge i gammel tid", in: *Tromura*, Tromsø Museums rapportserie, Tromsø, pp. 30–56.

Berglund, J. 1973/4. "På den yderste nøgne ø", in: *Skalk* 1973/4, pp. 11–13.

Berglund, J. "Europahavnen", in: *Skalk*, 1979, vol. 2, pp. 25–29.

Berglund, J. 1993. *GUS-journal* 1993, 18.June–17.July, Nationalmuseet in Copenhagen.

Berglund, J. 1995. *GUS-journal* 1995, 19.June–17.July, Nationalmuseet in Copenhagen.

Berglund, J. 1996. *GUS-journal* 1996, 11.June–16.July, Nationalmuseet in Copenhagen.

Berglund, J. 1998. "The excavations at the farm beneath the sand", in: Arneborg, J and Gulløw, H.C. (eds.): *Man, culture and environment in ancient Greenland*, Dansk Polar Centre, Copenhagen, pp. 7–13.

Berglund, J. 2000. "The farm beneath the sand", in: Fitzhugh W. ed. *Vikings. The North Atlantic Saga*, Washington, pp. 295–303.

Bjørgo, N. 1965. "Skipstypar i norrøne samtidssoger", in: *Sjøfartshistorisk Årbok 1965*, published by Bergens Sjøfartsmuseum, Bergen, pp. 7–19.

Blair, J. 2005. *The Church in Anglo-Saxon society*, Oxford.
Blehr, O. 1982. "Når villreinen løper dit du vil", in: *Tromura, Kulturhistorie* no. 1, Tromsø, pp. 1–29.
Böcher, T. and Jens B. 2000. *Det grønne Grønland*, Copenhagen.
Borgedal, P. *Norges jordbruk i nyere tid* I-III, Oslo 1966–68.
Born, E. 2005. *Grønlands hvalrosser*, Nuuk.
Born, E. and Böcher, J. 1999: *Grønlands økologi–en grundbog*, publisher Atuakkiorfik Undervisning, Nuuk.
Bratrein, H. D. 1989. *Karlsøy og Helgøy bygdebok* 1, Karlsøy.
Bruun, D. 1896. "Arkæologiske undersøgelser i Julianehåbs distrikt", in: MoG volume 16.3, Copenhagen, pp. 171–495.
(a) Bruun, D. 1918. "Oversigt over Nordboruiner i Godthåbs og Fredrikshåbs-distrikter", in: MoG volume 56, pp. 55–148.
(b) Bruun D. 1918. "The Icelandic colonization of Greenland", in: MoG volume 57, Copenhagen, pp. 1–228.
Buchwald, V. 2001. "Ancient Iron and Slags in Greenland", in: MoG, Man and Society volume 26, Copenhagen.
Bugge, A. 1898. "Handelen mellom England og Norge indtil begyndelsen af det 15de aarhundrede", in: *Historisk tidsskrift* volume 3.4, Kristiania, pp. 1–149.
Christensen, A. E. 2000. "Ships and navigation", in: Fitzhugh, H. ed. *Viking. The North Atlantic Saga*, Washington, pp. 86–97.
Christensen, K. M. B. 1989. "En undersøgelse af den norrøne areal og ressourceudnyttelse i Vesterbygden i Grønland", in: *Hikuin* 15, Århus, pp. 7–26.
Christiansen, D. V. 2004. "Fra Europa til verdens Ende. De grønlandske nordboers kulturelle kontakter over Nordatlanteren", in: *Nationalmuseets arbejdsmark* 2004, pp. 27–39.
Christophersen, A. and others 1994. "Et område av stor arkeologisk interesse", in: Christophersen, A. and Nordeide, S. eds. *Kaupangen ved Nidelva*, Riksantikvarens Skrifter 7, pp. 9–38. Copenhagen.
Clemmensen, M. 1911. "Kirkeruiner fra Nordbotiden i Julianehåb Distrikt, Undersøgelsesreise sommren 1910", in: MoG volume 47, Copenhagen, pp. 283–358.
Dahl-Jensen, D., Mosegaard, K., Gundestrup, N., Clow, G. D., Johnsen, S. J., Hansen, A. W., Balling, N. 1998. "Past Temperatures Directly from the Greenland Ice Sheet", in: *Science* www.sciencemag.org, volume 282, pp. 268–271.
Degerbøl, M. 1930. "Animal bones from the Norse ruins at Gardar", in: MoG volume 76.3, Copenhagen, pp. 183–192.
Degerbøl, M. 1941. "The osseous material from Austmannadal and Tungmeralik", in: Roussell, Aa. ed. *Farms and churches in the Medieval Norse Settlements of Greenland*, MoG volume 89, Copenhagen, pp. 345–354.
Diamond, J. 2005. *Collapse*, London.
Dugmore, A. J., McGovern, T. H., Vésteinsson, O., Arneborg, J.; Streeter, R. and Keller, C. 2012. "Cultural adaptation, compounding vulnerabilities and conjunctures in Norse Greenland", in: *Proceedings of the National Academy of Sciences of the United States of America*, volume 109, no. 10 (March 6. 2012), pp. 3658–3663.
E = Eastern Settlement. The Norse Settlement in the fjords east of present day Qaqortoq.
W = Western Settlement, the Norse Settlement in the fjords east of present day Nuuk.
Edvardsson, R. ed. 2006. *Archaeological excavations at Qorlortorsuaq (E74) 2006, field report*, published by the Nationalmuseum of Greenland.

Edwards, K. J. 2014. "Early farming, pollen and landscape impacts from Northern Europe to the North Atlantic", in: Gulløv, H. C. ed. *Northern Worlds*, Copenhagen, pp. 189–201.
Edwards, K.J., Gordon, J., Cook T., Nyegaard, G. and Schofield, J. E. 2013. "Towards a first Chronology for the Middle Settlement of Norse Greenland", in: *Radiocarbon*, volume 55, no. 1, pp. 1–17.
Eggers, H. P. 1794. "Om Grønlands Østerbygds sande Beliggenhed", in: *Det kongelige danske Landhusholdningsselskabs skrifter* 4, Copenhagen, pp. 239–320.
Ekroll, Ø. 1997. *Med kleber og kalk*, Oslo.
Ekroll, Ø. and Stige, M. 2000. *Kirker i Norge* I, Middelalder i stein, Oslo.
Elias, N. *Über den Prozess der Zivilisation* I-II, Frankfurt am Main 1976. First edition 1939.
Enghoff, I. B. 2003. ed. "Hunting, fishing and animal husbandry at the Farm Beneath the Sand, Western Greenland. An archaeozoological analysis of a Norse farm", in the series: MoG, Man and Society 28, Copenhagen.
Espelund, A. 2007. "Ancient ironmaking in Iceland, Greenland and Newfoundland", in: *Archaeologia Islandica* 6, Reykjavik, pp. 48–73.
Eythorsson, B. 2005. "History of the Icelandic church 1000–1300. Status of research", in: Thorlaksson, H. ed. *Church centres*, Reykholt, pp. 19–70.
Fredskild, B. 1973. *Studies in the Vegetational History of Greenland*, PhD University of Copenhagen 1973, printed as MoG 198.4.
Fredskild, B. 1978/9. "Palaeobotanical Investigations of some Peat Deposits of Norse Ages at Quassiarsuk, South Greenland 1978", in: MoG volume 204.5, Copenhagen 1978/9, pp. 5–43.
Fredskild, B. 1982. "Vegetationen i norrøn tid", in: *Tidsskriftet Grønland*, September 1982, volume 30 nos. 8–9, pp. 189–196.
Fredskild, B. 1992. "Erosion and vegetational changes in South Greenland caused by agriculture", in: *Geografisk Tidsskrift* 92, Copenhagen, pp. 14–21.
Fritzner, J. ed. *Ordbog over det gamle norske sprog* I–III, Kristiania 1886–1896; reprint with new volume 4, Oslo 1954–1972.
Fægri, K. 1958. *Norges planter* I-II, Oslo.
Gaborit-Chopin, D. 1978. *Elfenbeinskunst im Mittelalter*, Berlin.
Gaborit-Chopin, D. 1992. "Brugen af hvalrostand i Vesteuropa", in: *Viking og Hvidekrist*, published by Nationalmuseet in Copenhagen, pp. 204–205 and 389.
Gad, F. 1984. *Grønland*, Copenhagen.
Gensbøl, B. 1999. *Naturguide til Grønland*, Copenhagen.
Graah, W. A. 1832. *Undersøgelsesrejse til Østkysten af Grønland, efter kongelig Befaling udført i Aarene 1828–31*, Copenhagen.
Grønnow, B. 2008. "Verdens nordligste arbejdsmark. Ni år med SILA–Nationalmuseets Center for Grønlandsforskning", in: *Nationalmuseets Arbejdsmark 2008*, Copenhagen, pp. 9–24.
Grønnow, B., Appelt, M. and Odgaard, U. 2014. "In the light of blubber: The earliest stone lamps in Greenland and beyond", in: Gulløv, H.C. ed. *Northern Worlds*, published by Nationalmuseet in Copenhagen, Studies in Archaeology and History 22, pp. 403–422.
Grønnow, B., Meldgaard, M., and Berglund Nielsen, J. 1983. *Aasivissuit–The Great Summer Camp. Archaeological, etnographical and zoo-archaeological studies of a caribou-hunting site in West Greenland*, in the series: MoG, Man and Society volume 5, Copenhagen.
Gudmundsson, G. 1966. "Gathering and processing of lyme-grass (Elymus arenarius) in Iceland", in: *Vegetation history and Archaeobotany*, volume 5, issue 1–2, June 1966, pp. 13–23.

Guldager, O., Stummann Hansen, S. and Gleie, S. 2002. *Medieval Farmsteads in Greenland. The Bratthlid region 1999–2000*, Danish Polar Center publications 9, Copenhagen.
Gulløv, H. C. 1997. *From the Middle Ages to Colonial times. Archaeological and ethnohistorical studies of the Thule culture in South West Greenland 1300–1800*, in: MoG, Man and Society 23, PhD University of Copenhagen.
Gulløv, H. C. 2000. "Natives and Norse in Greenland", in: Fitzhugh W. ed. *Vikings. The North Atlantic Saga*, Washington 2000, pp. 318–326.
(a) Gulløv, H. C. 2004. "Arktiske hvalfangere" and "Kulturmøder i nord", in: Gulløv, H. C. ed. *Grønlands forhistorie*, Copenhagen, pp. 201–217.
(b) Gulløv, H. C. 2004. "Nunarput, vort land–Thulekulturen 1200–1900 e.v.t.", in: Gulløv, H. C. ed. *Grønlands forhistorie*, Copenhagen, pp. 281–343.
Gulløv, H. C. 2008. "The nature of contact between native Greenlanders and Norse", in: *Journal of the North Atlantic* volume 1, pp. 16–24.
Gustavsson, K. 1997. *Otterböte. New light on a Bronze Age site in the Baltic*, PhD Stockholm University, thesis and papers in archaeology B:4.
Hacquebord, L. 2014. *De noordse compagnie*, Zutphen.
Hagland, J. R. 1990. "Runemateriale som kjelde til islandshandel–ein formasteleg tanke", in: *Historisk Tidsskrift*, 69, Oslo 1990, pp. 106–109.
Halldorsson, O. 1978. *Grænland i midaldaritum*, Reykjavik. [Sources for Norse Greenland history with comments in modern Icelandic. Among the sources is Bjørn Jonssons "Grænlands annal" on pp. 1–73,]
Handbook of North American Indians, volume 5–Arctic, ed. David Damas, published by Smithsonian Institution, Washington 1984.
Hansen, B. U. 2000. "Klima", in: *Topografisk Atlas Grønland*, Atlas over Danmark, Series II volume 6, published by Det Kongelige Danske Geografiske Selskab og Kort og Matrikelstyrelsen, Copenhagen, pp. 26–29.
Hasterup, K. 2010. *Vinterens hjerte. Knud Rasmussen og hans tid*, Copenhagen.
Heggstad, L., Hødnebø, F. and Simensen, E. eds. 2008. *Norrøn ordbok*, Oslo.
Heide, P. B. 2012. *Kommunikation, bebyggelse og samfund–sociale dimensioner i norrøne samfund i Nordatlanteren i vikingetid og tidlig middelalder (ca. 800–1200)*, PhD thesis, University of Århus, Institute for Anthropology, Archaeology and Linguistics, vol. I–II.
Helle, K. 1974. *Norge blir en stat 1130–1319*, Bergen.
Helle, K. 1999. "Olavskirken 1250–1350–sognekirke og kongelig kapell", in: *Kongskyrkje ved Nordvegen. Olavskyrkja på Avaldsnes 750 år*, Karmøy, pp. 54–103.
Helle, K. 2005. "The position of the Faeroes and other "tributary lands" in the medieval Norwegian dominion", in: *Viking and Norse in the North Atlantic*, Mortensen, A. and others ed., Tórshavn, pp. 11–21.
Henriksen, P. S. 2014. "Norse agriculture in Greenland–farming at the northern frontier", in: *Northern Worlds*, Gulløv H. C. ed., Copenhagen, pp. 423–431.
Higham, N. 2013. *The Anglo-Saxon World*, Yale University Press.
Holm, G. 1883. "Beskrivelse av ruiner i Julianehåbs distrikt, der er undersøgte i året 1880", in: MoG volume 6, Copenhagen, pp. 57–145.
Holm, G. and Garde, V. 1889. "Beretning om Konebaads- Expeditionen til Grønlands øskyst 1883–85", in: MoG volume 9, Copenhagen, pp. 57–143.
Holm-Olsen, L. 1975. *Edda-dikt*, Oslo 1975, comments to his own translation into Norwegian of the poems.
Hunt, B. G. 2009. "Natural climatic variability and the Norse settlements in Greenland", in: *Climatic Change*, no. 97 (2009), pp. 389–407.

Imer, L. 2017. *Peasants and Prayers. The Inscriptions of Norse Greenland*. Copenhagen. Before her book was published in 2017 her unprinted manuscript *Katalog over grønlandske runeindskrifter* dated 2011 was available at Nationalmuseet, Copenhagen.

Indrelid, S. 2015. "Medieval reindeer trapping at the Hardangevidda mountain plateau", in: *Exploitation of outfield resources*, Indrelid, S., Hjelle, K.L. and Stene, K. eds., Bergen, pp. 29–36.

Ingstad, A. S. 1977. *The Discovery of a Norse Settlement in America*, Norwegian University Press, Oslo.

Ingstad, B. 2010. *Oppdagelsen. En biografi om Anne Stine og Helge Ingstad*, Oslo.

Ingstad, H. 1959. *Landet under leidarstjernen*, Oslo; reprint with different pagination, Oslo 2004; English translation: *Land under the Pole Star: a voyage to the Norse settlements of Greenland and the saga of the people that vanished*, Jonathan Cape editors, London 1966.

Ingstad, H. 1965. *I Vesterveg til Vinland*, Oslo; reprint with different pagination, Oslo 2002; English tanslation: *Westward to Vinland: the discovery of pre-Columbian Norse housesites in North America*, translator Erik J. Friis, St. Martin's Press, New York 1969.

Jakobsen, B.H. 1991. "Soil erosion in the Norse Settlement area of Østerbygden in southern Greenland", in: *Acta Borealia* 8, Oslo, pp. 56–68.

Jansinski, M. E. and Søreide, F. 2003. "The Norse Settlements in Greenland from a Maritime Perspective", in: *Vinland Revisited–The Norse World at the Turn of the First Millennium*, Lewis-Simpson S. ed., St. John's Newfoundland, pp. 123–132.

Jensen, K.G., Kuijpers A., Koc, N. and Heinemeier J. 2004. "Diatom evidence of hydrographic changes and ice conditions in Igaliku Fjord, South Greenland, during the past 1500 years", in: *The Holocene* 14(2), London, pp. 152–164.

Jóhannesson, J. 1956. *Íslendinga saga* I, Reykjavík 1956; English translation: *A History of the Old Icelandic Commonwealth*, Winnipeg 1974, University of Manitoba Press; Norwegian translation: *Islands historie i mellomalderen*, Oslo 1969.

Johnsen, O.A. 1940. "Marcellus", in: *Norsk biografisk leksikon*, first edition, volume 9, Oslo, pp. 70–71.

Jonsson, F. 1893. "En kort Udsigt over den islandsk-grønlandske Kolonis historie", in: *Nordisk tidsskrift för vetenskap, konst och industri* 1893, Copenhagen, pp. 533–572.

Jonsson, F. 1894. *Den oldnorske og oldislandske litteraturs historie* I, Copenhagen.

Jonsson, F. 1899. "Grønlands gamle topografi efter kildene. Østerbygden og Vesterbygden", in: MoG volume 20, Copenhagen, pp. 267–329.

Jonsson, F. 1924. "Interpretation of the runic inscriptions from Herjolvsnes", in: MoG volume 67.2, Copenhagen, pp. 273–290.

Jonsson, F. 1929. "Rune inscriptions from Gardar", in: MoG volume 26, Copenhagen 1930, pp. 171–179.

Jonsson, F. 1930. *Det gamle Grønlands beskrivelse af Ivar Bárdarson*, Copenhagen, 75 pages. Ivar Bárdarson's account is printed on pp. 17–32, the remaining pages are Jonsson's comments and discussions.

Kalkar, Otto: *Ordbog til det ældre danske sprog* (1300–1700), I–V, Copenhagen 1881–1916.

Kalland, A. 2014. *Hval og hvalfangst på Vestlandet 1600–1910*, Oslo.

Karlsson, G. 2000. *Iceland's 1100 years*, London.

Keller, C. 1983. "Gård og seter på Grønland", in: *Hus, gård och bebyggelse*, Olafsson, G. ed., Reykjavik, pp. 59–66.

Keller, C. 1989. *The Eastern Settlement Reconsidered. Some Analyses of Norse Medieval Greenland*, unpublished PhD dissertation, University of Oslo.

Keller, C. 1991. "Vikings in the West Atlantic: A model of Norse Greenlandic Medieval society", in: *Acta Archaeologica* 61, Copenhagen, pp. 126–141.

Keller, C. 2001. "Vinland etter Ingstad", in: *Leiv Eriksson, Helge Ingstad og Vinland*, Hagland J. R. and Supphellen, S. ed., Trondheim, pp. 67–90.
Keller, C. 2010. "Furs, Fish, and Ivory: Medieval Norsemen at the Arctic Fringe", in: *Journal of the North Atlantic* volume 3 (1), pp. 1–23.
Kjartansson, H. 2005. "Thin on the ground. Legal evidence of the availability of priests in 12th century Iceland", in: *Church centres*, Thorlaksson, H. ed., Reykholt, pp. 95–102.
Klepp, A. 1983. *Nordlandsbåter og båter fra Trøndelag*, Oslo.
KLNM = *Kulturhistorisk leksikon for nordisk middelalder* I–XXI, Copenhagen, 1956–1976.
Kolltveit, G. 1997. "Spor etter middelalderens musikkliv: To strengestoler fra Gamlebyen i Oslo", in: *Viking* 1997, Oslo, pp. 69–83.
Kolsrud, O. 1913. List of bishops in the Norwegian church province, printed in DN XVIIB, Christiania (Oslo), pp. 177–300.
Kristjansson, J. 2007. *Éddas and* Sagas, Reykjavík.
Kristjansson, L. 1982. *Islenzkir Sjávarhættir* II, Reykjavík.
Krogh, K. 1967. *Erik den rødes Grønland*, published by Nationalmuseet in Copenhagen. A revised edition appeared in 1982, see Krogh, K. 1982 below.
Krogh, K. 1974. "Kunstvanding–hemmeligheden bag Grønlandsbispens hundrede køer", in: *Nationalmuseets Arbejdsmark* 1974, Copenhagen, pp. 71–79.
Krogh, K. 1976. "Om Grønlands middelalderlige kirkebygninger", in: *Festskrift til Kristjan Eldjarn*, Reykjavík, pp. 294–310.
Krogh, K. 1982. *Erik den rødes Grønland*, published by Nationalmuseet in Copenhagen 1967, revised edition 1982.
Kuijpers, A., Abrahamsen, N., Hoffmann, G., Hühnerbach, V., Konradi, P., Kunzendorf, H., Mikkelsen, N., Thiede, J., Weinrebe, W. and shipboard scientific party of RV Poseidon, and surveyors of the Royal Danish Administration for Navigation and Hydrography, 1998. "Climate change and the Viking-age fjord environment of the Eastern Settlement, South Greenland. Review of Greenland activities 1998," in: *Geology of Greenland. Survey Bulletin*, no. 183, pp. 61–67.
Kuijpers, A., Mikkelsen, N., Robeiro, S. and Seidenkrantz, M.S. 2014: "Impact of Medieval Fjord Hydrography and Climate on the Western and Eastern Settlements in Norse Greenland", in: *Journal of the North Atlantic*, special volume 6, 2014, pp. 1–13.
Lamb, H. H: *Climate, History and the Modern World*, London 1995.
Landscapes circum-landnám: Viking settlements in the North Atlantic and its human and ecological consequences, unprinted final report 2007–2011, The Leverhulme Trust.
Lassen, S.J., Kuijpers, A., Kunzendorf, H., Hoffmann-Wieck, G., Mikkelsen, N., and Konradi, P. 2004. "Late-Holocene Atlantic bottom-water variability in Igaliku Fjord, South Greenland, reconstructed from foraminifere faunas", in: *The Holocene* 14(2), London, pp. 165–171.
Latham, R. E 1965. *Revised Medieval Latin Word-List*, London.
Lawrence, C.H. 2001. *Medieval Monasticism*, third edition, Longman publishers.
Louvre–Guide du visiteur, Les Objets d'art, Moyen Age et Renaissance, Réunion des Musées Nationaux, Paris 1993.
Løvberg, K. 1991. "En kvartærsedimentologisk analyse af GUS. Feltrapport 1991", udført for Grønlands NationalMuseum af Kit Løvberg, institutt for Almen Geologi, Geologisk Centralinstitut.
Lübben, A. 1888: *Mittelniederdeutsches Handwörterbuch*, Leipzig 1888; reprint Darmstadt 1993.
Lunden, K. 1975. "Potetdyrkinga og den raske folketalsvoksteren i Noreg frå 1815", in: *Historisk tidsskrift*, volume 54, Oslo, pp. 275–315.

Lund Jensen, E. 2014. *Rejsen til landets ende. Historien om 1800-tallets innvandring fra Østgrønland til Kap Farvel*, Copenhagen.

Lynnerup, N. 1998. *The Greenland Norse–A Biological Anthropological Study*, Ph.D. dissertation, Panum Institute, University of Copenhagen 1995; printed in: MoG, Man and Society volume 24, Copenhagen 1998, 179 pages. Jan Heinemeier and Niels Rud wrote pp. 44–50 in the printed version.

Lynnerup, N. 2000. "Life and death in Norse Greenland", in: *Vikings. The North Atlantic Saga*, Fitzhugh W. ed., Washington, pp. 285–294.

Madsen, C. K. 2013. *Farming in the Norse Fjords in the Comparative Island Ecodynamics in the North Atlantic (CIE)*. Interim Field report on surveys and sampling in the southern Eastern Settlement summer 2013.

(a) Madsen, C. K. 2014. *Pastoral settlement, farming and hierarchy in Norse Vatnahverfi*, PhD dissertation in archaeology, University of Copenhagen.

(b) Madsen, C. K. 2014. "Norse pastoral farming and settlement in the Vatnahverfi peninsula, South Greenland", in: *Northern Worlds*, Gulløv, H. C. ed., published by Nationalmuseet in Copenhagen. Series: Studies in Archaeology and History, volume 22. Copenhagen, pp. 95–114.

Mahler, D. 1993. "Shielings and their Role in the Viking-Age Economy", in: *The Viking Age in Caithness, Orkney and the North Atlantic"*. Proceedings of the eleventh Viking Congress 1989, Edinburgh, pp. 487–505.

Malmros, C. 1992. *Gården under sandet. Profiloppmåling og prøveudtagning ved en nordbogård i Vesterbygden, Grønland 1991*, NNU rapport no. 19.

Marquardt, O. 2000. "Kolonitiden", in: *Topografisk Atlas Grønland*, published as part of "Atlas over Danmark" serie II volume 6, by Det Kongelige Danske Geografiske Selskab and Kort og Matrikkelstyrelsen, Copenhagen, pp. 56–59.

Massa, C., Bichet, V., Gauthier, É., Perren, B., Mathieu, O., Petit, C., Monna, F., Giraudeau, J., Losno, R. and Richard, H. 2012. "A 2500 year record of natural and anthropogenic soil erosion in South Greenland", in: *Quaternary Science Reviews* 32, pp. 119–130.

Mathiassen, T. 1934. "Contributions to the Archaeology of Disko Bay", in: MoG volume 93 no. 2, 192 pages, Copenhagen.

(a) Mathiassen, T. 1936. "The former Eskimo settlements on Fredrik VI's coast", in: MoG volume 109 no. 2, 55 pages, Copenhagen.

(b) Mathiassen, T. 1936. "The Eskimo Archaeology in the Julianehaab district", in: MoG volume 118 no.1, 141 pages, Copenhagen.

Mathieu, J. 1998. *Geschichte der Alpen 1500–1900, Umwelt–Entwicklung–Gesellschaft*, Böhlau Verlag, Wien.

Mathieu, J. 2015. *Die Alpen, Raum–Kultur–Geschichte*, Reclam Verlag, Stuttgart.

McGhee, R. 1990. *Canadian Arctic Prehistory*, Quebec.

McGovern, T. 1979. *The Paleoeconomy of Norse Greenland: Adaption and Extinction in a Tightly Bounded Ecosystem*, unpublished PhD dissertation, Columbia University, New York.

McGovern, T. 1985. "Contributions to the paleoeconomy of Norse Greenland", in: *Acta Archaeologica* 54, Copenhagen, pp. 73–122.

McGovern, T. 1992. "The zooarchaeology of the Vatnahverfi", in: *Vatnahverfi, an inland district of the Eastern settlement in Greenland*, ed. C. Vebæk, MoG, Man and Society volume 17, Copenhagen 1992, pp. 93–107.

McGovern, T. 2000. "The demise of Norse Greenland", in: *Vikings, the North Atlantic saga*, Fitzhugh, W. ed., Smithsonian Institution Press, Washington 2000, pp. 327–339.

McGovern, T. 2011. "Vikings in the International Polar Year 2007–2009: Still bloodthirsty, but also ecodynamic and educational", in: *Viking Settlements and Viking Society*, Sigmundsson, S. ed. Papers from the Proceedings of the Sixteenth Viking Congress, Reykjavik, pp. 290–303.

McGovern, T., Amorosi, T., Bigelow, G., Perdikaris, S. and Woollett, J. 1993. "The zooarchaeology of E17a", in: *Narsaq–a Norse landnáma farm*, ed. C. Vebæk, MoG, Man and Sociey volume 18, Copenhagen, pp. 58–72.

McGovern, T., Amorosi, T., Perdikaris, S. and Woollett, J. 1996. "Vertebrate zooarchaeology of Sandnes W51: Economic change at a chieftain's farm in West Greenland", in: *Arctic Anthropology*, volume 33 no. 2, pp. 94–121.

(a) McGovern, T. and others 2007. "Norse Greenland Settlement: Reflections on Climate Change, Trade and the Contrasting Fates of Human Settlements in the North Atlantic Islands", in: *Arctic Archaeology*, volume 44, No. 1, pp. 12–36.

(b) McGovern, T. and others 2007. "Bone remains" in: *Archaeological excavations at Qassiarsuk 2005–2006*, Field report, ed. Ragnar Edvardsson, Grønlands NationalMuseum & arkiv 2007, pp. 22–36.

Medieval Scandinavia–an Encyclopedia, ed. P. Pulsiano, New York 1993.

Meldgaard, J. 1982. "Tjodhildes kirke–den første fundberetning", in: *Tidsskriftet Grønland*, Copenhagen, pp. 151–162.

Meldgaard, J. 1995. "Eskimoer og nordboer i det yderste nord", in: *Nationalmuseets arbejdsmark* 1995, Copenhagen, pp. 199–214.

Meldgaard, M. 1986. "The Greenland caribou–zoogeography, taxonomy and population dynamics," MoG, Bioscience volume 20, 88 pages, Copenhagen.

Mikkelsen, N., Kuijpers, A. and Arneborg, J. 2008. "The Norse in Greenland and late Holocene sea-level change", in: *Polar Record* 44 (228), Cambridge, pp. 45–50.

Mikkelsen, N., Kuijpers, A., Lassen, S. and Vedel, J. 2001. "Marine and terrestrial investigations in the Norse Eastern Settlement, South Greenland", in: *Geology of Greenland Survey Bulletin* no. 189, Copenhagen, pp. 65–69.

Miller, W. I. 1990. *Bloodtaking and Peacemaking*, Chicago.

(a) Mogensen, G. S. 1999. "Mosser", in: *Grønlands økologi–en grundbog*, Born, E. W. and Böcher, J. eds. Atuakkiorfik Undervisning, Nuuk, pp. 258–263.

(b) Mogensen, G. S. 1999. "Ammassæt", in: *Grønlands økologi–en grundbog*, Born, E. W. and Böcher, J. eds., Atuakkiorfik Undervisning, Nuuk, pp. 164.

Møller, N. A. and Madsen, C. K. 2007. *Gård og Sæter, Hus og Fold–Vatnahverfi*. Rapport om besigtigelser og opmålinger i Vatnahverfi, sommeren 2006. SILA report no. 25, 39 pages. Published by Nationalmuseets Center for Grønlandsforskning, Copenhagen.

Moltke, E. 1936. "Greenland Runic inscriptions", in: MoG volume 88.2, Copenhagen, pp. 223–232.

Munch, P. A. ed. 1864. *Pavelige nuntiers regnskabs- og dagbøger, førte under tiendeopkrævingen i Norden 1282–1334*, Christiania.

Muus, B. 1990. "Fisk", in: *Grønlands fauna–Fisk, fugle, pattedyr*, Muus, B., Salomonsen, F. and Vibe, C. eds., Copenhagen, pp. 23–158.

Myhre, B. 1982. "Synspunkter på huskonstruksjonen i sørvestnorske gårdshus fra jernalder og middelalder", in: *Vestnordisk byggeskikk gjennom to tusen år*, Myhre, B. and others eds., published by Arkeologisk museum i Stavanger. Skrifter volume 7, Stavanger, pp. 98–118

Nansen, F. 1911. *In Northern Mists* volume 1, London.

Naumann, E. 2014. *Diet, mobility and social identity in Norway 400–1050. An investigation based on 13C, 15N and 87Sr/86Sr analyses of human remains*. PhD thesis, Faculty of Humanities, University of Oslo.
(a) Naumann, E., Krzewiaska, M., Gotherstrom, A. and Eriksson, G. 2014. "Slaves as burial gifts in Viking Age Norway? Evidence from stable isotope and ancient DNA analyses", in: *Journal of Archaeological Science*, volume 41, Elsevier publishers, pp. 533–540.
(b) Naumann, E., Price, T. D. and Richards, M. P. 2014. "Changes in dietary practices and social organization during the pivotal Late Iron Age period in Norway (AD 550–1030). Isotope analyses of Merovingian and Viking Age human remains", in: *American Journal of Physical Anthropology*, volume 155(3), New York, pp. 322–331, available online.
Nedkvitne, A. 1977. "Handelssjøfarten mellom Norge og England i høymiddelalderen", in: *Sjøfartshistorisk årbok* 1976, published by Bergen sjøfartsmuseum, pp. 7–254.
Nedkvitne, A. 1988. *"Mens Bønderne seilte og Jægterne fór". Nordnorsk og vestnorsk kystøkonomi 1500–1730*, Bergen.
Nedkvitne, A. 1989. "Runepinner og handelshistorie", in: *Historisk tidsskrift* volume 68, Oslo, pp. 348–350.
Nedkvitne, A. 2004. *The Social Consequences of Literacy in Medieval Scandinavia*, Brepols publishers.
Nedkvitne, A. 2005. "Bønder og skrift i norsk middelalder", in: *Historisk tidsskrift*, Oslo, pp. 97–106.
Nedkvitne, A. 2009. *Lay Belief in Norse Society*, Copenhagen.
Nedkvitne, A. 2011. *Ære, lov og religion i Norge gjennom tusen år*, Oslo.
(a) Nedkvitne, A. 2014. *The German Hansa and Bergen 1100–1600*. Series: Quellen und Darstellungen zur Hansischen Geschichte 70, Köln.
(b) Nedkvitne, A. 2014. "Linguistic tensions between Germans and natives in Scandinavia compared to Eastern Europe", in: *Uses of the Written Word in Medieval Towns. Medieval Literacy II*, Mostert, M. and Adamska, A. eds. Brepols publishers, pp. 87–97.
(a) Nelson, D. E., Møhl, J., Heinemeier, J. and Arneborg, J. 2012. "Stable Carbon and Nitrogen isotopic Measurements of Wild Animals hunted by the Norse and Neo-Eskimo People of Greenland", in: *Journal of the North Atlantic*, special volume 3, pp. 40–50.
(b) Nelson, D. E., Heinemeier J., Møhl, J. and Arneborg, J. 2012. "Isotopic Analyses of the Domestic Animals of Norse Greenland", in: *Journal of the North Atlantic*, special volume 3, pp. 77–92.
(c) Nelson, D. E., Heinemeier J., Lynnerup, N., Sveinbjörnsdóttir, Á. E. and Arneborg, J. 2012. "An Isotopic Analysis of the Diet of the Greenland Norse", in: *Journal of the North Atlantic*, special volume 3, pp. 93–118.
Nenseter, O. 2002. *Å lære andre gjennom ord og eksempel. Augustinerklostrene på Vestlandets religiøse funksjoner*, Master thesis in history, University of Oslo.
Nielsen, N. 1930. "Evidence on the extraction of iron in Greenland by the Norsemen", in: MoG volume 76, Copenhagen 1930, pp. 193–213.
Niermeyer J. F. 1993 (ed.). *Mediae Latinitatis Lexicon Minus*, Leiden.
Nordal, S. 1953. "Sagalitteraturen", in: *Nordisk Kultur* VIII:B, Copenhagen.
Nordeide, S. 1994. "Handel og vareutveksling", in: Christophersen, A. and Nordeide, S. eds. *Kaupangen ved Nidelva*, Riksantikvarens Skrifter 7, pp. 243–260.
Nørlund, P. 1924. "Buried Norsemen at Herjolvsnes", in: MoG 67, Copenhagen, pp. 1–270.
Nørlund, P. 1926. Unprinted report in "Nordboarkivet" in Nationalmuseet in Copenhagen with the heading "Grønland" and signed "Poul Nørlund 1926". The report includes Ketilsfjord with a "superficial examination" of the Augustinian monastery E105.

A description of the Augustinian monastery E105 and a ground plan of its church were added by Svend Albrethsen in 1970.
Nørlund, P. 1927. "Kirkegården på Herjolvsnes. Et bidrag til diskussionen om klimateorien", in: *Historisk Tidsskrift* 5. rekke (= 5th series) 6. bind (= 6th volume), Oslo, pp. 385–402.
Nørlund, P. 1928. "En bispestav af hvalrostand fra Grønland", in: *Fra Nationalmuseets arbejdsmark* 1928, Copenhagen, pp. 61–66.
Nørlund, P. 1942. *De gamle nordbobygder ved verdens ende*, first edition 1934, second edition 1935, third edition 1942, and fourth edition 1967. All editions were published in Copenhagen and have 153 pages. English translation: *Viking Settlers in Greenland and their descendants during five hundred years*, Cambridge University press, London 1936, 160 pages. The edition from 1942 and the English translation from 1936 are referred to in the notes.
Nørlund, P. and Roussell, A. 1930. "Norse ruins at Gardar, the episcopal seat of medieval Greenland", in: MoG volume 76, Copenhagen, pp. 1–170.
Nørlund, P. and Stenberger, M. 1934. "Brattahlid", in: MoG volume 88.1, Copenhagen, pp. 1–161.
Norsk biografisk leksikon. First edition: volumes 1–19, Bull, E., Krogvig, A. and Gran, G. eds., Oslo 1923–1983. Second edition: volumes 1–10, Arntzen, J.G. and Helle, K. eds., Oslo 1999–2005.
Norsk ordbok. Ordbok over det norske folkemålet og det nynorske skriftmålet, Wetås, Å. and others eds., volumes 1–12, Oslo 1966–Oslo 2016.
Norsk stadnamnleksikon, Sandnes, J., Stemshaug, O. and Aune, K. eds., Oslo 1997.
Norske Gaardnavne I-XIX, Rygh, O. and others, eds., Oslo 1897–1936.
Nyegaard, G. 2009. "Restoration of the Hvalsey Fjord Church", in: *Journal of the North Atlantic*, special volume 2, 2009, Norse Greenland–Selected Papers from the Hvalsey Conference 2008, pp. 7–18.
Nyegaard, G. 2014. "Dairy Farmers and Seal Hunters. Subsistence on a Norse Farm in the Eastern Settlement, Greenland", Unpublished manuscript which Georg Nyegaard kindly gave me access to in September 2014. It is used with the author's permission. It is a data file without pagination.
Odess, D., Loring, S. and Fitzhugh, W. 2000. "Skraeling: The first peoples of Helluland, Markland and Vinland", in: *Vikings, the North Atlantic saga*", Fitzhugh, W. ed., Washington, pp. 193–207.
Olason, V. 1993. "Kvedskapur frá sidmidöldum", in: *Islensk bokmenntasaga* II, published by Mál og menning, Reykjavík, pp. 285–378.
Ordbog over det danske sprog, 28 volumes, ed. Verner Dahlerup and others, published by Det danske sprog- og litteraturselskab, Copenhagen 1919–1956.
Ostenfeld, C.H. 1926. "The flora of Greenland and its origin", Biol. Medd. Danmark, Vid. Selsk. 6, no. 3, Copenhagen, the entire volume.
Østergård, E. 2003. *Som syet til jorden. Tekstilfund fra det norrøne Grønland*, Århus.
Pentz, P. 2014. "Ships and the Vikings", in: *Vikings–Life and Legend*, Williams, G., Pentz, P. and Wemhoff, M. eds. Published by The British Museum, London, pp. 203–227.
Petersen, F. 1896. "Undersøgelser af ruiner ved Agdluitsok-Fjord", in: MoG volume 16, pp. 408–437.
Pilgrim, V. 2004. *The Greenland Norse: The hunt for wood in Labrador. A cross cultural perspective*, unpublished MA thesis, The Centre for Nordic Viking and Medieval Studies, University of Oslo.
Pinker, S. 2011. *The Better Angels of our Nature*, London.

Bibliography

Pitt-Rivers, J. 1965. "Honour and social status", in: *Honour and Shame. The Values of Mediterranean Society*, Peristiany J. G. ed., London, pp. 19–77.
Pontoppidan, E. 1752–53. *Norges naturlige historie* I, Copenhagen.
Porsild, M. 1919. "Hvor gammel er brugen af isgarn til sælfangst i Grønland?" in: *Tidsskriftet Grønland*, Copenhagen, pp. 9–16.
Raahauge, K. and Gulløv H. C. "Indsamling af får i grønlandsk middelalder", *Tidskriftet Grønland* 2005/5, 53. årgang, pp. 165–176.
Raahauge, K., Høegh-Knudsen, P., Gulløw, H. C., Møhl, J., Krause, C. and Møller, N.A. 2003. "Tidlig Thulekultur i Sydgrønland. Rapport om undersøgelserne i Nanortalik kommune, sommeren 2002", SILA, Feltrapport no. 9, 75 pages, Copenhagen.
Ramskou, T. 1966. "Ret kurs", in: *Skalk* hefte 6, pp. 27–29.
Rasmussen, K. 1906. *Under nordenvindens svøbe*, Copenhagen.
Rasmussen, K. 1938. *Knud Rasmussen's posthumous notes on the life and doings of the east Greenlanders in olden times*, ed. H. Ostermann, in: MoG volume 109 no.1, 215 pages, Copenhagen.
Reinton, L. *Sæterbruket i Noreg*; volume 1, Oslo 1955 and volume 2, Oslo 1957.
Robinson, J. 2004. *The Lewis Chessmen*, The British Museum Press, London.
Roesdahl, E. 1995. *Hvalrostand, elfenben og nordboerne i Grønland*, Odense.
Rogers, P. W. 1993. "Dyes and wools in Norse textiles from E17a", in: *Narsaq–a Norse landnáma farm*, in MoG, Man and Society volume 18, Copenhagen, pp. 56–58.
Rogers, P. W. 2003. "Fibre og farver i nordbotekstiler", in: *Som syet til jorden*, Østergård, E. ed., Copenhagen 2003, pp. 79–107.
Rollason, D. 2003. *Northumbria 500–1100. Creation and Destruction of a Kingdom*, Cambridge.
Rosing, J. 1988. "Rensdyrjegerne i Itinnera", in: *Palæoeskimoisk forskning i Grønland*, Mjøberg, T., Grønnow, B. and Schultz-Lorentzen, H. eds., Århus, pp. 69–79.
Roussell, A. 1936. "Sandnes and the neighbouring farms", in: MoG volume 88.2, Copenhagen, pp. 1–219.
Roussell, A. 1938. "Udgravninger i en afsides grønlandsk nordbobygd", in: *Nationalmuseets arbejdsmark* 1938, Copenhagen, pp. 55–64.
Roussell, A. 1941. "Farms and churches in the medieval Norse settlements of Greenland", in: MoG volume 89, Copenhagen, pp. 1–354; Also published as book by C. A. Reitzel publishers, Copenhagen 1941.
Sandgren, P. and Fredskild, B. 1991. "Magnetic measurements recording of late Holocene man-induced erosion in South Greenland", *Boreas* volume 20, pp. 315–331.
Sandnes, J. 1968. "Garder, bruk og folketall i Norge i høgmiddelalderen", in: *Historisk tidsskrift* volume 47, Oslo, pp. 261–292.
Sara, O. K. 1979. "Reindriftsnæringen", in: *By og bygd i Norge, Finnmark*, Reidar Hirsti, ed., Oslo, pp. 360–367.
Schirmer, H. 1886. "Beliggenheden af Gardar på Grønland", in: *Historisk tidsskrift*, 2. rekke volume 5, Christiania (Oslo), pp. 412–417.
Schulerud, A. 1945. *Norske næringsmidler*, Oslo.
Seaver, K. 1992. *The Frozen Echo*, Stanford.
Sigurdsson, G. 2004. *The Medieval Icelandic Saga and Oral Tradition*, Harvard University Press.
Sivertsen, E. 1947. "Selene", in: *Norges dyreliv*, volume 1 Pattedyr, Føyn, B. and Huus, J. eds., Cappelen publishers, Oslo, pp. 176–226.
Skaaning Høegsberg, M. 2005. *Det norrøne bispesæde i Gardar, Grønland*. Konferens-speciale, Afdeling for Middelalder- og Renæssancearkeologi, Århus Universitet.

Skaaning Høegsberg, M. 2007. "A reassessment of the development of the Cathedral at Gardar, Greenland", in: *Archaeologia Islandica* volume 6, Reykjavík, pp. 74–96.

Skaaning Høegsberg, M. 2009. *Materiel kultur og kulturel identitet i det norrøne Grønland*, volumes I–II, PhD thesis, University of Århus, Institute for Anthropology, Archaeology and Linguistics, Århus 2009.

Smiarowski, K. 2007. *Greenland 2007 Field Season–Preliminary report*. Unpublished report on excavations in Vatnahverfi, to the Greenlandic NationalMuseum in Nuuk, 18 pages.

Smiarowski, K. 2012. *Preliminary report on the 2012 archaeofauna from E47 Gardar in the Eastern settlement*. Unpublished report in Nationalmuseet in Copenhagen, read in November 2013.

Solberg, B. 2002. "Anne Stine Ingstad", in: *Norsk biografisk leksikon*, second edition, Helle K. ed., volume 5, Oslo, p. 33.

Sørensen, I. 1982. "Pollenundersøgelser i møddingen på Niaqussat", in: *Tidsskriftet Grønland* 1982, nos. 8–9, annual volume no. 30, Copenhagen, pp. 296–302.

Spurkland, T. 2001. *I begynnelsen var Futhark*, Oslo.

Steenstrup, K. J. V 1886. "Om Østerbygden", in: MoG volume 9, Copenhagen, pp. 1–39.

Steinnes, A. 1962. "Peder Claussøn Friis", in: *Norsk biografisk leksikon*, first edition, volume 14, Oslo, pp. 534–551.

Stoklund, M. 1984. "Nordbokorsene fra Grønland", in: *Nationalmuseets Arbejdsmark* 1984, Copenhagen, pp. 101–113.

(a) Stoklund, M. 1993. "Greenland runes, isolation or cultural contact?" in: *The Viking Age in Caithness, Orkney and the North Atlantic"*, Proceedings of the eleventh Viking Congress, Edinburgh, pp. 528–543.

(b) Stoklund, M. 1993. "Objects with runic inscriptions from E17a", in: MoG, Man and Society volume 18, Copenhagen, pp. 47–52.

Storm, G. 1884. "Harald Hardraade og Væringerne i den græske keisers tjeneste", in: *Historisk Tidsskrift*, 2. række, 4. bind, pp. 354–386.

Storm, G. 1890. "Om Biskop Gisle Oddsøns Annaler", in: *Arkiv för nordisk filologi* VI, Stockholm, pp. 351–357.

Stratford, N. 1997. *The Lewis Chessmen*, The Trustees of the British Museum, London.

Struman-Hansen, S. 2003. "The early settlement of the Faeroe Islands", in: *Contact, Continuity and Collapse*, Barrett, J. H. ed., Brepols publishers, pp. 33–71.

Thorlaksson, H. 2012. "Succumbing to secular chiefs. On secular chiefs in Iceland, their loss of ground to the church, c.1270 to 1355 and its impact" in: *Ecclesia Nidrosiensis and Noregs veldi*, Imsen, S. ed., Trondheim, pp. 261–281.

Valeur, H. 2000. "Havis", in: *Topografisk Atlas Grønland;* published as part of "Atlas over Danmark" series II volume 6, by Det Kongelige Danske Geografiske Selskab and Kort og Matrikkelstyrelsen, Copenhagen, pp. 14–17.

Vandvik, E. ed. 1959. *Latinske dokument til norsk historie fram til år 1204*, edited in the Latin original language and translated into Norwegian, Oslo.

Vebæk, C. L. 1941. "Middelalderlige bondegaarde paa Grønland. En sommers udgravninger i Nordboernes østerbygd" (E64a, b and c), in: *Fra Nationalmuseets arbejdsmark* 1941, pp. 39–48.

Vebæk, C. L. 1943. "Inland farms in the Norse East settlement", in: MoG volume 90 no.1, Copenhagen, pp. 1–119.

Vebæk, C. L. 1953. "Klostre i de grønlandske nordbobygder", in: *Tidsskriftet Grønland*, volume 1953, issue no. 5, Copenhagen, pp. 195–200.

Vebæk, C. L. 1956. "Mellembygden", in: *Tidsskriftet Grønland* 1956, no. 3, Copenhagen, pp. 92–98.

Vebæk, C. L. 1982. "Vatnahverfi", in: *Tidsskriftet Grønland*, 30th annual volume, nos. 8–9, Copenhagen, pp. 207–217.

(a) Vebæk, C. L. 1991. "Hunting on land and at sea and fishing in Medieval Norse Greenland", in: *Acta Borealia* volume 8, no. 1, London, pp. 5–14.

(b) Vebæk, C. L. 1991. *The church topography of the Eastern settlement and the excavation of the Benedictine Convent at Narsarsuaq in the Unatorq Fjord*, MoG, Man and Society volume 14, Copenhagen.

Vebæk, C. L. 1992. *Vatnahverfi. An Inland district of the Eastern Settlement in Greenland*, in the series: MoG, Man and Society volume 17, Copenhagen, entire volume.

Vebæk, C. L. 1993. *Narsaq–a Norse landnám farm*, in the series: MoG, Man and Society volume 18, Copenhagen, entire volume.

Vesteinsson, O. 2005. "The formative phase of the Icelandic Church ca. 990–1240 AD", in: *Church centres*, Thorlaksson, H. ed., Reykholt, pp. 71–81.

Vesteinsson, O. 2014. *Archaeological investigations in Igaliku*. Excavations at the meadow 2012–2013, Field Report, Reykjavik.

Vibe, C. 1981. "Landpattedyr", in: *Danmarks natur*, Copenhagen, pp. 477–499.

Vibe, C. 1990. "Pattedyr", in: *Grønlands fauna–Fisk, fugle, pattedyr*, Muus, B., Salomonsen, F. and Vibe, C. eds., Copenhagen, pp. 364–459.

Vollsnes, H. 2004. *"at minu borde má hæyra thiotannde strænglæica med sætum ok fagra tona". Musikk som en del av kulturhistorien i norsk middelalder*. Master thesis in History, University of Oslo.

W = Western Settlement. The Norse Settlement in the fjords east of present day Nuuk. Cf. E = Eastern Settlement. The Norse Settlement in the fjords east of present day Qaqortoq.

Wallace, B. 2000. "The Viking settlement at L'Anse aux Meadows", in: *Vikings, The North Atlantic Saga*, Fitzhugh, W. ed., Washington 2000, pp. 208–224.

Weidick, A. 1982. "Klima og gletscherendringer i det sydlige Vestgrønland i de sidste 1000 år", in: *Tidsskriftet Grønland*, 30th annual volume, Copenhagen, pp. 235–251.

Widding, O. 1976. *Islenzk–Dönsk ordabok*, Reykjavik.

Wold, H. 2004. *Querinis reise*, Orkana publishers, Stamsund.

Woodward, D. 2013. "Geography", in: *The Cambridge History of Science*, volume 2 Medieval Science, Cambridge, pp. 548–568.

Appendix I

Empirical material for Table 5.7

W54 Nipaatsoq

Bone fragments from meat-bearing animals

Seal	765	42%
Reindeer	357	20%
Sheep/goat	520	29%
Cattle	165	9%
Sum	1807	100%

Sources: McGovern 1979, p. 374; Enghoff 2003, p. 93.

GUS

Bone fragments from main meat-bearing animals

Seal	3098	44%
Reindeer	1192	17%
Sheep/goat	2156	30%
Cattle	659	9%
Sum	7105	100%

Source: Enghoff 2003, p. 22.

W51 Sandnes

Bone fragments from main meat-bearing animals

Seal	1561	48%
Reindeer	736	23%
Sheep/goat	556	17%
Cattle	378	12%
Sum	3231	100%

Source: McGovern et al. 1996, p. 106, table 3.

W59

Bone fragments from main meat-bearing animals

Seal	2740	64%
Reindeer	790	18%
Sheep/goat	575	13%
Cattle	166	4%
Sum	4271	99%

Source: McGovern 1979, p. 375.

W48 Niaquusat

Bone fragments from main meat-bearing animals

Seal	10,477	82%
Reindeer	693	5%
Sheep/goat	1,354	11%
Cattle	268	2%
Sum	12,792	100%

Source: McGovern 1979, pp. 371–373. W48's midden was excavated by McGovern in 1976–1977 (McGovern 1985, p. 84).

E34 in Qorlortup valley

Bone fragments from main meat-bearing animals

Seal	39%
Reindeer	6%
Sheep/goat	36%
Cattle	16%
Sum	97%

Source: Nyegaard 2014, section 6.1 "Totals for mammals, birds and fish from the 1997 and 1998 excavations". He gives percentages of other meat-bearing animals than the four in the table. The "Sum" is therefore lower than 100%.

Eight farms in Vatnahverfi (1)

Bone fragments from main meat-bearing animals

	Six farms (2)		E71 South		E167		Average (3)
Seal	612	51%	2102	43%	508	36%	43%
Reindeer	14	1%	82	2%	24	2%	2%
Sheep/goat	366	31%	2166	44%	545	39%	38%
Cattle	200	17%	564	11%	321	23%	17%
Sum	1192	100%	4914	100%	1398	100%	100%

Source: McGovern 1992, p. 95.

The "Six farms", "E71 South" and "E167" have been entered in three separate columns because the bone fragments excavated at E71South are so numerous that they would have dominated the "Average".

The "Six farms" are E64a, E64c, E66, E68, E71 North, and E78a.

The percentages in the column "Average" have been calculated by summarising the three percentages from "Six farms", "E71 South", and "E167" and dividing the sum by three.

E17a Narsaq

Bone fragments from main meat-bearing animals at Narsaq (E17a)

	Lower layer		Upper layer		All fragments	
Seal	440	49%	199	49%	639	49%
Reindeer	86	10%	22	5%	108	8%
Sheep/goat	243	27%	108	27%	351	27%
Cattle	127	14%	76	19%	203	16%
Sum	896	100%	405	100%	1301	100%

Source: McGovern et al. 1993, pp. 59–60; cf. Arneborg et al. 2012(b), pp. 129–130.

E149 Vágar?

Bone fragments from main meat-bearing animals

Seal	373	63%
Reindeer	23	4%
Sheep/goat	98	16%
Cattle	100	17%
Sum	594	100%

Source: Vebæk 1991(b), p. 72. His information on this point is taken from McGovern 1979, pp. 100–101.

E29a Brattahlid

Bone fragments from main meat-bearing animals

	1000–1200		1200–1410		All fragments	
Seal	135	53%	1476	73%	1611	71%
Reindeer	21	8%	62	3%	83	4%
Sheep/goat	54	21%	305	15%	359	16%
Cattle	45	18%	183	9%	228	10%
Sum	255	100%	2026	100%	2281	101%

Source: McGovern et al. 2007(b), pp. 23–25.

Appendix II

Maps of the Eastern, Western and Middle Settlements of the Norse
---

The location of the known Norse farms is given with the number assigned to them and used by the Danish Nationalmuseum.

Daniel Bruun created this numbering system with separate numbering for the Eastern Settlement starting with E1, the Western Settlement stating with W1 and the Middle Settlement starting with M1.

In this Appendix ten pages of maps are printed.

Maps 1 and 2 are from the Western Settlement.

Map 3 is from the Middle Settlement.

Maps 4–10 are from the Eastern Settlement.

The maps are copied from Knud Krogh's book *Erik den Rødes Grønland*, Nationalmuseets forlag, Copenhagen 1982, where the maps are printed as an appendix. The copyright to the maps then belonged to Geodætisk institut in Copenhagen. This institute no longer exists, and Nationalmuseet which published the book had no objections to my using the maps.

The map on this page shows which parts of Greenland are covered by the 10 following detailed maps. All ca. 280 Norse farms were situated in the areas covered by these 10 maps.

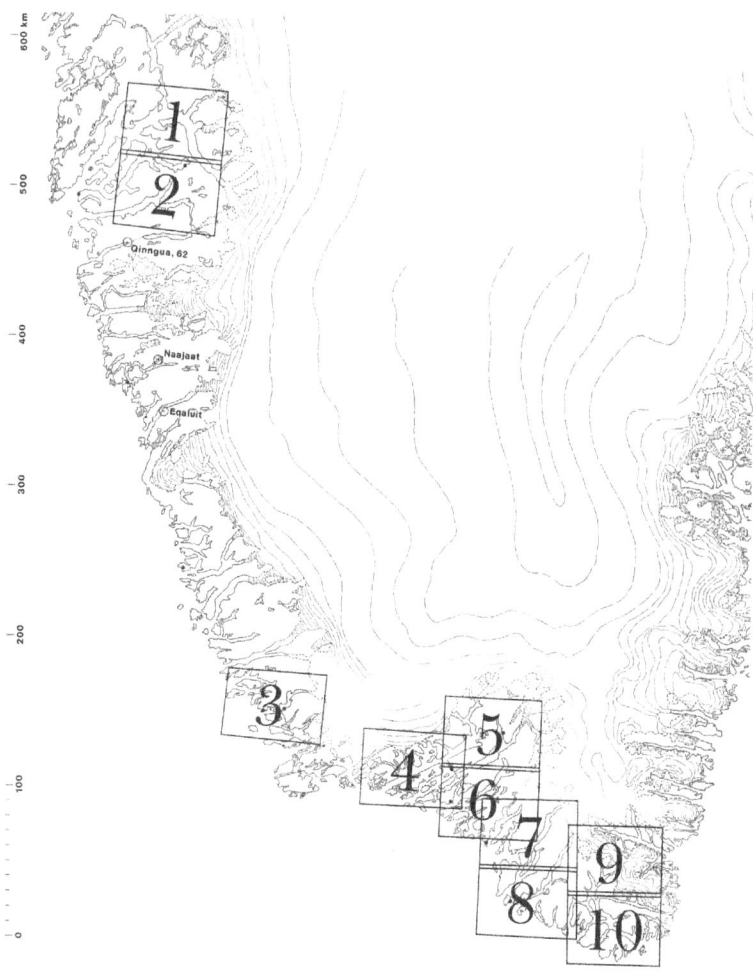

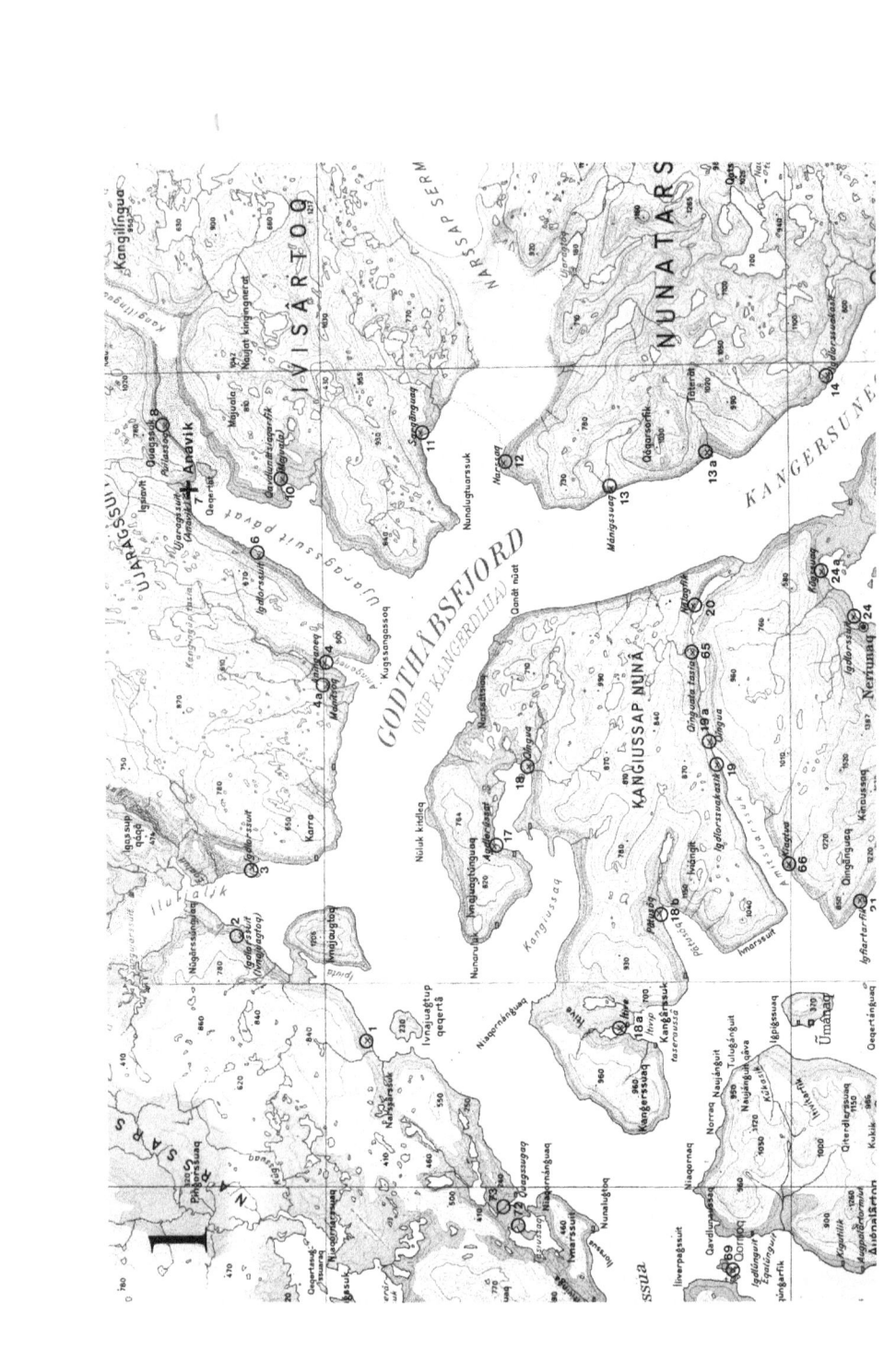

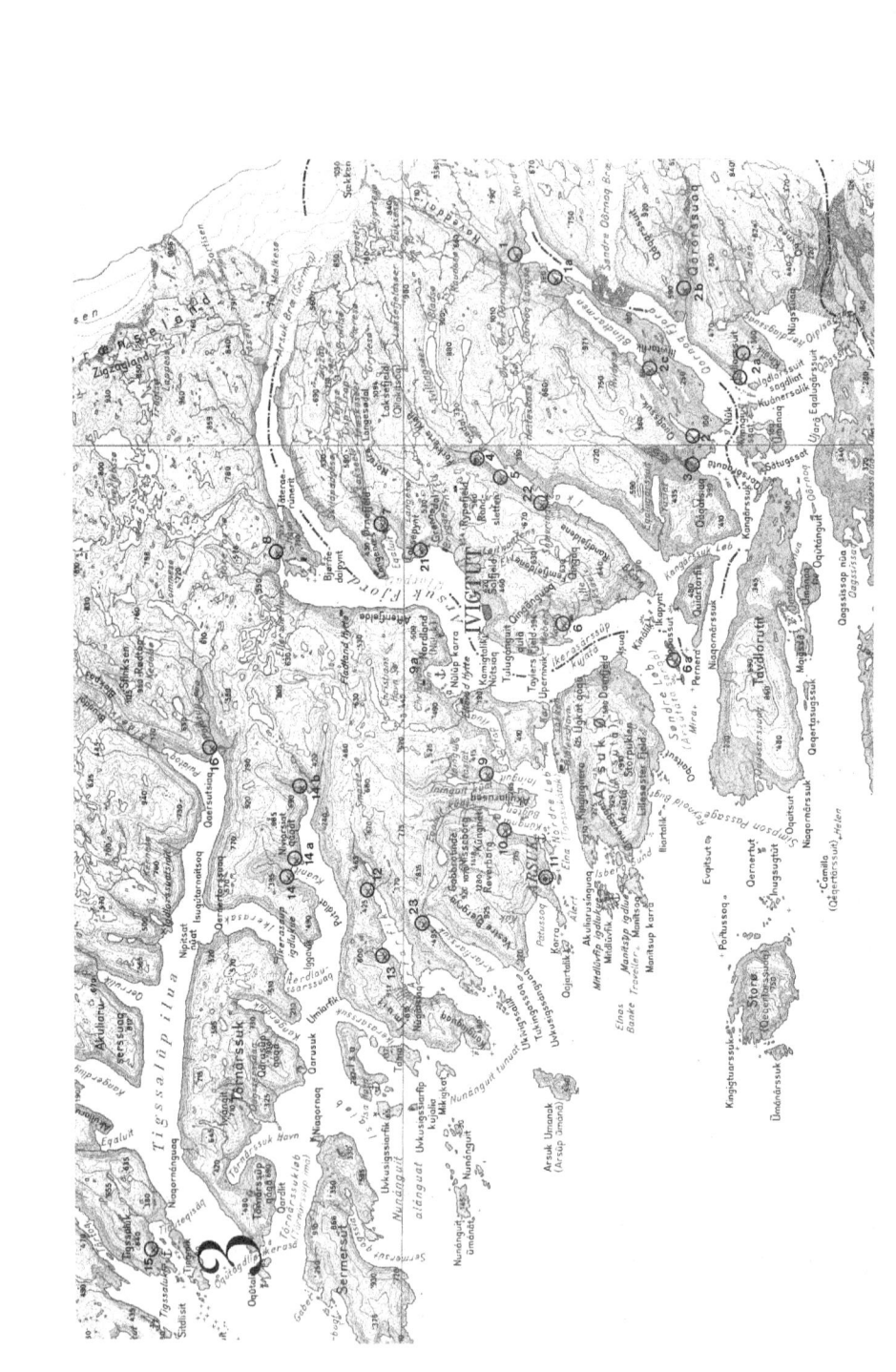

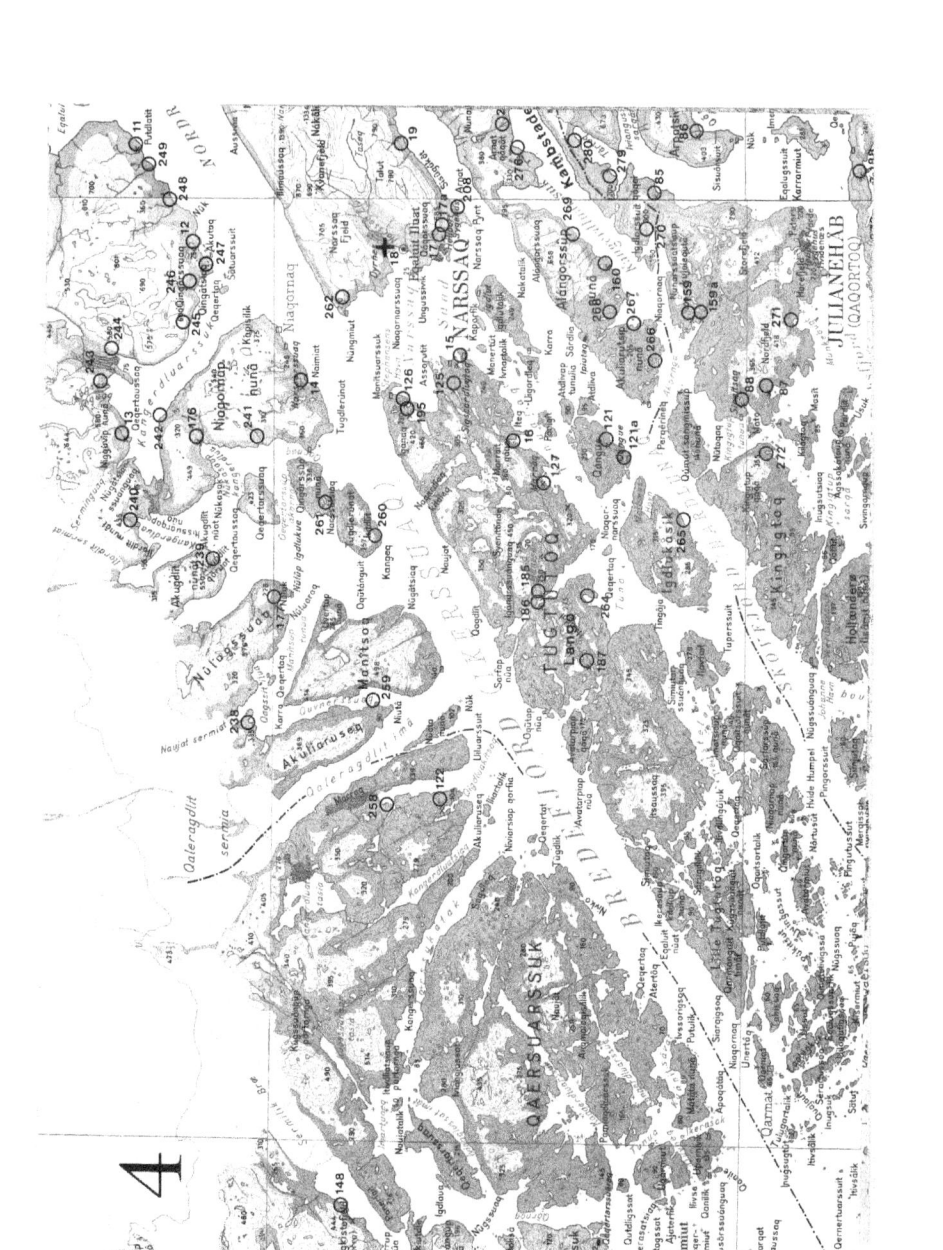

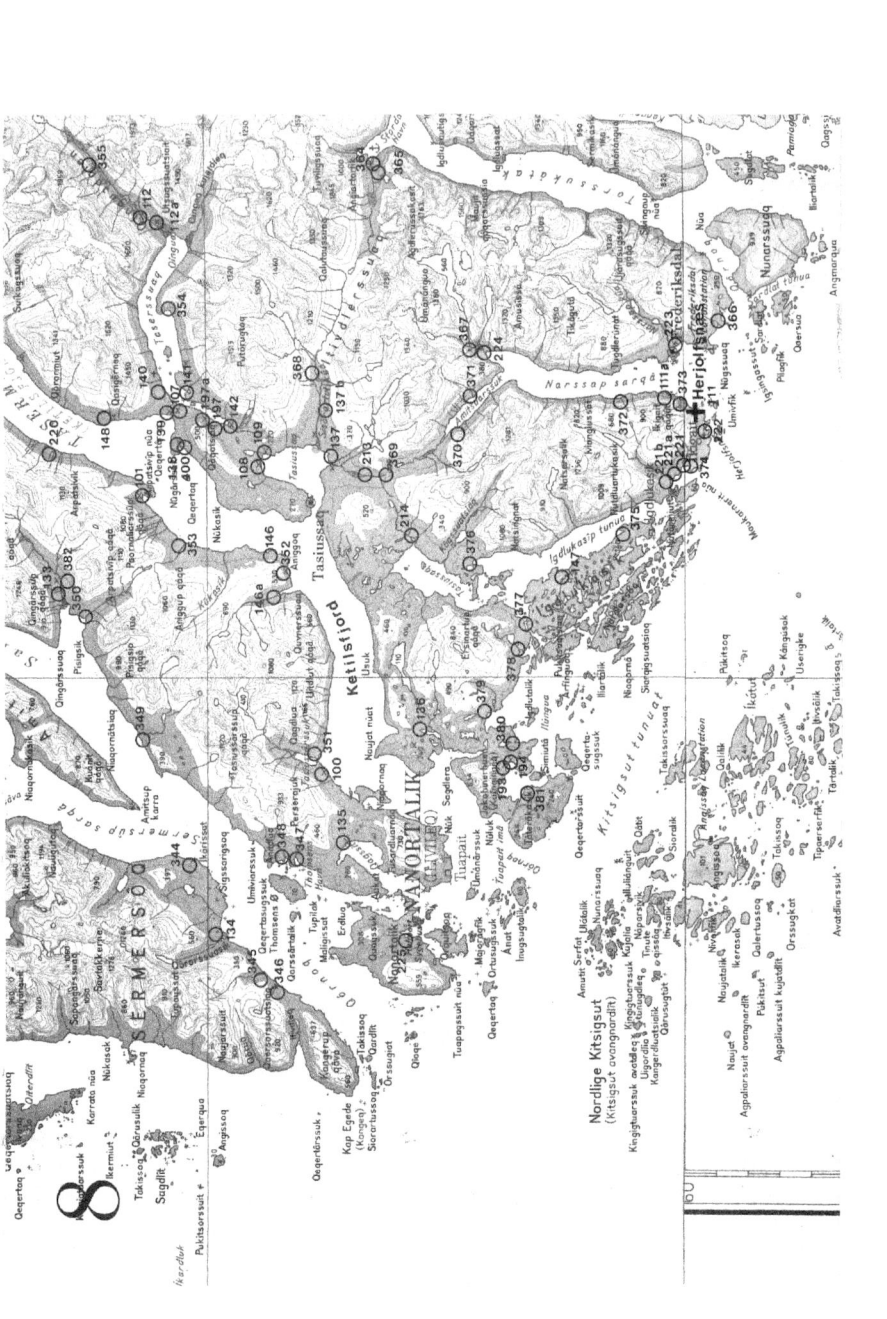

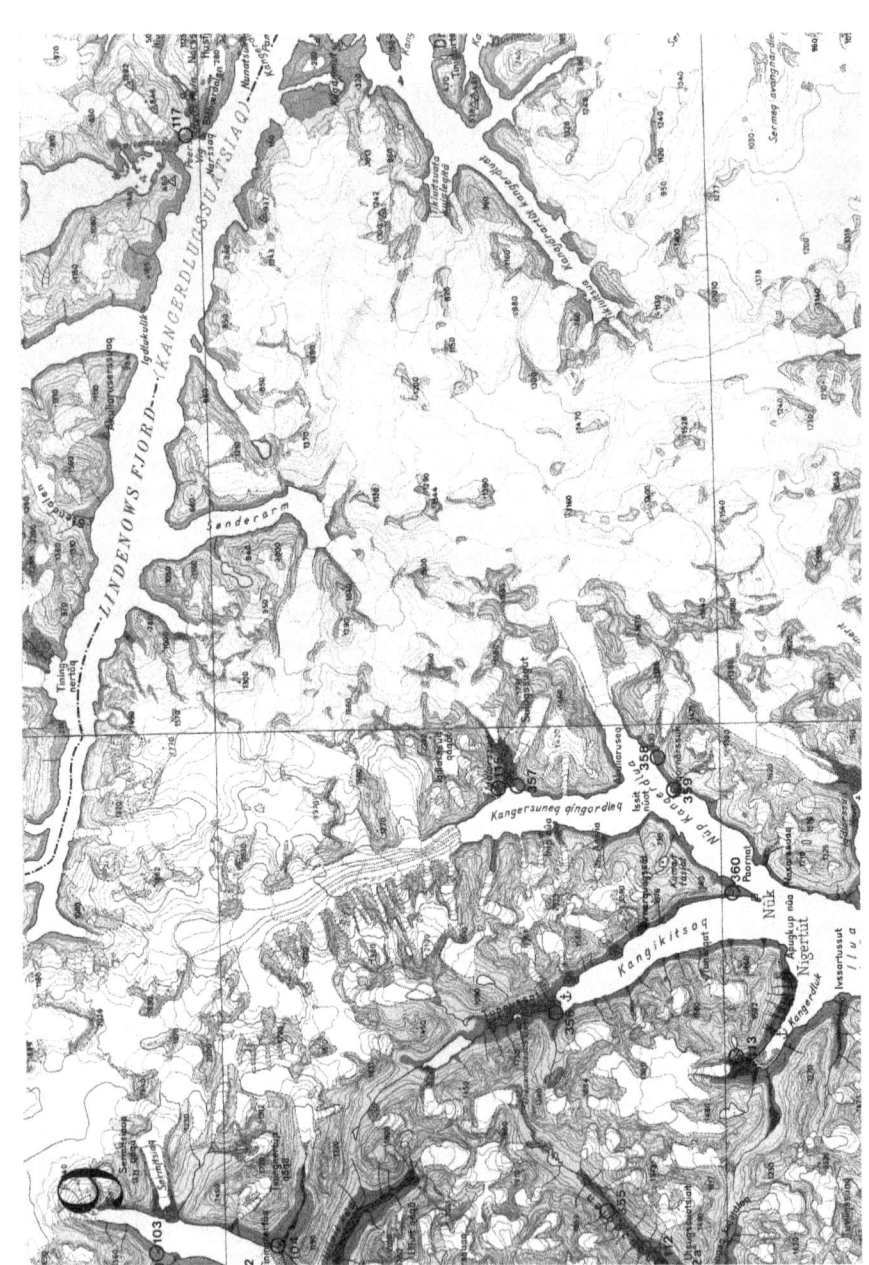

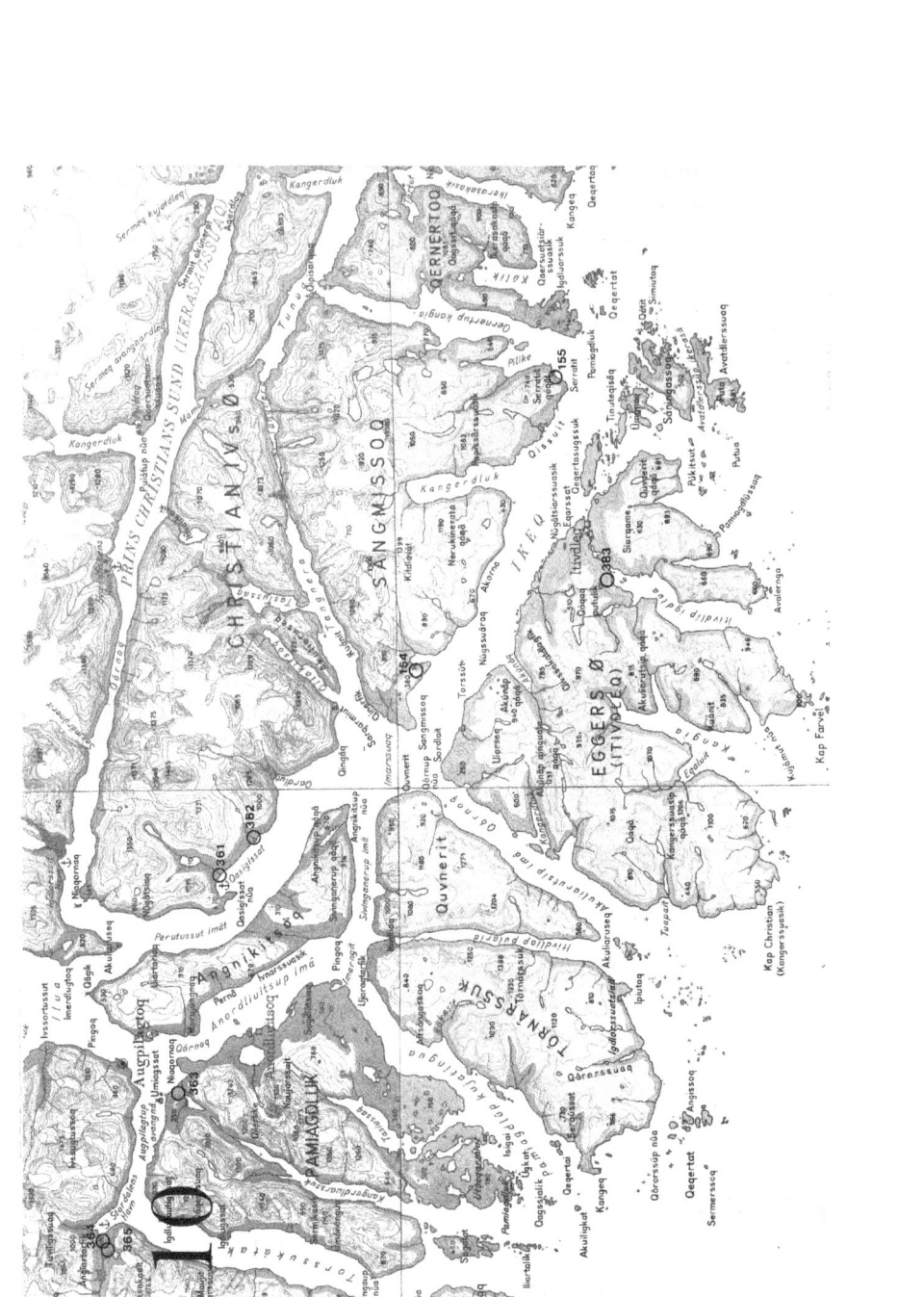

Index of matters

Entries which would have contained the same information as subheadings in the table of contents, have been excluded. The entries are selective. It is recommended to supplement the index with the table of contents.
Non-Scandinavian readers may not be familiar with Norse society. I have therefore added a few explanatory keywords at some entries.

after-boat (eptirbát), see lifeboat
agriculture 232–271, 26, 52, 298–300
alcohol 49; see also beer, wine
ammassæt (= capelin) 246, 251, 290, 292–295, 297, 330
angekok, Inuit spiritual leader 334, 336, 338, 364
angelica eaten as vegetable 251, 300, 363
anthracite, type of stone coal 169
anthropocene, definition 330; 330–331
archbishops
    Bremen 90
    Lund in Denmark 84, 91–92
    Trondheim 92, 102, 121–123, 115–128, 141–142, 172, 206, 343–344
arrow 163, 274, 278–281, 287, 312, 337, 370
Atlamál hin groenlenzku, poem composed on Greenland? 45–46, 108–109
austmadr, Greenlanders' name for Norwegians and Icelanders 44
axe 49, 55, 134–135, 137, 162–163, 165, 196, 206, 252, 280, 288

baptism 82–83, 94, 135, 144, 338
bard, see skald
barrel 111, 182, 288
beer 31, 49, 124, 161, 166, 169, 183, 285, 300
berries 116, 124, 301
bishops on Greenland, see also visitations, education, archbishops, Gardar
    organisation of Gardar diocese 81–146

bishops' biographies 115–120
    Gardar bishops' morale 120–121, 141–142
    appointment of Gardar bishops in Nidaros 122
    appointment transferred to Rome 142
Bjarkøyrett, the earliest Norwegian merchant and urban law 96
Black Death, consequences for Greenland 120, 128, 142, 212, 345, 360, 369
blubber, see seal
boatbuilding and ship repairs in Greenland 189–192
bog iron 161, 162
bog soil as fertilizer 252–253, 260, 270, 330
burials
    pagan 81–82
    Christian 51, 86–87, 89–90, 93–94, 144–145, 167, 168, 305–306
butter 71, 166, 232, 241–243, 246, 258, 297, 309
byrdingr, ship type 185
byres 233–240, 58, 231, 258, 262–263, 353–354

cannibalism 333
capelin, see ammassæt
caribou, see reindeer
cattle 231–261; cf. 46, 56
centralised house 235, 238–239, 349, 352–353

centre and periphery on Norse Greenland 31–32, 174–177
cereals 230, 232, 245, 247, 285, 298–300
  barley 251, 299–300
  oats 299
  imports 166–167, 169
chapel (a privately owned and used church) 68, 85–88, 96, 98, 100, 104, 345
char, Arctic 68, 187, 272–273, 290–291, 293, 295–298, 301–302, 307, 312, 329, 370
cheese 71, 232, 241–243, 246, 258
chessmen of walrus ivory 171, 173
chieftains, political and judicial role 30–31; cf. 22–36, 45–59; see also landownership
Christianisation of Greenland 81–85
church buildings, see chapels, minsters, parish churches, monasteries, royal chapels, Gardar
climate deterioration 268–271
cloister, see nunnery, Benedictine; Augustinian monastery in "Index of names"
cloth, Greenlandic or imported 107, 164, 167–168, 208, 244, 300
cochlearia, plant eaten to cure scurvy 244, 300
cod 68, 161, 166, 176, 178, 187, 230, 273, 289–295, 297–298, 302, 307–308, 312, 329, 370
common land, definition 250; 250–252, 258, 261, 270, 272, 274, 283, 312, 330; cf. outfield
compass 196, 198
confession, part of sacrament of penance 94, 131
courtly culture 45–48
courts of justice
  Gardar Thing 50–56
  the lawman 66–67
crosses as symbols and decorations 81, 93, 110–113, 144–146, 168–169, 186, 191, 289
crowberries for making wine 116, 124
crown administration centres in Greenland 66–73
crown monopoly in Greenland trade 214–217
crucifix 107, 113, 144–146, 352, 354
crusade ideology 110, 345–346
cultural identity, see ethnic identity, language, literacy, literature, music, religious identity

customs duties Bergen and English ports 168, 171–172, 179–180, 182, 211, 213–214, 217

"death sentence through exclusion" in Inuit hunting groups 332–335
decorations, Greenlandic aesthetics 106, 110–113, 172–173
demography 26, 32–35, 94, 127, 329, 336, 368–369
Det gamle Grønlands beskrivelse af Ivar Bárdarson, source criticism 342–349
devotions in laymen's homes 144–146
Dorset Eskimos 138, 340–342
dragons as decorations 113
drainage in agriculture 56, 255–256, 260–261
driftwood 145, 165–166, 169, 183, 189–192, 230, 352
drying of food for preservation 166, 176, 294–295, 297–298, 330, 336
dung as fertilizer 250, 252–254, 330, 354

earth seen as a sphere 140
earthenware 169
ecological versus ethnic model 1–2, 9–10, 26, 232, 302, 327, 368–371
education of
  lawmen 66–67, 122
  priests 84, 91, 114–115
  choir-boys 107–108, 112, 115, 347
  lay children 107
eelpout, a fish species 290
eggs 230, 289
Eiriks saga rauda, source criticism 15–18
erosion in agriculture 265–268
eskimos, see Inuit and Dorset
ethnic identity 43–45
excavation practices 2–9
exhaustion of agricultural land 265–268
exploration at Greenlandic and Atlantic coasts 21, 33, 135–140, 170, 175, 204, 342
exports, see walrus tusks, walrus ropes, hides, skin, falcons, polar bears, lamp oil
Eyrbyggja saga, source criticism 18–20

Fagrskinna, source criticism 83
falcon
  gifts to kings and lords 180
  commodity in trade 171, 180–182
  byname for bishop of Gardar (*Smyrill*) 116–117

fence/dyke between infield and outfield, definition 272; cf. 46, 56, 256, 259, 271
ferja, ship type 175, 185–186, 189, 191, 355
fertilisation of meadow 252–254, 354
feud on Greenland 22–24, 27, 30, 49–50, 54–56, 210, 339, 352, 368
fires in churches or houses in the final phase 145, 253, 352, 354, 361, 366–367
fishing
  boats 175, 176, 186–189, 292; see also sexæringr
  sea fishes 290; see also cod, halibut, herring
  freshwater fish 290; see also char and salmon
  handlines 291–292, 294, 296, 298, 312, 329, 335
  nets 251, 272, 278–279, 281, 288, 295–298, 312, 328–329
Flateyarbók, source criticism 17, 94–95
flax 167, 300, 301
Flomanna saga, source criticism 18–20, 200
fodder from common land 250–252; see also *utslått,* moss, seaweed, ammassæt
Fostbroedra saga, source criticism 18–20
funding for Greenland research 9, 261; see also Leverhulme trust
fur 167, 180

gangway to enter a ship 186
glaciers 3, 136, 138, 145, 188, 199, 269
goats 129, 231, 253, 301, 309–311, 329, 348, 353–354, 363
  fodder 248–253, 256–258
  milk 232, 241, 243–244
  meat 244–245, 282–284,
  hides171, 179,
Gothic church architecture 68, 104, 106,
Gottskalk, Icelandic Annals 202
Grágás, Icelandic law codex 53, 204
grapes (*vinber*) for making wine 16, 19–20, 124, 188
Greenland law 50–54, 206, 258, 272
Greenland right whale = the Bowhead whale 286
Groenlendinga saga, source criticism 15–18
Groenlendinga tháttr, source criticism 18, 48, 52, 132–133, 166
Groenlandsfar, ship sailing to Greenland 205
Grænlands Annal written in the 17th century 89, 94, 143, 165, 174, 212

Gulathing 50–54, 246, 258, 272, 277, 278, 285–286, 288, 345

hafskip (ocean ship) 184, 188, 192, 203, 208, 356; see also *knarri*
Hákonar saga Hákonarsonar, source criticism 18, 124
halibut 290, 294
Hansa merchants 179–180, 182, 209, 211, 217
hares 136
harpoon 277–278, 287, 288, 312, 328
Hauksbok, manuscript written ca. 1300 for Hauk Erlendsson 14, 16, 21, 137, 165
Hávamál, Norse poem 133
Heimskringla, source criticism 18–19, 84
herding domestic animals 9, 230, 256–258, 348
herring 294–295, 297
hides and skins of cattle, goats and seal 125, 167, 170–171, 179–180, 274, 282
high seat pillars 23
hird (retinue) of Norwegian king 22, 28, 46, 61–63, 65, 83, 91–92, 123, 205, 210
Historia Norwegie, source criticism 60–61, 84
Holy Communion 94, 101, 124, 144
Holy Mass 144; cf. 87–88, 93, 101–102, 107, 108, 114, 118, 125, 130–131, 141
honour in Greenland 16–18, 22–25, 45, 47, 49, 56, 83, 87, 116, 166, 209, 277, 358
horses 3, 68, 192, 233, 246–247, 249–250, 258–259, 329, 348
  as food 246
household farm, definition 232–233; cf. 34, 56–58, 66, 71, 234–235, 241, 248, 271
hunger/starvation
  Norse Greenland 232, 261, 292, 297, 335–336, 350
  Inuit society 249–250, 331–335
hunting expeditions of Norse
  walrus in Disco region 174–179
  seal in the two settlements 274–279, 281–283
  reindeer in the two settlements 279–285
  whales 285–288
  polar Bears east of Cape Farewell 288–289

ice
  ice floes and icebergs along the Greenland coast 174–175, 189, 197–198, 269–270

ice and navigation 25, 55, 68, 137, 174–175, 185, 192–193, 197–198, 199–200, 212–213, 217, 233, 343, 349, 352, 368
ice and hunting 32, 174–175, 246, 275, 289, 312, 332, 335
ice covering pastures 249
inland glacier on Greenland 2, 3, 8, 99, 135–136, 138, 200, 267, 352, 353
ice spurs with spikes 163
Icelandic Annals, source criticism 21, 200, 202, 356
immigration to Greenland 22–36; cf. 368–369
infield of a farm, definition 272–273; 56, 254–256, 259, 271; see also outfield
inheritance law 207, 358–360; see also courts of justice
insulation of houses 87, 106–107, 129, 164–165, 231
Inuit and Norse
 peaceful exchanges? 328
 seal-hunting technologies 328–329
 fishing technologies 329
 starvation 331–336
 violence 336–339, 366–368
 ideas of revenge and blood-taking 364–365
 social organisation 339
 Inuit memories of Norse society 363–366
iron 107, 137, 161–164, 166, 191–192; see also knife, scythe, sickle
 iron production 161–162
 smithies 162, 328
 rivets for ships 162, 163, 189, 191–192, 196
 iron weapons 162–163, 169, 183, 279–280
 iron fishing hooks 291, 292, 298, 312
irrigation 254–256, 261
Islendingabok, source criticism 14, 341
isotope analyses 247, 251, 302–310
itinerant priests and monks 88, 90, 102, 130–131

Jacob's staff, instrument for navigation 196
jewellry 111, 168
Jökuls tháttr Buasonar, source criticism 200
judicial protection for trade 209–214
juniper used as firewood, fodder and raw material 165, 169, 251, 265, 280, 363
jurisdiction, see settlement of conflicts
jury (*dóm*) 31, 51, 54, 55, 67, 207, 213

kayak 332, 338, 342
King's Mirror, source criticism 16, 133, 140
kitchen utensils 110–113, 163–164, 353
knarri, ship type 162, 184, 189, 199, 205–207, 214–217, 345, 355; see also *hafskip*
knife 110, 112, 113, 163, 169, 280, 288
Kroka-Ref's saga, source criticism 170, 172, 179

Landnámabok, source criticism 14–15
landownership
 church 57, 130, 264–265,
 chieftains/secular elite 31–32, 57, 71–72, 89, 103, 207, 261, 264–265
 the crown 57, 66–67, 69, 72, 212, 264
 the peasants themselves 32, 264
landøre customs tax paid in Norway 204
language on Norse Greenland 14, 42–44, 48
larch (larix) species of wood 191–192
Latin competence 107–108, 114, 143–144, 343
lawman
 education 66–67, 122
 appointment 66
 at Gardar Thing 51, 54, 57, 66–67, 72, 339, 345–349, 357, 367
 as individual judge 66–67
 at Norwegian Thing assemblies (*Lögmadr*) 54
 at Althing in Iceland (*Lögsögumadr*) 54
legal regulations of hunting and fishing 272–273, 312
leidang
 a tax on merchandise in Norway 210, 217
 a peasant militia in Norway 350
lendmann, Norwegian civil servants 72
Leverhulme Trust 9
lifeboat 188, 191, 197, 199, 275, 355
lime mortar used for church walls 104, 106–107
linen cloth 167, 300
literacy 107–109, 111–112, 365; see also runes, education
literature/narratives on Greenland 45–47
Little Ice Age 268–269, 294
Lögmann Annals, source criticism 202, 356–357, 360
loom weights 81, 108, 111, 113, 145, 296, 352
luxury consumption 123, 166–169, 173–174, 182
lyme grass 299–300

magic/sorcery, definition of concept 132
  Norse Greenlanders 132–135, 141, 172, 335, 356–358
  help from pagan Norse deities 81, 133, 134–135
  help from the devil 132, 135
  Inuit sorcery 200, 336, 337–338, 364
Magnus Lagabøte's National Law 66, 272, 357, 360
marketplaces on Greenland 207–209; see also Brattahlid, Gardar, Sand,
marriages 123–124, 144, 356, 358–360
meadow 24–25, 26, 68, 231, 252–256, 258–260, 264, 270–272, 302, 329–330, 348, 354
meat
  high quality – low quality 183, 281–282, 302–310
  conservation 166, 176, 297
  domestic animals 212, 213, 240, 241, 244–247, 249, 301
  hunted prey 232, 233, 274, 301; see also seal, reindeer and whale
meat forks 109, 163
merchants who were Greenlanders 203–204
midnight sun 139–140
milk production and consumption 233–245; cf. 71, 246, 258
millstones/quernstones 299–300
minsters on Greenland 87–91, 102, 105, 114
miracles on Greenland 132–134, 141
missionaries to Norse Greenland 83, 85, 89, 91, 114; see also Eirikr Gnupsson Upsi in "Index of names"
monastery, see cloister
Morkinskinna, source criticism, 18, 181
moss 251, 260–261, 270, 300
mounds for pagan burials 81
musical instruments (harp, lyre crowd) on Norse Greenland 47

name farm, definition 232–233; cf. 34–35, 56, 71, 94, 341; see also household farm
narrative and remnant, two methods for use of sagas 20
nationalism in historiography 3–8
Nationalmuseet in Copenhagen xii, 4
  in Nuuk xiii
natural sciences used by archaeologists
  14C radiocarbon dating 8
  13C isotope method, definition 302–304; 8, 245, 247, 251, 302–309

15N isotopes 309
pollen analyses 8, 21, 167, 299–300, 363
navigation 193–200; see also compass
  latitude 140, 194, 196
  longitude 197, 199, 357
"nordbo", Danish name for "Norse Greenlander", definition 44–45
Nordrseta, definition 174; cf. 137, 139, 168, 175, 179, 246, 329, 342
Nordrsetudrápa, poem probably composed on Greenland 46–47, 179
Norse identity on Greenland, definition 43; 42–48
Norse language, see language
"Northern Lights" *(nordrlios)*, a Greenlandic word? 140
"Norwegian model" in resource exploitation 230–232, 311–312
nunnery, Benedictine 97–99, 128–132, 264, 273

observation posts 349–350
ocean ship, see *hafskip* and *knarri*
Oddverja Annals 202
officialis, replacement for an absentee bishop 143, 346, 358–359, 366
ombudsman, the crown's representative for a particular task 213
outfield, definition 272–273; cf. 26, 57–58, 231, 250–252, 270–273, 283, 301; see also fence, common land

paganism 81–82, 86, 91, 133–135, 345–346, 348, 361
parish organisation 92–114, 143–144
pastoral services, definition 144; cf. 87–89, 93, 101–102, 130–131
pastures 24, 26, 68, 231–232, 241, 244, 247, 256–260, 268, 270, 302, 330
pax 107, 144
penance, a sacrament, definition 144; cf. 101–102, 124
periplus, aid for navigation 193
Peter's Pence 127, 207
pigments for cloth 167–168
pigs 245–246, 329
pine 192
plants as food 298–301
Polar Bears 137–138, 172, 177, 181–182, 273, 287, 289
Polar Ice/Great Ice 25, 174, 185, 197–198, 212–213, 269, 346, 368
Pole Star, "under the Pole Star" is north of Nuussuaq 65, 196–197

Pope
  organisational leader 90, 114, 117
  authority to interpret Christian doctrine 123–124
  taxation of Greenland 124–128, 171–172, 179, 204, 207, 346
  taxes to pope paid in tusks 126–127, 171
  assumes right to appoint Gardar bishops 142, 343, 361
  services to King Håkon 63–64, 124
prayers 83, 87–88, 90, 93, 101–102, 108, 111, 131–133, 141, 145–146, 201
preaching 83, 88, 90, 101, 130, 332, 334
professional merchants in Greenland trade 205–207, 209

rá, wooden transverse pole supporting the sail 185, 196, 198
redfish 294
reindeer
  hunt 9, 137, 272–274, 279–281, 288, 293, 302, 312, 332, 335, 348
  food resource 232, 246, 281–285, 301, 304, 307–308, 329, 370
religious identity 143–146
remnant, see narrative and remnant
Rimur of Skald-Helgi, source criticism 66, 177
Romanesque church architecture 104–106
rosary/counting stick 101
royal chapels 68, 98, 100, 102, 107, 169, 343, 345; see also Hvalsey and Foss
runes and their uses 101, 111–113, 133, 138–139, 174–175, 349–350
  dating 43–43, 139
  runic competence on Greenland 108–109
  ornaments 111
  religion 108, 109, 111, 198, 352
  magic? 133
  see also Kingittorsuaq in "Index of names"

sacraments, see confession, penance, Holy Communion, baptism, burial
sailing routes 193–196
salmon 68, 230, 272–273, 290, 293, 295–297, 301–302, 329, 370
sculpin, fish 290, 295, 330
scythe 163
seal/seal oil
  species hunted by Norsemen 276–277
  hunting methods 272–273, 275, 277–278, 302

  food resource 170, 232, 270, 274, 276, 278–279, 282, 301
  isotope analyses to quantify seal consumption 302–310
  skins used for clothes and ropes 125, 167, 170–171, 179, 276
  lamp oil 165, 170, 182, 235, 274–276, 281, 283, 287–288, 310, 364, 370
sea level changes 57, 59, 185, 259, 261, 268, 271, 302
seaweed
  fodder 251, 253, 270, 301, 309, 330
  fertilizer 252–253, 301
  food for humans 301, 330
sekkia gield, customs tax, definition 213; cf. 213–214, 217
sele-smolte = seal blubber or seal oil (= lamp oil) 182
sermon 102, 131, 144
settlement of conflicts, definition 54–56; see also feuds, courts of justice, Greenland law, lawman, jury; Gardar Thing in "Index of names"
sexæringr boat rowed with six oars 133, 137–140, 175–178, 186–188, 192, 189, 192, 292, 297, 341–342, 351
shears to shear sheep 164
sheds in stone 176, 243, 258, 297
sheep 69, 230, 232, 249, 251–252, 260, 266, 270, 329, 346, 348, 363
  housing 129, 231, 243, 250, 353,
  milk 244, 248, 253, 256,
  meat 245, 248, 282–284, 301–302, 307, 310–311,
  dung as fertilizer 253–354
  dung as fuel 253–254, 354
  see also woollen cloth
shieling, see sæter
ship and boat types, see sexæringr, skuta, ferja, byrdingr, hafskip, knarri
shipwrecks and problems at sea 196–200
  Norwegian coast 181, 206, 214, 216
  Icelandic coast 52, 64, 109, 118, 171, 184, 195, 203
  Greenland coast 33, 51–52, 84, 89, 96, 109, 162, 184, 199–200, 203, 205, 211, 289
  Atlantic Ocean 32, 191–192, 198
sickle 163, 251
skalds on Greenland 46, 65–66, 81, 84, 134, 179, 277
skaldic poetry, source criticism 19, 177
Skálholt Annals 119–120, 141, 202, 205, 355,
skin 170, 179–180, 208, 276, 289, 291, 294, 332, 355

Index of matters

skræling (= Eskimos and "native Americans") 43, 91, 137, 341, 344–345, 350, 365
Skuldelev I, ship excavated in Roskilde fjord 184–185,
skuta, ship type 175, 185–186, 188–189, 191–192, 355
skyr (= sour milk), see milk production
soapstone 81, 107, 111–113, 146, 163–164, 169, 235, 273–275, 279, 288, 291, 296, 300,
Sögu Eiriks, name of early version of *Groenlendinga saga* 17–18
sorcery, see magic
spear/fish-spear 134, 163, 278–279, 280–281, 286, 297–298, 312, 329,
spruce timber 192
stables for horses, sheep and goats 59, 71, 231–233, 243, 247, 250, 354
state growth in the Norse area 22–25, 30, 52, 63–74, 146, 211–214, 370–371
stoneware 169
Sturlunga saga, source criticism 18, 30, 123, 191, 195, 200
submission to Norway 63–66
sustainable ecological balance 230–312, 329–331
   sustainable agriculture 1, 8, 9, 249, 261, 266, 267, 271, 329
   sustainable population 330–336
   sustainable hunting 274
   sustainable use of drift timber 165
Sverris saga, source criticism 18,
sword 49, 163, 172, 280, 361
sword-stick in weaving 288
synod, assembly of priests or bishops 87, 114–115, 124, 144, 344
syslemann/syslumadr, Norwegian civil servant 71–72, 212–213
sæter, definition 256–257; 8, 68, 71, 233, 246, 256–260, 270–271, 302, 348

tar, made from seal oil 190, 275
taxes/tribute to the state 56, 60–61, 64–65, 69, 72, 204, 207, 210, 212–214, 217, 357, 370
temperatures 8–10, 232, 243, 249, 261, 267, 268–271, 292–294, 299, 302, 335, 368–369
thegngildi 65
Thing assemblies, see Gardar
Thorfinn Karlsefni's saga, original name of *Eiriks saga Rauda* 16–17

timber
   imported from Norway 161, 164–166, 184
   drift-timber 165, 177, 189, 190
   from Vinland and Labrador? 165
tithe to the Norwegian church 35, 93, 96–99, 100, 102–103, 130–131, 206, 264
toilet articles 168–169
Tournois, French coin from Tour 126
trencher for eating 110–113
Tristram and Iseult, French novel translated into Norse 171, 180
"troll", definition 335; Icelandic nickname for Inuit
"tunga" and "language", definitions 83
Tunit Eskimos = Dorset Eskimos 340

umiak 250, 332–333, 336, 342, 356
university scholars 3, 7–9, 340
utslått, grassland for haymaking outside the farm's fence 250, 258–259

Vatican Archives 124, 125
vegetation changes caused by Norse 24–26, 252–255, 265, 270, 300, 329
Vestustissimi, name of Icelandic Annals 202
vinber (grapes) 19, 124
Vinland sagas, see *Eiriks saga rauda*, *Groenlendinga* saga
violence
   individual violence 22–25, 30, 49, 55
   authorised by community 62–63, 73–74, 210
   Norse 30, 48–50, 337–339
   Inuit hunter society 327–356, 363–368
   pacification in Norse and Inuit society 50–59, 73–74, 336–339
visitations by bishops 95–99, 114, 143, 264, 343–345
visual decorations 106–107, 110–114, 169, 172, 291

walrus
   the hunt 32, 46–47, 174–179, 186–187, 289,
   one hunter's annual production 127, 178
   start and end of *nordrseta* 139–140, 179, 183, 217, 289, 351,369
   tusks Greenland –Bergen 66, 73, 109, 125, 171, 179, 193–196, 201–202
   exports of tusks and ropes from Norway 170–172, 193–196

tusks as gifts to kings 91, 170–171
tusks as tax payments 126, 171
ropes of walrus hide 91, 125, 170, 179
tusks as raw material for artists 107, 112, 168, 172–174
walrus meat as food 276
water supplies to dwelling 255
wax tablets 108, 109
weapons, see arrow, axe, spear, sword, iron
whale
   species hunted 285–286
   hunting methods 285–287
   the hunt 137, 230, 273, 275, 302, 312, 340
   food and lamp oil 166, 212, 232, 274, 276, 287–288, 301–302, 370
   teeth, bones and baleen 171, 253, 288
   rope of whale-skin 179
willow 26, 68, 165, 169, 250–251, 265, 363
wine 19–20, 116, 124, cf. grapes
winter grazing outdoors 247, 249–250, 260, 261, 266
wolves 46, 136
woollen cloth, Greenlandic or imported 161, 167, 208, 243–244

Index of names (places and persons)

Only names in the main text are included. Footnotes, table-notes, bibliography and texts to illustrations are excluded. Modern place names which were only used to explain the location of medieval places, are also excluded,
Medieval personal names are registered according to their first name, post-Reformation names according to their second name.
There is no consensus on the spelling of Inuit place names, and Danish names are often used on maps and in literature. I have normally kept to the spelling used in Appendix II.
Greenlandic ruin sites are identified by the numbers traditionally used at Nationalmuseet in Copenhagen. E stands for Eastern Settlement (maps 4–10), W for Western Settlement (maps 1–2) and M for Middle Settlement (map 3). Locations are marked on maps in Appendix II.

Adalbrandr Helgason, Icelandic explorer 136
Adam of Bremen 19, 59, 60, 90
Africa 2, 136, 266
Agdluitsup (= Lichtenau fjord, Appendix II map 6) 68, 98, 293
Agdluitsup Paa (Appendix II map 7) 249
Albrethsen, Svend, Danish archaeologist 90, 258, 260
Alexander III, pope 124
Alfr, bishop of Gardar 120, 141–143, 202
Alfred, English king 170, 286
Allumlenger/Öllumlengri, fjord near Cape Farewell 186, 289
Alptafjord, unidentified fjord in Greenland, another name for Siglufjord? 23, 28, 31
Ameragdla (= Lysufjord Appendix II map 2) 32, 95, 276, 279, 281, 294, 350
Ameralik fjord (Appendix II map 2) 276, 293–294, 299–300
America/Americans 165, 195, 248, 261, 296, 301, 312, 340, 344, 349
Amitsuarsuk fjord (Appendix II map 7) 67–68, 296
Ammassalik on Greenland's East Coast 331–333, 338

Anavik parish (W7) 21, 68, 95, 100, 104–106, 238–239, 293, 305–306, 350–351
Apostelkirken, King's chapel in Bergen 169, 346
Ari Thorgilsson Frodi 14, 15, 21, 22, 26, 27, 30, 32, 50, 51, 82, 341, 342
Arnaldr, bishop of Gardar 50–51, 53–54, 87, 94, 115, 120–121, 199
Arnaldr Greenlander, priest 123, 216
Arnbjørn, Norwegian merchant 201
Arneborg, Jette, Nationalmuseum archaeologist xii, 22, 44, 48, 89, 90, 92, 97, 121, 144, 165, 241, 246, 258, 267, 274, 278, 288, 304, 306, 309–310, 328, 339–340, 342–343, 362–364
Arngrimur Jonsson, Icelander d. 1648 35, 94, 97
Arni, bishop of Gardar 119–120, 122, 141, 142, 346
Arni, bishop of Bergen 123, 201
Arnlaug, settler in Arnlaugsfjord 29
Arnlaugsfjord (= North Sermilik/Ikersuaq? Appendix II maps 4–5) 29, 31
Arsuk island (Appendix II map 3) 90, 93
Asmundr Kastandratzi, skipper from Greenland 191–192, 198, 289
Asser, archbishop in Lund 92

Index of names (places and persons) 425

Audun from the Western fjords, Icelander 195
Augustinian monastery (E105) 90, 97, 100, 102, 105, 128–132
Auros parish (= Vatnsdalur) (E137, E198 or E109?) 52, 96, 99, 103
Austmannadal 5, 32, 113, 145, 192, 246, 250, 253–254, 286, 288, 351–354
Avignon 125, 127–128, 343

Bárdr Dies, Bergen and Greenland 72
Barrett, James, English archaeologist 303–304
Bautahlutanum, *gárdr* in Bergen 205–207, 216
Benedictine nunnery, see nunnery in "Index of matters"
Bergen is excluded because it is mentioned too many times. Main entry is on pp. 193–196
Berglund, Joel, Danish archaeologist 189, 203
"Besuk", one of Knud Rasmussen's Inuit informants 337–338
Beyer, Absalon Pederssøn in Bergen 162, 207
Bjarni, from Stokkanes (E44?) 162, 186, 206, 210, 263–264
Bjarni Greenlander, peasant 44, 346
Bjarni Grimolvsson, Icelandic skipper 33, 188, 190, 201, 204, 209
Bjarni Herjolvsson, chieftain at Herjolvsnes 17, 28, 62, 203
Bjarni Thordarson, Greenlander 139
Bjørn Einarsson, Icelandic skipper 143, 212–213, 334–335, 355–356
Björn Jonsson, Icelander d. 1655
 as author 143, 212
 demography 34–35
 burials 89
 ships 109, 165, 171, 203, 216
 distances on Greenland 174
 Nordrseta 175–177, 203, 275
Blehr, Otto, Norwegian archaeologist 280–281
Born, Erik, Danish scientist 266, 274
Brattahlid
 clan 17, 32, 54, 61–62, 82, 86–87, 90–91, 105, 305
 the initial "Viking Age farm" of Eirik Raudi 56–59, 208–209, 232
 "The North Farm" (= *Lijder*), the parson's seat 57–58, 70, 72–73, 85, 95, 99, 104–106, 240, 271

"The River farm", the lawman's seat 54, 57–58, 66–67, 72, 239, 271
 "The South farm" 57, 67, 271
 "The Mountain farm" 57
 Brattahlid as marketplace 208
British Isles 27, 85, 169, 196, 171
British Museum 173
Bruun, Daniel 4, 53, 67, 68, 86, 233, 243, 250, 257, 260, 282, 300, 349, 366–367
Buchwald, Vagn, Danish metallurgist 161
Burfeld (Itlerfissalik), observation post 349
Bærefjord, fjord for hunting close to Cape Farewell 273
Böcher, Jens, Danish zoologist 266, 274

Canada 7, 136, 279, 329, 340
Cape Farewell 136
 shipping lane 3, 193–195, 197, 199, 201, 208, 269, 357
 hunting 137, 179, 181, 191, 273, 285, 288–289
Celtic Britain 84–85
Christensen, Karen, Danish archaeologist 281
Christian, leader of Inuit hunting group 337–338
Christine, born on Greenland? 358–360
Clavering, English captain in Greenland 339
Clemmensen, M., Danish archaeologist 86
Copenhagen 145, 213–215, 365, 367
Cross Island (Kaarsø) east of Cape Farewell 181, 186, 191, 289

Dalir, farm in Einarsfjord 264, 273
Davis Strait 165, 174, 191–192, 276–277, 285, 292–294, 296, 355
Denmark
 political power 3, 4, 44, 61, 73, 211
 church 91–92, 121, 142
 trade 170, 179, 180–181, 184–185, 193, 196, 215, 217
 immigration to Greenland? 27
Denmark Strait 191, 194, 269
Diamond, Jarred, American author 1, 9
Didrik (Thithricus) at Gardar 143
Disco Bay 328, 336, 342, 349, 351
Disco Island (=*Bjarneyar*) 175, 287, 342
Disco region between Sisimiut and Nuussuaq
 journey 46–47, 65, 165, 186–187, 288–289, 355
 hunting 32, 127, 174–179, 183, 275
 Inuit 136–137, 342, 351, 355–356

Dugmore, Andrew, Scottish geoscientist 278
Dyrnes (=Hardsteinaberg) parish church (E18) 4, 95, 98–99

East coast of Greenland
  shipping lane 51, 89, 109, 162, 186,194, 200–201, 208–269
  hunting 163, 181, 186, 288–289
Edwards, Kevin, Scottish botanist 299
Egede, Hans, author
  source criticism 363–366
  search for Norse Settlements 2, 3, 363–366
  firewood 165, 190
  agriculture 232, 249, 299
  hunting 274, 279
  fishing 293–295, 329
  lamp oil 275, 278
  scurvy 300
  Inuit lack of empathy 327–339, 334
Egede, Niels, merchant on Greenland 197, 274, 282, 334, 337–338
Egede, Poul, parson on Greenland 334
Eggers, Henrik Peter von 3
Egil Skallagrimsson 22, 34
Eidsfjord parish church in Norway 104, 106
Einar, chieftain in Einarsfjord 28–29
Einar Sokkesson, Brattahlid 48–49, 54–55, 62, 91
Einar, Icelandic ship owner 199
Eindridi Andresson, officialis at Gardar 43–44, 143, 358–359, 366
Eindridi Oddsson, Greenlander 139
Eirik, earl and ruler of Norway 28
Eirikr Gnupsson Upsi, bishop on Greenland 91
Eirik, Norwegian king 118, 201
Eirik Raudi
  settlement on Greenland 14–35, 179, 341
  as chieftain 23, 30–31, 42–73, 166, 169, 264
  attitude to Christianity 61–62, 81–85
  descendants 16, 17, 62–63, 85–86, 89–90, 210, 370
Enghoff, Inger Bødker, Danish osteologist 243
England, church and religion 85, 107
  trade 167–182, 193, 196, 286
Eqaluit (E78) 86
Erlingr Sigvatsson, Greenlander 139
Eystein Erlendsson, archbishop of Nidaros 116, 122–123, 132, 194

Falgeir, Greenlander 49
Faroes 22, 62, 106, 109, 194, 207, 274, 286, 292, 366
  church 83, 118, 121–122, 124–125, 127, 201, 343
  Norse identity 14, 43–45
  state ties 3, 52
Fedje, on shipping lane to Greenland 194
Finn's booths, hunting station 186, 191, 289
Finnmark, comparisons to Greenland 60, 170, 172, 245, 251, 261, 281, 284, 297, 350
Flanders 125–126, 172, 193
Foss (E91) 67–69, 71–73, 96, 98–100
France 124, 131, 171–173, 180, 193
Fredrik II, Dano-Norwegian king 215
Fredriksdal (Appendix II map 8) 333, 337–338
Fredskild, Bent, Danish botanist 8, 21, 251, 252, 265, 266, 270, 363
Freydis daughter of Eirik Raudi 17, 50, 89
Friis, Peder Clausson, Norwegian parson 122

Gaborit-Chopin, Danielle, art historian 173
Gallium Kær, lake behind Brattahlid 255
Gamla, Greenlandic magician 31
Gardanes parish church (= E1) 95, 99–100, 104–106
Gardar, secular functions, see also bishops in "Index of matters"
  Thing 31–32, 45, 49–55, 63–64, 66–67, 93, 102, 110, 187, 201, 206, 213, 339, 349
  farm (E47 Igaliku) 28–29, 56, 71, 73, 88–89, 234–243, 254–255, 258–259
  marketplace? 122–123, 133, 193, 203–204, 208
Germany 45, 124, 196
Gisli Oddsson, bishop of Skálholt 344
Godal, Jon Bojer, boatbuilder 190
Graah, W.A., Danish excavator 367
Greenland Ocean 193–202, 109, 184, 188, 191–192, 216, 342
Grim, Norwegian skipper 162
Grima another name given to Gamla, see Gamla
Grimr, Greenlander married to Gamla 31
Grimr, Greenlander who had a prophetic dream 44
Gudbrand, Norwegian moving to Greenland 205
Gudrid, Icelander in Greenland 16–18, 33, 134, 135

Index of names (places and persons) 427

Gudrun, character in the Greenlandic Atlakvida 108–109
Gudveig, buried in the Greenland Ocean 109, 198
Guldager, Ole, Danish archaeologist 86, 260
Gulf of St. Lawrence 20
Gulløv, Hans Christian, Nationalmuseum archaeologist 328–329, 356
Gunnar, character in the Greenlandic Atlakvida 46
GUS (Farm under the sand; Appendix II map 2) 8, 21, 112–113, 167, 179, 189–190, 241, 243, 246–247, 250, 252–253, 267, 276–277, 282–283, 285–286, 290, 299, 310–311, 350, 352, 354

Hafgrimr, settler 29
Hafgrimsfjord, early settlement 29, 31
Hafsbotn, an imagined northern coast 136, 138
Halldis, sailing to Greenland 198
Halldor, Greenlandic priest 133, 137, 140, 216, 287
Halldorsson, Olafur, Icelandic philologist 133
Hamar, diocese in Norway 115, 118, 121, 125, 127, 201
Hamburg/Bremen church province 59, 90, 121
Harald Gilli, Norwegian king 52
Harald Hardrádi, Norwegian king 20, 48, 181
Hardanger, near Bergen 162, 205–206, 216, 280, 284
Hauk Erlendsson, author of Hauksbok 16, 137
Hauk ("Murder-Hauk"), immigrant to Greenland 30, 195
Hebrides and Man, diocese and earldom 14, 22, 27, 44, 60, 81, 118, 121–122, 171, 173
Heide, Baltzer, archaeologist Århus 6
Heinemeier, Jan, Danish physicist 274, 302–304, 306, 309–310
Helgason, Jon, Icelandic philologist 133
Helgi, bishop of Gardar 117, 121,
Helgi, Icelandic settler in Greenland 24
Helgi (= Skald-Helgi), lawman on Greenland 66, 117
Helgu-Steinarr, Icelander sailing Bergen – Greenland 44, 184–185
Helle, Knut, Norwegian historian 61

Helluland (= Baffin's land) 136
Henrik, nominal bishop of Gardar 142
Henry III, English king 180
Henry III, German emperor 181
Herdisarvik at coast of Iceland 118, 195, 203
Herjolv Bárdarson, settler at Herjolvsnes 28, 81
Herjolvsfjord 28, 31, 95
Herjolvsnes
    farm and parish (E111) 5, 42, 73, 81, 95, 96, 103, 105, 111, 112, 162, 164, 169, 193, 198, 199, 208, 293, 335
    chieftain 17, 28, 62, 96, 99–100, 134–135, 203
    burials 93, 109, 113, 144, 167–168, 305, 308, 362–363
Hermundr Kodranson, Icelander in Greenland 48, 132, 206
Hernar near Bergen, point of departure for Greenland 194
Hitranes at coast of Iceland 195
Hohler, Erla, art historian 145–146
Holar diocese in Iceland 92, 118, 121, 132, 141, 361
Holastadr, see Thiødhillestad
Holm, Gustav, Danish excavator 367
Holmedalen, *gardr* in Bergen 205, 207
Hop, parish in Western Settlement 95
Horn at south-east Iceland 193–194, 199
Hrafn, settler in Hrafnsfjord 29
Hrafnsfjord (early name for Uunartoq fjord/Siglufjord?) 29, 31, 39
Hunt, B.G. Australian climatologist 270
Hvalsey/Hvalseyfjord, see also Holastadr and Thiødhillestad
    farm, chiefdom, church, parish (E83 and 83a) 5, 28, 31, 81, 95, 99, 103–107, 256, 293
    crown property? 67, 69–73, 98, 107, 357
    the last visit 357–359, 361
    the end 367, 369
    excavated items 167, 291, 299
Hvarf, mountain, today Ikigait (Appendix II map 8) 193–194, 208
Hæthum (=Hedeby) port near today's Schleswig 170
Høegsberg, see Skaaning Høegsberg
Håkon Håkonsson, Norwegian king 47, 63–65, 117, 124, 180, 216
Håkon V, Norwegian king 107
Håkon VI, Norwegian king 211
Håkon archbishop of Trondheim 118

Icelanders and Norwegians are excluded from the present index because they are mentioned too many times in all chapters and most subchapters.
Igaliku (E47), see Gardar
Igaliku (E48) 86, 234, 237–239, 305
Igaliku South/Igaliku Kujalleq (E66) 95, 100, 103, 105–106, 234, 238–239, 271, 299, 306, 367
   sand erosion 265–268
Ikerssuaq (= Bredefjord) (Appendix II map 4) 99
Ilulissat, colony in Disco Bay 331, 336, 342, 351
Ingemund, Icelandic priest 109, 116–117, 122, 199
Ingstad, Anne Stine, archaeologist, Oslo 7
Ingstad, Helge 4, 7, 19, 49, 68, 91, 215, 249, 254–255, 260, 281, 293, 299
Ireland 85, 172, 188, 190, 196, 275
Isafjord, see Sermilik fjord (northern)
Isafjørdur parish church (E4?) 95, 99–100, 104–106
Isleif, first bishop Iceland 90, 181
Iterolaq (E64) farm with chapel 86
Itinnera, reindeer hunting site (W27a) 281
Ivar Bárdarson, see *Det gamle Grønlands beskrivelse af Ivar Bárdarson* in "Index of matters"

Jakobsen, B.H., Danish geographer 266
Johannes Treppe, nominal bishop of Gardar 142
Johannes d'Ypres, papal tax collector 126
Jon Knutr, bishop of Gardar 116, 120, 122
Jon Skalli, bishop of Gardar 119, 141, 201–202
Jon Smyrill (=Falcon) Sverrisfostri, bishop of Gardar 116–117, 120, 122–124
Jonsson, Finnur, Icelandic philologist 4, 42, 45–46, 70, 94, 98, 107, 109, 133, 179
Jæren, home of Erik Raudi's ancestors 22, 32

Kangersuneq Icefjord (Appendix II map 1–2) 269, 352
Kangilleq (E39) 86
Kapisillit (W28) farm, fjord, river 32, 192, 246, 249, 265, 279, 349, 351–352; fishing 293–294, 296–297
Keller, Christian, archaeologist, Oslo 8, 27, 84, 87, 96, 103, 257, 260, 278, 344
Ketil Kalvsson, Norwegian merchant 52, 206–207

Ketil, settler in Ketilsfjord 29
Ketilsfjord [=Tasermiut] 29, 31, 90, 96–97, 105, 129–131, 293, 296
Kimbavágr, farm in Alptafjord 23
Kingittorsuaq, island where a Norse rune stone was found 43, 138–139, 174–175
King's Lynn 169
Knarri-Leiv, the crown's envoy to Greenland 64, 216
Koch Madsen, see Madsen
Kolgrimr, burned for black magic 132, 358
Kristjansson, Jonas 15
Kristjansson, Ludvik 189
Krogh, Knud, Nationalmuseum archaeologist xii, 5, 8, 19, 25, 44, 82, 86, 97, 241, 255, 260
Kroksfjardarheidi, see Nuussuaq
Kuijpers, Antoon, Danish geologist 57

Labrador (= Markland) 19, 136, 165, 191–192, 197, 355
Lamb, Hubert, English climatologist 268–269
Langanes, seat of the chieftain of Einarsfjord 16, 29, 205, 224 (= E64? cf. p. 87)
Langhøø island (= Tugtutoq island, Appendix II map 4) 98
L'Anse aux Meadows, Norse site on Newfoundland 19
Leiv Eiriksson, chieftain 16–17, 33, 50, 56, 61, 82–84, 88–89, 165, 188, 203–204
Leksa, farm at the estuary of the Trondheim fjord 205–206
Leverhulme trust 9
Lewis, Uig Bay, where chessmen of walrus ivory were found 171, 173
Lijder parish church, see Brattahlid
Lindenow fjord (Appendix II map 9) 186, 289
London 173, 181
Louvre museum 173
Lucca merchants in the pope's service 125
Lunden, Kåre, Norwegian historian and agronomist 242, 245, 248
Lund, seat of archbishop, until 1658 part of Denmark 84, 91–92, 115, 121
Lynnerup, Niels, Danish physician 8, 274, 288, 302–304, 306, 309–310
Lysufjord, see Ameragdla
Löngunes, see Langanes

McGovern, Thomas 6, 8–9, 243, 261, 265, 267, 276–278, 343, 351

Index of names (places and persons) 429

Madsen, Christian Koch, archaeologist Nuuk 10, 68–69, 188, 243, 362–363, 368–369
Magnus Bareleg, Norwegian king 172
Magnus Eiriksson, king of Sweden and Norway 107, 216
Magnus Lagabøte, Norwegian king 123, 137
Magnus Markusson, Icelander in Greenland 30
Malmros, Claus, Swedish archaeologist 21
Man, see Hebrides and Man
Margrete, Queen of Denmark and Norway 211, 213–214
Markland, see Labrador
Marklandsbotn, an imagined northern coast 136
Mathieu, Jon, Swiss historian 270
Matheus Parisiensis, English monk 124
Mathiassen, Therkel, Danish archaeologist 328
Meldgaard, Jørgen, Danish archaeologist 85
Melville Bay in Greenland 46, 133, 136, 138, 140, 187, 341–342
Middle Settlement (Appendix II map 3) 87, 90, 93, 100, 102, 258, 351, 355
Mitfjord, section of Northern Sermilik? (Appendix II, map 5) 98
Moltke, Erik, Danish runologist 111, 133
Munch, P.A., Norwegian historian 125
Munkeliv, monastery in Bergen 141
Muus, Bent, Danish biologist 295
Mödruvellir cloister on Iceland 132

Nanortalik (Appendix II map 8) 2, 249, 296, 333
Nansen, Fridtjof, Norwegian zoologist and oceanographer 189
Narsarsuaq, today airport 249
Narssaq (E17a) 21, 42, 98, 112, 133, 167, 169, 191–192, 246, 250, 256, 280, 282–283, 291
Narssaq in Uunartoq (E162) 43, 97
Naumann, Elise, Norwegian archaeologist 303–304
Netherlands 180, 182, 196, 275, 285–286, 289, 328, 335, 339
Newfoundland 7, 19, 136, 197, 276, 277, 370
Niaquusat (W48) (Appendix II map 2) 167, 282–283, 300–301, 310, 351, 400
Nidarholm, cloister on islet in Trondheim 172
Nidaros, name for Trondheim as church centre, see Trondheim

Nielsen, Niels, Danish metallurgist 161
Nikolas, first non-Norse archbishop of Nidaros 142
Nikolas, Icelandic abbot and author 136
Nikolas V, pope 361
Nikulas, bishop of Gardar 117
Nipaatsoq (W54) (Appendix II map 2) 167–168, 246, 282–283, 296, 310, 399
Nordal, Sigurdur, Icelandic philologist 15
Northern Norway and Greenland, comparisons 34, 85, 87, 179, 185, 209
North Pole 25, 174, 269
North Sea coast of Norway, comparisons agriculture 240–261
fishing 289–295, 308–309
see also 1, 11, 176, 178, 206, 311–312, 369–370
Nup Kangerdlua = Godthåbsfjord 293
Nuussuaq = *Kroksfjardarheidi* 32, 137, 139, 174–177, 342, 351
Nyegaard, Georg, Danish archaeologist 310, 363
Nørlund, Poul, Nationalmuseum archaeologist 4, 6, 42, 44, 56, 57, 67, 88–89, 97–98, 113, 129, 133, 144, 161–162, 164–165, 169, 172, 208, 213–214, 216, 254, 259–260, 269, 271, 274, 352, 362, 366–367

Odd from Sjoltar, envoy to Greenland 64
Oddr Snorrason, monk and author 83
Odin 133, 135
Olav, bishop of Gardar 64–65, 107, 117–118, 123, 168, 203, 172
Olav Bonde, sailed Bergen – Gardar 128
Olav Haraldsson, Norwegian king 44, 62–63, 129, 134, 289
Olav from Leksa 205–206
Olav Trygvason, Norwegian king 61, 83–85
Ordericus Vitalis, English chronicler 60
Orkney 3, 14, 22, 43–45, 48, 60–61, 83, 90, 118, 121, 126, 142, 173, 207, 308–309, 343
Orm, Icelander in Greenland 198
Orm Eysteinsson, regent of Norway 345
Oslo diocese 118, 121, 125–127, 132, 201
Ossur, Norwegian merchant 49, 52–53, 55
Othere, Norwegian chieftain 170
Ökrum, farm in Skagafjord, Iceland 357–359

Pál Hallvardsson, priest at Gardar 143
Pál, bishop of Skálholt 116

Index of names (places and persons)

Pål, archbishop of Trondheim 119, 122
Paul Knutsson, lawman in Gulathing 345–346
Paul Magnusson, envoy to Greenland 64
Petersen, Frode, Danish archaeologists 67
Pettersvig/Vik parish church (E140) 95, 97, 99
Pilgrim, Valerie, Canadian archaeologist 165, 189
Pole Star 65, 196–197

Qaqortoq (= Julianehåb) 2, 3
Qaqortuq, Inuit name for Hvalsey church 106
Qolortorsuup, lake in Vatnahverfi (Appendix II map 6) 68
Qorlortup valley behind Brattahlid 8, 112, 246, 255, 260, 282, 299–300, 367
 the farm E34 in this valley 112, 256, 259, 282–283, 310–311, 363
Quebec 20
Quequertannguaq island (Appendix II map 2) 349
Quirino, Piero, Italian merchant 181

Rampnessfjord, see Sermilik fjord (southern)
Ramstadefiord (= Kangerluarsuk) close to Hvalsey 69–70, 98
Rasmussen, Knud 275, 331–333, 337–338
Ref, character in *Kroka-Ref's saga* 170, 179–180
Reinton, Lars, Norwegian historian 256, 160
Renø island (= Akia, Appendix II map 6) 273, 279
Reykjanes at west coast of Iceland 195
Rhine area 169, 172–173, 193
Roesdahl, Else, Danish archaeologist, Århus 169
Rogers, Penelope, textile expert 168
Rollason, David 32
Roman curia 114, 117, 121, 123–125, 127, 142, 171, 361
Rosing, Christian, parson in Ammassalik 332, 338
Roskilde fjord 184
Ross, English captain 339
Roussell, Aage, Nationalmuseum archaeologist 4–6, 71, 81, 88–89, 107, 129, 145–146, 189, 251, 254, 260, 269, 352, 366
Russia 135–136, 350

Sandhöfn/Sand, port close to Herjolvsnes 193, 205, 208, 356

Sandnes (W51)
 farm 71, 231, 235, 237–238, 240–242, 253–255, 265, 311
 church 32, 89, 91, 104–105, 107, 144–146
 hunting/fishing 276–277, 280, 282–283, 288, 293, 310
 other subjects 5, 42, 81, 95, 110–113, 135, 163–164, 167–169, 192, 246, 301, 305, 308
 end of settlement 351–352
Sandnes at Jæren in Norway 32
Sandnes in Northern Norway 230
Sarqarssuaq (W16) (Appendix II, map 2) 352
Schirmer, Hermann, Norwegian architect 4
Sciringesheal, Norwegian port near today's Larvik 170
Scotland 173, 182, 257
Sermilik fjord (southern) (= Rampnesfjord? Appendix II map 8) 67, 97–98, 129–130
Sermilik fjord (northern) (= Isafjord Appendix II map 5) 29, 98–99, 233
Shetland 3, 14, 22, 43–45, 61, 83, 121, 173, 194
Siberia 136–137, 189–192
Siglufjord, see Uunartoq fjord
Sigrid, landowner on Greenland 264
Sigrid, Greenlander, maker of a spindle whorl 109
Sigridur Bjørnsdottir, Icelander married at Hvalsey 357–360
Sigurdr of Bautahlutanum, Norwegian skipper 205–207, 216
Sigurdr the Jerusalem Crusader, Norwegian king 91, 93, 181
Sigurdr Kolbeinsson, Bergen and Greenland 72, 207, 212, 264
Sigurdr Njálsson, Greenlandic hunter 185–186, 289
Sisimiut, see Disco region
Skaaning Høegsberg, Mogens, archaeologist Århus 6, 43, 71, 88, 89, 114, 162–163, 254
Skagefjord (= Narssap sarqa?, Appendix II, map 8) 96
Skagefjord, North Iceland 357–358
Skallagrim, Icelander 34, 230
Skufr, living at Stokkanes 25, 62–63, 186, 195, 198, 203, 206, 210, 263–264
Smith Sound 136, 340, 342
Snorri Sturluson 19, 46, 62, 84
Snorri Thorbrandsson, Icelandic settler in Greenland 23, 28, 33

Index of names (places and persons) 431

Snæfellsnes, Western Iceland 193–195
Solefield (Undir Solarfiøllum) (E23) 95, 98–99, 104–106, 234, 238–239, 306
Stad at the North Sea coast of Norway 193–194
Stavanger diocese 117–118, 121, 126, 201, 207, 240, 346
Stenum/Sigridur, Icelander on Greenland 357–358, 360
Stokkanes, farm in Eiriksfjord (E44) 23, 25, 62, 206, 210, 263–264
Stoklund, Marie, Danish runologist 42–43, 111, 133, 139, 145–146
Storm, Gustav, Norwegian historian 207
Strait of Belle Isle between Labrador and Newfoundland 136
Straumsnes in Straumsfjord, parish church in Western Settlement 94–95
Streeter, Richard, Scottish geographer 278
Sturla Thordarson, saga author 65, 84
Styrkár Sigmundsson from Greenland 200
Svalbard 174, 190, 285
Sveinn, skald living on Greenland 46
Sveinn (=Svend) Estridsson, Danish king 170, 181
Sverrir, Norwegian king 52, 116–117, 123–124, 170
Sweden 27, 44
Sæmundr Oddsson, Icelander on Greenland 358–359
Sölvadal, chiefdom 29, 31
Sölvi, settler on Greenland 29
Sörli, Norwegian skipper in Greenland 162

Tasermiut, see Ketilsfjord
Tasersuaq, lake in Ketilsfjord 97, 296
Thiødhillestad, royal farm (= Holastadr?) 67, 69–71
Thor, pagan god 81, 134–135
Thorbjörn Glora, settler 28
Thorbjörn Vivilsson, Icelandic settler at Stokkanes 23, 30, 33, 198, 263–264
Thordis, owner of Löngunes in Einarsfjord 16, 134, 186
Thordr, bishop of Gardar 34–35, 94, 95, 118–120, 122, 201
Thorfinn Greenlander, peasant 346
Thorfinn Karlsefni, Icelander 16–19, 23, 33, 165–166, 195, 201, 204, 206, 208–209, 370
Thorgils, character in *Flomanna saga* 33
Thorgrim Trolle Einarsson 29, 33, 45, 50, 53, 62–63, 184, 186, 188, 194, 203, 205, 208, 277, 368

Thorgrimur Solvason, Icelander visiting Greenland 357
Thorhall, Icelandic skipper 33
Thorir, Norwegian merchant 33,164, 184, 204
Thorkell Farserkr, first settler at Hvalsey 28, 31, 70, 81
Thorkell Gellison, Icelander visiting Greenland 14–15, 341
Thorkell Leivsson, Eirik Raudi's grandson 31, 49, 56, 62, 166, 210
Thorlak, bishop of Skálholt 115
Thorleif Kimbi Thorbrandsson, Icelandic settler in Greenland 23, 28
Thorleif the Wise, Norwegian law expert 50, 51
Thormod Kolbrunarskald 25, 44, 49–50, 53, 62–3, 134, 162, 187–188, 210, 277, 292, 349, 368
Thorolv, Norwegian chieftain in conflict with the king 22, 230
Thorstein, skipper from Bergen 182
Thorstein Eiriksson, son of Eirik Raudi 16–17, 32–33, 56, 89–90, 135
Thorstein Olafsson, Icelandic magnate 357–360
Thorvald Eiriksson, son of Eirik Raudi 17, 33, 89
Thorvald Helgason, Icelandic explorer 136
Thorvard [Einarsson?] peasant at Gardar farm 29, 33
Thule, today American air-base in Greenland 180, 339
Thule, used in Latin texts for Iceland 84
Tjodhild, Eirik Raudi's wife 82–83
Tjodhild's church 59, 82–83, 85–86, 97, 107, 299
Tongarsuk, an Inuit protecting spirit 364
Tower of London zoo 181
Treppe, Johannes Petersson, nominal bishop of Gardar 142
Trondheim/Nidaros
  religion 81–146, 172–173
  ivory workshop 172
  trade 51, 171, 173, 193, 201–202, 205–207, 216
  other subjects 168, 181

Ulfljot, first *lögsögumadr* on Iceland 50–51
Umiviarsuit (W52a) 192
Umiviarsuk (W52) 101, 112, 280
Umivik on the East Coast 338

432   Index of names (places and persons)

Umivik farm in the Kangersuneq Ice Fjord (W15) 269
Upernavik 138–139, 174
Uthaf, an imagined World Ocean surrounding the land mass 136
Uunartoq fjord (Appendix II map 7) 28, 31, 86–87, 97, 130 (= Siglufjord, possibly Alptafjord)
Uunartoq, island 97, 130, 264, 273

Vágar parish church (E149?) (Appendix II map 7) 95, 97, 99, 103, 105–107, 275, 282–283, 291, 293, 306, 367, 402
Vatnahverfi (Appendix II, map 6) 6, 21, 26, 29, 68, 86, 98, 100, 146, 169, 188, 192, 242, 246, 280, 282–283, 285, 291–293, 296, 362–363, 368

Vatnsdalur (= Auros), parish in Ketilsfjord, (Appendix II map 8) 95, 99
Vebæk, Christian, Nationalmusem archaeologist 4, 6, 97–98, 129–130, 242, 266, 291
Verdsdal, locality in Pettersvig parish in Ketilsfjord 97
Vesteinsson, Orri, Icelandic historian 278
Vik/Vig, see Pettersvig

White Sea 162, 170, 350
Wilhelm of Sabina, Cardinal 124

Øssur Asbjærnarsson, buried in the Middle Settlement 90, 93
Østergård, Else, Danish archaeologist 167, 363

Printed in the USA
CPSIA information can be obtained
at www.ICGtesting.com
LVHW011233161023
761197LV00010B/257